The Future of Audit

Keeping Capital Markets Efficient

Towards a national strategy on the future of auditing

The Future of Audit

Keeping Capital Markets Efficient

Towards a national strategy on the future of auditing

Keith Houghton, Christine Jubb, Michael Kend and Juliana Ng

THE AUSTRALIAN NATIONAL UNIVERSITY

Cover design and layout by Teresa Prowse, www.madebyfruitcup.com

Cover image: "black and white of Shang" iStock photo # 1543492.
www.istockphoto.com/stock-photo-1543492-close-of-business.php

Printed by University Printing Services, ANU

CONTENTS

ACKNOWLEDGMENTS

We offer our appreciation to a large number of participants over the entire life of this project and in particular to the more than 40 contributors to the Future of Audit Symposium held at Parliament House, Canberra, on 20 September 2007. In addition, the authors would like to acknowledge the substantial contribution of a number of individuals who provided feedback, including comments on earlier drafts of this report, or parts of this report, distributed between September 2008 and March 2009. The most important of these comments came from Pat Barrett (former Auditor-General of Australia), Dr Gary Pflugrath, CPA Australia, and Liz Stamford. Funding for this project came from an Australian Research Council Linkage Grant. Funding and other assistance was provided by Deloitte, Ernst & Young, KPMG, PriceWaterhouseCoopers, the Institute of Chartered Accountants in Australia and CPA Australia. Thanks go, too, to Chris Ikin for his contribution, particularly in the early stages of this project.

Address for correspondence:

Director, Australian National Centre for Audit and Assurance Research, Copland Building, The Australian National University ACT 0200.
Telephone: +61 2 6125 3596; email: <ancaar@anu.edu.au>

EXECUTIVE SUMMARY

Overarching comments

With the onset of the global financial crisis, now more than ever the operation of the capital market has been put under pressure. A key objective of this research project is to make observations that might enhance and support the efficiency of the capital market through the information provided by auditors and its impact and influence. At the time of writing, there have been few negative observations about auditors and their role in the global financial crisis (GFC). While criticisms of bankers, regulators, directors and senior executives, advisory firms, hedge funds and other financial service organisations (among others) mount, little concern has been expressed about the role of audit. To some, this could be unexpected, but the presence of no news is to the eyes of some 'good news'. In some ways, the GFC can be seen as a stress test of audit where the stress has not resulted in structural failure.

In essence, the aim of this project has been to put a 'window' on a number of issues in auditing and its operation in the capital market. The scale of the project from the outset was large and has grown substantially. It is acknowledged that the data collection for this project predates the GFC and readers are warned of this limitation. There are, however, many instances where the underlying core issues existed before and will continue to exist during and after the GFC. Even now, the project is not comprehensive, but it is of sufficient scale to allow the opportunity to explore quite specific issues and gain considerable insight into the views of participants in the market for audit services in relation to those issues.

While the authors have provided a list of conclusions, policy issues and recommendations on actionable items, this is by no means comprehensive. We have sought to list actionable items that need to be considered by the relevant organisations and for these items to be considered generally in the context of a public policy debate. The Australian Research Council and the linkage partners have not endorsed this list. The authors have not attempted to be definitive or comprehensive but have simply summarised the positions that have been observed in the market and sought to bring them into focus so that those charged with decision making might appreciate this synthesis of information as having utility.

This report contains not only information that is survey generated; it includes the direct words used by many players in the market for audit services in face-to-face interviews and inferences drawn from those words. We have given over much of this report to direct quotations from these participants as the power and authority of much of what we describe is best conveyed, we feel, in the participants' own words. We have, however, in each chapter tried to synthesise these quotations into a more efficient summary for those who might desire a more concise summation of these views. The authors note that while there are summaries that precede the chapters and summaries within the chapters, there is no doubt that for an understanding of the issues, the reader needs to read in depth the parts of the report that are relevant to them. To aid this, Chapter 1 includes various directed pathways that will assist particular types of stakeholders (users, purchasers, suppliers and the like).

There is no doubt that this project could not have been undertaken without the contribution of a large number of individuals and organisations. The Australian Research Council is this nation's premier research funding body across many fields of inquiry and its participation in this project has been crucial. Also of importance has been the role played by two of the major professional bodies within the business community, the Institute of Chartered Accountants in Australia and CPA Australia. Their respective contributions—financially and in terms of expertise—are recognised. All four of the major audit firms—Deloitte, Ernst & Young, KPMG and PriceWaterhouseCoopers—have also made important contributions. These institutions and numerous individuals within them have played a significant role and we would like to formally acknowledge our appreciation for their contribution. In addition, there were the many individuals representing various stakeholders' views—including users, purchasers, suppliers, standard setters and regulators—who contributed to the statements contained in the report and to the overall depth and richness of the materials that have been presented. We would like to thank each of these individuals; we are appreciative of the time and expertise they gave so generously. A number of staff within the authors' respective institutions also contributed in different ways and at different times and their contribution is acknowledged also.

Considerable care has been taken in compiling this report, which has involved seeking comments from certain key individuals and organisations over the past several months. Any remaining errors and omissions, however, remain the responsibility of the authors. Any comments or observations can be made by contacting the research team at <ancaar@anu.edu.au>

In that connection, please be aware that we have used directly the words from a range of stakeholders in the various quotations included in the report. We note specifically that the perceptions, beliefs and even representations of facts that are described in the report and attributed to stakeholders are those of the participants and not the authors. Those who made them might think of some of these observations as factual, but in reality they might not be. The authors do not necessarily agree that all assertions made are true in fact. The authors remain responsible for the other components of this report, which are described as summaries, issues and implications, concluding remarks and recommendations. It is important to note that none of the industry partners to the ARC linkage grant has had a right of veto of the recommendations nor are these recommendations included at their request. The recommendations come as a consequence of the information gathered in the study and have been crafted by the research team.

We have attempted to ensure that no person has been or is able to be individually identified and no organisation has been named where there could be an adverse outcome from that identification. There are a few instances where specific firm and company names are referred to, however, this occurs in circumstances where we do not believe there will be any negative consequences for those organisations and generally these are a matter of public record. We trust that this report and any further papers, publications and public discussion of its contents will contribute positively to the market for audit services and as a consequence of that to the efficiency of the capital market. Others will judge its utility and the efficacy of its recommendations and of the report more broadly.

Summarising, the study can be characterised as exploring issues within certain major themes:

- expectations gap/informativeness of the audit opinion
- staffing, skills and social impacts
- public policy implications
- the audit and assurance service.

A brief discussion of the inferences we draw from participants' responses under the above themes follows. A chapter-by-chapter summary of issues raised in participants' responses and their implications, together with suggested actions to address these issues, follows this brief executive summary.

Expectations gap/informativeness of the audit opinion

From the responses of participant stakeholders, we conclude that the external financial statement audit is valued and that there is no call for change to its mandate. We note that in the context of the global financial crisis, its role becomes even more important to confidence in the capital market. As a starting point, this is a clear positive for the future of audit. On a less positive note, however, the audit expectations gap continues to exist (Chapter 3). Further, in our view, it is not possible that this gap can be 'closed'. This is so for a number of reasons, including the perceived complexity of financial reports, which is a function of accounting standards and for which auditors cannot be held responsible. The wide disparity between retail and more sophisticated investors in terms of their understanding of financial and related reports is another reason for our view that the audit expectations gap is not closable. We therefore conclude that efforts to minimise the gap should not focus only on retail investors, since the likelihood of success with this group is low, although we do explore ways in which auditors might make more of their process and work known to a general audience (Chapter 4). Rather, efforts should be focused on specific topics our research has led us to believe contribute to misunderstandings by even the more sophisticated stakeholders in the market for audit services. In particular, we observe a concerning expectations gap between suppliers and regulators and, in our view, this gap can be minimised given the common interests of these groups, and suggestions are made as to how this might be achieved.

In our view, the standardisation or 'commoditisation' of the audit and its expression through virtually identically worded audit opinions could have contributed to the expectations gap and to an undervaluing of the financial statement audit in the market for information. We suggest that those relevant stakeholders in the market for audit services give consideration to amended audit report wording and reporting formats to address this issue.

We infer from participants' comments that some audit committee members and even directors exhibit less than complete understanding of matters relating to the external audit and we make recommendations for ways that these cohorts might be better alerted to correct this. In particular, the issue of 'materiality', as this term is used in an audit context, appears to be poorly understood and a whole chapter (Chapter 5) is dedicated to this important issue.

Staffing, skills and social impacts

Many of the participants' comments, including from many junior auditors themselves, highlight the perceived 'menial' nature of much of the work of audit staff. We note that many of these individuals see themselves as stereotypical of 'generation Y'. We infer from their comments that this issue has been exacerbated by recent changes to the auditing regime in terms of documentation requirements, check lists and reduced opportunities to vary work by providing secondments to clients or engaging in non-audit service work for clients. The GFC might mask the implications of any decrease in the attractiveness of audit as a career in the short term, but the underlying image of auditing as a career option, intersecting as it does with the expectations of generation Y in terms of seeking a challenging and varied work role, needs to be addressed in our view. These issues and the issue of developing business acumen and client and industry knowledge are explored in Chapters 6, 7, 8 and 9 and suggestions are made to address the underlying issues that emerge.

Public policy implications

In terms of the conduct of audits, our findings reveal at the time of the interviews a common concern among suppliers about the increased level of prescription of audits accompanying the revised auditing standards and inspections by the regulator (Chapters 11 and 12). There is recognition that audit documentation quality has improved. If the changes introduced to the auditing regime as a result of 'CLERP 9' were made with a view to decrease the likelihood of unexpected corporate collapse or to increase confidence in financial statement credibility, there was little evidence that stakeholders perceived that they had succeeded. There is, however, consensus among stakeholders that these changes have added to costs (Chapter 10). Statements from those in the market provide a view that audit partner rotation and some of the constraints on auditor-provided non-audit services, often self-imposed by companies, are not maximising economic efficiency and suggestions are made to relax requirements in these areas (Chapter 9). In terms of competition in the market for audit services, many participants express concern about the potential consequences should one of the existing 'Big Four' firms not survive (Chapter 13). Suggestions for dealing with this potentiality are made.

The audit and assurance service

In terms of the provision of audit and assurance services, we observe from participants' comments mixed views on whether differential auditing standards based on listed/non-listed auditee status should be introduced (Chapter 14). We observe also that the value of internal audit is generally understated and that although opportunities for increased liaison between internal and external audit exist, there is little appetite by external auditors to undertake the incremental work necessary before the work of the internal auditor can be relied on (Chapter 15). We observe also from participants' comments in relation to the potential for provision of assurance on information outside the scope of traditional financial statements that there is extensive demand but little willingness to supply (Chapter 16). In terms of the provision of levels of assurance other than 'reasonable' as pertaining to financial statement audits, evidence of some demand but an inability to supply under the current international assurance framework (Chapter 17) is observed.

Concluding remarks

A detailed reading of this report will result in an uninformed reader concluding that there are many challenges and sub-optimalities of audit. This would not be a sound conclusion. While this report documents many opportunities for improvement, it is the case that auditing and other such professions rarely see the benefit of a 'good news' story. When, for example, would we expect to see a newspaper article with the headline 'Auditor does good job' or an investigative television report finding that an audit meant that shareholders were protected? The best auditing and other experience goods can hope for is the absence of bad news. This report needs to be read in this context.

SUMMARY OF REPORT CHAPTERS

1.0 Introduction

Many challenges for the profession of auditing are presented in this report, but we can conclude that the 'future of audit' is a positive one, with considerable ability to contribute to economic wellbeing. The report makes a number of recommendations across a range of issues. Some of these challenges are relatively simple to implement but others need deep consideration and much time. Several of the issues and recommendations are not original to the current authors. There have been other examinations of auditing and the authors acknowledge the work of those others and their ideas, which have been implemented. Nevertheless, it is hoped that this comprehensive study of the perceptions of stakeholders in the market for audit services can contribute to debate and policy making about the external audit.

When the project began, there was no global financial crisis; it had not even been imagined. The size of the project and therefore the length of time it has taken to complete this report have been major challenges. As a consequence, some of the issues and underlying circumstances of the market for audit services in Australia have changed. The presence of the GFC, however, does not change the underlying challenges facing the audit profession. It might change the timing of some of the issues coming to fruition, but it does not eliminate the issues. Notwithstanding changes to the employment market created by the GFC, it appears that the nature of the work of auditors is becoming less attractive, especially to generation Y, and the greater prescription around maintenance of auditor independence, audit documentation, regulatory inspections and legal backing for auditing standards is working to deplete the image of auditing as a career. While the GFC might mitigate the consequences of these events and occurrences in the short term, there are some aspects of our findings that at the least require deep consideration by the relevant stakeholders.

The next section of this summary of report chapters describes the research method used, very briefly, before provision of an overview of each of the remaining chapters and the issues and recommendations that flow from the content of those chapters. The summary concludes with a table that provides an overview of each recommendation reference number classified according to likely stakeholder interest.

2.0 Research method (Chapter 2)

This research project uses the voices of participants in the market for audit services to explore the current state of that market and gain insights to its future. It uses multiple methods (preliminary focus groups to focus the survey questions and interview protocols, telephone and mail surveys, face-to-face interviews and focus group interviews with more junior auditors) to elicit qualitative evidence of the perceptions of stakeholder representatives. The stakeholder representatives accessed include those who use auditor's reports (users such as shareholders), those who purchase audit services (purchasers such as chief financial officers and audit committee members), those who supply audit and other assurance services (suppliers), those who set auditing standards (standard setters) and those who regulate the market for audit services (regulators). The timing of the project coincided with the first year of administration of the legally enforceable auditing standards and other changes to the regulatory regime as a result of the *Corporate Law Economic Reform Program (Audit Reform and Corporate Disclosure) Act 2004* (*CLERP 9*) that were by then well entrenched.

The responses elicited from participants in interviews, which make up a large part of this report, have been coded and grouped according to themes using a qualitative software analysis tool and reported, along with the survey results, within these themes, grouped according to the category of the stakeholder. The authors provide 'summaries' of responses by each category, together with sections on resulting 'issues and implications' and 'concluding remarks'. In summary, the following issues and recommended actions arising as an outcome of this research project can be found in the chapters of this report.

3.0 Understandability of the audit (Chapter 3)

3.0.1 Inferences from survey findings

Suppliers believed there was substantial value added in the audit, but this was rarely replicated by other participants in the market for audit services. When asked whether the auditor had a good understanding of the business, again, suppliers provided a positive response, whereas purchasers and users were more mixed in their views. A large proportion of users believed that the audit provided a form of guarantee about the truth and fairness of the financial statements.

Users, purchasers and suppliers all reported self-rated understanding of financial statements as above the median. Purchasers and suppliers indicated that it was really the external auditor's responsibility to detect material fraud. Users, suppliers and purchasers all recognised that the auditor had responsibility to detect material error. There was a shared view that the auditor had responsibility to warn the audit committee about early signs of risk. There were mixed views about whether the auditor should act as a whistleblower to an appropriate regulatory body. Big Four suppliers were the only respondents who strongly indicated they disagreed that the auditor had responsibility to provide direct assurance about the adequacy of the internal control system.

From these survey findings, there is evidence that assurance is valued and there is no case to remove or limit the existence of an audit as it is currently known to the market.

3.0.2 Inferences from interview findings

Users report checking whether an audit report exists, that it is provided by a brand name auditor and is not modified. Such a simplistic categorisation could cause users to miss statements of emphasis of matter. Another implication is that the audit report is perceived as a 'commodity', which is simplistic, standardised and fails to recognise the diversity of expertise held by some users.

Purchasers perceive auditors to be doing 'the right thing' but some concern exists that the amount of regulation and bureaucracy is a distraction from the main objective of providing assurance on the financial statements. Suppliers are concerned that audit has suffered because of the complexity of accounting standards and believe that there is scope for enhancing what is communicated in the audit opinion.

What also emerges from all stakeholders is genuine concern about the level of complexity and information load jointly contained in the financial reporting and auditing disclosures, for which auditors cannot be held responsible, but which limits what can be done to enhance the understandability of the audit and audit process.

Issue 3.1

Perceived complexity of financial reports limits potential for communication solutions for auditors.

Suggested action 3.1

Policymaker recognition that enhancing the readability and understandability of financial reports is a multifaceted, multi-agency responsibility with no single body taking overall responsibility for monitoring more than technical compliance with accounting standards, and so on. A body, likely the Financial Reporting Council (FRC), should take on explicit responsibility for monitoring aspects of the quality and understandability of financial reports.

Issues 3.2 and 3.3

Audit report wording is standardised/commoditised, which hides the degree of auditor judgment involved in relation to a specific auditee, ignores the diversity of the audience in terms of motivation for and capability of understanding audit outcome information and uses terms that can be misconstrued (for example, material misstatement, test basis).

Suggested action 3.2

Amend audit reporting standards to encourage more nuanced and auditee-specific audit reports in order to encourage reading by target audience. Perhaps this should be in the form of appendices to a standardised report.

Suggested action 3.3

While audit reports need to fulfil minimum legal requirements, there should be positive encouragement by regulators to allow auditors to include nuanced and subtle explanations and observations in a way that adds value to the report for interested readers.

3.1 The audit expectations gap (Chapter 3)

3.1.1 Inferences from interview findings

The majority of participants acknowledged the existence of an expectations gap or gaps. Users, primarily large professional users, commonly perceive the existence of an expectations gap between themselves and suppliers, but also between regulators and auditors. Purchasers too observed multiple gaps, including a gap between auditors and regulators. Some purchasers were critical of regulators in their inspection and oversight functions. Other purchasers indicated that the audit expectations gap arose mostly in the presence of business failure and yet in a free market economy there will always be the presence of business failure. A number of suppliers indicated that they did not believe the expectations gap was closable, with several acknowledging there were different sorts of gaps with different participants in the capital market. In particular, retail investors were uninformed and probably uninformable. There were observations by many suppliers of an expectations gap between auditors and regulators. There was criticism by non-Big Four suppliers that audit expectations developed by regulators were based on their observations of the Big Four. Another observation was that the presence of a stronger regulatory environment had really added to the expectations gap. Suppliers observed that it was not well understood that materiality meant that the audit was undertaken at reasonable cost to give reasonable assurance.

There were few suggestions for resolving the gaps. One comment was that the scope section of the audit report described more fully that which was undertaken by the auditor and that which was not. One standard setter observed that much of the expectations gap was caused by regulators who might choose to deflect blame and negative market sentiment from themselves and on to the accounting profession. None of the regulators interviewed indicated that legally enforceable auditing standards would help solve the expectations gap, narrow it or manage it. In terms of policy implications, the authors observe that much has been done to encourage participation by investors in the Australian capital market, yet there has been no parallel public policy support mechanism to help educate and inform those participants in the capital market.

In summary, the audit expectations gap continues to exist, is complex and multifaceted (existing at least between users and suppliers, purchasers and suppliers and regulators and suppliers) and at the least is costly to the efficiency of the market for information within the capital market and could have many other costs associated with it. It goes without saying that the audit expectations gap should be minimised to the extent possible. There needs to be, however, recognition that the audit expectations gap will never be closed and that eliminating differential incentives for a gap to exist and 'educating' all stakeholders are not possible. Focusing on stakeholders who are motivated and have the capability to have their knowledge and understanding of audit and its outcomes raised and focusing on specific topics known to be the subject of misunderstandings (for example, materiality, use of the term 'test basis') are the best strategies. Because of shared objectives and sophistication levels, the gap between suppliers and regulators should be given the highest priority in terms of gap minimisation.

Issue 3.4

Generalised non-reading of the auditor's report—potential to miss emphasis of matter paragraphs.

Suggested action 3.4

Consider the current guidance on location and highlighting of emphasis of matter paragraphs to ensure they are conspicuous.

Issue 3.5

The standardised audit report wording uses terms that can be misconstrued and that can therefore contribute to the audit expectations gap. In particular, there is evidence of misunderstanding of the use of the terms 'reasonable assurance', 'material misstatement' and 'test basis'.

Suggested action 3.5

Change the wording within the auditor's report to minimise the audit expectations gap (for example, 'This audit is a certification of the X percentage probability of the absence of misstatement in the financial report above an absolute aggregate dollar value of Y' or 'We are X per cent confident that there are no misstatements in the financial report above an absolute dollar value of...').

Issue 3.6

Several suppliers' comments indicate that they do not understand that authorities in Australia view the external audit as a form of 'delegated regulation' (Knott 2002). In Australia, audit is privileged by a mandate in many cases (that is, is required by legislation), has the shareholder at its centre as the client and always is the beneficiary of restraint of trade policies (that is, only appropriately qualified people can sign an audit report). These aspects of the current framework are not well understood by some suppliers.

Suggested action 3.6

Creation and wide dissemination of an overarching, high-level, educational piece on the role of audit in Australian society, including content in plain English, on for which types of entities audit is mandated, the audit process and, for suppliers, a section reinforcing the privileged role that audits hold and the rights and responsibilities that level of privilege brings with it.

Issue 3.7

Regulators allegedly sometimes do not practice 'delegated regulation' in its purest sense, but instead dictate 'detail' to a point that interferes with audit efficiency, but even more seriously, with audit effectiveness.

Suggested action 3.7

Despite acknowledged existing mechanisms for communication, greater communication between regulators and supplier representatives from larger and smaller audit suppliers and wider dissemination of feedback to the population of audit suppliers are needed to enhance communication of what each party (regulators and suppliers) is seeking to achieve.

4.0 Communication of more of the audit process by auditors and/or by management (Chapter 4)

4.0.1 Inferences from interview findings

There was no support at all for management communicating more of the audit process to stakeholders; however, there was wide support from users and purchasers for auditors doing more of this than was the current case. In a large difference from users and purchasers, suppliers were more critical of this as a possibility and standard setters were mixed in their views. One purchaser observed that the current process undertaken in an audit was opaque. A purchaser and a supplier observed that the language used in audit opinions tended to contain 'jargon' and was not easily interpreted. Many participants, particularly purchasers and users, perceived the audit opinion as a 'blunt instrument' conveying only whether the opinion was modified or not. That is, suppliers seek the ability to exercise their professional judgment, but most of the audit observables are standardised or 'commoditised'. Several, however, observed that the audit report was currently not read, so any further disclosures would suffer the same fate, could add to confusion and would likely be written with litigation risk in mind. One supplier observed that those charged with governance sometimes did not want information about how the audit was undertaken because this might increase their own legal accountability. Others argued that encouraging confidence in the framework and professionalism of audit was more important than additional disclosures.

Issues 4.1–3

Many of the aspects of audit are not well understood by some users and purchasers.

Suggested action 4.1

Provision of collaboratively written, widely available educative material about auditors' work and process, focused on users as the audience, written in layman's language and spelling out important things such as the fact that the work involves sampling, could be particularly risk focused, deals with substantive issues pertaining to that particular industry or entity and describing what levels of materiality are used. For consideration is whether these descriptions should be specific to the company or might be more generalised for a particular audit firm.

Suggested action 4.2

Provide educational materials in plain English in relation to use of the words 'material' and 'materiality' in an audit context.

Suggested action 4.3

Consideration to be given to a government-funded public education campaign of the type administered to encourage understanding of the importance of superannuation contributions.

Issue 4.4

Information search costs for auditor's reports are high since these documents are currently available only by acquiring, and searching within, individual company annual reports.

Suggested action 4.4

For listed companies, auditors' reports should be mandated as a separately filed Australian Securities Exchange (ASX) document (as well as located within the annual report) so that they can be searched in aggregate as publicly available information individually or for a particular class of company or type of report.

5.0 Materiality (Chapter 5)

5.0.1 Inferences from interview findings

The issue of materiality was raised in the preliminary focus groups used to provide input to development of the survey instrument and interview protocol as a major source of misunderstanding in the market for audit services. The desirability of having disclosure of the level(s) of materiality was expressed by users and purchasers, but was less welcomed by suppliers, standard setters and regulators. That the financial statements were barely read anyway or that the concept would be confusing were major reasons behind unenthusiastic comments. Standard setters and regulators observed that misinterpretation, misunderstanding or miscommunication of materiality had not caused company failures. Others, however, acknowledged that even if a small minority of informed readers read and understood the disclosures, it would assist in making the market more efficient. Some suppliers argued that fostering more confidence in the existing process and framework was the key rather than explicit disclosures.

Among suppliers, purchasers and some users there was a view that providing disclosure of the existence of a materiality threshold influencing the audit represented a key ingredient in advising the market that the audit was not a 100 per cent guarantee. From users and purchasers, there was a focus on the quantitative aspects of materiality. Suppliers invoked both quantitative and qualitative characteristics. Some suppliers argued that at audit committee level it was common to have a discussion about materiality at an aggregate level, but when one discussed line items in the financial statements on the basis of materiality, occasionally the discussion could become 'heated'. Also, although not brought out in the interviews, disclosing materiality levels could facilitate fraud.

Issues 5.1–3

The concept of 'materiality' as it is used in an auditing concept is not well understood outside the profession and is a previously under-emphasised part of the audit expectations gap. As such, costs are imposed on the market for information within the capital market.

Suggested action 5.1

Apart from the inclusion of generalised information about materiality and its role within audits, create specific guidance for audit committees in terms of their need to inform themselves about audit materiality and their right to request disclosure to them by the auditor of the level of 'tolerable error' used in the audit.

Suggested action 5.2

The ASX to include in its Corporate Governance Guidelines and Recommendations a recommendation that audit committee members undertake structured education programs that include content related to the statutory role of audit, audit processes and audit outcomes and audit committee member rights and responsibilities in relation to these features. This could be a recommendation that such requirements be included in corporate audit committee charters.

Suggested action 5.3

Consider the integration of audit-related concepts wherever relevant into subjects/units within tertiary and professional business qualifications (as many institutions do with ethics education).

6.0 Developing business acumen and client and industry knowledge (Chapter 6)

6.0.1 Inferences from survey findings

In terms of the telephone and mail surveys, in response to a question about whether external financial statement audits were of value because of 'the specialist industry expertise of the auditor', 50 per cent of suppliers, 46 per cent of users and only 31 per cent of purchasers responded affirmatively. Among the suppliers, there was a sharp differentiation between Big Four and non-Big Four suppliers, with 77 per cent of Big Four suppliers believing industry expertise brought value compared with only 42 per cent of non-Big Four suppliers. This difference could reflect the relevance of industry expertise across the levels of market capitalisation and across unlisted companies. With respect to agreement with the statement that 'an external audit is of value because the auditor has a good understanding of the business', 55 per cent of suppliers, 33 per cent of purchasers and 40 per cent of users responded affirmatively. Chief executive officer/chief financial officer (CEO/CFO) respondents as a subgroup of the purchasers particularly denigrated the value of the financial statement audit as that subgroup perceived it.

In response to questions about an audit being of value because of the 'business acumen the auditor brought to the audit', 45 per cent of users, 33 per cent of purchasers and 55 per cent of suppliers responded affirmatively. Specifically with respect to audit partners, most users and suppliers saw the business acumen of audit partners as above the mid-point, with junior auditors not rated highly. Interestingly, overall, purchasers took a harsher view compared with users.

6.0.2 Inferences from interview findings

Purchasers' expectations were low in terms of the business acumen of auditors yet differentiation between expectations of senior and junior auditors was present. Purchasers acknowledged the lack of stability in audit teams, causing lapses in client knowledge.

It was acknowledged among suppliers that junior staff did not have the business acumen or the maturity of more senior staff, so they could ask clients the 'wrong' questions. There is, however, also realisation that 'dumb' questions can be very useful in uncovering audit issues. Less reliance on substantive testing compared with prior periods might have limited the opportunity of junior staff to become deeply familiar with how businesses operated. Suppliers make frequent observations that inexperience is not only evident among junior auditors; it is common among client staff. Regulators observe that business acumen is not necessarily one of the core attributes of a successful and competently completed audit. Comments were received on the size of the market in Australia as a constraint on gaining industry expertise in particular industries.

The issues relating to junior auditors and their ability to develop experience and acumen—requiring elements of 'emotional intelligence'—useful in a business career remains, and perhaps has implications for tertiary education.

One interesting insight that emerged from focus group interviews with more junior audit staff was the presence of remuneration schemes that rewarded client accounting staff based on the number or extent of audit adjustments. The authors note that these schemes could usurp the role of the audit committee and encourage conservative accounting rather than accounting that reflects economic reality.

Issue 6.1

The personal attributes of maturity, tenacity, self-assertiveness, resilience and integrity—many of which feed into the notion of 'emotional intelligence'—could be as important to successful audit outcomes as technical auditing skills, yet are seldom targeted explicitly as graduate attributes by tertiary institutions and beyond in their teaching and learning programs.

Suggested action 6.1

Collaboration between relevant parties to assess the best way to build the development of key personal attributes into subjects/units and courses.

Issues 6.2–6

Based on participants' comments, the present audit business model in some practices is under stress. It is seen in some instances as heavily pyramidal, tending to rely overly on junior staff—who are least likely to possess the ideal 'personal emotional intelligence' attributes—at the interface between the client and the auditor and depends on retention of staff with the appropriate personal and technical skills for future leadership.

Suggested action 6.2

Consider whether the current widely used audit business model is sustainable and optimal in the longer term.

Suggested action 6.3

Consider whether audit practices' current recruitment techniques test appropriately for the personal skills required of a successful auditor.

Suggested action 6.4

Consider developing more effective systems and processes for the management of client-specific knowledge and ensuring its continuity despite changes in audit team membership.

Suggested action 6.5

Consider developing more effective workplace flexibility practices to retain staff at points of major change in their personal lives.

Suggested action 6.6

Alter recruitment policies to encourage the hiring of many more accounting honours graduates (and others with higher-level analytical skills).

Issues 6.7–8

A number of stakeholders noted that opportunities for development of business acumen and industry knowledge in junior auditors had become more limited with increased independence requirements.

Suggested action 6.7

Consider development of a national database divided by industry groups and also geographic distribution including data that relate to audit, governance and risk issues relevant to auditees within the Australian market for audit services.

Suggested action 6.8

Enhance the adequacy of the teaching of auditing at tertiary level and in continuing professional education by developing high-quality, realistic multimedia and case-based teaching and learning materials.

Issue 6.9

Remuneration schemes that reward client accounting staff based on the number or extent of audit adjustments exist and can usurp the role of the audit committee and encourage conservative accounting rather than accounting that reflects the economic reality.

Suggested action 6.9

Include in the ASX Corporate Governance Guidelines and Recommendations a recommendation that audit committee members be advised if client staffers are, in part, remunerated based on the number of audit adjustments and how the scheme operates.

7.0 Attracting and supporting staff (Chapter 7)

7.0.1 Inferences from interview findings

Issues that were raised in the context of audit firm attraction of staff included the image of the auditing profession, the work/life balance preference of generation Y, the fact that the CA program no longer had to be completed within a public accounting firm, the attractiveness of other employers (especially organisations such as those in banking and finance), the comparatively low initial salary scale, the increasingly prescriptive and regulated nature of auditing, the available pool of graduates from which to recruit and questions about the continued attractiveness of achieving partnership.

Purchasers saw no threat to attracting appropriate talent to the profession, although they acknowledged the competitiveness (at the time) of the employment market. Some purchasers had reservations about whether the pool of graduates had, in relative terms, declined, while others observed that the CA in commerce program had affected the prior near-monopoly recruiting position of the Big Four. That is, accounting graduates entering other occupations are not necessarily lost to the accounting profession, although the Big Four might have lost their relative position. One purchaser observed that recruitment to chartered accounting via the CA in commerce program might be more attractive in view of the level of external oversight and inspection attached to public practice. Repeatedly, the observation was made that the accounting firms simply did not remunerate adequately.

With respect to suppliers, more questioning ensued about the total pool of graduates available for recruitment. Frequently, observations were made that the total pool seemed to be either small or at a 'tipping point'. Auditing was still seen as a good training ground but there was also a perception that it held less glamour and prestige than it once did. One of the attractions of the larger employers put forward was their multidisciplinary nature that could provide alternative careers to ambitious accounting graduates who sought diverse employment opportunities. Suppliers questioned the number of accounting graduates completing their degrees eligible for employment in Australia and their often limited knowledge of auditing. The pedagogy of teaching auditing is lamented if it is procedural in nature as opposed to thematic. Also, because auditing is often taught late in degree programs, applicants for graduate positions tend to have little or no understanding of the nature of auditing. The authors note that universities are under similar competitive employment pressures for staff as are accounting firms.

Standard setters observed that accounting did not have the glamorous profile it once had and that the prestige of accounting was declining. As observed by a standard setter: 'It is no longer possible for the auditor to be the trusted advisor.' There was also acceptance that many of today's generation were seeking multidisciplinary careers that were diverse and challenging. Questions arise about the sole use of Year 12 scores as university entrance criteria. The authors observe that other professions have broadened their criteria and that university entry scores are affected by factors that influence both supply and demand. If public accounting firms were more willing to take more graduates from universities without such high entry scores, and were more willing to recruit international students whose working visas were yet to be processed, perceptions of too few willing graduates might dissipate. One standard setter questioned whether firms tracked their selection choices at entry point to evaluate those who survived, prospered and contributed to the auditing profession in later years.

Regulators shared the view that accounting was not as glamorous as other employment opportunities and suffered as a consequence.

Issues 7.1–3

Many participants' comments indicate that in their view higher levels of prescription have led to more 'menial' work for junior auditors.

Suggested action 7.1

Consider greater use of mechanisms other than Year 12 scores for entry to university accounting degrees (for example, as has been done for entry to medicine) since the competitive forces to maintain university entrance scores as high as possible might not create circumstances for suitably disposed students to enter into accounting degrees.

Suggested action 7.2

Conduct research into whether the presence of alternative pathways (to CPA segments and the CA program) have a negative effect on entrance standards and the quantity of accounting graduates entering or exiting universities in Australia. If there are other alternative pathways then what would be the likely consequences?

Suggested action 7.3

Consider whether the 'best and brightest' really represent optimal audit firm recruits for the majority of appointments.

Issue 7.4

Auditing is perceived to have an 'image' problem and to have become less attractive as a career than it once was. The GFC could mask this fact in the short term, but it will resurface as an issue.

Suggested action 7.4

Consider how the profile of auditing can be made more widely known as an attractive career option.

8.0 Retention of staff (Chapter 8)

8.0.1 Inferences from interview findings

From the focus group interviews with junior staff, completion of CA and time commitments relating to fee reimbursement or when promoted to manager were frequently cited as trigger points for departure of staff. By and large, remuneration was not a key driver of the decision to leave. Often the departure of a colleague seemed to trigger departure. Perhaps after the interpersonal connectedness issue was the work/life balance and in particular the changing nature of the work, which was repeatedly described as either 'documentation' or 'admin'.

Again, from the focus group interviews with junior staff, the following emerged as reasons to stay: 1) having someone who was a key role model for them; 2) the quality of people and colleagues working around them, the level of friendliness and the functionality of that group; and 3) having good-quality clients. Opportunities for secondments, especially overseas, were also seen as reasons to stay.

In terms of the face-to-face interviews, users did not see audit firms as premium employers. Purchasers questioned the recruitment from outside public practice to partner as undermining the traditional business model for staffing an audit firm. Another level of criticism by purchasers of the audit firm business model was the relatively low pay, high hours of work and a disconnect with lifestyle for modern, younger staff. Purchasers also acknowledged that much of the work undertaken by junior staff was 'menial' and that this provided industry with the opportunity to recruit people who were experienced in business, especially at the completion of CA or promotion to manager trigger points. Purchasers see a short-term monetary gain for an audit firm employee to move to industry, but there is less clarity about long-term financial rewards.

Suppliers see the real challenge as being around retention, having in mind generational expectations and structural changes in the nature of the work brought about by regulatory reform and the perceived lessening of professional judgment as a key part of the job. There is a lack of empathy from some with generation Y expectations in regard to the desired rate of change in their working environment. The authors note that perhaps the audit business model cannot facilitate this desired variety of tasks, but it then comes to the point of recruiting the appropriate staff and managing their expectations. Some suppliers recognise the need for constant change and innovation in the working lives of generation Y junior auditors and seek to be proactive in providing this. Some suppliers recognise that the traditional incentive structures—in particular, the prized goal of partnership—are no longer the attractions they once were. Suppliers repeatedly lament that the nature of oversight of the profession has degraded it, with the high level of regulation and scrutiny having consequences for job satisfaction, employment and retention.

Standard setters are somewhat cynical that what is happening is anything but a desired outcome. There were very penetrating comments from a standard setter that even at partner level, there was a serious threat from attrition, which had system-wide implications, especially for highly specialised industry groups.

There was an observation that suggested some partners and managers belonged to a 'previous generation' and were not empathetic with generation Y, especially with regard to changes to documentation requirements. While some of the participants of the focus groups suggested that documentation was one reason to leave the profession, there were also some positive advantages seen to better documentation.

Issues 8.1–4

Widespread observations by participants at the time of questioning result in the conclusion that retention of staff is becoming more of a challenge than in the past.

Suggested action 8.1

Make sure human resource performance systems work optimally to reward merit and potential.

Suggested action 8.2

Consider secondments to regulators (and others such as 'policy' officers) since secondments to clients are no longer as possible, presuming any potential conflicts of interest can be eliminated or adequately managed.

Suggested action 8.3

Inform staff about employment opportunities and career development that exist within their firm and give benchmarked objective comparators with alternative employment.

Suggested action 8.4

Engage with audit firm alumni not just as potential clients but as potential returning employees.

9.0 Auditor independence (Chapter 9)

9.0.1 Inferences from survey findings

In terms of a survey question—'Are you aware of the following specific changes that have occurred in the regulation of audit services in Australia: reforms pertaining to auditor independence'—57 per cent of users, 79 per cent of purchasers and 92 per cent of suppliers were aware.

9.0.2 Inferences from interview findings: auditor-provided non-audit services

In the face-to-face interviews with stakeholders, users generally saw a balance between the advantage to auditor independence of more prohibitions placed on auditor-provided non-audit services (APNAS) and the loss of knowledge from the joint supply of several services. It was observed that there was much cynicism on the part of the public about the issue and there was a very clear need to be independent and to be seen to be independent.

Among the purchasers, there was scepticism about the efficacy of 'Chinese walls', while there was also mention of the potential loss if there was a blanket ban on any form of joint supply of services. Purchasers wanted a framework or systems to make choices about service provision from the incumbent auditor.

Suppliers questioned whether the current situation with regard to APNAS was optimal. A number of suppliers, particularly those with small to medium-range clients, spoke of the advantages and efficiencies of joint supply as being substantial and lost in the current environment. It was common for suppliers to comment on the expertise they brought—otherwise deficient within the client—and that efficient and cost-effective joint delivery was in the best interest of all. This includes start-up companies with a preference for a 'one-stop shop' including capital raising, tax advice and financial reporting expertise to be supplied from the one source. One of the suppliers indicated a concern with the differential investment behaviour of audit and non-audit staff. The authors note that this could be a deterrent to retention within audit divisions. One observation from suppliers was that tax services delivered were so integral to the audit that the distinction between the two could be artificial.

Standard setters varied in their belief about whether the current regulatory system was tuned optimally. One standard setter raised concerns that the independence debate had been 'hijacked', arguing that what was sought was objectivity rather than independence.

The authors note that the issue of joint supply of non-audit services by an auditor is a classic example of public policy and personal interest conflicting. The objective of regulators and regulations is to protect business from the potential negative outcomes of possible independence threats, whereas the role of individual boards of directors and auditors is to provide an efficient and effective supply of relevant services to enhance the financial and business outcomes of clients.

Issue 9.1

Discouraging auditor provided non-audit services for all sizes of clients creates inefficiencies and costs for shareholders.

Suggested action 9.1

Apply the ethical rules covering APNAS differentially to different sizes of company or according to some other criteria such as listed company size.

Issue 9.2

Companies' disclosures regarding non-audit service fee categories are inconsistent, reducing comparability.

Suggested action 9.2

Provide guidance as to appropriate detailed services that fit within specific APNAS classifications.

Issue 9.3

Audit division staff has reduced freedom with respect to investment opportunities compared with other public practice staff, but generally might not be as susceptible to losing employment in economic downturns because of the mandated nature of audit.

Suggested action 9.3

Investigate whether stability of employment characteristics compensate for forgone investment opportunities and, if not, compensate accordingly.

Issue 9.4

Although members of the three professional bodies in Australia (CPAA, ICAA and NIA) are bound by the IFAC-compliant APESB's APES 110, there remain registered company auditors who are not members of these bodies and hence who are not necessarily bound by an ethical code based on IFAC's code through membership of a professional accounting body.

Suggested action 9.4

Include ethical standards within the AUASB's legal mandate or else the FRC provides the AUASB with a strategic direction to issue ethical standards for auditors.

9.1 Inferences from interview findings: rotation

The issue of mandated partner rotation is one of the few issues on which there is agreement among stakeholders. A large number of purchasers and suppliers as well as a number of users, regulators and standard setters articulated the desirability of having a 'fresh pair of eyes' and the 'diversity of view' that audit partner rotation could bring. Purchasers noted that rotation was practised by many audit firms before the current regulatory framework, but that the period was typically longer than five years. Purchasers also expressed some degree of uncertainty about the quality of any partner rotating in. Among the purchasers representing companies within the top 50 or so listed companies on the ASX, there was deep-rooted concern about the speed of rotation. Purchasers also expressed concern that when senior partners rotated off, the next logical client could be a major competitor in the same industry.

Suppliers also agree with the principle of rotation but have concerns. Suppliers noted a significant trade-off between independence—real and perceived—and the erosion of client knowledge. It was common to suggest that a five-year period was too short, particularly for large, complex or highly regulated (particularly APRA-regulated) companies. One supplier noted that there was no similar requirement for directors to rotate off. Suppliers to larger clients observed that large clients felt they had the power to demand any particular partner of their choice. Consequently, there is increased pressure on the most expert partners and less ability to train more junior partners.

Some suppliers noted that the five-year rotation was a 'tipping point' for clients in a decision to put the auditor to tender; it was also a tipping point for some individual partners to reconsider their own careers. Suppliers also noted the time and energy needed to manage the partner rotation process with the need for 'shadow' partners for some complex clients in the year or more before rotation. The authors note the anomaly of this situation in terms of bringing a 'fresh pair of eyes'.

Regulators, standard setters and users agreed in principle with rotation, but also acknowledged a substantial trade-off between knowledge of the client and independence. Suppliers and standard setters recognised that, generally, the initial-year audit quality was lower than the quality of an audit where the partner had been engaged with the client for three or more years. The authors note that the balance between engagement time and perceived independence might need to be crafted conditionally on the size, complexity or regulatory framework within which the auditee operates.

Issue 9.5

Five-year audit partner rotations are reported as creating problems for large, complex, highly regulated companies.

Suggested action 9.5

Consider differential application of audit partner rotation requirements rather than a 'one-size-fits-all' approach.

Issue 9.6

Several participant suppliers commented on the audit partner rotation being a trigger point for decisions regarding whether to leave or remain in the auditing profession. No data are available about whether the point of partner rotation has increased the rate of exit from the profession.

Suggested action 9.6

Conduct research into movements of registered company auditors per capita before and after the introduction of the five-year rotation requirement, controlling for other factors likely to affect these movements (for example, retirement).

10.0 Regulatory reforms to audit: their impact (Chapter 10)

10.0.1 Inferences from survey findings

Several survey questions were asked about the regulatory reforms and their impact. In response to questions about awareness of the following specific changes that have occurred in the regulation of audit services in Australia, the percentage agreeing or strongly agreeing was:

	Users	Purchasers	Suppliers
awareness of introduction of legally enforceable auditing standards	54%	77%	90%
regulation will reduce the number of corporate failures occurring	28%	15%	15%
responses to high-profile corporate collapses have assisted in improving the general public's confidence in the capital market	21%	19%	20%
responses to high-profile corporate collapses have assisted in enhancing the credibility of financial statements	25%	21%	22%
responses to high-profile corporate collapses have assisted in enhancing the quality of an audit	33%	34%	42%
responses to high-profile corporate collapses have assisted in adding value to a company's business operations	37%	18%	20%
in your opinion, complying with the additional mandatory procedures will increase the costs of conducting an audit	81%	90%	92%

10.0.2 Inferences from interview findings

Some users took the view that as soon as a crisis emerged in what would otherwise be a free market; the political response was to increase regulation. There was concern about unintended consequences, which could in fact damage what would otherwise be appropriate public policy settings. Some users felt that, broadly, the market would not be well served by a change to the status of auditing standards. With respect to engendering more confidence in the capital market, users suggested that the market would continue to believe that auditors would undertake what they needed to do to form their audit opinion. Others supported this with a belief that the market would not see much impact from the changes. One respondent was somewhat critical of the profession's ability to enforce standards, implying that a high level of regulated enforcement would give rise to a higher-quality outcome. In terms of audit quality, some users praised the current regulatory requirements, suggesting that they provided a floor level of quality. Various users described the present regulatory system as giving rise to audits that were 'standardised', 'consistent', 'unbiased', 'objective', 'comprehensive' and 'methodical'. There seemed to be an implication in the minds of some that these requirements would give rise to higher-quality auditing and they took the view that this would mean that the auditors would be better able to comment on the credibility of financial statements. A few users suggested that the auditor needed to go beyond this and be inquiring and innovative in their understanding of a business and the risks that business faced.

Purchasers were split between whether or not legal enforceability was a positive initiative for the Australian economy. Some purchasers suggested that it could be worthwhile, while others were concerned that legal enforceability would result in auditors withdrawing from offering opinions and judgments and moving to fulfil compliance requirements. One purchaser lamented the loss of intellectual property rights for the profession. This purchaser also observed that the government had no-one to blame but itself and its own processes if and when there was another round of corporate failure. Few purchasers suggested there was a clear increase in confidence in the capital market, and suppliers also shared the scepticism that the market would be any different to that which had preceded it. In terms of audit quality, some purchasers felt that while the audit might not change much of what was done, the current regulatory requirements added considerable robustness to the audit, which might not have been present before. A number of purchasers suggested that, fundamentally, the audit they observed had not changed with recent amendments to regulatory requirements; however, it had driven up costs. Few purchasers were able to identify how the audit had been changed or whether the auditors provided new and valuable insights into the business. Those who were able to make direct comparisons between Australia's current position and the Sarbanes-Oxley legislation in the United States spoke favourably of the Australian position and somewhat harshly of the more prescriptive and compliance-driven US position.

Standard setters took the view that legal enforceability was good because it would give rise to improved quality. One regulator indicated that it would give substance and support and a more clarified approach than had previously been the case.

Users, purchasers and suppliers all acknowledged that costs had risen as a consequence of these changes. For users who were somewhat sceptical of the value-adding capacities of an audit, these added costs only intensified their irritation. Purchasers also acknowledged that costs had risen, but there appeared to be some acceptance of these costs being passed on—at least in part. Suppliers acknowledged increased costs and that in some instances margins had been squeezed. While recognising there was going to be a cost gravitation upwards with respect to legally backed auditing standards, some standard setters commented that this came about because of changes in the international standards, which called for higher levels of documentation. One standard setter also made the observation that the change to legally enforceable auditing standards could in fact substantially increase the threshold costs of becoming an auditor to the corporate sector—thereby limiting competition.

Related to but not directly connected with the increase to operating costs of conducting an audit under the new regulatory environment is the issue of the costs or potential costs to auditors of litigation risk. One regulator took the view that the presence of legally backed auditing standards would change the environment in only a relatively minor way—adding another legal pathway to enhance auditor accountability.

Issue 10.1

Increasingly, prescription of audits is seen to 'distract auditors' from their tasks.

Suggested action 10.1

Evidence should be gathered about whether the regulatory reforms of earlier this decade have been cost beneficial.

11.0 Increasingly prescriptive audits: a distraction for auditors (Chapter 11)

11.0.1 Inferences from survey findings

Respondents were asked: 'In response to high-profile corporate collapses, regulation now requires auditors to comply with additional mandatory audit procedures. In your opinion, complying with the additional mandatory procedures will distract auditors from the objective of a financial statement audit, which is to give assurance on the credibility of financial statements.' Nineteen per cent of users, 27 per cent of purchasers and 37 per cent of suppliers either agreed or strongly agreed.

11.0.2 Inferences from interview findings

Users, purchasers, suppliers, standard setters and regulators were all interviewed with a query about whether the additional audit procedures required as a result of the reforms distracted auditors from the objective of a financial statement audit. Many users felt that the current regulatory requirements had shifted the focus of the auditor away from the need to spend time understanding the business and the risks of the business. Some users took a different perspective, suggesting that the current regulatory requirements were not a distraction and that in fact an audit could be largely irrelevant anyway. Other users praised the current regulatory requirements, suggesting that they provided a floor level of quality. In terms of policy implication, the descriptors used ('standardised', consistent', and so on) by users might represent a necessary but not sufficient condition for there to be a high-value audit that attests or gives assurance to the credibility of financial statements.

Purchasers were also split between those who believed that the current regulatory processes were a distraction and those who believed they were not. Those who were critical of the current proposals suggested that for the audit to be of value it really needed to look at the substance behind the transactions and behind the documentation. Those who believed that regulation was not a distraction tended to share the view of users that the current regulatory requirements were there to ensure an appropriate job was done and that they represented 'demonstrable compliance'.

A number of purchasers suggested that, fundamentally, the audit they observed had not changed with recent amendments to regulatory requirements; however, it had driven up costs. Those who were able to make direct comparisons between Australia's current position and the Sarbanes-Oxley legislation in the United States spoke favourably of the Australian position and somewhat harshly of the more prescriptive and compliance-driven US position.

One purchaser questioned why auditors might find increased documentation requirements a negative development, alluding to an unwillingness to convey their 'true' beliefs. In view of this, when commenting on the increased requirements, auditors and audit firms need to be careful to explain the reasons behind their concerns and not give an incorrect impression of an unwillingness to commit their thoughts to writing. One purchaser observed that the US jurisdiction was very focused on prescription, with a rules-based environment, whereas the United Kingdom was conceptually founded on a principles-based environment. The commentator observed that in Australia, regulatory agencies had gone on to interpret these principles to create guidance, which in turn was interpreted as rules. This is not meant to be a criticism of regulatory agencies because sometimes they create this guidance at the behest of participants in the market to assist them. The commentator also observed, however, that the difficulty with rules was that they could become outdated as circumstances changed or even irrelevant because of environmental changes. The second difficulty with a rules-based regime is that rules can be used as a substitute for good judgment.

Similarly, suppliers were divided between those who believed the current regulatory requirements were a distraction and those who believed that they were an enhancement. Those critical pointed to the ever-increasing time spent on documentation, which had distracted them from committing to understanding the business while clients were reluctant to absorb substantially increased fees. Those who were critical suggested that some audit partners were becoming 'gun-shy' of the possible penalties and that they had to change their approach to being less principles based and reliant on judgment to being much more check-list oriented. Other suppliers suggested a 'heightened regulation risk'. One standard setter observed that the whole debate of rules versus principles was not helpful. Although Australia has come from a background of a principles-based environment, even principles-based standards have included an amount of prescription.

Standard setters see the current regulatory requirements as a useful part of the quality control of an audit and not as a distraction from the real, continuing operation of the audit. They observe that the requirements give rise to demonstrated evidence that a good job has been accomplished. One standard setter observed that although auditors called for audits to be judgment driven and principles based, when interacting within professional bodies, they sought greater 'clarity', which inevitably became something akin to a check list.

Regulators acknowledged that the current requirements could give rise to a loss of focus and audits could indeed become bogged down in some of the tedium. Given the scale of the change in the nature of the work, it has consequences for the working lives of many individuals who might be attracted to and retained within the profession (refer to Chapter 8).

Issue 11.1

There appears to be no agreed minimum documentation requirement between the regulator and auditors. It appears that, by default, PCAOB documentation requirements have been adopted by the Big Four in internationalising their audit processes and applied to PCAOB and non-PCAOB regulated audits alike. In turn, suppliers interviewed advised that they believed that Australian regulators saw this as the minimum and onerous when applied to Big Four and non-Big Four auditors in relation to the bulk of audits inspected.

Suggested action 11.1

Greater dialogue between auditor representatives and regulator representatives should take place.

12.0 The approach, operation and resources of the regulators (Chapter 12)

12.0.1 Inferences from interview findings

Both purchasers and suppliers recognise the need for regulatory inspections and their benefits, which provide quality control and potentially useful information to the capital market—albeit that the regulators' reports tend to highlight negatives only. Nonetheless, purchasers and suppliers were sceptical about the inspection process. One purchaser observed that there was never an opportunity to gain an understanding from working paper files of events as they unfolded in the real world. Purchasers and suppliers provided criticism that inspectors did not have sufficient 'real world' auditing experience and that inspections were limited because of this deficiency.

Supplier members of firms that had been inspected were mixed in their evaluation of the inspections process and some were overtly negative. Those in the non-Big Four observed that the process had been contaminated by inspectors observing resources available to the Big Four and expecting the non-Big Four to operate at the same resource level. There was, in the view of one non-Big Four supplier, a lack of empathy for the fact that they did things differently.

Users, purchasers and standard setters observed that the regulator was inadequately equipped to undertake inspections. One user expressed disappointment that there was a need to obtain greater interaction between practice and regulators and to attain more practical experience for regulators from those in regulatory environments. One purchaser observed that resources assigned to regulators were almost by definition inadequate for fully undertaking the task entrusted to a regulator and that the efficient operation of a regulator was to be selective and strategic about the work undertaken rather than attempting to be comprehensive. This purchaser also noted the beneficial use of secondments and sabbaticals from private sector suppliers into regulators, which was common in the United States but until very recently rare in Australia.

One standard setter observed that audit was in fact an outsourced form of regulation, but there was a potential disconnection between the outcomes of the audit and what the regulator might ultimately wish to be reported. This is not the responsibility of the auditor per se, but suggests a subtle re-engineering of regulatory objectives and outcomes.

It is interesting to observe that while participants in the market have their criticisms of audit documentation requirements, users, purchasers and suppliers and perhaps particularly standard setters all observe that there is a benefit to enhanced levels of documentation.

Issue 12.1

There was evidence of tension and misunderstandings between suppliers and regulators at the time of the interviews. The authors note that current forums such as the Australian Securities and Investments Commission (ASIC) Chairs Committee and various task forces, the Regulatory Discussion Group, APRA's Superannuation National Auditors Consultative Committee (SNACC), ASIC Accounting Liaison meetings, the Research Group and other informal as well as formal meetings and discussions did not all exist at the time.

Suggested action 12.1

Establish a new forum or make more effective existing forums for communication between suppliers and regulators and create wider dissemination of outcomes of those communications to ensure transparency and a comprehensive understanding of these communications by the supply side of the market.

Issue 12.2

It is difficult to encourage communication between suppliers and regulators when there is no peak body for registered company auditors.

Suggested action 12.2

Encourage formation of a peak body for registered company auditors.

Issue 12.3

It is noted that there has since been increased funding to ASIC, but at the time of the interviews several participant stakeholders perceived continuing under-resourcing of ASIC—in monetary and expertise terms.

Suggested Action 12.3

Adequate resourcing of and training in audit related matters of regulatory inspection staff so they hold relevant expertise and experience.

Issue 12.4

There is an alleged 'one-size-fits-all' approach by ASIC to inspections.

Suggested action 12.4

Introduce a more nuanced and informed approach to inspections, which might include engagement with the peak body for registered company auditors.

Issue 12.5

Reports on ASIC inspections tend to focus on negative aspects.

Suggested action 12.5

Introduce a more balanced approach to ASIC reporting on inspections.

13.0 Competition (Chapter 13)

13.0.1 Inferences from survey findings

In response to the assertion that 'for larger companies in Australia, there is a lack of competition in the market for audit services', 57 per cent of users, 52 per cent of purchasers and 55 per cent of suppliers either agreed or strongly agreed. In response to the assertion that 'an external financial statement audit is of value to you because of the brand name of the audit firm', 32 per cent of users, 34 per cent of purchasers and 30 per cent of suppliers either agreed or strongly agreed.

13.0.2 Inferences from interview findings

A significant number of users were concerned that with only four major audit firms there was a lack of competition. Users also observed that for a significant portion of the market, the Big Four were the only potential suppliers and that certain investors sought out and gave preference to global brand names such as the Big Four. One user made the observation that the sheer scale of the Big Four provided opportunities for training and skill development unmatched by the non-Big Four, which created potential dominance and quality-level implications.

Purchasers were more mixed in their views. A positive view was that the quality of the non-Big Four meant that the sector could be turned to for specific advice on certain matters. Other purchasers believed that, for the big end of town, the market was sufficiently competitive and that there was significant competition once one looked beyond the larger ASX-listed companies. One of the more complex observations was that too much competition could drive down quality. Other purchasers suggested that for some services the non-Big Four were stepping up and becoming more competitive. Purchasers noted that at the margin between the Big Four and the non-Big Four there was considerable competition, with the Big Four establishing 'enterprise' or 'middle-market' divisions that competed fiercely with non-Big Four firms. While some purchasers believe that the market encompasses self-correcting mechanisms, other observations suggest the difficulty of another large audit firm developing through natural market forces. One observer suggested nationalisation of the audit industry given the low level of competition. Others observed, however, that much competition existed, particularly at partner rather than firm level, and that the Big Four could move partners around the world.

Several suppliers observed heavy price competition and that tender battles were intense. There are repeated suggestions of tight margins and considerable fee pressures. On the other hand, suppliers recognise that purchasers at the upper end are limited in choice. One supplier commented that competition could be generated where a large listed company might have an inner circle of three of the Big Four in one way or another, but must have one not supplying it. Several suppliers observed that for some clients the market comprised three rather than four large suppliers. Suppliers also recognise that some of the mid-tier firms are moving up and some of the Big Four activity is moving down into smaller audit purchasers. One supplier suggested that the presence of the Big Four with work divisions that catered for middle-market clients effectively created a second brand name of the Big Four, with potentially different standards of quality and cost structure.

Other suppliers indicated that the Big Four competed with consulting firms since divesting their own consulting arms, which meant less work for the Big Four, placing pressure on all parts of the organisation, including on staff retention and the ability to interchange between audit and non-audit work. Some suppliers observed that more competition would mean some firms not having the expertise or skill set to undertake quality audits because of the pressure on recruiting qualified staff. Other suppliers expressed concern that the regulatory environment and the expectations of the standards of quality for audits meant that some suppliers were moving out of the market, thereby lowering competition. A related issue is that increased regulation has meant that the ability of each Big Four firm to differentiate itself on quality terms is limited and in fact the quality differentiation comes at partner level not at firm level. This in turn represents a challenge due to mandated requirements for audit partner rotation.

One standard setter also observed that in the 1980s audit firm fee competition was intense and initiated essentially by the audit firm in order to win consulting activity. Through regulatory change, this is now not possible but there is still considerable price pressure in fees, driven this time by clients rather than audit firms. Their motivation appears to be the desire for cost efficiencies.

There were repeated comments about the moral hazard for regulators should another large firm fail. As economic circumstances adjust with the GFC, the potential moral hazard could be more real—at least in some jurisdictions around the world. One regulator made the observation that the moral hazard problem had already occurred in Asia, where, while one firm was subject to regulatory sanction, sufficient concessions were given such that it continued to trade. The authors observe that despite sometimes intense competition, the majority of purchasers do not currently see financial statement audits as a value-for-money service provided to the market.

Issues 13.1–2

In the unlikely event that there is a failure of one of the Big Four accounting firms, it is probable that there will be adverse effects on the market for audit services and particularly for competition in that market. The continuing viability of these partnerships, however, cannot be observed and there appear to be no contingency plans by those who regulate this market.

Suggested action 13.1

If not already in existence—and although unlikely to be needed—a contingency plan to deal with the threatened failure of one of the Big Four should be established.

Suggested action 13.2

There should be regulatory oversight, perhaps on a confidential basis, of the financial statements of the Big Four accounting firms.

Issue 13.3

There is no single regulatory body responsible for oversight of the 'wellbeing' (for example, number per capita, level of activity, level of maintained competence) of the pool of registered company auditors.

Suggested action 13.3

A body responsible for oversight of the wellbeing (for example, number per capita, level of activity, level of maintained competence) of the pool of registered company auditors should be established. Alternatively, existing mechanisms could be adapted to deal with this matter. As a minimum, continuing registered company auditor accreditation should be dependent on carrying an appropriate amount of professional indemnity cover, complying with minimum annual continuing professional education requirements and subject to appropriate quality review processes.

14.0 Differential auditing standards (Chapter 14)

14.0.1 Inferences from interview findings

The notion of 'differential auditing' causes confusion in the minds of at least some participants and in particular users, who tend to confuse the issue of differential auditing standards with differential mandates. From users, there is a mixed view with regard to the advantages and disadvantages of differential auditing standards. Some of the motivation for the positive view comes from the perception that they will create cost savings. Some users, however, were adamant that they would cause capital market inefficiencies by enhancing the attractiveness of remaining private as opposed to going public. Also, there is concern that differential auditing standards will cause decreased understandability and increased confusion in the capital market.

Purchasers showed little support for differential auditing standards. They note that the criterion of listed versus unlisted is inappropriate, with a size-based criterion seen as more functional. Suppliers describe concern about the ability to effectively communicate what level of assurance is being given. Standard setters were also not supportive of differential auditing standards, although one drew a sharp distinction between differential auditing standards and differential accounting standards and suggested that the debate might be confused because of the intersection of the two. Regulators did provide some support for differential auditing standards. Much of the positive motivation focused on the costliness of obtaining assurance; however, the case against focused on the undesirability of large unlisted businesses being audited to a differential standard.

In summary, there was limited support for differential auditing standards and, if there was to be a discussion around this issue, it should focus on the size-based criterion rather than listed/unlisted.

Issue 14.1

Entities that require what might be called 'micro-audits' often are required by their constitution or by legislation (for example, incorporated associations) to be subject to an audit, when a review would suffice.

Suggested action 14.1

Consider reviewing with a view to amending (often state and territory) legislation so that the term 'review' rather than 'audit' is used—or indeed a choice between both, where appropriate.

15.0 Internal audit (Chapter 15)

15.0.1 Inferences from interview findings

Many users valued internal audit capacity—whether outsourced or inhouse—however, they saw little interaction between the work of external auditors and the role of the internal auditor. Additionally, there seems to be little support for the proposition that users value the internal audit as part of the value of a company. Purchasers do see a relationship between the internal and external audit functions. Purchasers also value internal audit as an important part of risk management. There is scepticism about whether the capital market has a view on the role and value of the internal audit function.

Many suppliers commented that not all clients maintained an internal audit function. Suppliers provide little evidence that external auditors rely on the work of internal auditors, but recognise that boards of directors, audit committees and management value the internal audit function. Standard setters do not support the proposition that external auditors rely on the work of internal auditors. Regulators do see external auditors as placing more reliance on the internal audit function, but they do not recognise that it is perceived as being valuable to the market, probably because its work is not observable to the capital market.

Issue 15.1

Reliance by the external auditor on the internal auditor requires procedures to investigate the competence and level of independence of the internal auditor that tend to negate any efficiencies involved in reliance.

Suggested action 15.1

Consider ways in which external auditor reliance on internal audit can be facilitated. This can emanate from the internal or external audit side of the market.

Issue 15.2

It is difficult for the market to perceive the value of internal audit when present in a company.

Suggested action 15.2

Companies should be encouraged or required to disclose details about the internal audit function, what level it reports to, the type of work it engages in, the number of personnel involved, and so on.

16.0 Other assurance services and reports (Chapter 16)

16.0.1 Inferences from survey findings

Survey responses to questions about whether the external auditor was best placed to provide reports on various forms of non-financial information resulted in the following percentages agreeing or strongly agreeing.

Levels of support for auditor provision of reports on:	Users	Purchasers	Suppliers
presence of material fraud in a company	81%	66%	69%
internal control procedures	80%	79%	81%
integrity of senior executive managers	50%	33%	27%
risk-management approaches of a company	75%	70%	63%
performance of senior executive managers	34%	14%	12%
environmental and corporate sustainability performance	44%	31%	32%
quality of corporate governance	77%	74%	68%
conflicts of interest of directors	74%	74%	53%
senior executive managers' projections	40%	32%	30%
reasonableness of non-financial information	48%	49%	47%

16.0.2 Inferences from interview findings

Users particularly expressed the desirability of reports on material fraud, internal control procedures, risk-management approaches within the auditee, the quality of corporate governance and reports on conflicts of interests of directors, but even then responses were nuanced. Purchasers and suppliers were not so enthusiastic, with positive responses in relation to reports on material fraud, internal control procedures, the quality of corporate governance and risk approaches of the auditee. It was observed that additional assurance around these disclosures might inhibit the provision of enhanced disclosure by directors and/or management. Users expressed scepticism about disclaimers that would accompany these assurances. Purchasers were concerned that they would result in 'second-guessing of the board'. Suppliers were sceptical that purchasers would be prepared to pay for these assurances. Some questioned whether these additional assurance services would be well understood. Standard setters were more positive but suggested the need for universal reporting and a framework within which to report. Regulators were sceptical, questioning whether there was value in these assurance engagements other than in the unrealistic circumstance of provision of real-time assurance, but were more positive with respect to additional assurance around the presence of material fraud. Regarding internal controls, again, more positive than negative views were expressed and suppliers saw a nexus between their current role and the provision of additional assurance around internal controls. Each specific type of potential report received comments, but the most universally disliked report was assurance over the integrity of senior management, which was generally seen as not possible when auditors worked so closely with management.

Issue 16.1

There is demand for assurance on various non-financial information types, much of which falls within a 'risk-management' framework.

Suggested action 16.1

Provide thought leadership by developing subject-specific guidance for assurance on certain types of non-financial information within an overarching framework of 'risk management'.

17.0 Differing levels of audit assurance (Chapter 17)

17.0.1 Inferences from interview findings

Users revealed some confusion about the level of audit assurance but did express a desire for higher levels of audit assurance. Suppliers were less enthusiastic, observing that users were not enthusiastic about even the current audit product, repeatedly describing it as 'a necessary evil' or seeing it as a compliance commodity that was not necessarily high value adding. Additionally, legal liability associated with higher-level assurance was raised. One supplier observed that there could be circumstances in which a lower level of audit assurance might be desired. Some suppliers believed higher levels of assurance were possible but only if privately communicated to directors. Also raised was the prohibitively high cost of higher than existing audit assurance. Generally, standard setters were not positive about differing levels of assurance, expressing that it was a challenge just to communicate adequately the current level of audit assurance. This viewpoint contrasted with that of one regulator, who believed that it was possible to have differential levels of assurance where those differential levels attached to different components of what was communicated to shareholders. In summary, in certain conditions, differential levels of audit assurance might be possible, but there is little enthusiasm for them.

Issue 17.1

The auditing standards constrain the level of assurance to 'reasonable' even when there is client need for something above this level and when the circumstances exist in which it can be delivered.

Suggested action 17.1

Provide a framework whereby higher than 'reasonable' assurance can be given within auditing standards, in circumstances in which there is client demand and an ability to deliver at that higher level. It is acknowledged that this suggestion would mean a departure from the present position of the assurance framework of the IAASB.

Issue 17.2

Agreed-on procedures engagements cannot provide any assurance.

Suggested action 17.2

Consider whether agreed-on procedures engagements should be able to provide a level of assurance. It is acknowledged that this suggestion would mean a departure from the present position of the assurance framework of the IAASB.

18.0 Conclusion

This summary of report chapters provides an overview of the whole report. It is not a substitute for reading the chapters in full in order to examine the issues giving rise to its 53 recommendations. With this number of recommendations, some of which would be relatively easy and quick to implement and others of which need a longer-term view, it might be helpful to consider which recommendations are likely to be of most interest to which set of stakeholders. The table below lists each recommendation and classifies it according to the authors' view of where the interest might lie. The concluding chapter, Chapter 18, includes a table that summarises all of the issues and recommendations and provides the authors' view of which party might best be given responsibility for implementation. It is important not to confuse the table below with author-perceived assigned responsibility, but rather to view it as the authors' attempt to assist stakeholders in focusing on recommendations most pertinent to them.

The reader might also find of assistance content towards the end of Chapter 1, which provides various diagrammatic pathways or 'road maps' to reading this report, contingent on reader interests and motivations.

Table A Summary of expected stakeholder interest in specific recommendations

No.	Recommendation no.	Users	Purchasers	Suppliers	Standard setters	Regulators	Academics	Legislators
1	3.1		√	√		√		
2	3.2			√	√			
3	3.3					√		
4	3.4				√			
5	3.5	√		√	√			
6	3.6				√	√		
7	3.7			√	√	√		
8	4.1	√	√	√	√	√		
9	4.2		√	√	√	√		
10	4.3							√
11	4.4			√		√		
12	5.1		√					
13	5.2		√			√		
14	5.3						√	
15	6.1						√	
16	6.2			√		√		
17	6.3		√	√				

No.	Recommendation no.	Users	Purchasers	Suppliers	Standard setters	Regulators	Academics	Legislators
18	6.4			√				
19	6.5			√				
20	6.6			√				
21	6.7			√	√	√		
22	6.8						√	
23	6.9		√	√		√		
24	7.1						√	
25	7.2						√	
26	7.3			√				
27	7.4			√				
28	8.1			√				
29	8.2			√		√		
30	8.3			√				
31	8.4			√				
32	9.1			√	√	√		
33	9.2			√	√	√		
34	9.3			√				
35	9.4				√	√		

No.	Recommendation no.	Users	Purchasers	Suppliers	Standard setters	Regulators	Academics	Legislators
36	9.5			√		√		
37	9.6			√		√	√	
38	10.1			√		√	√	
39	11.1			√		√		
40	12.1			√	√	√		
41	12.2			√		√		
42	12.3					√		
43	12.4					√		
44	12.5					√		
45	13.1					√		
46	13.2			√		√		
47	13.3			√		√		
48	14.1							√
49	15.1		√	√	√			
50	15.2		√	√		√		
51	16.1			√	√			
52	17.1		√	√	√	√		
53	17.2		√	√	√	√		

LIST OF TABLES

LIST OF ABBREVIATIONS AND ACRONYMS

AASB	Australian Accounting Standards Board
AGM	annual general meeting
AICD	Australian Institute of Company Directors
AIFRS	Australian Equivalents to International Financial Reporting Standards
ANCAAR	Australian National Centre for Audit and Assurance Research
APESB	Australian Professional Ethical Standards Board
APRA	Australian Prudential Regulation Authority
ASIC	Australian Securities and Investments Commission
ASA	Australian Shareholders' Association
ASX	Australian Securities Exchange
AUASB	Auditing and Assurance Standards Board
AQRB	Audit Quality Review Board
CALDB	Companies Auditors and Liquidators Disciplinary Board
CEO	chief executive officer
CFO	chief financial officer
CLERP 9 Act	*Corporate Law Economic Reform Program (Audit Reform and Corporate Disclosure Act (2004)*
CPAA	CPA Australia
FRC	Financial Reporting Council
FSR	Financial Service Regulation
GFC	global financial crisis
IASB	International Accounting Standards Board
IAASB	International Auditing and Assurance Standards Board

ICAA	Institute of Chartered Accountants in Australia
IFRS	International Financial Reporting Standards
IIA	Institute of Internal Auditors
IQP	internal quality process
NIA	National Institute of Accountants
P&L	profit (loss) statement or income statement
PCAOB	Public Company Accounting Oversight Board (United States)
SDM	staff development manager
SEC	Securities Exchange Commission (United States)
SOX	*Sarbanes-Oxley Act 2002* (United States)
UK	United Kingdom
US	United States

DIVISION A

INTRODUCTION AND SUMMARY OF FINDINGS 1

1.0 Introduction

This monograph is the culmination of an extensive project examining the value and future of audit in Australia. The objective of this study is to provide policy advice to key stakeholders in the market for audit services on the current challenges and future opportunities in that market. This advice is informed and enriched by a comprehensive survey of major stakeholder groups in the capital market of their concerns about and expectations of the market for audit services in Australia. The data form the backdrop against which the future directions of the Australian market for audit services are shaped to ensure that audit and audit-related services are of the highest quality and that the credibility of, and confidence in, the market for audit and audit-related services are enhanced.

1.1 Aims and background

The breadth of this project was scoped from the results of a preliminary study of the future of audit in Australia conducted in 2005 as a commissioned report to certain relevant participants. The preliminary study facilitated the identification of broad questions and issues, which were then pursued in greater depth in the current project, utilising a larger sample size and wider geographical dispersion.

In September 2007, the Australian National Centre for Audit and Assurance Research (ANCAAR) hosted the Future of Audit Symposium at Parliament House, Canberra. The purpose of this symposium was to communicate preliminary results from the survey and to use the results as a basis to encourage further discussion, thus supplementing the richness of the data set through additional insights from different stakeholders' perspectives.

This project has received the support of the Australian Research Council (ARC) through an ARC Linkage Grant. Additional support has been provided by industry partners, the Institute of Chartered Accountants in Australia, CPA Australia, Deloitte, Ernst & Young, KPMG and PriceWaterhouseCoopers.

1.2 Research method

This project utilised a mixed-method research design (comprising focus groups, telephone and postal surveys and in-depth interviews) to capture qualitative and quantitative data. By drawing on the strengths of the various data-collection methods, methodological triangulation facilitated the unravelling of dynamic and complex issues.

Focus groups are particularly useful to explore and generate ideas and issues through group interactions. The nature of the focus groups, however, presents limited opportunity to probe issues in greater detail. In-depth interviews, on the other hand, provide a source of data richness, as the researcher is able to probe further into the complexity of issues. The personal interaction that is required, however, restricts the number of interviews that can be conducted within a reasonable time frame. The strength of telephone and postal surveys lies in their capacity to reach a large sample of participants across diverse geographical locations. Surveys are, however, restricted in the extent to which issues that are raised can be explored. By drawing on the strengths of each technique, this mix of methods was the most efficient and cost-effective means of collecting a wide range of responses yet provided a rich and meaningful context within which to tease out and analyse underlying issues related to the value and future of auditing in Australia.

Views were canvassed from a wide cross-section of key stakeholders, representing the supply and demand sides of the market for audit services. Specifically, the project sought participation from the following major stakeholder groups:

- users of audit reports, including
  - users with accounting expertise (for example, accounting professionals)
  - professional (for example, financial advisors, financial planners, lenders, analysts, investment managers, stockbrokers)
  - private investors

- purchasers of audit and assurance services, including
  - directors and audit committee members
  - management (CEOs and CFOs)
- suppliers of audit and assurance services
  - Big Four
  - non-Big Four
- standard setters
- regulators of audit services.

1.3 Issues considered

This project covered a broad-ranging set of questions, enlarging on the themes identified in the 2005 preliminary study and incorporating themes of particular interest to the industry partners. Given this, the guidelines set at the inception of this project centred on: the expectations gap; business acumen; corporate law reforms; and the risks faced by suppliers and users. Specific issues within these broad themes unfolded during the course of the project, including:

- the value placed on the audit product
- understandability of the audit product
- expected deliverables from an audit compared with real deliverables
- the adequacy of communications surrounding auditors' work and processes
- auditors' use of 'materiality' and stakeholders' interpretation of that concept
- attracting, supporting and retaining quality staff in the audit profession
- development by audit personnel of business acumen and client and industry knowledge
- auditor independence issues involving auditor-provided non-audit services and audit partner rotation
- competition in the market for audit services
- the costs and benefits of the new regulatory regime for auditing introduced after the high-profile corporate collapses earlier this decade, including
  - awareness and understanding of the reforms
  - impacts of the reforms on financial statement credibility
  - costs
  - risk of being a distraction to the auditor
  - regulatory processes for monitoring and enforcement.

In addition, some other matters were addressed, including:

- the case for and against differential auditing standards
- the value of internal audit and the external auditor's reliance on it
- the case for and against provision of assurance on certain financial and non-financial information, not commonly subject to audit or review
- the case for and against provision of levels of assurance beyond currently sanctioned levels.

Each of the above issues is examined in the chapters that follow. Examination of some issues involves survey questions as well as interviews, whereas others involve interviews only. Focus group interviews with more junior auditors were incorporated for specific issues. In all cases where there were interviews, the stakeholder groups included users, purchasers (management and board), suppliers (Big Four and non-Big Four), standard setters and regulators.

1.4 Structure of this report

This report comprises eight divisions including this introductory one. The seven further divisions are: B) expectations and understandability; C) competency and expertise; D) independence; E) regulation; F) the market for assurance services; G) other issues; and H) concluding remarks.

Division B (expectations and understandability), comprises:

- Chapter 3: Understanding of the audit and perceptions of the deliverables
- Chapter 4: Communication
- Chapter 5: Understanding of materiality.

Division C (competency and expertise) comprises:

- Chapter 6: Developing business acumen and client and industry knowledge
- Chapter 7: Attracting and supporting staff
- Chapter 8: Retention of staff.

Division D (independence) comprises:

- Chapter 9: Auditor independence (which discusses auditor-provided non-audit services and audit partner rotation).

Division E (regulation) comprises:

- Chapter 10: Regulatory reforms to audit—their impacts
- Chapter 11: Increasingly prescriptive audits—a distraction for auditors?
- Chapter 12: The approach, operation and resources of regulators.

Division F (the market for assurance services) comprises:

- Chapter 13: Competition.

Division G (other issues) comprises:

- Chapter 14: Differential auditing standards
- Chapter 15: Internal audit
- Chapter 16: Other assurance services
- Chapter 17: Differing levels of assurance.

Division H (concluding remarks) comprises:

- Chapter 18: Conclusions and recommendations.

Since it is likely that different readers will be more interested in some topics included in this report than in others, the next few pages describe different pathways to reading the document that might be helpful in creating a road map to the topics and pertinent recommendations. Since the topics are interrelated and hence so are many of the recommendations, the following diagrams represent but a few ways in which the document can be dissected.

1.6 Road maps to reading this document

Topic orientation 1

Of course, interest in specific topics lies in the eyes of the beholder, but the first road map presented suggests dissection of the report into communication, technical, staffing and societal issues and suggests in the figure below the relevant chapters and recommendations to read under each issue.

Figure 1.1 Road map 1: topic orientation

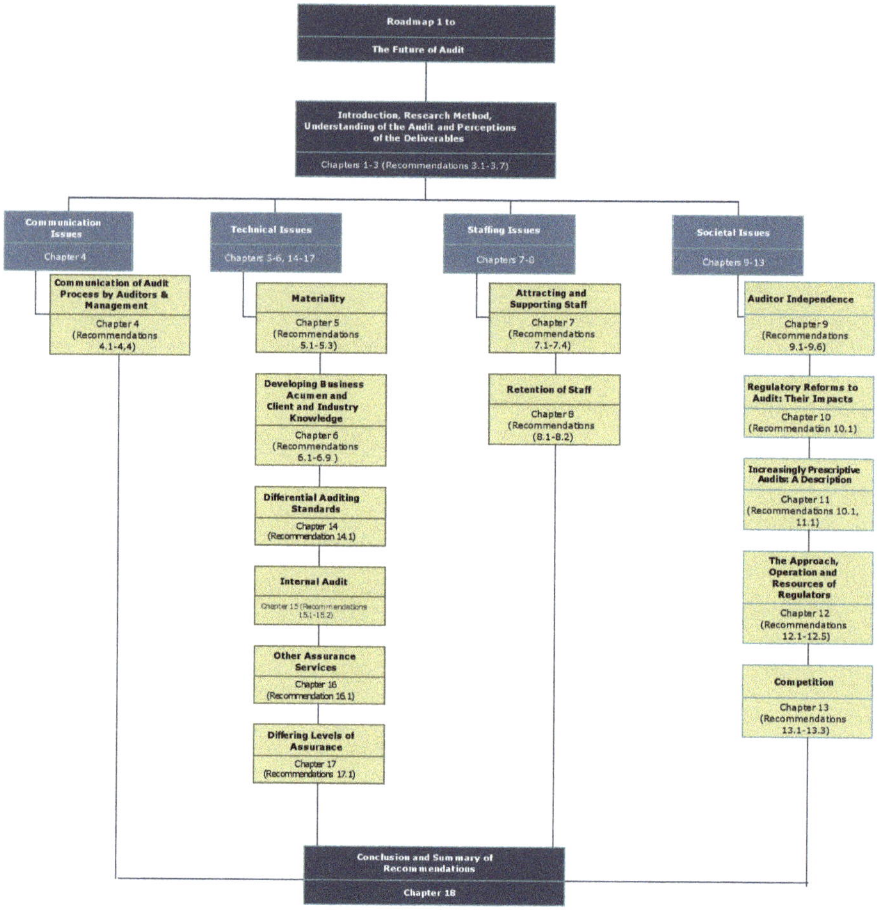

Topic orientation 2

The second suggested road map dissects the report into expectations gap/ education, materiality, staffing, independence, regulation and assurance on other than financial report issues, and suggests relevant chapters and recommendations under each topic.

Figure 1.2 Road map 2: topic orientation

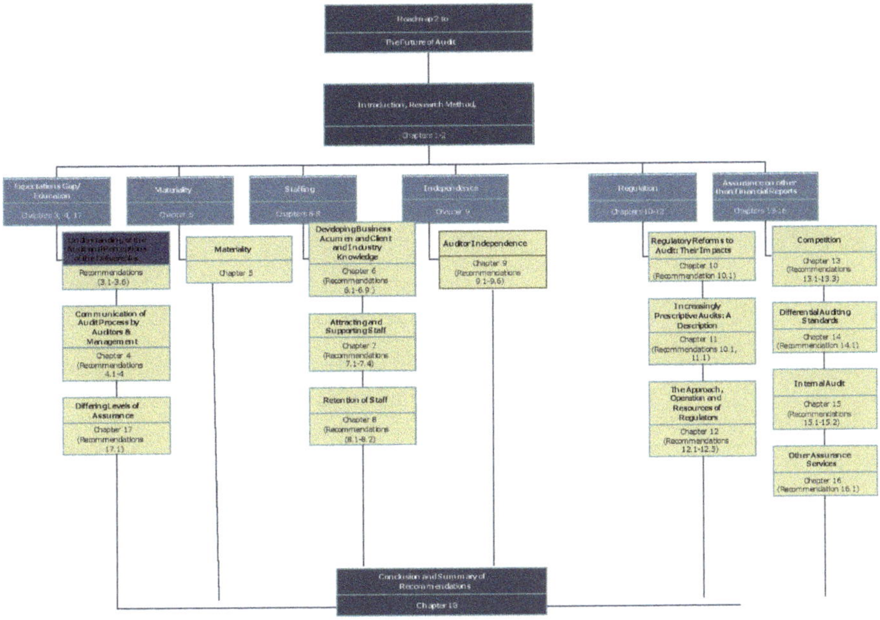

Topic orientation 3

The third suggested road map to reading this report takes a stakeholder approach and suggests the chapters that might be of interest to users, purchasers, suppliers, standard setters and regulators.

Also of assistance in reading this report might be the summary of expected stakeholder interest in the recommendations, which appears at the end of the executive summary.

Chapter 2 concludes Division A. It discusses the research method used in this study.

Figure 1.3 Road map 3: stakeholder orientation

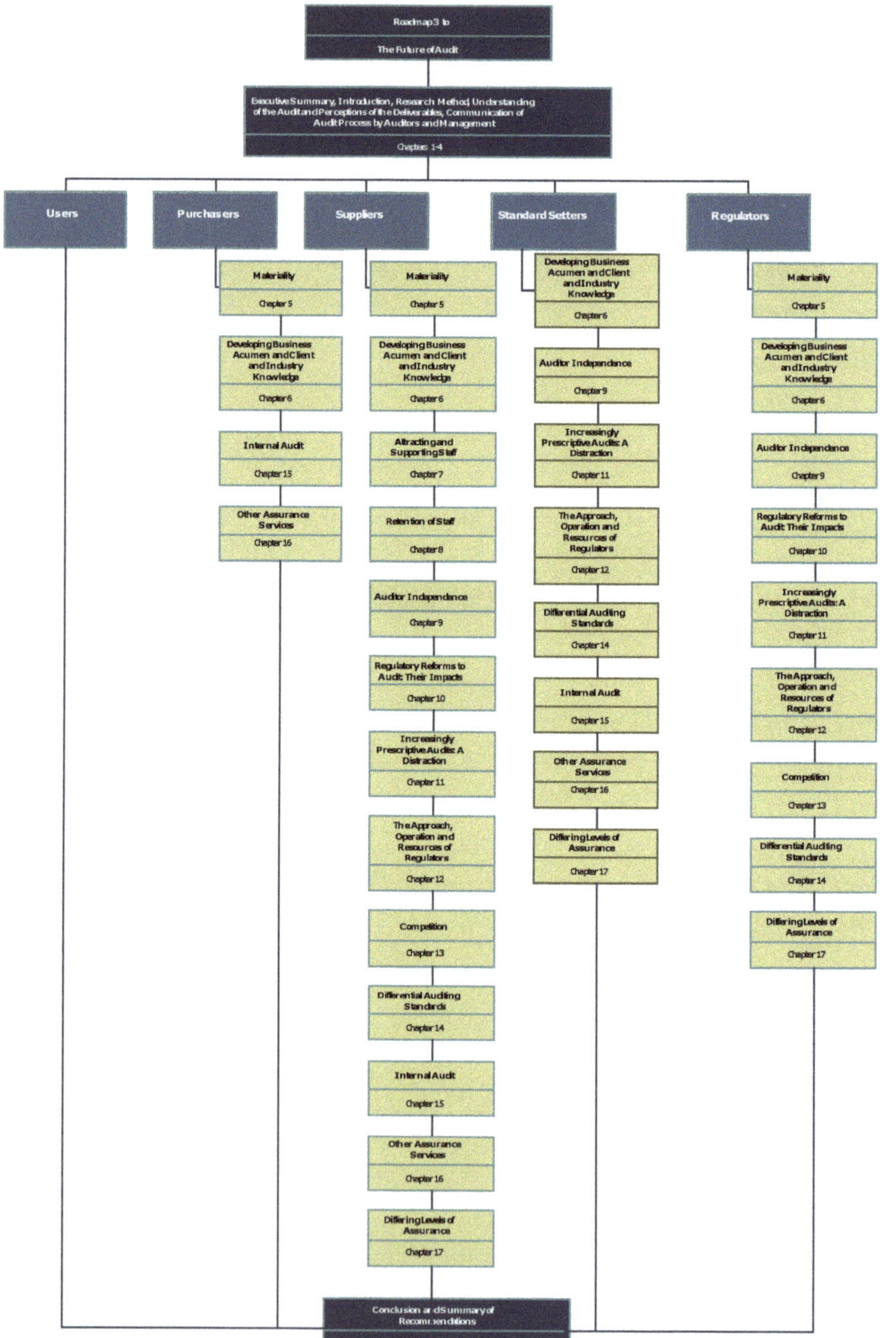

RESEARCH METHOD 2

1.0 Introduction

This study uses multiple methods to derive data in order to extract the richness of the experience of those whose working lives are connected in some way with the market for audit services and the audit product. Surveys, focus group interviews and face-to-face interviews are the methodologies employed to gather the data that are then analysed using various techniques—quantitative and qualitative.

1.1 Sample

To reflect as wide a range of opinions as possible, this project sought the participation of representatives of key stakeholder groups from the supply and demand sides of the market for audit services, encompassing: users of audit reports (for example, financial advisors, financial planners, lenders, analysts, investment managers, stockbrokers and private investors); purchasers of audit and assurance services (for example, management, directors and audit committee members); suppliers, representing the Big Four and non-Big Four firms; and regulators.

Participants were drawn primarily from the following sources: nominees from the industry partners, purchased databases, data collected from the *Connect 4* database and professional association membership lists. In total, 7296 records were purchased from the Fairfax and Accountable List Brokers' databases, covering finance professionals, chief executive officers and directors. An additional 2530 records on directors and audit committee members of listed companies were collected by the researchers using *Connect 4*. We also approached relevant professional associations for their assistance in securing the participation of their membership. Participating professional associations were: the Institute of Chartered Accountants in Australia, CPA Australia, Australian Shareholders' Association, Financial

Planners Association of Australia Limited, Securities and Derivatives Industry Association, the Association of Financial Advisors Limited, Australian Bankers' Association, Group 100, Australian Securities Exchange and the Financial Services Institute of Australasia. Typically, these professional associations contacted their membership on our behalf to participate in interviews or surveys.

As different sources were accessed, it was expected that there would be overlapping listings, as it was likely that stakeholders would belong to more than one group.

While effort was made to reduce the possibility of multiple listings, privacy legislation prevented us from eliminating overlapping listings. We also encountered difficulties in recruiting participants. There was reticence to participate in this project, with many of those contacted declining the opportunity to participate. The extent of our difficulties is clearly evidenced by the numbers reported in the following sections.

1.2 Research design

Data for this project were collected using a mixed-method approach, combining focus groups, telephone and postal surveys and in-depth interviews. The advantages of methodological triangulation were outlined in the previous section. These three techniques were conducted in four phases, using the strengths of each technique to build an understanding of the issues.

Table 2.1 Four phases of the study

Phase	Technique
Phase 1: July – November 2006	Focus groups
Phase 2: December 2006 – February 2007	In-depth interviews (pre-survey)
Phase 3: April – May 2007	Mail and telephone survey
Phase 4: May – November 2007	In-depth interviews (post-survey) and focus groups of junior auditors

The project was sequenced in this way to first allow the scoping of the project in the Phase 1 focus groups. While the broad themes had been identified at the inception of this project (that is, the expectations gap, business acumen, company law reforms and risks faced by suppliers and users), the focus groups provided the setting to explore issues of concern and to generate ideas within these broad themes. Since focus groups do not provide much opportunity to probe issues, in-depth interviews were also conducted (Phase 2) to develop a better understanding of the issues. To ascertain the views and concerns of a wider cross-section of stakeholders, mail and telephone surveys were conducted (Phase 3). Finally, as a culmination to the data-collection process, we allocated the opportunity for additional in-depth interviews and focus groups to consolidate the findings of the earlier phases.

The following sections outline the scope of the questions and the type of participants in the focus groups, in-depth interviews and survey.

1.3 Focus groups

Scope of questions

Phase 1 focus group participants were asked to consider three broad questions relating to:

- audit services
- the audit expectations gap
- the risks faced by suppliers and users.

The specific questions used as a starting point for discussion were:

- 'What types of audit or audit-related services are wanted by shareholders and management to enhance the credibility of financial statements?'
- 'Are there other audit or audit-related services that are wanted by shareholders and management?'
- 'Do you believe a gap in expectations still exists? If so, in what areas and among which groups?'
- 'Can the gap be closed? Does it need to be closed? What are the mechanisms that can help to manage expectations or narrow the gap?'
- 'What are the major risks faced by: i) audit suppliers, and ii) other participants in the market for audit services (for example, users, preparers)?'

Each session was approximately 1.5 hours in duration, and different approaches were used to elicit responses from participants, including individual assessment and group discussion. These procedures facilitated the identification of relevant issues, which were then developed and pursued further during the interviews and in the survey.

The purpose of Phase 4 focus groups was to glean the opinions of auditors of their perceptions of staffing issues and industry and client knowledge. The inclusion of junior auditors in this project is significant as these individuals provide the cornerstone of the future of auditing in Australia, and their views on the attraction and retention of quality audit staff are important. These auditors are also in direct interaction with audit clients and can therefore provide insights into the day-to-day auditor–client working relationship. The following questions were used to facilitate discussion with the junior auditors.

- 'How is it that you came to be employed at your current firm?'
- 'What are the factors that cause you to stay employed at this firm?'
- 'Do you personally know anyone who has left the employ of this firm? If so, what factors caused them to leave the employ of this firm?'
- 'Are you thinking about leaving the employ of this firm? If so, what are the factors that led to this thinking?'
- 'What factors are key to an audit firm retaining your employment?'
- 'Does your firm seek to retail all employees? If so, how do they do it? If not, why not?'
- 'Do you think it is important to have client knowledge in completing a quality audit?'
- 'How do you gain that client knowledge?'
- 'Are there any other ways to gain this knowledge not utilised by your firm?'
- 'In terms of your learning about client-specific issues through interactions with clients, can you share some of your experiences (both good and bad) or relate any examples?'
- 'Do you think it is important to have industry expertise (for example, in banking, media, marketing)?'
- 'How do you gain that industry expertise?'
- 'Are there any other ways to gain this expertise not presently used by this firm?'

Where permission was received from the focus groups, the sessions were tape-recorded and transcribed for analysis.

1.3.2 Participants

Phase 1 focus group participants were drawn primarily from the nominees provided by the industry partners and the databases. Five focus group sessions were held: two in Sydney, two in Melbourne and one in Brisbane. It was also planned to conduct one focus group session in Perth, but difficulties were experienced in obtaining a sufficient number of participants within a reasonable time frame. In total, there were 23 participants, though the numbers of participants in each session varied. The difficulty experienced in securing participation, however, was evidenced by the number of contacts that had to be made to secure these 23 participants. One hundred and twenty contacts were made, which reflected initial contact and follow-ups. Details of the focus group participants are provided in Table 2.2.

Table 2.2 Phase 1 focus group participants

		Stakeholder groups		
Location (no. of sessions)	**Total no. of attendees**	**Users**	**Purchasers**	**Suppliers**
Sydney (2)	10	8	1	1
Melbourne (2)	10	5	2	3
Brisbane (1)	3	0	2	1
Total	23	13	5	5

Phase 4 focus groups comprised junior auditors drawn from Big Four firms. Three sessions were held—two in Melbourne and one in Sydney. In total, 25 junior auditors participated in these sessions.

Table 2.3 Phase 4 junior auditor focus group participants

		Stakeholder group
Location (no. of sessions)	**Total no. of attendees**	**Suppliers (junior auditors)**
Sydney (1)	10	1
Melbourne (2)	15	2
Total	25	3

1.4 Interviews

1.4.1 Scope of questions

The interviews provided an opportunity to probe issues in more depth. In total, 58 interviews were conducted, providing 'richness' to the data that could not be accomplished solely through questionnaires and focus groups. Each interview was approximately one hour in duration. This time limit was set partly to provide scheduling certainty to the potential interviewees—all with limited time to devote to such a commitment—and partly to minimise fatigue for interviewers and interviewees. Given the volume of interviews to be covered, the interviews were staggered across two broad periods: December 2006 – February 2007 and May 2007 – August 2007. Spreading the interviews over time also facilitated the opportunity to refine questions as new ideas or issues came to light. Given the time constraint for the interviews and our aim to probe issues in depth, it was also necessary to be conservative in terms of the number of questions that could be asked. Hence, once we believed that we were in receipt of consistently similar responses for a question, the question was replaced. This facilitated greater circulation of a broader range of questions within a limited time frame, but did eliminate quantification of the percentage of interviewees whose responses to a particular question fell into particular categories (for example, agreement/disagreement) and any scope for statistical analysis of interviewee responses. Some questions were, however, maintained consistently across the periods.

The questions asked in the interviews were broadly classified as being about: expectations gap, law reform, business acumen and risks. The following are questions representative of those asked during the interviews.

- Materiality drives the levels of work external auditors have to do and affects the assessments they make. Given that potentially many shareholders do not understand the concept of materiality, should this be a concern for the accounting profession? Can you suggest ways to address this concern?
- To what extent, if at all, do auditors and regulators have different perspectives on how financial statement audits should be conducted? If there is a gap, what is its nature? If this gap is a problem, what changes need to be made?
- In your view, do external auditors have sufficient knowledge of their clients' business and operations? If this is an area of concern to you, can you identify ways in which it could be addressed?
- To what extent, if at all, do you agree that the current required regulatory processes and procedures distract external auditors from the objective of the audit, which is to give reasonable assurance of the credibility of financial statements?
- To what extent, if at all, is there sufficient competition in the market for quality audit services?
- To what extent, if at all, is attracting and retaining high-quality staff a concern for the auditing profession?

Where permission was received from participants, interviews were tape-recorded. The responses to the interview questions were analysed using content analysis techniques.

1.4.2 Participants

The participants were drawn from the nominees provided by the industry partner, the databases and the professional associations' membership. Three hundred and thirty-two initial and follow-up contacts were made, giving rise to 58 participants. Interviews were conducted in Perth, Brisbane, Sydney and Melbourne. Details of the interview participants are provided in Table 2.4.

Table 2.4 Interview participants

		Stakeholder groups			
Time	**Total**	**Users**	**Purchasers**	**Suppliers**	**Regulators**
December 2006 – February 2007	18	8	3	4	3
May 2007 – August 2007	40	7	15	15	3
Total	58	15	18	19	6

Interview data from the focus groups and the face-to-face interviews were analysed using a qualitative software package, *Nvivo 7*.

1.5 Surveys

1.5.1 Scope of questions

A questionnaire was used to garner the views of a wide section of stakeholders. The instrument comprised more than 50 questions. Section A of the instrument asked respondents to indicate the stakeholder group to which they belonged. Section B asked questions covering:

- the scope and value of external financial audits:
  - in this section, respondents were provided with a range of services that might be provided by auditors and asked whether they perceived that each service would be best provided by auditors and whether the value of the service warranted an additional fee. Respondents were also given the opportunity to list additional services. This section also asked respondents a series of statements pertaining to expectations about the external financial statement audit, including expectations about the assurance that the audit

provided, auditors' responsibilities, the aspects of an audit that provided value and the complexity of audited financial statements, notes and the audit report. Respondents were asked to rate their level of agreement or disagreement for each statement, using a five-point Likert scale.

- perceptions of business acumen:
  - respondents were asked to rate their perception of the business acumen of audit partners and also of junior auditors on a five-point scale, ranging from 1 (poor) to 5 (excellent). In addition, respondents were asked to rate how confident they were that an auditor would detect all material fraud and also all material errors. Respondents were asked to provide a numerical percentage for these two questions.
- the legal and regulatory environment for audit services:
  - in this section, respondents were asked their perceptions of the effect of regulatory and market changes on a series of items, such as improving the credibility of financial statements, enhancing the quality of audits, reducing the number of corporate failures and adding value to a company's business operations. Again, a five-point Likert scale was used to capture responses. As not all respondents would necessarily have been aware of the regulatory changes, respondents were also asked to indicate whether they were aware of: i) the introduction of legally enforceable auditing standards in Australia; and ii) the reforms pertaining to auditor independence.
- general questions relating to the provision of audit services:
  - these general questions asked respondents whether they perceived that external financial statement audits represented value for money, and whether there was a lack of competition in the market for audit services. Two open-ended questions were included to gain insights into the future directions of auditing in Australia. Respondents were also provided with an opportunity to comment on the issues that they believed the audit profession had to address to ensure that auditing was highly valuable and to comment on the way audit services were provided and regulated in the future.

Respondents were also asked a series of biographical questions, which were captured in Section C. A copy of the questionnaire is provided in the Appendix to this report. The questions were largely mirrored in the telephone survey.

1.5.2 Participants

The sample for the mail survey was drawn from the professional associations and the databases. Mail questionnaires were sent to 19 300 stakeholders. Of these, 335 questionnaires were returned to sender for various reasons, including wrong addressee details and the person no longer worked there. A total of 1202 completed questionnaires were returned, but 37 did not indicate the stakeholder group to which they belonged. Given the likelihood that stakeholders could appear on more than one listing, our introduction letter to respondents apologised for the duplication of requests that they might receive and instructed them to respond only once. We also relied on the professional associations to distribute the questionnaires to their membership, and therefore the timing of distribution was beyond our control. As the distribution of questionnaires would be done at different times, we could not reliably examine for non-response bias.

The sample for the telephone survey was drawn from nominees from the industry partners and the databases. The conduct of the telephone survey was outsourced to a social and market research firm with the expertise and resources to cater for the number of telephone calls. A sample of 3616 names and contact details was provided to the firm. When contacted, approximately 36 per cent of the sample did not wish to participate. Due to other reasons (for example, difficulties in contacting individuals, wrong numbers), the telephone survey resulted in 350 responses.

Table 2.5 provides details of the participants in the mail survey and telephone survey.

The difference in the mix of stakeholder groups between the telephone survey and the mail survey is not unexpected given that the telephone survey sample relied primarily on the databases, which contained more finance professionals and directors.

Table 2.5 Survey participants

		Stakeholder groups		
Survey	**Total**	**Users**	**Purchasers**	**Suppliers**
Mail	1165	769	204	192
Telephone	350	171	164	15
Total	1515	940	368	207

Despite this differing proportion of representation between the telephone and mail surveys, the majority of respondents came from users (62 per cent), with almost one-quarter of all responses from purchasers (24 per cent) and 14 per cent from suppliers to the market for audit services (Table 2.6). In all, more than 1500 people provided positive responses, suggesting there was considerable penetration into the market for audit services via the various survey techniques. As indicated, in addition to these telephone and mail respondents were those involved in focus groups and in one-on-one interviews.

Table 2.6 Number and proportion of total responses

		Number	Percentage
1	Users	940	62
2	Purchasers	368	24
3	Suppliers	207	14
	Total	1515	

1.5.3 Focus groups with junior auditors

During the initial focus groups, it became clear that it would be valuable to explore some issues with early recruits to the profession. For this purpose, peer groups of early recruits from three of the Big Four firms were made available through the auspices of the professional bodies partnering in this ARC linkage project. From the first Big Four firm, 10 suitable staff made themselves available; from the second Big Four firm, seven suitable staff made themselves available; and from the third Big Four firm, eight suitable staff made themselves available. A single focus group interview was conducted at each of the three Big Four firms' premises with these more junior auditor cohorts.

1.5.4 Biographical descriptive data

With respect to the large group of users, a substantial portion of them (approximately one-third) described themselves as private investors, while approximately one-quarter of the total represented users who were involved in advising or managing investment portfolios and might be considered as professional rather than retail investors. The members of a final large group of users categorised themselves as accounting professionals and differentiated themselves from financial advisors or analysts.

The private investors group represents what has been argued in the literature as generally those who are less sophisticated, whereas the other two groups might be regarded as more informed or expert.

Table 2.7 Number and proportion of user responses

	Users	Number	Percentage of total responses	Percentage of user responses
1	Accounting professional and other	388	26	41
2	Financial advisor, analyst, lender, planner, investment manager and stockbroker	237	16	25
3	Private investor	315	21	34
	Total	940	63	100

In regard to the responses from purchasers, approximately half were either the CEO or CFO of a listed company, with a little less than one-third of the responses from audit committee members or directors of the company. The remaining 19 per cent were other purchasers, who were typically members of the senior management of companies. This group, therefore, represented senior management and director-type individuals with decision perspectives reflecting those positions (Table 2.8).

Table 2.8 Number and proportion of purchaser responses

	Purchasers	Number	Percentage of total responses	Percentage of purchaser responses
1	Audit committee member or company director	111	7	30
2	CEO or CFO	186	12	51
3	Other	71	5	19
	Total	368	24	100

In all, with respect to the suppliers to the market of audit services, there were more than 200 responses. The majority of these came from the non-Big Four suppliers and were drawn principally from membership lists provided by two of the sponsoring organisations—the Institute of Chartered Accountants in Australia and CPA Australia. Privacy requirements were observed in the handling of these lists. Approximately 20 per cent of the responses came from the Big Four suppliers. As will be indicated later, there are some notable differences in responses to certain questions between these two groups of suppliers to the market for audit services.

Table 2.9 Number and proportion of supplier responses

	Suppliers	Number	Percentage of total responses	Percentage of supplier responses
1	Auditor (Big Four)	44	3	21
2	Auditor (non-Big Four)	163	10	79
	Total	207	14*	100

* Rounding error

1.5.5 Focus groups with junior auditors

All of the more junior auditor peer focus group members were currently working in audit in roles ranging from senior accountants to assistant managers. The average time with their firms was approximately three years, but ranged from one to six years, with the range for working in audit specifically ranging from one to five years.

1.5.6 Reading of and reliance on financial statements

With respect to the reading of and reliance on financial statements by users, the majority agreed with the proposition that they read annual reports and audited financial statements (Table 2.10). This was so even when the respondents were private investors. The extent of the reading of financial statements did, however, potentially reflect the research methodology used, which would have been biased in favour of sampling from those users who were more rather than less interested in financial statements. This is so because the lists from which potential participants are drawn come from within the business community, including professional accounting bodies.

Given this possible bias in the sample selection, it is interesting to note that there is some consistency in a relatively low professed reliance on or usage of audited financial statements for decision making. On average, approximately half of users indicated such reliance or usage.

With respect to purchasers, the level of reading of audited financial statements was high; indeed, the responses suggested near universal agreement. The level of reliance was also high, particularly among audit committee members and company directors.

With respect to suppliers, again, there was a high level of reading of audited financial statements, but a lower level of reliance or usage, with a particularly low level reported from non-Big Four suppliers.

Table 2.10 Responses on reading and reliance of financial statements

A. users' responses by subgroup (per cent)

Statements	Total users		Accounting professionals and other		Advisors, and so on		Private investors	
	No	Yes	No	Yes	No	Yes	No	Yes
Do you read annual reports and audited financial statements?	12	88	13	87	14	86	9	91
Do you use or rely on audited financial statements in your decision making?	47	53	52	48	46	54	41	59

B. Purchasers' responses by subgroup (per cent)

Statements	Total purchasers		Audit committee and directors		CEO/CFO		Other	
	No	Yes	No	Yes	No	Yes	No	Yes
Do you read annual reports and audited financial statements?	5	95	4	96	4	96	9	91
Do you use or rely on audited financial statements in your decision making?	38	62	30	70	41	59	43	56

C. Suppliers' responses by subgroup: firm size (per cent)

Statements	Total suppliers		Big Four		Non-Big Four	
	No	Yes	No	Yes	No	Yes
Do you read annual reports and audited financial statements?	6	94	7	93	6	94
Do you use or rely on audited financial statements in your decision making?	57	43	42	58	61	39

1.5.7 Demographic information with respect to respondents

With respect to age groups (refer to Table 2.11), the median age of respondents for users and purchasers was in the forty-five to fifty-four year old age bracket and this was true for those who professed to holding accounting qualifications or were professional users of financial statements. Private investors were typically older, with more than half of these respondents sixty-five years or older.

The median age of audit committee members and directors was also somewhat older, at fifty-five to sixty-four years, with CEOs/CFOs typically forty-five to fifty-four years old. Suppliers were typically younger, with the median age of all suppliers being thirty-five to forty-four years. The younger age group was particularly noticeable among the Big Four suppliers (see Table 2.11).

Table 2.11 Age demographic by respondent category: users' age bracket by category of decision perspective and by accounting credentials

Statement	Total users (%)							Accounting professionals and other (%)							Advisors and so on (%)							Private investors (%)						
	18–24	25–34	35–44	45–54	55–64	65–74	75+	18–24	25–34	35–44	45–54	55–64	65–74	75+	18–24	25–34	35–44	45–54	55–64	65–74	75+	18–24	25–34	35–44	45–54	55–64	65–74	75+
To which of the following age brackets do you belong?	1	14	18	20	23	15	9	2	23	27	26	14	7	1	1	12	23	23	32	5	4	0.5	3	5	11	27.5	31	22

Purchasers' age bracket by category of decision perspective

Statement	Total purchasers (%)							Auditing committee and directors (%)							CEO/CFO (%)							Other (%)						
	18–24	25–34	35–44	45–54	55–64	65–74	75+	18–24	25–34	35–44	45–54	55–64	65–74	75+	18–24	25–34	35–44	45–54	55–64	65–74	75+	18–24	25–34	35–44	45–54	55–64	65–74	75+
To which of the following age brackets do you belong?	1	9	26	29	27	6	2	0	3	10	22	45	15	5	0	7	33	33	24	2	1	4	23	34	29	6	1	3

Suppliers' age bracket by firm size

Statement	Total suppliers (%)							Big Four (%)							Non-Big Four (%)						
	18 – 24	25 – 34	35 – 44	45 – 54	55 – 64	65 – 74	75 +	18 – 24	25 – 34	35 – 44	45 – 54	55 – 64	65 – 74	75 +	18 – 24	25 – 34	35 – 44	45 – 54	55 – 64	65 – 74	75 +
To which of the following age brackets do you belong?	1	26	26	23	18	5	1	0	46	27	18	9	0	0	1	22	26	24	20	6	1

1.5.8 Educational credentials of respondents

With respect to the educational background of respondents in the telephone and mail questionnaire survey, not unsurprisingly, a substantial proportion of all users were university or college educated, with almost 80 per cent professing to have at least an undergraduate qualification (see Table 2.12). Again, this could be reflective of the sampling technique used in the study so that a disproportionate number of responses came from well-educated respondents. This same pattern is also true of purchasers, where again almost 90 per cent of all purchasers indicated that they held at least an undergraduate degree and more than half of the purchasers indicated that they held a postgraduate qualification. This was true also for the sub-categories of audit committee members and directors of companies and the CEOs/CFOs.

Similarly, suppliers in the market for audit services also possessed significant qualifications, with almost 90 per cent of suppliers claiming to hold at least an undergraduate degree. There was a marked distinction between Big Four and non-Big Four respondents, with very few Big Four respondents holding a postgraduate qualification (as distinct from a professional designation) and well more than half holding an undergraduate degree. With respect to the non-Big Four, the existence of postgraduate qualifications was more common. Overall, a very high level of qualifications was shown for suppliers in the market for audit services.

Table 2.12 Educational qualifications of respondents: users' educational credentials by category of decision perspective and by accounting credentials

Statement	Total users (%)						Accounting professionals and other (%)						Advisors and so on (%)						Private investors (%)					
	<10	10 – 13	TAFE	UG	PG	O	<10	10 – 13	TAFE	UG	PG	O	<10	10 – 13	TAFE	UG	PG	O	<10	10 – 13	TAFE	UG	PG	O
What is the highest level of education you have obtained?	1	6	9	37	41	6	1	3	5	37	48	6	1	5	9	41	34	10	0.5	9	13	35.5	36	6

Purchasers' educational credentials by category of decision perspective

Statement	Total purchasers (%)						Audit committee and directors (%)						CEO/CFO (%)						Other (%)					
	<10	10 – 13	TAFE	UG	PG	O	<10	10 – 13	TAFE	UG	PG	O	<10	10 – 13	TAFE	UG	PG	O	<10	10 – 13	TAFE	UG	PG	O
What is the highest level of education you have obtained?	1	3	4	35	53	4	1	4	8	33	50	4	0.5	3	0.5	37	55	4	1	3	6	30	55	5

Suppliers' educational credentials by firm size

Statement	Total suppliers (%)						Big Four (%)						Non-Big Four (%)					
	<10	10–13	TAFE	UG	PG	O	<10	10–13	TAFE	UG	PG	O	<10	10–13	TAFE	UG	PG	O
What is the highest level of education you have obtained?	0	2	1	36	52	9	0	2	39	55	4	0	0	3	1	35	51	10

<10: less than Year 10
10–13: Years 10–13
TAFE: TAFE or equivalent
UG: undergraduate degree
PG: postgraduate degree
O: other

1.5.9 Conclusion

The sample of respondents used in the research was drawn broadly from three groups: the initial focus groups were purposely sampled individuals; the in-depth interviews (both pre-survey and post-survey) were purposely sampled from individuals expert in the market for audit services, including purchasers, users and suppliers as well as standard setters and regulators; and the telephone and mail surveys, which were a (broad but not deep) mechanism to achieve large-scale responses.

The structure of the questions asked was developed principally from the input of the key stakeholders, who formed the partnership to create this ARC linkage grant, but were refined and more keenly focused through the initial screening of questions and the use of focus groups.

Ultimately, the number of responses was broad, with more than 1500 participants involved at some stage of the project.

In terms of sampling bias, the present authors acknowledge that the use of the sampling frames did induce responses from those who are more likely to have an interest in financial statements, are more likely to have financial expertise and are better educated generally than the wider population—at least in some instances. As is evident from the educational qualifications data, the data reported are beyond the educational credentials of the average Australian citizen and resident. With this potential bias acknowledged, it is argued that the sample is broad and deep and represents an interest group whose responses can help inform the debate about the market for audit services and policy surrounding this area.

2.0 Limitations

As with all research, certain limitations exist. For instance, in terms of the mail survey, there is no assurance that the addressee completed the questionnaire themselves, or that it was completed with due diligence, without fatigue and without the potential effect of 'socially desirable responses'. In terms of the telephone survey, there can be no assurance that the responder was indeed the target of the call or, again, that the phone survey was taken seriously and responded to without perceived 'socially desirable responses' being given.

In terms of the face-to-face interviews with stakeholders, not all participants were asked the same questions and even the same questions could have been asked in different ways by the same interviewer across time and by different interviewers. Again, the possibility that perceived 'socially desirable responses' were given was present, as was the possibility that the presence of the interviewer influenced the responses in some way and in differential ways depending on the identity of the interviewer. All interviewees were invited to make open-ended responses to all interview protocol questions and also, as part of the concluding aspects of the interview, were invited to raise any other issues. It is possible that these open-ended responses have been interpreted incorrectly by the authors as relevant to topics not intended by the interviewees. While all interviews have been faithfully transcribed, it is possible that not all intonations or emphases have been captured accurately. The authors obviously have not been able to represent hand gestures or other communications through body language in this report. These are all limitations common to the research methodology used in this study.

While every endeavour was made to ensure that there was representation of the identified stakeholder groups (users, purchasers, suppliers, standard setters and regulators), we were not able to test this statistically. We are, however, confident that a wide spectrum of opinion from within these stakeholder groups has been captured. If there is a bias in terms of participant selection, it could be that for some interviewees there is an over-representation of people with particularly strong accounting/financial expertise. This is so because of the self-selection process of people motivated to be involved in this type of study and because the organisations providing contact details tend to have more dealings with such people.

The quotations have been taken from lengthy interviews and while they have been placed in relevant contexts there has been need to edit or truncate some of these quotes for reasons of length and grammar.

Wherever relevant, the quotations have also been adjusted to ensure the interviewee, his or her related organisation and/or organisations within which examples have been used have been made anonymous. This is so other than when names of people or organisations have been identified as being on the public record.

DIVISION B

UNDERSTANDING OF THE AUDIT AND PERCEPTIONS OF THE DELIVERABLES 3

I have serious doubts whether you can ever close the expectation gap, because it's not so much the profession and how we actually communicate to the users of financial reports...the problem is that you've got such a significantly wide range of people who do read these financial reports...It's very hard to communicate to such a wide group and such a wide level of knowledge; people have got different levels of knowledge, et cetera...it's extremely difficult to close that gap to what we would consider to be an acceptable level, where basically the readers of the financial reports are fairly well in tune with what our process is, and understanding...when we do sign an audit report and attach that to financial reports...what that actually means. So I've got significant reservations that we could ever close that expectation gap significantly.
— Supplier

1.0 Key issues

Major challenges in relation to understanding the role of audit and the audit process continue to exist for stakeholders in the audit process judging by some of the observations made in response to the survey and interviews conducted as part of this project. These issues are inextricably linked with the audit expectations gap and include the following.

- Is it possible to communicate effectively with stakeholders of differential levels of sophistication and knowledge about financial reports and about the audit process and the existing single public outcome—the audit report?
- To what extent has the increasing complexity of financial statements and notes thereto added to the apparent misunderstanding of the audit process?

- To what extent does the level of comfort apparently derived from audit, particularly from brand-name audit firms, emanate from what is known as the 'insurance hypothesis' and the fact that auditors are seen to have 'deep pockets'?[1]
- Should access to and real reading of the auditor's report be facilitated and encouraged and, if so, how?
- Have the reforms since the corporate collapses of the early 2000s served only to move auditors and regulators further apart in terms of mutual understanding?
- Whose role is it to educate those stakeholders who are in need so that they become informed consumers of audit services?

2.0 Introduction to Chapter 3

The authors have included both understandability and the expectations gap in this chapter. This has been done in order to provide a more comprehensive description of the wider landscape of the issues around auditing and reporting of audit outcomes in the context of an efficient capital market. The overlap between the two concepts of understandability and expectations is important, as is the need to understand the interrelationship between the two. Understanding might be seen as a precursor to the removal of an expectations gap. Put another way, having understandability of the audit is a necessary but not sufficient condition for a path to lowering or eradicating an expectations gap.

The absence of an understanding of the audit, its processes, structures, incentives and its surrounds is but one part of the elimination of an expectations gap. Even in the circumstance in which there is complete understanding of the audit, it does not necessarily lead to the elimination of an audit expectations gap. In the circumstance in which this understanding exists, there still could be a mismatch of expectations around the regulation of audit, the framework in which auditing is conducted or indeed even the framework within which financial reporting is conducted; these all impact on the perceived expectations for the audit. Even when there is complete

1. The 'insurance hypothesis' refers to the fact that auditors must carry professional indemnity insurance in order to practice, and hence auditors can be seen to have 'deep pockets' if investors seek to recoup their losses.

understanding, an audit expectations gap can still exist. Obviously, if there is not shared understanding of key factors between stakeholders in the market for audit expectations, there is an even greater rationale for the presence of an audit expectations gap.

3.0 Introduction: understandability of audit

Understandability of the audit is one of the key issues that has arisen in the audit expectations gap debate. Understandability is largely in the eye of the beholder and it can be argued that self-evaluation of understandability is fraught with measurement error. Despite this methodological difficulty, asking key stakeholder groups about their understanding of the audit report and the related documents in the financial statements is a key first question for investigating the future of audit.

4.0 Survey

The telephone and mail questionnaire respondents were asked about several issues relating to the extent of their reading of annual reports and audited financial statements, the extent to which they were used and relied on in decision making and to what extent the respondents would rate their understanding of financial statements and the audit report.

4.1 Do external financial statement audits represent value for money?

One of the key questions to understanding present attitudes and positions with respect to financial report audits is whether the market sees this service as something of value. These questions are in the context of an external audit being, in most circumstances, mandated and outside the discretionary choice of users and purchasers.

Table 3.1 Responses: whether audits represent value for money (per cent)

	USERS				PURCHASERS				SUPPLIERS		
	Total	Accounting expertise	Professional users	Private investors	Total	Directors/ audit comm.	CEO/CFO	Other	Total	Big Four	Non-Big Four
External financial statement audits currently represent value for money	28	28	29	29	25	26	24	28	57	75	53

Percentage of respondents answering 'Strongly agree' or 'Agree' on a five-point scale.

In response to the survey, which asked specifically whether 'external financial statement audits currently represent value for money', a relatively modest proportion of users and purchasers responded positively. Approximately one-quarter and one-third of users and purchasers, respectively, reacted positively (that is, either strongly agreeing or agreeing) to this proposition. On the other hand, suppliers, particularly suppliers from Big Four firms, responded very positively, with three-quarters affirming that current financial audits represented value for money. Non-Big Four respondents were more equivocal, with approximately half responding positively by either agreeing or strongly agreeing. This strong differentiation between purchasers and users on the one hand and many suppliers on the other hand is one of the key challenging issues for the operation of the market for audit services and its regulation. This perception was subject to some comment in the interviews discussed below and has important policy implications for the future of auditing.

The next three survey questions probed why respondents felt that an external financial audit was of value. Allowing for the fact that respondents rarely respond with extreme values in surveys, there is a general positive view across all stakeholder groups that the audit opinion is something that is expert and therefore has the characteristics of expert advice. Much less positive is the view that the auditor has a good understanding of the company's business. Both Big Four and non-Big Four suppliers, on balance, responded positively to that question, but they were the only group in the market for audit services that took this perspective, with less than half of all other groups—including CEOs/CFOs and directors/audit committee members—responding positively. Indeed, about one-third of all purchasers and slightly more than one-third of users believe that the company's business is well understood by the auditor.

Table 3.2 Responses: why the external audit is of value (per cent)

	USERS				PURCHASERS				SUPPLIERS		
	Total	Accounting expertise	Professional users	Private investors	Total	Directors/ audit comm.	CEO/CFO	Other	Total	Big Four	Non-Big Four
An external financial statement audit is of value to you because:											
The audit opinion issued is an expert opinion	62	65	57	63	59	60	59	57	68	66	69
The auditor has a good understanding of the company's business	40	38	34	46	33	41	31	29	55	66	53
The auditor provides an unconditional guarantee about the truth and fairness of a company's financial statements	39	36	42	41	28	23	28	37	19	11	21

Percentage of respondents answering 'Strongly agree' or 'Agree' on a five-point scale.

With respect to the auditor providing an 'unconditional guarantee about truth and fairness', no group or subgroup of the stakeholders responded with a particularly positive response to this question and indeed the Big Four suppliers responded in a very modest way. The notion that there is anything of an unconditional guarantee in the market for audit services is not something subscribed to by the majority of stakeholders.

4.2 Understanding of the audited financial report

The telephone and mail questionnaire respondents were asked about several issues relating to the extent of their reading of annual reports, including audited statements, the extent to which they were used and relied on in decision making and to what extent the respondents would rate their understanding of financial statements.

As shown in Table 3.3, on a five-point scale from 1 = Poor to 5 = Excellent, respondents indicated that the rating of their understanding of financial statements was either at or above the mid-point. Overall, users rated their understanding just marginally over the mid-point at 3.6 (where the mid-point is 3.0), with private investors reporting the lowest level of understanding and those with professional accounting credentials the highest within the three subgroups. With respect to the same question, purchasers showed a noticeably higher level of understanding, with a rating of more than 4.0 on the five-point scale, with audit committee members and company directors, CEOs/CFOs and other purchasers at the upper end of the scale. With respect to suppliers, those from the Big Four subgroup and the Non-Big Four subgroup reported very high levels of understanding of financial statements.

As reported in Chapter 2, each of three respondent groups—users, purchasers and suppliers—rated their reading of audited financial statements very highly, but the level of usage among users was about the mid-point, with 53 per cent reporting that they used or relied on financial statements in decision making and 62 per cent overall of purchasers and 43 per cent overall of suppliers. These lower levels of usage or reliance reflect the different decision perspectives of these two respondent groups and the likelihood of access to information sets beyond audited financial statements as being useful in their own decision making.

Table 3.3 Respondents' self-rating of the level of understandability of financial statements

A. Users

Statements	Total users			Accounting professionals and other			Advisors and so on			Private investors		
	Poor %	Excellent %	Mean	Poor %	Excellent %	Mean	Poor %	Excellent %	Mean	Poor %	Excellent %	Mean
How do you rate your understanding of financial statements?	11	59	3.60	4	76	3.94	6	52	3.56	21	42	3.21
How do you rate your understanding of the external financial statement audit, which includes the level of assurance that the audit provides?	16	49	3.40	7	65	3.73	15	41	3.31	29	34	3.05

B. Purchasers

Statements	Total purchasers			Audit committee and directors			CEO/CFO			Other		
	Poor %	Excellent %	Mean	Poor %	Excellent %	Mean	Poor %	Excellent %	Mean	Poor %	Excellent %	Mean
How do you rate your understanding of financial statements?	2	81	4.08	5	72	3.87	1	85	4.15	1	86	4.26
How do you rate your understanding of the external financial statement audit, which includes the level of assurance that the audit provides?	4	74	3.95	7	67	3.79	4	76	3.97	1	80	4.13

C. Suppliers

Statements	Total suppliers			Big Four			Non-Big Four		
	Poor %	Excellent %	Mean	Poor %	Excellent %	Mean	Poor %	Excellent %	Mean
How do you rate your understanding of financial statements?	1	89	4.38	2	86	4.39	1	90	4.38
How do you rate your understanding of the external financial statement audit, which includes the level of assurance that the audit provides?	2	91	4.50	2	93	4.64	2	91	4.47

Poor = 1 and 2 and Excellent = 4 and 5 on five-point scale.

Table 3.4 Respondents' self-reported extent of reading of audited financial statements and the level of usage and reliance (per cent)

A. Users

Statements	Total users		Accounting professionals and other		Advisors and so on		Private investors	
	No	Yes	No	Yes	No	Yes	No	Yes
Do you read annual reports and audited financial statements?	12	88	13	87	14	86	9	91
Do you use or rely on audited financial statements in your decision making?	47	53	52	48	46	54	41	59

B. Purchasers

Statements	Total purchasers		Audit committee and directors		CEO/CFO		Other	
	No	Yes	No	Yes	No	Yes	No	Yes
Do you read annual reports and audited financial statements?	5	95	4	96	4	96	9	91
Do you use or rely on audited financial statements in your decision making?	38	62	30	70	41	59	43	56

C. Suppliers

Statements	Total suppliers		Big Four		Non-Big Four	
	No	Yes	No	Yes	No	Yes
Do you read annual reports and audited financial statements?	6	94	7	93	6	94
Do you use or rely on audited financial statements in your decision making?	57	43	42	58	61	39

4.3 Impact of complexity on understandability

As indicated in Table 3.5, aggregated to stakeholder groups and for subgroups within the users and purchasers groups, most respondents do not regard audited financial statements, the notes to those financial statements or the audit report to be too complex to understand. Indeed, of these three sets of documents, the audit report is seen as the least complex.

Suppliers, however, take a somewhat different view. On average, 50 per cent of suppliers believed that audited financial statements were too complex to understand and this was particularly so for the suppliers from Big Four firms. They also believed that, on balance, most of the notes to the statements were too complex to understand, but with respect to the audit reports their concern about complexity and understandability was markedly lower.

Interestingly, of the user group, the private investors, as opposed to the professional users and those with explicit accounting expertise, were more willing to agree to the statement that audited financial statements were too complex to understand. Similarly, they believed that notes were too complex and they had a high level of concern also about the complexity of the audit opinion. Their level of agreement with this concern matches the CEO/CFO group within purchasers more closely than it does the company director and audit committee member subgroups. Indeed, the lowest level of agreement with respect to the issue of understandability as a consequence of complexity is housed within users who have accounting expertise, professional users, directors and audit committee members. The long-held view that private investors are the 'problem' with respect to the expectations gap does not seem to be confirmed in these survey data.

Certainly, the survey data indicate that there are widely differing views on the understandability of financial reports and related documents, which are part of core disclosure requirements for publicly traded companies. This would suggest that the audit expectations gap is alive and well.

The richness and complexity of the interview questions unfolded a deeper and more meaningful story and this is described in the interview section below.

Table 3.5 Responses: impact of complexity on understandability of financial statements, notes to statements and audit reports (per cent)

	USERS				PURCHASERS				SUPPLIERS		
	Total	Accounting expertise	Professional users	Private investors	Total	Directors/ audit comm.	CEO/CFO	Other	Total	Big Four	Non-Big Four
Audited financial statements are too complex to understand.	36	32	35	43	41	39	41	42	50	58	48
The notes to the financial statements are too complex to understand.	37	33	36	42	45	36	48	52	51	55	50
The audit report is too complex to understand.	25	17	25	33	17	15	16	23	23	23	23

Percentage of respondents answering 'Strongly agree' or 'Agree' on a five-point scale.

4.4 Confidence that an auditor will detect all material fraud and error

As Table 3.6 shows, for all stakeholders in the market for audit services, there is a positive level of confidence with respect to the detection of material fraud and material error.

There was a markedly higher response rate with respect to material error compared with fraud. Once again, suppliers to the market for audit services had a noticeably more positive response with respect to error compared with all purchasers and all users.

Table 3.6 Responses on confidence that an auditor will detect all material fraud and error (per cent)

	USERS				PURCHASERS				SUPPLIERS		
	Total	Accounting expertise	Professional users	Private investors	Total	Directors/ audit comm.	CEO/CFO	Other	Total	Big Four	Non-Big Four
How confident are you that an auditor will detect all material fraud in a company's financial statements?	54	55	54	53	50	48	50	54	57	63	55
How confident are you that an auditor will detect all material errors in a company's financial statements?	65	66	65	63	67	66	67	69	76	80	75

Percentage of respondents answering 'Strongly agree' or 'Agree' on a five-point scale.

4.5 Responses: external auditor's responsibilities

Survey participants were asked for responses in relation to their perceptions of an auditor's responsibility to detect all material fraud and error, warn the audit committee of early signs of risk areas or to act as a whistleblower.

With respect to an external auditor's responsibility to detect all material fraud, there is some degree of shared understanding between purchasers and suppliers, with generally less than half responding positively to a survey question on that responsibility. Users, on the other hand, see this more positively as being the responsibility of the external auditor.

Similarly, with respect to a survey question on whether the external auditor has a responsibility to act as a whistleblower to an appropriate regulatory authority, purchasers and suppliers are more ambivalent about that being a requirement compared with users. So, with respect to responsibilities for detecting material fraud or acting as a whistleblower, there is some shared agreement between suppliers and purchasers and those two groups can be differentiated somewhat from users. With respect to detecting all material errors and warning the audit committee of early signs of risk, there is some degree of shared view on these two issues between all members of the stakeholder groups surveyed—again, with the user group being rather more positive in its responses to the survey than the supplier group.

Table 3.7 Responses: auditors' responsibilities to detect material fraud, material error, warn audit committees about risk or to act as a whistleblower (per cent)

	USERS				PURCHASERS				SUPPLIERS		
	Total	Accounting expertise	Professional users	Private investors	Total	Directors/ audit comm.	CEO/CFO	Other	Total	Big Four	Non-Big Four
An external auditor has a responsibility to:											
Detect all material fraud in a company's financial statements	66	57	68	76	45	49	41	51	35	48	32
Detect all material errors in a company's financial statements	80	75	82	86	76	79	74	76	68	75	66
Warn the audit committee of a company about early signs of risk areas	86	86	86	85	81	81	80	83	77	77	77
Act as a whistleblower to the appropriate regulatory authority	65	61	65	71	47	53	44	47	53	48	55

Percentage of respondents answering 'Strongly agree' or 'Agree' on a five-point scale.

4.6 Responses: what does the audit provide direct assurance about?

Each of the questions in Table 3.8 goes to the perception of the substance and shared understanding of various components of assurance for the audit opinion.

With respect to the question about whether an audit provides direct assurance on the integrity of senior executive managers, none of the groups (users, purchasers or suppliers) responded strongly positively, with suppliers being most reticent about the current financial report audit providing that type of assurance. Similarly, there was a generally negative response by all groups to the question relating to the provision of direct assurance on the prudence of business decisions, with a more positive view by all groups other than Big Four suppliers to the question about whether the external financial audit provided direct assurance about the adequacy of the internal control system of a company. In that question, less than 40 per cent of Big Four suppliers reacted positively, whereas with all other groups there was a majority view. Some would speculate that the Big Four suppliers have a more expert view on this particular issue compared with the rest of the capital market. Importantly, the question does refer to direct assurance so some might speculate that the other respondents have construed the question other than the way in which it is specifically worded.

Table 3.8 Responses: what does the audit provide direct assurance about? (per cent)

	USERS				PURCHASERS				SUPPLIERS		
	Total	Accounting expertise	Professional users	Private investors	Total	Directors/ audit comm.	CEO/CFO	Other	Total	Big Four	Non-Big Four
An external financial statement audit provides direct assurance about:											
The integrity of senior executive managers in a company	26	21	30	29	14	14	12	29	14	11	14
The prudence of the business decisions made by a company	22	21	29	20	12	14	9	17	12	7	14
The adequacy of the internal control system of a company that is relied on in the preparation of financial statements	64	65	60	66	61	61	59	66	53	39	59

Percentage of respondents answering 'Strongly agree' or 'Agree' on a five-point scale.

5.0 Interviews

No specific interview question addresses the understandability of the audit; however, in responses to many questions, several comments pertinent to this issue and to the issue of the audit expectations gap, which is discussed later in this chapter, emerge. These comments provide a wider context, which sets the scene for what follows in terms of explicitly asked questions, the responses to which are covered in later chapters.

5.1 Users

It is obvious from users' comments how much reliance is placed on the brand name of the audit firm and on the existence of an unqualified or unmodified audit report.

> I look to see [in the audit report]...who does [the audit]...I'm not really interested [in the audit report]—I don't think I've ever read one in full, but I look at who does it. And...you've got some... auditing firms that are credible and if their name is on the top of that sheet, then it does give us some comfort. So whether that's right or wrong I don't know, but I'd flick to the back of the annual report, have a look at who did the audit, and move on.
>
> You look at the firm they're from [that is, the audit firm]...there's an assumption of comfort under branding of the firm. You always read it, to make sure there are no qualifications in there, and...anybody relying on an audit report [is] looking for that.
>
> The key things for an investor when they look at that audit statement [are] who signed off on it and whether there's anything in there that says 'is there anything wrong with the statement', so if there [are] any qualifications or anything that's been highlighted, any limitations that they've put on the audit report, or anything like that.
>
> I don't spend too much time on the audit report...there [are] so many other figures to digest. I'm one of those who's mainly looking [for] 'is there any problem', 'have the auditors any concerns'? It is looking at the exceptions rather than any details because most of it is just standard stuff and a certification that everything is in order.

As acknowledged in the first quote above, however, and in the one below, the audit report is seldom read:

> [I]t would be interesting to line up 100 shareholders and ask them have they ever read an audit report. I suspect [they have not].

5.1.1 Summary

Users' comments indicate the comfort they derive from the reputation of the audit firm that is signatory to the audit report. There is not a lot of indication that the audit report is read in full; rather, it is scanned for an indication of a modification and more particularly of a qualified or adverse audit report.

5.2 Purchasers

The degree of assurance that purchasers derive from the audit and auditors is evident in the following illustrative quotations; however, what emerges is dissatisfaction with the form of the financial statements themselves.

> [W]e get...comfort that the auditors are doing the right thing, but it might just be [a] function of the economy...we appreciate that post things like HIH, there has been a tightening of what [auditors have] done. We generally have a high opinion of the depth of what they do...I suppose the key issue that we've got with accounts quite often...doesn't really come back to auditing per se—it's more what they actually say and what they communicate, which is quite often not user friendly.

> [T]he accounting policy notes now run to 10, 15 pages. Related party notes run to 10 to 15 pages...it's just a joke and it's now a case of everyone's focusing on this 80 [per cent] that pays 20 [per cent], not the 20 [per cent] that pays 80 [per cent] and the auditors have to deliver into all these disclosures. And boards are unhappy and management's unhappy because, for the cost and the effort, it doesn't add value and actually probably distracts auditors from focusing on what's important, which is the financial health and the sustainability of...a business. You spend so much time chasing the disclosures and all the other incidentals, you can miss focusing enough time on the core stuff—and that's where I see a significant issue.

This last quotation suggests that not only are there concerns about the financial report complexity, the auditor might be positively distracted from the 'real task' because of this complexity.

5.2.1 Summary

Purchasers indicate the degree of comfort that comes with the audit, but allude to a dismay with the content of the financial report more generally.

5.3 Suppliers

Criticisms by suppliers of the audit report wording as a contributor to a lack of understandability of audit and the audit process emerge in the following quotations.

> [M]aybe one option is to try and reword the audit reports into plain English. But I don't think you'd want to add too much, because... one of the issues we've got at the moment is [that] there's just so much data out there—financial statements now run to 200, 250 pages. [If] you now make your audit...sign off four or five pages, the question is does anybody really read it? Do they really understand it? Because it's very difficult to put a very complex process into a couple of pages.

> [T]he audit report formats which we're obliged to comply with seem to be bogged down with legalese rather than plain English explanations.

> [T]hey've started down that track [of better understandability] with the wording in the audit report. I'm not sure that too many people read it...they determine whether it's qualified or not and then move on.

> The audit standards do not allow a lot of scope for variation in terms of an unqualified and a qualified report. Perhaps that could be looked at. You can have an emphasis of matter, but that's also fairly specific in when you can apply that.

> [T]he audit opinion, although it's distinct...explains the materialities at play and there's sampling, and if someone read that carefully they should get a sense of...what an audit is not.

One of the suppliers points out the inevitability of reduced understandability of audit in light of the increasing complexity and sophistication of the underlying financial representations and instruments:

> If you look at the auditing profession, you look at the financial accounting profession over the last 10 years, and you look at the financial products in the market, and the level of sophistication across all of those has ramped up significantly. And therefore you have to get a much more complex reporting framework, a much more complex auditing framework to try and deal with the additional complexities of doing business in a sophisticated financial market today.

5.3.1 Summary

In comments made during face-to-face interviews, suppliers point to the wording of the audit report as one issue influential in the understandability or otherwise of the audit product. For suppliers, there is some unease with the wording of the audit report itself. It is clear that this issue remains 'live' despite the longstanding convention of adhering to the suggested wording included in the auditing standards. This issue is returned to in Chapter 4 when the potential for additional disclosures, either by auditors themselves or by management, is explored.

5.4 Standard setters

Reliance on the integrity and honesty of the communication that takes place between auditor and client emerges in this standard setter's comments:

> [It's like saying I didn't know about it so I didn't go and look for it.] That's an interesting one because...if you take a scenario, for example, say you're doing your half-year review and you sit down and you read the management reports and you go through everything else and...you've done all that, then you go and have a meeting with management and talk about what's happened in the business and it turns out, for example, something's happened and they don't tell you about it. It's not in the management reports, it's not even, from reading anything else—a legal claim, for example. They don't tell you about it. We're being sued by party X...You've asked questions and you've probably even asked the

'[H]ow do I know all your stuff's in the shoebox?'

> question 'Is there any major litigation from partners?' No, there's no major litigation. Nothing's come to my attention. He could tell me that.

The same standard setter continues with a simple analogy that highlights the dilemma of the auditor:

> I'm of a completely different view...the greatest example I always give of trying to get someone to understand the concept of an audit would be if you went along with a shoebox with all your financial transactions in it for one year and go over to someone off the street and said: 'I want you to write me a letter that I could give to anyone else that tells me that my income, all of my income, and all of my expenditure that's in that shoebox is everything I did in the year financially; if you could just write that down and put down my revenue, my expenditure, my final cash balance, and I'm done, I'll pay you to do it'...And then the person says, 'But how do I know all your stuff's in the shoebox?' It's very simplistic but the concept becomes bigger but...there is a fundamental reliance on the transparency of the process and the integrity and honesty of communication that is fundamental to the audit process and without it I believe the whole process is flawed.

6.0 Issues and implications

With respect to understandability, the researchers use survey and interview techniques to investigate a series of related questions: first, the issue of whether the audit is of value. This question is asked against the background of the audit being generally mandated and outside the discretion of purchasers of audit opinions. While generally suppliers believed there was substantial value added in the audit, this was rarely replicated by other participants in the market for audit services. This would be consistent with other forms of 'compliance' goods and other markets where there is compulsion. The ability to value add and to be seen to value add is always a challenge. Perhaps equally as concerning are the responses about whether the auditor has a good understanding of the business. Again, suppliers to the market provided a very positive response whereas purchasers and users were more mixed in their views. Finally, a key issue about understandability—which also relates to the whole issue of the expectations gap, to be addressed later in this chapter—is whether the audit provides any form of guarantee. While all respondents reacted positively in the minority, a disturbingly large proportion of users, including those among whom one might expect relevant expertise, believed that the audit provided a form of guarantee about the truth and fairness of the financial statements.

It is noteworthy to acknowledge that while levels of understandability of financial reports might not be high among users and purchasers of financial reports, when asked about self-rated understanding of the financial reports and related documentation, they rated the audit opinion as the most easily understood. This does not necessarily mean there is not some room for improvement, but it shows more acceptance of the level of complexity of audit reports as opposed to financial statements and notes to the accounts.

Users, purchasers and suppliers all professed a self-rating with a level of understanding of financial statements above the median point, with users generally being more modest on that scale. Given this level of self-reporting for understandability, more worrying was the fact that the majority of surveyed respondents indicated that although they read annual reports and audited financial statements, their use within decision making was markedly lower.

Respondents of all types were more rather than less confident that auditors would detect material fraud and material error. Purchasers and suppliers were much more circumspect, indicating that it was really the external auditor's responsibility to detect material fraud. Users, suppliers and purchasers all recognised that the auditor had responsibility to detect material error. There was also a considerable shared view that the auditor had the responsibility to warn the audit committee of early signs of risk. There were mixed views about whether the auditor should act as a whistleblower to an appropriate regulatory body.

In terms of whether the financial statement audit provides direct assurance, one interesting deviation is whether the auditor has the responsibility to provide direct assurance about the adequacy of the internal control system of the company. Big Four suppliers were the only respondents who indicated they strongly disagreed with this proposition.

With respect to the one-on-one interviews, the user group could be typified by the proposition that they check whether an audit report exists and that it has been provided by a brand-name auditor (or someone in the view of the market who has the credibility to conduct the audit) and for qualification or modifications to an otherwise 'clean' audit opinion. Their interest in going beyond these three basic elements seems to be very limited. For purchasers, there seems to be comfort in that the auditors are perceived to be doing 'the right thing' but some concern that the amount of regulation and bureaucracy is a distraction from what they see as the main objective of the audit, which is providing assurance on the financial statements. Suppliers, on the other hand, have concern about the audit opinion itself—that it is not overly lengthy, that in some ways the audit has suffered because of the complexity of accounting standards and that there is scope for enhancing what is communicated in the audit opinion, including, but not limited to, plain English statements.

As indicated above, this chapter has been structured so far to set the scene and a number of these issues are picked up more directly when we refer specifically to stakeholders' statements about the audit expectations gap later in this chapter and beyond. The second half of this chapter explores more deeply what lies behind some of these misunderstandings in relation to the deliverables that can be expected of an audit.

7.0 Concluding remarks

There are three areas in which policy implications have arisen from the discussion thus far: 1) the value of the audit; 2) the wording of the audit report; and 3) the complexity of the material that is provided for the consumers of information in the capital market. The first policy implication relates to the value to the capital market of the assurance given by an auditor. There is evidence that this assurance is valued and the policy implication is that there is no case to remove or limit the existence of an audit as it is currently known to the market. Put another way, sceptics of the audit are unlikely to find any comfort in the material provided to us.

The second issue is the wording of the audit report. It seems there is no doubt that at least a proportion of users in the capital market will view an audit report and judge it virtually by its length and categorise it into one of two groups: 1) modified (qualified), or 2) other (clean). Policy implications are involved here. For example, such a simplistic categorisation based on casual observation (with no reading of the audit report undertaken) of the audit opinion could in fact cause users to miss important but short statements of emphasis of matter. Indeed, with respect to emphasis of matter paragraphs, we observe later in this publication that understanding of them and their intent might not be universal.

The second policy implication is the type of wording used in the audit report in that the standardised wording, which in the minds of some includes legal jargon, is received as a 'commodity'. If the auditing profession seeks to be seen to exercise a considerable amount of professional judgment then it has the difficulty that the principal outcome it delivers to the market for information is highly standardised and not fulsome in terms of its contents. The parallel that might be drawn here is where an oncologist diagnoses a patient as having contracted cancer or not having contracted cancer. The professional judgment leading to such an outcome cannot be standardised in a simple statement of the presence or absence of cancer. There is a need to elaborate further by the explication of the exercise of the professional judgment of the oncologist. Is the cancer developed? What type of cancer is it? Has the cancer metastasised? Where is it located and is it operable? The standard form audit report is perceived as a 'commodity', which is simplistic and standardised rather than subtle, nuanced and fulsome. The subsequent policy implication in this circumstance is that a standardised audit opinion fails to recognise the diversity of expertise in the market for audit services and hence the ability to understand more complex information is ignored—at least for some users. While audit reports need to fulfil minimum legal requirements, there should be positive encouragement by regulators to allow auditors to include nuanced and subtle explanations and observations in a way that adds value to the report for interested readers.

The final policy implication is the reference to the complexity and burdensome nature of financial statements. This complexity and its challenges for understandability of financial statements are outside the scope of this project and indeed auditors should not be held accountable for this complexity. There are, however, consequences for the audit process and for the information-handling capabilities of users, since the extent of this complexity can pose a limitation to what might be done to enhance what is reported in the audit opinion and audit information presented elsewhere. The receipt of audit information by the market will of course occur simultaneously with receipt of information within the financial report and therefore policy setters must recognise this as a joint burden.

We would conclude that there is very genuine concern about the level of complexity and information load jointly contained in the financial reporting and auditing disclosures. Our inquiries reveal that no-one seems to take responsibility for or accountability of this. This joint level of complexity makes the probability of significant reduction in the expectations gap improbable. We recommend that the Financial Reporting Council (FRC) gives consideration to setting up a task force that examines the competing challenges of comprehensive and technically accurate financial reporting and auditing information together with the need for understandable disclosures that have genuine utility to the capital market.

While we appreciate that in a purely technical sense only a small number of people need to read and interpret the financial report in order for there to be a share price reaction, there is also a political and societal aspect that should not be any longer ignored and it is for this reason that we recommend a single body takes responsibility for enhancing the utility of these joint auditing and accounting disclosures.

In terms of policy issues, the three issues that have emerged in this chapter thus far are: 1) auditors and auditing should not be held accountable for the complexity of financial statements and notes; 2) the assurance given by an audit has value to the market; and 3) consideration might be given to allowing and encouraging more diverse and fulsome wording of the audit opinion in terms of outcome and in terms of process.

8.0 Introduction: the expectations gap

Among the stakeholders, there are few who protest that there is no such thing as the audit expectations gap. Rather, although not universal, there is acknowledgment of the gap not just between the public and auditors, but between regulators and auditors. Common issues raised among user, purchaser, supplier, standard setter and regulator groups include gaining a more definitive understanding of who the users of financial reports are and their diversity in capability of accurately receiving the message sent by financial statement preparers and auditors, presuming that message is appropriate—which in itself is by no means agreed. Another common issue raised relates to varying expectations of the auditor's responsibility for fraud detection. Materiality, as that term is used in an auditing context, is another area that emerges as commonly misconceived. This issue of materiality arose in the initial focus groups too and a separate chapter is dedicated to it (Chapter 5). Regulators in their comments remind us that deliverables from an audit are price sensitive, but confirm that their expectations of the audit are often not met. The gap between regulators and auditors appears to have widened with recent reforms and particularly the ASIC inspections, and so much rich material on this issue has been forthcoming that only a taste of it appears in this chapter, with the rest dealt with in later chapters on regulation (Chapters 11–13).

8.1 Interviews

In the conversations in the individual interviews, there were innumerable references to the 'audit expectations gap', even though there were few explicit questions or prompts raised by the interviewers. Many of the observations about the gap, its existence or otherwise, which parties the gap falls between, whether the gap is resolvable or not and suggestions for ways to reduce it presuming it exists, are included in this chapter. These observations were made in many different contexts during the course of extended conversations between the interviewer and the interviewees. As a consequence, many of the observations described below are also relevant and should be borne in mind when reading other chapters on more specific or technical issues.

8.2 Users

Users in their interview responses make it clear that an audit expectations gap continues to exist. Further, the illustrative responses below signal that regulatory reforms introduced after the collapse of HIH Limited in 2002 and other noteworthy collapses elsewhere in the world have made little impact on the way in which this group perceives the auditing profession.

> You've probably got more sophisticated people in the regulators... be it ASIC [or others]. They're probably a bit more aware about what auditors do and what the auditor's responsibilities are. I don't see as big an expectation gap between the regulator and the auditor as between the auditor and the general public, the user.

The diversity among users of audit reports in terms of understanding of the audit process is elucidated in this next user's comments:

> [A]s far as professional investors are going to go, they're quite aware about what the audit statement is actually saying, but for the general retail investor they'd probably take more comfort from the audit statement than maybe some of the professional investors do. We accept it for what it is, which is a sign-off to a certain degree, but it's certainly not giving you blanket coverage as to this is a great investment, go out there and invest in it.

Somewhat disturbingly, one user sees the expectations gap as having been lessened by the corporate failures in a perverse way:

> '[T]he naive expectation from an analyst and shareholder point of view is that the auditor is there to make sure that what the company says is based on fact rather than arbitrary decisions by management.'

> [I]n terms of what is debated as the audit expectation gap, if anything, those collapses have lowered the public's perception a little bit and thereby closed the gap in terms of lowering their expectations, but I don't think that they've got more confidence in the auditing standards than they had before. And...I don't think the broad public is that aware of the regulatory responses, the tightening of regulations, and rather would, if anything, if you mentioned to them an Enron or an HIH, they would mainly see that as a failure of the audit profession, and it would undermine their confidence rather than say, 'Okay this has led to a regulatory response and a tightening up of standards that now makes us actually more secure than we were before.' We just didn't know how unsecure[d] we were. But in terms of perception, I don't think it's improved really...The...naive expectation from an analyst and shareholder point of view is that the auditor is there to make sure that what the company says is based on fact rather than arbitrary decisions by management...gilding the lily in terms of their accounts. The auditor is there to stop them doing that—fudging the numbers.

8.2.1 Summary

Users confirm the presence of an audit expectations gap. Perversely, far from the regulatory response to the corporate collapses of the early 2000s having increased confidence in the profession, one user's perception is that the collapses in themselves have lowered the public's expectations of the audit profession. This is arguably not the way the regulators or the profession would prefer to see the gap narrowed. The responses also confirm that there is diversity of competencies between different subgroups of users.

8.3 Purchasers

Purchasers, perhaps because some of them have been auditors in past lives, tend to be sympathetic to the notion that too much is expected of auditors, particularly by retail investors and the media. The idea that part of the expectations gap lies between regulators and auditors also receives some sympathy—in favour of the auditors. This next quotation emphasises the commonality of goals that exists between auditors and regulators, but also perceptions of divergence in the means to achievement of those goals:

> I don't think there's an expectation gap or a different perspective [between regulators and auditors] on how [auditors] should do the audit...they're both trying to achieve the same end. The difference is in how you go about it: if the regulators are trying to drive a higher degree of certainty, or if the auditors are trying to achieve through their own audit...they want to achieve it in different ways. The auditors want to achieve it in the most cost-effective, least wasteful way for them and the regulators are trying to push them down a different path.

'The auditors want to achieve it in the most cost-effective, least wasteful way for them and the regulators are trying to push them down a different path.'

The means to achieving goals is alluded to in the following quotation, too, with the alleged check-list approach of the regulator coming in for criticism:

> [D]oes the general public care? I think they have an expectation of what...the financial statements are and I don't think that that will have changed. Maybe there was a bigger gap before in that expectation and maybe the gap has closed a little now...there is a gap between what the regulator thinks the auditor should be able to pick up and what the auditor realistically can...it's very dangerous having a check-list kind of approach being [used] by regulators.

The same purchaser goes on to provide an analogy of directors' relationships with management and that between regulators and auditors—in terms of delegating tasks to achieve a mutually required goal:

> When you study the practice of directorship versus management of an organisation, one of the first things you learn is that directors don't tell [managers] how to do things. They...should be saying to management what [they] want to be achieved, what's the outcome and what don't you want management to do and then let management be innovative in how they get about achieving those objectives. And I would say the similar kind of thing should apply between regulators and auditors. The regulators should be specifying what's the outcome that they require. The auditor ought to be able to come up with the most appropriate way of achieving that outcome.

The different world views of regulators and auditors are blamed for the perceived gap between these parties by this next purchaser:

> 'The problem...[that] arises is that regulators, and particularly the legal profession, are trained to think in a prescriptive sense.'

> [I]f there's an expectation gap between regulators and auditors...broadly speaking...regulators understand what auditors do...people I've spoken to in ASIC and APRA...understand that. The problem...[that] arises is that regulators, and particularly the legal profession, are trained to think in a prescriptive sense. They do not think in terms of generalities or principles—at least that's been my experience. And...that's where the difficulties arise, in that they look for prescription and they tend to not see the value as much in informing...judgments based on subjective information.

Public expectations surrounding the level of scrutiny of transactions when an audit is conducted are pointed to by this next purchaser:

> [Y]ou've got to do it at a material level and I absolutely understand the concern is...going back to the fact that...there's an expectation in some people's minds that auditors would review every single transaction and I don't think they understand what that would cost...I don't know how...you educate them because when you look at Sarbanes-Oxley and all the rest of it...[the] general public was wildly enthusiastic and it plugged a political gap at that stage

> and it's now turning out to be one of the worst interventions that I can think of.

Misperceptions of how an audit is conducted in terms of the thoroughness of the coverage of transactions are alluded to in this next quotation:

> One of the problems...with the auditors is that there's this perception in the general community that the auditors are there to catch every fraud and to detect every single issue that goes wrong and...they're never going to be able to do that... so I don't know if disclosing more information makes any difference at all...because where you'd disclose it would be in places like the annual reports...and I don't actually think anybody reads it. I quite honestly don't.

'[T]here's this perception in the general community that the auditors are there to catch every fraud and to detect every single issue that goes wrong.'

A reminder of the link between corporate financial failure and the audit expectations gap emerges in the following quotation:

> I have a reasonably sanguine view of what an audit is or what an audit can do and...we can set our expectations too high. Whenever there's a failure in the country...there's a cry put out: 'Well, you know it shouldn't have happened, they should do this, they should regulate that.' And the reality is failure happens and...the expectation of the auditing profession is too great among the mum[s] and dads and the media, and of course the sophisticated investors will pull the lever and press the button when it suits them. Maybe I'm too cynical, but the altruism of the institutional investor is [that] they just want to get recompense... or sue a deep pocket. We're all partners in this model that has now developed to where it's at.

'[T]he altruism of the institutional investor is [that] they just want to get recompense...or sue a deep pocket.'

The same purchaser continues, expounding on the current model under which auditors conduct their work and about how a more adversarial model would need to be adopted before an auditor could give an alternative representation of company performance.

> [W]hat I'm getting at is that unless you have some radical view as to what the model should be, and frankly you have to create a more contentious model, a model that in fact became more adversarial... then you talk about the type of people that would be in that model. If you want...the auditor to stand up at an annual general meeting and give an alternative representation of the performance of the company to the shareholders and to point out the weaknesses both in the business model and in the financial statements, then you'd move to a completely different model.

An explanation of this different model is given as the same purchaser continues:

> If you're looking for a model that moves from 2 per cent of qualified[2] reports in the top-200 companies over the last 10 years to a model that is 25 per cent qualified then you're going to have to define what qualification means. It's going to have to have various graduations on it. It'll become totally burdensome and then you say, 'What kind of people do you want?' Do you want [audit] partners who are advocates who effectively become shareholder activists...That will require a different kind of person.

One purchaser, despite acknowledging the link between corporate financial failure and the audit expectations gap, still does not perceive the gap, if it exists, to be a pressing issue:

> [M]y question would be is there really an expectation gap today that is crying out for some particular area? Typically this comment gets made when there's a series of financial disasters and people are saying well, what happened? And the last time it occurred was when there was a series of failures back about the early '90s. Now if you turned around and said 'Is there an expectation gap at the moment that's got to be solved?', I'd query whether there is...I don't see in the literature great drama...saying people don't understand what the auditors are doing.

2 Under the revised auditing standards effective from 1 July 2006, the correct term is 'modified' reports.

8.3.1 Summary

Purchasers are not as sure that the expectations gap persists as the illustrative comments suggest. Those who continue to acknowledge its existence tend to see the public and regulators' expectations of auditors as being excessive and beyond that which can be achieved. There is acknowledgment of misunderstanding, particularly on the part of retail investors, but also on the part of regulators—in particular of the concept of materiality and of the role of judgment as opposed to prescription. The difficulty in overcoming this misunderstanding through education is acknowledged also.

8.4 Suppliers

Suppliers, from their comments, take for granted the fact that the audit expectations gap exists. Their comments indicate a preoccupation with the gap they see as existing between regulators and auditors in an emphasis that the research literature pertaining to the audit expectations gap has not previously emphasised. The next quotation alludes to the link between corporate financial failure and the audit expectations gap. It is a link that appears in several quotations by suppliers in this section.

> [T]here's just always generally an audit expectation gap...it more happens when you get fundamental financial failure and people just say, 'Well, the auditor should have predicted that.'

The role of the audit report in conveying what it is that the audit represents is the topic of the next two quotations.

> '[I]f shareholders and if the financial markets are relying on auditors...to make sure that the accounts are not materially misstated, it's just made for disaster, because that's not what we do.'

> [W]hat's in the audit opinion now [is] in terms of explaining to people that we don't test everything, there's a judgment involved. We're not out there looking specifically to identify fraud per se, so we're not on the trail—we don't set the whole audit up on the basis of looking for that...there's probably enough in there...we could add more but I don't think they would read it; I really don't think they even read it. So we could make a five-page thing but would they read it? It doesn't help that whenever there's a disaster they'll all go sue the auditor because that automatically makes people think that the auditors are ultimately accountable for the financial statements, which is absolutely not right. So the

> perception they've got is from a whole host of things that happen in the environment, and when your regulators come out and say well 'we're going to make the auditors do...'—everyone seems to focus on the tail end of the chain of events. Look, we're the people that come in right at the end and we do a sample of things, we look for things, but...if shareholders and if the financial markets are relying on auditors—100 per cent on auditors—to make sure that the accounts are not materially misstated, it's just made for disaster, because that's not what we do.

The next quotation also emphasises that auditors examine only a sample of transactions and balances, but, like many suppliers, refers to this process as a 'test' rather than a sample, which in itself will be confusing to some in the market for audit services. This is so because the word 'test', which is used in the recommended audit report wording, could mean testing 100 per cent of the population of items or a tiny proportion of that population.

> At the moment whilst...in the audit opinion reference is made to the scope and that it deals with tests rather than absolute assurance, there's probably still a little bit of a gap there...that could probably go some way to being addressed by maybe stating...in a little bit more detail what constitutes the scope of an audit and...what might be excluded from the scope of an audit.

The difficulties of having a wide range of knowledge levels among users of the auditors' output are evident in some of the comments that touch on the audit expectations gap. The first quotation points to a deficient understanding by the public of the context of audit.

> '[T]he general public probably thinks that an auditor is just simply a policeman.'

> [There are] a couple of issues. One, the expectations gap from the point of view of the general public. I don't really think they know much about the audit profession, and I don't really believe that they understand the context of audit within the profession...the general public probably thinks that an auditor is just simply a policeman acting on behalf of someone, but they don't really know who they're acting on behalf of...And consequently the expectation is that they should uncover anything that's wrong with the company on the financials or the reporting obligations of the company.

Another supplier reiterates the assertion that the public does not understand what it is that auditors do:

> [T]he public don't quite understand what we do. And we specifically state in the scope section of our audit reports the work that we do, but the expectation...of the public, of...investors, is quite often 'Well, the auditors are the people who are in there and they're meant to be checking what's going on, and if they're not doing the checking, if they're saying that there are certain things that they don't give an opinion on, that they don't check, well who is meant to be doing that?'...there's that expectation that everything's being checked. And the reality is that if everything was being checked to the 'nth' degree, that...is unrealistic. Then the company's management will be tied up for months on end answering inane questions and you wouldn't necessarily get anything of great value.
>
> [T]he concern I have is that when something goes wrong, no matter how you've tried to explain it, and you say 'Well, actually, our audit wasn't designed to pick it up, et cetera'...the expectation gap is there. The same way if a bank were to collapse, the expectation in the Australian public would be that the government through the RBA is going to pay out.[3]

A non-Big Four supplier laments ASIC's regulatory approach, which he or she sees as unfair:

> So ASIC have been very critical of the mid-tiers and I think unfairly...they need to understand that it's a relative issue. The mid-tiers, in my experience, do a pretty good job auditing businesses which are of the right level for them, perhaps with turnovers of $10 to $200 million, that sort of thing. Yeah...there's an expectation. I don't think the regulator properly understands their role.

'ASIC have been very critical of the mid-tiers and I think unfairly.'

Recent reforms to the regime under which auditors operate are not seen as a solution, as the following illustrative comments demonstrate. More commentary on this issue is included in Chapter 11.

3 The interviews were conducted at a time before the Federal Government introduced the bank deposit guarantee.

> [Legal backing for auditing standards has] done nothing for [the expectations gap]...because the public don't read the auditing standards. So no, from their point of view, they would have no idea...from that point of view, it's done nothing for the expectation gap.

A perceived gap between regulators and auditors was the subject of comments by suppliers. The next two quotations signal a perception that this gap is not large, but other comments after these are less sanguine about this gap.

> '[T]he debate is around where an auditor can or can't exercise judgment.'

> [T]he expectation gap between regulators and auditors is the smallest expectation gap...auditors have understood for a long time how to do audits... [With regard to] the audit quality argument and the legally enforced auditing standards, the debate is around where an auditor can or can't exercise judgment...I don't believe that the legally enforceable auditing standards have changed the substance of what we're doing...a lot of what we're doing we were already doing...Maybe it's a little bit more prescriptive in certain areas to give some certainty to it and take out that judgment.

A perception that regulators have a tendency to extract from the external audit more than is warranted given the circumstances under which it operates is suggested in this next quotation:

> '[T]he regulator's trying to draw as much as possible from an external audit that's probably not really there.'

> [T]here is an expectation gap with regard to an external audit between the accounting profession and the regulator...the regulator's trying to draw as much as possible from an external audit that's probably not really there and...there is danger in that for the accounting profession in that if something does go wrong then the regulator will try and draw more from the audit than it should do and it will also try and defend itself and use the accounting profession to defend itself, to deflect blame...and HIH is probably a prime example. Things have tightened up considerably since then as well...But... all the accounting profession should actually work closer with the regulators to manage expectation gaps. Without a doubt that will happen too through ASIC's regulation of the auditing standards.

> No doubt, there'll be lots of liaison and discussions. What that will show too is what the regulators' expectations actually are because I don't think we really have any evidence of them. We have a sort of understanding of what they are.

A perceived disconnection between what auditors see as the key issues within a particular engagement and what the regulators see is elucidated by this next supplier:

> Is there a gap? Look...if there's a gap in terms of expectation... there...[are] more files...being subject to ASIC review. As you know, a lot of other financial partners as part of their own review process... look at what [ASIC's] focusing on and what they do is what ASIC focuses on as part of their surveillance program...At times, I am a little bit surprised at what they are focusing on versus what I see as the key issues...there might be a bit of a disconnection. Why does that occur? I'm not 100 per cent sure...they probably have their hot spots as to what are the indicators of some anomaly...they're trying to achieve ultimately the same thing in true and fair reporting, transparency, the provision of information to shareholders, all those things, which is what we effectively are trying to do through our audit process. So I'm sure there's a big disconnect, but...at times I do see that and I may even see it by the question that I get asked from the regulator when they go through a file. Their focus is on something which I don't see as important—issues that they raise a question [about]. I don't know why that is. It probably goes to... the level of experience that...some of those within the regulator [possess] to be able to implement.

The regulators have created the perceived gap between regulators and auditors according to this next supplier:

> [T]he expectation gap between regulators and auditors has been created by the regulators. The regulators have taken a position as to where they think...an audit should necessarily be conducted, and what their expectation [is] on how an audit should be conducted. And primarily we're talking about things like documentation, and the way we maintain an audit file and document procedures that have been done. So I'm of the view [that] they've actually created the expectation gap.

The same supplier continues along the same theme:

'I'm not sure whether the regulators really know what they're trying to achieve out of this whole exercise that they're going through now.'

> Has that been of any assistance to the capital markets? In my opinion, no. I'm not sure whether the regulators really know what they're trying to achieve out of this whole exercise that they're going through now…But to form an opinion on how an audit should primarily be done is…not the role of the regulator. And because they've taken what I would…describe as this high moral ground, then they're going to be disappointed, absolutely. But that doesn't mean that what we're doing is wrong, or is not the right way to conduct an audit. And that's the problem. And this is where I say you've got this almost expectation gap because they're saying this is the way we think you should do things. But [what] we're also saying is well you're not actually doing it wrong, but this is the way we think you should do these things. And…that's the problem.

The issue of materiality as a component of the audit expectations gap featured among suppliers' comments that were pertinent to the expectations gap. Below are two such illustrative comments, with Chapter 5 dedicated to the issue of audit materiality.

> The thing I think is well and truly misunderstood is the concept of materiality, probably across a lot of users not just mums and dads—but for big…multinational groups that…obviously can be a very big figure and…a lot of shareholders would struggle if you said to them 'We can still sign a clean audit opinion but the audit error might be X many tens of millions.'…that would stun them…so there is still this expectation gap between what an auditor knows an audit opinion actually is versus what a reader of accounts might expect an audit to be.

> [T]here is certainly a disconnect between what we do and what the general public would perceive an auditor does. I'm sure there's no disconnect really between what the analysts believe we do, and certainly there's probably not a super disconnect between us and what management believes we're doing, although I would imagine in some cases the materiality might be a surprise to some people. However, there's been more disclosure of that with management,

but certainly not with outsiders.

8.4.1 Summary

Suppliers' comments indicate little ambivalence about whether or not a gap exists between shareholders and auditors. There is virtually unanimous support for the proposition that it does exist. Further, there are few suggestions as to how that gap can be reduced. Tellingly, many suppliers see a gap between regulators of the market for audit services and auditors—and some auditors see regulators as primarily responsible for this gap. Perceived discrimination by regulators against the mid-tier firms compared with the Big Four comes through as an aspect of the perceived gap between regulators and auditors. Some suppliers lament the difficulty of having all users of financial reports—no matter what their background or level of business sophistication—read and understand the audit report and what it is that the audit can achieve.

8.5 Standard setters

Standard setters tend to take a philosophical view of the audit expectations gap and position it relative to many other gaps they perceive in stakeholders' grasp of an informed view in relation to companies in which they hold an interest.

> [T]he audit expectation gap isn't the only gap...what we're acknowledging [is] that clearly there is a whole raft of issues around how much or little shareholders know about the company. So do they read the annual reports? Do they look at who the directors are and have a sense of their capacity or reputation, or the management team for the same thing? Do they understand the strategy of the company and what it's about...Fraud?...that's a classic example of does an audit report sign-off mean that no fraud has been conducted. Clearly, it doesn't. There's an expectation I suspect on the demand side that certainly a substantial fraud would be found. But the auditors...?

An expectations gap exists not only between auditors and stakeholders in the audit process but between regulators and stakeholders in the regulatory process and the reader is reminded through the next quote of the pervasive nature of the gulf that can exist in perceptions of what can be achieved.

> Over the years there's been lots of debate in the US and discussion... that we should explain more about what the audit process is, and [the] expectation gap and all that stuff. It doesn't matter...you can write books on it and it makes no difference...apparently in all the cross-examination in the [HIH]...case they can't find anybody who actually can claim they read the audit opinion. Not one person from any of the claimants can categorically say they actually read the audit opinion.

This same standard setter goes on to point out that auditors are not the only group subject to an expectations gap. Regulators too can be the focus of such a gap.

> '[A]ll of a sudden... they're now the victims of this expectation. Where was ASIC? Why didn't ASIC stop this from happening?'

> [T]he body that I believe is now focusing on this expectation gap for themselves is ASIC, who are struggling right now with the [name of a company failing at the time of the interview] and all of a sudden...they're now the victims of this expectation. Where was ASIC? Why didn't ASIC stop this from happening? It's always why didn't someone stop this from happening? So an audit shouldn't stop something from happening. It should stop something from continuing...I don't think there [are] different expectations around what can be achieved in an audit... ASIC themselves are now victims of the expectation gap...[and] they now are perhaps more sympathetic, but they have a job to do and once you're a regulator with a role to review, you've got to work to a standard and so they're looking for a standard to work to. And remember when you come in after the fact to review something it's very different to being there during the process. Imagine if a surgeon conducting brain surgery also had to...document what he was doing as he did it at exactly the same time.

That all stakeholders, including regulators, need to work closely to minimise the gap, which is seen as unresolvable by this next standard setter, is drawn out:

> [I]n some ways, it's not so much an expectation gap...it's also [that] there [are]...elements of different interpretations of what responsibilities are and what would be reasonably expected. So whether you say that's an expectation gap or whether you define it

> more as an interpretation issue...those fundamental issues have not been dealt with. And so what we loosely call 'expectation gap'... [hasn't] gone away...I don't think you can solve the overall or the broader expectation gap, but...it's incumbent on all the stakeholders in the process to...work hard with the closer stakeholders...the regulators, the politicians.

Just which categories of stakeholders can be said to represent users of financial statements is eloquently drawn out in the following quotation:

> [W]e're saying or implying that we can never close [the expectations gap] because you've got a moving target or perhaps a difference in perception, but the real question is, who are the real users of the financial statements when we come to what is the expectation gap? And is it the mums and dads or is it the analysts, the brokers, the superannuation funds et cetera...those groups of people are not idiots and they pick up a set of financial statements that most of these analysts have their own assessment of the areas of judgment, hence, the questions they ask off the record and on the record. [At m]ost of the AGMs you go to there are one or two key questions around the business. The reasons I would assume there aren't any more is they've already received the responses outside of that arena.

The same standard setter continues, questioning how there can be reliance on the audit report when research shows that few actually read it:

> '[T]he statistics showed that most people don't even read the audit report.'

> [W]e come to this issue of how do you narrow or manage the expectation gap? Perhaps one of the key factors is—and it's clear in most investor relations-type publications—if in doubt, consult your financial advisor or accountant...one of the more interesting...studies...was a project done on the use of audit reports and...the statistics showed that most people don't even read the audit report when they read a set of financial statements. If you take that at face value, then fundamentally you would ask the question when something did go wrong and someone then sought to find someone that they might like to be responsible, you'd ask the question, well if they didn't read the audit report in the first place, how could they have a reliance on the report and then, more importantly, how could there be an expectation gap? Because if you're not actually even using

> the report, the question is well, how...do you have an expectation gap because you've got no expectation in the first place because you haven't even seen whether the auditor's qualified [the report] or not.

The same standard setter goes on to explain that in his or her view, it is the fact that investors want certainty in their investments but are not prepared to accept the commensurate low returns that gives rise to the expectations gap:

> I would suggest that the expectation gap lies in...what I call the classic syndrome of people wanting to know the answer before they know the question and we see that...in our profession, with people wanting advice, is this going to work and you haven't got all the facts, and...the expectation gap is that people want a certainty when they invest...People want 'guaranteed'. Now if everything was so certain, the returns would be very low.

A standard setter highlights the concept of materiality as an area in which misunderstanding by stakeholders occurs—as this illustrative comment reveals (the topic of materiality is returned to in Chapter 5):

> '[T]hat expectation gap is not necessarily something that can actually cost you as an accounting firm.'

> Potentially, many shareholders do not understand the concept of materiality and they'd be the retail shareholders. Should that be a concern for the accounting profession? I mean, it might be a concern for the retail investors. Should it be a concern for the accounting profession? Only if...that creates an expectation gap that could result in retail investors feeling aggrieved for something that happened subsequent to the audit that impacts them financially in a share price or whatever. If I was an accounting firm...I don't know that I'd be too concerned about it because...with good quality-control processes within an accounting firm with a good methodology, with sound basis for conclusions, that expectation gap is not necessarily something that can...cost you.

The practical difficulty in appropriately signalling corporate failure is highlighted in this comment from one of the standard setters:

> This whole concept of trading whilst insolvent is going to become greyer and greyer...because what you're going to be faced with is businesses that are one day going reasonably...the automotive industry's a classic. A customer who then turns around and says, 'No, we're going to change supplier but in the interim, can you keep supplying us?' And they keep them going. The question is, at what point does it tip?

'This whole concept of trading whilst insolvent is going to become greyer and greyer.'

8.5.1 Summary

Among the standard setters' comments is one that compels us to view the audit expectations gap within a wider perspective of a much more fundamental gap—a presumed gap in shareholders' knowledge and understanding of companies in which they invest. Interestingly, attention is drawn to another gap—between what is expected of regulators and what they can reasonably be expected to deliver. The thorny issue is raised of the auditor's responsibility to detect fraud and shareholder understanding of the auditor's role in that respect. Some exasperation comes through in terms of how infrequently the audit report is actually read; however, how important this is when reports are standardised is another matter. The issue of stakeholder misunderstanding of materiality in the context of auditing is raised in an illustrative comment among those above, but from the initial focus groups this issue took on such prominence that a subsequent chapter is dedicated to exploring perceptions of this concept and the communication of it by auditors. Despite some pessimism that the audit expectations gap can be resolved, there is evidence that standard setters have not given up striving to bridge it.

8.6 Regulators

Regulators do not flinch in acknowledging the expectations gap—not just in terms of expectations of audit by the public, but between themselves and suppliers.

Comments relating to public expectations of audit and auditors include the following.

> [T]he expectation gap between what people think an auditor should do and what they really do is probably a bit wider than I had first imagined before I came to this job.

> [I]t seems as though there's a vast amount of effort going into the audit process but it doesn't seem to turn up things that people are actually interested in. And...that's of course the audit expectation gap and...the auditors say, 'Well, you can't expect us to have found that.'
>
> There is certainly a huge difference in expectation between what people understand audited accounts to mean [and] what auditors think they mean and obviously what regulators mean. So probably it's partly a function of auditors to explain what it is that [they have done or]...they haven't done and what they're really willing to say is the true position with respect to a company...A professional class of investor who makes the vast majority [of] investment decisions in Australia in terms of value—well, they probably don't need any more education. I'm not sure how much reliance they place on audited accounts anyway. But...for ordinary people who are trying to run their own super funds or whatever...they probably would need quite a bit more help.

An illustrative comment regarding the regulator–auditor expectations gap follows. This topic is returned to in a Chapters 11–13, in which the issue of 'regulation' as it impacts on auditors is discussed in detail.

> [T]he first thing is that there is a huge expectation gap between regulators and auditors. [The regulator's] view of what an auditor should be turning up in an audit was radically different to what auditors thought was reasonable...so we would look at numbers of examples where it would seem to us to be fairly glaring problems seemed to have slipped by. Whereas the auditor would say, 'Well, you know you can't expect me to find all of these things.' Partly as well is of course what underlies all of these issues...money—in the sense that...how much do you want to spend...If you want to spend vast amounts of money on audits, well—that's what auditors used to say to us. You've got to be realistic about how much people are willing to spend on an audit, and if we had unlimited resources we could find all of these things, but otherwise...

Again, the mystique surrounding the auditor's use of the materiality concept is identified as part of the gap:

> '[T]he shareholders would absolutely be staggered at that...and they wouldn't understand the correlation between that materiality level and in a sense the cost of the audit.'

> There would be very few shareholders who would understand materiality as applied by an auditor. And...some of them would be quite staggered to learn...if you take [one of the top-100 listed companies], the materiality on that job might be 20 million—I'm just picking a figure—and therefore the numbers are right, plus or minus the 20 million. Well...the shareholders would absolutely be staggered at that...and they wouldn't understand the correlation between that materiality level and...the cost of the audit...if you were going to be dropping that down to just say five million then you're going to have to be doing four times the amount of work that you presently do...therefore that concept hasn't been well put out there because...it's started to get into the audit report.

8.6.1 Summary

From a regulator's perspective, the gap in their expectations of what an audit can achieve and that of auditors is evident. Similar distinctions between sophisticated and unsophisticated investors' capacity to understand emerge, as is the case with the comments of other stakeholders earlier in this chapter. One of the comments draws us back to the reality that, among other things, it is what can be achieved for a given price that constrains the audit deliverable. Again, an illustrative comment about the auditor's use of the materiality concept is included, completing the mention of this notion by all stakeholders as part of the audit expectations gap. Chapter 5 is dedicated to analysis of stakeholders' views about this important topic, which has not been identified particularly as a component of the audit expectations gap in the research literature.

9.0 Issues and implications

In the detailed individual interviews of users, purchasers, suppliers, standard setters and regulators, the majority acknowledge the existence of an expectations gap or gaps. Only a relatively small proportion of the interviewees believe there is no expectations gap or that it is limited, and the majority believe there is an expectations gap and indeed many argue there are multiple gaps.

The users interviewed were by and large professional users as opposed to retail investors. It was common for users to perceive the existence of an expectations gap between themselves and the suppliers of audit opinions, but it was common for them to express a concern that there was a substantial expectations gap between regulators and auditors. Some users commented that the expectations gap had narrowed but in a way that might not be consistent with increasing the prestige of the profession. Some users commented that the failures that occurred earlier in the past decade caused expectations of what the auditor could achieve to be lowered and therefore the gap narrowed. Interestingly, some users took the view that the changes to the regulatory environment meant that the expectations gap had lessened because auditors were now working more closely with regulators.

Purchasers too observed that there were multiple gaps and in some cases commented at length about the expectations gap between auditors and regulators. Purchasers expressed some criticism of regulators. Much of this criticism centred on the fact that there was a belief that regulators needed to specify the objective of the audit in their inspections as well as in their oversight of the auditing profession rather than just tell them how to achieve that outcome.

There was a series of perceptions within the purchasers that auditing involved undertaking validation of the financial statements to a level of materiality that was healthy and achieved within a reasonable cost. One purchaser observed that while the Sarbanes-Oxley legislation in the United States had 'plugged a political gap', it had done so at enormous cost to the economy. One might argue that this legislation has gained little benefit for the efficiency of that country's capital market.

Other purchasers indicate that the audit expectations gap arises mostly in the presence of business failure and yet in a free market economy there will always be the presence of business failure. Concerns are raised about the auditing profession, which might be motivated by false expectations, due in part to an attempt to gain some economic recompense from a party who has 'deep pockets'. There was also critical comment with respect to the media reaction to business failure and the role of auditors.

One purchaser indicated that if we wanted to change the role of auditing one would have to adopt quite a different model. Rather than having an audit process that yields a small proportion of audit opinions that are qualified or modified, one might have to increase modifications to, say, 25 per cent to present a more varied set of outcomes for the market to consume and absorb. Possibly, then, there might be a more active interest and readership in the audit opinion.

Leading from this is the issue that standard form audit opinions could in fact generate a lower level of interest by participants in the capital market and indeed could result in the users of financial statements looking at the length of the audit opinion rather than really reading the opinion itself. Suppliers confirmed the expectations of certain other participants in the market. Their assessment is that the expectations gap is focused on essentially two aspects: 1) materiality; and 2) that an audit opinion does not guarantee all transactions and all events.

A number of suppliers indicated that they did not believe the expectations gap was closable, with several acknowledging there were different sorts of gaps with different participants in the capital market. In particular, retail investors were uninformed and probably uninformable. There were observations by many suppliers of an expectations gap between auditors and regulators, although comment was made that regulators were aware of what it was that auditors did, they just chose not to believe that this was the ultimate objective of the audit process. There was criticism by suppliers from the smaller audit firms that audit expectations developed by regulators were based on their observations of the Big Four and that those expectations were inappropriate in different parts of the capital market—in particular, for those companies that were smaller in market capitalisation.

Frequently, suppliers observed that auditing could be cast in many different ways, but the presence of materiality meant that auditing was able to be undertaken at reasonable cost to give reasonable assurance and this in itself was not understood by a large proportion of the market.

There were few observations from any of the interviewees about how the audit expectations gap might be resolved. One positive comment nominated was that in the audit report the scope of an audit could include comment on that which was undertaken by the auditor and that which was not, so that there was a more fulsome description of the scope of the audit process.

Another observation was that the presence of a stronger regulatory environment had in fact added to the expectations gap. This could be so because if regulators undertake their inspections with a particular purpose, as a consequence, they might miss the key issues of an audit engagement compared with those identified by the auditor at the time of the engagement.

One standard setter made the observation that many investors paid little or no attention to the audit opinion unless there was a business failure involved. Hence, there should be no expectation on auditors by those who did not use the audit opinion in their investment decision making. Others reading this report might conclude that such a view is naive and slightly condescending, as one does not have to read an audit opinion comprehensively to be able to understand what it says. As observed above, one might reasonably conclude the contents of a standard form audit opinion by its length.

There was also a comment that audits had a further type of expectations gap in that they could not stop the existence of certain behaviours (such as directors continuing trading while a company was insolvent); the best they could do was to terminate or minimise that behaviour once it had been discovered. One might say that they can also disclose information about this behaviour to the investing public.

One standard setter observed that much of the expectations gap was caused by regulators who could choose to deflect blame and negative market sentiment from themselves and on to the accounting profession. One might also observe that the expectations gap between the accounting firms and the regulators can be particularly damaging to the suppliers of audit services and to the efficiency and credibility of information available to the capital market.

Regulators also took a 'big-picture' view. None of the regulators interviewed indicated that legally enforceable auditing standards would really help close the expectations gap, narrow it or manage it. There was also a view that many players in the capital market did not require assistance in understanding the role of audits, but some players did.

We would like to comment on an issue not expressly raised by any of the regulators—that in the Australian economy, much has been done to encourage participation by a wide spectrum of investors in the Australian capital market. There have been many government floats and increased participation by a wide section of the public in various pension plans. There has, however, been no parallel public policy support mechanism to help educate and inform those participants in the capital market.

10.0 Concluding remarks

This second part of Chapter 3 touches on the often-quoted issue of the expectations gap. While this part is linked to the earlier part of this chapter, focusing on understandability, there are also certain distinct differences.

Among a large and disparate group of stakeholders there is widespread but not universal recognition of the audit expectations gap and one can conclude that with few exceptions no-one believes that this issue has been bridged. The policy question becomes: does it matter? From one perspective, the view is that the presence of an expectations gap or gaps is not costly to audit firms, but there is evidence that it is costly to the efficiency of the market for information that operates within the capital market. It is therefore still an important policy issue that warrants the investment of time and effort by those interested in the efficiency of the capital market.

Importantly, as a policy consideration, there was reference to the existence of three potential gaps: 1) between users and suppliers—the traditional gap referred to frequently in the literature and in discussions more broadly; 2) between regulators and suppliers; and 3) between purchasers and suppliers.

In terms of the policy considerations, these issues will be dealt with in turn.

First, the expectations gap between users and suppliers is dealt with. In this study, as there has been with previous studies, there is recognition of a wide diversity of expertise among users. One policy consideration not widely contained in the literature is that the diversity of expertise is not played to by the current provision of audit information. Many users have high levels of expertise but the same commoditised audit report is provided to all. A second policy issue is that for the less expert users of financial reports, the population is poorly defined and probably constantly moving. As such, there is a serious question about the feasibility in a public policy setting of building that expertise or educating those users to a point where they will not have an expectations gap, but rather a full or at least reasonable understanding of the audit process and outcome. The question becomes, is it worth embarking on any process to close an expectations gap with such a population of users? This does not presuppose that nothing will be done, but that we do not have as an expectation that this gap can close completely.

Additionally, with regard to the expectations gap between users and suppliers, there is the issue of diversity of incentives. Where corporate collapses occur there is the possibility of an enhanced or even 'manufactured' gap existing. On the one hand, we have users who might not have ever relied on an audit report claiming such reliance to access the 'deep pockets' or economic substance of large audit firms. On the other hand, we have suppliers to the market for audit services claiming that the limitations on what they seek to undertake in an audit are not understood, thereby attempting to avoid accountability in the circumstance of corporate failures. Put another way, from a public policy perspective, the audit expectations gap will come and go depending on economic circumstances. If this is the case, there is the question of what is the legitimacy or validity of the expectations gap in a stable or neutral setting?

With respect to the expectations gap between regulators and suppliers, the policy issue is: what is an audit? It is well understood that auditing in a free market economy is a form of delegated regulation. The presence of an audit comes about because of legislation in order to provide some form of assurance of the disclosures made by companies and others trading in the market. Is it the case that suppliers and regulators understand that this is in fact a form of delegated regulation? The implication for auditors is that the audit process is a form of regulation that they are asked or required to undertake for and on behalf of a client who is from neither the directorship nor the management of the company. For regulators, do they understand that delegated regulation means they must pass on that delegation in a fulsome way? Put more directly, do regulators understand that the role of regulation is to specify the objective or outcome of the audit process rather than to specify the means and processes by which the audit is undertaken? Do regulators need to withdraw from the specifying process and more clearly specify the objective and outcome? If they do specify the process, do they have unintended bias about specifying that the processes used by the Big Four represent best practice and therefore should be used as the benchmark?

There is also reference to an expectations gap between purchasers and suppliers, but this is not seen in the same dimension or at the same level of complexity as the other two. If there are some issues around this expectations gap, they could relate to particular topics that are dealt with in the next paragraph.

One possible policy implication of a discussion of the audit expectations gap is a need to attempt to obtain greater focus on the gap by specifying which topics of the audit process or outcome are subject to an expectations gap. From the evidence available to us, there are three issues that are clearly of substance: 1) the issue of forward detection and whether this is an expectation and, if so, whether it should be expressly removed from the expectations of users by way of scope paragraphs; 2) the issue of materiality and the extent to which there is no or insufficient public description of materiality in an audit context and the consequences on the audit process and outcome; and 3) the use of certain language. The key in this last category is the use of the word 'test' in the audit report. A test can be a test of 100 per cent of the population of items or it can be a test of a much smaller proportion. The word 'test' does not in and of itself suggest that the work of the auditor is on a sample basis. Substitution of the word 'sample' for 'test' might be a simple action, but it could provide much greater shared meaning of a key part of the audit process.

Another issue with respect to the expectations gap is whether we can expect removal of the expectations gap when there is evidence that the audit report is much less than universally read. Again, this returns us to the issue of what incentives, behaviour or actions would help ensure that the audit report is more frequently read rather than scanned, and we refer to comments made in the earlier part of this chapter in relation to this matter.

Another policy implication is whether the legal backing of auditing standards will assist in the eradication of the expectations gap. That is, based on conversations with stakeholders, those responsible for public policy should not expect that legal backing of auditing standards will have any consequences for the audit expectations gap.

There were some alternative propositions put by various stakeholders. For example, do we want to adopt a quite different model to the current audit model? For instance, one in which auditors may be given the responsibility of providing an alternative set of financial reports to those of management. This is an extreme alternative and possibly not worthy of any consideration, but it does illustrate the point that there are alternative models to the existing audit process. Whether these models are acceptable or even remotely achievable is not so much the case as that there are alternative models available. Another model might be to undertake a much more comprehensive sampling of items in the financial reports, but that would come at a significant cost, which in turn would result in much lower returns to shareholders.

The policy issue here is that the current model is based on certain parameters, which include reasonable costs and the absence of a guarantee. Are these the parameters we want to live with in the future? Because these parameters are now so universally accepted, do we have any choice in the matter?

In conclusion, the biggest single policy issue in this part of the chapter is that the expectations gap is alive and possibly is not subject to closure. Indeed, it is complex and involves multiple gaps. With respect to the gap between regulators and suppliers, the observation made is that these are clearly defined populations of stakeholders, which one would expect to have considerable shared levels of expertise and understanding, and that it might be efficient in public policy terms to work on the expectations gap between these two stakeholder groups as a matter of urgency.

COMMUNICATION 4

> I would question how useful...[detailed information about the audit process and outcome] really would be, because...if there was an agreement amongst the audit firms or a direction from government... that they're required to make more disclosure...it would literally be lawyers sitting round a table working out how to word that disclosure, and the wording would be similar amongst all the firms, and very soon it would be pointless in terms of adding real value... to the reader of the financial statements...It would be a motherhood statement...that says we've conducted this, this, this and this, and my guess would be it would be fairly similar between each audit client...They [would] put a lot of effort into getting the words right initially, but they wouldn't be putting a lot of effort into tailoring the words for each audit...so I'm not sure that it would really provide that much value to a sophisticated user of the statements.
> — Purchaser

1.0 Key issues

Responses to the proposition that either auditors or management should be charged with the responsibility to disclose incremental information about the audit process and/or the audit opinion are mixed, within and across categories of stakeholders. Key issues include:

- is there value in further disclosure in the audit process and/or outcome that is subject to regulatory requirement
- if either auditors or management provides additional disclosures in the context of audit, what would be the most appropriate content and location
- if such disclosures are to be provided by either management or auditors, what mechanisms could be used to monitor the disclosures to ensure that they are not misleading or deceptive?

- if such disclosures are not to be provided by auditors or management, what other mechanisms might be introduced to provide that content, presuming the content is deemed desirable for distribution
- will additional disclosures, no matter where they are located, merely exacerbate information overload to the point that a counterproductive effect occurs?

2.0 Disclosure of the audit process by auditors

Within the literature, some commentators have suggested that, at least in aggregate, one way of helping overcome differences of view in the market for audit services is to provide more disclosure to the market on audit processes. This, it is suggested, will enable users of audit opinions and other participants in the market to be better informed about what occurs within an audit. While there was not a specific survey question about this issue, the individual interviews revealed a rich and diverse array of opinions in this regard.

Interestingly, there were many comments from users, purchasers, suppliers, standard setters and regulators, including some that were introspective and possibly even self-interested. For example, purchasers tended to focus on information potentially provided to management of auditees rather than to the wider stakeholder group of shareholders. Even standard setters tended to think of their own position rather than that of the efficiency of the capital market. Typical comments are provided below.

2.1 Users

Several of the users felt that having auditors disclose information about the auditor's work and processes would be useful, particularly at the individual client level, but overall there was scepticism that this information would be taken advantage of as a useful resource, especially by retail investors who some might argue were most in need of this type of additional information. The following quotations reveal reactions among users when the question is put to them about the worth of auditors disclosing more about their work. Several made suggestions about the type of information thought desirable to be disclosed by auditors and suitable outlets for it. This first quotation provides the interviewee's perception that as long as the information is presented in a highly readable way, it is of merit:

> I can see some merit in...[a] statement that's included in the annual report if that...gave a few more details about what's actually done... at the moment all you're looking at is 'have they signed the dotted line?' 'Is there any qualification?' That's all you're looking for. So people may not spend all that much time...reading if you put more details in it, but you could imagine that if it's set out nicely and easily readable, people would actually at least scan and see this is what they've done...Yes, there's some merit in that.

This next quotation suggests content, including verification of the existence of assets and liabilities and their value and whether internal controls are reviewed to ensure accurate capture of data:

> I actually think [auditor disclosure of the audit process is] a really good idea. I don't think they [provide] enough [explanation] of what they've [done], how they arrive at their opinion and...it would help people who read the assurance statements to formulate in their mind what's been done. Things like 'we've verified the existence of assets and their value, we've undertaken an internal controls review of the business to ensure that the capturing of accounting data is accurate, we've verified assets and liabilities where we can, we've got independent views'...If they went through all of that process... it would be really good and it doesn't need to be hugely wordy... obviously it's going to take up a bit of space, but it wouldn't be a bad thing...even if that was something on a company's web site.

More suggestions for content are included in this next user's comments, as well as disclosure of whether invoices and contracts have been examined, the level of testing of subsidiary ledgers and the materiality level:

> [M]ainly the confusion arises when the reader of the audit [report] doesn't really know how much work or how much background checks or information the auditor has actually done to come up with the response. So whether it's...the level of testing of things like debtors, creditors, ledgers, whether they actually checked invoices, whether they've looked at contracts, what the materiality has been et cetera, because...from a [lender's] point of view, when you're looking at a balance sheet, have they really gone behind the numbers to validate things or have they just relied on the data given to them by the customer and then perhaps [a] random sample of that particular testing and if so, that's okay, but what's the level

> of confidence [that] can be gained from that...if you knew what sort of testing they have done or what...methods they've used, you can then draw your own conclusions [about] whether you need a further assessment on that particular aspect or whether you can rely on it totally.

This next user would like to see the auditor's views on matters that go well beyond what is included in the financial audit, such as the operational efficiency of the audited organisation or the transparency in obtaining information relative to experience with other organisations.

> If I'm referring to our own organisation, probably things like if they come across operational issues where they feel...there's something behind it that's not quite right, or if they come across [issues] that aren't necessarily just related to the figures but...in actually getting hold of figures or getting hold of data and they find either... unnecessary complexity or difficulty in obtaining that information, or that it seems to be not documented or any of those sorts of things...that would be a good concept to disclose...So just from their point of view in operating, in going and auditing a number of organisations, a view as to maybe the operational efficiency or the operational transparency in actually obtaining that information relative to other organisations.

The next user seeks greater disclosure by the auditor of his or her subjective assessment of the financial position of the company:

> [W]e deal with clients who have shares...[and] the majority wouldn't have any idea of some key measures that you'd like to think that they'd know about the company...when you look at... company reports a little bit more, you really have to look hard and unless you're a specialist or you know what to look [for], it's hard to get certain kinds of information. You get the core information but any more detail—which...sometimes gives you a feel[ing] of what the company [and] its financial position is—it's a little bit harder. So I would like to see a lot more [disclosure by the auditor].

One user feels the venue for enhanced disclosure by the auditor should be the AGM and the importance of the independence of the auditor needs to be more conspicuous:

> [I]t probably wouldn't be a bad thing. You could probably do it at an AGM, run through the financial reports, say, potentially even have...a statement read out from the auditors to say, 'We've actually read through these financial reports and they're in compliance with standards', any events, extraordinary events or whatever it might be that need to be read out—need to be read out as well...that would be a good thing. Just to heighten the awareness of people at AGMs of what's happening with the financial reports. Because quite often you get read out the financial reports from the CFO and they're brushed over pretty quickly...And it doesn't give a feeling of independence...at an AGM, which is shareholders' only real avenue to management, there's always a bit of a feel[ing]...of spin doctoring, et cetera, by the company to say, 'Listen, this is fantastic, we've had a great year'...and there's no real clarification of reports by the auditors at all.

This next user implies that it is the financial statement and note presentation, not the audit, which needs attention:

> [P]eople just need to understand in general...terms what's gone on, but...I do think that they just assume it's right...what the frustration of the capital market is, is not with the audit itself, but with the way in which the information is then presented.

Less supportive comments by users include concerns that any additional material will not be read, especially by retail investors:

> It would help, but [for] the retail market, reading accounts is such a small part of their life.

> [T]he retail investor does take comfort from the fact that an audit firm is doing the audit, that gives...a level of comfort. But I don't think they really want to know too much more...[and] nine times out of 10, everything is right...for listed companies anyway.

'They don't read what they've already got.'

> [T]hey're really pushing it uphill to start with. I don't think they need to disclose any more, because when things are going well, people don't read it. They don't read what they've already got...it would be interesting to line up 100 shareholders and ask them have they ever read an audit report. I suspect most would say no. Because...most retail shareholders struggle to read the accounts. It's a real reflection on the accounting profession, how poorly we present financial information.

The next user raises the issue of information overload, with the auditor's responsibility for detecting fraud being singled out as a worthy disclosure:

> [T]here is already so much information out there that it's difficult to digest...if the concern of auditors is that there's a gap...people are expecting them to pick up fraud when they're not, then perhaps in general that needs to be addressed. I'm not sure how you do that exactly, but in terms of audit by audit, whether that needs to be paraphrased in some manner at the end of the financial statements. I just don't think people will read it.

'I don't think the average person would look at it.'

> I don't think the average person would look at it. I mean, if you read the audit report, it tells you what they're looking at anyway. If you've got any understanding of financial statements, you can take quite a lot away from that. The issue is that the average person doesn't have that knowledge about the financial statements, so that's when it becomes more difficult...it's the general view that if the auditor signed off on it then it all must be okay, and that's the layman's understanding about what an audit statement is. It's probably something that's going to change over time. It's a bit like superannuation—people don't understand superannuation, even though they have to put 10 per cent[4] of their salary towards it each year...the education of investors will happen slowly over a period of years.

4 In Australia, the statutory minimum employee contribution to superannuation is 9 per cent.

There were several other comments, not reproduced here, to the effect that the annual report itself was not the place for such further disclosures by auditors.

2.1.1 Summary

Although some users are enthusiastic about the notion of greater auditor disclosure of the audit process, reservations are expressed about whether one part of the user group—the retail market—would find the time or motivation to read such additional information. As to what type of information about the auditor's work and processes would be useful, users suggest a variety of things—from detailed information about assets and liabilities, operational issues and difficulties encountered in accessing the underlying needed information to unnecessary complexity or difficulty in obtaining that information, or required information that is not documented and further information about the company's financial position. Each of these disclosures is well beyond the current requirements of auditors.

2.2 Purchasers

As with users, purchasers provided mixed responses to a question put to them about the worth of having auditors make additional disclosures about the audit process. Some, as illustrated below, were quite enthusiastic about this type of communication as an educative process—but more for company insiders than for shareholders, as suggested by this first quotation.

> [F]ace-to-face is the way to go. Certainly, an audit-wide perspective to a selected audience...I'd appreciate that very much. I wouldn't expect too many changes between the audit firms, especially the Big Four, but...you do understand there are different cultures. So I would be very interested [if], as one of the first things that our new auditors did, would be to say, 'Look, this is how we're going to be approaching the audit and these are the key areas that we're looking at.' I guess not just as a start-up to the audit, but...wherever they head out.

The next purchaser suggests disclosures from the auditor about changes to regulations and standards as potentially useful:

> [T]here would have to be a constant education to shareholders on the changing regulations and what auditors are doing...there were some new standards coming out for the auditors a few years back, [and] it's definitely an education process to shareholders.

> I mean, to the extent that they don't know, then…they should know, and…it would be up to the accounting profession, or the auditing profession, to be in a position where they are educating the wider community on exactly what they're doing and how they're doing it, and where things are heading and changing.

Information sessions run by the auditing firms to which purchasers and users are invited is the suggestion of another purchaser:

> Even me, for example, I'm not fully sure of what those new auditing standards meant. I've got the perception that there's a lot more red tape that auditors are going through now, and there [are] a lot more sign-offs and qualifications, and peer reviews and all these sort of things. But I'm not really sure of what is meant and how that's reflected in the audit work that's now being done in our organisation, or in our audit fees or any of that. So education…I definitely want to know a bit more and in some more succinct environment to do that. We get invited to plenty of forums that our auditors give… whether it's [on] tax updates or accounting updates and all that. But I've never seen a general two-hour session in the afternoon… with maybe drinks afterwards, or tea or coffee, talking about the profession and where it's heading and what the new standards mean. If…shareholders and the wider community [are invited to that type of activity]…that could be worthwhile.

Information about the client-tailored expertise of audit personnel would be a worthwhile disclosure from this next purchaser's point of view:

'[I]t's not just simply a process, it's also…how do they ensure they've got the right people?'

> [T]here needs to be a certain level of disclosure from accounting firms about how they approach things, the expertise that they've got—because it's not just simply a process, it's also…how do they ensure they've got the right people? If you're basically going in and you're auditing, for example, the resource entities that are cropping up now in Western and South Australia, well a lot of the audits of those kinds of organisations probably require some kind of resource expert… somebody who's basically had two to three years post-university who's doing the audit doesn't have that skill…so how do auditors get the right blend of skills for the different types of organisations?

What comes through in this next quotation—which includes suggestions for enhanced disclosures around accounts or the processes used to verify them that the auditor is not comfortable with—is the ability for insiders to converse with auditors about these issues. Shareholders have this potential at AGMs, but rarely use it to elicit this type of information from auditors—at least according to views expressed in this chapter by all categories of stakeholder.

> [W]e're reasonably happy on this front...the key thing for us is, if there is something [that] is not a straightforward matter...say, a reserve...[which is] normally what happens now, it either gets signed off or it gets signed off subject to qualifications...We would like just a bit more description as to the particular...fields in the accounts that [they]...maybe aren't as comfortable with, or they've gone through a rigorous process to verify the accuracy [of]. There's not a lot of description, so what we don't really know is how much time has the auditor actually spent looking at a particular reserve or a particular accounting number and how comfortable they are with it...[and] particular items in the accounts where auditors might have a particular issue rather than having a qualification instead of a sign-off. Just maybe some more colour around how they've verified...or even just...at the beginning of a set accounts...a statement of what they've actually verified. Because at the moment what we get is 'true and fair' or whatever [as a] sign-off from the auditor. It's...very broad...we don't actually know what have they actually verified. How close do they look at things...we talk to the auditors in detail and we find that out afterwards, but we can't tell that from the actual accounts.

'It's...very broad...we don't actually know what have they actually verified. How close do they look at things?'

> I'm a firm believer that the annual report should...give a shareholder a good understanding of the organisation, not only its financial statements, but its operations and its business. So I would punt for greater disclosure in the annual report over [an AGM]...not everybody can make an AGM, not everybody has...access to the web or even wants to sit there and listen to broadcasts,

'[N]ot everybody can make an AGM, not everybody has...access to the web or even wants to sit there and listen to broadcasts.'

> and let's face it, if you're actually sitting there listening to an accountant talk about how they audited financial statements, it's not going to be the most exciting thing to listen to.

The same purchaser continues, explaining that whatever information is provided needs to be linked to potential implications for the shareholder:

> [A]ny additional disclosure, especially in these sort of areas...needs to be kept simple. There's no point having disclosure in the annual report that is...caught up in jargon. And what I mean by simple is, you should be able to give the average shareholder out there a nexus between... 'this is why we're auditing, this is what we're doing, so this is what it means to you, and this is what it doesn't mean to you'...I don't know how you would do this...but linking that to the financial statements...instead of just having a page on the auditor saying, 'We did a controls-based audit and we looked at this, this and this and we judged that their revenues are recorded accurately and their expenses have been recorded accurately and everything's capitalised that should be capitalised'...That's all well and good, but [it should be linked] back to what...it mean[s] for the shareholder, reading that, as opposed to just getting a blurb?

The next purchaser would prefer to see enhanced disclosure by the auditor about how the firm goes about preparing and undertaking the audit in the audit engagement letter—again, a medium that capital market participants are not privy to.

> 'I'm constantly trying to struggle to understand what they call their audit approach, the proprietary approach that they adopt for each audit.'

> As a manager in a business, and being a CPA but not an auditor myself, and not having an audit background, I'm constantly trying to struggle to understand what they call their audit approach, the proprietary approach that they adopt for each audit. And as a customer of the audit firm, I'd like to understand more about how they go about that, so that I can evaluate whether we're getting the right level of service; whether they're undertaking processes that with a little bit more information and insights as to how they go about preparing and doing their audit... I could actually say, 'Do you realise this or that?' And 'that's not ever going to be material', and 'you don't really need to worry about this'. And it could actually drive efficiencies in the process

> that way because, obviously, with the purchase of these audit services we've got a big interest in keeping the fees down. So... I'd like...some more information in that regard to be disclosed. And...the logical way for them to disclose that to their customer is through the engagement letter process in almost a couple of pages of explanatory memorandum about their audit process and how that ties back to specifically what we're going to do for you, rather than just the normal engagement letters, which are pages and pages of just canned information, disclaimers and those sorts of things.

Enhanced disclosure by the auditor about materiality is the suggestion of this next purchaser:

> So the people that are interested can actually seek it [from the company's web site] without cluttering up [the audit report]... maybe something about materiality...might be of interest.

Making the management letter public is the preference of another purchaser, who has capital market participants in mind in responding to this question:

> [W]hen you look at the bland innocuous report that appears in the annual report and when you look at the fact that very few auditors are actually ever questioned at AGMs, one really wonders what people get out of the report other than the brand name of the firm, the brand name of the individual that's auditing the firm and the clean certificate... the management letter that is disclosed to the board should be made available to shareholders on the web site. The auditor should be required to present it and take questions on it at the AGM. There will be the usual complaint that it contains confidential information. The reality is that if the matters are significant enough to be brought to the attention of the board, then as the proxy of the shareholders, the board should be comfortable with that being disclosed.

'[T]he management letter that is disclosed to the board should be made available to shareholders on the web site.'

As with users, several of the purchasers, however, are sceptical about incremental disclosure of the audit process by auditors. This next purchaser points to the potential for information overload as a reason to maintain the status quo:

> '[A]nnual reports, financial statements, have probably already got too much information.'

I would generally say that annual reports, financial statements, have probably already got too much information. So I'm not in favour of...putting more and more information about more and more things that many people won't want to read. But, having said that, I also recognise the fact that there needs to be an avenue for people to get information if they want to. So perhaps the issue is the halfway house.

From the financial service industry point of view, the disclosure, of itself, is actually quite onerous. It's quite extensive already... both in preparing the financial statements and other audit work that the external auditors have to prepare for the regulators or for management or for the external managed [funds]. So there's actually quite a bit of information and on top of that they also present at the various board meetings on what they do, how to do it and it's up to the individual boards to ask them.

The same purchaser continues, pointing to the AGM as the opportunity for shareholders to ask questions of the auditor:

[A] simple answer, if there is a simple answer...to this question is [that the auditors]...have discussed quite a bit in terms of what they do, how they do it and also there's always opportunity for key stakeholders to ask them more questions, especially if it's a listed company. Nowadays external auditors have to actually attend the annual general meeting...so obviously it's up to ordinary shareholders...And I must say that obviously a lot of the information might be verging on too technical, too complicated and could be confusing and misleading to the uninformed or un-technically trained readers. So...especially from the financial service industry aspect...the current level of disclosure is...quite extensive already.

Another purchaser similarly invokes the AGM as providing an opportunity for shareholders to learn more about the audit:

They have the information. They can come to the AGM, and the auditors come to the AGM.

One purchaser, responding to this question, makes clear his or her feelings about the worth of existing disclosures by auditors as 'jargonish...mumbo-jumbo statements':

> '[C]urrent disclosures and the opinions that are provided are jargonish...mumbo-jumbo statements. So no-one understands them and no-one reads them.'

> My initial reaction to that question was no, they shouldn't, because I've got no idea what they would actually disclose...and why they would disclose more information...it comes back to a further question, which is what's the role of the auditor? What are they actually trying to achieve? What I do think is that the current disclosures and the opinions that are provided are jargonish...mumbo-jumbo statements. So no-one understands them and no-one reads them...there is an expectation in the...public arena, and that's what people measure auditors' performance against. So I don't think additional disclosure in their report actually addresses that expectation gap, if you want to call it that. I don't think it is the expectation gap.

The suggestion for a 'simple English' report stating what the auditor has done is the reluctant suggestion from this next, unconvinced purchaser:

> [Auditors] should just state...in simple English what they did. What does it add? I suppose I'm very in favour of a simple English-type report, but I'm not sure what [more disclosure] adds.

This next purchaser enunciates the likelihood of a 'motherhood', 'boiler-plate' generic statement, vetoed by lawyers, if the suggestion is to go ahead, with little or no tailoring to the specific circumstances of each audit engagement and hence with limited value:

> [E]ven if I was an active retiree investor in the habit of reading financial statements, which...is probably a very small minority, would I get value out of reading a statement that said exactly what sort of work was done and, more importantly, would I make investment decisions or be guided by that? I still don't know that it would add a lot, unless there was a requirement somehow to tailor those words very specifically to that audit and that organisation...if it was a generic statement about the processes that were undertaken, I don't think it would add a lot, but if it was a statement that was very specific...[it might].

Three purchasers point to the importance of users being able to rely on the professionalism of the auditor and the professional nature of the conduct of the audit, rather than any need to rely on enhanced disclosures:

> [M]ost people probably could understand but I don't know if they're really interested. They can go and read the auditing standard...and we don't get anybody doing that...all they want to know is do the auditors tick it off or not and then there's an assumption that if they've ticked it off there's a professional level and standard to that which applies. So it's really...that integrity around the profession which is the...critical one.
>
> I don't know where else it could be disclosed quite frankly. I don't know what [the disclosure] would be. I don't think you want auditors busy explaining sets of accounts to the investors or anything...that's up to the companies...and the other thing is...these are professional firms and...you've just got to rely to an extent on [their] professional nature. That may be a bit of an old-fashioned concept.
>
> I don't think it's really necessary for auditors to disclose any more than they do today...what shareholders have got to have confidence in is the selection of the auditor, the auditor's independence, and [that] the company through its audit committee has processes to ensure auditor independence. At the end of the day, auditors will give an opinion that is also based on certification and representation letters from management...when you stand up there at an AGM, or sit on the stage like I do, shareholders today are really looking at that CFO and saying, 'You're accountable for all those numbers of disclosures and we're trusting you that they're right.'

The same purchaser continues, arguing that what is more important than auditor disclosures about the audit process is transparency by the organisation about auditor selection and mechanisms the organisation uses to enhance auditor independence.

> [Y]es, auditors will give an opinion, but auditors give disclaimers. And, as you've seen from the various litigations around the world, CFOs go to jail first. Now, would there be any greater protection for a CFO if the auditor was required to disclose more information about their audit? Probably not. So I don't think it's necessary. But what is necessary, and we are required to disclose this now as part of good governance, [is] that you have a good process in place for your auditor selection, that there are good processes in place to ensure their independence. And...once you've got that, that should be adequate comfort for shareholders.

The same purchaser explains the content of his or her organisation's disclosures about auditor selection and independence-affirming mechanisms. Of concern is this purchaser's last observation—that even analysts do not read the financial statements.

> 'Analysts today don't even read the financial statements and disclosures. They wait for a CEO and CFO to get up on announcement day and distil it for them. They can't understand it all.'

> [The auditor's independence declaration] does help, but if you read our disclosures…you will see we have in our governance attachment to the directors' report the process we actually go through as a company to ensure the auditor is independent. So, yes, the auditor's got to give a certification they are, but we're disclosing how we also verify their independence. And we have a cap on how much other work they can do. We've got a process of approval for non-audit services. We list the prohibited services and so on. So to disclose more I don't think is necessary. And I happen to be one of those people who believe that we've gone over the top with disclosure. And I'll give you an example why I say that. Analysts today don't even read the financial statements and disclosures. They wait for a CEO and CFO to get up on announcement day and distil it for them. They can't understand it all.

The explicit or implied claim of these next few purchasers is that enhanced disclosures by an auditor of the audit process will not achieve anything.

> It just won't help. [The reality is n]obody's interested…and I just don't think you can…make people interested, that's the trouble. I don't think you can legislate…what you've got to do…is make sure that there's…a professional standard that goes on there, which people can generally rely on.

> No, I think current disclosures are fine.

> I presume…you're talking about in a set of statutory accounts, should the auditor…provide a 10-page report rather than a one and a half page report like they do at the moment? And my view would be no.

> [M]y view would be the auditor's got to follow auditing standards. The standards are a public document. Why would they need to do anything more?

'[T]ypically, a set of accounts now is over 100 pages and I don't believe the majority of shareholders either read them or understand them.'

I strongly don't believe that by providing a lot more detail they'll get that information. As a side comment, the published accounts at the moment have gone crazy with the amount of disclosure we do under the new accounting standards. Because, for a company like the ones I'm associated with, typically a set of accounts now is over 100 pages and I don't believe the majority of shareholders either read them or understand them. So...in that context, if you actually say, do they need another 10 pages to explain...if you actually said they're going to provide a document which was a proper description of the way the audit was conducted in detail, you wouldn't do it in under 10 pages. It would be...very dense material and I just don't think it would actually help the situation at all.

2.2.1 Summary

Few of the purchasers feel that it would be useful to disclose more information about audit work or audit processes, wherever disclosed. Several make reference to the extensive disclosures in annual reports and the fact that few users understand these, without adding more. Three refer to the AGM as an opportunity for financial report users to ask questions of the auditor. Three refer to the auditing standards as being available for reference if information is needed. A fear that such disclosures, if made, would become standardised or 'boiler plate' was also expressed. That such disclosures might lead to negative outcomes for auditors is a concern expressed by one of the group. Interestingly, in this group's comments, there is a high degree of knowledge demonstrated of what is entailed in an audit and sympathy for the auditor in terms of unrealistic expectations of what an audit can achieve.

2.3 Suppliers

Suppliers were generally, although not universally, against greater disclosure of their audit processes than that already existing. Added 'confusion' and difficulty in explaining the exercise of judgment was the verdict that filtered through in comments such as those reproduced below.

> [D]isclosing more information potentially runs the risk of creating more confusion around people in the marketplace understanding

> what the auditor does or what he doesn't do…there is a large amount of judgment involved in the conduct of an audit, and the procedures you would undertake and the work you would do vary significantly from entity to entity, and can differ from entities even within the same industry sector, depending upon their risk profile, depending upon their individual circumstances. So…to come up with some form of disclosure [about]…the work…undertaken…would be quite [hard] in my view to try and create something that would be meaningful, other than something that would be fairly generic, if you were to say well, this is broadly conducted across any financial statement audit.

The next two suppliers allude to the likelihood of generic disclosures: should auditors disclose more of their audit process than is the current case?

> I doubt it. In fact, you're much better informed about the structure of an audit opinion and what's supposed to be in there and you know to look for a heading called 'qualification' or 'modification'…Most people don't know that. But there [are] two or three other paragraphs around directors' responsibilities, scope, et cetera…so whether we extend that to three pages of discussion around [a] director's responsibility and our processes, it's just three pages of boiler plate that no-one's ever going to look at. And the other question I'd put…is, well to whose benefit would it be for us to disclose more about our work and our processes? I don't think the users really get any benefit from it. All they seek is our assurance. So long as they've been given that clearly…that's all they would want to know.

'[I]t's just three pages of boiler plate that no-one's ever going to look at.'

'External auditors do phenomenal amounts of work and end up with...one page in the annual report that basically says nothing much.'

> I can't see that it would add much value...When we do internal audit work or a[n]...assignment or whatever, the typical outline of our report...is an introduction and context, if you like...that has the genesis of this job, and then obviously has scope, and particularly any limitations thereto, and then you have work performed. So, when we are writing a report to a client or to whoever it is, we would give that context. External auditors do phenomenal amounts of work and end up with...one page in the annual report that basically says nothing much...If we are going to change that and have the auditors explain what work they do, you'd probably have a lot more to disclose. The auditor will then... either want to say a lot, or say as little as they do now. It sounds a bit like opening Pandora's box...It would either be a very generic statement that I don't think anyone would read, or it'd be a genuine description of everything they did, which would be voluminous, and written with a view to the defence lawyer further down the track, rather than to...informing the capital markets.

Like the previous supplier, the next one cannot see a happy medium between saying little and saying more than enough to cause confusion in order to explain the audit process adequately. Succinctness in the explanation is not a characteristic that suppliers see as possible because of the complexity and ambiguity of the audit task.

> [M]y concern in disclosing more information is that does that then create even more confusion? The question is whether there's a happy halfway house between disclosing nothing and just saying we do an audit in accordance with auditing standards to a disclosure which lays out in gory detail exactly what steps we take. And I'm not comfortable that there's a halfway house between the two.

Confusion is the theme in this next supplier's reaction, too:

> [T]he investors in the street probably...don't understand financials, and therefore if you start to add more information to that framework...you create more confusion rather than less confusion. There probably is a need to create some form of simplification.

The difficulty in adequately articulating the application of professional judgment in the audit process is the concern of another supplier:

> '[T]here still is an element of professional judgment that goes into the way we conduct it. So it's very hard to articulate that sort of thing.'

> The only reservation I have...about that is...how far do you go, and what information do you disclose to them...whilst we certainly need [to] try and do something to close the expectation gap, I'm not convinced that giving them more information about the process that we go through is necessarily going to close that expectation gap [to] any great degree. The way we conduct audits...[is] particularly regulated by standards, et cetera...but there still is an element of professional judgment that goes into the way we conduct it. So it's very hard to articulate that sort of thing into further information to disclose to the reader. So I would find it very difficult to see that particularly closing the expectation gap to any great degree.

Determining what it is that is relevant to disclose is the dilemma as far as the next supplier is concerned:

> [I]t's near...impossible to succinctly explain that to someone...so my concern would be if you go away from what we've got now—which is a straight page, a page and a half that says we've done an audit according to the standards, the directors are responsible for the accounts, we've done an audit—where do you go? Because obviously there's the full audit manual as to what an audit is, but where do you draw the line [on] what is relevant for them to know?

The next supplier is of the view that there are accessible sources of information about the audit process for those who are interested:

> I would've thought that the capital market, which is allegedly relying on the work that these auditors have done, should have a statement, which would be fairly general admittedly, but [which] would explain what the role of the auditors was and what level of reliance people could place upon it...if anyone really wants to find out, we have the Internet nowadays. If anyone wants to find out what the role of auditors is, it's actually very easy to find it out. If anyone wants to understand assurances, there's a plethora of published information that people can go and look up and understand.

Some of the suppliers' responses are more nuanced, conveying that the notion has merit, but also that there is difficulty achieving effective communication in this respect.

> I guess they've started down that track with the wording in the audit report. I'm not sure that too many people read it...they determine whether it's qualified or not and then move on...therefore it's got to be in fairly simple words...The one [audit report] in Australia...I think they've made a good attempt [with]. It's easy for an auditor to read and understand. I'm not sure that anyone who hasn't had any auditing training would really understand that. And then it comes back to who's going to read it and what would they gain from that...if you could put it in simple language that makes sense then...that would be good. But the ability to do that, it's easy to say, it's probably a little bit harder to work out what the wordings could be. But...there is an ability to disclose what an audit really is in somewhat layman language, and...that would be a help.

The difficulty of explaining the auditor's use of the concept of materiality is explicitly and eloquently referred to in the next quotation (the issue of materiality is returned to and analysed in more depth in Chapter 5).

> [I]t's a difficult question because if I say yes they should [disclose more], the way in which you would do that then becomes awfully complex...but obviously professional judgment is a strong part of what we do and if you then try and explain...everyone's going to have a different view about what an audit should be...I've had experiences where I've just worked through materiality with boards of listed entities and while they might agree with what the materiality is in regards to the financials as a whole, when we then try and apply that and talk them through how we apply that to different line items or captions in accounts, even that discussion with board members who are well educated, often with a finance background, becomes quite a heated debate and people have different views.

The same supplier gives the example of 'sampling' to illustrate how difficult it is to explain that concept in an auditing context to the average shareholder:

> [I]f we put this question and applied it purely in regards to materiality to try and take that debate into a forum and a broader group so shareholders, maybe the institutional investors, could get that...the mum and dad investor I don't think will have the ability to do that...if you then say, 'Well, what about the audit as a whole and forget materiality. Tell us what you do and when you do it—sampling and how that might work', I cannot imagine how you could possibly explain that to an average [shareholder]—and professional judgment is the main reason. As long as we're able to apply our professional judgment while working within the... standards and the relevant regulations, I can't imagine how you could properly explain that to a broad user base.

More disclosures by the auditor around the issue of accounting estimates would be the somewhat reluctant preference of this supplier:

> I suppose the area in the accounts that...can cause a lot of issues is in terms of accounting estimates within balances. And perhaps the audit report could have a framework that allows comment in relation to those estimates. Other than that, I haven't got any other specific changes that I would recommend.

The diversity in reader sophistication is raised by another supplier as an obstacle to greater disclosure by the auditor of the audit process:

> The issue there is that of course [greater disclosure of the audit process] is being read...by a knowledgeable audience that knows what they're looking for in reading that and how to interpret that. I guess the challenge we've got with the public financial statements, if we begin to try and explain in an audit, it's to retail investors [and] mums and dads. Is it any more helpful for them to...[get more] more detail? I'm not sure whether that will actually narrow or manage the expectation gap.

There is, however, some support for disclosing more information about the audit and its processes. There is also acknowledgment that even professional training in related financial fields (for example, financial planning) does not always encompass other than high-level information about audit and its processes. The implication for those with no financial training is left unsaid, but is clearly implied in the following quotation:

> Someone I know is actually going through the Certified Financial Planner course, and there's really nothing in there…to any degree about accounting and auditing in a way that would allow [that person] to really understand what we do or why it might be important to have an audit…the focus tends to be more on the higher-level stuff…the logical place is the audit report to explain what we do…So…it would make sense but you'd need to have it in layman's language so it's able to be understood.

Among suppliers, even though there is not support for auditor disclosure of work and processes, there is acknowledgment of the lack of transparency surrounding the audit process. One suggestion to overcome this is to seek other means of engendering confidence in the process—for example, through external reviews of the audit firms, as indicated in the following quotation:

'I'm quite sensitive to… the apparent lack of transparency around audit and how it's done.'

> [T]he simple answer to that question…is the disclosure about process might actually beg more questions than it provided answers or clarity on, but what I'm quite sensitive to is the apparent lack of transparency around audit and how it's done. So, in order to address that issue about the lack of transparency…[there is a] need to ensure that the market is aware that there is confidence, or give them a basis rather for having confidence in what it is that auditors do. And it's in that context that…the external reviews of the auditing firms that are taking place make sense…it's about confidence that an appropriate process is taking place. How do you deal with it? Well, you could try and explain it and explain it and explain it and…without an appropriate background, you won't necessarily increase understanding but…it's more in confidence than understanding, which is actually why I go back to what KPMG did with the Houghton and Trotman[5] report. It was to say to people that [there is awareness] of their concerns and [a willingness] to have what [is done] open to external scrutiny. So, the profession is required to do that now. ASIC is doing that. The firms also have both the Institute [of Chartered Accountants in Australia] and this body called the AQRB [Audit Quality Review Board]…doing it.

5 These were reports about quality reviews of one of the Big Four firms undertaken by K. Houghton (one of the current authors) and K. Trotman.

> And…[external oversight] is an appropriate response…as opposed to trying to explain even more about the audit process, because I think it's about addressing confidence.

Interestingly, suppliers speak of this type of information being demanded by and available to those charged with governance, including members of audit committees. Outsiders such as shareholders, however, are not privy to the same type of information.

> Some audit committees, some individuals or groups within those charged with governance, have an interest. Why do they have it? Probably because they believe that's the way they need to discharge their duties. The mechanism…our firm and others [use is] we present them with an auditor plan of some sort at the start of the year and that's generally well received. For even this small group of legally trained…legally focused individuals, [they] still appreciate…receiving an audit plan. It's a question of just how it's presented and what level of detail is in it and what they might struggle with. So that's the mechanism for doing it for that group of stakeholders in the audit process and those other people who basically pay us, and they are the subjects of our audit, of course. So they're informed. But remember they have an agenda as well, which is [that] they effectively carry the same if not more responsibility for the financial information put into the marketplace as the auditor does. Our objectives should be totally aligned.

'So that's the mechanism for doing it for that group of stakeholders in the audit process and those other people who basically pay us, and they are the subjects of our audit, of course. So they're informed.'

2.3.1 Summary

Suppliers voice concerns that disclosures of the audit process by them beyond those already existing would confuse rather than help and might in fact exacerbate the audit expectations gap, particularly for retail investors. Fears surface that further explanation is unlikely to be read, that it would manifest only as a generic statement in view of the potential for litigation and hence it would be of little value. A preoccupation emerges with the difficulty of articulating the nature of professional judgment integral to the audit process. A reminder is given that 'deep pockets' make auditors a target in the event of a corporate failure, regardless of the level of information available about the audit or understanding of that information. In summary, suppliers' perceive that there are many people in the capital market who have no interest in understanding the audit work and processes. There are a small number who want no information about it. There is a smaller number that do have some interest, but the conventional vehicle of the audit opinion is not the way to communicate the work and processes involved in the audit.

2.4 Standard setters

Standard setters reiterate the doubts expressed, especially by suppliers, about how valuable greater disclosures can be when they are likely to be poorly understood by users. One (immediately below) even suggests that exposing more of the limitations of an audit might be counterproductive in terms of reducing confidence in the process rather than increasing it.

> '[T]he more detail you put down, probably the more evident it will be that audit is just a test of a small proportion of a large population.'

> [W]e actually know what auditors do and for those who don't know what auditors do, how much do they really need to know and what would it add if they did [know]...if there was disclosure then how much would it be understood by the general users of financial statements anyway? Not being experienced...in the accounting or the auditing world, would the extra disclosure actually mean a lot? Now, if there was more detail on the principles behind an audit and maybe some of the limitations of an audit, that might be useful, but it may also be dangerous because if you start using that disclosure as a kind of liability limitation thing then you could actually reduce confidence in the audit rather than increase confidence, because the more detail you put down probably the more evident it will be that audit is just a test of a small proportion of a large population.

Disclosures will not necessarily increase confidence, according to this next standard setter's response:

> [There are] a lot of pitfalls potentially with further disclosure that don't necessarily add to the confidence of the investment community, but on the other hand I'm not convinced that [investors] actually want it—that they're actually asking for it.

> I don't know whether it would be meaningful going forward on a regular basis for an entity...you would be finding you would have quite voluminous reports, which...I [would] question whether there would be an advantage for [the general user] in that...in the abnormal situation where something's going wrong, I could imagine that being the case, but in the day-to-day thing, probably not.

> '[W]hat we will get is a more complicated report which for the... users...may raise more questions because they just don't know the process.'

> My initial thoughts are that I don't think an auditor should need to disclose more because there is what I clearly believe [to be] an appropriate framework...I balance that up against certain situations where I've found in practice...you can have specialised audit approaches. That needs to be weighed up against whether in fact the reader, if I could say, the un-knowledged reader, of the financial reports is going to get any benefit from it...what we will get is a more complicated report, which for the... users...may raise more questions because they just don't know the process [rather] than the outcome. So I see that as a downside. So having thought about it...I don't know whether I would...support a more detailed response in the audit...of the individual steps which you've gone through. I don't think that's the case...the auditors should give a very clear and precise opinion that the accounts are true and fair or a review opinion, the negative opinion. So my feeling would be in that vein more than [that] we need to provide more detailed scope...that's probably outside...an audit. That may be into another engagement.

> I don't think it's going to achieve very much. For some of the other stakeholders—regulators, directors—I think that's a good thing to do because...you can educate and you can change some of those views. But...it's that subset that it's worthwhile [for]...trying to do it[for] the...millions of retail shareholders, I just don't see that that's ever going to happen.

Perhaps not unsurprisingly, some standard setters point to the public availability of the suite of auditing Standards as a source of information about the audit process.

> 'I'm not sure it would add anything to the financial statements. [I wonder] whether it could be made available on request.'

> I don't know that it's really needed and...the only people that could really answer that would be the users of the accounts. But the thing is... that all the firms use similar audit techniques and procedures, so...they'd probably gravitate to a standard [disclosure] and if they gravitated to a standard one then it would just be a bit like an auditing standard and what [the standards] do say is that we did the audit in accordance with Australian Auditing Standards, so if you want to read the Australian Auditing Standards you'd get an idea of what [the auditors] did. So in theory it's available.

The fear of another of the standard setters is that more disclosures would involve 'second-guessing' users' views of important and non-important audit procedures:

> [I]t becomes a question of how much information do you provide and where do you stop...[and] it becomes a question of the auditor... second-guessing what the users' view as being important procedures or non-important [procedures]...the standards are specific enough in terms of the requirements of an audit and if a user of the financial statements was that interested in understanding the conduct of an audit then presumably they would familiarise themselves with the standards or at least the core standards that sit behind the scope of an audit, what the objective of an audit is.

> '[I]t really raises the question of who actually reads the audit opinion in the first place, assuming you believe the audit opinion is the appropriate forum for making this disclosure.'

> [W]hen I look at this question—should we disclose more information about work and processes—it just raises a lot of questions as to how far can you go and who is it going to be any use to when you do it? And it really raises the question of who actually reads the audit opinion in the first place, assuming you believe the audit opinion is the appropriate forum for making this disclosure. The auditing standards...in some ways have taken us along the path of disclosing more about our processes to our client base [and] those charged with governance, and...there is a general move in the audit profession...probably...progressively over the last 10,

> 20, 30 years to give those charged with governance more information about the audit process.

The next standard setter draws attention to the various reports available from the range of bodies that provide oversight of the audit process:

> I've got a very particular perspective, but...there's been a lot of discussion about the oversight of the profession. We're in the...year of reviews by ASIC. We're in the...year of reviews by AQRB...the PCAOB will come and visit Australian audit firms with ASIC in the future...So...for those who are sensitive to that, there's information out there and...the FRC oversight, [and] what it is that ASIC is doing in this space. So I think there's enough there.

Interestingly, one standard setter makes reference to those with legal training who prefer not to be informed of the audit process:

> [T]heir view appears to be, look, I need you to assure me you've done what you must do, but please don't share with me how you did that because I don't want to...assume any responsibility for that.

2.4.1 Summary

Standard setters in general are not in favour of greater disclosure by auditors of their processes and work. Perhaps predictably, they are confident in the auditing standards as a source of knowledge about the audit process. That few outside the profession read these standards does not seem to perturb them; their point is that the standards are publicly available. Faith in the various review processes of the regulatory and professional bodies is also expressed as being enough to provide confidence in the processes and also as a source of reports on audit. There is great uncertainty among the standard setters about whether greater disclosures in the audit report or elsewhere will be read, understood or valued by users, and there is even a suggestion that it could be counterproductive in drawing attention to limitations of the audit process.

2.5 Regulators

Regulators had mixed responses when asked the question in relation to the desirability of auditors disclosing more details of their audit work and processes. At least one did not feel such disclosure would be particularly valuable. One alluded to the flagship nature of the audit product and the existing understanding of it in the community. The other felt the content of the current audit report gave sufficient detail.

> On the financial statement audit, I think that's a fairly tried and tested product...I see that as the flagship product in the sense that it's not one of these newer areas that auditors tend to work in...in terms of procedures...people understand what an audit is—right?
>
> In their view, an audit is something that the auditor does fairly rigorously and...as a diligent person, and...they do all the procedures that are necessary to come to an opinion. So it's the highest level of assurance and...in terms of procedures...that becomes more relevant when I compare an audit with a review rather than when I look at an audit...with the financial statement audit, it is more communicating the outcomes of the audit which is an issue, where people actually use an emphasis of matter when a qualification would be more appropriate.

Another regulator, however, does seek greater disclosure:

> [T]hat's a good idea. I can see a lot of merit in that so...you narrow the expectations gap. As long as the language is...easily understandable, I would subscribe to that.

'[T]he public really needs to know that it's not a ticking bomb...it's more of a risk-management exercise.'

> I would like to see some kind of education campaign or some way to get to investors generally to explain what an auditor does...there is quite a gap in terms of what the public think auditors do and what auditors actually do. In terms of process-driven risk-based approaches, the public really needs to know that it's not a ticking bomb...it's more of a risk-management exercise...Something that maybe an independent organisation could try and get across to the public, rather than the company itself.

2.5.1 Summary

The regulators interviewed expressed mixed reactions to the notion of auditors providing more information than was currently available about their processes and work. Regulators see the audit as an already well-understood product compared with the review engagement, and one takes the opportunity to emphasise how important it is to provide an appropriate audit opinion as a form of communication.

3.0 Where should auditors disclose incremental information?

In responding to a question from the interviewer about whether more information should be provided by the auditor about the audit process, several of the stakeholders provided suggestions about where any such information, were it to be provided, should be located. This section analyses these suggestions.

3.1 Overview of interviews with stakeholders

Suggestions in relation to the positioning of additional information provided by auditors about their audit work and the audit process include corporate, auditors', regulators' and professional bodies' web sites, the audit engagement letter, publishing of the management letter to the auditor, in the annual report, in the auditor's report (with a suggestion to file the auditor's report separately from the annual report with the ASX) and in recordings or web-casts of annual general meetings.

3.2 Users

Users made various suggestions about where more information disclosed by auditors about the audit process might be positioned. Some of the quotations in the previous section, which focus on perceptions of the merit of having auditors disclose more information, mention potential locations for this information and should be borne in mind when reading this section.

The first user thinks the company's web site is the appropriate location:

> It may be that they can cross-reference...to something a bit more detailed on their own [company's] web site about the typical sorts of procedures.

Professional body web sites are the solution for this next user:

> '[T]hey should have available on the ICAA web site...a clear description of what [audits] are.'

> I don't think you want to add pages to the annual reports...Perhaps that's more a financial education process that the auditors should be doing themselves...most people who have become professionals in this space go through commerce or economic[s] or an accounting [course] that...is a big part in the education of young financial professionals [so] that they understand the limitations of an audit and what they're doing...they should have available on the ICAA web site...a clear description of what [audits] are, and then telling people you can go and find that. But then in the annual reports they're referring to places where you can go and see what the scope of an audit is, and...If you want more information on what we've actually done, go and find it. You could make that available on companies' web sites, but I wouldn't be encouraging making those annual reports any thicker.

Two users suggest placement within the annual report as part of the audit opinion or linked to the opinion.

> I tend to think that you'd have to put it in an annual report as part of an opinion or at least a reference back into an opinion...if it's on a web site, it's unlikely to be read or...it may not really have enough prominence for those that probably have the greatest need to know what an audit constitutes...I'm not advocating that it should be reams and reams because...that goes to the other extreme and probably wouldn't be relevant...the more information you provide...in terms of scope, the less likely it is that it's going to be understandable and you can put it into some context, but...there probably needs to be something a little bit more than is there now.

Another suggestion for the location of this additional information is the audit opinion itself:

> I look at things like the American 10K, which is much more information than we have even in our annual reports...[However,] you can still achieve it without necessarily overwhelming...the reader with more information...it's more just to provide clarity, it's not really changing anything in terms of what gets performed, it's

> more really just to define a little bit for the reader to understand what does get performed...whether that gets read within the context of an audit opinion...the readers probably read the factors and a clean opinion or otherwise and maybe [leave] out a bit of the scope, but...if it's there for those that want to know, [they] can probably refer to it.

One user, who suggests the audit report is the place for the additional information, also has a suggestion about provision of access to audit reports that is somewhat left of field. The suggestion is that all audit reports should be lodged separately from the annual report with the ASX so that they can be referred to.

> '[T]he audit statement should also probably be released to the market.'

> You tend to see a lot of...statements come through in company announcements, around AGM time. You get the AGMs, you get the chairman's address, which will come through the ASX news wires. You get the CEO's address, but you don't ever get any qualification of those reports unless you go into the actual annual report itself...the audit statement should also probably be released to the market. I'm not 100 per cent sure whether it is or not, but that should be something that probably pops out, that the company is obliged to release as a company announcement...the actual audit statement, with the figures that come out post the AGM—just...to build awareness that there is someone reviewing and auditing the company...that's probably fairly important, because the audit function is probably a little bit unknown...me being an accountant...in terms of the undertaking of an actual audit, what it's supposed to achieve and what it's supposed to prevent is still a little bit hazy for me, and I would imagine even more so for the everyday end user of a financial report. How you go about clarifying that, I'm not too sure. Other than publishing the... auditor's report into the company news wires, and just [having] that as part of the whole process to build credibility.

Several other users suggest the audit report as a suitable location for incremental auditor-provided information.

> [It should be] in the audit report because you like to think...that the audit report gives something that is a little bit more—I'm trying to think of the word—not neutral...[in comparison with the directors' report].

> [T]he actual form of the audit report has changed in the last 12 years or so and…there is more being put in there—what is not done and who is responsible for what—so…that's probably helped a little bit. Maybe there's something else that could be put in there, but I wouldn't know. [It] might be helpful.

> You always read [the audit report] to make sure there are no qualifications in there and anybody relying on an audit report's looking for that…probably, if they are qualified, that's where you have the opportunity to perhaps provide more information than there is at the moment. But other than that…it does get back to educating expectations, and I don't think the annual report should be the vehicle for that.

Yet others' suggestions for a location include the ASIC or ASX web sites.

> In terms of whether they should actually disclose [information about the audit process] or not, possibly…as a separate document to the actual audit and financial statements; maybe just as something that could be on the ASIC web site, that you can say okay what's an auditor looking to do or what's their role? And, as a shareholder, if you're really interested, you can go and read up on that. But…these annual reports are getting large anyway. To add something like that in there…most wouldn't read it. But if you wanted to, maybe there could just be a link to a site where…whoever runs the auditing of that company can just say look this is what we're aiming to achieve, we're bound by this and this is what we're going to be looking at, and then you cover both bases.

> [M]aybe the answer is through the regulators or the stock exchange, or through their shareholder information sessions or the like…I don't know which is the best way because there's going to be an extra cost obviously associated with this sort of marketing exercise.

One user suggests placement of the information in the recording of the annual general meeting and a transcript of proceedings:

> I'm not aware if [questions of the auditor at the AGM are recorded and available], but that would be…quite a simple [exercise]…it's a record of meeting anyway. Many meetings are web-cast, but not for all companies…you could have a transcript of the meeting made available, but that's an additional cost for small public companies,

> listed companies. It's surprising that that avenue has not been addressed...There's an opacity regarding what is the work of the auditor. And, as organisations become immense, the understanding of what an auditor does is very difficult for shareholders to comprehend, particularly at certain levels of shareholder interest.
>
> [N]ot only through the AGMs but through their web broadcast would help.

3.2.1 Summary

Users were quite inventive in their suggestions of where to locate incremental information provided by the auditor about the audit process and auditor's work. Suggestions range from company web sites and the ASIC web site to audit reports, annual reports, recordings and transcripts of annual general meetings. Perhaps one of the most lateral thinkers suggests it be included in the audit report, but the audit report itself should be filed with the ASX as a separate document rather than having to be found within an annual report.

3.3 Purchasers

A variety of sources were suggested for greater disclosure than exists currently of the auditor's work and processes.

Audit firms' web sites were suggested as a source, as per the following quotation:

> If you go to PWC's web site there [is]...a statement about, in broad terms, how they approach audit. What is their philosophy around audits...in fact, materiality was another question, but perhaps these issues...[are] more an [opt in]. Giving [opt in] capability and ease of accessibility for that information to retail shareholders in particular...is the way to go. I wouldn't want to be putting more information into my financial statements and making [them] even longer and bigger than they are already.

One purchaser wants to extend the disclosures to results of an audit of the audit firms themselves and their procedures:

> '[A]n audit of the audit firms themselves and their procedures... being publicly available is clearly very relevant.'

I wouldn't put in financial statements the statement...of what they do...there's obviously their audit statement in terms of their opinion on the accounts. There's their independence opinion that goes in there. Personally, I'm okay with that, but... perhaps all we do is...add a line...in that statement at the bottom that simply says, 'Look, if anybody would like to know the approach to the audit, et cetera...here is the relevant web site', and you can go and look up KPMG's link and you can basically look at and get a full disclosure on their site of their philosophy and how they approach audits, what they cover, what they don't cover...given...the key role [that audit firms] play...once we feel that whether ASIC gets to a level of maturity or whoever it is...an audit of the audit firms themselves and their procedures and...that being publicly available is clearly very relevant. I wouldn't have an issue with that per se.

This next purchaser makes the point that several stakeholders would need to be involved in creating the wording:

> [I]n conjunction with quite a number of key parties...the regulators probably have to...play a certain role. It depends on the...industry itself because I speak on behalf of the finance service industry, which is heavily regulated. And I do believe that APRA and ASIC would need to play a certain role, without being too prescriptive, especially because you'd be talking about education and here is not a pure disclosure issue. And...the audit profession probably need to play a certain role because they are the expert[s] and they have to be comfortable with the actual wording and sign-off and the company management [and]...the board has to be comfortable as well. They have to play a certain role because they will expect their readers to be not mislead and to actually understand what we are trying to disclose in here and, again, hopefully try to becom[e] a bit more of a marketing concept as well for the particular company, because... we invest the time and the money and actually try to...educate our shareholders, for example.

The audit report as a source of this information is popular with some purchasers.

> [I]t should be in a report in the sense that there should be a separate section perhaps on what procedures and what sort of sampling or what materiality is being used, et cetera, and what they've actually checked against and what reliance they've placed on...directors' information...perhaps a page...unless we see [it] on a web site which talked about audits or...a CPA web site or Association of Chartered Accountants web site...which talked about what the rules were and what the expectations were...maybe that's one...place [where] you could have that sort of information.

3.3.1 Summary

Purchasers are very familiar with the web sites of those audit firms that place information there about their audit product. Other suggestions from purchasers include the financial report, references within the annual report directing readers to web sites and the web sites of the professional accounting bodies.

3.4 Suppliers

Since suppliers did not, in general, support provision of incremental information about the audit, few made suggestions about where such information, if provided, should be located. Below are suppliers' suggestions, beginning with the audit report as a location.

> [I]n terms of how do you disclose the information...there's been some development in the audit report...maybe one option is to try and reword the audit reports into plain English. But I don't think you'd want to add too much, because...one of the issues we've got at the moment is there's just so much data out there. Financial statements now run to 200, 250 pages. You now make your audit report or your audit to sign off four or five pages. The question is does anybody really read it, do they really understand it, because it's very difficult to put a very complex process into a couple of pages.

The suggestion of another supplier is that the professional bodies could do more:

> I don't think our professional bodies do enough. The institute and the CPAs—their profiles in terms of these sorts of issues out in the market are very, very low...the regulators [also] need to be making

> the market informed of what it is that the auditors are doing...if that would enhance the market, that should be part of their role as well.

3.4.1 Summary

The auditor's report and the various available output locations of the professional bodies and of regulators are suggestions made by suppliers in relation to where incremental audit product information made available by auditors might be located.

3.5 Standard setters

Only one comment by a standard setter touches on the issue of the location of auditor-provided incremental information: making such information available on request or on the audit firm's web site.

> '[T]he audit report actually does say in itself anyway that it's not designed to pick up all weaknesses in internal control.'

> I'm not sure it would add anything to the financial statements. Whether it could be made available on request...[is] something that could be quite possible or practical and you could make a statement in the accounts...[that] something could be made available on request, but it would still be a standard kind of document that they'd just keep in a drawer for anybody, or they could put it on [the audit firm's] web site. So, if the audit firm was to, say, give more detail, they could basically give a summary of the audit process on their web sites if they wanted. You could...refer to the auditor's web site...it would be a general statement...the audit report actually does say in itself anyway that it's not designed to pick up all weaknesses in internal control.

3.5.1 Summary

Audit firm web sites and the auditor's report itself are the suggestions from the lone standard setter who canvassed this topic, although he or she does not really support such an idea.

4.0 Issues and implications

Generally, users and some purchasers were in favour of some form of extended disclosure by auditors of those processes that occurred within an audit. Suppliers were more guarded and even critical of this as a possibility, while standard setters were more mixed in their views. Importantly, the gap in the perspective of suppliers on the one hand and users on the other was quite significant, as were their relative views of the current situation of disclosures. One purchaser of a major listed company made the observation that the current process undertaken in an audit was opaque and not viewable by the capital market or indeed by many other interested stakeholders.

A purchaser and a supplier both made reference to the fact that the language used in audit opinions tended to contain 'jargon' and was not easily interpreted by many stakeholders in the market for audit services. Many observers, particularly from purchaser and user groups, perceived the audit opinion essentially as communication of a single item of information—that is, whether the opinion was unqualified or not. In that sense, it is a 'blunt instrument', which essentially conveys a simple message without the nuances or details of how that conclusion has been reached. There was some recognition that current audit opinion wording was better than it had been in the past. The presence of jargon and the carefully crafted words that are standardised, however, do not represent an opinion in the same way that an opinion is crafted by an expert witness for a piece of litigation or for the conclusions and outcomes described by auditors when they complete an agreed-on procedures engagement. Put another way, on the one hand, suppliers seek the ability to exercise their professional judgment, but on the other, most of the observables provided by suppliers to participants in the capital market are standardised (or, as cynics might say, 'commoditised') without any regard for the individual circumstances of the auditee.

The notion that the audit opinion is currently crafted as a simple statement with very little information about what underlies it is a common theme among users and purchasers. One supplier, however, suggested that any more detailed wording was probably going to be written by lawyers and the additional disclosures would need to be crafted with an eye to exposure to litigation risk.

The respondents to the questions and their conclusions can be divided into three groups.

- Group 1: Those who believe there is merit in the proposal to make further disclosures about the work undertaken by the auditor.
- Group 2: Those sympathetic to the need to more fully inform the market but who believe that there can be a more subtle alternative of achieving this by supporting the current framework and processes.
- Group 3: Those quite dismissive of further disclosures and possibly even cynical about the prospect.

The third group dismissed the idea on a number of grounds. Several questioned whether anything could be gained by further disclosures. Some would argue that the audit report is currently not read, so any further disclosures will suffer the same fate. Those who take this view also frequently add that further disclosures will add confusion to the market rather than clarification. Several made the observation that if one was to make further disclosures, how was one to judge how much was enough and that the sheer weight of further disclosures would contribute to a situation of information overload, which already existed with financial reports? Finally, another criticism was that if there were to be further disclosures they would almost inevitably be written with litigation risk in mind rather than being useful in decision making for the capital market.

A more subtle observation made by one supplier was that in his or her experience those charged with governance sometimes implicitly or even expressly did not want information about how the audit was undertaken. This is because if they are fully informed about the processes and procedures used, they might expose themselves to accountability for those processes, which could involve their own legal accountability. Interestingly, aspects of the audit related to difficulty in accessing required information are generally recommended by corporate governance guidelines as a discussion to have with audit committees, but not as the subject of communication with the public.

The group that was somewhat supportive of the fact that more needed to be done in this area of disclosure took the view that the current audit opinion could be broadly acceptable as it was. The key is not in disclosing more, but in ensuring that the current framework is one that has the confidence of those in the capital market. Specifically, they suggest that the confidence in the processes undertaken can be gained through the public disclosure of inspection reports (such as the current regime of the ASIC inspections), which gives overarching support to the processes used by auditors. This transparency and oversight of the process could cause the capital market to have more confidence. A purchaser commented that companies might do more to describe for themselves how they chose their current auditor. Again, this level of disclosure and transparency would give reason for shareholders in particular to have confidence in the choice and in the outcome of the work of the individual signing auditor of that company.

5.0 Disclosure of the audit process by management

The researchers conducted interviews with users, purchasers, suppliers, standard setters and regulators with regard to the role of management in explaining the audit process and opinion since it was one of the topics that had come up in earlier discussions in focus groups as well as in the Future of Audit Symposium held in Canberra.

5.1 Overview of interviews with stakeholders

Overwhelmingly, there is opposition from all stakeholder groups to the proposition that management should be charged with responsibility for conveying information to stakeholders about audit processes and the auditor's opinion. A common objection is that it is not management but the board or audit committee that should have this responsibility. The objections to the idea are, however, unlikely to disappear even if responsibility is ceded to these parties. The objections relate primarily to potential conflicts of interest and potential misrepresentations—especially if management is the conveyor of the information. Other objections relate to management not having sufficient time or interest to be involved in this task and the argument that the financial statements should stand alone. Those few stakeholders who support the idea see management's reach to stakeholders compared with that of auditors as an advantage and see the annual general meeting, or a web-cast of it, as an appropriate forum in which management can take the opportunity to inform shareholders of these issues.

5.2 Users

As the comments below reveal, users are overwhelmingly against management providing information about the auditor's work and processes or the audit opinion. The sentiment expressed in the first two users' comments is that it is the auditor's and not management's responsibility to provide information about the audit process.

> No, I think it's...the auditor's report, it's the management's accounts, it's the auditor's audit report and I don't see that it's up to management to inform people about what the auditor does. The auditor's the best placed to do that.

> I don't think it's the management's responsibility to educate investors on how to understand...financial statements, so their job is to prepare it and to run the company. Maybe another group [can] create awareness out in the greater community by having seminars... for those that are interested in finding out more or learning more about how to understand financial statements. But I don't think it's the management's responsibility.

Another user, who feels that statements by managers about the audit would not achieve a great deal, raises the issue of information overload:

> I don't know that it would be helpful if management went out and said, 'Our auditors—this is what they're doing.' I don't know that shareholders would care that much. One of the problems that I have with a lot of the measures that are proposed about widening the scope of the audit is that we already have an awful lot of information and we're suffering, if anything, from information overload. So an annual report that has more and more sections about reports that essentially say everything is fine—and only once in every 100 reports...would you read a critical line in there—isn't very helpful. So...a regular statement in the annual report [saying] this is what our auditors do—I don't know that that would achieve very much.

Several users feel that if information about the audit process is to be provided from the client rather than the auditor side, it should come from the board of directors rather than from management, as the next three quotations indicate.

> [T]he board should be more involved in providing that information rather than management...in the way in which it communicates to the shareholders. But...the shareholders need to feel that the board is actually really representing [them]...it's really the board that through their communication have to show their leadership in this role by not only showing that they're doing a required audit, but they're actually doing audits which are perhaps relevant also to the particular type of business or the sector that they're [in], to ensure that they are actually receiving or that they have the ability to receive information.
>
> I don't know if managers are allowed to provide that information independently of the directors.
>
> The financial statements should be able to stand alone without having to speak to management...they should give a clear picture, because you've got two years of what's happening. [Management's]... ability to get to all its investors...is through written or some communications means...they're never going to be able to speak one-on-one to all...the stakeholders in the investment market. So...in explaining the numbers, the annual report becomes very important...I've followed companies for years where you can read the annual report, and if people bothered to read it, it is exactly what the company is doing. [For o]thers, the annual report is so poor it's complete marketing, or there's no information in it, in the descriptive bits, and maybe that is where management needs to play a role. But again, the board comes over that to ensure that there is full and fair disclosure and all the rest of it.

Only one user is in support of the proposition that management should disclose more about the audit process or the audit opinion:

> [T]here's merit [in it]. We have to provide a copy of our audited financials to our people that have invested with us. And at the moment we just provide them, without any cover note or letter or any explanation or anything like that...there would be merit in that to probably give more confidence... So to reassure the investors that the information that they're being presented with has been audited, has been signed off, has been through a rigorous process

'The information that you're receiving is being provided after a rigorous and lengthy audit process.'

> and reviewed prior to them receiving information. 'The information that you're receiving is being provided after a rigorous and lengthy audit process.' We don't do that, but I can see merit in it.

5.2.1 Summary

Users are overwhelmingly opposed to the notion of management disclosing more information of the auditor's work and processes. Reasons given include a perception that management is not responsible for the auditor's report, that the auditor's role is to prevent management from manipulating earnings—so implying a potential conflict in having management explain the audit outcome—that it is the board of directors, rather than management, that should have this role if a party external to the audit takes the role on, that the financial statements should be capable of standing alone without the need for management explanations and that there is already so much information available that more can only lead to information overload. The only user supporting the concept felt that such disclosures by management could increase confidence in the integrity of information included in financial reports.

5.3 Purchasers

Although not a great number of purchasers responded to this question, as with users, purchasers were overwhelmingly against management providing incremental information about the auditor's opinion and processes. Disbelief that management would even be interested in providing this information is the reaction in this first quotation:

> I just can't see why management would be interested in doing that. Management wants to talk about what the company is doing, and what they're planning...to do in the future. In my experience, with the management teams that I've dealt with, I just can't see that they'd be very interested in doing that.

> 'I don't perceive that there is that risk or gap, or lack of information that is actually causing any market dysfunction.'

> It's not in management's [interests]...to do that...the second reason for my initial response, and maybe as important a reason, is that I don't actually see the education gap there. I do think that taking this trickle-down view of the market as the people who have the most knowledge of the company, of the processes, publishing analyses or media material, and

> just going down further to the enthusiastic amateur, I think at the top level those...leaders in the market know (and obviously there [are] a lot of ex-accountants, ex-auditors in that level anyway)... entirely how important an audit is. And I don't perceive that there is that risk or gap or lack of information that is actually causing any market dysfunction.

Only one purchaser saw merit in the concept of management-provided information pertinent to the audit process and opinion and pointed to corporate web-casts as a useful device to achieve this.

> [T]he answer to this is, yes. One of the things that...was a very good development was the web-casting of briefings that were given to the financial analysts. Public companies often have these every six months or so, and every quarter, and then [they are] put out on the web so that every investor has equal access. As part of that, the chief finance officer normally presents fairly detailed analysis of the financials, and...the questions and answers that come from it, so the combination...is quite good. But we tend not to do these things at annual general meetings. Some companies do, but very few. Normally, the CEO gets up and gives an overview, but you don't get any of that other information.

5.3.1 Summary

Purchasers are divided about the idea of management provision of audit-oriented information. The lack of a reason or incentive for management to take on this task is the main reason behind the opposing purchaser. The supportive purchaser sees this type of management activity taking place in the same way that analyst briefings are web-cast.

5.4 Suppliers

Two suppliers saw a great deal of merit in the idea that management should convey the audit processes and issues surrounding the auditor's opinion to stakeholders. Their responses to this question appear below; the first points out how much more reach with shareholders management has compared with auditors.

> Yes [there is merit in the idea]...because it's very difficult for auditors...our engagement is with the members of the company, but we don't have access to them, we don't have the day-to-day access or the regular access to that group of people. And they really do need to understand—and the market as a whole really needs to understand—what exactly are we getting when we read an audit opinion? And you'll notice in recent years the way the audit opinion is drafted is a lot better, it goes more towards explaining to readers and users of the accounts, right here's the responsibility of the auditor, here's the responsibility of the company, this is what an audit is, there's judgment involved. So...a lot has been done in terms of what's in the audit opinion. It would be great if management could do more. I'm not quite sure what more that they could do, but...users probably flick to the audit opinion to make sure it's not qualified. I doubt they even read it [which] is probably the real problem.

The next supplier makes the point that the external audit is just part of a wider assurance agenda that management needs to meet and communicate to its stakeholders:

> '[T]he question of how risk management and internal audit and external audit and anything else they might happen to do [fit] together...is management's responsibility.'

> The avenue through which we can do it is limited to answering questions at the AGM. If we're talking about listed companies, [it is by] answering questions at the AGM, either on the day or on notice and under the act, or through our audit report...it is from our audit report, so it [is] clear [that it is] from us. Management's slightly different because they've got two options. They can either attempt to do it through the financial statements themselves, and in the public area through an AGM or a shareholder information session, or they could do it through the company's web site and explain what happens on that...there is scope for that because...what management and the board are across is a broader degree of assurance.

The same supplier articulates further what he or she means by 'a broader degree of assurance':

> We, as external auditors—and this [is] half the problem...have responsibility in certain areas and there are caveats around that. But management have a much broader responsibility for risk management generally, and the question of how risk management and internal audit and external audit and anything else they might happen to do [fit] together...is management's responsibility. And if they are describing—partly under the ASX guidelines—the 10 Corporate Governance Guidelines, number 7 [is] on risk management, [and] there [are] good descriptions they're beginning to put in...with the increased disclosure on how the business manages risk and so on; there's quite a neat nexus between that and what internal audit does and what external audit does. So I suspect there's more scope for doing that because they can explain the external audit in the context of assurance overall and who does what. Whether it's management or the board, I'm not sure. I tend to think it's the board because it's the board that communicates with the shareholders on that. But management would do it. So I can see that in the same way that management try [to] communicate in more voluminous documents...if you go to a number of web sites now they do have their codes of conduct, audit committee charters, quite a list of things. So...it would give better context to what the external audit does, rather than just a list of here's what we do and what we don't do.

Two suppliers, however, are quite strongly opposed to this suggested role for management, as the quotations from the interviews below show. The first quotation reveals doubts about the capacity of management to convey accurately what has transpired:

> I would have a real issue with that because you've got an issue of how well they actually articulate what's...transpired and what's been done, and I don't think management could adequately deal with that...[And] you've got real problems from, potentially, misrepresentations et cetera that might come through. So I don't think that that would help in any way, shape or form.

Another feels that this task is not among management's priorities:

> [M]anagement will feel they have a lot of more important and urgent things to do than publicising the role of financial statement audits.

This final quotation from a supplier reveals his or her belief that boards and audit committees rather than management have responsibility for communication with shareholders about the audit:

> I don't think management should [have responsibility]—if you mean management as management within the company. I think boards and audit committees should...it is incumbent upon them. At the end of the day, the board, the chairman of the board and the audit committee are appointed by shareholders. They're the ones that have the responsibility to really appoint the auditors, [and] direct the auditors. They're the ones that should be ensuring that there's effective communication back to shareholders as to what an audit is and how that operates.

5.4.1 Summary

Suppliers' responses are mixed about whether management should be charged with the responsibility to explain the auditors' processes and/ or audit opinion. Arguments used in support of the notion include the fact that management has greater access to the stakeholders than do the auditors, and that management has a good grasp of the nexus between internal and external audit and risk management and is best placed to convey these concepts in a holistic way. Reasons given by suppliers in opposition to this suggestion include the possibility that management will misrepresent the situation as it pertains to audit-related matters and the possibility that management will not agree to undertake this task because it is fully occupied with other matters. Finally, one supplier baulks at this being management's role rather than that of boards and audit committees.

5.5 Standard setters

Like suppliers, standard setters are equally divided between support and opposition for the proposition that management be charged with the task of conveying to stakeholders information about the auditor's processes and audit opinion, as the quotations below show. The first comment is supportive, but implies that it is only through a trickle-down effect from sophisticated market players that this information might be picked up:

> [T]hat's desirable. The question about this is, if management or directors can put information out, whether it's actually picked up by shareholders directly, maybe it's picked up by the analysts as part of the information flow that impacts on the analysts' recommendations.

> Because you've got so many levels of shareholders, from sophisticated institutional and sophisticated high net-worth individuals, down to mum[s] and dads who are in a different space altogether...through the formal reports out to the market [is the way it would manifest]. [*In response to whether it is desirable for management or the board to do it*:] Well, isn't it going to be a combination, because the releases to the market are overseen by the board...again, management does the work but the board also oversights the output.

The second supplier echoes the view that it is the board of directors' responsibility rather than that of management:

> I would substitute directors for management firstly...it's much more the directors' responsibility, as being the delegates of the shareholders...it's very difficult to do that and...the only forums... realistically are AGMs and financial statements or annual reports. Conceptually, it's a good idea but...in practice, it's very hard to do.

5.5.1 Summary

One of the standard setters, who is in support of the proposition, recognises that although this management-provided information is targeted at those with less understanding of the audit process and opinion, it might be the analysts who become the primary recipients of the information, which then 'trickles down'. The other standard setter responding to this question would prefer it to be a board role and sees the AGM as the only practical implementation device.

5.6 Regulators

Perhaps predictably, regulators are opposed to management being charged with the responsibility of conveying information about the auditors' processes or audit opinion, as can be seen in the following quotations from the interviews.

> '[K]ey financial and... investment decisions by and large are made by professionals only...and they won't need that sort of thing.'

[I]t's an interesting question about who is really looking at these financial statements, because your average person on the street who buys or sells shares, they're probably not really buying or selling shares on the basis of information in those financial statements. But...the people who are looking at those documents are the analysts and...more sophisticated investors like fund managers and people like that, and those people probably don't need someone to explain to them what it is that the documents mean. What I mean is that the key financial [and]... investment decisions by and large are made by professionals only... and they won't need that sort of thing.

The same regulator continues, articulating further on the differentiation in the marketplace between sophisticated and unsophisticated stakeholders and how the first group does not need the information and the second is unlikely to read it:

[T]he reason why I'm a little wary about it is because...[of] the cost of going through all of that division of resources to...[provide] information to a fairly select class of people. I'm sure there are some people who invest in shares who actually get out the annual report and read it from cover to cover, but...I haven't come across...that many, and people seem to invest on the basis of other...market releases...if they're interested in companies, rather than the annual report...and, in a sense, you're probably talking partly about two entirely different groups of people, because if you're talking about people on the street who are buying and selling shares, they're not going to understand much about any of these issues...A professional class of investor who makes the vast majority [of] investment decisions in Australia in terms of value, well, they probably don't need any more education. I'm not sure how much reliance they place on audited accounts anyway.

The next regulator sees management provision of information about the audit process as a conflict of interest:

I see that as management wearing two hats, because management prepares the financial statements and then it sounds as though the question is directed towards them selling the financial statements

> to people, and I would see that as a conflict...AGM's substantially are a waste of time and are quite cynically dated and timed for when investors can't turn up...auditors are hardly ever asked the questions and, if they are asked a question, their response is unsatisfactory. But...because it's management who prepared the financial statements, they try to market them anyway, try to put themselves in a good light in terms of the year's results and I can't see that they would be the appropriate people to give an explanation of the financial statements.

5.6.1 Summary

Regulators oppose management-provided information about audit processes and/or opinions. One sees such an eventuality as a conflict of interest for management. The other believes that the retail investors—the group most in need of a deeper understanding—would be unlikely to gain much from it while the more sophisticated investors would not need it.

6.0 Issues and implications

In summary, there was a generally negative reaction among all stakeholder groups for the proposition that management had a significant role in explaining the nature of the audit process and its outcome. A small number of users took a more positive view, stating that this could be done at the annual general meeting, in that the role in explaining the audit process and outcome pointed more to the board of directors as being the appropriate body to undertake such a task.

In terms of how this might be achieved, one observation was that as a very minimum the auditor needed to play a more significant role at the annual general meeting and possibly read out a statement about the audit process or at very least read out the audit opinion. One purchaser suggested the possibility of further disclosure occurring via web-casting related to analysts' briefings or other important events. Those who had negative views about management's role observed that this approach might cause a conflict between the role of management and the role of the auditor. It is the auditor who comments on the representations made of management and to then make management an advocate for the role of auditing sets up a potentially conflicting relationship.

On the whole, there was more enthusiasm for auditors, audit firms and the accounting profession more generally, together with more overarching organisations, including the accounting bodies and the Auditing and Assurance Standards Board, playing a more positive role in explaining to the market about the role of auditing, its processes and outcomes.

7.0 Concluding remarks

There was a substantial group, particularly among users and purchasers, who supported the idea of added disclosure in relation to auditors' work and processes. The questions arising of their support were:

- what to disclose
- to whom
- by whom
- where should the disclosure occur
- when should the disclosure take place
- what is the nature of the disclosures to be made?

In terms of what to disclose, in general, interviewees suggested a description of what work the auditor undertook. Generally, in layman's language and spelling out important things such as the fact that the work involves sampling (arguably a less ambiguous word than 'testing'), might be particularly risk focused, deals with substantive issues pertaining to that particular industry or entity and describes what levels of materiality are used. There is diversity of opinion about whether these descriptions should be specific to the company or might be more generalised for a particular audit firm.

There was also some diversity of view about the appropriate audience for these further disclosures. By and large, there was an underlying assumption that the ultimate risk taker in the capital market was the investor and this was the primary audience for these additional disclosures. There was a further view that the key audience was in fact those charged with governance in the company who in turn might seek to disclose it by some mechanism to the shareholders. Embedded in this is the issue of who will understand these additional disclosures and whether these additional disclosures need to be understood by everybody or in fact only by those who are 'price makers' rather than 'price takers' in the capital market.

By and large, there is little support for further disclosures by auditee management. Rather, stakeholders see that responsibility for these disclosures rests with the body that undertakes the work—that is, the auditor—albeit that existing publicly available information (for example, auditing standards) might have a role.

There were a number of innovative suggestions with regard to where these disclosures should be made. A substantial view was that the financial report was already overly complicated and represented 'information overload', so there was some scepticism about whether this would be the appropriate vehicle for additional disclosures. Additionally, while some suggested that the annual general meeting might be a means by which this information was described, those who had a user perspective were more likely to suggest that AGMs were sparsely attended and auditors were rarely asked questions at these meetings, so that too might not be an appropriate vehicle. If one accepted that those charged with governance made up the appropriate audience, there were a number of suggestions about how that disclosure might be made, including in the detailed audit plans presented to audit committees or boards of directors or in a detailed management letter. There was one suggestion from a user that those charged with governance should, as a matter of obligation, publish the management letter on the company web site and have it available for shareholders to ask questions about at the AGM or some other appropriate point. Several suggested that further disclosures could be on the individual company web site or on the web sites of audit firms or even of professional bodies or regulators and quasi-regulators. Obviously, if one is publicising these additional disclosures on an audit web site or on a professional association web site, they would tend to be more generalised than specific to the individual auditee. This, in the eyes of some, would limit their value.

There was also another body of thought that there was not enough known about what the audit process entailed, public education documents had fallen into disrepair and that, as a public policy issue, there needed to be more time, energy and resources spent on informing the public of the work of an auditor.

There was overwhelming support by all of those who made comment about it that the language used in disclosures should be jargon free and be able to be read by an intelligent but not necessarily professionally educated individual. The reference to jargon and technical language by respondents made it clear that because the responsibilities are to communicate with the capital market, there is a need to communicate in plain English.

One issue that was raised was when these disclosures should be made. There was one suggestion that one might make these added disclosures where an auditee was experiencing a particular set of circumstances. One presumes what is meant by this is financial distress, but it could also be at a time when a particularly substantial transaction occurs or when the auditor believes there are particularly pertinent transactions or events that need to be described or attention drawn to.

In concluding this chapter, we must observe that there are important public policy issues relevant here. We have seen changes in public policy on a number of matters relating to the financial circumstances of individuals within our society and our economy in the past several years. We draw as a parallel the fact that there have been substantial changes in policy position on superannuation (otherwise known as pension plans) and the fact that there has been a significant investment in informing the market about superannuation paid for by both the public and private purse. These education and information programs have helped inform the market of the circumstances and changes that have occurred in the market. While there have been substantial regulatory changes and a focus that is said to be an important public policy debate in relation to audit, there has not been a parallel investment in informing the market in the same way as there has been in regard to superannuation. The striking difference between the regulated response with respect to auditing and the public policy response with respect to superannuation is remarkable. One policy issue here is to ensure that those responsible for undertaking public policy fulfil their responsibility in ensuring that the market is informed, that the public expectations of auditing are understood and that the changes and enhancements to the capital market through auditing are appreciated by all relevant stakeholders. At a practical level, having audit reports filed with the regulator in a form that enables searching comprehensively across any and all audit reports rather than individually by auditee would be one small step.

We observed in the conversations that whether it was standard setters or purchasers—that is, management of listed corporations and others—they did not particularly focus on shareholders as being the ultimate clients of auditors. Rather, there were either implied or explicit beliefs expressed that the key stakeholders for these additional disclosures were those charged with governance. At present, the legal position in Australia is that the ultimate client and consumer of the audit opinion is the body of shareholders and this can be compared and contrasted with the US position (after Sarbanes-Oxley), where those charged with governance are formally the client of the audit firm. Given this legislative position, it is hard to argue that the ultimate client of the auditor is anything other than the shareholder of the auditee.

UNDERSTANDING OF MATERIALITY 5

> [A]nother question is: 'Do they actually understand that they don't understand what materiality is?' Because if it's never actually mentioned to them, they may not be aware that they don't understand this term...So...rather than just the concept of materiality, if you...start disclosing what your materiality level is... in simple terms...if your materiality's 10 [million], that means that the auditors will want accounts restated if they find errors that total that sort of money, for example.
> — Purchaser

1.0 Key issues

The contribution to the audit expectations gap of the issue of the level of understanding of the concept of materiality in an auditing context might be one of the most important findings from this study. The issue presents many challenges for the profession and for regulators, including:

- how can the role of auditor judgment surrounding the auditors' use of materiality in the conduct of the audit be best explained
- what are the mechanisms used for auditors to determine the level of materiality (tolerable error) and when and to whom is this information communicated
- can information about materiality be articulated effectively to users of the audit product of varying levels of sophistication
- is developing deeper understanding of quantitative materiality alone sufficient, or must it be accompanied by developing deeper understanding of qualitative materiality
- should the real levels of materiality used in conducting the audit be disclosed publicly or could this be 'dangerous' to the audit product

- is developing greater understanding about materiality of a higher priority than developing understanding of other aspects of audit
- is board and/or audit committee member understanding of materiality sufficiently well developed
- if educative material about audit materiality is to be made available, which party/parties should take responsibility for it and where should it be located?

2.0 Introduction: shareholders and materiality

The notion of materiality arose frequently in interviews and, to a somewhat lesser extent, in focus groups. Its importance to the debate after the interviews seems to be unquestioned and indeed might be one of the more underdeveloped issues in the whole audit expectations gap debate.

2.1 Users

Most users favour auditor provision of more information around the issue of materiality in the context of audit conduct, as the following comments illustrate. The first user foresees a day when disclosing materiality thresholds is required:

> They [users] probably don't understand the materiality and [for]... large organisations, the materiality threshold can be quite large. So maybe a bit more work can be done there to inform about the material. And I could even see a day when you have to disclose your materiality thresholds.

The difficulty of explaining to those earning modest incomes the size and application of materiality thresholds for the audit of a very large company is the subject of this next user's quotation:

> '$200 000 is a vast sum of money, and for someone to say: "Well, in the scope of the BHP accounts, it's totally irrelevant"—it's a very hard concept for them to grasp.'

> [I]s it just materiality that drives the level of work, or is it risk...it's very hard to explain to a schoolteacher that a $200 000 difference is irrelevant, because to a schoolteacher, to a taxi driver, $200 000 is a vast sum of money, and for someone to say: 'Well, in the scope of the BHP accounts, it's totally irrelevant'—it's a very hard concept for them to grasp. But...I would question how many retail shareholders even know the

> word exists. Yes, there is an audit function in there, that's in [their] checking, and they probably think they are doing far more checking than they really are, but they do take comfort from the fact that the auditors are in there. Well, at least the big firms, they have a chance of recognising the name when the auditor has any issues.

The same user continues, highlighting his or her understanding of the personal responsibility involved when an audit partner signs an audit report:

> When all's well...I don't think anyone's concerned. But the auditor of [a recently collapsed company] must have had worries. It didn't just all happen overnight and go down the gurgler. And I'm not sure how you would do it...I don't have an answer, but the audit partner who signs off on [one of the largest blue-chip companies] is a lot more relaxed than the audit partner who signed off the last set of accounts for [a recently collapsed company].

The need to explain the concept of materiality in layman's terms is articulated by this user:

> [M]aybe [materiality] just needs to be explained in layman's terms, or less accounting type of terms, because...from experience, it's something that if you don't understand, you just go over it and it could be quite crucial in the scheme of things.

This next user believes that auditors should bring material issues to the attention of investors before issues cause problems; otherwise people tend not to identify problems until they have emerged.

> [Auditors] should [explain materiality]...investors understand it intuitively in the sense that if you've got something major in accounts and it has the... potential to impact a company's performance, then they understand it. But...people don't identify the problem until, typically, it's already emerged. So that's why...while [accountants] understand the concept...the auditors should be striving to identify those issues, so [as to] at least to bring those issues to the attention of people prior to them causing problems...people have an intuitive understanding of that without understanding the technicalities of the accounting, if you like.

> '[I]f you've got something major in accounts and it has the...potential to impact a company's performance, then they understand it.'

Lack of understanding of the auditor's use of materiality by retail investors is one thing, but if boards of directors are struggling with the concept, it could be of greater concern.

> Yeah, it is a concern [that potentially many shareholders do not understand the concept of materiality]...it's even not well understood by a lot of boards either. There's always a bit of...an explanation required to the board as well.

The interviewer then asks whether that communication to the board is effective and the response given is negative, with the claim that the audit profession should take action to create better understanding:

> Not necessarily, no. I'd say with issues like that...the audit industry could probably go a long way in trying to clarify some of those things a lot better to everybody. I don't think they're well understood.

The interviewer then asks whether this issue is a major driver of expectations gaps between suppliers and purchasers and this user does not seem to think so, but it is difficult to see how it would not be, given the full context of his or her response:

> [A]t the end of the day, when you get the outcome, it leads to either a better or a confused understanding of the situation. So, you can be in meetings where you'll be going through something and these issues come up and...it's news to people how that is actually defined or how it's clarified.

2.1.1 Summary

Users, when asked whether auditors should explain more about their implementation of the concept of materiality in the conduct of the audit, feel that this would be a positive, but somewhat difficult, thing to do in layman's terms. Comment was received about the likely incomprehensibility to some of the large threshold dollar amounts of audit materiality used in the conduct of audits of the largest companies. The need to explain the concept in layman's terms, if it is to be explained, and the foreseeability of required public disclosure of materiality thresholds are raised also.

2.2 Purchasers

Remembering that in a past life, purchasers had sometimes been auditors, two purchasers expressed a perception that there was not a problem with the understanding of the concept of materiality as used by auditors.

> [T]o me, it's...not an issue at all...I can't speak...for retail shareholders, but...I used to be an auditor myself [and] I don't think there is an issue with materiality at all.

> [A]s a concept, no, I don't think so. Because... the auditor's approach of applying materiality I don't think has led to any of the significant audit failures...it's a valid approach that says we can't look at every single transaction that the company has undertaken in the past 12 months. We have to determine where to focus the audit effort, and we're going to make that determination on considering the risk associated with any particular aspect of the client's business and, providing we're satisfied that an error that we miss in our audit is not going to have a significant effect on the financial statements, then that's acceptable, and that probably should be acceptable...the big audit failures have not really been materiality driven. They've been driven by either incompetence or just a lack of understanding of the client's business and/or the clients themselves not properly disclosing what's happening in their business—and the nature of risks that they're undertaking.

'[T]he auditor's approach of applying materiality I don't think has led to any of the significant audit failures.'

Another purchaser feels that developing deep understanding of the concept of audit materiality is not high on investors' agendas and that what is more important is having faith in the professionalism of the auditor. He or she alludes to disclosures around subjective judgments as raising concerns:

> '[T]hose subjectivity-type areas on what you disclose and what you don't, and more around the nature of what's material…would possibly raise a concern [as to] where it's headed.'

> [A]s far as the wider community [is concerned], it's important to have more education and have that information out there so that people are well informed…if you're well informed of materiality and what auditors are actually doing and how they're going about it…you'll have more comfort in the work they're performing…otherwise…a couple of those subjectivity-type areas on what you disclose and what you don't, and more around the nature of what's material…would possibly raise a concern [as to] where it's headed.

The same purchaser continues with the theme of the importance of confidence in the professionalism of the auditor:

> [A]t the end of the day…materiality is just…a mechanism, of how auditors go about their work…and do investors want to know that or do they just want to know that they're doing a good job and they're doing what they should be doing? I can see how it plays a role internally, but…for investors, as long as they have confidence in the auditing profession—the professionalism—then…that's probably more of just another mechanism of how they go about their work, which they should have confidence in.

The remaining purchasers, however, constituting the majority, did feel that there was a problem with understanding materiality and that greater disclosure by auditors of the level of materiality to which they worked and/or around the concept of materiality more generally was desirable. Some, as in the next three quotations, want more detail of materiality as it pertains to the conduct of specific audits.

> '[Q]uite often, I'm sitting there explaining to people what an auditor actually does and how they review things.'

> [W]here they might be signing something off…tell us a bit more about the issues you do have a material issue with and what you [have] done around it and how you've satisfied yourself. Just doing a more generic statement in terms of 'this is a process we've undertaken to review these accounts'. [What I would want] from the generic statement would be…to try and explain to people what the account is doing if you haven't been an expert, haven't been

> familiar with the process of what they do...quite often I'm sitting there explaining to people what an auditor actually does and how they review things...it just gives the reader of the accounts a bit more feeling as to...materiality and does it actually get explained in the accounts, what materiality thresholds are, et cetera...even the standards are a bit broad in terms of 'is this material?'...if it's going to impact on users' economic decisions...I haven't looked at the statement in detail for a while but...the [auditor's] sign-off... does it refer to materiality or not...it's not really a high order of priority-type issue that we've got.

That different risk tolerances exist among key stakeholders to the audit is articulated by this next purchaser as a reason for disclosure by the auditor of the materiality level used.

> [M]ateriality affects everything external auditors do in many ways. How they disclose, how they make a decision, determine whether certain adjustment needs to be made or need[s] to be disclosed, so materiality is definitely... going to affect the way that certain financial information's being interpreted...there is some need to actually incline towards disclosing some more information on that particular part because materiality is basically...a risk-tolerance level, and therefore slightly different shareholders or key stakeholders would have a different level of risk appetite, so they need to be able to make an informed decision. They need to understand what materiality the auditors use. I work in a company and...I therefore understand what materiality our external auditors use in respect of my own company. But, obviously...[the] general public perhaps may not be aware of that. There will be a need for them to understand it.

'[M]ateriality is basically...a risk-tolerance level, and therefore slightly different shareholders or key stakeholders would have a different level of risk appetite, so they need to be able to make an informed decision.'

The same person goes on to articulate a dilemma in explaining the materiality concept in an auditing context. Could it raise more issues than it solves?

> '[O]bviously we don't want to suddenly ring the alarm bells; not 100 per cent correct—what does it mean? Is it only 50 per cent correct?'

Having said that, materiality itself is not...simple. A lot of the time we're not talking about just 5 per cent, 10 per cent of P&L [profit and loss] items because obviously external auditors also make their own judgment based on materiality...so there will be some judgment call required [about] how to actually disclose it without...misleading the audience because [there's] nothing worse [than] when we just give information and it's actually misleading...So, rather than just give...figures—because probably a certain number of figures may not actually apply in most situations...people would therefore need to understand when they read the financial statement, they need to be a bit more informed in what they actually read. It may not be, for example, 100 per cent correct [which] is probably one of the main things they need to be aware of and...is probably important. But then, obviously, we don't want to suddenly ring the alarm bells; not 100 per cent correct—what does it mean? Is it only 50 per cent correct...that's probably not what we are trying to drive...people need to understand perhaps what we're talking about [with] materiality is anything maybe under a certain level or something which is a little bit more important to the readers.

The next purchaser's comments reveal that he or she sees more explanation around materiality as useful not for retail investors, but for professionals who can use that information more effectively.

> '[I]t's just that much easier if it was disclosed: what have we looked at, what haven't we looked at, et cetera?'

[Y]ou need to maybe spell out what percentage or what level of due diligence or materiality have been put into it, as against just a standard statement that 'we've done audits based on section something that says [what] materiality is'...that needs to be further clarified...as a note as to what you've really done and what you haven't done. If you're looking at a normal, common shareholder...they're pretty sceptical anyway overall, so it's not going to help to that extent. If you're looking at professionals using the information...you can ask the question and it's just that much easier if it was disclosed: what have we looked at, what haven't we looked at, et cetera? And then, say somebody is looking at that or analysing the balance sheet, whether

> it's a fund manager or a banker, maybe the questions have been answered in those notes, or if they haven't then they could [drill in] to a particular aspect.

In the following comments, purchasers make clear the way in which misunderstanding or miscommunication of auditors' use of materiality (otherwise thought of as the level of 'tolerable error or omission') in the conduct of the audit can feed into the expectations gap.

> [T]here is quite a big expectations gap on the materiality threshold, which is, in a very big company...a very big number, and I don't think that number is really stated clearly enough...most people in the [name of a major ASX-listed company] issue didn't realise that that very big number—was it [a] $120 or $140 million...hole in the foreign exchange—might've ended up being higher in the end, but that it was under the auditor's threshold of what they actually said they would catch. So I wonder if that number should be stated. Obviously, that number...[is] approved by the audit committee each year, and obviously also that number is very sensitive for the audit fee...if they bring down the threshold, there's the implied assumption that there'll be an increase in the fee, which obviously the auditee never wants.

The same purchaser continues, concluding with a positive affirmation of just how much the insider knowledge that the auditor possesses is appreciated and valued:

> [T]he auditor may be seen as a warrior for the P&L as well as the capital...on the balance sheet, and...that is an expectations gap and probably could be better communicated...the reason I say that is, talking to...people in the market, whether they're on the buy or sell side...the market has a very lively knowledge of just how deeply the auditor understands the operations and risks of the company.

Constantly reiterating the cost consequences of failing to set a materiality level to which the auditor works is the suggestion of this next purchaser as a means to educate the public about the materiality issue.

'[T]here's an expectation in some people's minds that auditors would review every single transaction and I don't think they understand what that would cost.'

> [Y]ou've got to do it at a material level and I absolutely understand [that] the concern...[goes] back to the fact that [there] is an anticipation... there's an expectation in some people's minds that auditors would review every single transaction and I don't think they understand what that would cost and I don't know how...you educate them because when you look at [Sarbanes-Oxley] and all the rest of it...[the] general public was wildly enthusiastic and it plugged a political gap at that stage and it's now turning out to be one of the worst interventions that I can think of...it's just caused billions of dollars of impost with virtually no return and it would be the same with materiality...I know this business about letting the people regulate themselves is a tricky one politically, but...you've just got to drive to a materiality level and I don't know how you do that except at every instance suggest what the consequences of not doing it [are]. So...if our audits...are costing over a million dollars, well, if we did it to a materiality level of zero, we probably wouldn't make a profit. And what would be achieved? I don't know how you do get that whole management-of-risk concept across.

That it is not feasible to expect that retail investors can be educated about the role of audit or audit materiality comes through in this next purchaser's quotation:

> The ordinary person cannot in any genuine sense understand the auditing framework, so when we talk about this issue of materiality or any other issue, you really have to segment the audits. Let's abandon the mum and dad because, frankly, an annual report is beyond their comprehension...So let's move to the sophisticated end. The problem is that an audit is limited assurance[6]—we all know that—so what's the problem? It is not a thorough investigation of every transaction. It is effectively looking at the control posture of a company, looking at the risks and seeing if those risks and the

6 An audit provides 'reasonable' assurance and reviews provide 'limited' assurance in the language of the auditing standards; however, it is, in the authors' opinion, reasonable to presume that this purchaser uses the word 'limited' here to signal less than absolute assurance, given the context of the remainder of this quotation.

> controls are properly reflected in the financial statements and in the narrative that's given to the shareholders—that's what an annual report is about.

The same person goes on to allege that auditing firms are 'captured' and he or she asserts that the regulatory model under which they work is flawed in that the contract effectively becomes one between directors and auditors rather than between shareholders and auditors, as is the legislative intent. It is therefore not regulatory capture that is being spoken of here, which is the way in which the word 'capture' is often used in the research literature. Rather, it is capture of auditors by the auditee that is alluded to.

> [T]here's a sense that, frankly, audit firms are captured. There are four big ones and they deal with the top-200 companies...The auditors are—it's almost a rote that they go through... the appointment and the contractual model is...flawed in today's world. It's a contract with the directors—understand [that] it used to be a contract with the shareholders—it's no longer a contract with the shareholders even though the words say it is...I don't have a problem with that, but don't try and create any link between auditor and shareholder when in fact the auditor directs literally 99 per cent of their attention to the management and the directors and 1 per cent of their time to the shareholders when they now, for the first time in years, turn up to an AGM and can be subject to questions...this question of materiality—how many top-200 audits have been qualified in the last 10 years? It's not even a fat tail on a normal distribution curve. It's such a low number...So then when you get down to materiality it is only the sophisticated end that understand what the materiality concept is. There is no mum and dad shareholder who has read the relevant accounting standard on materiality or the relevant auditing standard, so how can they possibly understand it?

'It's a contract with the directors—understand [that] it used to be a contract with the shareholders—it's no longer a contract with the shareholders even though the words say it is.'

This next purchaser implies that even when the concept of audit materiality is understood, it is conveniently overlooked when something goes wrong and a scapegoat is sought—often the auditor.

> '[T]here's almost a selective amnesia about it. If something goes wrong and the managing director is being hauled over the coals...the default response is to look for someone to blame.'

> Yes, [the audit concept is] easy to explain. There are certain things that are too small to worry about. But...there's almost a selective amnesia about it. If something goes wrong and the managing director is being hauled over the coals because of problems in his organisation, the default response is to look for someone to blame. And generally the person to blame is the auditor, on the assumption that they're checking 100 per cent every process, every account balance, every whatever, and they miss the fact...[of] what the auditors are trying to achieve in an audit.

Another purchaser alludes to the same tendency of management to selectively ignore the application of audit materiality levels if something goes wrong. This purchaser also indicates that non-accounting or finance-specific management personnel need education with regard to materiality as auditors apply it.

> 'I don't know if that's indicative of the fact that they don't understand materiality or selectively they choose to ignore it when it suits their own ends.'

> [N]ot being a listed business and not having to think too much about shareholders, I guess I'm changing the word 'shareholders' for 'general management' and use them as my reference. Outside of the accounting and finance people, the general management, in this business at least, doesn't understand the concept of materiality. They know about it, but they seem to selectively forget about it if ever issues arise. And there's a general presumption that the auditors are actually checking that we're 100 per cent right. And if anything goes wrong, the default position is to blame the auditors—be that even not just external auditors but internal auditors for missing something. I don't know if that's indicative of the fact that they don't understand materiality or selectively they choose to ignore it when it suits their own ends...addressing the issue of materiality...as the customers of the audit firm, purchasing their service...if they were to provide more information about how they conduct the audit in terms of the process, and their proprietary method, that would probably

> address materiality at that point. So...that would be useful as an educator for management in the purchase of these audit services as to what materiality is and how it fits into the whole process.

Several other purchasers also differentiated between sophisticated and retail users of financial reports in terms of their level of understanding of the auditor's use of the materiality concept.

> I did a quick search on our annual report from last year...just on the word 'materiality', and the only place it was really mentioned was in the corporate governance disclosures. So, you'd have to...[ask whether] materiality really [is] discussed out there in the public forum, being through annual reports or whatever. You'd probably say no. Does that mean people don't understand what it is... if you're an experienced or a sophisticated shareholder then you would understand these types of concepts, especially since those corporate governance principles have come in and three or four of them specifically mention material misstatement, or words to that effect. So if you were...a sophisticated shareholder...and you didn't understand something, you should research it and find that out yourself. The ones...[who] maybe...don't really understand the concept...[are] some of your mum and dad investors...or maybe ones who have just become investors through demutualisations or things like that.

One apparently knowledgeable purchaser observes the profoundly different attitude of the regulatory regime in the United States. He or she points to the more conservative approach in the United States, where all errors are treated as material because a user might be affected if they are not corrected.

> We're talking about someone making an assessment. So people make assessments for a variety of reasons—and not all of them are financial. So, if we just stick with financial analysts and funds...the big end of town have a good handle on the concept of materiality. So, I would suggest you have to stratify your shareholder base to answer this question. And then [ask] should this be a concern? Well, yes...it should, because...what you do get is

'[W]hat you do get is the situation in the US where everything's material in the view of the regulator. If it's a mistake, it's not appropriate not to correct it, because you don't know if that would change someone's view.'

> the situation in the US where everything's material in the view of the regulator. If it's a mistake, it's not appropriate not to correct it, because you don't know if that would change someone's view. And so you err on the side of caution and say that everything's material...I'm not sure how you address the concern around materiality...the only way that you cannot backslide further is to maintain a substance-over-form framework.

One purchaser felt that information about materiality should be available, but only for those interested and on an 'opt-in' basis.

> [S]hareholders have to have an avenue that's made clear where they can find [information about materiality]...what I'm saying is...that, effectively...1 per cent should actually opt in to...be able to have a very efficient way through an information market to be able to find out their answer to their question, as opposed to working [to] a scheme that sends the information to all 100 per cent [of] them—for 99 [per cent] not to read it.

As is the case with some of the above quotations, several purchasers' comments, illustrated explicitly by the next two quotations, go to the desirability of providing educative material around the issue of materiality.

> [M]aybe it's more an education and disclosure issue than actually changing the way an audit is done, or changing the use of the concept of materiality. Maybe you do have to educate people to say we undertake our audit under the umbrella of materiality, and this is what that means. It means that we will miss things, or we may miss things, that are not appropriate, but the implication of that is not going to have a significant effect on the wellbeing of the company or the share price or other aspects to do with the audit.

> There is a group of shareholders that do understand materiality, but...there still needs to be materiality thresholds...Rather than try and address materiality, let's try and address the education of the shareholder, [provide] an explanation to the shareholder, without just standing up at an AGM...[or] a shareholder meeting and just saying 'it wasn't material', [which goes] straight over the head. So just explain what we mean by that...it's a fine CFO trick to say 'it wasn't material'. It's not a trick, but it's true. You don't help a shareholder by not explaining what you mean. So if you

> actually say, 'The impact of that court case was only $3 million on this company and you all know the cost of it, you all know our expenses are $12 billion'—sorry, that's why it's not addressed...So, my point is this: the way to address the question is to explain it better to the shareholders.

The difficulty of providing effective educative material alluded to in some of the preceding quotations is, however, explicitly pointed out in this next quotation:

> [I]f you'd never ever bumped into any of this before but you had a whole series of shares and companies and things, I really do think there'd be an expectation out there that you wouldn't have a clue that it's been done to a materiality level, although it's put in this statement. I don't know how you do educate people that way, I really don't.

The same person, when pressed by the interviewer about whose responsibility it was to educate about materiality, saw that squarely in the remit of auditors, but pointed out that the concept needed to be placed within a risk framework and there was also the danger of it being seen as an attempt to absolve the auditor from responsibility.

> Auditors collectively...probably [have] a responsibility [to educate on materiality]. But...what you don't want...is...a perception with everybody saying, 'Oh well, they're just absolving themselves from everything', and then they lose confidence in it. So there's the balance of perception that, yes, we are detailed, we are following it up, because...having that mind-set out there probably has a governance role in itself. But...maybe it's trying to drive the fact that they're managing risk, which is what they're all doing now...they're auditing to risk...and...that's—certainly at our board meetings—all well understood...But I wouldn't anticipate it to be [understood] at the...general shareholder level.

'[Y]ou don't want a perception with everybody saying, "Oh well, they're just absolving themselves from everything", and then they lose confidence in it.'

The next purchaser points to a wider perspective of materiality and how it needs to be applied to many engagements to maintain cost parameters and obtain meaningful information.

> [Y]ou've got to put it into a context. If you say, 'Do people understand the issue of materiality?', it's like all things in the literature and the auditing and accounting standards. I don't think many readers would understand most of the accounting standards or the auditing standards in detail. So the fact that...they might not understand the materiality issue in great detail, that's not surprising. But you've got to have a notion of materiality just to be able to do a job within a reasonable boundary of economics and the cost of doing it, and a reasonable exercise as to what does the information mean.

The next purchaser raises the subjectivity of the more qualitative aspects of materiality judgments. This purchaser, unlike an earlier one, feels that there will be more confidence in the audit process if the wider community is well informed about this issue:

> [T]he main area of materiality that would probably cause some concern is that area where there's subjectivity...there's not as much subjectivity if we're just talking pure numbers—if you find an issue worth X amount. But when we talk about perhaps the nature of some items, or disclosure...and what's material and what's not, and where subjectivity creeps into that decision, there could be some concern there as to what's disclosed and what's not and should it be...as far as the wider community [is concerned,] it's important to have more education and have that information out there so that people are well informed...if you're well informed of materiality and what auditors are actually doing and how they're going about it...you'll have more comfort in the work they're performing.

Purchasers were also asked explicitly about audit committees and boards' understanding of materiality. Their responses indicate perceptions of a much deeper understanding of materiality by the members of these bodies compared with retail investors and even average sophisticated investors.

> [E]verybody who sits on an audit and risk committee should understand the concept at the very least, if not the board...from a shareholder's point of view, do they need to know what materiality is...It's probably questionable because if the auditors have signed off the accounts then they're saying everything...is true and correct... Does a shareholder need to know that it's true and correct to a certain level of materiality? For example, that's why the audit firms have materiality. It's because anything below that would generally

> mean that it's not going to affect the financial performance of the company. So does the shareholder need to know about it? You'd probably question that and maybe say no. But certainly management and the audit risk committee should definitely know what that is. Although I don't think they have a lot of input in setting the level of materiality, they should understand why it's set at that level and how it's set at that level. At least ask the questions.

The next purchaser provides a suggestion that it be within the charter of the audit committee that committee members become educated about audit materiality.

> 'Perhaps...there ought to be an obligation on the external auditors to be educating members of the audit committee and likewise the audit committee should have on their charter that they should get education...from the external auditors on their process and what materiality is.'

> [T]hey do [understand materiality]... because audit committees generally are made up of people who've been around the traps for a long time...they've been involved in a lot of discussions on financial statements. They understand and also they're seeing the unders and overs and things that haven't been adjusted...again, it comes down to how does the audit risk committee function? What does it see? And that's all around governance and what is... best practice in terms of [the] audit committee as to whether directors are really on top of the game—and that, to me, is best addressed through that avenue...But the ones I've been involved with...I don't think there's any issue about people understanding what materiality is and at what levels it's applied because it's very transparently advised by the auditors to the audit committee...Perhaps...there ought to be an obligation on the external auditors to be educating members of the audit committee and likewise the audit committee should have on their charter that they should get education...from the external auditors on their process and what materiality is and all the other bits and pieces. There's a two-way obligation there.

The next purchaser points out that audit committee members who do not understand audit materiality are in peril:

> Certainly in respect of the way that auditors report to audit committees now, I'd be surprised by [a lack of understanding of materiality] because of the fact that—and I'm not sure if this is

> a requirement of the auditing standards—but certainly the whole reporting of audit differences is pretty much standard now, and that's been driven largely out of the US. Tell us if you've got an audit difference, and we want to know the audit differences that were there and [were] adjusted as much as anything. So if you're dealing with audit committees...that's a 'horses for courses' issue...if you're a director and you're not understanding the financial report and you're on the audit committee, well, you've got bigger problems than the auditor does.

Explicit in this next quotation is the fact that in some circumstances audit committees demand to know and are aware of the level of audit materiality to which the auditor is working:

> I don't understand why it's a concern because when the issue comes up of materiality, on the audit committee, we're very specific about...what level of materiality they're working towards...for example, recently I was in a board meeting and they said they were working to a broad materiality—hundreds of thousands. And that was in theory, but in practice they were working to a much stricter [level]. And we said we want it spelled out—what you're working to—because it's important for us to know exactly, so we can present to shareholders what materiality means. And that point of it's so broad that you could have a major problem and it wouldn't be... covered in the sense of having been considered to be material under their much broader guidelines.

'Now...$1 million might only represent 1 per cent, but I still want to know about it because I think it's not so much that it's material as such in final accounts, but it becomes significant to me in managing the process by which those accounts are prepared.'

> [T]hat can sometimes happen because you get to a situation...typically it arises where you get something that's gone wrong, and let's just say there's been an error or a defalcation or something of that description and if someone says, 'Well, gee, that's material', in their mind it's a material number because it's more than a certain dollar impact. And...in my own mind when I'm looking at accounts, I say forget about the 5 per cent test...tell me the items that are over $1 million. Now...$1 million might only represent 1 per cent, but I still want to know about it because... it's not so much that it's material as such in final accounts, but it

> becomes significant to me in managing the process by which those accounts are prepared. So the context in which people can raise it is different.

The same purchaser continues, explaining that in his or her experience, even among audit committee members, differential levels of understanding of the concept of audit materiality exist:

> [A]n audit partner might say to me, as a chairman of an audit committee, 'But that's not material', and I say, 'I don't care.' I want to know about it because it is important [to] me understanding the process of what's happened. He might then turn around and say, 'Well, you're trying to put too fine an interpretation on something.' Well, so be it, but that's something you agree with the audit engagement team up front about what's a reportable item. You'll get different people on audit committees that have different levels of knowledge and expertise. And on the audit committees I chair, I have people who have a very high level of financial sophistication and knowledge and others that are more business oriented and not so much into financial issues. And the ways they approach things, and the questions they ask, and the way they get to their comfort, [are] entirely different. So you can get differences in terms of people understanding it or not.

2.2.1 Summary

With the exception of an ex-auditor purchaser, there is general agreement among purchasers that the concept of materiality as used by auditors is not well understood by retail users of financial reports and even, as some observe, by some auditee managements and even audit committee members. Some purchasers in their comments, however, make it clear that the situation is complex, with the more sophisticated readers of financial reports much more able to grasp and understand the concept and its utilisation in the conduct of an audit. Directors and audit committee members create another level of sophistication and accountability again and are seen generally by purchasers as competent in their understanding of auditing concepts surrounding materiality.

Given purchasers' comments about the concept of materiality and the perceived potential of a failure to fully understand it to exacerbate the expectations gap, several advocate the need for education of users about the audit product. The use of materiality in terms of 'tolerable error' emerges from purchasers' comments as particularly misunderstood, although two comment that this could be a deliberately selective, self-interested misunderstanding.

2.3 Suppliers

Suppliers' comments about their application of the materiality concept and their perceptions of users' understanding of that concept range from those asserting that materiality is of little interest to shareholders to those who believe it is crucial that understanding of the concept becomes more widespread.

The first two quotations below express suppliers' perceptions that there is little need for shareholder concern or interest in the concept of materiality as it is used in the conduct of audits, although education about the issue is desirable.

> [P]robably all shareholders wouldn't care about materiality; all they care about is the value of their shares and whether or not their investment is going to be returned to them at some stage with a reasonable interest or capital improvement. So they probably don't even care or know about the concept of materiality. But from the audit point of view, we still have to recognise materiality and we still have to recognise risk assessments and so on, and I don't think the auditor should change. But the educational process to the end user should be beefed up so that if materiality should be an issue to the reader of the financial reports, or the stakeholders, or the shareholders or whoever they are, they should be educated more about the concept of materiality, or whether they should even concern themselves with materiality. Materiality should be a tool of part of the audit; it shouldn't necessarily concern the end user. But...there must be much more education [of] the end user of financial reports than exists at the moment about the whole concept of financial reporting in the disclosure [area].

> I don't see [materiality] as a major concern. Occasionally, you do get questions, but if they are answered...I haven't seen it as a major issue, no. Yes, it can be explained to [mum and dad investors]. I don't think it's a difficult concept...I would've thought a lot of people do understand it. I don't see it as a major issue...the people

> that I see are quite accepting of the concept. Once you explain it to them, they can understand.

The potential for lack of understanding of materiality to exacerbate the audit expectations gap is, however, acknowledged by the next supplier:

> '[T]he numbers are sort of right, plus or minus the 20 million. Well... the shareholders would absolutely be staggered at that. And they wouldn't understand the correlation between that materiality level and...the cost of the audit.'

> [I]t is part of the expectation gap, because... there would be very few shareholders who would understand materiality as applied by an auditor. And...some of them would be quite staggered to learn...if you take [one of the top-100 listed companies], the materiality on that job might be 20 million [dollars]—I'm just picking a figure—and therefore the numbers are sort of right, plus or minus the 20 million. Well...the shareholders would absolutely be staggered at that. And they wouldn't understand the correlation between that materiality level and...the cost of the audit—that if you were going to be dropping that down to just, say, five million then you're going to have to be doing four times the amount of work that you presently do. And I think therefore that concept hasn't been well put out there because, again, it's started to get into the audit report.

Another two suppliers agree that the concept of materiality is not well understood, but they express the belief that articulation of more information about the concept is likely to be of limited usefulness because of its technical nature.

> [Ordinary shareholders] don't understand the concept of materiality. Materiality doesn't just come in numerical form...which is largely the way we would do it, but there are other non-numerical concepts which apply to materiality. If it was on a just non-numerical form, it probably wouldn't be difficult to communicate as to what our materiality [is]—whether you call it materiality, whether you call it tolerance, whatever you like to call [it]. Quite possibly, that could give them some level of comfort...I don't know...How we communicate it...where we have, let's say, non-numerical materiality. And what I mean by non-numerical [is] it's really where something is just absolutely material by nature regardless of what the amount is. So how you articulate that might be a little bit difficult. Would

> it give them any more comfort…it might give them some comfort… to know what the tolerance level is, but I'm not sure how much comfort that would give the users on those financial reports.
>
> [I]t's such a technical issue, I don't think that we necessarily expect the public to understand it…materiality always comes down to commonsense. If you've got a million-dollar profit and there might be $10 000 of dubious revenues, well, why would you spend any time at all looking at that? You would just simply say, 'Well, look, I'll accept that because it makes sense to me, because I expected them to make some money on that particular little venture', or whatever it was. It might be donations or it might be reimbursements or something like that. But…that's an easy commonsense-type thing. It gets a little bit harder when, obviously, the numbers get bigger. And the auditor does in fact need to have empathy…[he or she] needs to put themselves…pretty much in the shoes of the investor, or the member of the company…or prospective investor even, and just say, 'Well, if I was going to be investing here would I be concerned about whether the profit was X or X plus 100 or X less 100?' Does that make a difference? We can come up with all the statistical analysis in the world but it doesn't necessarily give us the answer as to whether something's material or not. And of course one of the age-old problems with the materiality is that something might be material for the profit and loss statement, but not material for the balance sheet…that's a technical issue, which I don't think most people necessarily get.

The perceived difficulty of articulating understandable explanations of the auditor's use of materiality and its association with the degree of auditor judgment is demonstrated in the next few quotations.

> '[Y]ou could speak to four different people and you'd get four different interpretations of what materiality is in a particular context.'

> Both within the accounting standards and within the auditing standards there are standards of what is materiality and guidelines to materiality, so if you really are concerned [about] getting people to understand it, I don't think that those standards are overly complex. What they do outline is that materiality is a particularly complex issue that is made up both of quantitative and qualitative factors. There are some broad guidelines, but… it comes down to individual judgment around

something as material and...you could probably start to address the broad concepts of materiality with users of the financial statements, and with shareholders if you did that through some form of education marketing campaign. But is that really a concern for the accounting profession? Even within the accounting profession... you could speak to four different people and you'd get four different interpretations of what materiality is in a particular context...it's a very complex issue, it requires judgment that is particular to an individual circumstance, and therefore...you can give some broad guidelines, but...you've got to leave it...to individual practitioners to exercise their judgment.

[I]t's a huge area, materiality. And we all struggle with it as professional accountants. So how the hell people who are not accountants can look at materiality and properly understand it, I don't know.

[T]he issue of materiality is no more a concern than shareholders understanding what an audit does and doesn't do...the materiality effectively drives that and how you apply things...Whether...and quite how you're able to articulate a materiality...it's quite difficult for me to stand up in an AGM in front of 700 people and try and explain the principles of materiality. If they ask me, that's what I'll do, but... you'll lose people after a while, and...you'll get into a philosophical debate about well 'gosh, shouldn't you do more to give the comfort', which comes back [to] the heart of what an audit is and what an audit isn't.

'[I]t's quite difficult for me to stand up in an AGM in front of 700 people and try and explain the principles of materiality.'

[I]t's a difficult question because if I say yes, [auditors] should [explain materiality], the way in which you would do that then becomes awfully complex...Obviously, professional judgment is a strong part of what we do and if you then try and explain...everyone's going to have a different view about what an audit should be...I've had experiences where I've just worked through materiality with boards of listed entities and while they might agree

'[W]hile they might agree with what the materiality is in regards to the financials as a whole, when we then try and apply that and talk them through how we apply that to different line items or captions in accounts...that discussion... becomes quite a heated debate and people have different views.'

> with what the materiality is in regards to the financials as a whole, when we then try and apply that and talk them through how we apply that to different line items or captions in accounts, even that discussion with board members who are well educated, often with a finance background, becomes quite a heated debate and people have different views.

The same supplier continues, expanding on the complexity of explaining not just 'materiality', but 'sampling' to a broad user base:

> [I]f we put this question and applied it purely in regards to materiality, to try and take that debate into a forum and a broader group...maybe the institutional investors could get that, but the mum and dad investor I don't think will have the ability to do that. So, if you then say, 'Well, okay what about the audit as a whole and forget materiality, tell us what you do and when you do it, sampling and how that might work', I cannot imagine how you could possibly explain that to an average [investor]...and professional judgment is the main reason. As long as we're able to apply our professional judgment while working within the accounting standards and the relevant regulations, I can't imagine how you could properly explain that to a broad user base.

The same supplier goes on to explain the nexus between the audit materiality concept and the audit expectations gap:

> [T]he audit opinion, although it's distinct...explains the materialities at play and there's sampling, and if someone read that carefully, they should get a sense of maybe what an audit is not. The thing [that]...is well and truly misunderstood is the concept of materiality...across a lot of users, not just mums and dads. For big...multinational groups, that obviously can be a very big figure and...a lot of shareholders would struggle if you said to them we can still sign a clean audit opinion but the audit error might be X many tens of millions...that would stun them...so there is still this expectation gap between what an auditor knows an audit opinion actually is versus what a reader of accounts might expect an audit to be.

The divide between retail investors and more sophisticated players among users of financial reports is apparent in several of the preceding suppliers' comments and is made explicit in the next quotation:

> [I]f you ask most...mums and dads...who knows what they know? But if you were to ask most analysts, most brokers, most lawyers...what's... material, they'll say 5 per cent...[so] that kind of quantitative threshold is capable of being reasonably well explained...whether...you mandated putting some extra disclosure about that in the audit report so everyone understood it, I don't know. Where it gets harder of course is...[where] in the auditing standard it talks about the quantitative and then the qualitative threshold and the qualitative threshold will always make you lower your materiality. It will never say ignore the quantitative, go higher. And so there's always judgment around that...[but] I'm not a big fan of making things more prescribed, so I don't know how big an issue this is...most people other than mums and dads would say 5 per cent is material in anyone who deals in financials...Whether you'd want to go to the next step of highlighting that, I don't know.

'[T]he qualitative threshold will always make you lower your materiality. It will never say ignore the quantitative, go higher.'

No suppliers are explicitly in favour of disclosure of the real level of materiality used in the audit and one voices his or her express wish that this not be done since it could be detrimental:

> [W]hat we need to do is get a better understanding out there of how the audit works and what does it mean, because I still think that generally people think that we are there to stop fraud. And...they don't understand materiality...I'm not sure how you get to the average shareholder...I don't think you'd be smart to be [saying] this is our materiality on this job...you need an educational process of somehow putting information out there which allows the people to get a feel for materiality, and then you can be starting to maybe allude a bit more to that in the audit report...But I doubt that they'd ever get to the point of actually putting a dollar figure [on it].

'I doubt that they'd ever get to the point of actually putting a dollar figure [on it].'

> [I]f people actually sit back and think about things, they ought to understand materiality and that that 5 per cent threshold's not a big concern. So, now the audit report as it currently stands talks about things being material...whether you'd actually want to go [to] the next level and prescribe the amounts—I don't know. I think that would be unwise and probably detrimental.

Several of the suppliers' comments—some prompted by a specific interviewer question—turned their attention to directors and audit committee members' understanding of materiality in the context of an audit.

Generally, suppliers are positive about board understanding of the concept, as is revealed in the next few quotations. The first comment also reinforces doubt that the materiality level should be publicly disclosed:

> [There are] often some significant items that are left on our unadjusted schedule that the board concurs with or is happy to lean with—unadjusted—but [which] never see the light of day either in value or in the quantum of errors...I [would] like to put those on the table now, or I have an obligation to anyway, but...not in terms of just the value, but the fact that if you've got pages and pages of unadjusted differences it also goes to show that there are other deficiencies—potentially control deficiencies. So from that point of view, I know that you come back to the question of materiality...I would never get to the point...of necessarily disclosing that to shareholders because it's not just quantitative, it is a qualitative assessment and...if you start talking quantitative, it does take away the qualitative. But...in terms of the amount of...the profile materiality...has now maybe to what it did five–10 years ago, I can certainly say the board is more conscious of it now, management is certainly more conscious of it now. Sometimes they use it as a bit of a tool themselves as to what they can and can't do.

The same supplier continues, explaining his or her perception that, increasingly, management is using the materiality concept to say to the auditor 'don't worry about that, that's not material':

> [O]ne thing that I would hate to think would happen is that companies start to think materiality in their own right. I've seen that creep in a little bit more over the recent years where management will say,

'Don't worry about that, that's not material.' And our view is well, that's your objectives, you should really get it right; materialities has [sic] just become more of an audit function rather than for in the first instance not to address something because you don't believe it's material. So as long as there's not a disconnect there as well.

Generally, suppliers are also positive about the skills of audit committee members in understanding the concept of materiality as pertaining to audit. The next quotation, however, makes the point that understanding it does not mean approving of its use:

I don't know if [audit committees] don't understand [materiality]; they just don't like it. So they will understand that the audit's done to materiality, but nevertheless they expect you to know everything. So if there's a million-dollar fraud, then why didn't you pick it up? If there's something like the wheat board type of thing, with all those facilitation payments...would they necessarily have come to the auditor's attention based on materiality? No.

'[T]hey just don't like it. So they will understand that the audit's done to materiality, but nevertheless they expect you to know everything.'

The next supplier's comment points out that even audit committee members can be surprised by the numbers involved in audit materiality:

[W]hen you deal with audit committees and things like that, when you start talking about materiality and you put [out] ball-park figures, you still get a bit of a reaction from people. 'What does that mean—that's a big number?' And it's the complexity of the systems...which requires you to do testing of a representative sample. But because of the volume of transactions, that's why we end up with materiality. Yes, it is a concern...because that's part of that. I don't think they understand that.

The next supplier explains what he or she sees as one of the reasons for the level of audit committee understanding of materiality:

> 'Probably what's given them a greater appreciation as well, just in the context of materiality, is the kind of factors that we as the auditors are grappling [with] as well—whether something might be material from a disclosure-deficiency point of view.'

[T]he audit committee has certainly elevated their understanding or the level of inquiry that they make beyond just the normal reporting mechanism—being the kind of... board reports. Probably what's given them a greater appreciation as well, just in the context of materiality, is the kind of factors that we as the auditors are grappling [with] as well—whether something might be material from a disclosure-deficiency point of view...that's certainly something and we've moved down that path in the last couple of years...We're not just reporting financial statement errors in terms of [the] quantitative, but we're also reporting disclosure deficiencies...We won't qualify because of that deficiency, but it's certainly not preferred practice. It's not enough for us to give a qualified opinion, but certainly a preferred position would be to have more disclosure and therefore...even there, you're starting to see boards in particular start to think...[about asking] the question of management: 'Well, why not? Why haven't you gone down that path?' And if there's not a reasonable explanation there then... that's where we think you should take it. You should move towards the preferred position...there's a general view that more disclosure is better than less.

Not all suppliers, however, are complimentary about the knowledge levels of management, boards and audit committees, as the next few interview quotations show.

> '[I]f there is one area...[where there is] still...confusion between even boards and audit committees, and something that we've got to decide, [it] is making them abundantly aware of the standard on materiality and what that means and how it's been set.'

Now, the shareholder doesn't have any idea on a particular entity whether we're working to $1 million [or] $10 million. Right, so a shareholder—a big perception—may think that we're auditing everything and even though we say an audit can't test everything, they may still [think] that. Would it help to say that we've used a materiality of $10 million? The only issue with that is, do they really understand the concepts around materiality and how that drives it? So you get caught either way. But

> if there is one area...[where there is] still...confusion between even boards and audit committees, and something that we've got to decide, [it] is making them abundantly aware of the standard on materiality and what that means and how it's been set. Because often a board will say, 'Well, how come you didn't spot that 200-grand adjustment?' Well, you're never going to spot the 200-grand adjustment if you're working with a materiality of 10 million. It's just not how an audit will work...[that area is] still fraught with danger as to how you explain that to the general public.

The next supplier has experience with a board that understands that to lower the materiality level below that set by the auditor will increase the cost, with a preparedness to pay that incremental cost to acquire the requisite level of assurance.

> '[C]ould we reduce our materiality to come to that benchmark? And I said, "Yeah, absolutely", because that's an extension of the scope of the audit. There's a cost element to it, which the board understood and were comfortable with.'

> [Q]uite often management and the board don't have a good appreciation of materiality and how it works and how it fits in. And I'm very keen to set out my materiality to the board so they understand exactly where it is, how we've applied the...standard on materiality. But firstly...it actually helps me when you're selecting the benchmark to confirm that's where they view it. I recently had an example where we had a good discussion with a very major listed company, and I'd set the materiality absolutely in accordance with the standard and judgment and so on. And they accepted that that was the benchmark, it was a right benchmark, or a benchmark. But they actually had another benchmark that was important to [them] and [they wanted to know] could we reduce our materiality to come to that benchmark? And I said, 'Yeah, absolutely', because that's an extension of the scope of the audit. There's a cost element to it, which the board understood and were comfortable with. So we varied that. And both materialities in fact are acceptable under the standard, which actually shows that the standard itself can lead you down to different answers. So...the first point I have is that I want to make sure that the board understands the concept of materiality and therefore what is or isn't going to get picked up in an audit. And that leads us into another one, which is extending the audit and so on.

2.3.1 Summary

Several suppliers position the understanding of audit materiality within the context of other understandability challenges presented in the form of complex financial reports more generally, the issue of audit sampling and what it is that can and cannot be expected of an audit. Suppliers are eloquent in expressing the qualitative as well as quantitative nature of materiality and the role of their judgment in applying materiality, leading to the difficulty they perceive in articulating to unsophisticated users of the audit product their use of materiality in their audit conduct. Most suppliers are positive in their comments about the level of understanding of the materiality concept displayed by directors and audit committee members; however, this is not a universally held view. While there is little dispute that retail investors do not understand adequately the concepts involved, there is not agreement that this situation can be resolved, even with more disclosure. There is no support by suppliers for public disclosure of the real level of audit materiality employed, but it is evident that there are many instances—although not universally so—where the materiality level is disclosed to clients, either auditee management or audit committees. Suppliers are particularly knowledgeable that the level of materiality and the related use of sampling have consequences for the cost of the audit.

2.4 Standard setters

Like the comments of suppliers, those of standard setters range from conveying no discomfort with existing levels of understanding of audit materiality to those who see further education being required.

One standard setter reminds us that there are many aspects of audit that are not well understood and uses an analogy to convey the point that not all the intricacies of a product or service need to be known before use can be made of that product or service.

> 'Does a brain surgeon need to explain to me every intricacy, or do I just need to know that he knows what he's doing and he's going to fix me up?'

I challenge what is it that they need to know. I don't want to get too off the track here, but we can joke about using inappropriate analogies around brain surgery and nuclear physics or whatever, but if I went to a doctor and needed to be fixed, how much do I need to know about the process and how he goes about fixing me? Does a brain surgeon need to explain to me

> every intricacy, or do I just need to know that he knows what he's doing and he's going to fix me up? So I could equally talk about shareholders not understanding the difference between controls testing and substantive testing, understanding what we report to audit committees or those charged with governance. I could pick up lots of individual aspects of an audit in addition to materiality and say 'people don't understand'.

One standard setter claims that it would be 'dangerous' to disclose the materiality level itself, and believes that the auditing standards should be the source of information about materiality, with education about where the standards can be found as a potential solution.

> '[I]f you can increase their awareness of what the Australian Auditing Standards actually are and where they can be found then...that's probably a good thing.'

> [The disclosure of the materiality level itself is] probably dangerous and you don't really want to dig those kind of holes for yourself because it's subject to interpretation and you get a dollar above or a dollar below. Who knows what kind of impact that's going to have in the minds of some investors...the auditing standards do set out materiality pretty well and...maybe there's scope for increased awareness of the auditing standards to some extent. So we say that we have conducted this audit in accordance with Australian Auditing Standards and maybe some reference to key elements of auditing standards...[with] materiality—probably the risk standards around assessing the risks of an organisation, the risk of material misstatement and procedures designed to address those risks. That's a general [statement], which you could include and then refer to the main body of standards and where they might be found...It makes them aware that the information's available but now they'd probably just read the word in accordance with the Australian Auditing Standards without any concept of what that actually is...So if you can increase their awareness of what the Australian Auditing Standards actually are and where they can be found then...that's probably a good thing.

Several standard setters make it clear that in their view there are more important audit issues than materiality for which understanding needs to be clarified, as the quotations below demonstrate.

> [C]ertainly, wherever I've worked, yes, [materiality is understood by boards of directors]. And it's now absolutely the norm for the auditors to disclose their level of materiality in terms of the work they're doing. That seems to me now to be standard practice at audit committees and then [there is] potentially a robust discussion around whether that is an appropriate level. In terms of shareholders...it's just another facet of the difficulties of understanding the complexity of the work that auditors are expected to do. So yes, I'm sure that's not well understood, although it's not a difficult concept to grasp if you can engage someone and have a discussion. But how do you do that with the shareholders?

Education about the fact that a financial report audit does not give absolute assurance, which is a corollary of the application of audit materiality, is seen as the way to tackle the issue, according to the next two standard setters.

> [T]he profession would benefit...by having a greater understanding in the marketplace about the fact that an audit isn't absolute assurance, so I would perhaps focus more on not so much defining materiality, but defining just what an audit is...So an audit provides reasonable but not absolute assurance. What does that mean...more discussion and disclosure [are needed] about the fact that it's not a 100 per cent review, but...the message to convey there is more one of concept than the fact that it isn't absolute assurance, rather than getting into the detail of describing materiality and what your thresholds are and the technical concepts...[it should be] the reinforcement that it's not absolute assurance.

In discussing the materiality issue, this standard setter also comments on the issue of probability and the lack of desirability of disclosure of the dollar value of materiality:

> [A]s long as people understand that the opinion an auditor gives is not an absolute opinion, but [that] really it is done within a range and you're up in that 94 [per cent range]...If they understand it's in that area that the opinion is given...that would be of benefit. I don't know how you'd go around better educating the user base out there...it's a task which you will never get a satisfactory answer [or] outcome on. In other words, there will always be someone who believes you're giving absolute assurance, which is clearly not the case, and

> I notice that in the review opinions where you're giving the negative opinion...there is the level of confidence which is being expressed... that is probably even less well known. And so [for] the materiality level, my preference would be that...we give a general recognition to it, but I wouldn't like to see the number being flagged or disclosed because...the materiality does vary. In other words, you might have one materiality for an area but in terms of, say, the related parties and the materiality in terms of that may in fact be less than what you've used for receivables and payables because of the...qualitative nature of the materiality, and materiality is based on both quantitative and qualitative...so therefore it's just not one figure.

The same standard setter continues, affirming the need for greater understanding of the concept of audit materiality:

> [W]hile I would support...a greater recognition, it would be interesting to see how that is done in terms of the...general or whether in fact it should be [in] the audit report...[in] my opinion... the audit report [doesn't need] to give any more than what it's currently got on it, but...the general kind of awareness in terms of what an audit is about and the role of materiality...would be good and...that goes generally without saying. We've got to increase users' understanding of those concepts. Whether it's achievable or not, it's probably hard to say, but...we have to certainly devote more in that area.

The same person goes on to infer, as with certain other comments cited in this chapter, that there could be negative consequences for the public's views on auditing if there is universal understanding of materiality and its implications for 'reasonable' assurance.

> [F]rom a public interest point of view, it probably would be helpful for the retail investors to understand more about materiality. And I'm trying to think of the wording of the audit report...in terms of whether it helps investors understand that we're not saying the accounts are correct to the dollar—within reasonable limits...there are statements about reasonable assurance. But...the retail investor probably doesn't understand what reasonable assurance

> '[T]he other side of that coin is that it may lead to a negative view of the audit opinion in the invested community. It's a doubled-edged sword really. How much do people need to know?'

actually is…it could be helpful if something was said that this audit report is not a cast-iron guarantee. But there's always a pro and a con and the other side of that coin is that it may lead to a negative view of the audit opinion in the invested community. It's a doubled-edged sword really. How much do people need to know…Having said that, if you make these disclosures, you make them across the board…an audit report is what it is, so…one firm's audit report's going to be the same as another firm's audit report. So if investors are not happy that they don't get [a] cast-iron guarantee down to the dollar, they're still not going to find that anywhere. Even if they want it, they're not going to get it. So…awareness is always a good thing…I always believe in being transparent about things…that's a good principle in itself, but you've always got to do things with caution and think about whether you're achieving the right objectives, because [what you're trying to do is] objectives driven.

The next standard setter expresses the difficulty of dealing with tiers of sophistication among users of the audit product and having all tiers understand materiality:

'[A]nalysts [and] brokers…understand materiality because they look at the risk. Your average punter on the street probably [does] not, but then again, research would show they don't read audit reports.'

[W]ho are the…core users of these reports? And you go back to analysts [and] brokers—they understand materiality because they look at the risk. Your average punter on the street probably [does] not, but then again, research would show they don't read audit reports, so you ask the question, 'Well, would they even understand what the basis of an audit was before you get to materiality?' And the fact that the audit scope actually discusses the concept of materiality and the risk of material error and the risk of collusion and breakdowns in controls and all sorts of things that can lead to problems…materiality is one element of variance that could result. I actually query…whether materiality is the real issue or whether what we're looking at here is in terms of the assessments people make. My concern would be that…businesses are projecting, forecasting, communicating their outcomes and it's achieving those outcomes that then becomes the focus and…the audit becomes the verification of whether they did achieve that forecast, and does materiality come into that?

The same standard setter goes on to argue that it is qualitative materiality that could end up having a more important consequence than quantitative materiality:

> '[T]hat segment in its own right may not necessarily be material today in terms of its relevance to the business, but going forward, it may be what everyone's betting on.'

Materiality has two elements—qualitative and quantitative—so you've got your two branches. You're probably dealing with the qualitative aspect...more than the quantitative in a lot of these types of situations, because you can get some fairly significant variances of earnings over a period...[about which] arguably no-one would have done anything different even if they'd known about it. But let's just say you've got a new start-up in your business, [a] new segment, et cetera. The qualitative aspect there is, is that segment delivering what you said it would deliver based on a forecast basis? And, that segment in its own right may not necessarily be material today in terms of its relevance to the business, but going forward, it may be what everyone's betting on. And qualitatively that information is far more important than anything else you would read in the accounts or want to know about and...that's probably where materiality is of greater importance than [whether]...earnings per share [were] 11 cents or...10 cents or nine cents.

Among the standard setters, there is confirmation that board and audit committee members are conversant with the concept of materiality as used by auditors and that there have been improving levels of understanding among these parties in recent years.

We [auditors] have probably driven that discussion in the sense of... [having] consciously put it fairly and squarely on the table, going back a little bit, and built a discussion around what that means in that framework, and that has then engendered, in some cases, an ongoing discussion around materiality and what does it mean. What does this issue mean in the context of materiality? So, yes, absolutely. It's been a bit of push/pull...The auditors have pushed that issue more front and centre into the board at some places...[but] what's happened is...you get these cross networks of directors...it actually filters through the director network over a period.

> [Materiality does not cause confusion in their minds]...not within the audit committee environment...We give them the audit plan at the start of the year and we explain our process and...the auditing standards make it fairly clear these days. Not that audit committees are familiar with them but...you've got to aggregate a number of issues. On the other hand, you've got qualitative aspects of issues to be addressed by management and by others charged with governance as well. So we have a professional obligation to report a number of things that we would never deem to be individually or in aggregate material. But now under the standards we must still make those charged with governance aware of these issues. So... over the last three to four years, between ourselves and our clients, everyone's become quite educated on that.

2.4.1 Summary

Standard setters, many of whom are suppliers also, tend to position the issue of understanding of materiality within a broader perspective of other aspects of audit that need to be understood just as much, if not more. Addressing these understandings among an audience comprising varying levels of sophistication is perceived as a difficult issue to overcome. Several standard setters are not convinced the issue needs to be given high priority, even though it might be contributing to the expectations gap. Confirmation that directors and audit committee members, on the whole, have appropriate levels of understanding is forthcoming from interviewed standard setters.

2.5 Regulators

Not unexpectedly, regulators' comments focus on the application of auditors' judgment around materiality considerations.

> [I]f you see the review-level reports...that the big firms produce today—and this is closely related to materiality—you're very limited in terms of what they've done, and the audit profession uses materiality all the time. The thing with materiality is, where do you...draw the line...I don't expect an auditor per se to detect every error. I expect an auditor to pick up all the big-ticket items... And there's a commonsense test...let me [give] a simple example...If you've got a balance sheet with assets of 100 million and you find a $10 or $20 million asset...is misstated—that's material. It gets tricky

> when it's five...[which is] in the grey area...When you're in the five to 10 area...the auditor needs to actually justify quite clearly in their work papers at least why they've reached that conclusion and how they've made that conclusion.

This regulator goes on to advocate more information being provided in the audit report if further testing does not resolve an issue that is in the 'grey' 5–10 per cent quantitative materiality range. Adding content to the audit report over this type of issue is currently not encouraged by the auditing standards.

> 'If you can't reach that conclusion and you believe in aggregate they're material...you should state it in the audit report.'

> [T]he idea of prudence with professional judgment seems to be lost on an auditor sometimes...if you're dealing with an issue, and there's a material issue and it's in the grey space. If you adopt a very prudent approach—let's put aside the cost considerations of the audit—in a perfect world, the auditor will do further testing and satisfy themselves that that's not going to cause me concern going forward. So that grey area will become either black or white. So you'll do either more procedures or whatever, in the 5–10 per cent [range]. If you can't reach that conclusion and you believe in aggregate they're material...you should state it in the audit report. If you've got three errors, on its own it's not material, but in aggregate if the three of them are material, you should...communicate that.

When asked whether it would help just to disclose the quantitative side, this regulator's response is:

> No...you need to disclose both.

2.5.1 Summary

The grey area of quantitative materiality where the item at issue is found to be between 5–10 per cent of the relative base preoccupies this regulator's comments, with a call for more disclosure in the audit report when such issues cannot be definitively resolved with more testing.

3.0 Materiality: responsibility for and location of disclosures

In making comments about the level of understanding of the auditor's use of the materiality concept, several stakeholders made suggestions as to where incremental disclosures or educative material might be positioned and who might be made responsible for provision of this information. Some content relevant to this section appears in the comments in the previous section too, but below are stakeholders' comments dedicated to this issue of responsibility and positioning.

3.1 Users

Only one user makes a comment with respect to responsibility for provision of information on audit materiality:

> [W]hen you have a concept like that, that auditors rely so much on...the education needs to come out there. The Auditing Standards Board [is the body to provide it]. Impose that consistently across the profession...the problem is that it's not just quantitative it's also qualitative judgment...and also can be cumulative.

3.1.1 Summary

One user comments that it is the role of the Auditing and Assurance Standards Board to provide educative information about the role of audit materiality.

3.2 Purchasers

One purchaser is wary of any more disclosures made in the financial report:

> [T]he way to educate shareholders is not through more disclosure in financial statements. That's not the place to do it...that has to be just clear, simple, to-the-point opinions...that's the right way to go, and where it is at the moment, I'm happy with that as a general statement. But...there needs to be the ability for shareholders very easily to be given explanations of materiality and how it operates.

Another purchaser would like to see a general educative statement that explains materiality, presumably in the financial report, although this is not made entirely clear:

> [A] general statement in terms of educating shareholders or [the] general public especially, who are not familiar with the term materiality, is probably...important—as to what is materiality in the first place and what does it actually mean...when the reader's reading the financial statement...that is probably [more] important than anything else...[It shouldn't be just] a figure, because probably a certain number of figures may not actually apply in most situations...people would therefore need to understand when they read the financial statement, they need to be a bit more informed in what they actually read. It may not be, for example, 100 per cent correct is probably one of the main things they need to be aware of and...that is...important.

One purchaser wanted disclosures to be made by the auditor, presumably in the auditor's report, tailored to the audit. This same type of comment also featured in purchasers' quotations detailed previously in this chapter.

> [W]hen there is a material number, we'd rather have more disclosure on material numbers rather than [less.] And...it comes back to material in terms of...signing this off, but it might be worth saying, 'Well, it's a very generic statement that the sign-off is well'...and it might just be a bit more detail as to this is the process that we've undertaken to review the account.

3.2.1 Summary

From purchasers' comments, it is clear they want auditors to have responsibility for disclosing more about materiality. The content of the disclosure ranges from a wish to have audit engagement-specific information in the auditor's report to a wish to have educative material made available somewhere other than in the financial report.

3.3 Suppliers

Few suppliers made suggestions about which party should take responsibility for provision of more information about materiality in an audit context. One who did suggested the location should be within the financial statements:

> [M]aybe the solution to this is...[and this is] where certainly the International Accounting Standards Board has been going, and I know the PCAOB in the US has been going...and this is why financial

> statements are blowing out, but more disclosure about some of the judgments, more disclosure about the estimates, more disclosure about some of the qualitative factors behind the financials and behind the actual companies you're putting to that is...as important as the quantitative numbers themselves.

The other supplier making a comment in the context of which party might be responsible for incremental information surrounding auditors' use of materiality suggested the professional accounting bodies or the Australian Institute of Company Directors, but acknowledged the difficulty in making it highly readable.

'How you make that interesting so people will read it I have no idea, because that would be the hardest thing.'

> [I]t's the professional accounting bodies and the directors' association, [the] Institute of Company Directors...[who are responsible] so that people understand a bit more about what auditing is and how it works. How you make that interesting so people will read it I have no idea, because that would be the hardest thing. And that's why you then come back to a simplistic way of saying...if you know materiality, mention [it]. And there's mention of it already in the audit report, but there [are] no parameters or context...Mr Joe Average...might think anything over 100 000 is quite material without relating it to the company. So that's the problem at the moment, because everyone has their own concept of materiality. And...there is an issue there and how you overcome that I'm not actually too sure. But...there needs to be more information out there, more articles and a variety of things. And maybe a bit more prescriptive description of what an audit is and what it can achieve.

3.3.1 Summary

Suppliers suggest the professional accounting bodies and/or the Australian Institute of Company Directors (AICD) as appropriate parties to take responsibility for generalised provision of incremental materiality information. A suggestion for location of the material is in the financial report disclosures.

3.4 Standard setters

One standard setter believes the audit report or the publications of the accounting firms would be the best locations for incremental materiality information:

> [There are] two options...One is in the body of the audit report, which is in the auditor's responsibilities...if it was reasonably brief and, in terms of managing the expectation gap, there's obviously a cost associated with everything and the cost of more than reasonable assurance is increased costs [to] the organisation. So it's assurance at a reasonable cost as well as reasonable assurance. The... only other place to basically educate the community...is in the publications of the accounting firms...or somewhere in the financial statements. But it's not a client entity's issue...for them to disclose. So the only places auditors can disclose things really are in their own reports and in their own web sites... You don't want to make the audit report too long.

'[I]t's not a client entity's issue...for them to disclose. So the only places auditors can disclose things really are in their own reports and in their own web sites... You don't want to make the audit report too long.'

Another standard setter believes the profession—presumably through the accounting bodies—would be best to take responsibility:

> [The accounting profession] could do [it], but they tend to communicate more with their own constituency than anything else. The accounting profession communicates with accountants around the place. They don't really put pronouncements out to the public. The public probably would never look at them or read them or be interested in them.

Another standard setter suggests the incremental materiality information be placed within reports by regulators, or through forums such as those held by the Shareholders' Association or the professional accounting bodies. The Auditing and Assurance Standards Board is mentioned also as playing a potential role.

> I don't have a simple answer for that because...we do it in the audit opinions at the moment, but that's really a statement that it's not absolute assurance...when we're providing a statement of the scope of the audit opinion...How would I demystify the process a little bit

> more...[and say] it's appropriate? Perhaps through reports from the regulators around how they assess whether an appropriate piece of work is done or not, but...if it's shareholders generally, how do you [do it?]...the retail people are difficult. Institutional investors and larger interest groups are...more easily touched...forums through the Shareholders' Association and obviously bodies that represent assurance practitioners are forums [where] we can do this, but only if we touch the people who are interested in the message...how do you get a message out...it's more about confidence in the process and that it's applied appropriately rather than having to understand the process in detail. But perhaps there's a role here for the Auditing and Assurance Standards Board as well.

3.4.1 Summary

Standard setters vary in their suggestions as to which party might be given responsibility for providing incremental disclosures surrounding the auditor's use of the materiality concept and where such disclosures might be located. Suggestions for responsibility range from auditors themselves and audit firms to the AUASB, professional accounting bodies and the Australian Shareholders' Association. Suggestions for positioning range from the audit report and forums held by the above-mentioned bodies to the publications of the audit firms.

4.0 Issues and implications

The issue of materiality in the audit was discussed during the interviews both as a consequence of specific questioning and more broadly. The notion of having some form of disclosure of the level(s) of materiality was common among users and purchasers and was mixed among suppliers, standard setters and regulators. Those who did not support some form of disclosure of materiality included those who believed that participants in the capital market did not read financial statements and therefore would be disinclined to inform themselves about issues of materiality or that the majority of the participants in the capital market would find the concept confusing and it would contribute to the audit expectations gap rather than assist in closing it.

Those who played a standard setter's or regulator's role also observed that while there had been audit failures in Australian corporate history and elsewhere, none related directly to a misinterpretation, misunderstanding or miscommunication on the matter of materiality, but went to more fundamental issues. There were some responses to these more negative positions, including the notion that while not all those who participated in the market would necessarily understand the concept of materiality, even if disclosed or discussed in some form, there would be more informed users who represented the price makers in the capital market and even if that small minority was informed it would assist in making the market more efficient.

Some who were negative about further disclosures in this area made the observation that the real thrust of what was needed was more confidence in the existing process and framework—for with this came a reduced need for further disclosures.

While this argument is held with some degree of passion, particularly by suppliers, it runs the risk of being interpreted as patronising. By this statement, the authors mean that the supply side within the profession might be viewed as providing information and therefore accountability only when they believe it is in their interests to do so and those people expert in the market know enough to be able to protect all market interests. The parallel might be a distinguished surgeon who has such great knowledge of surgery that he or she makes all decisions with respect to the surgery, doing away with informing the patient of key aspects of the procedure. Of course, the parallel here is the issue of informed consent. If those participating in a capital market know key issues about an audit that would more fully inform the capital market then why is this not provided? It might represent the equivalent of informed consent in surgery.

A large majority of all interviewees suggested that some form of disclosure would be useful, however, suggestions about the nature of that disclosure, to whom the disclosure was made, where the disclosure was made and what form the disclosure would take were quite varied. There were various innovative ideas as to what could be achieved. There are, however, some important caveats that need to be considered before any final decision is taken.

Among suppliers, purchasers and some users, there was a view that providing disclosure of the existence of a materiality threshold influencing the audit represented a key ingredient in advising the market that the audit was not a 100 per cent guarantee that the representations made in the financial statements were entirely accurate. That is to say, if the market is informed that there is a materiality threshold, the notion of a 100 per cent guarantee is immediately removed.

There is a key set of issues around what type of disclosures are necessary or useful with respect to materiality. Users and purchasers focus on the quantitative aspects of materiality. When discussing this issue with suppliers, there was considerable debate surrounding the fact that materiality involved both quantitative and qualitative characteristics and hence the complexity of materiality judgments could not be underestimated. This gives rise to an important choice in terms of disclosures between some aggregated, quantitative, estimative materiality or a more simple conceptual disclosure of the presence of materiality. Further, some suppliers argued that at audit committee level, it was common to have a discussion about materiality at an aggregate level, but when one discussed line items in the financial statements on the basis of materiality, occasionally the discussion could become 'heated'. Another factor to bear in mind with respect to disclosure of quantitative estimates of materiality—although not brought out in the interviews—is that this might present a useful piece of information (that could have damaging consequences for the auditee) for those who might seek to commit fraud to a level below the materiality threshold against the auditee.

Those who favour disclosures of the concept of materiality make a compelling argument that the qualitative characteristics are a key aspect to the determination of materiality. For example, materiality levels over related-party transactions might be very different to materiality levels over accounts receivable. The nature of these two items is different, which drives dissimilar relevant materiality levels.

There is also active debate about to whom and when the materiality disclosures should be revealed. On the one hand, there is strong argument that boards of directors/audit committees are the appropriate audience for this information and the appropriate time is at the audit planning stage. In this circumstance, both qualitative and quantitative issues could be discussed at considerable length. There is a strong argument that the existing best-practice guidance, including the ASX corporate governance guidelines, could explicitly make reference to the fact that audit committees have a responsibility to be informed on matters of materiality and that audit committee charters should reflect this.

The more controversial disclosure would be to shareholders and therein lies the debate about the level of understanding and potential confusion these disclosures could cause. There were, however, persuasive comments that more complete discussion about general aspects of materiality could be included on an auditee's web site or on the web sites of the audit firms, the AUASB or professional associations.

Some of the more experienced and sophisticated interviewees were strongly of the view that better communication of materiality was an area where action could and should be taken. The authors of this report note that successive governments have encouraged retail shareholders to participate in the capital market but this encouragement has not been matched by equivalent public support mechanisms to assist them into this participation. There has been an implicit assumption that the free market behaviour of Australia's capital market will ensure their rights and interests are protected. Disclosures, including that of materiality, might be a key factor in effective participation in the capital market. Not informing participants is a public policy issue. Put more directly, some widespread understanding that materiality levels exist within the audit poses a significant benefit in reducing the audit expectations gap if, by virtue of its disclosure, it removes the notion that the audit is somehow comprehensive and is a guarantee that the transactions and financial representations made are 100 per cent guaranteed by the auditor.

5.0 Concluding remarks

If the capital market had information about materiality then it seems certain that it would use it to enhance market efficiency. This can be illustrated by reference to two examples. The first example is a hypothetical one, in which we have two absolutely economically identical companies trading on the stock market with assets, profitability and prospects as well as risk, which are identical. One company, however, is audited with a materiality level of $2 million and the other with a $6 million threshold. In an efficient market, investors would gravitate to the first mentioned company because of the prospect that its financial statements are likely to be more 'finely tuned' than the second company's. A second example is more realistic in a sense that one might have two companies that have different asset structures and different prospects for the future. One company, however, has a governance structure that ensures it has a very low level of materiality as part of the audit process and the other company is more aggressive in its behaviour and has agreed with its auditor to a much higher level of materiality. The second company represents for an investor a higher level of information risk, which would need to be incorporated into the investor's decision making. If investors have a large appetite for risk then they are more attracted to the second of the two potential investments. These examples imply that the absence of information about materiality results in a cost being borne by the capital market.

Despite the efficiencies that would flow to the capital market, we find little if any empirical evidence of the public disclosure of materiality. We also find significant diversity of practice among audit committees in asking for or being provided with materiality information. There is little direct guidance available for audit committees on this issue. Some—perhaps many—audit committees seek direct and substantial information on materiality from their auditor. One or two might seek to avoid that knowledge. Others might not know of its availability and its role within decision making on the quality of the audit—hence, our observation about diversity in practice. This variability is troubling from a public policy setting. An implication is that guidance or even requirements for boards and/or audit committees could be enhanced to make express reference to the desirability of having a conversation with their auditor about materiality, if not their right to ask for disclosure to them of the level or levels used. In the same vein, board and audit committee educative processes could mandate the inclusion of a discussion of materiality.

Who could be responsible for providing this guidance? Clearly, the AUASB could be a vehicle for providing this guidance, as could be the ASX and/or the AICD. Each would have varying attributes and bring varying qualities to the provision of such guidance.

Clear communication with management—as opposed to boards and audit committees—with respect to the materiality level has some potentially disadvantageous effects. It is the case that some managers might use knowledge of the materiality level as 'pushback' on the auditors and it might be used to dissuade auditors from pursuing a line of inquiry if the matter in question is under a pre-specified materiality level. In other words, management might use this knowledge to dissuade auditors from following their own preferred line of inquiry. Similarly, if materiality levels become known within an auditee, those who wish to commit fraud or engage in other opportunistic behaviour could have valuable information with which to work that would not be available in the circumstance of uncommunicated materiality levels.

Despite the fact that the capital market is a global one, any specific guidance on materiality has to recognise that there is a sharp difference between the US regulatory style—to which some of Australia's companies are exposed—and the common experience in the Australian capital market. It would seem that in the US system, if there is error, the tolerable materiality level is zero. This comes about because of accounting standards that are interpreted to mean that any error might affect the decision making of users and hence needs to be corrected. This is not the application in Australia. One consequence of this is that there is a higher proportion of modified audit reports in the Australian jurisdiction than in the United States and it would seem that there are more restated accounts in the US system. Some might argue that the Australian system is more tolerant of imprecision.

In the eyes of retail investors and possibly even some more sophisticated users and purchasers of audit services, as well as accounting students who might be useful surrogates for some of the above, there is the possibility of materiality being misconceived because some of the dynamics of materiality are counterintuitive. In common language, the convention is that the 'more material, the better'. In its application to auditing, however, the higher the level of materiality, the 'weaker is the audit'. That is, where materiality levels are higher, the screen through which the auditor puts the transactions and balances is coarser. Put more directly, more gets through the screening device undetected. As noted above, the alternative expression to materiality is 'tolerable error'. The authors would speculate that usage of the term 'tolerable error' in guidance or elsewhere might be received with more clarity than the term 'materiality'.

Some respondents made the suggestion that the key to understanding materiality was to turn to the auditing standards. These standards, even in the hands of experts, are insufficient in order to calibrate levels of materiality for any given engagement. The rationale that all can be found in the auditing standards is, in the view of the authors, false because so much rests on the proprietary audit models of the audit suppliers. This further supports the necessity for clear guidance.

The evidence we have gathered, either expressly or impliedly, refers to quantitative materiality thresholds, but there is also reference, particularly from suppliers, to qualitative materiality. This introduces a level of subtlety and complexity that is hard for even sophisticated stakeholders in the capital market to get a good handle on. Further, it makes the audit more opaque, less understandable and more mysterious.

In addition to the complexities introduced by qualitative aspects to materiality, it is the case that there are multiple levels of materiality that apply in any given audit and so a conversation that talks about a (singular) materiality level is in many instances overly simplistic and makes the difficulties of communication to relevant stakeholders on materiality more complex than might be represented.

Among the unforeseen consequences of this project have been some observations about undergraduate auditing education and its placement within the curricula and the perspective with which it is taught. Conventionally, because of the perceived need to have a fulsome education in financial accounting, auditing is taught towards the very end of a commerce degree. A non-conventional alternative would be the early introduction of auditing so that a student's exposure to financial accounting issues can be informed from an audit point of view. This could give the student a more subtle and insightful perspective on their education in financial accounting.

It is also possible that with auditing being taught earlier in the curriculum, it might be less technically focused and more conceptual. This being the case, the use of case studies could lend itself more positively to the educational experience of the student. The consequence of this would be lower levels of technical knowledge of auditing standards; however, one might speculate that those students who go on to auditing are re-educated on these through their professional training.

From our discussions, it would seem that materiality is crucial to the quality of the audit, is never expressly referred to in the audit report and is less than universally discussed even among audit committees. This being the case, we would argue that materiality has a significant role in the existence and extent of the audit expectations gap. It is the case that auditors use materiality as a crucial screening device for the conduct of their professional work. Closely related to this is their use of sampling. Sampling and materiality are keys to audit quality and to cost. This, together with the quality of the staff undertaking the audit, the methodology employed, the wider availability of expertise and mechanisms for ensuring independence are keys to the completion of a satisfactory audit.

As conventionally worded, the audit report makes no explicit reference either to the level of materiality or to sampling. Materiality can be represented by reference to the aggregate absolute dollar value that applies generally to the engagement. Sampling has direct consequences on the probability that misstatement will occur. Note particularly that current conventional wording to 'test'. 'Test' could mean that 100 per cent of transactions are tested or that some smaller proportion is examined. It gives no hint that it is a proportion or sample that is tested or that there is existence of a probability around that test.

One wonders if an audit report that, among other things, states that 'this audit is a certification of the X percentage probability of the absence of misstatement in the financial report above an absolute aggregate dollar value of Y', would be subject to the same level of misinterpretation that has been attributed to the current wording in the audit expectations gap literature.

The fact that materiality levels and the cost of an audit are so inexorably linked is known by a number of purchasers, and probably every supplier in the market for audit services. The fact that it is not seen as an express part of the negotiation over the quality of the audit (and as an opportunity for an added assurance service) is, however, an important oversight in the market for audit services. We found little evidence that there were negotiations over materiality levels and that this aspect of quality and price appeared to be treated as independent from each other in all but a handful of cases. Surely, as part of an efficient market for audit services, this should be more explicit.

DIVISION C

DEVELOPING BUSINESS ACUMEN AND CLIENT AND INDUSTRY KNOWLEDGE 6

> You will always have some clients who say you don't understand my business. Is it getting worse? At the junior end, it probably is because you have the mindless drones who aren't enjoying their work, turning up [and saying], 'Oh yes, just another audit. What is it today...last week it was a car dealer, do I care? No, I just fill out this check list.' So if it is getting any worse—and perhaps it is, perhaps it isn't, I can't make a general statement really on that—at that lower end that will be why. At the more senior end—partner and director...it's actually less likely to be getting worse because you are increasingly getting...industry specialisation and that has been the case for a number of years now.
> — Supplier

1.0 Key issues

All stakeholders to a greater or lesser extent recognise the importance to audit quality of a supplier having business acumen and client and industry-specific knowledge. Some of the key issues for the profession around development and maintenance of these knowledge bases include:

- does industry expertise add value to the provision of auditing services
- to what extent do industry categorisations remain valid between different sized levels of market capitalisation
- does auditor industry specialisation add to potential conflicts in terms of independence
- to what extent does specialisation in a specific accounting standard(s) overlap and/or conflict with auditor industry specialisation
- how is it best to develop client-specific knowledge
- what is the role of audit working paper documentation in effectively conveying client-specific knowledge

- what is the best way in which to convey client-specific knowledge to more junior auditors
- how frequent is the occurrence of client staff bonuses being tied to few or no audit adjustments being required or made and are there consequences for financial reporting or audit quality of this practice
- how can it be reconciled that those to whom the client is most frequently exposed and those who do most of the day-to-day audit work—the more junior auditors—are those least likely to possess the business acumen many clients expect to be present
- is audit personnel turnover becoming an issue among seniors and partners when this group was considered stable previously
- what are the most effective training techniques for audit personnel
- how can auditors best communicate to clients the engagement issues presented by high client staff turnover and/or lack of knowledge
- how can auditors best communicate to clients that at times asking the seemingly 'dumb' questions can uncover areas that need to be the subject of audit investigation
- is the quality of initial audits different from that of subsequent audits
- are there characteristics beyond industry expertise, client knowledge and business acumen that individuals could usefully hold and/or develop?

2.0 Introduction

An important aspect of auditor competence is the development of skill in understanding the client's industry and the client's business within that industry. Indeed, gaining this understanding is a requirement of Auditing Standard ASA 315: *Understanding the Entity and Its Environment and Assessing the Risks of Material Misstatement*. This chapter examines survey, face-to-face interview and peer junior auditor focus group responses to issues including the development of client and industry-specific knowledge, whether it is valued by clients, how it is applied to clients and the role of business acumen in the delivery of audits.

While, as acknowledged later, some responses from interviewees intertwine the issues of industry expertise, client knowledge and business acumen, it is the case that the three have differentiating and distinctive characteristics. Business acumen is about having a commercial sense and a general insight into the operations of business; industry expertise is having knowledge and appreciation of the particular characteristics, risks and critical issues of an industry or group of industries that share similar characteristics relevant for an auditor; and client knowledge is a more specific understanding of the issues, risks and characteristics of a particular auditee, its management and its operations. It is evident that these three are intertwined; you could not, for example, have particularly acute client knowledge without having well-developed business acumen; it is unlikely that you would have business acumen if you had well-developed industry specialist knowledge. That being said, we use the three terms below in the contexts of the three descriptions given above.

3.0 Survey

One of the questions asked of survey recipients tapped into perceptions of the value of industry and client knowledge. In response to a question about whether external financial statement audits were of value because of 'the specialist industry expertise of the auditor', as shown in Table 6.1, the most positive of the groups was suppliers, with 50 per cent of them rating this as being valuable. A similar proportion of users and a more modest proportion—at slightly less than one-third—of purchasers responded affirmatively to this question. Among the suppliers, there was a sharp differentiation between Big Four and non-Big Four auditors in their level of agreement, with in excess of three-quarters of Big Four auditors believing industry expertise brought value compared with less than half of non-Big Four auditors. This could reflect an issue of industry expertise and its relevance across all levels of market capitalisation.

Table 6.1 shows that, with respect to knowledge or understanding of the client's business, purchasers and users were more guarded in their responses, with less than half responding positively. CEO/CFO respondents were particularly harsh, with about only one-third indicating that the audit was of value because of the auditor's understanding of the client's business.

Industry knowledge is valued over client knowledge by users, but purchasers and suppliers place a higher importance on client knowledge than on industry knowledge.

Table 6.1 Value of financial statements audits because of the industry and client knowledge of auditors (per cent agree)

	USERS				PURCHASERS				SUPPLIERS		
	Total	Accounting expertise	Professional users	Private investors	Total	Directors/ audit comm.	CEO/CFO	Other	Total	Big Four	Non-Big Four
An external financial statement audit is of value to you because:											
Of the specialist industry knowledge that the auditor brings to the audit	46	43	47	48	31	37	26	34	50	77	42
The auditor has a good understanding of the company's business	40	38	34	46	33	41	31	29	55	66	53

Percentage of respondents answering 'Strongly agree' or 'Agree' on a five-point scale.

As observed in Table 6.2, there is overall concern about the business acumen of auditors within some quarters. In response to questions about an audit being of value, a minority of purchasers expressed a negative view about the business acumen that the auditor brought to the audit, while a majority of suppliers responded to the same question in the affirmative. Specifically with respect to audit partners, most users and suppliers saw the business acumen of audit partners as above the mid-point, with junior auditors not rated highly. Interestingly, overall, purchasers took a harsher view than users.

A superficial description of these results, however, might not tell the full and rather complex story with respect to the market's view of the business acumen of auditors. With reference to users, the comments below illustrate that while there is genuine concern about the level of business acumen, there is a sharp distinction between the acumen of partners and more junior auditors and a realisation that turnover, particularly at the junior level, is a part of the audit firm business model, and that juniors have to learn.

Table 6.2 Responses on the business acumen of auditors (per cent)

	USERS				PURCHASERS				SUPPLIERS		
	Total	Accounting expertise	Professional users	Private investors	Total	Directors/ audit comm.	CEO/CFO	Other	Total	Big Four	Non-Big Four
An external financial statement audit is of value to you because:											
Of the business acumen that the auditor brings to the audit	45	44	41	49	33	32	33	37	55	68	51
In general, how do you rate the business acumen of:											
Audit partners	57	64	55	51	60	54	63	61	81	88	79
Junior auditors	9	10	9	8	6	7	27	4	14	16	13

Percentage of respondents answering 'Strongly agree' or 'Agree' on a five-point scale.

4.0 Interviews

In the face-to-face interviews conducted among the user, purchaser, supplier, standard setter and regulator stakeholder groups, several questions relating to client knowledge, industry specialisation and the business acumen of auditors were asked. Interestingly, many of the interviewees interlaced their responses with comments about all three issues and there was interdependency in these responses. As a consequence, in the comments made below, we will tease out observations about these three important, distinct but interrelated concepts.

4.1 Users

Among users, there was some scepticism that accounting firms could be viewed as business experts at all.

> [Industry expertise is a] bit of a joke. I'm...quite amazed at the projection of accounting firms as business experts at all...The [professional body advertisements] I find quite amazing. Having worked at [name of organisation] and knowing how much involved the accountants were in all the projects we developed...the self-

> promotion of that has been very successful, but…[it is] very made up and fabricated and I don't agree with it at all.

There is acknowledgment of the need for development of industry specialist knowledge, but recognition also of conflict between the development of this knowledge in a small market such as Australia and maintenance of independence, as the following comment reveals:

> [T]hat's probably a fair criticism [about auditors' business knowledge]. But…in a small market like Australia, you're going to have to run that [independence] risk, because there are many, many industries. What do you do? Do you want an auditor that's an expert in auditing just one industry? They're going to lose their independence, because you can get too close…that's a cost they just have to bear. I don't know how you get around it. They can probably get around it in bigger capital markets, [such as] Europe or the States…And where does the real knowledge rest? It's only really with the audit partner, because everybody else is changing so much. I mean, it's a training ground, auditing. So where does the real industry knowledge rest anyway? It's with an audit partner who directs the work [and] all the rest of it, but it's the minions doing the work, and they're going to be turned over every year. So I'm not quite sure it's a good argument.

Auditors possessing core product knowledge within specific industries is the desire of this next user when responding to the question 'Do you think it's important that auditors have that sort of specialist-type knowledge of the clients; so we're talking beyond the industry expertise—a client-specific knowledge. And, if that's important, how would they develop and maintain that?'

> I can…understand a client being frustrated if an auditor comes in—and, using a bank as an example—doesn't understand what a derivative is, or can't get their head around a structured transaction, a foreign exchange transaction, whatever it might be. That…would be unacceptable…core product knowledge is essential on the part of the auditor. I can see that leading more to auditors becoming sector specific—industry specific—in terms of their knowledge, particularly in more complex industries like insurance, for example.

The same user continues, differentiating between senior and junior auditors in terms of their client-level knowledge:

> As to whether they need detailed knowledge of the client...at the more senior level they would definitely need that familiarity and ability to talk to senior management in a...knowledgeable, strategic way. At the junior level...that's the age-old problem, isn't it? Everybody has to start somewhere and they're not going to be the world's best auditors on day one, so every audit team has its juniors, and...a client simply has to accept that...But they should expect that that person has the product knowledge that they could have gained through their studies.
>
> The senior staff [is] pretty good but the junior ones are...learning the ropes all the time and they're doing quite important things.

Another user responds:

> [I]t's still hard for the auditors sometimes to be on top of all the different areas of business, particularly if you've got a complicated business, or an international business, or you've got numerous transactions going on. Obviously, the greater complexity in the business, the harder it is for people to understand it, and...it opens the door to transactions going through that people don't necessarily understand.

An interesting interchange takes place, which has relevance for the subject of Chapter 9 (independence) and the issue of audit partner rotation, but is positioned here to maintain the context of the question. The interviewer asks: 'In your opinion, do external auditors have sufficient knowledge of the client's business and operations? If this is an area of concern to you, can you identify ways in which this can be addressed?'

> I'd have to say no [*and the interviewer confirms that this is in relation to the sufficient knowledge of the client's business*]...No, they don't and that's probably of concern too...for the shareholder...No, they don't and they can follow a certain formula, follow a procedure, but the depth of actual understanding and therefore the depth of being able to identify other issues is perhaps limited.

The interviewer then asks how this situation might be improved and the response is:

> [I]t would only be improved if before you get into an auditing position, you [are] required to spend time inside [corporations], actually operating in a reasonably senior role inside that sector... you'd need to have that sort of experience level.

The interviewer comments, 'So, what you're saying is the life cycle of an auditor is not the traditional [one]: you graduate, you go to work for a Big Four firm, you get promoted to a senior and manager, but in fact cycling through different employment circumstances', and the interviewee agrees. The interviewer continues, saying:

> So, a profession that facilitated cycling backwards and forwards and audit firms that actually encouraged interchange. See, I'm interested in your reflection on this. I mean, the regulatory changes have probably made that more difficult rather than less because of audit rotation if you have industry expertise. By and large, for big clients, partners and their families have to move interstate periodically because there is no...

The interviewee responds in the following way:

> Yeah, it seems like a good thing on the surface—the rotation—but in practice...it's another one of those situations where you're having practice and...theory and...in practice...[there are] a lot of negatives about it as well and I can understand why, but at the same time...it leads to other issues...unless you do have that grounded experience in the industry sectors and understand the operations of what's really going on then to do the audit is really more of a calculating exercise at a very high level and...a good management team can manipulate that process very easily.

In this next exchange too, the issue of audit partner rotation is addressed as detracting from the ability to know the client's business and operations:

> No, they never [have sufficient knowledge of their clients' business and operations].

The interviewer then asks, 'Is that across all levels, or partner and managers?', and the response is:

> I think so...it's more extreme—and obviously with junior staff turning over like they do, it's just physically impossible. Obviously, it's nowhere near as noticeable at the manager partner level,

> because typically the partner in particular has been exposed to that industry. He might do a number of audits within that industry and also [has] been exposed to your company for a longer period... within audit partners, there's a huge variability in answering that question. Some guys are significantly better than others.

The interviewer then asks: 'So, in your opinion, do you think that trying to maintain the same audit team members on a continuing tenure with one client would help?' The response is:

> Well...getting rid of these silly rules about audit partner rotation would help.

4.1.1 Summary

Users display awareness of potential independence conflicts that could arise when auditors become specialist in a single industry, but acknowledge the difficulty of avoiding such conflicts in an audit market the size Australia's. There is also acceptance that client-specific knowledge is more important for senior audit personnel than for more junior audit personnel and tolerance for junior auditors acquiring this knowledge and business acumen on the job. Users are in the main tolerant of the need to train junior auditors on the job, but point out that it is these auditors who conduct much of the audit work. They recognise the lower personnel turnover and higher industry expertise of audit partners. Comment is made about the reliance on the audit partner as a relatively stable constant and as the source of the real industry knowledge. Understanding is present too in terms of the complexity of business and how difficult it is for auditors to be across all areas of business.

4.2 Purchasers

Several purchasers spoke of the importance of selecting an audit firm that could supply the appropriate industry knowledge at the various levels of personnel. One person from the purchaser group spoke of the importance of proactively managing the process by requesting as part of the audit tender documents or negotiations that audit staffers with skills in specific areas were made available.

> [The level of client knowledge is] not of concern to me because this gets down to your selection of the auditor. As we go out to tender... one of the criteria is industry knowledge. That means that virtually

> restricts you to four, because when you think about it...we are virtually the industry...there are others, but you wouldn't want the auditors of the competition, right? So that limits us to really global firms. And...we've moved from [firm X to firm Y] over the last 10 years. And when we changed one of the criteria was [the] industry experience, which they had, and you have the people here in Australia who have the experience. I don't want to be given advice from [a major US city]. And that's part of the selection process. So for a big firm like ours, I haven't experienced any difficulty in getting the industry experience, and I guess it's a bit of a plum job.

The same purchaser adds:

> If I was to ask my people to deal with the more junior staff, they would probably say that [the auditors] don't know what they're talking about, or they don't know, so they don't ask the right questions. You're going to get some of that. I mean, where do you get your experience? You've got to start somewhere. And can I expect that every one of that audit team has industry experience...that's an unrealistic expectation. And we go through the selection process; we go through at partner level, at...director level, manager level, [to ensure] that there is sufficient mix...it's part of the selection. But of course you're going to get some people who are going to be learning on the job.

Perhaps surprisingly, some of the purchasers made it clear that they did not expect a great deal of business acumen to be displayed by their auditors and did not believe it was necessarily part of the job of an audit. The following quote reveals the thinking behind this perspective:

> Auditors do not understand business models. That is not their job. Their job is to understand internal control over financial reporting. They want financial reports to reflect the bad, the good and the indifferent and, as long as they do, then their job has been done.

The interviewee goes on to comment on the relative client knowledge of the auditors versus the management of an auditee:

> [A]t the audit partner level...there is what I call broad experience and broad knowledge [about] how to apply the audit regime to a given company. Do they really understand the business of the business? No, they don't get into the business in the same way, to

> the same depth, as management [does] or the directors do. No, it's not possible.

Nevertheless, among some of the purchasers, there were very positive comments about the client knowledge of the auditors, about how at a senior level they tried hard to keep up to date with client circumstances—particularly where stable audit teams could be maintained. The following quotations give a flavour of some of these positive comments.

> I don't have any concerns [about auditors' business knowledge]. But that comes from having a very stable team, and having a really long-term involvement of key people in the job. I'll give you an example...we had a senior manager on the job when I started [a number of] years ago. He was the senior manager at [one of the Big Four firms]. He got promoted to partner and came back into the job as the partner in charge. He was in the job for five years or whatever their rotation period was. He moved out of that role and took up a regional consolidation role, or a regional partner role to coordinate [one of the Big Four's] functions for our operations in Asia-Pacific. So he's still the same guy as I was dealing with 12 years ago, and I was the junior here. I deal with him every quarter when we do a regional wrap-up...quarterly audit call...In our specific example, we've had great continuity of...staff and they understand the business very well. So I don't have any concerns in that area. They get in there, they try and find things every year to help us. But...generally they don't find things because we've got a fairly stable business model anyway. But they do understand the business very well.

The interviewer probes further about the turnover of audit staff. The same purchaser responds:

> [I]t could be a lot worse than it is. It happens at the junior level, but that's...a little bit of noise and it's not the end of the world. If one of our junior staff is having to think about something to answer an auditor's position, well our guy's probably only been in the role less than a year anyway, and it's [an] education exercise for him to have to figure out the answer so he can tell the auditor. So I don't think there's a great cost to us; [there is] a little frustration, but I don't think there's a great cost to us because of that turnover at the coalface. If it was at a more senior level, it would be more of an issue, but we haven't had that problem.

Another purchaser is also enthusiastic about auditors' client knowledge:

> [T]hey do have a good idea…it's very difficult when you're immersed in this day in and day out. This is the world you live in, that's a totally different environment to something where you parachute in for a couple of months a year…I can only talk for ourselves, but… they generally have a good understanding of our business…they read quite extensively, they ask quite broadly and…with finance… in a strange sort of way, there's quite a lot of cut-over from company to company and…that sort of broad industry perspective is…quite good.

Probing further, the interviewer inquires about the business acumen of junior staff and the same purchaser's response is:

> Well, it's a bit unfair to say, 'Oh well, they don't know how to do it' and they've only just stepped out of university…there's got to be a training process and I accept that.

Returning to the issue of client knowledge, however, and the stability of audit teams, some see this as a real issue, as the following quote indicates:

> From a trained perspective…they're definitely improving…when I first joined the industry…the external auditors would just come in, do whatever they need to do and then pull out, but nowadays they're actually spending…a bit more [time]…try[ing] to build an ongoing relationship and…the bigger the client, the bigger the size of the account. They…spend a lot of time, not just because they have to be here doing the quarterly or the half-yearly reporting, but because they're also spending time…especially in the beginning… to speak to all their key stakeholders within the company and try to understand what the business is like, what's going forward, anything they need to be aware of from a [business] point of view. So they are definitely getting more and more understanding of the particular business.

The interviewer probes further about staff turnover and the response from the same purchaser is:

> [T]hey're always changing their staff, from one year to another, especially the more junior level, they tend to change every year… basically, the one who is really doing the brunt of the work will be

> changing. Hopefully, the more senior, the manager's level, they're less likely to change. But having said that, when I say less, maybe two to three [years], not forever. And we don't expect forever, but continuity is always a bit of an issue with the external firm...it's something I don't think they can help too much.

Probing further, the interviewer asks: 'What kind of costs do you see because of that continuity issue, from your perspective?' The response is:

> Obviously, we may have to backtrack a little bit more in terms of what we do, what we discuss to get the new person [understanding]... if it's a new staff [member]...fairly junior...they are likely to ask exactly the same question they asked the year before. So this is the comment I tend to get...especially [from] the finance managers, and they feel like they have to repeat themselves because [the auditors] don't understand perhaps how we do certain things within the finance department and so that's where they think that—whether the time is wasted is probably one thing—[it] is more like...they feel like they have to repeat themselves...Why can't we do it better, or why can't we actually move forward? And then perhaps try to quicken the process...or not waste each other's time...[that's] probably where everyone is coming from.

The same purchaser continues with respect to ways in which to minimise the effects of auditor staff turnover:

> [T]hey are trying their best...they maintain their documentation just like any auditors and every one of them now use[s] electronic work too, so hopefully there's a slightly better maintenance of the records...But having said that, the record is only as good as the person taking the minutes. It depends on how detailed, how extensive [they are]...and the quality of the minutes...but we're still finding from time to time that someone may have to repeat the actual process or conversation they may have undertaken.

The interviewer continues on the same theme and asks about the proportion of new staff in the audit team:

> It varies [from] one year to another sometimes. Just talking about... the last, say, five to 10 years, sometimes the whole junior team might have changed, but sometimes even the manager would have changed, so...we are more concerned if the management team

> change[s] because...they would be the one likely to have all the knowledge or corporate memory. And if they change and they don't have a proper handover period then management will start thinking 'Do we need to start...repeating what was said to external auditors before?', because a lot of the knowledge might have been lost with the person. We have the situation this year that external auditors will be changing their manager on sites of all the subsidiaries...this is a staff turnover issue [not a rotation requirement].

Among the purchaser group, there were those who were quite scathing of the client knowledge of auditors.

> [I]t's fair to say out of 10, I would be looking around the four mark...there's huge improvement in this area needed...it's one thing having the partner and the senior manager having knowledge and understanding your business, which is generally the case, but it's really the core individuals who are performing the work that we find have a big lack of knowledge. And...that's where there's huge improvement needed by the firms themselves. Now whether that's more regular contact [or not]...there's always a problem with rotation of staff, which obviously affects the broader knowledge.

The same purchaser continues:

> [There are] different reasons [for audit staff turnover]...I know that the profession is...under a fair bit of pressure on staff turnover. If you are constantly changing your staff over, asking the same questions the next year, and then the next year...it builds up a bit of animosity within the organisation. And the auditors...get annoyed and then that'll lead towards these sort of shutdown questions... if you can build a good relationship, it's going to help. If you can try and maintain consistency of staff...those two are critical areas which should stand you in a better position and move [you] forward and you can grow together.

The same purchaser talks about gaining client knowledge more succinctly if audit staff come from non-accounting education backgrounds:

> [Having spent] some time in the UK, it's interesting seeing [that] what they do at university has nothing to do with what their next job is. So a lot of our auditors, junior auditors and senior auditors, when I was working in the UK, their background is something

> in geography or engineering. It was just a complete[ly] different background to what you get here in Australia...which is just your standard. And...to some extent that worked well because you did get a different view and a different perspective from the auditors. They did [not] ask...robotic questions. They asked...a lot more commonsense-type questions, whereas...a lot of people coming just from [an accounting] background...it's almost a standard question without giving as much thought behind it. Now, whether that came from different backgrounds, it would be interesting to look at that.

Many of the purchasers distinguished between senior audit personnel and more junior personnel and had praise for the senior staff's business acumen and client knowledge. The following is illustrative of such sentiments:

> [M]ost of my interaction with auditors these days is at the partner and very senior manager level, so I couldn't comment below that... But I'm very impressed with the knowledge that all of those people have of the business. They seem to have a much more strategic kind of focus than we did...back in my days as an auditor...they seem to come to grips with the issues for the business very quickly and, in many cases, where you're having a change in CFO or that kind of thing, they provide a very, very valuable service and background in helping a new CFO get up to speed.

Others, however, were not so tolerant in relation to the issue of client knowledge and business acumen more generally.

> I would argue in broad terms that external auditors don't have sufficient knowledge...and it's no fault of the individuals, it's just... structurally in the way that the teams are put together...generally most of the partners I've come up against have been pretty good... because they've been working in the field for quite a few years. But the trouble is [that] 80 per cent of the people on the audit are fairly green and inexperienced and they wouldn't necessarily...see the warning sign[s].

Troublingly, there were comments that the lack of client knowledge of junior staff was increasingly being experienced at even the higher ranks. This is an example of such a comment:

> [The more senior audit staff] don't have time to get amongst the business and to understand it...ten years ago, I would have said

> look, it always happens at the junior level because you're still learning, right?

The same purchaser continues on the same theme:

> [The lack of client knowledge is] starting to creep up to the senior or supervisor level...But now...in pockets it's starting to creep up to the manager and director and sometimes the partner level... [perhaps] because they've got too much to do so they can't get an intimate knowledge for businesses. And why do they have too much to do? Because they're chasing...disclosures and other requirements. You look at all the regulation that's come out on top of AIFRS...All the ASIC requirements, ASX requirements, changes to the *Tax Act*, [the] GST. There has been just a boom of additional work for the accounting or finance function full stop, let alone technological change, let alone a skill shortage. You've had more to do with less people and people with...net less experience. I just don't think this has been approached very strategically and our capital markets were fine pre-AIFRS. In fact, I can't see how we're any better off.

One interesting comment by a purchaser related to a trend towards accounting standard subject matter expertise (by one individual in the audit team) in addition to industry expertise (by another individual). The share-based remuneration accounting standard (AASB 2 *Share-Based Payment*) was given as an example, with the need to value options and opine on that valuation requiring specific expertise that few among either purchasers or suppliers possessed.

> For instance...I've mostly operated in the financial services area and...basically in the big firms you can't be an audit partner of financial services clients unless you've had experience in the financial services industry. People have got to specialise. So then you get to an issue of you're within the financial services area, you get trading banks and you get investment banks and you get insurance companies and the like, so you can always [go into] sub-specialisations and you've got to make sure the expertise is appropriate...the big firms generally do a pretty good job of trying to address that.

The same purchaser continues, giving an example of an accounting standard that requires specialised expertise:

> It's always a bit of a struggle because as industries are moving rapidly and particularly, say, financial services, it's hard for the people in the profession to keep up. You keep up-to-date with what's happening on a product basis and all the rest of it, but it's particularly hard at the moment because of the change in the accounting standards. For instance, if you…took accounting standards at the moment and said, 'How many people are experts in the application of the standards in relation to executive compensation to a public company with share options and everything else?', I would guarantee that of the top-200 companies in Australia, probably less than 10 per cent of the CFOs would be expert in that area themselves and certainly less than 10 per cent of the partners in the firms would be expert in that area because it's such a tricky area that you need experts to do it. So invariably, the way that gets done is someone who's a specialist in that area gets called in to look at it.

> '[I]t's particularly hard at the moment because of the change in the accounting standards.'

A comment was made among the purchasers about highly specialised valuations (for example, gas and oil reserves) for which auditors were heavily reliant on technical specialist experts.

> A very important measure in our world is…our oil and gas reserves…the extent [to which]…we get that wrong has significant financial statement impacts…the auditors come in and check and see if that reserve statement has been verified independently, but they're essentially relying on the qualifications and the expertise of the reserve estimator…you know if they've got it wrong—well, certainly, auditors don't have the expertise to assess that…They just…rely on the process, but have no idea whether the process is a good one or a bad one. So in that regard, [in] certain specialist areas, basically the auditors do not have the expertise. Is it an area of concern for us? No, not really, because we have our experts in the area. And the market expects that as well…[The] ASX [has] regulations around how you go about measuring reserves and things, so you know that is covered in another way.

The same purchaser laments a 'tick-the-box' approach being practised by more junior auditors. The 'check-list' issue is returned to in depth in the chapters dealing with regulation (Chapters 11–13).

> '[W]hat you get now is... very junior staff who don't really understand the business asking a significant amount of questions, spending a significant amount of time, and you wonder for what end.'

> I began to think about expertise and knowledge and understanding of operations, and it's an age-old [problem], but what you get now is...very junior staff who don't really understand the business asking a significant amount of questions, spending a significant amount of time, and you wonder for what end...Are they actually adding to the audit or are they just really filling in a form, checking off a box? And...if you asked around...you'd get a lot of the latter—that there's this checking...the box...one time out of a hundred that check-a-box approach might pick up something, but in the end you know the big issues are dealt with at the partner and the senior management level. And it's a question of whether those two are up on the business and understand the business and understand the risks and are focusing on the risks, and asking the right questions around those risks as to whether the audit is of a high quality or not.

4.2.1 Summary

With respect to purchasers, many of the comments have potential implications for business acumen, industry expertise and client knowledge. Specifically, in regard to industry expertise, the observation is made that the requirement for having industry expertise is something that is expressly requested and indeed demanded at the inception of an engagement with a particular audit. Additionally, implied in a number of comments is an expectation of industry expertise at least among the most senior of the audit team. Working against developing industry expertise is a 'tick-a-box' procedural style, especially among junior staff. Importantly, one purchaser observes that in addition to the necessary presence of industry expertise, there could also be, at least for some clients and in some circumstances, a need for the development of accounting-topic expertise or expertise in particular transactions and how they are reported.

Generally, purchasers are able to praise the business acumen of senior members of the audit team. While there are a number of negative comments about the business acumen of junior members of the audit team, there are observations that the audit process relies heavily on such junior people, who are in some circumstances described as 'green'. There is also considerable sympathy for the fact that these individuals have little life experience and cannot be expected to have developed the business acumen that those more senior in years have acquired. Purchasers observe that the business model of an audit firm really demands that a large proportion of the staff on an audit engagement have limited exposure to businesses either in their industry or elsewhere. It would be reasonable to conclude that purchasers understand and in many cases are tolerant of the absence of highly developed business acumen in many junior staff. In one case, a purchaser saw a potential advantage to this because a 'dumb' or repetitive question might be asked of relatively junior client staff in a business in which they too were new and needed to know.

Many of the comments made related to client knowledge. Again, there is a sharp distinction between the level of client knowledge of junior and senior members of the audit team and there is a degree of tolerance for more junior staff—albeit with the recognition that there is a cost to the client due to an absence of client knowledge. There is also recognition of high staff turnover on audit teams and that there are ways of minimising the cost to the client, particularly with respect to documentation and the quality of handover from one group of individuals on an audit team to a new team. The level of auditor client knowledge can in fact be advantageous in the circumstance of a high-level turnover within the accounting staff of the client (such as a new CFO). There is also an observation that insightful questions can sometimes be asked by people who have non-traditional (non-accounting) educational backgrounds.

4.3 Suppliers

Suppliers emphasise the importance of understanding the client's business, as the following quotation illustrates:

> [Client knowledge is] one of the most critical things you can... have...in conducting an audit. It's absolutely critical that you have knowledge of your client's business...what you find is at the higher end of audit teams, the knowledge of clients' businesses is usually fairly high because we need to understand where the risks are, particularly around that business, and to do that you need to... understand what [the client does] and how they transact.

Suppliers, however, recognised the concerns of purchasers of audit services associated with the lack of client knowledge among more junior staff. Some suppliers also alluded to the problems created by rotation. The issue of rotation is returned to in a later chapter.

> [Rotation is] less likely to be a problem—well, it jolly well should be less likely to be a problem—at the partner level and the manager level...this rotation thing is interesting because it does take time to build up a knowledge of a business and operations. That's why all firms have brought in the fact that in your fifth year as a partner, your successor will shadow you. He can't say anything at board meetings or whatever, but he's there to absorb and try and pick up on that learning curve rather than have a gap.

The same supplier continues with respect to client knowledge and industry expertise:

> [S]ometimes at a partner level, it [comes down to]...the individual... you have some people who are deeply skilled and really understand the industry very well and are gurus in that...we'd like to think at [name of one of the Big Four], as with the other major houses, and indeed some of the smaller firms, that you've got those specialists in there, that they do understand the industry first, and then the client's business and how that works in the industry. You're never going to know it as well as the client because they're operating in there, but perhaps you'll bring a different perspective...we do have sufficient knowledge and sometimes that's a collaborative effort between a number of partners and managers and directors running that.

The same supplier continues, acknowledging that client knowledge is not present at the beginning of an engagement but is systematically responded to:

> [T]here is sometimes a start-up on that...we're transitioning onto the audit of [name of client], which is fantastic, but there's a lot for us to do to learn the historical issues, how the business works and so on. So it's a very steep learning curve and very enjoyable, but we know that in some time we will have got to that plateau...I think we do that well...at the junior level, some people do...well and pick it up and have...knowledge...others don't. And...it's a fair criticism that some clients have when we don't achieve continuity—that they're forever

> training our staff and [audit staff] ask the wrong questions...what's important is that the people who need to have the knowledge have the knowledge. You could argue that for some of the more junior staff, where they're doing some specific tasks...it would be helpful if they had...knowledge, but sometimes it's not critical.

The same supplier uses an analogy to explain his or her point further:

> As an analogy, if you're looking at payroll testing and setting out some prescriptive tests on how to test payroll...those payroll tests will be the same whatever the industry, whatever the client. And you could argue that you don't really need to have a lot of knowledge of the client's business to be able to do that work properly...the danger is where the knowledge of business and operations...can impact the efficiency. So be it: it annoys the client and it annoys you, but the issue is where it impacts the effectiveness and that's the challenge...[and] it's important we [meet it]. And where you've got to build it up quickly when you take on a new client or you bring in new people, you have to factor that in.

The model and resulting cost structure that audit firms use to bring in new graduates and then progress them through a career path were acknowledged by some in the supplier group as creating difficulties in terms of allowing for understanding of client businesses.

> [A]s long as the audit model is appealing in structure, and it's becoming less so given our work is changing, but we do need the cheaper arms and legs to be out there doing the field work. So at times questions will be asked that maybe shouldn't be, but if their on-job training is sufficient and they're well educated, the programs are right, then really those circumstances should be minimal.

One supplier argued that the structural arrangement of industries in Australia had changed and consequently auditing had changed.

> [T]here's been...a quantum shift in the economy. And...auditors are trained to use their knowledge of accounting standards and auditing standards, external financial reporting issues, to apply that. But they're not necessarily trained to understand businesses and to understand industries. And as much as we do our best to really get a fundamental understanding of what we're doing...it's probably a fair criticism of auditors, because I hear it from potential clients

> '[I]t's probably a fair criticism of auditors, because I hear it from potential clients all the time: our auditors are idiots, they don't know what they're doing and they ask stupid questions.'

all the time: our auditors are idiots, they don't know what they're doing and they ask stupid questions. And part...of that is always going to be there because in order to do this job we need to bring in graduates. Now graduates have got their three-year degrees and they're twenty-two, twenty-three. They've got no real life experience and they're given jobs which are appropriate for their level, but the reality is that they will ask questions. As much as you supervise your staff and you try not to have them doing things which are going [to] upset your client, they will ask questions which might appear a bit dim because they don't quite [have] the understanding.

The same supplier continues further with respect to client knowledge and expertise in the relevant industry:

> [P]erhaps the issue for us is to ensure that we have very well-documented audit plans, which deal with not just the actual business itself but deal with the industry. And we need to really discuss those sorts of things. And I know, for instance, what we're doing here at [name of audit firm] is we've got a planning day coming up in a couple of weeks' time, and we're going to run through every major client of ours with the 30 June balance date. And we're going to have all the audit team here and we're going to discuss the fraud and error-type issues in the financial report in accordance with the new standard so that we can really cover off on the requirements of the auditing standards; that we have properly planned the audit; that we'd have discussion in a group; and that we've considered these possibilities for fraud and error. But in our particular case, that'll be four to five hours worth of meeting with our entire audit division going through all of our clients. And we've just worked out that is the most efficient way of doing it. And it's good because it means that people who aren't necessarily working on other jobs get a bit of an understanding. So if we have to move the staff around, at least they have a better understanding of the client and the issues. But wherever I've been, it's always been an issue that clients have complained that the auditors don't understand. And the reality is we're in there for a week or two weeks of the year, if that. We

> don't actually spend all that much time conducting the audit. These people who are actually working in the particular industry of that entity...work there all the time...and we can never quite get to their level of knowledge. So...it's a bit harsh on the auditors, but there's probably also an element of fairness there that we need to properly consider whether we can get a better understanding of the business.

The same supplier continues about client knowledge as it relates to the 'corporate culture':

> '[A] lot of the opinion is actually based on your feeling about the enterprise. Corporate culture...is an extremely important issue.'

> I always enjoy the walk, the tour of the factory... even if they don't actually manufacture anything, I always say...can you take me through the building and I want to meet the people in marketing, and dispatch, or whatever it may be, distribution, printing, that sort of thing. Because...when you see things for yourself and then you talk to the people who are actually responsible, and it doesn't matter how unimportant it is in the organisation, you just get a better [feeling] for what they're doing...an audit opinion...[is] not a certificate, it's actually an opinion. Who knows if it's right or not? But a lot of the opinion is actually based on your feeling about the enterprise. Corporate culture...is an extremely important issue. And if you look at the nature of failures in Australia, you look at HIH—there was a massive corporate culture issue going on there. And I don't know whether the auditors picked up on that one. But what I have seen of late is the Big Four in particular are knocking back audits if they think there's a corporate culture-type issue, because...the risk profile is off their scale, they're not prepared to take on that particular business as a client. And that's actually come as a bit of a shock to me because...I've seen different Big Four firms knock back some fairly useful size audits simply on the basis that they thought it might've been a bit risky for them.

Suppliers pointed out the difficulties for the auditor if the client representative being questioned about the business was inexperienced.

> [H]olistically...we do [have sufficient client knowledge]...as you go down the...levels...ultimately what you've got is...a team

> that's leveraged in a certain way...[in which] you'll have partners, managers, seniors, juniors. The further...you go down the tree, probably the less appreciation there is of the business, as much as you try to instil that in people. Unless you're out there and you've got some experience, it's very, very difficult to have that commercial awareness and to put things into context. You might want to understand—[and it's] not through a lack of desire of wanting to understand, but some things are complex. And what tends to happen is that the more junior people probably have the greatest amount of time at a client and as you go up the tree the partners have the least amount because they're managing several engagements at one time. The key is can the more experienced people on the team get that knowledge through the team; can you do it in a way that you don't compromise the way that you...undertake your audit through planning, through regular meetings, through the partners being involved in the crucial aspects of the work, whether it's a risk assessment, their evaluation, the reporting...that's the model that you try to achieve...the big issues—we pick them. Where the frustration tends to come [in]...is more at the edges and the people asking the stupid question, which [they wouldn't ask] if they knew a little bit more about what we did...it's like anybody, it doesn't matter how well trained [you are]...you can't have an expectation of people [that] they're going to have this high level of knowledge of the business.

The interviewer then comments:

> If the client doesn't have patience for juniors and they're just answering the question in a way to brush them off so they go away then they're going to be coming back asking the same questions again because they really didn't get the answer they should have got in the first place.

The response is:

> That's right. Or what happens is you ask one question and...the answer gives rise to three more questions and four more questions and then there's another, and it keeps going. That's just a fact of what we do. Our job is really to get information and analyse it, and then what you expect to come out of that is a further analysis, further question...this may be a bit of a generalisation, but...the

> criticisms that are levelled out in, say, the audit profession by... corporates could very well be levelled by the audit profession [at] the corporates. And just as we may be essentially asking a lot of questions and sometimes the same question...the quality of the response—and not just the response but even competency and understanding—has probably diminished in organisations. And that would only be fair to say as a generalisation, but what tends to happen is [that] it's more complex than it used to be. There's more to be done by less people, there's a leverage within organisations so those that know are in higher positions versus those that know less being in lower positions. So the people that you're dealing with sometimes at those lower levels only know a little bit and they don't know the context, just as the overlords don't know the context... Their roles have changed from being pretty much processing and reporting to being more holistic [in terms of] responsibility and sometimes they don't have the level of competency to be taking on the task that they are—but that's within their portfolio [and is] what they need to do. So...it does cut a little bit both ways.

One non-Big Four supplier opines that there is less industry expertise than is optimal other than where there is an appropriate portfolio of clients in the same industry:

> [W]ith the calibre of the staff...there's always going to be that issue [with client knowledge]... We are very system driven so we try to find out the systems and identify the controls. And... we have...[an] overview of the firm's business, but...we [need to] get into that a little bit more... So, if I do one shop, one retail unit...then I'll overlay my general knowledge into it, and so will the auditors. If we do a number of retail outlets then we're more likely to put a bit more effort into understanding the retail industry and getting research so that can be better equipped...there's an element of truth there that an audit process can be overlaid on any business, but you really need to find the hot points in the business. And I don't think we tend to do that as well, and then we have less-experienced people. And that's also a major issue at the moment with the staff—in the inexperience of the people...But their inexperience doesn't allow them to put

'[T]here's an element of truth there that an audit process can be overlaid on any business, but you really need to find the hot points in the business.'

> any overview. And, in a sense, if you're looking at that, some of the key things are performed by graduates...maybe they should be performed by the partners, but that's the way we tend to operate... that's a fair criticism in that we probably don't do enough research about the industry or really find out what the hot spots are. It's very [much] driven by the systems. So it's where do the forms go and who does anything with them, and who then is the control, what is the control to make sure that those get correctly processed? Now, you could do all of that without understanding anything about the industry because it's systems driven. And that's part of the issue.

The issue of cost structures comes to the fore with respect to industry expertise, as the following comment demonstrates:

> [W]e're under audit fee constraints. So the concept of really overlaying a huge industry knowledge—hell, who's going to pay for that sort of scenario...occasionally with the clients we have, you'll talk to them and they'll say, 'Fred didn't seem to really have a good understanding of what we do'...so you...talk to Fred and encourage him to really understand the business as part of the process. But... what we've tried to do is very much target information on certain of the Internet sites about an industry, and get that put into the audit file. We've done it with training of the staff to say, 'Look, you know it's important for you to understand what's the key driver in that business, because if sales are just getting sales without relative to margin then that's going to be short term and we need...you... to understand those things, and what are the risks that they're facing, and things like that.' So we build it into the training, but the difficulty...is that the young kids nowadays, they don't know what they don't know, and in fact they think they know everything. And...that's impacting on a bit of it too.

The same supplier notes that the personal skills of the inexperienced audit staff also pose certain challenges to the quality of the audit:

> [S]ome of the people [in the client's company] give them the first answer that comes into their head. And the problem you've got is the...inexperienced [audit] staff are maybe not confident enough to challenge that until they go back and check with the in-charge. And then when they do, they then go back and challenge because they'd said, 'Well, that doesn't seem right.' And that's a bit of confidence

> thing. It's also the person going and asking the question without having thought about it before they ask the question, and that's a real issue. We try to tell the staff [to] think about what you're...asking about, and what do you think the response might be...because then you've got context...[and] that's [how] you know part of the problem too...they don't think because they know, and then they get an answer that's totally left field and they have to go back. And some of them then struggle to go back to the in-charge and...say that. So they might write something down on the work paper, and it's only when you review the work paper [that] you think...that's nonsense, we need to go back and get that...there's a lot more for the clients to [cope with]...that's saying that the quality of [the client's] staff quite often...they're struggling to get staff all the time and so the newer people aren't as knowledgeable as the others... so it's a combination. Certainly, from our point of view, we've got to really work on training the auditors to think about the response, get context about it and think about it in relation to the business. But... the clients also have to make sure their staff understand that it's better to give the auditors more information than less information, rather than just kind of brush them off.

'[T]he clients also have to make sure their staff understand that it's better to give the auditors more information than less information, rather than just kind of brush them off.'

Others among the suppliers saw the need to develop client knowledge exacerbated by the cost pressures facing audit firms.

> Certainly, more knowledge would help an audit. The difficulty there is in a market environment, clients are not always prepared to pay for that extra knowledge that an auditor will get through spending the time. So that becomes difficult. If anything can be done to benchmark audit fees or something along those lines then that would allow an auditor to spend more time with a client. In a market environment which is competitive, it's difficult to justify that.

4.3.1 Summary

Suppliers do not question whether industry specialist auditors exist—particularly among the Big Four. Among the supplier group, there are comments regarding the cost of nurturing industry-specific knowledge and the effort involved in updating and maintaining it, especially in highly specialist industries. Suppliers acknowledge the challenges of putting inexperienced auditors into the field, but do seek to support them with appropriate training and with mechanisms to help them develop client knowledge and industry expertise. In part at least, this could be a function of the audit firm business model. Suppliers point out another side to the dilemma of inexperience and staff turnover—that affecting their staff auditors in the field when client positions remain unfilled, client staffers turnover or do not have adequate understanding of their tasks or roles. Nevertheless, they acknowledge the crucial importance to risk assessment of an auditor possessing superior business acumen skills and understanding the client's business. The issue of client reluctance to recompense for the time needed for an auditor to develop appropriate client knowledge and industry expertise is raised also within suppliers' comments.

4.4 Standard setters

Standard setters cited banking, insurance and mining as industries requiring industry-specific knowledge, especially of the relevant regulatory regime. The role of the Australian Prudential Regulation Authority (APRA) in recognising only 'approved' auditors with senior-level experience in the audit of certain industries and hence constraining supply was noted also. Beyond that, there was the perception that a competent general auditor would be able to cope in auditing other industries.

> For heavily regulated industries—banking, insurance—clearly, you need a great degree of industry regulatory knowledge and to do that you need to understand the operational…aspects, but you'll never have the same industry knowledge as someone who works in that industry. Therefore, if I was to say…we need a lot of industry knowledge, I'd have to say: 'Well, how do we do that other than bring people in from the industry?' Generally speaking, I don't think that will add a lot to the audit process.

Standard setters acknowledge the importance of client knowledge and industry expertise, but observe that the current prescriptive requirements could impact on the application of this information.

> '[T]here's a real focus on documenting how that assessment's been done. So there's a danger that we get a form-driven response to this issue rather than a substantive response.'

> [G]enerally, auditors do [have sufficient client knowledge]. And this has been an experience... coming from a large firm where we would use the term 'face the market' on a line of business or an industry expertise basis. So we've got, in theory, the capability to obtain an understanding... the audit standards appropriately direct people to understand the [client's] business and to understand risk, although...a danger or an impediment in getting an appropriate understanding is that the approach to assessing risk is increasingly becoming...formula driven at the front end of an audit. There [are] some reasons for requiring that though. The standards have become quite explicit to demonstrate that you've considered things because, in some instances, where there've been failures, it's arguable that that understanding wasn't obtained...this is all about getting the right balance, but there is a high degree of prescription around risk assessment and because we've got the external oversight and the need to document, there's a real focus on documenting how that assessment's been done. So there's a danger that we get a form-driven response to this issue rather than a substantive response. But...generally, the industry knowledge is there.

There was comment on how the audit itself and training of audit personnel and the development of their business acumen had changed in the move away from a fully substantive approach.

> [A]cross the board, audit teams don't have enough knowledge and maybe you never can have enough knowledge...The one area where...auditors should be generally more proficient in is financial systems, financial accounting internal control systems and... auditors are probably less proficient now than they were 20 years ago on that.

The interviewer asks why this is and the standard setter responds:

> Because...methodologies 20 years ago were looking for audit deficiency and cutting out understanding systems was the way it was done, jumping to the substantive and...what it...means—you cut out your knowledge of what's really happening and it's very hard to reintroduce it when you no longer have the audit budgets to

> do it with. Therefore [the issue of] the training of the junior staff... at the time I had in the late '70s out at clients, wasting a lot of time on transactional testing but learning a lot, absorbing, not realising how much I was learning as I was doing it. And the younger auditors these days don't have that luxury and I don't think our training processes [have] kept up with that lack of on-the-job access exposure.

The standard setter adds with respect to the possibility of interchange between industry and the audit profession:

> [W]e need the balance of industry knowledge and awareness versus auditing knowledge and auditing skill and once you get out of auditing for a few years, it's very difficult to come back into it.

Having acknowledged that banking, insurance and perhaps mining are industries that require specialist knowledge, the standard setter is questioned about whether 'knowledge industries' also require in-depth industry expertise:

> I don't think so. They require a bit of knowledge and it helps, but not specialist expertise that is beyond...[what] any general well-qualified, competent...auditor could easily pick...up.

This standard setter, having acknowledged the role of client knowledge, industry expertise and business acumen, also asserts that we should not forget the importance of technical knowledge of the business of auditing:

> Perhaps [clients are] looking for more from their audit firm to bring more value to them, and they see value in terms of their industry and that's still there despite a change in the last five years. There is still this pressure on audit firms to justify their existence beyond the audit sign-off. But as far as part of the actual audit process, the area where...our lack of knowledge...impacts the audit is our junior staff's lack of understanding...of accounting control processes.

While there is a common criticism of junior auditors asking 'dumb' questions, the importance of the 'dumb' question is noted by the following standard setter:

> There will always be the questions and...we shouldn't underestimate the dumb question... that's the question which needs to be asked and you...find the problems from sometimes the dumb questions...therefore I, in part, am sympathetic to the comments you make, but I also believe that an audit is about interaction, communication and...asking the right questions...clients will always have their day-to-day business to do and then have the auditors there for part of the year asking questions and they have to devote time to them. I can understand that they can sometimes get a little bit annoyed with that, but that's part of life. So, provided... the individuals have brought their staff up to the appropriate level...and that should be the objective to make sure that there's enough planning and enough question[ing], enough bringing the individuals up to speed before they get there, but there will always be a bit more [of] that on the job...it's probably an area for improvement but...we will always get that comment because an auditor has to ask questions and therefore sometimes it will always be people who will be a little bit put out by it or [will find] a little bit of annoyance to it.

'There will always be the questions and...we shouldn't underestimate the dumb question... sometimes...that's the question which needs to be asked and you...find the problems from sometimes the dumb questions.'

The interviewer raises the issue of the personal characteristics of the auditor and their tenacity in a situation where an answer is provided to an auditor and the answer is unsatisfactory. Does that mean the auditor has to go back and ask further questions, sometimes to the annoyance of the client's accounting staff?

> Yeah, well, that's right. Now if you...don't get the right response, you've got to ask the question. And nor should you be put off... if someone doesn't want to answer you, because if it doesn't stack up, you've got to keep going back...[There are] always those types of situations there and people may not like to be asked, but... that's part of what a good audit is all about. In other words, does it stack up...when you sit back and look at it...does that lead to a further question, you know, I need a bit more evidence or a bit more understanding of another part of it. So, in other words, it's a process you go through.

The next standard setter observes that even at senior levels, the industry expertise of auditors cannot be at the same level of those working in the industry—at least with respect to the highly regulated industry groups:

> 'Do they have enough knowledge of the operations? Well, I don't think they can because they're not here often enough.'

> [I]n our industry, which is financial services, at the senior level, at the partner level, yeah, they do understand the business because they're involved in financial services across the board, so our business isn't that different from our competitors' business, [at] a macro level. So, at a macro level, the senior staff members are up to date with changes in regulation. They see what a number of organisations are doing, which gives them a very good overview and perspective of the industry. So...in terms of the business, they're pretty strong on industry knowledge and that's good; operations is a different thing. So they probably do have sufficient knowledge of the business but only at a senior level. Do they have enough knowledge of the operations? Well, I don't think they can because they're not here often enough and...when you're in and out and you're here for... three months of the year or whatever, then you can't have a really detailed knowledge of the operations.

The standard setter does observe that even with senior audit staff with considerable expertise, the business model is reliant on junior staff elevating important issues:

> Do [junior staff] understand [a complex issue] and the context of it, and do they really understand what they're documenting, or do they understand the context of what they find in order to evaluate it and then bring it up to the right level of attention? No, probably not. So, if anything would keep me awake if I was a partner or a senior manager, [it] is...are my guys good enough to bring to my attention what I need to know? There's a danger there in terms of using inexperienced staff that things can occur that don't get elevated and that's the biggest danger.

The standard setter observes that managing the risk involves supervision of staff:

> [T]he only thing you can do really is pretty close on-the-job supervision...the key to success in audit...is having the right

> management team, and with the right management team then you can...effectively supervise those managers who are prepared to get involved in the detail and understand the detail and educate the staff on the job. Then...you can cover that risk. But...it's a bit like the regulators. Your biggest risk is what you don't know and it's how you make sure you get to know all the material things that you need to know.

This standard setter suggests industry expertise can be gained from the client:

> I don't see any reason why the external auditors couldn't attend some of the organisation's training...But you know you're paid a limited audit fee. There's a limit to how much of this stuff you can do.

The importance of the business acumen of the auditor and personal attributes, including integrity, is drawn out in the following comment from one standard setter:

> Clearly, the more commercial acumen that the auditors have, they're able to relate to both management and the board and be seen to really understand the business and be a trusted source of advice, if you like, in part sort of outside the audit process even, subject to independence, the more valuable they can be. They still need that...fearlessness about standing up to management if they're pushing the envelope too much. But...as a trusted advisor to the business, they're more likely to be able to do that than if they're perceived as being weak or not sufficiently commercial. They're the auditors that a management with some kind of, not necessarily ill intent, but even just trying to fudge things a bit, are more likely to be able to get around.

The standard setter notes that there is variability with respect to industry expertise and client knowledge and that those with particularly well-developed skills in each will command higher fees:

> What I'm trying to say is...it's variable...the ones that are highly regarded will be the ones that are, and [do,] command a premium.

The standard setter observes that staff exchanges and secondments would aid development of industry expertise, but employment practices in audit firms are not conducive to this:

> [Employment practices] hinder it. I don't think that whole sense of exchange is welcomed. There is a sense that you keep the people as long as you can and that you're always going to lose a proportion who don't want to go on to be partner or aren't good enough. Other than that, you try and hold them...It's not that sense of going off and working in other places, be it the private sector or indeed in government...Or the regulator [*at the prompting of the interviewer*]. And it's short-sighted.

One of the standard setters emphasised that the existence of industry expertise and client knowledge, together with a high level of implicit business acumen, was not sufficient. A necessary condition is that clients communicate honestly and comprehensively about the issues in their business. This standard setter emphasises that, without this, no matter what the level of understanding of the industry or the client, problems can arise:

> [G]enerally, when you...understand the business, there are probably what you'd call industry issues which are pervasive to the industry within which businesses operate. The businesses then have their own issues as a subset of the industry within which they operate, and a significant proportion of those issues [is] known to management...it goes back to this transparency of communication... you'd probably sit back and say: 'Well, if you'd told us about that, and given us a bit more information, we would have looked at it differently.' So you can have the...industry issues...you know what they are, you go deep, dive down into the business and you go through them...how does this affect this operation? And you only get half the story. You do some digging around, a bit more cross-checking. Great story, going around the business, everything's fine and, six months later, ooh bang, problem, and it's because they chose not to tell you.

4.4.1 Summary

Standard setters' comments convey a sense of the limit of what industry expertise can achieve. While it is seen as crucial to some targeted, highly regulated industries, there are other industries where it is not seen as crucial and where audit conduct has more generic application. Also raised is the difficulty for expertise at any level to overcome client secrecy or lack of transparency. The standard setters believe that audit teams generally do not have sufficient knowledge of the business, but knowledge at the senior levels is sufficient. Perhaps not surprisingly, the audit standards are seen as appropriately directing people to understand the business and to understand risk. There was, however, comment that an impediment to achieving an appropriate understanding was that the approach to assessing risk was increasingly becoming formula driven at the front end of an audit. There was also the observation that audit firms did not facilitate the interchange of staff between audit firms and other organisations and more flexibility there would aid in the development of industry expertise. Such interchange might be contemplated between external auditors and the internal audit functions[7] of key industry players. Regulatory requirements about independence pose a challenge here.

4.5 Regulators

One regulator expresses a view that business acumen is developed through managerial skills rather than through auditing, which is more compliance driven:

> [I]t's a question of training and perspective. When an auditor goes in, they think in terms of compliance, right? And when you are running a business, you think of profit. You think of growth. You think of risk management...there's a need for balance, commercial balance. You take on risk, you take on compliance and you take on growth, otherwise you won't succeed. So [to acquire business acumen] it's more a management issue rather than an auditing [issue].

In response to a question about whether audit partners know enough in the highly regulated specialist industries, this regulator notes, 'Not really.'

7 We are not able to include a direct quotation on this issue as the suggestion was made in a manner that would directly identify the individual who made the comment.

With respect to the expertise and use of junior staff, the regulator observes:

> I just get a feel[ing] that the junior levels...they end up doing a lot of the [hack] work...and that's how they make their profits. They keep their cost down. So the point is a lot of this really complex stuff, you can't really get junior people to do it.

4.5.1 Summary

The only regulator suggests that there is room for improvement with respect to industry expertise and the auditing business model puts heavy reliance on junior (inexperienced) staff.

5.0 Issues and implications

In terms of the telephone and mail surveys, in response to a question about whether external financial statement audits were of value because of 'the specialist industry expertise of the auditor', 50 per cent of suppliers, 46 per cent of users and only 31 per cent of purchasers responded affirmatively. Among the suppliers, there was a sharp differentiation between Big Four and non-Big Four suppliers, with 77 per cent of Big Four suppliers believing industry expertise brought value compared with only 42 per cent of non-Big Four suppliers. This difference could reflect the relevance of industry expertise across the levels of market capitalisation and across unlisted companies.

With respect to agreement with the statement that 'an external audit is of value because the auditor has a good understanding of the business', 55 per cent of suppliers, 33 per cent of purchasers and 40 per cent of users responded affirmatively. CEO/CFO respondents were particularly harsh and, again, there was differentiation between Big Four and non-Big Four suppliers.

In response to questions about an audit being of value because of the 'business acumen the auditor brings to the audit', 45 per cent of users, 33 per cent of purchasers and 55 per cent of suppliers responded affirmatively. Specifically with respect to audit partners, most users and suppliers saw the business acumen of audit partners as above the mid-point, with junior auditors not rated highly. Interestingly, overall, purchasers took a harsher view compared with users.

Across most interviewee groups, there was recognition of the importance of auditors possessing business acumen and yet also an understanding of the reality that auditors did not have the same perspective as those running the businesses that were subject to audit. Recognition of the difficulty of creating truly deep understanding at the more junior levels was present also. There was recognition of cost pressures impacting on the use of junior auditing staff. There was also recognition that some of the responsibility could be placed on clients for their use of inexperienced staff to answer auditors' questions. Two commented on the size of the market in Australia as a constraint on gaining industry expertise in particular industries.

As indicated previously, while purchasers in terms of survey data are harsher in their criticism of audit firms, there is a real sense from the interviews that purchasers' expectations are low in terms of whether business acumen is a critical part of the role of auditors. Purchasers also acknowledge that there is a sharp distinction between senior and junior auditors. There was also acknowledgment of a lack of stability and that this caused lapses in client knowledge. Purchasers make a number of observations in regard to the business model of the audit firms and perhaps the profession more broadly, which means that the life experience and business acumen of more junior auditors are limited.

Suppliers, including those who have a role in standard setting, probably have the most detailed comments with respect to the issue of business acumen. It is acknowledged, at least in some quarters among suppliers of audit services, that junior staff do not have the business acumen or certain of the personal characteristics, including maturity, of their more senior colleagues and, as a consequence, they might ask clients the 'wrong' questions. There is, however, also realisation that sometimes asking 'dumb' questions can cause considerable insight and the 'dumb' questions can be crucial.

Suppliers also volunteered that less reliance on substantive testing and examination of a business through its transactions had limited the vista of some junior staff on how businesses operated and how core activities of an auditee were undertaken. Additionally, suppliers made frequent observations that inexperience was not just in the hands of junior auditors.

Regulators observe that business acumen is not necessarily one of the core attributes of a successful and competently completed audit.

On balance, while the survey statistics suggest that business acumen of some audit staff (most notably the more junior staff) is limited and might potentially be seen as a criticism of the profession, the interviews reveal that the issue is more complex. The issue relating to the experience of junior auditors and their ability to develop experience and acumen useful in a business career, however, remains unresolved in the current debate and perhaps has implications for tertiary education.

6.0 Focus groups with more junior auditors

As part of the Big Four peer focus groups with more junior audit staff, questions were asked about the importance, development and use of client and industry-specific knowledge.

6.1 Client knowledge

Within each of the three separate focus group sessions, there was near universal agreement that client-specific knowledge was important to designing an appropriate audit approach, however, qualifications to this ideal then followed.

> [Having client knowledge] definitely helps. It makes it easier... because in financial services we quite often have very complex systems and the technical issues as well, so having that client knowledge as a base going into the audit...definitely helps a lot.

> [I]t's good to have specific client knowledge but sometimes you just can't have it. You do not have staff continuance...people [leave] and with that documentation, you cannot have [the] knowledge you need. Sometimes it's very discouraging...and to be honest, for the financial statements, all the captions look similar...you know what you need to do, all the basic audit techniques...you can just apply them to all of them...You ask this for reconciliation and you ask another one for some sort of [similar] reconciliation, but with a different name. This one may be a general ledger one, that one may be from some kind of strange system you've never seen. That's the most knowledge I would have. Even if you have a very tight budget only for one week or two weeks for a client, you can't even get all [the] documentation done. How can you just go on and ask for client knowledge? It's just not possible.

The point of this focus group member's comment is that client-specific knowledge might not be present at the beginning of an audit—without great harm other than to audit efficiency—but it should be present by the completion of an audit:

> [Y]ou do [need client-specific knowledge] to complete an audit but not to commence one... part of an audit is coming to terms with the client and knowing their risk areas and even knowing which staff they have in which jobs and making some judgment on how competent you think different people are in their roles...that's essential to complete your audit because you need to focus time and effort and energy where you think there [are] going to be problems coming up. But obviously you don't need it to start because you can go out to a client never having heard of them before. But you need to spend that time in gaining the understanding of their business, who they are, what their culture's like, whether they're perfectionists or whether they're not...[so] it's more efficient if you have the client knowledge beforehand, and...you need it to complete an audit...but not...necessarily to commence one.

'[I]t's more efficient if you have the client knowledge beforehand, and...you need it to complete an audit... but not...necessarily to commence one.'

The same theme of not being expected to have client knowledge at the beginning of the audit is repeated in this next quotation:

> When you start at the bottom level, you're not expected to have... knowledge on the first day you walk out there, which is good, because you generate that knowledge in your first...couple of weeks or however long your engagement goes for. Even in our division, especially the bigger clients, you have an opportunity, and then... you have...knowledge of the client and you get more of an exposure to their personnel, which is good.

A question put to one of the focus groups was: 'So, how do you gain client knowledge?' Responses included that knowledge was gained from managers and partners, from the previous year's experience with the client and/or prior year files, site tours, the Internet and from clients with similar systems and processes.

[A] manager can pass on the knowledge if you're new to the job; the manager or the [partner] can pass on the knowledge.

[Y]ou talk to the people who were on the job prior to you. If you haven't been on it, you speak to the partner who's on the job, because often they'll have contact with the guys at the top level, so they'll know the details [of the] work papers. And then talking to the client, going out...seeing what they're doing...If they're listed...there's quite a bit of information you can get from internet places about them.

[*In response to the interviewer's request for examples of what a manager might say*:] For one of my clients, the manager took last year's file and basically just explained to us what they do, key areas we need to focus on and blah, blah. And they went through the files, what needs to be done...and some of them...when you're there...talking to the client, that's when you gain more of your knowledge of the client.

I suppose from working on your previous years.

[T]here are a number of documents we are required to fill out which will cover understanding the business and prior issues and issues we expect going forward, and all these things that are done at the beginning and end of [an] audit...a lot of people [are] encouraged to be reading those...[to] understand the risks that have been documented in prior years, the build-up of knowledge, to then go through, suck what you can out of that for the audit going forward. So that's where people tend to get a lot of that risk, and you have to address it because you have to fill out the audit boxes.

It depends who you're working with. Sometimes, if you're in a job, someone will go out and they'll spend the first hour saying so this is what they do, they'll walk you through it, and...they'll take you on a site tour, and then...it becomes a lot clearer.

[S]omething that's more handy than I think a lot of people give credit to, with manufacturing firms especially, is simply a site tour. Because when you're thinking about raw materials to a work in progress, finished goods, seeing that actually happening at any site...makes it so much easier when you come down to describing all the controls and quality controls and processes and all the ins and outs of the business.

> [W]e're sectorised…in our groups so a lot of the clients are peer clients…there [are] systems and processes you can [access].

> No, I don't think [transferring knowledge of systems and processes between clients creates a conflict of interest]…on the flip side…it gives you the ability to…add value to your clients…everyone's so similar that there's not a process out there which one person's doing and everyone else isn't, but…there [are] certainly small refinements and improvements.

> [There are] all sorts of knowledge [*when pressed on the type of knowledge gathered*]…one is knowledge of the people who actually work there and who's driving the…process, the financial reporting process.

Clients in the same industry are interested in the auditor's inside knowledge of industry developments:

> Our clients…prefer it if we have multiple clients in…very much the same industry. I work on the [name of client] and I also work on [another client in the same industry]…when we got the client first this year…[the first-named client] was so interested in what everyone else in the industry was doing. We've actually set up a whole bunch of networking sessions and training sessions for the clients for all our [name of industry] teams so that they can meet each other and discuss all the things that they…want to…we can actually add value as a firm by doing that.

There was, however, consciousness of the potential conflicts of interest:

> [T]here is confidentiality and professional integrity not to be providing other companies with information.

Understanding the politics inside the client is often as important as understanding the business, as is drawn out in this next quotation:

> [I]t's all of those things [*'competency', 'integrity', prompted by the interviewer*] you want to know. Whenever you go out to the client normally, you'll [ask] staff: 'We're going out here, this is who does this, this and this, this is how I think this person performs, this is how this person performs.' So they can manage their dealings with them, and so that they know where to look for errors or whether they're likely to make errors as well, so that's definitely a part of

> it. But…there's also understanding the politics of what goes on in organisations. [It's] important to understand what not to say…and what to say…to get the information that you need.

The interviewer asks whether it's harder in the middle market to gain client knowledge. Responses included this:

> Our clients are that diverse…some of my clients go from [industry] to [industry] and that's how diverse mine gets, so client knowledge is recurring.

Recurring engagements with the same client come through as important in understanding the client's business:

> [Y]ou need to know that individual client, how it works. That's the most important thing…working on it, you do get…some clients [who] are similar. We have a multitude of [types of] companies, for example, but the most important thing is definitely [having worked] on that client before.
>
> Continuity is pretty key. More continuity is better.
>
> It makes it so much more efficient.
>
> And that's why staff retention helps, when the people who were there last year are there again the next year.

Recurring engagements are important not just to audit personnel, but to the client:

> [T]he clients demand [the same staffing]. They want…to know who they're dealing with; they don't want different people going out every year.
>
> So they can form relationships as well.

More probing and other comments reveal that documentation does not have to be filled out at every staff level; there is a document for each client and staff at all levels are encouraged to go through and read it. When probed on what happens for a new client, the interviewees respond that the document has to be created from scratch:

> [I]f you went…for a walk through, you don't have that knowledge of who does what…and you generally just start with your main

> contact and you work downwards in terms of...process knowledge. In terms of overall business...your top management are the ones that are going to know the most about the ins and outs of the business.

When asked whether documentation is a substitute for either industry knowledge or client knowledge, the responses are mixed. One answers in the negative, but another answers:

> [D]ocumentation means an experienced auditor can just pick up a file without any previous client knowledge [and] can still do [the] audit.

The next junior auditor confirms that documentation has improved in recent years:

> [T]he quality of our audits has improved with the new methodologies and the new requirements for work, sample sizes and all that kind of stuff...I've even picked up an audit file for a client we had three years ago, a file from three years ago and a file this year: this year's file will be a lot more comprehensive.

The limitations to documentation as a source of client knowledge and input to audit quality, however, are also acknowledged:

> [T]hat's a question of the quality of an audit file compared to [the] quality of an audit...documentation is much more important now.

> [J]ust because it wasn't documented doesn't mean those financials are materially misstated.

> If it's not on file, it's not done.

The interviewer then asked whether the AUASB's documentation requirements had caused difficulty.

> [M]aybe to a really small degree but I don't think documentation... means that people are working hours later than they otherwise would be. It's just the client base.

> [The budgets] are more [realistic] these days.

Responses to the question 'Do you think there are other ways that you can get client knowledge that do not happen to be used by this Big Four firm?' include:

> [W]ith a lot of my clients, there's a lot of industry knowledge... For instance, I have a...client, and there [are] certain accounting policies that are used, and rules that are not applicable to any other jobs I work on...they are having quality sessions going forward... [to] discuss that with [staff] before an audit begins...these specific things that relate to that industry.
>
> But that's more for young [staff] because as you go up you find them out through experience.

'[T]hat knowledge is in-house to us, so it's got to be passed on or documented in our files.'

> [T]he sort of information we use, the client knowledge we gain because we get out there and do the work... that information is ours. We don't publicly put it out there. Say, for instance, you can go look at [a company's] web site and you can figure out that if they're mining...they're going to have problems... because they've made a mess of the place...But if you're out at a little manufacturing firm, you're not going to know what their problems are until you start speaking to them, until you start looking at what's going on...Oh, they've made a mess of the ground around their area, or they're very, very good at what they do and everything's nice and neat and there [are] absolutely no problems when you get out there...that knowledge is in-house to us, so it's got to be passed on or documented in our files.

A point made in this next quotation is that more use could be made of managers' and partners' well of knowledge:

> [A] manager...stays on the job and it might be the senior accountant, the juniors that come on for the first time. And this is something I've raised...[that] I don't think we spend enough time tapping into that manager's and...that partner's knowledge...that's a way that we could build a bit more client knowledge by really allocating time and sitting there and going look, let's get a two-hour run-down of this client...at the beginning, right off the bat, just to get that up front.

As to good or bad examples with interactions with clients that have been revealing in terms of that client, one response is:

> [Y]ou work...for a new person who's employed at that job [in the client], you figure out their capabilities and...those people who really shouldn't be doing that job, because they're just bad at it... you just learn, you go to someone else. But there are bad experiences, when people just can't do their job.

There is general agreement that the above scenario involving client staff is common. The interviewer then asks: 'Are there any particular examples where [at the end] the client told you a profoundly different story to where you started from; you walked in and you learnt something and it profoundly changed the way you did the audit?' Responses include:

> The client changed their information systems and made a mess of it and it very profoundly changed everyone's job when we were out there, because we were out there for a lot longer than we expected and...we knew that they were...changing their information systems. And we knew that they had already warned us that there were problems because they delayed by a week, but when we got out there is when we truly found out how much of a mess it was.

> For one of my clients...they promised us to be really efficient because they were getting a Big Four manager to [head their] finance division, so we thought okay, they'll be really efficient and they had a merger during [the] last financial year and everything was just a mess, so it changed...because when we were going, we're confident this guy, with his background...they'd be more efficient, but when we got there and realised that things were...different...we spent more time and we incurred a lot of overrun.

A further question was: 'So if you came across in a client an accountant that had come out of one of the Big Four, would you immediately assume they must be reasonably competent?' Views were generally in the negative, with comments that competence would still need to be assessed.

> It depends why they left the firm. I know there's someone from our division who went to one of our clients, and when he was working here he used to be super, he used to work so hard, he used to get everything done. The people who came back in for the client said: 'Oh, he's hopeless, he'll work nine to five, won't bother helping me doing anything', so he's just like anyone else. So in that kind of case, it didn't really matter.

When the interviewer responds, 'So do you think a partner that's done manufacturing…', the response is:

> Could go into a bank? No. I don't know if that happens. I know I couldn't go into a bank…it depends on the experience and their skill set, doesn't it…I could go [to] manufacturing, to media, with no problems.

Another question about initial audits took the form: 'Do you think the first time you do an audit for a particular client, a new client, the quality of that audit is as good as if you were doing it for the fourth time?' The research literature tends to report findings of lower quality on initial audit engagements so focus group participant responses are of some interest here. Responses are mixed:

> No, it's not…the reason…[is] it doesn't matter if it's a new client. You've still got two weeks and I know it's wrong to say this, but you don't have all that prior year documentation and the work done to roll forward…All those check lists to roll forward, so you've got to spend more time doing the admin instead of understanding the client and doing the work and…it's hard to fit in everything.

> Based on your current knowledge of the client, you would think it's quality work, but on subsequent years, you realise that you can still improve on the work you did for the client…It makes it better [the second time around]. Not that you didn't do…quality work the first time, but…it's a process of improvement…because of client knowledge.

'[W]hen I've audited clients which are new clients to the firm, I found that there's much more focus on understanding the business.'

> I would disagree…when I've audited clients which are new clients to the firm, I found that there's much more focus on understanding the business and everyone on the audit team having a good understanding of the business and the key transactions and the like. And probably less on documentation and, we'll improve the audit file next year. But in terms of understanding what's going on and making sure that it's correct…there's much more focus on having an understanding and probably it's better quality because you have to do all the work yourself. You can't just kind of…roll something forward without really thinking about it. So, possibly, it could be better quality the first time around.

> [I]t depends on how you can consider the idea of quality. I wouldn't consider that doing the audit cheaply is a measure of quality... quality in an audit is whether you're going to pick up errors and... we're providing an audit report to say that a financial statement has errors or doesn't have errors...the quality in work the first time around or the quality of that opinion the first time around would be equal...maybe other, what I would consider sideline things, such as file documentation...can be improved or would be improved in future years just because you can lever off work that you performed previously.

The same participant goes on to explain how in his or her experience, partners new to engagements, whether or not new to the firm, are demanding in terms of their own and others' work effort:

> [I]n terms of the opinion...partners are probably more demanding in how much work you perform and looking at things more completely the first time around on a client... [but] in future times, partners are able to spend less time themselves on an audit because they feel that they have an understanding of what's going on. And...I've worked on audits which are brand new, or audits which we've had but the partner has changed so the partner's new to it, and each time I find a partner, when it's new, will spend a lot more time themselves—[and] in the second or third year [will then spend] less time to look at it.

'[I]n terms of the opinion... partners are probably more demanding in how much work you perform and looking at things more completely the first time around on a client.'

In the context of a general discussion about the demise of Andersen, the following comment is made:

> [I]t seems that as we go on, the cases like Enron and HIH and all the rest of it...regulatory [processes] become...stricter, and there's a lot more focus on corporate governance as well. It's almost like our job gets harder, and there [are] more things that you need to think about all the time, and auditing standards are becoming more [complex].

There were negative responses from the interviewees when asked whether they thought clients were taking them more seriously now that auditing standards had the force of law. It was acknowledged, however, that some clients, especially the smaller ones, really did appreciate the audit function and its capacity to add value. This was acknowledged as especially true of client personnel who understood that auditors checked processes rather than thinking that their job was being reviewed in a search for mistakes they had made. When the interviewer then asks how to approach these latter types in a non-threatening way, the following responses are given:

> That's pretty hard. Being an auditor.

> [There are] different personalities...and you kind of figure [it] out... but it changes from person to person.

> [I]t can be threatening...because there was a recent client in our group, the CEO got asked to go [by the board] then the acting CFO got asked to go...because of the issues the audit came up with. There were a whole lot of underlying issues, and generally the smaller [capitalisation] listed...clients have these problems where they've gone from less [regulation] up to all these regulations they have to meet...so that can happen. And...some people...do feel threatened, and occasionally it does come through.

One of the participants, in an exchange that reveals that some client staff receive bonuses linked to minimising required audit adjustments, then volunteers:

> I've got a couple of clients...[whose] bonuses are directly linked to [adjustments].

This participant is not alone in his or her experience. An observation is made by another interviewee:

> [T]hey get quite funny and try and get rid of all of [the adjustments].

From another comes the comment that:

> They chase you out the room.

And from another:

> Usually they do a better job, but at the same time they can get quite pig-headed with an adjustment...so if they get seven audit adjustments they get X amount of the bonus.

Another then comments:

> I've got clients whose bonuses are linked to the audit overruns, so if there [are] overruns on the job then it comes—directly proportional [to their] bonus.

This scheme applies to the person below the CFO. General discussion then follows about how many of their clients' bonus schemes are linked to profit and how lucrative these bonuses can be.

6.1.1 Summary

The younger audit staff generally believe that having high levels of client knowledge is appropriate and necessary for the execution of a high-quality audit. How to begin involves reading the previous file, talking with the various people who have been involved with the audit previously, whereas knowledge of new clients comes from site visits, talking with the people and detecting the key drivers within the business. There is also discussion about understanding the organisational politics within the client.

Several people comment that the level of staff turnover removes understanding of many of the 'soft issues' of a client—that is, organisational politics and individuals, their temperament, their expertise and the interrelationships between key executives.

In the case of a new client, having previous experience on clients in the same industry is seen as a real positive in gaining client-specific knowledge.

Several of the younger people comment that the lead-in to a new client is well managed by their firms, with entire teams having 'initial mobilisation time' to help them understand the client, the issues, the risks and the way the audit is expected to be approached. Others report that they have little time to understand a new client and it is very much a matter of learning on the job.

One interesting conflict between the expectations of the auditors and the clients does arise. There is a very strong view that the ultimate objective from the junior auditors' perspective is ensuring that one understands the client at the end of the audit. As will be seen in Chapter 8 (retention of staff), however, clients repeatedly comment that they expect the auditors to understand their client from the time that they begin on-site visits. This schism is understandable and probably exacerbated where a particular audit firm has been in a multiple-year engagement, because the client's expectations are that the same audit firm has been around for some years and therefore it should know the client, whereas the individuals working on the audit team might be new to the engagement.

Importantly, junior auditors report that the accounting staffers of at least some clients are remunerated with bonuses based on the number of audit adjustments required. This poses an important threat to the quality of an audit.

All of the junior staff members report that the audit firms have important databases and information sets about industries and sometimes even clients. This tends to be the larger listed clients, however, and there is something of a dearth of information about the smaller clients, which in some cases includes a substantial part of their portfolios.

6.2 Industry expertise

The conversations with the peer focus groups of more junior auditors encompassed the issue of industry expertise as well as client-specific knowledge. What follows is the gist of these conversations.

First, there was general agreement that industry expertise was important.

> [Industry expertise is] vital—[the] same as client knowledge. You can't fully understand the risks of a client or...of clients in that industry if you don't understand what's happening in the industry and...the key balances. You can't understand the risks and therefore where your potential [risk is] going to be and where to focus your time.

> [Industry expertise is] quite important because sometimes auditing is all about commonsense. You will know whether it's reasonable or not. If you do not have industry knowledge you wouldn't know. It's really important.

> [Y]ou have different accounting standards for different industries... which means you would have different auditing techniques for different industries. That makes sense.

> [It is important to have industry expertise] because when you're at the client they...expect you to know how to account for things. If

> you're doing funds for fund managers, they expect you to know the related accounting standards for that area and if you're doing all sorts of things, I don't think you'll get the same experience or knowledge.
>
> I had [a foreign exchange] guy working on one of my jobs, which was a manufacturing firm, and...I had to do his inventory. I gave him one of the smaller divisions and I had to do the inventory section for him because he just did not have the skills to do it. But... he said it straight away so it wasn't an issue, but the fact is that he needed that skill to be able to do that section. And if I went to one of his clients and tried to do a hedge fund, I'd struggle.

When pressed about the issue of industry expertise and how it is acquired, the following comments are made:

> The critical issues that our clients come upon are more to do with the size of their industry, so that's why...[they are] grouped [according to] size. So it...[is] difficult to [know the] industry...there are a lot of documents that we fill out which cover industry knowledge and competitors and so there's basically a quick snapshot of our company and where they sit in the business that you basically try and pick up as quick[ly] as you can...if you're spending two or three weeks on an audit, which is pretty standard for us, and spending two or three days getting your head around the industry and knowing everything about it, it's a pretty inefficient expense of time, so it's a matter of getting it done as quick[ly] as you can.
>
> Often the partners aren't [knowledgeable] because they're not working so many jobs. They do have a lot of industry knowledge specific to that client and...even the senior managers and the managers...take a lot of time to read the review so they're up to date with what's going on.
>
> The more you work on, let's say...the consumer markets, you start to get the general understanding...[that] they are doing a fairly similar thing, they're marketing things to people, they're selling things to people so you know that if they're selling cosmetics or alcohol or bread...[there are] the same sort of drivers...the same process is driving what these people do. It just happens to be a different product, but if you're...comparing bread and banking, it's two very basic needs but [it's] very different in what drives them.

Another, in response to the above observation, adds that there are 'very different risks and different regulations as well':

> You need to know. It's not because they expect more from us in terms of just applying the audit standards, there are other aspects… because the bread manufacturer also has to apply health standards and…if they don't apply those quality standards they can…become a going concern problem. Then there [are] the banking licences and it just goes on.

The interviewer then asks: 'How is that knowledge getting captured in the audit process?'

> [B]efore you start, you have a plain reading [document] and every person on the job comes in, including the partner, and they'll discuss what key risks they think have come out of industry changes from the year before, and they'll let you know.

The interviewer then asks how long the meeting is that is held at the beginning of every audit:

> [It] depends on how big and how many people.
>
> Between an hour and a couple of days.

The interviewer then asks whether the firm has a database on industries:

> Yeah, it does—not so much a database, but there [are] lots of technical releases and industry-specific releases that get sent out.

Then the interviewer asks about who is responsible for making sure the industry-specific releases are captured within the audit process:

> [T]he whole team, generally. It would normally be the manager or senior, but sometimes the partner will grab them and send them around to the team as well.

The interviewer asks whether there are other ways that interviewees think they can gain industry expertise:

> [I]t's difficult because we're all in so many different industries. I have three clients and they're [in] three completely different industries.
>
> One thing that they are introducing just recently is they're going

> to have these...seminars on certain industry errors...real estate and consumer products and that sort of thing, which is almost voluntary, you can go to one if those if you've got time.

The interviewer probes more deeply, asking whether being across different industries is frustrating:

> I find it better. I like...variation. They're three completely non-related industries [that I am in]. In any way, shape or form, you couldn't connect the dots between them. So every time I go to a new client I have to learn about that industry...it's difficult to get industry knowledge when you have a different industry on every client. Because really it's client knowledge as well that you need, so you need to link the two together.
>
> [I]t's very broad. Financial services is very broad so you've got your banking, funds management, insurance, treasuries, superannuation, so there [are] 10 specific areas within [that].
>
> [W]hen you come in as a graduate, you...have a broad range across the different industries and after you've been here for about a year or two, you're given a choice to...specialise in [one] industry or two.
>
> [I]t's getting that perspective on different clients which...gives you that industry perspective rather than that single-client perspective.
>
> [You] always struggle [with industry expertise in the middle market]...you'd hope to have at least a broad understanding. You have a higher demand so you should, in the majority of cases, be able to get an idea of what the major risks are just by that high level of understanding. But...there are some risks that you might miss if you don't have that detailed level of understanding.
>
> [T]he smaller companies are an industry in themselves...so even though they're spread across actual industries in terms of what they do...maybe the risks associated with that size of company is why there's a division, which is allocated rather than just picking the right thing out.

There is confirmation of the interviewer's observation that industry is quite narrowly defined:

> We have people who specialise in the superannuation industry, for example, because there [are] a lot of specific regulations...[from] accountants right through [*in response to a query about at which level this applies*].

The interviewer then summarises: 'So, what they're saying is just because the ASX has a bunch of industry categorisations, it doesn't make it necessarily relevant within the audit market...The differentiation is across sides.' There is some agreement with this:

> I never actually thought of it that way...[that] the middle market has its own inherent risks and knowing that as its own industry is its own benefit.

> I'd feel more comfortable if...I could specialise in an industry within [the] middle market.

> [W]e have business development groups within our group...I'm in resources services and government, so we have about eight different industry groups and I'm in the property group because that's what I specialise in and there [are] probably eight or 10 people in a BD [business development] group and we meet once a month and we talk about potential new clients and stuff. So it's a way of going out and sourcing new clients and servicing the ones that we've already got, but it's also [that] we have industry-specific training in those times as well. And...the people in the BD group will...receive any of the publications that we receive that are industry specific.

The interviewer asks: 'Are there any other ways of inculcating industry knowledge that the firm does not use that you can think of?'

> [I]n other offices...they have a lot more specialised industry knowledge, like industry training sessions that go for days...but they're not used by all of the offices...each of the offices...tends to be quite discrete in terms of the training, industry specific and just generalised...there could be potentially more sharing amongst different people.

The interviewer then asks: 'Are the offices really run almost independently of each other? It sounds as if there are quite different practices in different offices.'

> By the sounds of that, not only offices but divisions.
>
> [T]raining across the board, although good, could be better and more timely...sometimes, you're not receiving the training that you required until 12 months or six months down the track. [*In response to the comment 'until after you've had to use it':*] Yeah, which is just the nature of the beast in a sense...[that in] a large organisation, you can't tailor it to everyone and everyone...enters at different times.

The interviewer responds: 'So there are some industries where industry expertise is crucial and there are others where really audit expertise is more generic. Is that right? Is that what you're arguing?' There is general agreement:

> Especially in our division...with [state] audit too—we've been divided up into industrial markets, consumer markets, to travel [and so on].
>
> [B]ecause I'm in consumer markets, if I had to go and work in [another] job, I don't think I'd face too many issues in picking up. It might take me a day or two to get up to speed with whatever the specialisations are...and that's the same with a...partner, probably even less time. But to go from consumer markets to financial services would be a completely different kettle of fish. I'd have to get up to scratch on whatever standards these guys focus on.

6.2.1 Summary

There is widespread agreement among the more junior staff members that industry expertise is a crucial component of the quality of a good audit. Observations were made that with different applicable accounting standards requiring different audit judgments, knowledge of the industry and the regulatory aspect around it was crucial. One of the benefits of higher-quality levels of documentation occurs when staff turns over and, even with partner rotation, good documentation can assist with understanding the client as well as industry expertise.

It is acknowledged that there are wide differentiations in the amount and nature of expertise required by certain industries. Clearly, an industry such as financial services is regarded as requiring a high level of industry expertise, and there is a view that there are other industries that have aspects that are particular to them—for example, industries subject to regulation other than conventional business regulation. An example is the healthcare industry. Indeed, for this industry, an auditee might have critical going concern issues not because of corporate regulation but because of health regulation issues. Aside from where there are high levels of regulation, there is a general belief that understanding the audit process can be transferred from one industry to another.

It is widely acknowledged that firms are providing high levels of industry training (perhaps at the cost of further specific technical auditing training). This means that people from a number of divisions or a number of offices can take part in the same industry training to build their expertise on an industry-level basis rather than on a technical basis. Most people tend to view it as beneficial to have a portfolio of clients that are in one or two industries as it helps build industry expertise. It means that one understands the risks of the industry better and indeed helps in terms of understanding client knowledge. This view is not seen so much in divisions that look at the middle market, where there are large numbers of clients across many industries.

There is a view that much of this training is helpful but it could be better. There are several observations about the level of relevance of some of the industry training and, in particular, its timeliness. The extent of training seems to depend somewhat on the client base with which one is working.

There are a small number of people with a wide variety of different industries included in their portfolio of clients. While some indicate a degree of frustration with this, it is seen as a positive to the individual's working environment because it provides interest through variety.

7.0 Issues and implications

One of the major changes in the business of auditing has been the development and marketing of industry expertise by both Big Four and non-Big Four audit firms and the recognition by some purchasers and regulators of the importance of industry expertise, particularly in selected industry sectors. With respect to survey data relating to the question about whether external financial statement audits were of value because of 'the specialist industry expertise of the auditor', the most positive of the groups was suppliers, with 50 per cent of them rating this as valuable. A similar proportion of users and a more modest proportion of slightly less than one-third of purchasers responded affirmatively to this question. Among the suppliers, there was a sharp differentiation between Big Four and non-Big Four auditors on their level of agreement, with more than three-quarters of Big Four auditors believing industry expertise brought value compared with less than half of non-Big Four auditors.

The interview data showed a complex set of circumstances around the views of purchasers and suppliers in particular. There was widespread acknowledgment that auditors sought to develop and apply a sound understanding of the clients' business (client knowledge) as a part of the delivery of a quality audit. Despite the fact that a number of users saw industry expertise as adding value, there was scepticism, with some users taking the view that for some industry expertise there was less underlying substance (and development of knowledge) than marketing of such expertise.

Purchasers recognise that knowledge of a client's products—that is, the products of the industry in which the client is engaged—is crucial to the audit because this is where understanding the risks of the business will lie. Others see industry expertise as being a crucial factor in the selection by a purchaser of an auditor, implying that value is added and provides the audit firm with an advantage in that selection process. While there were positive comments with respect to audit firms having industry expertise, there was also recognition by purchasers that auditors needed to rely on industry expertise from those outside the profession and indeed that reliance could be substantial. Interestingly, some purchasers see specialist expertise from a different perspective. While the audit firms portray industry expertise as providing specialist knowledge in terms of conducting the audit, this is not necessarily seen as valuable to the client. Some clients identified that an audit firm having specialist accounting standard expertise was of value, implying that the larger audit firms had expertise simply because of the scale of their operations.

Suppliers generally had a more positive attitude towards industry expertise with recognition of a hierarchy of expertise including industry expertise, client knowledge and knowledge of how the business works within the industry. While the positive attitude, particularly among Big

Four suppliers, was evident, there was a genuine concern about how the substantial overhead cost of developing this expertise was funded by client fees. Additionally, there is recognition that much of the 'lower-end work' is routine and is not necessarily industry specific or indeed even engaging. It became apparent that suppliers saw industry expertise as more important among upper-level staff involved in an audit.

The presence of industry expertise, the need for it and value of it represent challenges for managing the rotation of audit partners.

Standard setters appear to be acutely aware that industry expertise is of a much higher value and of more importance in certain industries where there is a significant overlay of regulation, such as in banking and insurance. There is a much lower level of added value in industries that can be audited with more generic skills.

These individuals also acknowledge that even for an audit partner with a high level of industry expertise, the likelihood of that partner having the same high-level expertise as a senior person operating within the industry is not good. On the other hand, they also recognise that bringing someone who works within the industry into the audit firm is not necessarily going to add value to the audit, because of the need for auditing expertise as well as industry expertise.

Finally, some suppliers were quick to point out that having industry expertise was no guarantee that the audit would fulfil all of the users' expectations. For some industries, that expertise might be a necessary but not sufficient condition for an audit that is both comprehensive and far reaching. Overlying this, they concede the need for open and comprehensive communication between the client and the auditor. The overarching view is that industry expertise can be an advantage, particularly in some industries, but the story is more complex than this and purchasers and users, in part, take the view that some of the specialist expertise claims have been over-marketed.

Auditing staff possessing client knowledge prompted less discussion than industry expertise; however, some important issues were raised. These include the mechanisms used to inform audit teams when a new client is acquired and how to familiarise new staff with an existing engagement. Additionally, it is understood that client knowledge might not exist at the start of the engagement but will become a necessary condition of the successful conclusion of each year's audit.

The most important implication of all of this is that those audit firms that develop abilities to familiarise audit teams with client knowledge effectively, efficiently and systematically could give themselves a competitive advantage in the market for audit services.

While referred to only in the focus groups, the apparent presence of bonuses to client accounting staff based on the frequency and/or severity of audit adjustments poses some serious challenges to the environment in which the audit is conducted and potentially to the quality of the audit. There might be good reason to have such a remuneration scheme—such as reduction of errors and opportunistic practices—and it might generally induce greater care on the part of the client; however, there could be unintended consequences that damage the quality of the audit. A remuneration regime such as this could enhance secrecy and obfuscation on the part of the client's management and could circumvent the oversight by senior management, the audit committee and those charged with governance. This will not add to the efficiency of the capital market.

8.0 Concluding remarks

There are policy implications with respect to several matters raised in this chapter. At its outset, this chapter focuses on the development, use and value of industry expertise, client knowledge and business acumen. Each of these plays a role in the demand for and supply of audit services. What emerged also, however, was the extent to which the personal attributes and characteristics of staff assigned to an audit engagement play a role. These attributes include but are not limited to maturity, tenacity, self-assertiveness, resilience and integrity—many of which feed into the notion of 'emotional intelligence'. The existence and development of such attributes appear to have key policy implications with respect to the selection of new employees for audit firms, the training and education before their selection and the professional skills development and training of the accounting professional bodies.

Throughout the interviews, the supply and the demand side of the market for audit services commented on the importance of these various personal attributes. There is, however, little evidence from suppliers that psychological testing to measure these skills is part of the selection process. Additionally, from the authors' own knowledge, the specific development of nurturing and attainment of educational outcomes for these graduate attributes are not uppermost in educators' minds in the construction or delivery of degree programs relevant for the accounting profession. Similarly, the principal accounting bodies do not seem to have these personal attributes as things that are nurtured or tested in professional development courses, at least for those in the early years of their membership of their professional bodies. This is the case even though it is these junior people who are most exposed to the interface with clients. One important policy implication is that the supply side and the professional bodies together with the universities need to examine their recognition of, enthusiasm for and support of the development of these personal attributes. It could be that the inclusion of psychology subjects or at least their encouragement as electives to be taken by commerce and business students during university degrees should be explored.

The fact that junior staffers are so essential to the supply of audit services is a direct function of the business model that the principal and some of the smaller audit firms rely on. This business model requires that junior auditors with modest levels of life experience and, in some cases, self-assurance undertake a large proportion of the work. The sheer size of some of the audit firms and the underpinning cost structure make reliance on this group of individuals key to the commercial viability of this business model and yet reliance on these individuals is clearly a stress point in the operation of the current business model. In some smaller audit markets, where clients do not have the scale of the client base that has been the particular focus of this inquiry, we find that smaller audit firms that have adopted a different business model are becoming successful. For example, small audit firms with comparatively experienced staff and little reliance on junior auditors have often won the audit of local government authorities where this has been outsourced. It is the case that the larger audit firms are the only ones with the scale to successfully undertake many of the audits of Australia's larger business organisations. This business model has been in place for decades and yet many of the interviewees observed that the market for audit services and the products and processes in place have had to undergo profound change and development in recent years. The question is: is the business model still right for the modern market for audit services? Is it the case that such heavy reliance on a large proportion of junior auditors is still applicable? Is it the case that universities produce the optimal type of graduate who has been nurtured and developed in a way that suits the current audit environment?

Another aspect of the business model of audit firms comes from the issue of the acquisition and retention of client knowledge. Finding an effective, efficient and systematic way of acquiring client knowledge in the first place and then passing it on to new audit teams or new members of existing audit teams seem to be crucial and high value-adding characteristics for audit firms. The firm that finds the mechanism for systematically, effectively and efficiently achieving this goal will give itself a significant advantage in the market. We have observed anecdotal attempts at obtaining it, but conclude that there is a higher degree of variability between partners and within firms as to its success.

With respect to industry expertise, there is clear acknowledgment that this is very highly value adding, but only for a limited number of industries. There is also evidence that purchasers are somewhat sceptical, even cynical, that industry expertise is high value adding, seeing it in a number of instances as being 'over-marketed' by accounting firms seeking to argue the existence of a comparative advantage when one does not exist. Care needs to be exercised in marketing industry expertise and in the way that the industry expertise is structured. Do these structures mimic the capital market or are there in fact different structures that can be created because of the nature of the risks of business or the nature of transactions?

Another set of policy issues relates to those who are entrusted with educating the junior auditors of the future. Australia's universities have for many decades had degrees in accounting normally embedded in commerce or business degrees, which have a long history of quality education and development of technical expertise. The development of industry knowledge as well as personal and analytical skills might need to be revisited. For example, it might be possible to develop educational programs that are more theme based (the development of analytical skills and interpersonal skills such as tenacity, self-assertiveness and the like) and these skills might be better brought out in team-based educational experiences and the understanding of the business environment. The development of business acumen might be better developed through case-based study rather than through thematic or topic-based education, which is at the core of most of Australia's educational opportunities in business and commerce—although there are notable, innovative exceptions.

The nature and operation of the supply of audit services and the increasingly compliance-based approach to audits are also having an effect on those who seek to remain within the profession. This issue is dealt with at greater length in a later chapter dealing with retention of staff. One area that is specific to the retaining of the interpersonal characteristics such as maturity and experience also goes to the business model of the audit firms. We see evidence that the firms are unable (or in some limited cases unwilling) to provide employment opportunities for those who want to break away from the traditional full-time (or in some cases more than full-time) employment opportunities. Experience in other professions including law and medicine shows that excellent and highly expert employees are more likely to be retained where flexibility of employment is possible and encouraged.

Finally, there is recognition of the value of client and industry information and yet there is no systematic development of industry-wide databases designed for the use of the audit profession. The existing data tend to be intra-firm rather than Australia wide or generalised. One policy implementation that could be undertaken is the development of a database across the nation divided by industry groups and also geographical distribution, including data that relate to audit, governance and risk issues relevant to auditees within the Australian market for audit services. This important policy development is within the reach of Australia, would give it a structural advantage and provide a comparative advantage for suppliers of audit services and purchasers of those services, as well as adding to the efficiency of the capital market.

An important policy implication for those charged with governance relates to the existence of remuneration schemes that reward the client's accounting staff based on the number or extent of audit adjustments. While there might be good reason to have such bonus schemes, there can be unintended adverse consequences and, as a minimum, the audit committee needs to be aware of the existence of such bonus mechanisms, and guidance on best practice in audit committees should include reference to such disclosures.

Another educational policy issue relates to the auditing firms' demonstrated unwillingness to systematically attract honours degree graduates. As a general principle, some of the most desirable employers in other disciplines seek out and pay a premium to honours graduates. Honours graduates in these fields are widely seen as having advanced attributes including analytical ability, maturity, confidence and self-assertiveness—characteristics that we understand are desirable in junior auditors. Work that fulfils the higher intellectual capacity of honours graduates needs, however, to be available if more recruitment of them takes place. As a side benefit, some of those encouraged to remain for the honours year might decide to join the ranks of accounting/auditing academics—a field with insufficient recruits in an ageing workforce.

ATTRACTING AND SUPPORTING STAFF 7

> But that's [staff turnover] okay in a sense unless they want to grow their firm because they don't actually want everybody to come up to partner level...maybe they'd like greater retention, but then they'd have to grow their business to satisfy that retention. So the model is actually a good model from a talent-flow point of view...It's...still...a fantastic...ground to learn...the job of a young professional, particularly up to manager level. They learn about companies, they learn about communication, they learn how to argue their case, they learn how to document, they learn how to think on their feet. Now those are all personal development things, but what about value to society? The answer is there is still value to society because even though there may be only 1 per cent or 2 per cent [audit report] qualifications...that level [of learning] is always there for the partner. If the partner of the firm is not satisfied with the explanations that are given, he or she ends up having to put that down on paper. Now firms...are more prepared to support their partners in arriving at difficult, contrary decisions because their business model is at stake.
> — Purchaser

1.0 Key issues

The issue of attracting and retaining staff within the public accounting profession raises some serious challenges for the profession, including:

- is the common perception that the number of accounting major graduates available for recruitment is falling factually based or a myth
- what is the position for recruitment of international students who graduate with an accounting qualification

- do high university entrance scores for some commerce and business degree courses mean that recruits to the profession are not suited to it
- are there further alternative entry pathways to the auditing and accounting professions
- are there better ways of developing personal attributes, including communication skills, that might be of use in the supply of audit services—both during and after university study
- to what extent are the starting salary levels within the auditing and accounting professions a deterrent to attraction of staff
- has the lure of partnership lost its gloss as an attraction to the profession
- has growth in the number of chartered accountants through the CA in commerce program undermined the traditional entry path through public accounting
- to what extent is the training provided to new recruits to public accounting firms valuable to them
- is the performance appraisal system in place once new recruits join constructive and seen by them as fair?

2.0 Introduction

This chapter deals with the issue of attraction of staff to the public accounting profession and to audit in particular and also support for them once they have been recruited. It synthesises the views of stakeholders expressed during face-to-face interviews and the focus groups with more junior auditors. No survey questions directly addressing the issue of attracting staff to audit firms were included because the preliminary focus groups conducted before design of the questionnaire had made it clear that this issue was complex and not susceptible to investigation via broad survey techniques. This section starts with the interview comments from each of the groups in relation to this important issue for the future of audit and then proceeds to the focus group content dealing with attraction and support by way of training and the performance appraisal system.

3.0 Interviews

No users commented about the attraction of staff so this section begins with the views of purchasers.

3.1 Purchasers

Among the purchasers—who, at the time of the interviews, were facing a skills crisis themselves—there was recognition of the difficulties that public accounting firms faced in attracting (and retaining) staff. There are mixed views on the continuing attractiveness of the profession for luring new graduates:

> [I]t must be a concern for them because...the nice thing about it is, if they're trained by the profession then they become very desirable out there in...companies...attracting high-quality staff? Given their structure...they are right up there. If people are going around the universities and looking to grab talent...a lot of people would still see...the auditing profession as being a good place to start.

There is, however, acknowledgment of the quality of the training public accounting firm staff receive and the attractiveness of those staff to industry and commerce more generally:

> [I]t is a bit of a concern...because...it does affect even internal audits...because we also have [a] problem try[ing] to retain or attract quality staff...especially in the financial service industry, it's just getting more and more concentrated and therefore there's also a little bit of a specialised knowledge required. And they are commanding a bit of a premium to start with. So if we want someone experienced...then we tend to be actually poaching other firms' experience or auditors...unless we're prepared to actually invest the time to train someone who has no experience, so it's becoming a bit of a catch-22. But then the person, once they acquire the knowledge, they're likely to be walking out of the door to go to somewhere else...So where do you invest?

The same purchaser continues, commenting on a perceived image issue from which the profession suffers:

'[N]ow gen Y obviously is the generation we're looking at...and they are the ones who want to be out there and be promoted in two years' time.'

> I'm listening to some of the [audit] partners and also witnessing the fact that they do have quite a bit of staff turnover...to actually retain them is probably...the issue. First of all, the external audit environment is quite harsh...they expect everyone to perform...Some people [who] join will probably naturally leave, but then they walk out with the knowledge as well...at the same time, I do believe both [for] external and internal audit to a large extent, the profession suffers a bit of [an] image issue and...this...hasn't changed...now gen Y obviously is the generation we're looking at...and they are the ones who want to be out there and be promoted in two years' time, for example...Work–life balance is very important on [the] gen Y agenda. Is audit really the image they...want to put on themselves?

The salary levels paid by the public accounting firms are seen as not attractive, with financial rewards easily used to lure staff away from the profession:

'[T]heir problem with staffing is pretty much of their own making.'

> [E]veryone struggles to get good staff. We compete for the same staff as the auditors do. But...the auditors particularly struggle...because they just simply don't pay enough. They're not competitive in the market...for those more junior staff, and there's three years, three to five years of work experience, and a couple of years post[graduate] qualifications.

There is a perception that less accounting majors are being graduated from universities. This perception, however, really has to be challenged when universities are graduating more students—many of them international—from masters and other accounting conversion degrees.

> [W]hen you say the auditing profession, I put into that category my own risk-management assurance group...I have a hell of a trouble staffing that and, unfortunately for them, the source is the Big Four firms, but they can't get them. I can't get them. So there is a skill gap right now. And I don't know what it's like in the unis, whether less people are doing it, less people are interested in going into chartered firms. Whether the [number of] accounting-qualified people that are coming out of universities is dropping...But...the staff aren't there—well, all the people interested in the profession are not there.

Change in the way the CA program is administered is also cited as a reason for the difficulty in accounting firms' attraction of staff. No longer the monopoly province of chartered firms, the CA program can now be undertaken within commerce and industry. This and the attractiveness of the investment banks and similar organisations as employers of choice are seen by purchasers to have detracted from recruitment to the public accounting firms.

> '[B]ecause you can do your CA in commerce, that has removed a fundamental barrier to entry.'

> [Y]ou've got a lot of the investment banks taking on graduates out of uni, right? So, because you can do your CA in commerce, that has removed a fundamental barrier to entry because before the Big Four or the big six, the big eight or all the accounting charter firms had it sewn up. You had to get your charter with the firm. And you had to spend one or two years after you'd completed your exams and then that was the point of peak turnover—supervisor/manager. Now, where you can get CA in commerce…[it has turned some enterprises into] in-source chartered firm[s] and a lot of the senior guys would be partners at any one of the Big Four firms and they work centrally and they service the business. It's an excellent function. They pay very well. They recruit very well. So they are absolutely able to deliver into a training and cadetship-style environment for bright young graduates—not only in that finance area but now in the wider businesses.

Perhaps the most insightful comment from a purchaser is taken from a longer-term reflection on the quality of partners going forward:

> If you don't get the right staff initially, you'll never get the right quality people getting through in the profession to become partners later on.

3.2.1 Summary

No user comments address the issue of attracting auditing and accounting staff. Purchasers understand the problem audit firms have in attracting and retaining quality staff because they experience the same difficulty within their own firms, especially in relation to generation Y recruits. They acknowledge too that they are often the beneficiaries of training provided by the audit firms in conjunction with the professional bodies—particularly the CA program—in that they frequently hire these accounting firm alumni. There is observation that the CA program can now be done from within industry and commerce too.

There are mixed views about the attractiveness of the auditing profession to new graduates, with some citing an 'image' problem or lack of attractiveness compared with employment within banking and finance, but others see it as a 'good place to start'. The salaries paid by audit firms to new graduates are seen as an issue in attracting and retaining staff, with the lure of partnership no longer as attractive since partnership is increasingly eventuating on return to the profession after a stint in industry anyway—at least that is the perception. There seems to be a perception that less accounting graduates are being produced by universities at a time when universities probably have never graduated more people with accounting degrees.

3.3 Suppliers

Suppliers confirm as an issue the 'image' problems of the auditing profession raised by the purchasers. Again, the perception comes through that the pool of accounting graduates out of universities is shrinking at a time of record commerce graduations—many of whom are international students who seek permanent residency and employment.

> '[W]e also have a large amount of regulation, and a lot of people look at the audit partners and say, "We don't want to be that."'

> The more fundamental [issue] is about an image of what is the profession in public practice, and getting university students, because… if you look at the demand now out of the Big Four firms for graduates out of university, and you start stripping out and saying, 'Well, how many students are coming out of university with financial business degrees?', you strip away the foreign students who are here on a visa that [doesn't] allow them to stay and work, you take out those people who are really not interested in going into a Big Four, who want to go to merchant banking or to commerce…we're probably at that tipping point with the pool that you're left with; the Big Four will soak [them] up in their entirety…if that situation gets worse because the profession is not an attractive place to go and work or to seek a career longer term, you are going to have significant shortages just in getting the numbers in—forget about retaining

> them...it's a combination of a lot of things, it's a combination of some of the characteristics in the marketplace, it's a combination of...the fact that we do have full employment, we have shortages of accounting professional people, we have fairly sophisticated marketers in offering people opportunities in merchant banking... we also have a large amount of regulation, and a lot of people look at the audit partners and say, 'We don't want to be that'—because it's not an attractive profession.

There is a belief that prospective accounting students view the audit profession as a career in which information is gathered rather than one in which doing something with information is required.

> '[M]aybe the commerce degrees and business are [not] the degrees of choice that they might have been some time ago.'

> [I]f they find that they are interchanging with themselves that...whoever can follow a set of instructions could perform their role, then they become less valuable.... in an environment where it's called a finance or forensics [function], or somewhere where you have to exercise a fair degree of judgment and you negotiate, and you *do* rather than you get information...that's how a lot of prospective accounting students view the audit profession...I'm not sure, but maybe the commerce degrees and business are [not] the degrees of choice that they might have been some time ago.

Another supplier believes that fewer undergraduates are undertaking the prerequisites to complete the CA program:

> '[O]ur pool of potential candidates is actually shrinking.'

> [T]he attraction is an issue and, for various reasons... there are less people doing the prerequisites for their CA, so we've got less people in our pool of potential candidates...the options are broader so fewer people [are] doing that. Actually the overseas student numbers, because they've increased and not all of them have residency status...we're losing out because of that as well. So our pool of potential candidates is actually shrinking. The unis in Melbourne also...some of them do the audit module in the third year...and we recruit in the beginning...some are second year, so that candidates haven't necessarily studied audit when they apply and...that's an issue for some of them.

The way in which auditing is taught at university is also blamed for reducing its attractiveness as a career, as this next supplier's comments reveal:

> '[T]he ones that have done audit at times think it's dead boring so why would they take that career path?'

> Some of them, if they have studied audit, it's taught in a way that's very old school and it's purely teaching them the auditing standards. It's not helping them see how those standards live and...[does not use] the corporate collapses and debate about what might have gone wrong and trying to make those auditing standards live in the real world, so that the ones that have done audit at times think it's dead boring so why would they take that career path? So, [it's difficult] just to get them in the door, and their career options are much broader...when I was a graduate, for someone that had done a bachelor of business or a bachelor of commerce and was interested in accounting, the natural progression would be [to] join one of the Big A's chartered firm...[but] because the opportunities are much more diverse now, with being able to do CA in industry for instance, or doing the CPA and forgetting the CA, the number of people...going into the big firms is probably less, the pool that [is available] is [smaller] as well. And there [are] the generational issues...do I want to go to a big chartered firm and work long hours? And some still see that if you go to a big firm...you must have a passion to be partner.

Suppliers also acknowledge that the myriad other opportunities for graduates and trained public accounting staff contribute to the attraction issue:

> Interestingly enough, we find it very difficult to recruit ex-Big Four people because they are just burnt out. So that's a problem. And... there [are] so many different opportunities out there now, it's amazing, absolutely amazing. And there are some really good jobs out there... in industry, and really attractive stuff for them to go to. So...once auditing...starts to lose its flavour, they start looking around.

Some suppliers draw attention to the increasingly prescriptive nature of a highly regulated audit profession as a deterrent to attraction:

> [T]he grad comes in the front door, which is always the audit door, and then goes out the back door, which is business services and tax consulting and so on, and then goes into industry and commerce

> and makes a fortune. Audit's generally been regarded as being very much a training ground and then once you get your CA you branch out into the more exciting areas of a practice...audit's a great space to be in and I really enjoy it, but...we're finding it more and more difficult to convince grads that audit [is] a good place to be in because they think it's a training ground...it's harder to keep auditors inspired because of the prescriptive nature of the work—particularly if they're not signing off the audit.

> [A] general observation would be that clearly all of the stakeholders involved would like talented, intelligent individuals in the audit firms for... the quality of [audit], what it means to the capital markets [and] reliance on the financial information...all stakeholders—be it the regulators, the government, the actual companies, the shareholders—everybody wants...talented, intelligent people doing it...[There is a risk] with too much regulation...yes, we've got a role to play, but we're client facing, client serving, you're going to attract different types of individuals. And the risk...is that you lose your ability to attract talented, intelligent people when all they're going to be doing is filling in check lists and completing [them]. And that...in a holistic sense, is one of the biggest issues facing [attraction]—you've got to have the talented people...you've got to attract them and you're not going to attract them if they're going to be filling in check lists and just following rules.

'[T]he risk...is that you lose your ability to attract talented, intelligent people when all they're going to be doing is filling in check lists.'

This issue of the increasingly prescriptive nature of audit and the extent to which this issue has implications for attraction of audit personnel are explored further in reporting on the focus group interviews held with more junior audit staff.

3.3.1 Summary

Several suppliers make pejorative comments about the attractiveness of auditing as a profession to enter. The increasingly prescriptive, check list-type nature of audit work is cited as one reason for this fading attractiveness. Again, as with purchasers, suppliers hold the misinformed view that there must be less people with accounting majors emerging from universities. The issue of how auditing is taught at university and at what stage in their degrees this subject is taken relative to the firms' recruitment cycle emerge as other potential issues in the attraction debate. Also raised are generational issues, the potential long hours of work and a fall in passion to become a partner.

3.4 Standard setters

The standard setters interviewed raised the interesting issue of university entrance scores and whether those students with high scores were necessarily the 'right' recruits into the accounting profession. Not all university accounting courses, however, have high-scoring entrants, so if this is an issue for the profession it is a soluble one. This standard setter speaks of more lateral entry paths to the profession through bridging courses for non-accounting graduates as an alternative:

> [I]f we had...a TV show like *Chicago Accountant* instead of *LA Law*, that might make [the profession] a little bit more glamorous, but...a lot of the more senior people in the firms would say...the ability to be this trusted advisor doesn't exist as much now in auditing... because we're telling people that auditors can't have friends. They've got to be adversarial...That's relevant to a point. I wouldn't overstate it, but...to...attract good people we've got to offer good careers and good career prospects otherwise the danger is that...it's a race to the bottom in attracting the lowest common denominator... [so] something that does make sense...is being able to run multidisciplinary firms which offer career choices for people...The other thing is the quality issue that...is being discussed with some of the unis at the moment and different people would have different views...a concern for me is...the determination of [university entry scores, which] is effectively being driven by demand. [It] doesn't necessarily mean you're getting the right people into the right courses.

The same standard setter continues, expanding on what he or she hears in the marketplace about the lack of skills found in new graduates:

> What...amplifies that as well is the experience of some of the senior partners...saying the people that we're hiring just aren't good with clients. They can't deal with people. They're very much...book driven...Do they have the people skills...whether it's emotional intelligence [or something else]...we would like to attract some

> 'What...amplifies that as well is the experience of some of the senior partners...saying the people that we're hiring just aren't good with clients. They can't deal with people. They're very much...book driven.'

slightly different people with the base skills... the Big Four firms have got a good name and a good reputation in terms of a place to go as a graduate, so perhaps we need to be more discerning then as to who we seek to get in... you don't just want people there who've got credit greater or distinction averages and they've got 95. Maybe we need to be more discerning. But they're not coming through as rounded [is what]...people would say is the other area that's a concern...one of the solutions to that is... widening the funnel. You can start the CA program with the institute now from a non-accounting background, but you've still got to do a conversion course and so effectively notwithstanding that you followed one line through your university degree, you've then got to stop, bridge and get into it. But that's one of the alternatives that...we're following. Whether that'll be popular, I don't know, but that's tended to be the way the [United Kingdom] has worked for as long as I know that people have done that conversion course.

They could come in from somewhere else. The question then becomes, why would they leave what they were doing...and you may get people moving from one country to another because of the cultural difference and the opportunity, but the upside for them is the move to the new country. The question then becomes, how long do they stay in the profession [before they]...move on to something else and use it as a springboard to another area of the financial world?

You need...bright [people]; they don't need to be the best; it's not rocket science. You need people with good communication skills... fairly good thinking skills, but not necessarily high-level academic skills. I don't think you necessarily need those at all.

There is also recognition of the need for systematic research by public accounting firms of the outcomes of their selection methods.

I don't think we're particularly good at analysing our selection methods and looking back through history...to say, 'Well, if we actually look at how things transpire, does that tell us something about what we should be looking for and even when we know

> what we're looking for, which we do...are we seeing it [as] the real issue?'...quite often, what you're looking for you think you're seeing and then you're quite surprised six months to a year later when these individuals no longer seem to be demonstrating what you thought you saw in your somewhat superficial assessment processes.

3.4.1 Summary

Standard setters raise thought-provoking issues related to the skills and academic calibre of recruits to the profession. They lament what they perceive as the lack of sound communication skills and argue that the academic skill level required to work successfully in the profession probably could be reduced below the current level implied by university entry scores.

3.5 Regulators

The one regulator commenting on this issue maintains the theme of the relative unattractiveness of auditing as a career and perceptions of diminishing accounting graduates:

> I don't think they're going to be attracted to auditing, quite frankly... They'll want to be merchant bankers or something like this, or managers...a key indicator of that is...the number of accounting graduates...versus management graduates in universities.

3.5.1 Summary

Only one regulator commented on the issue of accounting firm staff attraction—and the comment reiterated perceptions common to the purchaser, supplier and standard setter groups in terms of a denigration of the attractiveness of a career in auditing to new graduates and a perceived reduction in the pool of graduates available to be recruited.

4.0 Introduction: focus groups with more junior staff

The focus groups of more junior staff were working in the offices of the Big Four. For this group, attraction to the auditing profession was fresh in their minds while how they entered the profession, why they were focused on obtaining useful professional and business experience, international experience and credible professional training supported by an employer varied.

4.1 Focus group participants and recruitment to their firms

In terms of recruitment and selection, for the first Big Four firm, most had been recruited out of university, but one had started as a temp and one had worked overseas for the same firm. Most had started in audit, but one had moved from the finance department to audit. All but one had come to the firm with accounting degrees; one had a finance major. Two of the second Big Four firm focus group interviewees came straight from university, but the other five had been recruited between second and third year of university into a graduate program. None had joined into a cadetship program after Year 12. Of the eight taking part from the third Big Four firm, two began after Year 12 through a cadet scheme and undertook university part-time for two years and then a third year of study full-time, working during vacations. One came from a non-Big Four firm. Four had come straight from university—one with experience of three placements during the degree, including one with the current employer. Finally, one had worked overseas for a Big Four for a year and a half during an Australian-based degree and had then returned to Australia.

Interviewees provided various reasons for their recruitment to their Big Four employer:

> I applied to most places but [this Big Four firm] was the quickest in answering letters and getting you into interviews and giving you the job. The rest were still doing the interview process.

> [This Big Four firm] was the only one that offered me [a place], so that was the only offer I got.

> I got a couple of offers, but I chose [this Big Four firm because] I didn't like the attitude of the people down the road.

> I went through the summer clerk program, so I worked, I applied for that at all the Big Four [firms] and received a few offers, but decided that I liked the people and the clients as well at [this Big Four firm] in the area [in which] I wanted to work.

Those present were then asked whether they felt that the Big Four firm for which they worked had made the right recruitment choices from among them compared with others they knew who had not been recruited.

> [G]enerally the calibre of people they recruit is really high... probably there [are] people who, for whatever reason, have... slipped through the net, like people they never made an offer to who I...was surprised [about] and remain so even having met who was recruited.

The interviewees were asked whether there was any defining thing that differentiated their chosen firm from other firms or any audit firm from other employment choices open to them as graduates.

> I wanted an international experience. I'm from [location outside Australia] so one of the Big Four was what I felt [was] the easiest way for me to get that opportunity and I have been able to [get it]... That was why I chose a Big Four, but...I always wanted to go into accounting.

> My Dad was an ex-auditor and he used to work for [name of firm] and he recommended me to join the Big Four...The range of opportunities in the Big Four office was one of the key drivers why I came to [this Big Four firm], plus my brother is an accountant, and when I was at uni I was looking forward to working for the Big Four...so that was partly the reason why I came here. But upon coming to [this Big Four firm], my plans have...changed. I'm looking...more overseas...getting overseas experience, which I will do here...when [I] finish...[my] CA.

> I decided when I was at uni that I wanted to...work...for a professional services firm, whether it was a merchant bank or a Big Four accounting firm. I didn't want to go commercial and the reason I chose a Big Four was because [of] the opportunities and [this Big Four firm] offered also at the time the internal training for CA.

> I was already working [for this Big Four firm] as I finished my uni degree, so I thought I'd throw [in] my hat...I thought it would be easier to transfer than go through the whole process of applying and all that and, as it turns out, they still made me jump through all the hoops.

> [I joined for] the experience. I thought the experience that you would get working with a Big Four accounting firm would be great, like the training, [and] the exposure.

> [*In response to whether a non-accounting firm job was considered*] Well, not really...I considered it, but when I was doing vacation work, I thought it's a good place to start, to get a feel[ing] for [it]...I wasn't quite set on what exactly I wanted to do and I thought auditing would give you some exposure to a broad range of different things.

> [I]n audit you get to see different industries and then in the future if you want to move somewhere you can say, okay, I like financial services.

> [W]hen I was applying for jobs I got offered...work in a mid-tier firm and obviously a Big Four firm and I chose [this Big Four firm] because I thought it looks good on your resume and because it's a Big Four everyone knows [it]...And then I also got offered [a place] at another Big Four, but in tax, and I thought tax would pigeonhole me, so I...[chose] audit.

> [I]t's relatively easier to go into [a] Big Four than to go into those commercial firms. I'm not saying that Big Four has less demanding requirements, but they have huge demand for people...I'm not sure about Australia, but back in [location outside Australia], we have new graduates—almost 100 to 200 per year—and it's impossible for those commercial firms...You've got more opportunities and [the Big Four] need people.

The group was then asked: 'Why did you join this firm as opposed to other Big Four firms? Why did you pick the Big Four versus the others?'

> I...picked the Big Four from a training point of view. You probably get more opportunities to get training and support there as well [as] future travel and that kind of thing. [It was a] bit of a matter of elimination with why I ended up with [this Big Four firm]...my

> dad worked at [another of the Big Four], so I didn't want to go there…I had a couple of mates that were [at another of the Big Four] and weren't overly happy with it, and…you start thinking if you're going to go Big Four, you may as well go big, Big Four. That's why I chose [this firm] initially.
>
> [My decision] was more…that I left applying…[until] very late, and [this Big Four firm] was the only one that was still open…So I applied and then I got a job, and my sister used to work here, and she enjoyed it, so I got feedback from her, and she's a pretty honest person, and I thought it would be a good place to work.
>
> [T]he reason that I stay is—or stayed till now—what I enjoy about it, [as] opposed to other accounting career paths, is that there is a clear career path set out, and clear progressions set out along the way. So you've got a defined plan of where you're actually heading, and where you could end up…[as] opposed to [being] in industry, where you could just float about at the same level for a while; it's not as clear. And then…the other thing that's attractive about it is the training that's provided, and the exposure to so many different issues.

There is general agreement in response to an interviewer prompt that the level of training and support for the CA program is high:

> [T]here's a good structure that you can follow, and there [are] just opportunities for anyone and everyone. If you told me that I'd be working directly with a partner in my first year, when I first started…I wouldn't have believe[d] it…when I first went through this process of selecting, I was in a fortunate position…selecting which firm to choose. [This Big Four firm] presented probably the best [opportunity] because of the people—I identify with the people. And you know you've made a good decision when you meet other people from…not even in the same division, on a very divisional basis…But if you're out and about, obviously I know [others in the group] from the graduate camps that they have. And you hold those friendships the whole way through, so it's the people aspect as well that keeps you here. It's not just the small group of people you're in contact with eight hours a day; it's outside of that as well.

Reputation was a very big [issue] for me...It was firm specific rather than going straight down the line of wanting to be an auditor. That was a big factor as well...For me, coming out of university, it was all about getting the best opportunities and...the bigger the firm and the better the reputation, there was going to be more opportunities from within not just an audit field, but a whole sector and that's one of the main reasons I came.

[W]hat links closely with that too is clients and the client base that [this Big Four firm] has [as] opposed to some of the other firms. And obviously one of the benefits of being in audit is the ability to see a wider range of firms. So if you can see what the best firms are doing...that's certainly a contributing factor.

I've...done a double degree in Arts/[Language] and then also majored in accounting on the business side and my university set up a placement for a year up in [name of company]. But I was more an 'explorologist'—it's that kind of role, but also working with a few chartered accountants and it was from that that I realised that probably going into chartered first after my university degree would give me some more opportunities to get more technical knowledge and understand how other businesses operate. So from that I decided that chartered was what I wanted to do.

[W]hen I was in high school...[I] wanted to go into law and that had been my plan...since I was about three years old...[I] did work experience with [this Big Four firm] when I was in Year 11, and I had also done work experience at a couple of law firms as well. I originally...only applied for the traineeship for interview experience, but when I got in, I thought well, I've got three months before I start my degree so I'll give it a go and I found with my three months at [this Big Four firm], and the same with the work experience that I did, compared with the law firms that I was working at, I found it was just a much better environment...It was a lot friendlier...there was much more of a team-focused kind of environment...I only saw two different law firms, but the focus really seemed to be very much individualised and it was more competitive against each other rather than working as a team to get things done. And I much preferred the kind of environment and the culture that I saw at [this Big Four firm] and that's what made me switch focus.

[I]nitially, the choice was part of my course. I ended up at [name of industrial company]...I was working in the general audit there. Then I worked at [another of the Big Four firms], where I also ended up in audit...and then I ended up in audit here and basically...that suited me just fine because...I wanted to...understand how all these big businesses work...and then why did I choose [this Big Four firm]? I pretty much chose [it] because when I was working here as opposed to the other Big Four firm. I just found the team to be friendlier and the hours I was working [were] a bit more reasonable, and that...was the only point of difference in terms of the work you're doing. It's fairly similar.

I chose Big Four because I thought that's where I'd get the best experience. I had quite a few different offers, so then it was a decision as to which firm I go to. And it came down to pretty much attend[ing] the cocktail parties and getting to know people and I found that the people at [this Big Four firm] were very friendly and were the best fit for me. And I was also very impressed with the client base and found that from those clients I'd get a really good experience and auditing is definitely an area where, as other people touched on, you get to see how different companies operate and you get a really good understanding.

When I was at uni I was working part-time at a manufacturing company in their accounts department and we had the auditors come in and...just speaking to them and the work that they did... [made me decide] to go into audit just for that whole experience and getting to see how other companies work rather than doing the same thing day in, day out.

[I]t was a...toss-up between industry and a Big Four accounting/ auditing role. Either I go into industry, I'd do the same thing day in, day out for the next year...before I'm promoted to the next level and then I do that role for another year or two before I get promoted. So...just the challenges that auditing would provide... the learning curve is very different to what you'd get if you were in industry. That's probably why I joined audit.

The interviewee who had moved from a mid-tier firm had the following to say:

> [T]he ease of the graduate recruitment program was a lot easier at mid-tiers and it was a lot more friendly so you got to meet a lot of partners and managers because they're the people you're working for. And I looked into maybe one or two top tier but then chose [name of mid-tier firm] as my first preference.

4.1.1 Summary

A number of purchasers make the observation that recent changes giving more diversity to graduates entering the profession have been good and have worked elsewhere in the world for some time. There is no real issue with respect to quality control in the profession because of the professional examinations, which are seen as the 'barrier' to entry. There are a number of diverse views about training and the relative attributes of training within the Big Four versus commerce. One interesting set of comments relates to the widespread belief among purchasers and suppliers that initial training within a typical large accounting firm is a highly efficient and effective way of attaining a widespread, diverse set of experiences that are useful in developing the foundations of a career in accounting and, more broadly, in business. The training and experience beyond say, the first five years, however, shows a more divergent set of views. For example, some take the view that several years in commerce after those initial foundation years are preferable because of the deeply embedded industry experience one has. Also, the experience of being on the 'receiving end' of interactions with accountants in professional practice assists in developing certain personal attributes for the individuals involved and perhaps their sensitivity to needs and wishes of clients. Thus, the relative benefits of training and experience at different levels within a career are more complex and the quality of that experience is not simply linear.

In terms of the more junior auditors, various reasons are given for their recruitment to the public accounting profession and to the firms for which they work in particular. Many of the reasons appear serendipitous rather than planned, although sometimes there is a connection to auditing through family. There is awareness among participants that their peers are ill informed about what auditing is and its role. Opportunities for training, international travel and secondments are given as reasons for attraction to the profession and to the Big Four in particular.

Having decided to join public accounting, credibility and reputation of the firm seem to be key drivers in the attraction process. Another key driver that arose in the interviews with more junior staff was the importance to them of people. Many report that it is the ability to connect with those in the recruitment process and those within their working environment that is key in both attraction and retention within the accounting profession.

5.0 Issues and implications

Issues that were raised in the context of audit firm attraction of staff included the image of the auditing profession, the work/life balance preference of generation Y, the fact that the CA program no longer had to be completed within a public accounting firm, the attractiveness of other employers (especially organisations such as in banking and finance), the comparatively low initial salary scale, the increasingly prescriptive and regulated nature of auditing, the available pool of graduates from which to recruit and questions about the continued attractiveness of achieving partnership.

In all of the interviews with users, no observations were made about issues associated with those entering into the accounting profession; however, purchasers, suppliers, standard setters and regulators all made observations relevant to the issue.

With respect to purchasers, no acute feelings were evident of the existence of a threat to attracting appropriate talent to the profession, although they acknowledged it was a competitive employment market. A key part of the stability of attraction into the profession is the large graduate intake that accounting firms, big and small, undertake each year. While the numbers of entering students seem to be sufficient, there are questions among some of the participant groups about the quality of these graduates. With regard to purchasers, they had reservations about whether the pool of graduates had, in relative terms, declined. Counter to this, some purchasers observed that members of the Big Four had lost their monopoly position as the training ground for membership of the Institute of Chartered Accountants in Australia because of the presence of the CA program within industry. As one purchaser observed, the large commercial organisations now had such good recruitment, training and development processes that they were equal to at least some of the Big Four.

From this, one can conclude that even though some accounting graduates enter other occupations (banking is by far the most frequently mentioned employment alternative), they are not necessarily lost to the accounting profession, although the Big Four might have lost their relative position in the employment market. A related issue comes from one observer who is a purchaser: recruitment into chartered accounting via the CA in commerce program now has the added appeal of not having the same level of external oversight and inspection as the public practice part of the profession.

On balance, purchasers believe the market is competitive for entry-level accountants and that commerce in a relative sense has some advantages over traditional public practices as the entrance point. Of course, this could change with the conditions in the economy changing so profoundly. Repeatedly, the observation was made that accounting firms simply did not remunerate adequately, so if they did not get the entry-point fundamentals right then significant long-term consequences would ensue and the total pool of professional people, including those with experience at all levels, would decline and atrophy as time passed.

With respect to suppliers, more questioning ensued about the total pool of graduates available for recruitment. Frequently, observations were made that the total pool seemed to be either small or at a 'tipping point'. Once one takes into account international students without the appropriate visa to work in Australia and those who choose to go into industry, commerce or banking, the pool of students available for audit is too small.

There was extensive belief that auditing was still seen as a good training ground, but there was also a perception that it held less glamour and prestige as a long-term career than it once did. Several suppliers indicated that one of the attractions of the larger employers was that they had multidisciplinary firms that could provide alternative careers to ambitious accounting graduates who sought alternative careers and diverse employment opportunities.

Some suppliers made a number of observations about the accounting degrees that many of the students undertook. First, there is some question about the number of accounting graduates who are completing their degrees and are eligible for employment in Australia. Even if the quantity is the same, many of the students who suppliers interview are seen to have limited knowledge of auditing. Indeed, the way in which auditing is taught is lamented, if it represents a type of education that is procedural in nature (following the auditing standards, for example) rather than thematic (tracing the history of a major corporate failure). Also, the fact that some universities teach auditing in a limited way and very late in the degree means that accounting students applying for entry-level positions in accounting firms have little or no understanding of the nature of auditing. While not directly stated by respondents, one might speculate that the reason why auditing is not taught in the manner suggested is because universities are struggling to recruit academic staff in the quantity and quality necessary for the education process of auditing and its precursor subjects. That is, universities are under similar competitive employment pressures for their staff as are accounting firms.

Standard setters made the observation that accounting did not have the glamorous profile it once had and this in turn was a challenge to recruitment into the profession. A related fact is that the profile and prestige of accounting are declining, as observed by one standard setter: 'It is no longer possible for the auditor to be the trusted advisor.' This has damaged the public perception, profile and professional image of auditing. There is also acceptance that many entry-level people of today's generation are seeking multidisciplinary careers that are diverse and challenging.

Again, there were questions about the degrees that were used as entry points to auditing and a direct assertion that consideration could be given to selecting not on the basis of Year 12 entry scores but by utilising a wider set of criteria. In this connection, attention is drawn to the fact that certain other professions, including the medical profession, have broadened their set of criteria. Is it time higher education in business does the same? Additionally, university entry scores are a function of supply and demand. If public accounting firms are more willing to take more graduates from universities without such high entry scores, and are more willing to recruit international students whose working visas are yet to be processed, perceptions of too few willing graduates might dissipate.

While it has been recognised that the existence of conversion courses and foundation programs improves the opportunity of recruiting staff from outside accounting degrees, there is incomplete evidence about whether these programs are sufficiently attractive or of high quality. We need to know if the quality of the educational offering is such that it delivers educational equivalents to traditional pathways so we can judge whether this is a successful way of widening the entry point for those seeking to join the auditing profession.

One standard setter questioned whether firms within the accounting profession tracked their selection choices at entry point to evaluate those who survived, prospered and contributed to the auditing profession in later years. This would represent a substantial longitudinal research study to examine the attributes of those who enter the profession and their contribution to the profession in later years. Parallels of this type of study have been undertaken in the field of sociology on a wider general population basis.

Regulators share the view that accounting is not as glamorous as other employment opportunities and suffers as a consequence. They also suggest that graduates who might be attracted into the accounting profession—particularly auditing—are perhaps being induced into other careers, including banking and business management. Again, this emphasises the need for a substantial longitudinal study beginning in high school and continuing through to post-graduation experience and contribution to the profession.

6.0 Focus group participants: the nature of their work and performance appraisal

It was generally agreed that performance appraisal was a useful experience and that feedback on performance was received, but comments were also made about it being very judgmental and having a few flaws.

> [I]f you work with the same person for the majority of the year and they give you that one review or two reviews for the whole year, you may have a completely different review to someone who works with nine or 10 different people…giving you separate feedback.

> And it depends on your personality. If you get along with someone great guns, and the job's really good, then you get a good review, generally speaking.

> And then you're rated against someone who was rated based on a lower expectation.

When pressed on whether a recalibration took place, there was a negative response and the following specific comments.

> They discuss issues round the table, so they try and get that together.
>
> [P]art of it's quite perception based as well. If the partner's reached a certain perception of somebody, whether or not it's actually supported by a lot of the work...often the partners don't see the detailed work—then that's going to be reflected in their rating and pay as well.
>
> And if you have a job that has no problems...if you have a job where you've got a really good client and they give you things and you tick them in, and it's really good, and you get it done quickly and you don't go over budget...it's easier to get a good review.
>
> [If] things go wrong and they've got a lot of errors and there's a lot...more management needing to come in, then often you won't get a good review, not because of your performance, but because everybody got a lot more stressed.

The interviewer then asks how the good performers are distinguished from the not-so-good performers:

> You get appraised for each job and then we have an annual review process.
>
> Every job over a week we get appraised for.
>
> You do your own personal [appraisal] and then whoever you're directly working with will sit down over a coffee and have a chat... [for] quarter of an hour, half an hour.
>
> But sometimes you don't get to do that straight away—I've got a little bit of a backlog.
>
> I've had times where I've just done five in a row and just got them all over and done with.
>
> They're quite...particularly [in my division]...proactive in doing them, and it's driven from the top down as well so it's an important part of it all.
>
> Our group...has what we call development days. So once a month, except during the busy seasons...we have a day where it's mandatory for everyone to come into the office and we have a couple of group

> meetings...and then there [are] designated times for...probably two hours during the day on a Friday...where you have to just do appraisals and your business plans and you sit down and have [staff development manager] meetings and that sort of thing.
>
> We're not allowed to do any client work...so they've really made... efforts to try and keep us focused.

The interviewer then asks whether progression is pretty much automatic:

> It seems very structured...I don't know what happens in other divisions, but especially with us...after a certain time period, six months, you get up a level, an extra 18 months you go up another level and then it's two and a half years, that sort of thing. It doesn't really deviate at all from that.
>
> [A]t the higher levels...from that point onwards...almost when you get to the manager's level in going up, that's when it's a bit more [centred] on the person.

The interviewer then asks whether there is satisfaction with the appraisal process and whether it is seen as fair and reasonable and helpful for morale and in understanding work performance better:

> Yeah, it does, but I don't think it helps morale that much.
>
> I like the appraisal process, but...the fundamental thing that's missing from the process is setting really clear expectations up front—not just on individual jobs—but there being a really clear communication about what's expected of each level...what you need to be able to do to make it to manager. Just setting expectations...is the main thing that I'm missing.
>
> [S]ome managers do a good job of telling you what they want from your job, but I don't think it's communicated—just generally as a senior accountant [that] this is what you should be doing.
>
> In our division, they...have a guideline that they distribute and it says at this level, at an accountant level, you need to start displaying these qualities, and when you get to senior accountant, you need to be able to show these qualities. So, overall, you get a very good picture of what sort of things you need to be looking at.

[Y]es, we do [get feedback that relates to those guidelines]. A lot of the times we use those and we write objectives for jobs based on those overall performance requirements, so then we can show that we've fulfilled them and we can see how well we've done it.

[I]t can be [good for morale]. It depends on who's writing it...a lot of the time, especially for us [with] lots of smaller jobs...they do tend to focus on the negatives a lot rather than positives and they probably don't write things in a constructive kind of way.

It probably depends on the manager or whoever's writing it as well. Some are better than others.

[*In response to a prompt about whether it depends on the client portfolio:*] I've got a few headache clients, which I'm worried about how it's going to reflect [on me].

[*Defining a headache client:*] I'm up to my eleventh outstanding list and the client not being prepared, the actual accountants at the firm, at the company, and then you go [to] the director saying they still want to meet the...October 31 deadline to ASIC and it's just like making sure...we've got everything documented. It's hard verifying numbers when there [are] no [reconciliations].

[*In response to whether this will affect the appraisal:*] I'm not sure yet. I'll find out.

If I was doing an appraisal for that kind of job...you know that the client is a problem client and I had one that was a shocker earlier this year. The client was badly prepared and [there were] short deadlines and the client was just not really up to the task, but it's more you need to manage it as best you can, to the extent that your level can do that. But if I was going to be appraising someone, I would definitely keep that in mind. You don't blame anyone for what the client does.

You'd think you'd get appraised on the fact that you're able to keep following up on it and trying to make that deadline...I've got a bad client like that as well and I didn't get penalised because of it.

[T]he sign of a good manager or a good senior will be someone who gives you informal feedback throughout the audit rather than just slinging you with a shocking appraisal at the end of it, which you

> had no idea of, instead of giving you chances to improve throughout the audit. And that's what I've found has happened with most of my jobs. I've been lucky.

When asked 'Does your firm do a lot of lateral hiring, or is it mostly in at the bottom and gravitate up?', the following responses were given.

> We have a lot of secondments. We have a lot of secondees...and... that's how we're filling in the gaps. We're not laterally hiring. We're not hiring from another Big Four firm. We're accepting resources from another country and bringing them.
>
> [*In response to 'Are there many people going out the other way?':*] No, not that many. Not nearly as many going out as are coming in.
>
> At my assistant manager level, they're all secondees. Every single one.
>
> Definitely at the manager level as well for us.
>
> A lot of the local resources are leaving by the time they get to [assistant managers] and then...in our division, audit too, we have more secondee assistant managers and at one stage we had more secondee managers than local managers.
>
> [*When asked how long secondments generally last:*] Two or four years usually...There [are] a lot that extend and there might be the slight minority that might...stay here permanently, but the majority come here for the two years, possibly extend for one and then move on.
>
> [I]t might be that they want to get into the country, [have a] better opportunity to maybe get a visa and this is their avenue to get in.
>
> One secondee manager I know told me that the only reason she came here was to see Australia, so [this Big Four firm] paid for that, [for the] costs of her moving here and...when her [secondment] finished she went back.
>
> [I]n my division, financial services, there's been an increased focus on lateral hires. We've had people come in from another Big Four firm at senior management level...and also they've had people come permanently from overseas. Quite a lot of people...[at] a senior or an assistant manager level move permanently from overseas.

Comments on any other issues were invited next.

> [T]here's a difficulty at the moment in getting the right people—at a graduate [level] and whether that's…a few of the competing industries and big organisations are pulling in more people, but… there's certainly a bit of a shortage out there.
>
> [A]t the senior level as well, because our division lost quite a few and they had to go international to try and recruit some seniors because there just wasn't the demand in Australia…We hired a few from India, Europe, Asia.

Pressed more, the interviewees respond that the recruits come from within and outside their firm, and from industry too:

> Which has its own implications because…a lot of those are here for two years, so then they come in for two years and then you lose them. So…in the next couple of years there [are] going to be some real problems because there's a lot of…lost continuity and even though those people are coming through and going…to manager… then they go…I've lost continuity on clients, lost continuity on culture, so that's…a big problem facing the firm in the next five years.

When pressed on why this is so, the interviewees explain that it is the nature of the secondment arrangement:

> Some people stay, but…we had such a shortage with seniors…just on my client alone, we had four seniors come in from the [United States] just for the three months and then they went back…so obviously we have the same problem for next year.
>
> I know people from uni who are having problems getting [jobs]. It's just that they don't know what audit does and what is audit…a lot of my friends, even when I told them, I'm an auditor, they're like 'What's that?' I'm like an accountant and they're like, 'Can you do my tax return?' I'm like, 'I don't do tax returns. I'm an auditor.' They don't know what it is, so getting people into a field where they're so unsure is going to be difficult.
>
> [T]he firm's being really, really proactive with trying to find people…I hear…our people partner or whatever you call him, who's on the phone half the day talking about trying to resource

> staff and finding them from wherever. You can tell they're making an effort; it's just hard.
>
> We get plenty of new grads, [but] they just...tend to disburse. I don't know where they go.
>
> I'm the only one left out of my grad group now in our division. So that's after three and a half years...people disappear so you don't get that continuity.
>
> It's happening before they get to senior as well now.
>
> Before you finish CA as well. People have left...to go into industry and finish off their CA there.

In response to a question about time off in lieu, one of the interviewees responded that the firm used to have it, but ceased doing so about four years ago. The interviewer then asked whether the bad clients had an effect on the work/life balance. There was broad agreement with this proposition:

> [I]t's just because...they've got bookings and if these clients go over and over forever and ever, you're often not booked for when the deadline is...So you're trying to do this work in your own time and you've got a job that you're doing for another client. [*In response to a query about whether this time is booked to the client:*] Oh, no, you charge...but they've got a booking schedule. So it might say this week you're out at this client, but when things go over time—months sometimes—you're still chasing up on that work whilst doing other work. So that's where the work/life balance...can be compromised greatly.

The interviewer then asks: 'If you were assigned to an audit, would you go in with an expectation that what you are expected to do can be done in the time allocated?'

> [I]t depends on the client. You generally know when you're not going to, when something will happen pretty much at the start. You know whether the time frame is reasonable...you've got that historical basis and you also just know how much time things... take, whereas a manager probably hasn't done it for a few years and they sometimes forget.

> [A] lot of us would be at the point where we're the ones setting the time to do things. And I'm terrible for always underestimating. So I'm probably guilty of committing [underestimates] myself, but… everyone's fairly realistic.

> [*In response to a query about whether hours over budget are charged to the client:*] Of course, you do charge time. [You] charge what you're doing so that next year [the record is there]. That's certainly the attitude which is being pushed out there [but]…a couple of years ago, it was, no, you wouldn't charge that.

'So there's been a cultural shift in recent times?' asks the interviewer in relation to the recording of all hours of client work. There is general agreement.

> Because it's not a matter of charging the client, it's [recording the hours]…and then you'd get less recovery…stuff but…[under-recording] was leading to a lot of people not charging their time and then people were saying, well, people aren't working that many hours because they're looking at the stats and then that's why we're still working at 3 o'clock in the morning. So now…there's been more of a focus on job margins rather than recovery…so people are starting to charge their time a lot more and we get into trouble if we don't.

> [I]t's shifting. I still think there's some of that but it's going…in the right direction.

The interviewer asks: 'But what about working from 7am Saturday until 3am Monday without going home?'

> We do get time off in lieu, but it's capped. We're not allowed to take more than three weeks a year.

> But you have to work a minimum amount before you can start accruing.

> It's 100 hours for every six months and then after that it's hour for hour, but you can only take three weeks and most of us would accrue at least that for the three months.

> [O]ur department has tried—we can see the effort is there—but they're trying really, really hard to make the work/life balance better. They've got those development days. They're trying their hearts out, but they really can't help client delays.

In response to how many clients would be included in an individual's portfolio at any one time, responses varied between two to 12 in a year. The number, the interviewees agreed, was the luck of the draw and a matter of which team needed a new member when the graduates were recruited.

> [S]ome people left in my division recently just because the jobs take them away from their families too often...I work on a job which is in [a rural town] and I'd spend about a month in [the rural town]... I don't have kids...but if someone did have kids it...wouldn't work for them.
>
> At some point in people's lives...[family needs become] more important than others.
>
> And some people get sent overseas in our division very often...For lengthy periods, or they'll go for three weeks then come back for a week and then go again, and you don't even get your weekends... you might get a day off while you're over there, but you're still with your colleagues, you're not with your family, and other people don't like that.
>
> We've probably had a few people leave in the last year or two. They've gone to do other work, transaction work and that kind of stuff...they've got a bit of a taste for that and moved away from audit, so still within [this Big Four firm] or one of the other Big Fours, but it's been another attraction, just the type of work.

The interviewer then asks whether the interviewees have any control over the choice of client portfolios or they are just assigned them?

> There's some control. You can preference what you do and what you want to be on and what you don't. It's all pretty much dependent on whether you're a high performer...as to how much flexibility you get on your portfolio.
>
> I don't think that I've got much flexibility with mine. Given that some of the clients are a bit larger and...you're resourced onto only that one client. And it's very hard to get off that one client once you've been on that and then they recognise that you've got the knowledge and the continuity to keep going with that job, so it's just a cycle that goes on...I have voiced up and tried to get a change

> but nothing's happened...in the future, that might be something that I consider as being a reason why I'd leave because...I can't see anything outside the boundaries of that client that I'm currently working on.

The interviewer asks: 'So is that cutting away from your previous statement about training and the opportunity of developing and learning?'

> I've been given opportunities to work—there are things that I can do—but...diversity is something that I haven't been given.

Next the interviewer asks how many clients each of the interviewees has. Responses range from three to 15 for the middle-market tier.

Returning to the issue of what factors besides the work/life balance have driven colleagues away, responses include:

> Challenges. I know a number of people in the audit space specifically who have just got bored and it...[becomes monotonous] doing the same thing over and over again and...they've just got over it.
>
> [*When pressed about where movement has been to:*] A lot have moved into more transaction jobs...having that...audit knowledge behind them...Some have moved within [the firm]. Some have moved external to [the firm]. Some have moved into more advisory roles, but [boredom] was a major factor.
>
> [*When pressed on what type of opportunities—overseas, clients, other firms:*] Opportunities which draw people...[A] bit of everything, but probably...more money, less hours and different roles.

When pressed, several interviewees state that a lot of colleagues go to work for clients:

> [T]he opportunities come to you. You've always got someone asking what you're up to, whether you'd like a change...This year, I've had a lot of recruiters [contact me]...So you're always getting thrown something anyway. So whether you're at that point in your career and you go 'Maybe I'm ready for a change'. That could be a big factor.
>
> [I]t's also the circle that you're in, so if other people have changed jobs that you know. I don't know how your name gets out there but somehow it does.

> [The work/life balance is] the main [reason], particularly when—I don't want to be sexist—but particularly with females who are in their late twenties when they want to go and start a family. They will go to industry for less hours where they can potentially work part-time because...I don't know if you can do it or not, but there's just the consensus that you can't really do that at [this Big Four firm], or it's hard to anyway.

Next the interviewer asks whether there is an expectation that the interviewees do not report the hours worked on the above 'messy' sorts of clients:

> No comment.
>
> Generally, for the very messy ones, you're in a position where you will just bill the client whatever it takes, because it's their fault. But it's where you've got the in-betweener—they're not a brilliant client, but they're not a messy client, but there's this tight budget because they want to reduce fees. And you have this pressure to keep your hours to the efficient ones and keep it at that.
>
> You know how long it took you though.
>
> You know how long it took you, how long it should have taken you.
>
> I don't understand divisions...and I don't think there's as big a push in our division to not report hours as in some of the other divisions.
>
> I charge all my hours. Because the thing is that if the managers... do well in budget, they'll get a bonus. So it's in their best interest for their staff to charge seven and a half hours a day so their job doesn't go over-budget and then they get a bonus. And it works the other way...if you have a job that goes completely over-budget, often they're financially impacted, like higher up...But I just charge my hours...If I want to get up a job, I just charge all my hours... Because it's very discretionary. One job is different to another, and one manager's different to another.
>
> You're also being rated by these people, too.
>
> It's very much a balancing act.

When asked about when they are able to take annual leave, the responses are:

> Whenever you can squeeze it in.
>
> Two weeks over Christmas.
>
> [I]f you've got good clients, you're more willing to stay...a friend of mine, who started the year before I started, and he was the reason, or one of the reasons why I came...he left before I even started. Within a year, he'd been on that many bad clients, he [had had enough].
>
> [*Responding to the interviewer's request to define a bad client:*] Difficult, difficult, the work's not prepared, it's not ready, so you're always following them up, and that just increases your workload. And because you've got other jobs running at the same time, you're chasing up on jobs that are outstanding [as well as] the job at hand.

The interviewer then asks whether the interviewees think they're going to make partner. For one firm, the interviewee responses are all negative. For a second firm, two raise their hands:

> [A]t this stage, it's just too hard to tell, and there's so much that you want to experience between now and the time when you [might] make partner
>
> It's a lot of work as well.
>
> [The work/life balance] doesn't work, but there are enough benefits that I can live in spite of [that].
>
> I'm going to New York [for] opportunities for secondment...I'm enjoying the work that I'm doing at the moment, [it] is challenging and I can see that I'll progress.
>
> [T]he work/life balance might be the one thing that may result in me not wanting to be [a partner].
>
> [A] lot of people wouldn't want to go overseas with their families to live there, so you've got to take that. But a partnership is a good idea, or even an executive director. But I'm not going to be a partner.

Discussion then turns to partners' salaries; estimates range between \$200 000 and \$350 000. General discussion then takes place about positions with high salary levels inside and outside public accounting and the comparative length of tenure of partners and CEOs:

Interviewees were next asked whether people could have a honourable position at the Big Four firms other than partner:

> If you're manager or senior manager...obviously I'm not in that position, but it just seems that you could go to something with much less pressure and time and stress and more money....It seems like those positions are for people who are looking to move to something else, not to sit and stay.
>
> We are paid less than commercial because there is that potential increase every year and you will get more if you stay, so why stay for that lower salary if you're not actually going for more.

The interviewer comments that 'one issue that's arisen in some of our discussion is for someone who doesn't want to be partner, is there a honourable position you can stop at?'. The response comes, naming the executive director, the level below partner. Other comments follow:

> Some people come in and make partner, some people are advised to get up to partner.
>
> I'd take their pay to do what they do.
>
> No, I wouldn't.
>
> And there [are] people who you know aren't going to make partner, but they do the same work.
>
> There [are] not that many jobs that are above the executive director in the industry in Australia, to get more pay.
>
> [A]n executive director starts on 140 [thousand].
>
> No, the lifetime one's about 200, isn't it?
>
> And there wouldn't be many jobs, many industries where you can earn...much more than that.

> [A] lot of the directors, if you stay at directors' [level], you have... expertise. So you're there as an expert...you're not there as an overall partner who's got a bit of expertise, but got a lot of relationships and brings in the work and things like that. So your directors are more—they'll come in and sort out specific problems and they'll be known for those.

The interviewer makes the comment: 'And they tend to be back room? You know, they tend to be technical in a particular area rather than interfacing with clients or selling services or whatever?'

> For that reason as well, we've had a few directors that have...been known to say that they don't want to become partners. They're quite happy being directors so it's just not on their agenda.
>
> [*In response to questioning about whether directors exit to work for clients:*] They still work in the same clients, they're just not pushing that step further.

6.1 Summary

More junior auditors convey some inconsistencies in their performance appraisal systems, where a great deal can depend on the clients to which they are attached and some managers will take this into account while others will not. There appears to be variation in the skills of managers to conduct these appraisals. Interestingly, there is little to no evidence of pressure to not record real hours worked. There is, however, evidence of compromise to the work/life balance with a system that does not compensate adequately in less busy times for hours worked above standard during busy times. The 'audit readiness' of clients, who are arbitrarily allocated and then appear hard to move on from, is not factored into time budgets and often these junior staffers are coping with a new client simultaneously with a tardy one. The heavy use of secondees from overseas and the lack of continuity in staffing that accompanies that is discussed, as are mixed views about ambitions to become a partner.

7.0 Issues and implications

The appraisal system, which is normally part of the mechanism to retain people and provide them with a clear pathway to the future, received very mixed ratings. While there was praise for the attempt to undertake an appraisal, there was concern that it did not exhibit the signs of objectivity that would be expected within the auditing profession; it was arbitrary, it might not be supported by fact and, in particular, it was very client dependent. For example, if you had continuingly problematic clients who caused overruns and were unable to keep to time schedules that then gave rise to or at least the perception of an unreasonable appraisal. It was noted that some managers and seniors gave continuing clear feedback about progress while others did not. There was a more generalised concern that the statement of expectations and the clarity of that communication were key messages for development in the appraisal system.

8.0 Concluding remarks

The central focus of this chapter is on recruitment of people into public accounting and particularly into the practice of auditing. A key driver is the ability to attract the 'right' people into the profession because people are the key resource in the practice of auditing. An important part of the recruitment process lies in the attractiveness of the profession. The practice of auditing, reputation, esteem and desirability of employment in this part of the economy feed off a whole range of issues. In this connection, recruitment into the profession of auditing is not a closed system because, in part, the ability to recruit depends on the quality of the work experience of those who are already in this line of employment. The experiences of these people feed back into the ability to recruit and with generation Y the desirability of work and the nature of that work is, relative to the value set of older generations, disproportionately important. Also, the information flows between those who have been recruited and those the firm is seeking to recruit are much more active than in previous generations with the advent of active and substantial social networking, which is contributed to by the technology surrounding it.

The ability to recruit has also been influenced by the fact that Australia's universities have broadened their commerce and business degrees. Where once a commerce degree in one of the sandstone universities was seen to be dominated by those majoring in accounting, the options available to business and commerce are now many and varied, ranging from those who major in actuarial science to those who undertake one of the multiple majors in zoology. Australia's universities therefore no longer shepherd people into public accounting firms, as they might have done a generation ago.

The structure of the funnel into the profession has changed and, so it would seem, has the work of auditors. The relatively recent advent of high levels of prescription and regulation has had an effect on the type of work that is done, particularly by more junior auditors. There is also seen to be less variety, with public practices being required to separate some of the types of practice into other firms and independence requirements forcing auditors to have less diverse careers with less choice about options during their career path.

The changes to options within university degrees and to the nature of the work are just two of the significant changes that have occurred in the profession. As some would argue, however, the nature of the recruitment process has not changed to reflect these differences. In some other professions—for example, medicine—very different strategies have been adopted. Once, to undertake medical education one aspired to extraordinarily high university entrance standards and was educated in an elite environment with elite levels of employment options at the end. Entrance to the medical profession has, however, undergone profound change with graduate entry (as opposed to undergraduate degrees in medicine) now common and selection into medical training being based less on elite scores at high school level and much more on core knowledge and psychological suitability for the profession. The policy questions for the auditing profession are: should auditors also be selected on different grounds? Should selection be 'fit for purpose'? Is the nature of auditing now such that a different pool of recruits is required? Is it now the case where there are high levels of prescription that we need recruits who are more capable of undertaking highly detailed, repetitive but highly prescribed work? Is the level of independent thinking that is no doubt needed at some levels within the firm, such as partner, now a prerequisite for all employment within the firms, particularly at more junior levels?

Recruitment strategies might adopt more diverse pathways targeting those who do not come from a commerce or business degree—those who might be mature age or who have taken a more selective educational pathway (such as honours) or who might come from an international background. The key question is: does recruitment still match the task of the auditor?

If there is a mismatch between the current contemporary work of an auditor and the recruitment strategies, is it the recruitment strategies that need to change or is it the nature of the work? Either option might be possible.

The acute recruitment crisis that occurred in the years before the global financial crisis has now passed, but lower levels of competition in recruitment of new staff might only mask an underlying challenge for the auditing profession and, once competition starts again, the challenges in recruitment might simply resurface.

If the profession continues to recruit the intellectually gifted, strong, independent thinkers and those who seek intellectual challenge and require diversity of employment then consideration needs to be given to providing work that is of that type and that fits the generation Y work philosophy, as well as a substantial shift in the image profile of the accounting profession. The gloss of possibly becoming partner in 12 or 15 years might not be what it once was and the need for generation Y to have a passion and an interest must be fulfilled. An image enhancement or possibly an image makeover is needed.

The mechanisms used to attract staff into public accounting and, in particular, auditing appear to be many and varied. There are various mechanisms used to recruit and select individuals, including 'accessing' potential staff before graduation. The rationale used by individuals to select audit as a career also vary while there is widespread appreciation of the available training and support once in the profession. The one common theme seems to be mechanisms for recruitment and obtaining some degree of traction and bonding with other people within the firm. The use of cocktail parties, leadership seminars, information sessions, syndicate participation opportunities and the like are perceived as mechanisms for attaining interaction at a people level rather than specifically about the work or career opportunities within the profession. Many individuals interviewed indicated that they joined the profession for any number of reasons and it would appear serendipitous, but all were linked with interacting and obtaining traction with people within the profession rather than any perceptions about the general status or prestige of the profession, perceptions about income derived from employment or other aspects of auditing that were not 'delivered' via personal interactions.

Two important policy issues—one relating to the accounting firms and the other to the profession more broadly—were also common themes among suppliers. First, the nature of a career in a major accounting firm is no longer the lure that it might once have been. For example, an individual might enter one of the accounting firms, qualify with a professional designation and then exit the profession into a relevant industry. This person likely will continue to make a name as a competent and hard-working individual with relevant industry expertise, but is now perceived to be just as employable as if he or she had stayed in the employment of the firm throughout their career. The fact that the individual left an accounting firm at some point makes the possibility that this individual will not return to professional practice and auditing a real likelihood.

The second issue is a common policy statement voiced in various ways, but which in essence can be distilled to the point that if the profession does not acquire the right quantity and quality of those interested in auditing into the profession at the start, it will not have the right pool of people to draw on for more experienced positions in the future. This has implications not just for suppliers of audit services but for the purchasers of those services and indeed the regulators of that market. If our economy simply does not have the talented people with the right experience in sufficient quantity then the market for audit services will not be able to match community expectations with regard to the quantity and quality of services undertaken. Standard setters also enunciated similar comments.

Many comments made elsewhere in this report go to the whole issue and ethos of training and experience and there are various specific observations made by purchasers that support this view. While there was considerable welcoming of the opportunity of a wider set of university graduates into the profession, there was still the public policy question of the effect this would have on the traditional university accounting degree program. Would the presence of alternative pathways have a negative effect on entrance standards and the quantity of accounting graduates entering or exiting universities in Australia? If there are alterative pathways then what will be the consequences? This could be the basis for another potential long-term study on the effect of the training and labour market in accounting, which might be of benefit to the profession going forward.

RETENTION OF STAFF 8

> There's always going to be a retention problem at Big Four accounting firms...and you just hope that you retain the best; the ones who want to stay. You just hope that they're the...good ones...who want to be directors and/or partners...they can't have them all going to manager, a senior manager or director either—unless the business is growing that much that they need another 30 managers this year, or whatever the number comes in [at]. So this whole thing about retention is, sometimes they actually don't want to have 100 per cent retention, because the business isn't growing big enough for them to...promote everybody that year, which is another reason why people leave. Because you might have missed out on a promotion, you don't want to wait another 12 months to get your manager, and even in 12 months' time, then you've got the next lot of people coming up through, so not only are you competing with your peer group, you're now competing with the peer group that was behind you. And who's to say the business has grown enough in the next 12 months to warrant more managers or more senior managers?
> — Purchaser

1.0 Key issues

The audit firm business model and its association with staff retention present some challenging issues for the audit profession going forward. The challenges raised by interviewees included:

- to what extent is an increasingly regulated auditing profession and prescriptive audit task hindering the retention of staff
- how best can the nature of the work and the workload model within the auditing profession be adapted to enhance continuing variety and challenge

- what adaptations, if any, are necessary to retain generation Y within the profession
- how can the work/life balance be enhanced within the profession
- if the lure of partnership is losing its gloss as a factor in retention, how can this issue be best addressed
- if completion of the CA program is a 'trigger' for separation, what mechanism can be developed to assist in staff retention
- if promotion to and then success at the manager level are triggers for separation, how can further progression along the audit professional career path be better managed?

2.0 Introduction

Elsewhere in this report, we have discussed the need for auditors to have certain expertise. Given the importance of business acumen and client and industry knowledge to the profession of auditing, it is clear that retaining expertise, once it has been developed, is crucial. This makes retention of professional staff within the audit firms a key resourcing issue and an important protection of quality. This chapter explores perceptions of the factors behind the level of staff turnover that exists within the profession.

There are no survey questions directly on the issue of retention of professional staff with audit suppliers. Given the complexity and sensitivity of the issues around staff retention, these matters were best dealt with in face-to-face interviews and focus groups.

2.1 Users

Among the users, there was recognition of the array of work opportunities open to junior auditors:

> [I]t's not very exciting...people just want to get out of it as soon as they can and do other things—[go to] investment banks or... corporate [work].

The next user perceives a problem with public practice employers who do not identify staff with excellent potential and reward them early in their careers:

> '[E]ven today... audit firms aren't very good at [staff retention].'

> [I]t's a big concern...because high-quality people want to be challenged and rewarded, and they know there [are] plenty of opportunities for them outside; high-quality people don't have a problem getting a job...even today...audit firms aren't very good at [staff retention]. I joined a group of 30, fresh out of university, and three years later not one of us was in the firm, because audit firms are, or certainly were, conservative, and no-one said to you after three years, 'You've just qualified, we're going to fast-track you to partnership, we think you're a star.' You were just sent out on the next audit. And the world's full of opportunity... the big firms are better at it today in terms of giving people the opportunity to work overseas, but investing in good people is the smartest thing you can do...If you think someone's a star, you've got to pay them more than you pay someone who...is...what I call a good tradesman.

2.1.1 Summary

From the few users who provided comment on the issue of audit firm staff retention, it is clear that the audit role is seen as unexciting and that the audit firms are seen as deficient in strategies to encourage retention of staff.

2.2 Purchasers

Among purchasers, too, there was high recognition of the audit firm business model.

> [R]etaining high-level staff is an ironical point really, because a lot of the...qualified people who get into the firms, who leave the firms, are leaving them for career progressions...In other words, they're getting a chance to be a junior partner or partner in a smaller firm or they're getting into industry...they're getting into banking or they're getting into manufacturing, et cetera...not wanting to continue to work in the auditing field but to...work in real business.

The next purchaser sees the pyramidal structure at the heart of the public practice business model as one of the problems for the profession:

> [P]eople tend to go for job satisfaction and for pay generally and… it's a pyramid structure within the audit profession, so there's just a senior partner, a couple of senior managers and quite often the reason people turnover is because there's not enough room to move; that's why they leave.

The next purchaser feels that the Big Four firms have an advantage in retention because of a perceived capability to transfer staff between departments:

> There is more scope in the Big Four…to retain because of the various departments that they can push them off to and give them challenges, et cetera.

This next purchaser observes that it might have been counterproductive for the profession to recruit to partner level straight out of industry:

> And they still rely on the lure of the career ladder within the firm to become partner. And you do your time, you work really hard…and there's this lure of making $500–$800 000 a year as a partner. But… they've shot themselves in the foot a little with that because, more and more often, you see people go out of industry straight into a partnership level at the audit firms…so I don't find it surprising that their junior staff is…saying, 'Well, I can earn 25 per cent more if I go into industry today. And if I build a name for myself in the market in a particular niche, a particular area, it doesn't preclude me from going back into an audit firm and becoming a partner in the future.' So…their problem with staffing is pretty much of their own making.

The next purchaser observes that 'really they have exactly the amount of retention that they need':

> '[T]he hours that they make the juniors work for what they get paid—the balance is wrong.'

> [T]hey do work people really hard. They work their people harder than we work our people. They probably pay them 25 per cent less than we pay our people. They probably can offer a better career path than we can offer some of our accounting staff. But…in a job market where there's 4 per cent unemployment, people maybe aren't prepared to look 20 years ahead and make sacrifices now for the future…that's why they struggle…There [are] just

> too many other options in the market now for instant pay increases. I'm not surprised people don't look years and years ahead...the hours that they make the juniors work for what they get paid—the balance is wrong...Gen X, gen Y, whatever preferences...all these different generations [have]...I see their staff working on our job doing weekends and getting emails at 1 o'clock on a Sunday morning. They've worked all Saturday and Saturday night...that's for a twenty-two, twenty-three, twenty-four year olds—that's not interesting if you're also being underpaid. And maybe they complain about retention, but really they have exactly the amount of retention that they need, which is: we've worked out the cost of training them is X, and the cost of giving everyone a pay rise is Y, and we're at an equilibrium where we're happy to bring them in, keep the good ones, get rid of the average ones and train them some more.

This next purchaser does not see how a program of having more junior auditors work in industry and then return to public practice could work to provide deep and widespread skills, and sees audit work itself as a source of extensive exposure to industry.

> '[I]f you take junior people and put them into junior positions in industry you're not necessarily going to develop industry expertise.'

> [Junior auditors working in industry and coming back to the profession has] been talked about for a long time, but I don't know that it actually would work...because if you take junior people and put them into junior positions in industry you're not necessarily going to develop industry expertise. The typical accountant who does this stuff...they're not going to get an oversight of an industry. They're going to go and do a particular job for a particular period...So it's actually very hard to construct a program where you can build up wide experience. In fact, one of the best ways of doing it is through the auditing profession because you see different clients and you move around and you see different experiences. And that's why the profession for years has been regarded as a very good training ground for people to move from there into commerce...The best way of getting someone who was grounded and of wide knowledge was...to go and get someone out of the profession that had four years, five years experience in... the accounting profession.

Those in the purchaser group did not necessarily see the high staff turnover rate in audit firms as unhealthy. These next two quotations note how important it is for young people not to do 'menial' work for too long and how other industry benefits from the training these personnel have received.

> In a full economy, it's what we all have, but…in the accountancy practice there's always been a breeding ground for people. They take in a lot of graduates, it's their model that they have…[they] take on a lot of people and then lose quite a lot during the process… it just means you get a good turnover of young people…And the jobs they do are menial jobs right through the audit process, so… high staff turnover is a good thing for auditing.

> [*Is attracting and retaining staff a problem?*] No, because…as long as the intake is there, you're always going to have that… level of movement from the industry and vice versa. And that's healthy because that means you're getting people account trained. Accountants are then going into industry…where else is industry going to get them from? Obviously, they need the finance people in the companies and that's where they're getting them from.

The next purchaser points out the benefit of a defined career path, albeit at lower salaries in the initial stages than other careers:

'[T]he Big Four firm…[offers] a definite career path…there's a definite structure. You're a consultant, then you're a senior consultant, then you're a manager, then you're a senior manager, then a director.'

> I'd gone out of the [auditing] profession and then gone back into the profession, and one of the things I said to our recruitment guys a few years ago was 'You don't realise—until you go out into industry—you might initially make that extra 20 or 30 000 a year, when you first jump out…for that similar sort of job, but I'm not going to be giving you 10, 12 per cent pay rises each year.' And…your bonus structure may not be that great at those…lower levels. And the Big Four firm…[offers] a definite career path…there's a definite structure. You're a consultant, then you're a senior consultant, then you're a manager, then you're a senior manager, then a director, and you know that if you work hard, you don't stuff up, you're well respected, all that sort of thing…you will go up, and you know you'll go to those next levels…Whereas you come out

> into industry and you may not be looked after as much as you...are in that career path...in the Big Four...We did a...retention drive... around the senior consultant level and put some of those graphs up, because they were the most profitable grade to be at, but they're also the guys who have probably just finished their PY or their CPA. They're also the guys who have just finished that and want to take their six months off to go and do their overseas travelling and they're a very vulnerable employee, because they're very valuable. They've got five years experience, they're now chartered accountants, they've got all sorts of recruitment firms knocking on their door promising them the world.

The next purchaser points out that retaining staff is not a problem specific to accounting firms:

> '[A]ccounting firms are struggling to retain staff, but so are law firms, so are banks, so is everybody.'

> In terms of how to attract people...it's a cyclical thing. The accounting firms have always and will always be an attractive employer to staff. Where we're at right now in the economic cycle is such that accounting firms are struggling to retain staff, but so are law firms, so are banks, so is everybody. It's not anything...that's peculiar to the accounting profession, so I don't think it's a crisis in terms of looking at the accounting profession in isolation. But it's a crisis for the community generally...in terms of attracting and retaining the right people. So that's something...that every firm has to address in as innovative a way as they can in order to differentiate themselves, not just from their direct competitors, but also other alternative opportunities for graduates and for people in the market...different firms come up with different, really good and sensible ways of approaching that.

That purchasers understand the problem of retention of audit personnel is made clear in this next quotation:

> [W]hat's happening [is] they're going into these firms, doing their CA program and then after five years they're leaving. And [the firms] need to offer something, don't they? They need to reinvent the perception of what it's like...I've got friends who are exactly the same—they'll tell me now they're just...there to get their qualification and then they're out.

2.2.1 Summary

Purchasers express little surprise about the extent of the problem of staff retention for audit firms. For a start, they too are experiencing difficulties in a full employment market. In fact, several openly acknowledge that they are only too happy to lure staff trained by the accounting firms into industries hungry for skilled workers and to use pay incentives to do this. Some are highly critical of the accounting firms for not providing attractive pay and conditions conducive to retention, especially for generation Y employees seeking a work–life balance. In their comments, it is clear that the pyramidal nature of the structure of audit firms is well understood and, with that, the limited scope to progress through the ranks to the top echelons.

2.3 Suppliers

The comparatively uncompetitive salaries within the accounting firms, despite the long hours, coupled with constrained audit fees, mean that other mechanisms need to be found to create conditions conducive to longevity in the profession. The following quotations reveal the state of the tangible and intangible rewards within the profession.

> [S]taff retention is a major, major issue for the profession as much as for the firms. And our level of documentation has never been higher. But we're still under fairly significant fee constraints and, as a profession, we're not doing much about that. While it's becoming a greater risk, it's becoming harder to get staff—you have to pay them a lot more. The increase in audit fees is barely [keeping pace with] inflation. So I don't think we're helping ourselves.

The cost pressures when audit is seen as a commodity and the remuneration restrictions that creates is alluded to by this next supplier:

> [Y]ou'll get someone who's...say third year and they might be on 60 grand or whatever...They'll go out to the market and they can get a job for 120 [thousand]...[that] does not fit into our cost structure. Because the product is a commodity, we're viewed as a commodity. We can't push any costs on...we just can't compete. And that is the other big fear: the amount of extra hours that need to go into a file under the new regulatory check list...It's hard to manage that with a workforce that's constantly turning over and constantly leaving.

A non-Big Four supplier suggests that the Big Four's perceived heavy workload requirements lead to churn for that sector:

> [M]oney is not always the issue. We don't have a lot of people who leave for money. They will generally leave because they want to go and do something else, or they've had enough of audit…We run on a different model than the Big Four. The Big Four certainly work their people very hard…that's something that we try [to recognise]…we have…times of the year where things are quite busy, or very busy, but you've got to appreciate that. And also when we're not as busy, then they get the opportunity to just relax and make sure they're leaving at the right time and things like that. I don't necessarily know that that's the same sort of culture at a Big Four…so they tend to have…quite significant churn rates in relation to that.

'We run on a different model than the Big Four. The Big Four certainly work their people very hard.'

Several suppliers mention the need that auditing firm employees have to experience challenge and variety in their work, and the consequences for staff turnover when those features are lacking. The following extracts from the interviews reveal the importance of employers providing these job satisfaction in order to maintain the continuing engagement of their staff.

> [A] lot of them just…want the time with us on their CV and want the skills that we can teach them for a few years and then they want to move on. I talk to people at length and say, 'Look, I've been here for years and I've been able to keep reinventing myself and do new things and get involved in new things…and at very senior levels…I keep learning and growing…so why are you bored after three years?'…Their learning curve actually slows down and they just don't seem to be able to accept that. So they want to race off and do something completely different rather than explore those incremental things; so it really is quite tough.

The next supplier suggests the vast number of alternative opportunities available creates a lure if interest or engagement within the current position is lost:

'[T]he biggest thing you can do is give them variety and give them career development. If you can give them those two things, they will continue to be engaged.'

> [T]he pressures that we're getting...from the market, as far as keeping auditors is concerned, [means] that the biggest thing you can do is give them variety and give them career development. If you can give them those two things, they will continue to be engaged. And once they start to lose that engagement...they've got so many opportunities open to them, they'll just go like that; it won't take long. So you've got to keep them engaged and you've got to keep the variety up and...have a career plan for them and make sure that they're...progressing.

The next supplier suggests that those with good communication skills might feel most keenly any restrictions on the variety of tasks they undertake and leave because of that:

> [T]hat skill set [good communication skills] is the one that's probably least appreciated, but it's probably one of the most important and that differentiates people...those that are good, or better than good, are the ones that have got the ability to deal in it. And they're the ones that are the most vulnerable in saying, 'Well, if you're going to limit me and what I can do here, then I'll have to go elsewhere to get that challenge.'

As far as this next supplier is concerned, the perception that there are fewer to no opportunities for secondments to clients is one of the reasons behind issues with staff retention:

'[T]here are opportunities that no longer exist because of the independence requirements.'

> The retention thing is a real issue...Part of it is generational and it's an attitude about what an employee's role should be versus employer and almost what an employer owes their employees. So there's...certainly a huge change in mind-set from when I was a graduate and coming up through the ranks. And it is this...getting the diversity of experience. They don't want to—and nor should they—do audits year after year, potentially on the same client base, without significant opportunities. So how do we manage so that... they do get that diversity of experience? And it's been restricted because of the independence requirements. We used to cross-sell far more significantly to our client base than we can now, so that's

> had an impact with things. Examples would be secondments to clients. There used to be the ability with the auditor…for some sort of accounting assistance…or other assistance, and we could manage that. So there are opportunities that no longer exist because of the independence requirements. But we still very actively try and manage the diversity of their experience and send them offshore and do various things.

The same person continues, explaining the remuneration structure if a longer-term perspective is taken:

> One of the issues with retention…is how our remuneration sits compared to industry. At that CA level and…just prior to being a manager, if they leave…they could get a very significant pay increase if they moved to the corporate world and then potentially have it remain fairly static for quite a period after that. They don't appreciate the leap in the income stream if they do progress through the managerial ranks and into the partner group. So we've become more transparent in explaining to them what it means. If it's financial reward that does it to them, [we explain] what that actually means and what their future might look like if they stay.

Remuneration rates early in careers are also an issue as far as this next supplier is concerned:

> [A]t the moment, you get very few people coming back in [from industry] to become audit partners. They really have to have gone right up through the ranks…the biggest problem we have here is not so much at the graduate stage, but you go probably two and a half to three years after that where they've qualified. They're relatively underpaid compared to commerce and industry…and they leave in droves. So you lose that heavy senior experience, or the junior experienced auditor, the ones in the middle, the ones who actually do a lot of the work. And they're as rare as hens' teeth in terms of keeping them in the profession. If they stay they can go [to partner]…but it looks like a long road for them there. And a lot of them are at a stage in their life where they might've just got married or just had kids…and they… want a higher disposable income…one guy went out for twice the

'[Y]ou lose that heavy senior experience, or the junior experienced auditor, the ones in the middle, the ones who actually do a lot of the work.'

> money recently…what do you say to a twenty-five, twenty-six year old who's just [been] offered twice their salary? 'Thank you for your contribution,' is what you normally say, and, 'we hope you remember us later.' That's a problem. To some degree, it's always been there…To some degree, it's part of life. In [other divisions]… we have a much better degree of staff retention. And the main reason for that, despite what people may allege…is because we can give them a diverse and interesting work experience. There are other subsidiary reasons, but that's the main reason…You can't do that in audit and that's a problem.

Additionally, the lure of partnership is no longer as attractive as it once was—apparently as a means to maintain interest, engagement or incentive:

> [T]he attractiveness for our people to become a partner is significantly less than what it used to be. When I started my career, getting to a partner was an aspiration…if I surveyed most of my staff now, I'd probably get maybe 10 to 15 per cent who want to become a partner. So that's a problem for us because what that means is that they're not necessarily in here for the long haul. Therefore they can differ as to what they want to get out of their experience working in audit. They might be just getting knowledge and then they're off…they've got so many opportunities. And…investment banks in particular—the money they can throw around is quite phenomenal.

Some interviewees allude to the impact on clients and audit quality, as the next two quotes reveal:

> [W]hat we…have to do is pretty much tier our clients and say at the top end of town you want to have the highest level of continuity…at the lower end…maybe that's where you do have a lot of the turnover because you don't have these bigger teams, apart from the partner [who] stays on. He's a little bit closer to a smaller client anyway, so that's where your continuity of knowledge remains intact.

> [T]hat's the Y generation. We're not getting people staying with us for as long, and that makes it harder to keep the continuity, the audit quality.

This next supplier mentions limitations on the variety of work available due to independence concerns and the tendency to specialise early in their careers as reasons for the difficulty of retaining personnel:

> [T]he other thing that also is an issue for us with retention in the audit field is the independence issue, and the fact that it has... limited the variety of work that the individuals can do. In the past, you used to be able to do a wider range of jobs for clients. And this is not a comment on whether independence is right or wrong, but the fact that it's more constrained; that with a channel-one client there's not a lot more than audit you can do in many situations, apart perhaps from tax compliance and so forth... coupled with the fact that you have to be very knowledgeable about the audit process and the requirements means that people are specialising earlier. So...when you're coming in you are choosing to lead a potentially professional life as an auditor.

'[S]ometimes it helps people to have a bit of a check list, because that's the way in which...you execute. Does it stop an airline pilot flying an aeroplane because he or she has that check list they go through?'

The same supplier continues, expanding on his or her point about early career specialisation:

> [P]reviously people would come in and they'd get a flavour of a variety of different things and that of itself would keep the interest going...the reason people leave us is more around the ability they have to learn, rather than the boredom of the work they're doing. They're perhaps opposite sides of the same coin. But...it's drawing quite a long bow [to say that our retention problem is because of]... the fact that we've got some very prescriptive check lists...there are some other things that come into the pot. That check-list mentality... is there, but...sometimes even before the prescriptive standards, we as professionals, or as firms, went through different phases...it's a little bit more prescriptive but sometimes it helps people to have a bit of a check list, because that's the way in which...you execute. Does it stop an airline pilot flying an aeroplane because he or she has that check list they go through?

Suppliers repeatedly raised prescription, check lists and intrusive reviews as motivations for accounting firm personnel to question their continued involvement in the profession. Invasive file reviews and prescription to the level that the interest evaporates are the concern of the next supplier:

> 'I worry…[about] two things: 1) going more prescriptive and taking all of the interest out; and 2) anyone who's been through a file review—it's not a pleasant experience, and… it will put people off. Those kind of invasive reviews that feel like a witchhunt.'

> [I]t's not so much attracting [staff]…it's the retention that's the problem…there are lots of reasons why, even if you look at…gen Y and what they want and what they don't want and how demanding they are…being in a Big Four firm in an audit, it sounds pretty attractive if you're coming out of uni…Yes, you're an accountant but you're at a different client every week or every month. You've got all that sort of thing that they want: a constant change and interest and growth and learning, and you've got all the travel. So…attracting them is still reasonably okay… there [are] other professions throwing too much money at them, which is a problem.

The same supplier continues, explaining why it is that he or she sees retention as the issue:

> [M]oney aside…attracting is not particularly the problem but retaining is a problem…I worry…[about] two things: 1) going more prescriptive and taking all of the interest out; and 2) anyone who's been through a file review—it's not a pleasant experience, and… it will put people off. Those kind of invasive reviews that feel like a witchhunt and feel like they're not looking to see if you've got your audit opinion right; they're looking to see if they can trip you up—that kind of mentality from outside regulators. If staff see that and are touched by it…they'll find it quite off-putting and quite threatening…retention has long been a problem for us. We're doing all sorts of things with work–life balance and flexible hours…to try and keep people longer, and some of it's working. But it's becoming a less attractive long-term career opportunity for people.

The weight of regulatory scrutiny is the theme of this next supplier's comments, too:

> [I]t's a great environment because you're dealing with a whole lot of different companies and the challenges that that gives. But, yes… for the risk you take and where you put yourself, the rewards are not where you'd be saying that it would be good to be…therefore why would I want to stay in the profession…why would I want to have someone looking over my shoulder from a regulatory point of

view and crucifying me if I didn't tick every box? That's not an environment conducive to having people really operating at the top level. And... if they want us to do that then our fees have got to go up a lot...And I've got to be able to work with the regulator in such a way that I'm not feeling that I've been picked on, that...everyone's looking over my shoulder and that's creating an environment that is not as pleasant as it used to be. And therefore the staff are saying, 'No, I don't want that.' So... there's a combination of factors, but certainly the regulator coming down hard doesn't help at all.

> '[W]hy would I want to have someone looking over my shoulder from a regulatory point of view and crucifying me if I didn't tick every box?'

The next supplier points to the constant pressure of scrutiny and monitoring and risk of errors in judgment as creating a disincentive to remain in the profession:

[T]here are significant adverse and long-term consequences for the profession in retaining key people. In effect, not even in retaining; people look at the audit partners now and go, 'Why do I want to work in an industry where I'm constantly being reviewed, where everything I do...potentially could be a breach of the *Corporations Act* [and is] subject to sanction; when I could be publicly hung out [to dry]...not because my audit client failed, but because I made a judgment decision that was wrong...why do I want to live in an environment like that?'...therefore they make a choice to move out [to] where commerce—the merchant banks—are offering them careers with share options. They're offering them opportunities to work in dynamic capital markets, with very little regulation, very little oversight and no restrictions on holding shares...longer term, how does the profession compete? And if you can't keep the right people, that has to have an impact on quality...do you then start moving towards a model where it becomes a second-tier career and you actually contract the right level of graduates?

To some extent, the problem of staff retention did not come across as so pressing among the non-Big Four firms. An impression of the creation of a 'sense of community' within the non-Big Four compared with the situation in the Big Four, and the ability for these employers to vary the client base and work for their employees, appeared to be the reasons for this.

> [T]he smaller...second tier probably didn't have the same level of turnover; you're working with a smaller base. Maybe you don't have the...volume of staff that some of the other firms have. It's probably a little bit more working together, maybe a little bit of... variety, where you can perform more than one function without having to transfer to another division or transfer out of a firm.

The next supplier refers to a perception that Big Four staffers who have recently completed their CA are more marketable than non-Big Four staff in the same situation:

> [A]nyone that's had a Big Four experience—and generally they do their CA and that's the key point [at which] we could lose them—they've got an unbelievable level of experience and training that makes them incredibly marketable out there...Maybe if they'd... grown up in a much smaller practice, their marketability is somewhat less and therefore maybe the retention side could be [better]. Maybe they're better managed when it's a small practice too and they don't feel like they're lost.

Another supplier speaks to the additional challenges—apart from sought-after clients—that might be presented to staff who have recently completed their CA to interest and motivate them:

'What do we invest in that period after CA in training and the non-client basic activities that will keep those individuals with you for another three years?'

> [W]hat the big accounting firms struggle with is that, whilst you're doing your CA program, you're kind of all but locked in. Once you finish that CA program, it's 'What's the next challenge?'... There's a little bit of a void there and...the challenge for us is, what do we provide outside of the career that will keep somebody there? What do we invest in that period after CA in training and the non-client basic activities that will keep those individuals with you for another three years? Because then—and obviously we don't necessarily want everybody to stay—the attrition rates from time to time run over what you ideally want them [to be]...to have that continuity...so we're starting to think a little bit more cleverly around what can you do...and it's not just saying to somebody, 'I've got this great challenge. I'll put you on XYZ Co. for the next two years'...that's great and it gives me a career so I can work towards manager, but what else? What else? Well, I'll put you

> on that and you participate in this training program. In a year's time, we'll support you through an MBA or we will get [you] involved in other non-client-facing work, some community...work...which allows you to network...it's for your personal development outside of just your technical development. What other things can we do? And that's where the thinking is now.

2.3.1 Summary

No supplier feels there is a problem with attracting graduates. Many, however, acknowledge the problem of retaining them—not necessarily because of salary levels, although that issue is present, but rather for a variety of reasons to do with job satisfaction. These reasons include long hours, the 'career levelling' routine of form-filling the check lists induced by the new auditing standards and internal and regulatory scrutiny, and the lack of opportunity for secondments, for provision of little if any service outside audit to audit clients, for challenges that maintain the interest in a career in an accounting practice. Suppliers are left to find creative ways to maintain interest and engagement. The more innovative use the prospect of client rotations, overseas postings, more postgraduate training, community networking and personal development opportunities to induce engagement, especially at the times known to be most vulnerable for exit. It is, however, much harder to find mechanisms to retain partners who are exiting the profession in increasing numbers, according to some suppliers.

2.4 Standard setters

The standard setter interview group reinforces the suppliers' comments about the need to keep the auditing role varied and challenging in order to retain staff. The first standard setter looks to the implications of the high turnover of staff within accounting firms for the issue of knowledge management by those firms:

> [Y]ou need a culture that's attractive. And one of their problems is that they have a culture that requires a work/life balance that's not attractive: the hours that are required to be worked by each individual within the profession to maintain the margins and the profits and the business model. They're not something that's sustainable for a lot of young people. They can

'[O]ne of their problems is that they have a culture that requires a work/life balance that's not attractive.'

> do it for a limited...time and then people are going to move for lifestyle reasons...These are the high potentials that are going for lifestyle reasons and that's the issue about [the audit firms] retaining the right people...they've got to think carefully about skills and knowledge retention...I don't know that they're very good at knowledge management, so they don't...say, 'Well...we've got a body of knowledge within the organisation, in the people, not just in the database or whatever. How do we optimise and maintain that body of knowledge within the organisation? So these are key people for us in terms of their skills and experience, which are specialist skills and experience, therefore we want to keep them.'

The same standard setter continues, emphasising the importance of leadership and having partner role models whom others aspire to be emulate:

> [T]he other problem is that people just go in there to get the qualification and you're never going to change that. So even if they're good, it doesn't mean that that's what they want to do for the rest of their life; and it's a leadership thing as much as anything else. If people in there see the leaders that they...aspire to be then there's more chance of retaining them...a lot of the problem is that people look at the partnership and say I don't want to be like them... And the partners are pretty focused...on profit share and, as long as that's their key driver, then the people will always come second... But it's just an indication of this conflict between—or the balance you've got to get right between—business imperatives and looking after the people...the people are their money-making machine and that's why the more hours they work and the more productivity they get out of one person, the bigger [is] the profit share growth. And that's what drives people away...that's what drives behaviour in the partners and their decision-making processes that turns people off...being a partner.

The next standard setter's comments go to the heart of the business model used by accounting firms and its dependence on attracting many people in to the firm who will stay to go on and build up knowledge and expertise:

> 'Where we are going to find a real difficulty is retaining the registered company auditors.'

> Retaining them becomes more problematic...because people may say, 'Well, what have I got to do to have a rewarding career?' And part of that is being able to give them choice...[This is] why...multidisciplinary firms are still a way forward to give people... different paths...[to] follow. They might finish up coming back to where they started from, and that's fine, but how do we retain them...being able to go and do a [piece of] work on an investigating accountant's report, to do a piece of risk-management work as opposed to doing a piece of audit work—that's what I mean by that...we've found retaining people tougher, but...that's part of the market. And...everyone half jokes, is half serious, about gen X and gen Y...in particular... but people have a different perspective on their career generally... people coming to firms and staying with them for 20, 30 years is not the norm anymore...and that's the case for any employer. But the problem with audits and the way the audit business model is set up is it is dependent on getting a lot of people to come in. Yes, we can cope with attrition, but we've tended to build the expertise and the knowledge and to get well-grounded, solid, registered company auditors by keeping people. Where we are going to find a real difficulty is retaining the registered company auditors.

Another standard setter says that if a person is suited to assurance and auditing, they will thrive no matter what the changes to the environment are:

> I wouldn't have thought the variation in the audit, the way it will be undertaken, will necessarily mean that an individual won't be challenged on an audit. If you're a person who is suited to assurance and auditing...you'll thrive in that environment no matter what the changes. What it may do is for those who get by and who are, long term, probably not in the [right] industry might find out a bit quicker...I've found it quite exciting and quite a challenging role so...there will always be individuals who are like that. You can come across some quite interesting and challenging assignments whereas some other ones are quite [routine], very simple and sometimes those have a danger of...[posing the problem of] how does an individual remain focused, whereas [with] the other one... you've got to make sure you're on top of everything. So in each situation in an audit it can vary.

The increasing trend for partners to depart the profession early is highlighted again and the issue of prescription and regulatory scrutiny is alluded to as one of the reasons behind this relatively new phenomenon:

> I get partners who are five years into their careers as partners saying, 'Well, what do I do next?' Maybe I want to move and, unlike other businesses where people or businesses recruit at every level within the organisation [and] from outside the organisation, it's not as easy to recruit a registered company auditor at that level. So retaining people, not just to get them to partner—because I don't think we have that issue—but keeping them through their careers as partners [is the issue]...we would expect that when people are made partners, they've got at least a 20-year working life ahead of them. It's becoming increasingly common for partners to leave, so how do we [stop] that? How do we keep them? And part of that is that the changes disenfranchise people.

The same standard setter continues, discussing what he or she sees as 'leakage' from the profession rather than movement within in it as the most troubling aspect:

> When I talk about the changes in some of the rules and people becoming disenfranchised, it's been at the more senior levels, saying, 'Well, where's my career going to go, what am I going to do?' I know people have moved from one firm to the next because the firms have had a need, but...what I see happening overall is... leakage out of the profession at an increasing rate at the senior levels. And we need to work out how we manage that...For example...if we were to lose two or three of the approved auditors that APRA consider can do the audits of insurance companies...[you] can't go and manufacture one of those people inside five years...[They need] to have worked as partners on engagements like that without signing those audits. And if we lose those people to other audit firms, that's less of a concern—if the people are just moving around within the firms for whatever reason...But if we lose those people [from] the profession, then that's a problem and...that is what we're starting to see.

Another of the standard setters speaks of 'leakage' from the profession and what he or she perceives as the tendency for this leakage to come from the higher levels within firms. This standard setter sees 'regimented processes' as part of the problem:

> 'If we're going down processes that are so regimented that it's like doing the milk run every day...I don't see a lot of people staying in it.'

> I don't think it'll just be the junior levels...you'll start seeing the leakage coming [from] higher up... and potentially all the way to the top, because... you'll find that if...we're going down processes that are so regimented that it's like doing the milk run every day, the only thing that happens is someone tells you that the house up the street needs four bottles today, not three, and that's the only change that happens in your life—well, I don't see a lot of people staying in it. And then your issue becomes one of...you need people to be able to do complex valuations... we have to integrate our audit approach by bringing in corporate finance specialists, capital market specialists, IT specialists—those sorts of people will be involved, but they will be involved because they can do other projects outside of audit, not with audit clients but with non-audit clients. Your typical auditor...will do work in those areas as well, until it becomes too complex for them. So they can't get involved in that. They'll come in, probably get the basic training and move on, and all that means is that the upper levels will [suffer] because there'll be nothing left to come through.

The sentiment expressed by the next standard setter is that, ultimately, the quality of auditors will decline because they are limited to audits:

> [W]hat are the costs and benefits of auditors being, [and] companies being, prohibited from buying out the services...when I looked at that, I said, 'Well, to me the fundamental costs...will be [that] the quality of the person doing the audit will diminish ultimately.' If it continues the way it's going, that will diminish and the...level of service will diminish. Presumably, the level of reliability may diminish.

Finally, one standard setter points to the business model used by the accounting firm and focuses the dilemma not on retention of personnel, but on retention of the 'right personnel':

> It's a dilemma that [the accounting firms have] had for a long time and...they've probably improved but...they weren't known as being

> great people managers, being great people organisations. And there was always a lot of lip service to 'our people are our biggest asset', but the behaviour never...[reflected] that...so they're expected to have high turnover of staff. It tends to be the model they work on because once people...get their qualification and then get to a certain level, there has to be a certain amount of fall-out because of limited opportunities higher up...they need to keep moving graduates through to maintain their business model, their cost base. They can't train all these people and retain them all, otherwise their cost base would increase, so they've got to keep replacing...if you look at any big firm in town, you might have 2000 staff in the office; they don't want to grow [the] overall head count, but they want to maintain the proportion of partners to senior managers to managers to trainees and whatever. So as you bring in a new graduate intake, you've got to shed the other levels to maintain the proportion. So their key is retaining the right people.

2.4.1 Summary

The standard setter interviewees, who themselves often are also suppliers, make comments reminiscent of those of suppliers. Comments about accounting firms as less than optimal at making their personnel feel valued can be seen again. Similarly, comments about the need to provide variety and challenge in the work tasks are present. What is new is the insight that perhaps partners do not always portray the role-modelling that leads to aspirants seeking to emulate them. What emerges also is the cost to the profession in terms of industry-specialist expertise when highly skilled audit staffers exit, especially if they are expert in the highly regulated industries that APRA monitors and approves auditors for.

2.5 Regulators

The few regulators who commented on this issue repeated the stereotype of auditing as an unexciting activity, but also commented on the quality implications of the loss of personnel from the profession.

> [T]here are exterior perceptions that going into a firm, or going particularly into auditing just isn't exciting.

> [Retention is] always going to be a concern. If you don't have high-quality staff...given the size of audit teams that go in, it's going to be a real problem to do the work.

2.5.1 Summary

Regulators reveal a concern with audit quality if retention issues mean insufficient high-quality staff to undertake audits.

3.0 Focus group interviews with junior auditors

Given the importance of the retention issue, extensive conversations were held within the peer focus groups of more junior auditors about this issue. With no other firm personnel in the room, conversations flowed freely and with candour about individuals' own turnover intentions and those of others they knew.

Focus group participants were asked about factors that kept them with their firms. The clearly defined path to progression within the firm featured prominently in responses, as can be seen in the following illustrative comments.

> [One factor is] knowing that there are a number of sideway[s] opportunities. Whether that's out of audit into another division or whether that's overseas or secondments to clients. So...they are certainly appealing factors to stay. [*In response to a comment that it is diversity in work opportunities that keeps you at the firm:*] Yeah, definitely and...also too...the clear path of promotion. [*In response to a comment that a clear structure in terms of employment exists:*] Yeah, you don't have to wait five years for someone to keel over...before you can move to the next level. There [are] always opportunities and there's a lot of movement.

> Everyone's going to get to the point of our level or around about where you finish your CA and then it's 'the stay or move away' [question] and...the thing that kept me here was...you get to see an industry and there was actually a trainee who started in my year and who is now working at the client who I spend most of my time at. I see that she's still in the same role and she just doesn't get a chance to do anything else because the people above her are not going anywhere either. It's just like a giant backlog whereas...I can almost map out my future for the next years where I just stay here. There's just a defined progression path so that was it for me.

> I like it because you have a clear career path. In a commercial firm, you can't get promoted until your boss has left or something else... for the first 10 years you know where you are...After the first 10 years, maybe you can consider whether you want to stay here or not.

The opportunity to continue to learn and the challenges that presents also featured in responses.

> [I]t's the challenges that are always presented to you. I feel that after each job I've learnt something new so I'm never bored. That's pretty much what it comes down to and...[there are] still a lot of things to learn so that's definitely something that keeps me [here].

Firm and cohort support in undertaking the CA program was a common thread in responses too.

> [T]he learning environment definitely [is a factor]. I'm doing CA at the moment so the experience that I'm getting...I can put into use with the studying.

> They support you [with CA] much more so here than they do in industry. We get leave, we get...external study assistance.

> [*In response to a query about whether CA fees are paid:*] Yep, all that sort of stuff and from what I understand again, the girl that moved to industry...they give her textbooks and stuff. She's actually doing her CPA even though she wanted to do her CA, so they don't actually give her a choice. They just don't get the same amount of support and one of the guys who was halfway through his CA at the client actually called up and asked if he could join our...study group because he had no-one to learn with.

> [T]hat's one of the factors as well—in our division alone...we've got five or six people studying the same subject at the same time, so you've always got that support group.

The interviewer establishes that it is not a requirement to pay back a bond to the Big Four firm.

> [S]ome of the other Big Four [firms]...actually [go] so far as to, every time that someone passes a CA subject, they get $1000 up front and if you get a merit then they give you $5000 as well.

3.0.1 Summary

Once within the profession, considerable effort either intentionally or otherwise is spent on the bonding of people. Social events are a common mechanism used to help bond people, often with the use of alcohol (which has intended or unintended consequences for those people who do not imbibe or those with religious views about the consumption of alcohol). The fact that there is a high turnover of staff is one of the reasons this bonding mechanism requires so much effort. The mere churn that exists at lower levels in the firm breaks these bonds and indeed it has been expressly stated that one of the triggers for leaving is if one of your close colleagues decides to leave.

3.1 What triggers for separation exist?

Interviewees were asked whether any of them or any others they knew were thinking about leaving the employ of the firm:

> The reasons I came was the people...and, trying to put a different spin on it, one of the reasons I'm not considering staying...is that those people change...so that is something that I'm considering... The people that I did initially enjoy working with have now all left the firm and there's a very different dynamic here.

> [I]f the people I started with at [name of mid-tier firm] were still there, it might have let me stay a bit longer but the fact that they'd all gone was the real last straw—there was no connection to stay with them...We actually had so many resign...not enough people were being replaced. And when I was working seven days a week for six months...I burnt out. But the fact that my friends or the people I had started with, the graduates, had left also played a big part in me being able to let go a lot more easily.

> I don't think...I'd go [to another public accounting firm]...if you want to stay in accounting, I wouldn't go to another firm...that certainly wouldn't be in my thinking at all.

> I'm thinking of...leaving. Not so much because of the admin, I just think...out of the last two and a half, three years...in terms of building up a technical base that will sustain my career...I've done that to some extent but I'm looking for more experience...I'm looking to change the area I work in. I want to try and move into

> more of a merchant bank kind of situation. I want to try something else…I don't know if I'll get pigeonholed after three years, but I want to try something else before I really dig in hard at something.

> [I]t will be when I feel I've had enough of audit. [*In response to the interviewer's quip about the excitement and passion of audit:]* It does die…we cannot go on forever, so whenever the different experiences, secondment and all of that…will be the time I'll probably consider is the time to move on and do something else.

> [T]he thought did cross my mind, but…I'll probably leave only when I start getting really bored with audit or when/if I find a position that I like in the market and the salary's attractive.

> I probably will stay—at least until I'm promoted to manager. I want to see whether I can be a manager or not.

Several mentioned the search for a work–life balance as a motivating factor for leaving.

> [M]any of my colleagues left because they want a more stable life. As auditor, you have to travel around quite often and sometimes… there are tight deadlines. After [you] get married and have children, you want a more stable life. They just want to settle down and share more time with their family. [*When pressed on whether that observation was gender specific:*] [It's] more applicable to female[s].

> I know some people who felt that they were being taken advantage of. Like they're in there working long hours a lot of the time and then when they needed some sort of flexibility it might not have been forthcoming or when there was down time and they potentially could have…eased off more and maybe turned up a bit late or left a bit early when it wouldn't affect it, people were still driving them to…turn up at 8.45 and work til 5.15 and sit there doing nothing… So it's kind of all take and no give in the work hours. *[In response to a question about how common this is:*] [I]t's quite common.

> [W]here they feel they're getting worked pretty hard and maybe not appreciated for it or maybe not getting what they would perceive as the flipside of working the long hours when you're busy…When you're quiet you should be able to take the foot off the accelerator and even up the score.

> [W]ork/life balance has got to be a big one in that...you can burn out if you're doing very long hours and there [are] only so many busy seasons that some people can take. And obviously different things make different people leave, but...work/life balance is definitely [one reason].
>
> [O]ne of the key [reasons why people leave]...is the work hours... they just get sick of the constant work weekends, work nights... whatever you do you get the work done, and no, [there is] not necessarily any additional recognition for it at all.
>
> [A]lso your client base can determine if you will stay late.
>
> It's the same here [having to work nights, weekends and so on if called in], but you just don't get the time off in lieu.
>
> It's voluntary.
>
> You can decide not to do it, but...
>
> [The number of hours worked in a week] can depend on...which clients you're on, and how...big the workload can get.
>
> With us, [the number of hours worked in a week is] very seasonal, so July to end of September is very busy, but then once we get October, November, December...you'll be working nine to five again, and then January to March is busy again.

When pushed on the number of hours worked in a day, responses range from eight to 12, and below are some of the elaborations on this point:

> It depends on the situation. We had a particularly tough one this year, but...some busy seasons are going to be super flat out because you've got big technical issues, for example, so you've got to put more time into it; then others may not be quite as bad.
>
> [A]lthough it is still seasonal...the season's flattening a little bit, so it almost still seems like it's busy 12 months of the year instead of that three or four months.
>
> [*In response to a query about whether that is harder to take:*] It probably is. It's a bit of a luck of the draw with your clients whether you've got 30 June then 30 September then a 31 December, so it's individual by individual.

Others mention the nature of the work itself and a lack of variety:

> I know of two people that left and...they didn't leave because of the money. They...left because of the work. They weren't enjoying the work...I work in audit too so we get consumer/industrial markets, [and] it can all depend on the client mix you have. Some people are lucky; some people aren't as lucky. I know the people that left were just working long hours, working weekends [and] weren't enjoying it.
>
> [It was the] same client, day in, day out and it was a grind and they were over it.
>
> [*In response to a question about how long it took to be 'over it':*] Some people: six months. Some people: two and a half years.

The interviewees were then asked what it was that kept them with their current Big Four employer.

> I feel that I'm still learning and I've got a lot to learn and...this is... as good a place as any to continue learning the tools of the trade. Also...I enjoy working with the people. The people in my division, my teams, they keep me in touch with the job.
>
> [I]t's a number of things. The people are good, the opportunities are good, the training's good and...I've never seen a job at a clients' that I would want to do. They're doing the same reconciliation every month...[Here] you're not at the same desk, which has its downfalls, but it's also good in the way you work with different people. You're not pigeonholed; you can move around.
>
> [I]n our job, we have the ability to manage our own responsibilities, which is something I enjoy...if you've got to come in late one day, no-one's really going to kick up a storm as long as you get your work done. If you have to stay back that night, well so be it...I haven't had a set timetable of hours I have to work. As long as you get the work done then everyone's happy, which is something I enjoy.
>
> [*When pressed on whether 10 years is the time horizon for most people:*] [T]here's a mixture between three [years]...After the CA a lot of people leave and then...A lot of them take career breaks...There [are] quite a few people in my division that have just left to travel...And they...never seem to come back...the firm will give them leave, like a career break, for a year, but I haven't seen anyone come back yet.

[I'm carried] development-wise because the firm pays for your CA, which is really great. And at the same time you get a taste of different industries because you have a property client, a banking client, an insurance client. So it gives you a feel[ing] of what they do and what they're about...it develops you, develops your skills and, in the future, if you want to move elsewhere—definitely this is what I want—and this is how I'm going to get there.

[H]ere, you look at the average age in those divisions...and there [are] a lot of young people your age to work with...it's just a benefit [*in response to whether this represents a benefit or a threat*]. You're working with people who are [at] about the same point in their lives as you and have the same issues and go through the same jobs.

It seems to be a historical trend of about three years.

Generally...after you finish your CA you start thinking about it and then, if you don't do it then, you'll probably do it just after you become manager.

Historically...in our group, it's been because people say it's career suicide if you leave before [becoming] manager, because you don't get as many opportunities with senior accountants on your resume as you do with 'manager' on your resume.

[I]t's a combination of travel, money, different things to do...A lot of people leave the employment and do their own thing overseas.

It's a bit of a trend. Those that go to the UK leave the firm. Those that go elsewhere stay with the firm initially, and then venture out.

Usually the lower levels...step across as an accountant or a senior accountant into industry, earning a bit more.

[T]hat element of finishing the CA and your obligation of your three years with the firm can quite often go [with a sense] that you're free from the firm and that could be a trigger point for a lot of people... it was for our division about two years ago.

[CA] opens all these other doors that were...not quite there before.

You also have an obligation to repay monies that you owe to the firm for the training of the CAs...So people generally leave one year after completing their CA, because they've paid back their time of service.

Yeah. The pyramid just relies on people exiting in that time.

You...learn a great deal when you're here, but...people are under the impression that the longer they stay, the more highly qualified they become, and the more valuable they are outside of the firm. So...people hang on for...certain levels and trigger points, be it CA or senior or manager, so they can then step back at the height of them.

It doesn't involve you to sit down and go well...this is what I want...you still can fasttrack yourself, but it's pretty much laid out on the table as...if you meet these points, and you're performing how you're expected to, then you get [this].

I don't know if [the career path is] more [desirable than in industry]; it's more desirable the longer you stay. If you don't stay as long, the industry's more desirable once you get to a certain level, so at that three-year point with the CA, someone's offering you more money than what you can get here, and better hours...or more...reasonable hours throughout the year.

[I]t depends where you go in the industry. If you go to a small... company, then you cannot progress until someone quits half the time. If you go somewhere like [a large corporation], they've probably got the same kind of structure as we do, and you have a career path there as well.

[T]he day that...I rock up to work and I don't really learn anything anymore, or...there [are] no opportunities...if I'm sitting at my desk punching out the same stuff as I was doing the same time last year, I'm going to look at myself and go well, am I actually gaining anything by doing this? I mean, you're doing it eight hours a day, and if you talk the hours that we do, sometimes 10, 11 hours a day, if [at] that point I sit there and I say to myself, 'Am I actually learning anything here anymore—no', then that's when I'll say, 'Yep, time to go.'

It goes back to the structure of how the firm's set up, in that every year you do something different, just by how the structure works and you keep moving up, and someone keeps coming in below you.

> I'm in the...division [that] deals with small business, so...we do a mixture of businesses, so I like dealing with different companies and different sizes and different natures...And the people and that kind of thing, which is obviously the HR [human resources] recruitment line, but it...tends to be true.
>
> Quality people that can support the learning because...if there [are] no role models or people you want to aspire to be like or learn from...you're [not] going to stick around for very long at all.
>
> [T]he key thing as well is just opportunities to...change it up—like a secondment, maybe overseas for six months or a secondment into another division.
>
> [*In response to a query about whether secondments are common:*] Yeah, they're very common in our group. I don't know about other groups.

Several interviewees then said that they were off to locations in the United Kingdom or the United States.

> [F]or now, it's the international experience, but after that it will probably just be as long as I could tolerate it, just that I wouldn't want to look for something else...because I don't know what else I want to do. I don't know if that is what I want to do, but there's nothing else either.
>
> In saying that I want to try something else, what will keep me here is if [this Big Four firm] offer me a short-term secondment—to be able to have that opportunity [of] trying something else. [*When asked whether they want a secondment to a client:*] To another division... within another division, so out of audit...first of all...[this firm is] a good [firm] to work for...there's no point in leaving [this firm] unless you try something else...[This firm] has a lot to offer, like all the other Big Four firms. They have a lot to offer before you jump ship, so if they give me the opportunity to try other things while I'm here, they'll definitely keep me at the firm longer.
>
> [J]ob stability [is also]...one of the...retaining factors. I don't know what's out there.

In many of the comments above and throughout the remaining responses, the importance of friendships and networks of people to these groups of junior auditors comes through—as it does when they are asked what are some of the things they find attractive about the profession.

> Some of the little things they do like audit dinners or opportunities to catch up with the guys you have worked with in the past. That does…count for a lot for some people.
>
> [E]veryone mentioned that one of the things that they were here for is because of the people and…in our division [community activities are] one thing they haven't been doing as much and that's a reason why people have left.
>
> [B]eing interested in what you're doing…the day that it becomes…a real hard, boring grind is the day that I don't want to do it anymore. If it's something slightly different or new, or a new place or a new client…it's just got to be different and interesting at some level…[so you can] use your brain.
>
> [I]f you feel appreciated and valued in the firm, it will help you stay.

The interviewer then asks whether anyone is staying because they really want to be an auditor:

> I don't think anyone's proud to be an auditor.
>
> [*In response to a prompt about career progression:*] [Y]ou would just wait and see…the work does get better as you go along further, definitely, so that's a plus…also, the longer you stay, the better opportunities you'll get…if you go elsewhere.
>
> That was my number-one choice of what I wanted to do [promote other opportunities]. It was initially a training ground as such to come in for three years around about that sort of time and get the knowledge and experience of what we've all talked about and have that behind me and then be able to move sideways or go overseas or do something like that.

Remuneration was a factor in some of the answers, but did not feature prominently.

> [T]he people that I know who have left, they left because the salary's more attractive on the promotion side...including bonuses.

> Yeah, I've heard of 20–30 per cent more.

> I suppose a promotion, secondment, salary.

One of the issues the interviewer prompted comments about was whether the Big Four firm for which the focus group participants worked had recruited people to retain them or whether there was an inbuilt 'we don't actually want everyone to stay' mentality.

> I agree...they take in a big group of people and they hope that out of that 20 or so that they [take] into a division, there [are] going to be five there that are keepers to manager and then...they'll weed out the rest and hopefully every couple of years they get a partner out of the recruitment.

> I don't know if that's what they hope but that's what happens...it's a natural attrition; people leave.

> From their perspective, I don't know. I couldn't say what they think [*in response to 'So is your perspective that every person they recruit is a potential partner?*].

> I don't see them recruiting people thinking, 'I hope these three leave and these four stay.' I just think they recruit a whole bunch of good people knowing people are going to leave.

Does the firm seek to retain all its employees?

> They'd like to think that they do.

There are generally negative responses when the interviewer asks whether interviewees think their employer intentionally sets out to retain everyone:

> I don't think...they do...if they identify someone who's at manager level, and they say...realistically, they don't have a huge future with this firm, or don't think they'd be partner material, I wouldn't say they actively try to retain them.

Is it managed so that there are no gaps when people leave?

> No, I wouldn't say so...there's still a shortage.
>
> They like to keep the best people they can, and they can't always keep those people.
>
> It's the rate of pay.

Some interesting comments about the issue of partnership occurred during the discussion about triggers for separation.

> [T]here was one guy that...didn't see himself as a partner so he got to assistant manager and then he said, 'I don't have the personality to become a partner so there is no point for me to stay here.' So he just decided to go somewhere else. So personality sometimes [is an issue]...He went to...[an] investment bank...he said that sometimes to be a partner you have to be a little bit mean and...on the presentations [you need to] have a kind of charisma.
>
> A bit of charisma doesn't hurt.
>
> Partners are definitely charismatic.
>
> And motivational as well.

4.0 Prescription, documentation and junior auditors

One of the most interesting aspects of the conversations in the peer focus groups revolved around the perceptions of these more junior auditors about the regimented nature of much of the work in which they were engaged as a result of increasing prescription. Below are some of the most revealing of the comments. The cohesiveness within these firm-specific focus groups is manifest with the participants often finishing one another's sentences. For this reason, the authors have added few of their own comments in this section.

> [The work is] just ticking off the boxes. Definitely, if the admin work keeps on going up it could be enough to make me go 'stuff this', because if I'm just going to be ticking boxes to say that I might have thought about something, it's kind of really pointless. There's no...value in that.

[As a] senior accountant...you're kind of stuck in the middle. There's a lot admin stuff and...the way audit's going, there just seems to be more and more and more admin and less and less and less audit work being done. [*In response to 'What is meant by admin?':*] [T]here [are] check lists for check lists. There...are silly amounts of documentation...and...that's a contributing factor. They weren't enjoying what they were doing...even sometimes I find myself doing a check list and I'm like, 'Well, how is this value adding to that client? What purpose is this serving? Is anyone actually going to look at this check list ever?'

And some of [the check lists] are so big that it is a temptation to just sit there and just to click all the way through them, because you... know that 90 per cent of it's just not going to apply to what you've done because these check lists cover every[thing].

[The check lists are] comprehensive, but they're too comprehensive.

It just feels like the numbers aren't important anymore.

It's about having a file there that's going to protect you, more so than having a file that's proving...

[*Completing the previous interviewee's sentence*:] ...all the aim and the methodology.

It certainly increases the frustration levels.

It makes it feel quite useless—like what's the point?

[This can impact on one's own motivation] because certainly when you're planning a job, it doesn't always get the attention in terms of [the] time it needs, which means that you've got to cram [the documentation] in somewhere.

[M]y perception of it a lot of the time is that the partner or the manager want to see if there's a check list on file, but they're not going to look at it or think about it. They're just going to be concerned about the numbers.

Yeah and whether it's been done correctly or not is not important because they don't really value the contents of the check list. They just know that they have to have it there in case someone else looks in over their shoulder.

I feel…there's an attitude [of] well, whether I've looked at the check list or not…from managers and partners, I'll pick up whether there's an error when I'm reviewing whatever I'm reviewing…I'll pick up whether they're meeting the requirements or not and the check list is just something that has to be done that does not yield any further benefit.

[In response to '*Does it mean that someone can retrace your steps better?*'] Theoretically, possibly.

Some commented on a generational problem in that the more senior people had never had to go through the current documentation requirement regime.

[I]n the last three or four years there's been a generation gap in terms of the documentation requirements—more so [with] the partners and the managers, maybe even senior managers. They never had to deal with all this documentation. They see a check list and they think, 'Oh, this should take 40 minutes to do, half an hour to do but'…

[*Finishing the previous interviewee's sentence:*] It can take a day.

[I]n practice…they were never exposed to these kind of documentation requirements.

When it comes to some of the admin…doing the technical work obviously, not but just in regards to admin and putting together an audit file that has …

[*In response to the comment, 'That sounds like really quite important in terms of your working lives':*] Yeah, it's called breaking it.

4.1 Summary

The most junior auditors, within focus groups, expressed frustration with the level of documentation and check lists with which they were involved. They could see no value added to the audit and the time it takes is insufficiently budgeted for, with partners trained in a different era having little appreciation for the time impost.

5.0 Stakeholders' comments on the impact of prescription on retention

In asking about perceptions of the level of prescription as a distraction for auditors, several stakeholders made comments that touched on the potential impact of prescription on staff retention. Users did not make such comments, so this section begins with the words of purchasers.

5.1 Purchasers

One purchaser comments on the attractiveness of the profession in light of check lists:

> [T]here are issues that have come into the profession that—you reference the share one. But there are others that have made it less attractive. You feel like you are in a box, let alone ticking the box.

5.2 Suppliers

A supplier observes, more in the context of ASIC inspections than documentation or check lists:

> '[T]he approach of seeing how many auditors you can ban from signing in a year is not going to really lift the standard. It's going to drive people out...of the profession.'

> [I]f I can give you an example [of] where...the regulator doesn't think. When they went and did the review of the independence issues at the Big Four, what did they do? They looked at process. Well...blind Freddie would've said that the process would've been reasonable. Why didn't you go and select a whole range of listed company accounts where they had to delineate their services, and pick a few of those and go back and say, 'Well, how did you think that you were independent when you did that service?' But they didn't do that. This is where...it's driving the compliance, and that's why...they should be talking more. They seem to have a very closed mind...they've moved a little bit because there's been such a significant backlash to their approach. But they've got a way to go too...[to] really achieve what they're looking for. And...the approach of seeing how many auditors you can ban from signing in a year is not going to really lift the standard. It's going to drive people...out of the profession. So if you're going to go [after] people on those sorts of things, why would [anyone] be part of this?

Several suppliers made comments about the attraction and retention of staff as being negatively associated with the increasingly prescriptive nature of auditing.

> But if that's the perception, you know, perception equals reality, so…the question is if ASIC are coming in and doing reviews and doing it to get a true and fair view, to plagiarise from somewhere else, people accept that. But if they're coming in and they're picking up the minor points that actually don't drive to the heart of the integrity of the audit of those financial statements…that's problematic and they've got a genuine complaint. And it threatens where…you haven't got enough evidence, how did you get there? That's fair game. That's what they're doing. But if it's stuff that they're criticising that actually doesn't really impact the thing… that's an issue. And…you come back to this retention question: retention, entrance to the profession and retention. A lot of it is around the interest, the independence, and what's watching…why would people now come into it when it's that tough to get to grips [with] and understand that you can't…do a lot of the stuff you might want to do? And even when you've done it, someone independent is going to come along and say, 'Well, actually you haven't done it quite right, I'm going to penalise you'…all this helps swing a pendulum away from the attractiveness of audit.

The same person goes on to emphasise the same point about the attractiveness of the profession:

> [I]f the principle of audit is to underpin the capital markets and have good, competent people doing that, there's a difficult discussion around are you then turning off some able people who would come in…there's a risk that you begin to drive at the heart of the attractiveness of the profession in getting people into it and therefore it loses something in the translation.

The same person concludes, expressing misgivings that generation Y staff will necessarily stay with auditing until the perceived upheaval of the recent changes to accounting and auditing standards and to the regulatory regime 'settling down'.

> [W]e're going through an interesting period, having got the legal, enforceable auditing standards, the new accounting standards, the questions around independence...But it is tricky...We need to see it professionally strong and attractive to people who are doing the right job...we'll get there, but...there's also a risk that you can lose some of that on the way through, and we'd lose our way. And whilst the intent was noble, you lose some of that. Interestingly, I suspect the baby boomer who's into status and security would probably get through that and get to the right point of work...Gen Y maybe, who are more intellectually agile, less patient with some things...they may think, 'Well, I don't like the look of that and I'm going to wait till it settles down.' So...we've got some interesting times coming ahead.

'Gen Y maybe, who are more intellectually agile, less patient with some things...they may think, "Well, I don't like the look of that and I'm going to wait till it settles down."'

Another supplier reiterates the same point about what it is that generation Y wants from a career:

> I haven't been subject to the AQRB personally, so I can't really comment on the other regulatory forms...there is now too much checking up on the checkers and all of that will just lead to... young people leaving because it takes any free thought out of doing the audit, any commonsense out of the audit and it just drives a tick-the-box mentality and that's not what gen Y people want to do. They're creative, they think for themselves, they want to do that and we ought to be creating a framework where we work in a team with appropriate direction from the partner to use judgment to cover the risk properly, not tick the box.

'[W]e ought to be creating a framework where we work in a team with appropriate direction from the partner to use judgment to cover the risk properly, not tick the box.'

This next supplier looks to the future and who might be left in a profession that is increasingly compliance driven.

> [I]t's increasingly difficult to retain staff who are increasingly going mad as they fill out ever longer check lists and tick boxes, and that's a serious threat to the future of the auditing profession in that you don't want only dunderheads to stay in it, or people who have just got the physical and emotional strength to survive, banging their head against a brick wall for the rest of their lives.

5.2.1 Summary

Several suppliers make pejorative comments about the impact of increased prescription and the use of check lists in the conduct of the audit on the attractiveness of audit as a profession and on staff retention. The constant scrutiny and reviews from multiple sources, internal and external, are perceived to be turning able people away from the profession—potential newcomers and existing professionals. Generation Y is perceived to be particularly put off by recent developments.

5.3 Standard setters

One standard setter emphasises the need for audits to be productive and efficient, suggesting that form filling is not the best way to achieve this.

> [T]here's a required level of balance and...where we could find ourselves with the reviews of audit firms and areas like that is that the focus could become too much on ticking the box, writing down certain things that...may not be material to the conduct of the audit...the problem is that until something goes wrong, everything's fine and...'all is well until it's not'. And...where we're at is we've got to have a framework...that enables sufficient interest in the work, rather than form filling, for audits to be productive and by that I mean efficient.

The same standard setter goes on to elucidate the essence of the issue as he or she sees it; growing staff capable of dealing with complex issues when they come from a training ground in which compliance with what it is that regulators look for is the norm.

> For audits to be relevant...that means focus[ing] on the real issues, and for audits to add value to the business, which should come from the first two, and if we go down the path of saying well the only way we're ever going to really satisfy a regulator is to have such detailed programs for every aspect of the audit that we would need to have and need to complete because if we didn't do them we will always run the risk of breaching an auditing standard black-letter requirement or some other requirement, albeit it may not be material to the audit. The question then becomes one [of] well, are you going to encourage people who want to be innovative, deal with complex issues, work through them, grow and learn by having them go through a process that requires that? I don't know the

> answer to that but my gut feel[ing] is probably not, to a large extent, because they'll go somewhere where they can do that. And then what you start doing is, you start lowering the bar on the quality of individual that you're asking to come and evaluate risk, design relevant approaches to those risks, deal with senior management who are explaining those situations, identify risks that management haven't seen and then apply what are becoming far more complex accounting standards on fair value, financial instruments and so on, to those situations. Asset impairment, the judgments, what's a cash-generating unit? Do I tick the box…that's where I see the risk.

5.3.1 Summary

One standard setter notes the difficulty of encouraging innovative people with high-level skills to deal with complex issues to enter and stay in the profession and the danger that the quality of individuals will drop as a result.

6.0 Issues and implications

There were certain trigger points for public accounting staff leaving such as completion of their CA and having fulfilled undertakings with respect to repayment of time relating to fee reimbursement or when they were promoted to manager. When it came to other opportunities, however, there seemed to be extensive headhunting activity within the firms—possibly triggered in part by the departure of close colleagues for other employment. There was some reference to short-term pay benefits by leaving the firm, but by and large, remuneration was not a key driver in the decision to leave. Perhaps most important after the interpersonal connectedness issue was the work–life balance and in particular the changing nature of the work, which was repeatedly described as either 'documentation' or 'admin'.

Some reasons why staff remained with their existing audit firm included the possibility of international experience and/or secondment to other divisions within the firm or other locations within the firm. Also, the clarity of job security was attractive if they felt valued and appreciated by those who supervised their work. Remuneration was indicated as a reason to stay, as was the clarity of a career path. The three points indicating real interest in staying were: 1) having someone who played a key role model for them; 2) the quality of people and colleagues working around them and the level of friendliness and the functionality of that group; and 3) having good-quality clients.

Users do not see audit firms as premium employers. For some of the users who might have been employed with the accounting profession, this view could have been coloured by their own experiences as a former employee of a supplier.

Comments by purchasers reveal sophisticated questioning of the traditional business model for staffing an audit firm and, by virtue of being more flexible in their recruitment strategies, they undermine one of their core tenets: the hallowed route to partner. Another level of criticism by purchasers of the audit firm business model is the relatively low pay, high hours of work and a disconnection with lifestyle for younger staff.

While purchasers can be somewhat cynical of the accounting firm employment model, they do see, relative to themselves, enhanced opportunities for understanding by accounting firm personnel of not just the transactional, but the operational activities of business. At the same time, purchasers acknowledge and understand that much of the work undertaken by junior staff is 'menial' and that this provides industry with the opportunity to recruit people who are experienced in business.

Although some purchasers are critical of the quality of the work of audit firms, they see the work within the Big Four as very well managed, well defined and that there is an unambiguous career path. In contrast, industry employment holds more uncertainty and possibly a less well-managed career process. While there might be a short-term monetary gain for an audit firm employee to move to industry, there is less clarity about the long-term financial rewards.

Purchasers also recognise and, in a way, are grateful for the key point in accounting practice careers at which staff is both valuable and vulnerable. They see the employment situation of accounting firms as being not in crisis in relation to other professional areas and that innovation will be the way to make sure the accounting firms do not find themselves systematically disadvantaged.

Among suppliers, there is a general perception that the recruitment process is stable and in a healthy state—albeit with some concerns about salary levels in a competitive market. The real challenge they see is around retention—having in mind generational expectations and structural changes in the nature of the work brought about by regulatory reform and the perceived lessening of professional judgment as a key part of the job.

Within the supplier group, there is a perception of a lack of empathy with generation Y's expectations in regard to the desired rate of change in their working environment. Perhaps it is the case that the audit business model cannot facilitate this desired variety of tasks, but then it comes to the point of recruiting the appropriate staff and managing their expectations.

Some suppliers seem overtly envious of other careers, seeing them as less invaded by regulators and accountability. They believe that if the quality of the work no longer has the capacity for professional judgment then practice becomes more of a compliance career. If graduates who are 'fit for purpose' for a compliance-oriented career are recruited, their particular comparative skills in the management of detail and the ability to undertake routine and competitive tasks leave open a gap as to where the leadership of the profession will come from, as the comparative skill set for this group of graduates is not necessarily overlapping with the 'leadership class'.

From a 'where to from here' perspective, some suppliers recognise the need for constant change and innovation in the working lives of junior auditors—in particular, generation Y—and, importantly, recognise that they need to feel engaged in their occupation.

The key role played by the need for engagement will drive the search for innovative solutions. Some suppliers recognise that the traditional incentive structures—in particular, the prized goal of partnership—are no longer the attractions they once were. There is also a sophisticated recognition that different staff will have different incentives and motivations in their jobs at various stages in their lives, which has a consequence for managing and motivating staff performance. Employers recognise that the employment model itself is not at the higher end of remuneration for staff.

Among suppliers not in the Big Four, there seems to be acute awareness of the differential employment opportunity they can provide. There is recognition that they can use that differential to their own advantage in staff retention by using 'variety' in work tasks and the nurturing of a 'sense of community'. There is recognition among the Big Four that this sense of community is not as evident in their own firms as is the case for the non-Big Four.

Suppliers lament that the nature of oversight of the profession has degraded it, with the high level of regulation and scrutiny having consequences for job satisfaction, employment and retention.

Some suppliers are seeking innovative ways of adjusting employment practices by managing staff turnover between different categories of lower and higher importance clients. Firms are creatively innovating and re-engineering employment practices for staff at high risk of dissatisfaction. There is very sophisticated recognition by some that client-based opportunities that can provide challenges exist, but there are also changes that go to formal and informal innovations to create the components necessary for staff retention.

Standard setters are somewhat cynical that what is happening is anything but a desired outcome and question whether accounting firms are at the leading edge of building a community based on people. There is cynicism about the efficacy of a business model that places far too much emphasis on relatively superficial financial mechanisms and not enough on qualitative, community characteristics. In a people-driven business, if the right people leave, the business will ultimately suffer. There were very penetrating comments from a standard setter that even at partner level, there was a serious threat posed by attrition, which had system-wide implications, especially for highly specialised industry groups.

With respect to documentation, the view of the more junior staff was that the requirements to document hours worked, which historically were a problem, were no longer causing the generalised problems they once did, as firms had in general adjusted audit time budgets to be more realistic. The general view is that in recent years all firms have moved towards a process whereby the real hours of the engagement are recorded and there might be a decision not to then recover those hours, but that the number of hours consumed in undertaking the audit is now a true and fair reflection of the work undertaken. That is, the phenomenon known as 'eating hours' is part of history.

There was an observation (possibly only by a minority) that some partners and managers belonged to a 'previous generation' and were not empathetic with generation Y. For these individuals, documentation and the time constraints they caused were less important. As a consequence, time budgets—at least with respect to these partners and managers—are not realistic and do not reflect the amount of time necessary to fulfil documentary requirements. While some of the participants of the focus groups suggested that documentation was one reason to leave the profession, there were also some positive advantages to documentation. In particular, it meant that the quality of the audit file was better and, with the possibility of staff turnover, more information was routinely available to incoming staff on an audit, thus providing continuity. On balance, however, there were very mixed messages about documentation. On the one hand, there was a belief that it limited the amount of time available to execute the audit and, on the other hand, it was seen as a positive because it meant there was more continuity and more detailed information provided about the client in the file. One person even suggested that the quality of the audit was better because the documentation forced people to contemplate aspects of the audit more thoroughly.

7.0 Concluding remarks

While extensive interviews were held with users, purchasers, suppliers, standard setters and regulators, the level of innovation over alternative solutions to the challenges facing audit suppliers with respect to employment and retention of staff at all levels was relatively unexceptional. There is, however, some innovative thinking and the following synthesises the various views.

Users and purchasers provided a number of insights. There was repeated reference to the differences between generation X and generation Y and that much more care needed to be given to understanding these differences and the consequences for employment. Additionally, several better-informed users were assertive with respect to the issue of audit firms learning from some of the practices within law firms, which in the view of one interviewee, were better able to differentiate between 'star' performers and those who were perfectly adequate in the task. He cited the case of a young lawyer in a major law firm who was promoted to partner by his twenty-fifth birthday. Other observations from the user and purchaser groups were that audit firms needed to do more to encourage women—particularly those women who were star performers—to remain in the profession even if on a fractional basis. It is preferable to have 25 per cent of a star performer than nothing. Similarly, purchasers of substantial audit services made the observation that reward systems in audit firms seemed to be strictly bound by periods of service rather than merit. It is important to separate out particularly meritorious employees and promote, recognise and reward them in ways different to others. The implication is that accounting service providers need to have high-quality human resource systems that can differentiate between adequate and above-adequate performance levels by staff.

Related to this is the fact that audit firms at least, as perceived by purchasers, are shy about recognising stars even if they are able to observe them. The need to celebrate differential performance and support those genuine high performers is a necessary condition for a change in culture. Purchasers were also quick to point out that audit firms must be able to recognise staff as individuals and work with them as individuals not just as people employed at particular levels. Audit firms can no longer rely on the prestige of the auditing profession of the past. The role of the honourable auditor and business advisor is now in conflict with the public policy position of the role of auditors and the previous reliance on this notion of prestige is not an option. In terms of positive suggestions and as part of the recognition of generation X and generation Y, purchasers suggested more extensive utilisation of travel and training, careful use of secondments, particularly to commerce, and recognition that interchanges between commerce/industry and the profession, particularly at senior levels, could happen and needed to be given a more honourable place. While the notion of secondments and exchanges has traction among purchasers, it is acknowledged that the building of expertise in commerce tends to be rather narrow and that secondments must be carefully selected, especially at levels of seniority. Additionally, there was recognition by purchasers of secondments into and from regulators. Another observation was that lawyers seemed to have particular traction with corporate regulators in a way that accountants had yet to achieve.

Two observations that warrant special attention are that accounting firms might do well to inform their staff not just about employment opportunities and career development that exist within their firm but give benchmarked objective comparators to other alternative employment.

Additionally, purchasers took the view that accounting firms needed to interact more frequently with alumni. One solution would be to actively build alumni contacts not just as people who might be potential purchasers of services from large and small accounting firms, but as potential recruits for positions within these firms.

Suppliers also recognised the need to interact more with the alumni networks and that alumni relations within the Big Four were sometimes fragile and might not be as well focused as they could be. Alumni operations within some audit firms are fragile because they rely on a few individuals and are not always focused on the alumni as individuals who can be recruited, but more importantly as potential purchasers of their services. Many interviewees recognised the change in the work culture of numerous employees of audit firms. Among the bigger employers, there was recognition of an increased need for flexibility and work–life balance. Many also observed, however, that their business model and the cutting of margins limited the capacity to deliver on this increased flexibility and the ability to fully and appropriately make the most of the work–life balance. An example is where a particularly able 'in-charge' might be present, this usually results in several managers seeking the services of this 'in-charge' person. Ultimately, this person left the firm because of the pressure of work from so many different directions. Subsequently, that particular firm missed out on this rising star altogether. The implication here is that audit firms have to understand their working practices and their structure ought to attend to the fact that the work–life balance is a key determining factor in the employment of younger auditors.

Generally, there is recognition that audit firms could be more people-driven businesses and that employees need to be treated as individuals and recognised for their unique abilities. Further, more flexibility is required in the working environment and diversity in the work undertaken. Mainstays that should not be forgotten are overseas secondments and a strong culture and brand name for the organisation. None of these is a new solution, but their re-emphasis warrants consideration. An overarching issue among suppliers was that auditing needed to be something beyond 'ticking the box', and the importance of judgment, decision making and expertise development were key to ensuring that jobs were interesting, useful and engaging for people. There is genuine concern that these important requirements are increasingly being lost because of policy decisions within the Australian jurisdiction.

One of the challenges is that certain individuals in senior positions within audit firms do not necessarily empathise well with more junior staff. An example given was that senior managers who aspired to become a partner could actually look, feel and behave more like a partner than a partner and did not empathise and interact well with more junior staff, which was crucial to the continuing performance of the supplier.

In terms of specific solutions, some suppliers believe that a better relationship with the regulator is needed and there ought to be positive engagement with regulators to ensure they do not feel that there is a separation or large division of views between audit suppliers and the regulator. Similarly, careful management of clients and possibly management of those clients with preferential treatment are needed, so that in effect there is the creation of two products within the same brand name.

Again, among standard setters, there was broad recognition that audit firms should acknowledge the work–life balance and the fact that increasingly auditors were leaving the Big Four rather than the Big Four seeking to remove employees. The consequence is that the quality of people leaving the Big Four is seen to be of a very high level, which is good for the broader business community but potentially reduces the quality of individuals among audit suppliers. Interestingly, among standard setters, there was a belief that the most important marketing tool for employment was word of mouth. There is, however, a perception that the Big Four do not come out well in this regard.

Another observation from standard setters, which warrants further consideration, is that there are various levels of work within an audit and an audit firm's business model is to move people up the value chain by transferring them from one client to another. So, from an audit firm's perspective, they are developing the employee and providing a broader expertise with a diversity of clients. Of course, this same strategy viewed from the auditee company's perspective represents 'churn', with a series of fresh faces at short intervals. Within some employment markets, this degree of 'churn' is overcome by enhancing job specifications and the diversity of the skills required. In the Public Service, sometimes it is referred to as 'broad banding' and involves moving an employee up in their career rather than moving the employee away from a particular employment location. Naturally, this produces tensions because one of the values of moving an employee from one client to another is to provide diversity of employment experience and, as documented elsewhere, generation Y audit firm employees appear to crave diversity of work.

Perhaps overall, user, purchaser, supplier and standard setter groups recognise that auditing is under significant challenge due to the change in the nature of the work, fee pressures and pressure to perform, which have occurred simultaneously and are viewed very differently by generation X and generation Y employees. The mix has put considerable pressure on quality and the future. Staff lost to the profession now will, by and large, be less likely to become available to hold senior positions in the profession in the future.

One of the potential policy implications is that audit firms could be intentionally or unintentionally dividing their portfolio of clients according to those from whom they see a positive advantage in minimising employee turnover because of particular complex issues or because that client requires or has been provided with particularly high-quality service. This high-quality service might be more easily or more effectively delivered by a stable team. These premium clients might exist because of the complex or controversial accounting issues within them or because the client is prepared to pay a premium not so much for industry expertise per se but for the stable employment force that knows their client issues very well. If the market is dividing between these premium clients and other clients, the policy implications for regulators will be significant.

It can be concluded that overall, even before the recognition of the global financial crisis, those already in the system had keenly felt a shock to the system—played out in terms of overfull employment, scarcity of human talent and the presence of high staff turnover. At that time, equilibrium in work expectations and capacity to adapt to change were not reached. It will not be possible for those who find this change disagreeable to transfer out of the profession immediately and it will take some time for these forces to work through and for the system to adapt. Now we have a second shock to the system in the form of the global financial crisis, which is likely to lower the demand for the talent pool. This crisis, however, is likely to mask a continuing underlying trend; it might provide an opportunity for structural change that will place the accounting profession on a better footing for the future of audit.

The question must be asked, however, where the employment model is heading. Suppliers recognise that they have been under price pressure, which leads to pushing down staffing costs, which in turn means higher staff turnover, which in turn means higher costs and, potentially and more importantly, a lower-quality product. This business model is unsustainable in the long term and a solution needs to be found. Could a radical change to business processes, such as that which XBRL[8] or some other technology might induce, create a further shock that assists in remedying what appears to be a system near to crisis?

As noted above, we have heard some penetrating comments that, at all levels, including that of partner, the audit business model faces a serious threat from the attrition rates of professionals, which has implications for the entire market for audit services and even touches on the much discussed creation of specialist industry groups. The threats to a high-quality audit product as a consequence are foreseeable. For some levels of expertise, the question of attrition is highly costly, not just in monetary terms but in terms of the time lag before remedy. While this penetrating view has resonance, there is no obvious solution to what is a profoundly important question for the future of audit. While there might be some diversity of work for audit staff across clients, for the majority, it is at relatively low levels of expertise and is not going to solve this aspect of the problem.

It cannot be emphasised enough that care needs to be taken with the effects of the global financial crisis on the employment regime, particularly among more junior auditors. While the employment market might be less competitive, underlying trends are unlikely to change and the global financial crisis is likely to simply mask underlying challenges. The global financial crisis could in fact be an opportunity that can be seized to change employment practices and business models so that when full employment returns, the auditing business model as it pertains to employment can emerge with greater effectiveness and efficiency.

8 eXensible Business Reporting Language

DIVISION D

AUDITOR INDEPENDENCE 9

> [T]here are synergies when an audit firm goes through a company and performs the audit. They develop a great deal of knowledge about the way the company works and who the people are in the company and...there is an integration of knowledge when those firms also do the tax work and perhaps corporate services consulting work. But on the other hand, ...the audit's fee is generally a lesser percentage, a more minor percentage, of the total fee when a firm does all the other corporate-type work as well and...there are dangers with that. I can see there would be a loss; I see there would be an increased cost, but rather than prejudice or taint the performance of the audit, I would prescribe to the view that auditors should be prohibited from offering other services.
>
> — Regulator

1.0 Key issues

The issue of auditor independence has many facets. This study focuses principally on two key facets: auditor-provided non-audit services and audit partner rotation. Auditor-provided non-audit services is one of the most debated aspects in the maintenance of auditor independence. Audit partner rotation is tied inextricably to the continuity of audit teams and client and industry knowledge dealt with in Chapter 6. Challenges for the profession and regulators in these areas include:

- are the majority of participants in the market for audit services aware of changes to the auditor independence requirements as a result of the *CLERP 9* and related reforms
- is the focus on maintenance of independence confused with maintenance of objectivity

- can rules or guidelines be invoked to ensure maintenance of independence and objectivity, to the extent that they differ
- where does the balance lie in the trade-off between the potential for knowledge 'spill-overs', compromised independence and public cynicism as a consequence of auditor-provided non-audit services
- can the auditing profession learn from other professions in which similar potential independence conflicts arise
- is the management of separation of personnel successful in maintaining audit as independent from non-audit services
- to what extent can reliance on the personal integrity of the personnel involved in the provision of audit and non-audit services be relied on and how can that personal integrity be supported and evidenced
- are the requirements for independence in terms of clients and financial interests disproportionately harsh on audit personnel compared with other public accounting firm personnel and, if so, what are the potential consequences of this
- to what extent is avoidance by personnel of public accounting firm requirements and quality controls regarding independence an issue
- where does the balance lie between initial audit engagement quality and creating sought-after challenges for partners when they rotate to a new client, hence assisting in their retention
- where does the balance lie between enhancing independence and the potential for loss of clients and perhaps industry knowledge when partners rotate off an engagement
- are partner rotation requirements making it crucial to have a critical mass of partners and hence discouraging smaller firms from auditing listed entities, and does this give rise to changes in the level of competition in the market for audit services
- is the potential cost to personal career aspirations too high for those skilled in audits of highly complex entities where few industry participants exist
- is five years appropriate for the duration of audit partner tenure in all industry categories or is it too costly in terms of creating inefficiencies in some instances
- how do firms manage the partner rotation requirements while maintaining partner satisfaction and audit quality?

2.0 Introduction

The issue of auditor independence is examined in this study through specific questions asked in the survey and the interviews. The survey involved a general question in relation to whether stakeholders were aware of reforms pertaining to auditor independence. For the interviews, stakeholders were asked specifically about their perceptions in relation to auditor-provided non-audit services (APNAS) and audit partner rotation; both issues were affected by the *CLERP 9* and related reforms.

3.0 Survey

Participants in the mail and telephone surveys were asked about their awareness of certain changes to the regulation of audit services in Australia. One component of this was about changes relating to auditor independence. Their responses are reported in Table 9.1.

Table 9.1 Responses on awareness of changes in regulation (per cent)

	USERS			PURCHASERS				SUPPLIERS			
	Total	Accounting expertise	Professional users	Private investors	Total	Directors/ audit comm.	CEO/CFO	Other	Total	Big Four	Non-Big Four
Are you aware of the following specific changes that have occurred in the regulation of audit services in Australia?											
Reforms pertaining to auditor independence	57	69	53	45	79	79	76	86	92	96	91

Percentage of respondents answering 'Strongly agree' or 'Agree' on a five-point scale.

As one might expect, those who are most active in the market for audit services are the most aware that there have been regulatory changes with regard to auditor independence. Allowing for minor errors in responses, one can reasonably conclude that the population of suppliers of audit services is aware of these changes and that the majority of purchasers in that market are also aware of these changes. Again, as might be expected, the empirical evidence is that private investors are the least well informed, with less than half responding to an awareness of these changes.

4.0 Introduction: auditor-provided non-audit services

Users, purchasers, suppliers, standard setters and regulators were asked during the face-to-face interviews about their attitude to APNAS. Prompt questions revolved around the relative costs and benefits of companies being prohibited from buying other services—such as tax services and management consulting—from auditors and whether, if they were prohibited, that would be a concern or there might be a risk of a loss of synergies.

4.1 Users

Users are mixed in their views about whether prohibition of APNAS purchase is a concern. These first quotes reveal users who approve of the separation and have no concerns about potentially lost synergies.

> I don't see any scope between that...they can start providing tax and consulting and...that's probably been a good thing.

> I don't know, but then I'm quite comfortable having that separation of duties...that's probably a push by some of these larger accounting firms...[which] are missing out on huge business, because, for example, at the auditor of Telstra, and they can't do various corporate work for Telstra...that's fine. I don't see any issues with having that separation of duties at all.

The same person goes on to fully support regulation that maintains separation, arguing that there are many skilled people who can conduct the other services:

> [There are] enough people around these days...sure, it's going to be probably a little bit more expensive and [there will be a] loss of... having internal knowledge of things, but...if you've got external advisors that know what an annual report is and know how to read it, they can pick up from where the auditors have left off...it's a

great thing…it's probably a push from maybe some of the major accounting firms—because they're obviously missing out on a lot of business—to try and dull some of those laws down a bit. But… they're probably the most necessary laws there are, because it shows independence.

A similar theme is evident in the words of another two users:

> [I]n that particular case…even if you're a small company, I don't think it's difficult to quickly brief and get someone else…to actually understand your operation in terms of what they would need to know to assist you in that decision making, even if you're a small company…We're in that situation here and I would certainly not go to our auditors.

> No [to prohibition on auditor-provided other services]. Maybe on the surface. The ones…that have gone broke, the organisations… you might argue there's some conflict of interest.

The same person responds specifically in relation to APNAS relating to tax:

> Maybe [having shared audit and tax services]…works well. But it's the cases that go bad that you can see that maybe those things weren't being taken to the proper degree…for example, if you had a different analyst working on your company, theoretically, when you value your company, you'd have more information from all different sources. But if that's not passed with the auditor, for example, or to the end user, then maybe you're only getting half the information. So it works both ways, doesn't it?

Several users comment on how their audit firm manages the potential conflict by maintaining strict separation of the personnel involved.

> We do that. We do buy tax services from the same company but it's generally a different group. And they obviously say if you're buying tax services you're talking to the tax department within that firm, which is [a] completely different group of people that come to do the audit and they don't talk to each other, and they probably don't even know each other. So, yes, we do buy those services from the same auditing company.

> [T]he firms obviously have to manage that issue…as long as it's not one kind or one audit firm, or one accounting firm…that's totally

> reliant on where all their services are coming from...as long as they don't take it too far. There's a logic to...providing tax services and some of the related services. I'm not stressed about that...it's more with some of the chunkier fees, things in terms of advisory-type roles where there is obvious conflict between making, for instance, a transaction successful as opposed to the guardian[ship role] of ensuring that that transaction...complies with accounting rules and that people understand what's going on there...it has to be carefully managed.

> It depends on the size of the firm. For example, with [name of a Big Four firm], we get the tax services from the tax guys and the audit services from the audit guys. The only time they ever discuss the account is when the audit needs tax sign-off for the financial statements, and often that's the only involvement they'll have with each other.

> [T]hey have been managing the conflict of interest very well...we've appointed a foreign auditor, for instance, for one of our foreign accounts, and each year they will write to me and get me to confirm who our external auditors are so that we don't have conflict...so long as they manage it in that way, I can't see an issue with them continuing to provide other services. But there's definitely got to be that split between the different business units, and those Chinese walls, and they have to operate efficiently. And there are definite benefits that come to a firm with having access to that knowledge, probably more from an internal-audit perspective. To get a sign-off on changes to tax regulations or whatever it is, you wouldn't be able to just go to a generalist; you need to have that expert tax advice. So it's good for the internal auditor to be able to refer back to an expert in the area...there [are] probably more positives than there are negatives.

This next user explains that it is not an issue that causes concern to him or her, but the capital market focuses on it:

> [I]t doesn't concern me...because I know how it works in the real world. They're such big firms and the people are so different, [and] separated...that there is a level of independence. But having said that, it is something that the markets do focus on a little bit...you [have] just got to be a bit careful about how it looks...Although [there] was a big focus post-Enron and it's probably, over time, faded a bit.

Another user, an analyst, points to similar types of independence conflicts in his or her industry:

> There are perceived conflicts...you're providing tax advice and wanting to make money on this, and then you're going to audit the outcome of that...there is an inherent conflict unless you can prove that internally you've got these fantastic Chinese walls...I work in a business that's constantly dealing with these issues, and you get a very cynical public out there if we float a company that our corporate team has floated, and then write research on it; there's a perceived conflict.

The same person goes on to point out the cost of cynicism, if APNAS encourages that reaction from the public:

> We deal with it by full disclosure...which I know the accounting profession does, but does it benefit the company...and its cost of capital, and how it's viewed...People just get cynical. And there's a cost to cynicism, isn't there?

This next user would be happy to see more paid for audits by companies in which he or she is a shareholder if that is necessary to maintain a prohibition on APNAS:

> I'm more in favour of prohibition of the other services. I'd like the auditor really to—now this would probably mean that you'd have to pay more for the audit, but I'm prepared to live with that as a shareholder, because for me the independence of the auditor is supreme. I want as few...potential conflicts of interest between the auditor and the company as possible because...the prime function of the auditor is to...make sure that the company isn't telling me too many porkies, to put it bluntly. And anything that compromises the interests of the auditors—if we, a nudge and a wink if we don't do this, don't say this, will we have a better chance of getting other services—to me is fraught with dangers. Conflicts of interest are rife and...it's better that those other services are provided by other firms.

The same user continues, reiterating other users' comments that other providers can be found for consulting-type engagements:

> The risk of the auditor not being aware of all the details [of] the company—for example, of the tax arrangements...is relatively small because, particularly if you're talking [about] the big auditors, they would all know...what innovations the other ones are coming up with...it's like in research: imitation is the sincerest form of flattery. If somebody comes up with a good idea, we all adopt it, and so it would be in terms of those type of services. So I doubt that there's too much knowledge that would be lost, and it certainly wouldn't... outweigh the risk of a potential compromise of the independence.

Other users, however, have no problem with APNAS, do not want to see any prohibitions on it and can see the benefits of having an auditor provide these services.

> I can't see why they shouldn't be allowed to offer those other services...you've got someone that spends a week or two weeks, or however long it takes, inside your business, so they're going to get a pretty good handle on it. And so they're probably one of the best people to be able to offer the management consulting-type service... they should be allowed to do it. And you know they're professional so they're going to do it in a professional manner. I can't really see a conflict of interest.

The same user goes on to conclude:

> And I don't know how to fix [the independence conflict], but they would be the best people to give you advice on your business because they know it backwards. So I don't know how we get around that, but...the benefits potentially outweigh the costs.

This next user has great respect for the integrity of the profession and feels there is no need for further prohibitions:

> '[T]here are benefits in having the same firm that does your accounts doing your tax...and often doing other things like secondments and a whole host of different things. There are synergistic benefits for the business, and for the auditor.'

> [T]his really falls to the integrity of the auditor. Independence...is a state of mind, it's not a state of prescription. You can't prescribe independence. I'm a chartered accountant, I've been one for 30 years...the auditing profession in Australia has got a very high level of integrity...they are capable of being independent...the issues are, if the auditors [are] getting $200 000 in tax work as well as

> $500 000 for doing the accounts, as well as $50 000 for advising on something else, that client is a very important part of their business...so if your ability to be impartial when you're doing a job—because you're worried about losing that client—gets in the way of [how] you do your job, that becomes a problem and it's really...hard to measure that...the auditing profession in Australia is as good as anywhere else in the world and the right level of independence and integrity rests with the partners of the firm and the people that work with them. And there are benefits in having the same firm that does your accounts doing your tax...and often doing other things like secondments and a whole host of different things. There are synergistic benefits for the business, and for the auditor for that matter, in doing that, and it's a shame to lose those things. But I do understand why some people would think you can't let the auditor get too close to the company. That's the whole issue about rotating and all that sort of stuff as well...there's probably a fine balance there between the two.

The interviewer asks: 'What are the benefits of being able to share the business knowledge, like the tax people being able to share their knowledge with the auditor/audit teams?' The user responds:

> [I]t's just simpler, really. Just logistically simpler.

The next quotation shows a similar logic:

> [I]t's useful in that you would get at least the same answers. For example, when you buy a service from [say] PriceWaterhouseCoopers, are you getting the same answers, the same results as if you would've bought that service from [say] Ernst & Young, who are your auditors, who then audit...that service or that paper...it would be handy because we would only have one service provider, or one consultant...so we wouldn't have to get whatever paper we asked to be prepared...audited by a different firm. And so then there's a risk of coming [up] with different answers, which we've seen happen with the last firm.

4.1.1 Summary

Users are mixed in their views of whether a higher level of prohibition of APNAS brings desired benefits in independence. One user, an investor, is prepared to pay more for audits if that is the consequence of greater prohibition. For other users, however, the simplicity of having a single provider for audit and non-audit services is compelling. The lower risk of receiving differential advice, their superior knowledge of the business and the professionalism of the public accounting firms are offered as justification for APNAS. The perception that many other providers could service the need, the difficulty in managing separation of personnel, the expectations of the markets and public cynicism if auditors are seen as self-serving are the arguments raised by those who feel there needs to be more rather than less prohibition of joint provision.

4.2 Purchasers

Taking first those who are comfortable with the current situation and do not want greater prohibitions placed on APNAS, these next few quotations provide the purchasers' reasoning for their views.

> [T]here is a big potential loss to companies of synergies if you were to make it a complete blanket ban.

One purchaser reminisces about a time when even legal services could be provided by the audit firm and the benefits he or she perceived to have flowed from that:

> 'I really saw some advantages—particularly for small acquisition work, where often the auditor will work on an acquisition—to have people who knew and understood the audit function, as well as the legal function.'

> I'll give an example…which…certainly in these days…would [be] very, very unfashionable. In one of my roles…arguably even unfashionably…back in a '99, 2000, 2001 kind of world, I saw a definite synergy, even in getting legal services from [one of the Big Four]. They had some good lawyers who I knew had come in from good firms. So they had not an enormous law firm, but a quite talented firm of good people. And I…saw some advantages—particularly for small acquisition work, where often the auditor will work on an acquisition—to have people who knew and understood the audit function, as well as the legal function. And so that's one example—probably a rare example… that's certainly one of the things that's the deadest of all out of the non-audit services audit. The lawyers, of course, typically left the accounting firms…And the liquidations people is [sic] one that we probably took a bit of a de facto view the other way. Our loans

> management guys were relatively careful not to use [one of the Big Four]...there might be certain reasons why you did, but generally it was not a reason, whereas...the lawyers could see some definitive advantages.

The same purchaser continues, emphasising the importance of personal integrity on the part of service providers, whether audit or non-audit:

> [T]hen you go the other side. Was it changing our auditors' independence and robustness in telling the board that there was a problem, and I'm very confident, and obviously the example of one, I rely on the personalities of those auditors—not a chance in the world. I mean [Person X] would have told the audit committee any time, and did, his concerns no matter what was coming on the other side.

Another purchaser sees tax work as inextricably linked to auditing, so that it might indeed be seen as part of the audit, and is concerned that wider prohibitions to include tax might be implemented.

> I am concerned about it. I understand the reasons for the reporting and I certainly agree that auditors can't audit their own work or... get themselves into conflictive positions. But...the provision of taxation advice is so integral to the operation of the preparation of the accounts and, from a purely cost-effective point of view, it seems...that's one area which is often classed as a separate service that could be...treated more appropriately, as linked to the audit itself. That would be my preferred position.

Another purchaser provides a tax dispute as an example of where having auditor-provided tax consulting would be helpful:

> I'm quite agnostic as to the rules on non-audit services...a lot of the non-audit services, particularly...tax...helped the auditor to know more about you...[I]n our...fortunately small list of issues, we have a...tax dispute, and...five years ago [name of Big Four firm] would've had a bigger role in that matter and...they obviously know as much as they need to know as an auditor, where they would probably have known factually more about it prior to some of the non-audit service requirements.

The same person goes on to speak of another potential independence problem: having an ex-audit partner as a board member.

> [T]he downside risk...was [that] the auditor is too much in your pocket...for example, the HIH one that I found a bit freaky was that the guy on the board was an ex-audit partner of the place... that was obvious and I found that quite problematic from a genuine audit independence point of view.

The same person continues with the theme of the independence of board members.

> [*In response to the question: 'But it does depend on personalities. An ex-partner can have little sway or pull with the current audit team, but there are exceptions:'*] Yes...it's interesting you put it that way and of course that's absolutely 50 per cent of the risk, but the other 50 per cent is that he's...defending his old brand, his old reputation, given some of his old work...So we haven't even gone to the pension fund, you're articulating to levels of the complexity that I don't usually think about...the first risk, just sitting around board tables, is that there will be an emotional bond from that director for the old mob.

An insight into a purchaser's policy in relation to commissioning of APNAS is provided by this next quotation:

> '[O]n all my boards, we have pitched it somewhere in the middle. We haven't gone down the path of having rigid multiples of audit fees or just...a total ban...either.'

> [I]f you consider the full spectrum between a total ban on the auditors doing anything other than the audit...at one end and the total ability to do whatever they want on the other, on all my boards, we have pitched it somewhere in the middle. We haven't gone down the path of having rigid multiples of audit fees or just...a total ban...either. We've actually come up with policies that say the external auditor will only be selected to do other services in the following instances and we've listed a series of dot points that talk about where they're the best person to the do the job and taking into account a whole lot of factors and where it won't impair their independence and where it's not a service that's been banned. And so we will usually ban probably 10 or so services and then in the rest of the cases, we'd say to management well you prove to us why you think they're the best one for the job and how it won't impair their independence. If you can do that then you can use them.

One purchaser enunciates a view on the requirement to report non-audit services. He or she points out that auditors might, in their attempts to be independent to regulators, minimise amounts classified as audit work, which increases the value of the apparent non-audit service work and the eternal appearance of the threat to independence.

> [A]s a result of all of these organisations like [name of Big Four firm], for example, take all of the taxation advice and classify it as being other services. And they're just following that classic line. If it's going to be regulated, let's be absolutely safe about it and make sure there can't be an argument...so the effect of that is to increase the amount of other services, which then in turn promotes justification for reporting all of this stuff.

The interviewer then asks: 'Do you think there's a role for audit-only firms? There are one or two niche audit-only firms arising in some markets across the world...There are a few pension scheme audit firms that have arisen, and all they do is auditing, and all they do is pension schemes, so they're really good at doing that, but nothing beyond that.'

> [A]t first blush, [audit-only firms] seems attractive to me because it solves the problem of the Chinese wall, doesn't it? Because everybody's cynical about [Chinese walls] there [are] bound to be some problems with it, presumably perhaps in recruiting people or retention of people...But it has a certain attraction. It is an attractive proposal because it's very tempting under the current structure for other services to try to piggyback onto the audit process, which is fundamentally wrong.

4.2.1 Summary

Most purchasers do not feel there is a need for extensive prohibition of APNAS. Reminisces to a past era when even legal services were provided by the audit firm, and the benefits of that, are given, plus an insight into how the purchasing approval for APNAS is sometimes handled. Another purchaser reminds us—with the example of an ex-audit partner as a board member—of independence issues associated with other than the APNAS question. Another purchaser alludes to the importance of the personal integrity of those providing any service.

4.3 Suppliers

Suppliers show no appetite for increased restrictions on APNAS. The first supplier's comments indicate his or her certainty that clients prefer the current situation regarding APNAS and do not seek greater prohibitions.

> [A]nything with turnover of one million to 200 million...like a one-stop shop, and they like to know that their auditing is speaking to the tax professional and that they're coordinating their work in terms of the tax-effective accounting in the external financial report. Now it's an absolute reality that these organisations don't have the skills to produce an external financial report in accordance with the accounting standards because it's too...hard.

The same person continues, expanding on why clients prefer a one-stop shop for audit and other services:

> [The client relies] on their auditors. They provide the numbers, they say, 'Here's our trial balance, here's all the information that needs to be disclosed, now can you just assemble that into a financial report structure?' And that's been done by the Big Four, mid-tiers...since day dot because they tend to have management experience and management accounting experience, and they have various financial skills, but they don't necessarily have the external financial reporting knowledge. So it makes a lot of sense for us to be able to just go in there and deliver a seamless service, which says here's your external financial report; here's your tax return; here's the tax planning matters; here's your auditor opinion...our clients are demanding it. We see it from start-up companies; start-up companies in particular prefer—and I'm talking [about] companies here which might need capital raising as well—they love the idea of just having one firm that can do the whole lot for them.

One supplier enunciates, quite passionately, an example of the financial cost to him of having to comply with discarding personal financial interests when there is a potential conflict in terms of independence from a client of the firm:

> The whole independence issue as currently regulated globally is a complete farce. It doesn't achieve what it set out to do. I've only recently become a partner and I've spent most of my life bumming around and having a wife and kids and doing things. So I'm one of

> these wealthy people who's come all the way up. So fairly recently... I went to my bank and I invested in some particular investment. After six months, I am forced to dispose of that investment within five days because someone I've never met, and will never meet, and don't know, and don't influence...is also...[the person who] won the compliance plan of that audit in wherever in the world. How does that affect their independence? How does it affect my independence? All it does is penalise people...It is utterly stupid. There are any number of examples of this...the deceitful people will do things to get around these rules, and do.

The same supplier continues, explaining how deceitful audit personnel can evade the spirit of the rules regarding financial interests:

> I don't have any family over here, but people with big a family, they can say they're [their] brother-in-law's shares. No-one would ever know who put the money up, until the family falls out and then everyone dobs everyone else in. But deceitful people will find ways around it. It is complete crap and it hasn't been thought through at all. You also have the problem of global differences in legislation... So the restrictive services under Sarbanes-Oxley, and there's a whole list them, that doesn't apply in other places.

The same person continues:

> There are some things that...should be prohibited—for instance, I remember standing up at [one of the Big Four firms] in the late '90s and making myself extremely unpopular with the main partner... when he said, 'Look boys, you're talking about a total assurance solution of external needs...auditing', and I can tell you now having been an internal, where the external went off the rails, that this is an actual conflict of interest, and we should not be...[providing] the external and internal audits of this [client].

The same person continues, arguing that prescriptive rules penalise everyone when not all need to be penalised:

> In other cases, the auditor...despite people's comments about their lack of knowledge of the business, is actually well placed to do that work. [*An example is given where both services are jointly provided without an apparent problem.*] But I don't see a problem with that. So it does very much vary. But the problem with putting in prescriptive

> rules is that you take away people's judgment and you just end up making a rule that penalises everyone, when in fact you're only trying to stop the two boys at the back from fighting, and in fact the whole class has to stay in...It's counterproductive and it...does not preserve audit independence. I can think of situations where people in other parts of the firm, not in auditing, have gone into clients and sold their shares immediately when they see how those clients work, or bought more shares. Now...that is [a] far greater... conflict...And obviously at the extreme of things if the Arthur Andersen partner of Enron is getting $50 million through the door in one year and only a small proportion of that is audit, that is ridiculous...But that's arguing from the extreme. If you argue from the general, I can't support it.

The same person implies that there is enough non-audit work available from the clients of other audit firms to keep fee growth alive:

> [Y]ou need to completely rethink all of that. It's just [not a] working practice...people out there think it is working. And as with any of these things, we just get used to that, we work around it...not being in the audit division it's great for me, I can go to any of the other big firms' audit clients and get decent fees...out of it. So we all find a way of coexisting and living and it's okay. And the pie [grows] ever larger. Well, to put it another way, the cost of business grows ever larger. Would there be great synergies by the audit firm doing it? Probably not much; maybe a little. So [that's] a bit of a problem.

The interviewer, pursuing this theme of potential wealth impacts on individual auditors forced to comply with rules in relation to financial interests, elicits another anecdotal example from a supplier:

> I heard a story—and forget which firm it may have been...where a partner totally innocently went to Disneyland with his child. And you can buy a share in Disneyland...Walt Disney with a picture of Mickey Mouse at the kiosk and so on. Without thinking, he bought it for his kid's wall...And that was...deemed to be a breach of independence. And that's just ridiculous. And the Americans, bless them, many good things come out of America, but some stupidity comes out in very much the form rather than the substance.

The same person continues, arguing that form rather than substance characterises compliance with independence requirements.

> [W]here you get into independence, it is form rather than substance...I hasten to add I don't—but if I had a credit card with [one of the banks], which is one of our audit clients, does that distort the independence, does that breach our independence, where I have no involvement in the audit and no way of impacting it? It's difficult. But maybe it's one of those things. You've got to draw the line somewhere. The question is where do you draw it? I find this question of divesting—one sells the shares and all that sort of thing—is a problematic one.

Another two suppliers in the next and subsequent quotation provide insight into just how frequent are requests to disclose within the firm any potential conflicts that arise in the case of potential clients.

> [I]t should be up to the auditor to determine their own independence...the guidelines that are out there now are sufficient. The rotational aspect of auditors is probably okay...in my context, the independence requirements are contained in the codes of professional conduct and the regulators are relying on those codes for the auditors to ensure that they are independent. If an external regulatory audit discovers that the auditor is not independent...they should be slammed down like a tonne of bricks, and...that's happening...I'm happy with that. As a matter of course, if we're tendering on a large audit or any audit we circulate amongst, not just this practice but the other...practices in our group...We go through the full routine of 'are there any conflicts of interest', et cetera...Probably at least once a day all of the principals in this organisation would get an email asking [about] conflicts of interest.

'Probably at least once a day all of the principals in this organisation would get an email asking [about] conflicts of interest.'

> [I]t's probably not as much of an issue from a non-Big Four scenario because our brief doesn't go quite as far as what theirs do. But also the companies that we deal in tend to be more of the small to medium cap in particular. So the likelihood that someone in our Brisbane office, for example, has got shares in a company that we're auditing is less likely. But having said that, what we do from an independence point of view now is vastly different to what we did...

> [a few] years ago. And it's an extremely serious thing that's taken across our whole group across Australia. I'm getting independence checks almost every couple of days.

Another supplier speaks about the complex task involved in firms' maintenance of systems and procedures ensuring their independence from clients, and requests stability in the rules governing auditor independence:

> Our independence list is frightening in its length and complexity... the other thing that concerns me is that sometimes with the independence...it's a little bit like complying with the auditing standards. It's almost impossible to do the perfect file. It's almost impossible therefore if a regulator comes in says, 'Oh, you haven't done that.' Is that helpful, does that damage the form? The same with independence: it's almost impossible to keep everything up to date in terms of independence, it's so complicated, therefore you've only got to slip here and the whole framework comes crashing down. And that focuses people's mind and people are concerned [about] that. Therefore...it's right that there is independence. And perhaps it's right there should be prescription. But...it's difficult where you draw the barriers...the trouble is if you keep changing the rules then people don't quite know where they are.

In this next quotation, another supplier enunciates the complexity of the independence management task:

> I've got no problem with it and think that it's all good from our perspective. But...what it does do is it drags things into a scenario where you've got to...assess [those] that perhaps you wouldn't necessarily think you would have to. We get a number of queries. And most of the independence for our network is run out of Melbourne...there's no issue there, but it's got that person thinking. They've asked the query because they know that 'well, I'd better make sure that there's not an independence issue'. So... our sensitivity towards independence has heightened significantly. And...it takes...up administrative time...that's the problem with it. But I certainly think for where there are genuine independence issues then absolutely we need to have a process in place to make sure that they're prevented from happening.

The same supplier continues, expanding on the management of compliance with independence requirements:

> It's still a burden, don't get me wrong...because of...the client base more than anything else, it's not as much of an issue, put it that way...with the Big Four and particularly because they're so vast and they have client bases that are dealing in let's say ASX 200 or all of those sort of companies, and they've got so many people as well...it's more of a task for them to...make sure that independence is monitored. So from a resource point of view, it doesn't take us [as] much as what [it does] the Big Four...But it doesn't mean that we don't need to have those processes in place, because we do.

This next supplier approves of the current independence regime, but concedes that his or her consultant colleagues likely do not agree:

> We do segregate...and there's money with consulting. There's tax work we can do, [and we] still do quite a bit of tax work around compliance. Tax advising—okay you can't, but tax compliance you can. So...as an auditor, I'm looking at it solely from an auditor's point of view...it costs the firm money. But it would be worse if we were put into a position to sign something that came undone later on and cost us more...if you speak to a consultant, they'll totally disagree with me, but from an auditor's point of view, I'm glad that there is that independence line and it doesn't get crossed.

4.3.1 Summary

Several suppliers speak of the complexity and cost to their firms of monitoring potential independence conflicts. Other suppliers speak of the personal cost of forced, hasty divestiture of securities necessitated by a firm's acceptance of clients who create a potential independence conflict. Another issue raised is that some use deceitful practices to evade firms' policies. For suppliers servicing the smaller audit clients, anecdotal evidence is presented that a one-stop shop for service provision is preferred. Overall, there is little evidence of a pushback against the existing regime, but there is also no taste for extending it to prohibitions greater than those that currently exist.

4.4 Standard setters

Some interesting insights are brought to the issue of APNAS by standard setters. In particular, the distinction between 'auditor independence' and 'auditor objectivity' is raised, as the next quotation reveals.

> [T]he real question there is does the auditor doing other work inhibit their independence? Sorry, inhibit their objectivity... 'independence' is a word that's been somewhat hijacked...in all my experiences, the answer to that is absolutely no. [*in regard to the purchase of APNAS*] [This is] a bit like...risk-based versus prescription...There [are] clearly some things that the auditor should not do. So anything which gets you in a position of auditing your own work as a concept...you should not do.

Attempting to 'mandate objectivity' is how this same standard setter sees many of the independence rules:

> '[T]he rules that have been put in place are a prescriptive attempt to mandate objectivity, which...is the real issue. But the thing is, you can't mandate objectivity.'

> [C]learly, you can't do anything which involves management of the company. So there [are] clearly some buckets of things that absolutely... [you cannot do]. But once you take those things out, which are relatively few in number...the real issue is does it inhibit the auditor's objectivity? And my experience has always been that it hasn't. Instead...it's been that the rules that have been put in place are a prescriptive attempt to mandate objectivity, which...is the real issue. But the thing is, you can't mandate objectivity, so...that's why I say independence has always been hijacked...this attention and focus and concerns about breaching independence rules...have no impact whatsoever on the real issue, which is objectivity...it's been a whole lot of hoo-ha and carry-on and effort and cost for all sorts of people that was just [avoidable]...[also] it doesn't even go close to achieving what's being desired, which is quite laudable...it's this whole thing about the difficulty of auditing, and...it isn't particularly precise. There's a lot around mind-set and understanding what's going on...This is a good example of what happens when you try and mandate something in the audit space: you end up creating a whole set of rules that...don't go to the real issue.

Continuing, the same standard setter reinforces the point that the concept of independence has been hijacked:

> [I]ndependence has got hijacked. Objectivity of the auditor is paramount...it's an absolutely fundamental part of a robust assurance process...I absolutely agree with what I think is the concept behind this, which was trying to strengthen objectivity. I just think [that] in trying to do that, because objectivity is about a state of mind to a very large extent...so trying to create rules that mandate that, you end up with a set of rules which don't...achieve what you set out to achieve.

The same standard setter continues after the interviewer mentions the issue of perceptions in relation to auditors and financial interests in the client:

> Absolutely there is that. And I agree with financial interests, this perception issue. And so I actually support the concept that financial interests are out...also the other good thing that that does is it takes away...mostly a perception issue, but it takes away insider trading...for a number of different reasons...a blanket ban on financial interests is a good thing...some of this other stuff around...services is missed.

The same person continues, putting forward the notion that incremental involvement in an organisation can assist the audit process:

> [There are] synergies in the sense of their cost, but also there's a knowledge loss for the auditor. And we go to what a good audit is... it understands the risks and what's going on. And so some broader involvement though the organisation can actually help the audit process.

Another standard setter enunciates the complexity of the arguments for and against APNAS:

> [S]ome of the costs are...[related to] having to get another firm in that doesn't have the background knowledge about the organisation. So at times the auditors will be best placed to provide advice. Clearly, if you go too far that way you've got the risks of auditing their own work or becoming too close to management and not being sufficiently objective...that's the nuts and bolts of it. And they're both real issues.

The same standard setter continues, lamenting an overly prescriptive approach to APNAS:

> I worry about...completely slavish rules that the auditors can only do an audit for example and no other services, but...there should be proper processes around audit committees oversighting what sort of non-audit services the auditors are able to provide and having a framework in which to judge that. So some things will be 'no-go' areas, but others might be [related to] judgment, which either needs to be reported to the audit committee, or some things would need to be...approved by the audit committee in advance... At a higher level perhaps there is some place for the regulator too, or for there to be some rules. But I worry about that all being too prescriptive. Because otherwise you're implying that effectively the boards aren't...competent.

4.4.1 Summary

The distinction between independence and objectivity dominates the comments of one standard setter, who argues that the independence issue has been hijacked and that objectivity cannot be mandated. Another of the standard setters is wary of an overly prescriptive approach to APNAS, preferring that audit committees and boards make the judgment calls in this context. The benefits for risk assessment in an auditing context of an auditor being involved in an organisation in an additional service capacity are discussed as well as the risk of becoming too close to management.

4.5 Regulators

One regulator expresses scepticism about the potential synergies of APNAS, as revealed in the following quotation:

> I'd just be a bit wary about the synergies, because the reality of this is that you're talking about very large service providers providing services, and...a good example is...an IT consultant. Well, the reality there is that the fact that...some [part] of your empire is working on an IT consulting contract probably isn't going to add a lot of synergies to the audit. But a very aggressive audit approach can stuff up all sorts of relationships across your business...if you're going to do your job as an auditor properly, you're probably not going to be the most popular people, and I can see how, even in a very subtle way...being in that position doesn't tend to encourage

> you to be very independent and aggressive if you think there are very large chunks of business being done in other parts of the organisation, or the organisation that you work for.

The same regulator expands on the point, arguing how difficult it is for auditors to 'serve two masters':

> [F]rom a commercial perspective, that's what people think. If you work in a company and you think to yourself, 'Well, we're giving [one of the Big Four] or whoever it is a lot of work in one part or other of their business and why is this guy giving us such a hard time?'...it's very difficult to serve two masters like that.

4.5.1 Summary

The initial quotation by a regulator at the beginning of this chapter, together with the comments of a second regulator in this section, reveals strong opposition to APNAS.

5.0 Issues and implications

When survey respondents were asked about their level of awareness of changes to the regulatory environment with regard to auditor independence, the majority of users, purchasers and suppliers indicated that they were aware. One of the issues is the supply of non-audit services—specifically, auditor-provided non-audit services (APNAS). Detailed interviews with users, purchasers, suppliers, standard setters and regulators were conducted. There were as many positive observations from users as there were negative observations with respect to the current amended rules to APNAS. Some were not comfortable with the current provisions; a number of users wanted to see a higher level of limitation on APNAS, while others wanted a more flexible and less-restrictive environment.

By and large, users as well as purchasers and suppliers saw a balance between the costs of limitations and prohibitions, which were simply in the form of the cost of getting audit and non-audit services delivered to the company in addition to the limitation or loss of knowledge from the joint supply of several services. Counterbalancing these costs was the advantage of independence—real and as perceived by the market.

Those comfortable with the current level of limitation suggested that the market contained much cynicism and there was a very clear need to be independent and to be seen to be independent. These sentiments were echoed by those wanting to see further limitations and even a prohibition of joint supply.

Of the purchasers, again, there was a mixture of those who believed the current regulatory environment was favourably received and those who did not. Those believing that the current regulatory level of limitation was right spoke of scepticism about the 'Chinese walls' that are often used as a control device in audit firms, while also speaking about the potential loss if there was a blanket ban on any form of joint supply of services. Purchasers who believed there were still some enhancements to be made to the current regulations spoke of the need for boards of directors and audit committees to potentially have more power to pick and choose among the possible services supplied by the incumbent auditor. There were, however, also perceptions of the need for a framework or systems in order to make those choices.

Of the suppliers interviewed, there was acceptance of the current rules as being the environment in which they had to operate, but there was considerable questioning of whether it was optimal. The concerns raised were varied and were in some respects much like the balance referred to earlier between the costs of provision and the loss of knowledge as opposed to real and perceived independence. A number of suppliers—particularly those with small to medium-range clients—spoke of the advantages and efficiencies of joint supply as being substantial but lost in the current environment. It was not uncommon for suppliers to discuss the fact that they brought considerable expertise that did not previously exist within the client and that efficient and cost-effective joint delivery was in the best interest of all. This also includes start-up companies with a preference for a 'one-stop shop', including capital raising, tax advice and financial reporting expertise to be supplied from the one source.

Certain suppliers perceived that the market believed the current regulatory structure was going well, but others gave a less favourable response. One of the suppliers indicated a growing issue within a firm in which there were both audit and non-audit staff, which related to behaviour that was acceptable and tolerated but varied significantly between the two types of staff. While audit staff members can learn much about the client from being the auditor, they are prohibited from holding investments, while consultants from other divisions within the firm who might similarly gain knowledge about the client may buy, sell or hold shares based on that knowledge.

Standard setters also varied in their beliefs about whether the current regulatory system was tuned optimally. They believed there was a clear set of guidelines relating to those functions that should not be jointly supplied and, in particular, aspects that involved the potential review of their own work and the elimination of any possible financial interests in their activity with clients. There was, however, also acceptance that work undertaken by other parts of the firm would not pose a threat to independence.

One standard setter took a particularly subtle view of the independence debate and argued strongly that the ultimate goal was objectivity rather than independence and that rules should be set in place to keep objectivity as the key outcome. He or she raised concerns that the independence debate had been hijacked.

There is also a quite sophisticated set of observations around the fact that auditors develop knowledge of the business and so do non-audit service providers, who may deliver tax or consulting services. In fact, in the eyes of some, the tax services delivered are so integral to the audit that the distinction between the two can be artificial. There is a genuine yearning by audit suppliers to know as much about the business as possible and some feel that the loss of this alternative view of the firm is a genuine concern. One standard setter also puts forward the proposition of providing audit committees with strong frameworks to choose for themselves and then disclosing what has and has not been provided by the audit firm as a potential way of proceeding. This would provide efficiencies and advantages for the audit client without robbing shareholders in the market generally of knowledge of potential threats to independence.

More generally in all of this debate, there is a conundrum. On the one hand, it is common for purchasers and suppliers to state that there is a loss of knowledge, efficiency and logistical simplicity by dividing the provision of audit and non-audit services between multiple suppliers. On the other hand, there are those who are unhappy with the current regulatory environment, arguing that those who supply consulting and tax services often have little interaction with the auditor. These two perspectives appear inconsistent. Once again, they might go to the differential size of audit clients and the differential size and number of audit firms (refer also to Chapter 13, which deals with competition) and the consequential effect this has on the relationship between auditor, non-audit service supplier, the board of directors and the management of the company. This issue of joint supply of non-audit services by an auditor is a classic example of where public policy and personal interest conflict. Regulators and regulations are there to protect business from the potential negative outcomes of possible independence threats, whereas individual boards of directors and auditors are there to provide an efficient and effective supply of relevant services to enhance the financial and business outcomes of clients.

There is one consequence that is evident within interviews at this point and elsewhere in this document: the effect of this issue on the attraction and retention of staff in the audit divisions. As observed above, the potential investment behaviour of audit division staff and staff from other parts of the firm can be different. They may invest differently, trade on those investments differently and undertake varied work over a range of clients. These actions all have a consequence for the audit divisions of the firms and their ability to attract and retain highly competent, motivated and effective auditors.

6.0 Concluding remarks: APNAS

With respect to issues that could or perhaps should be acted on, there are several that come from the issue of independence. As acknowledged a number of times throughout discussions with stakeholders, there is no doubt that there is 'knowledge spill-over' between audit and non-audit services provided either now or in the past to an individual client. These knowledge spill-overs provide economic benefits to the auditee and indirectly to its shareholders. To the extent that there is prohibition of joint supply, there is a loss of this economic benefit. Arguably, the knowledge spill-over is not linear across all sizes of companies and could be proportionally less at the upper end. In these circumstances, the benefits of the prohibition of certain joint supply could outweigh the benefits of knowledge spill-over. In small to medium enterprises (SMEs), however, including listed SMEs, it could be the case that the knowledge spill-over outweighs any costs—and potentially significantly outweighs these costs. If there was to be a reduction in the prohibition of joint supply, it could be substituted by a policy position that dictates that audit committees and/or boards of directors have the discretion to permit joint supply of currently prohibited types of auditor-provided non-audit services (APNAS), where this would be also disclosed in a timely fashion to shareholders. This would be a change in the policy settings but one that would give rise to efficiencies for the Australian economy.

Somewhat related, as certain stakeholders have strongly noted, is that certain APNAS—specifically, certain forms of taxation services—are so integral to the audit as to be indistinguishable. The argument is that these forms of taxation services might be inappropriately labelled as APNAS when in fact they are an integrated part of the audit. Interestingly, their classification as APNAS could in fact add to the misguided perceptions of there being a threat to independence in circumstances where this does not exist. This therefore leads to the policy position of clarification of where these types of services end and audit begins. By extension, it leads to an important policy position on the absence of guidance of the definition of classifications of APNAS. At present, Australian companies are required to provide disclosures of APNAS across certain classifications. Because of the absence of classification guidance, the disclosures made by companies vary widely and make the use of this information much more limited to the market for audit services than is or perhaps should be the case. One policy outcome of this is that the Auditing Assurance Standards Board (AUASB) should be directed to provide clear guidance on the classifications of APNAS so that the market is better informed.

While several stakeholders commented on the presence of audit-only firms in the market for audit services, there is no prospect of any recommendation that would give rise to the creation of such firms. This needs to be a market-driven outcome. It is the case, however, that the barriers to entry have been enlarged by the presence of *CLERP 9*, and the prospect of audit-only firms seems remote.

This is a cost that has been created by the current regulatory framework; however, it is not the only cost. Indeed, the present cost of the regulatory framework is not easily or directly observable by examining aspects of the market for audit services and the presence or absence of demand and supply within that market. The cost of the current regulatory settings is in fact borne by increased costs for audit and other services provided by accounting firms and these costs are borne directly by Australian companies and indirectly by the shareholders of those companies.

One aspect of independence that operates internally within the audit firms is the effect on the attraction and retention of staff and their remuneration. It would appear that the staff in accounting firms who happen to be employed in the audit divisions have significantly less investment opportunities compared with their peers in other divisions. It seems probable that this has consequences on the attractiveness of those divisions. An investigation into what the effect might be and how it is compensated is perhaps overdue. Perhaps higher salaries within audit divisions offset the absence of these opportunities or perhaps they are compensated for by way of the stability of employment; this is unknown but researchable.

Finally, it has become evident from this examination that there is an important but subtle distinction between objectivity and independence. Objectivity is a state of mind and cannot be subjected to mandated regulation. In the minds of some, however, this seems to be possible. Somewhat related to this is the fact there is also an interaction between the notions of objectivity and independence and the ethical standards as practiced by auditors. It is the case that the ethical standards that apply to auditors in Australia at present do not have legal backing since they are issued by the APESB. It seems that this is a serious oversight. It is our recommendation that the Financial Reporting Council (FRC) expressly and in a timely fashion provides direction to the AUASB to include the development and promulgation of ethical standards. It is the case that the AUASB has in fact withdrawn from providing ethical standards with the withdrawal of AUP32 *Independence*. This matter is actionable and would provide a clear framework so that we can overcome the present situation of auditors not being bound—other than through optional professional body memberships—by any legally backed ethical standards.

7.0 Introduction: audit partner rotation

One impact of the reforms to the auditing regime after the HIH collapse in Australia was to reduce the period in which, in most circumstances, an engagement partner could serve on an engagement—from seven years under previous professional requirements to five years. The issue of audit partner rotation was raised by stakeholders, often in the context of the stability of audit teams and retention of staff generally (refer to Chapter 8), and an analysis of the comments received follows.

7.1 Users

The two users who commented on the issue of partner rotation clearly had little regard for its efficacy. The first is speaking in the context of the stability of audit teams and in response to the interviewer's question:

> [G]etting rid of these silly rules about audit partner rotation, would help [the stability of audit teams]...audit partner rotation just kills it...The guy's just starting to get on top of your business...he's seen something five years ago start, he's seen how it's developed, and then he's got to go...it's all this prescriptive answers to problems. Yes, there can be independence problems, but writing a rule that applies to every company and every auditor is never the answer.

Another user implies that rotation can lead to lower understanding of the business and more susceptibility to management manipulation of the accounting numbers:

> It seems like a good thing on the surface, the rotation, but...in practice, it's another one of those situations where you're having practice and...theory...[I]n practice...[there are] a lot of negatives about it... and I can understand why, but at the same time...in practice, it leads to other issues...very definitely...unless you do have that grounded experience in the industry sectors and understand the operations of what's really going on then to do the audit is really more of a calculating exercise at a very high level and...a good management team can manipulate that process very easily.

7.1.1 Summary

Users are not enamoured of the requirement for audit partner rotation. Their comments indicate that they see it as unhelpful to the effectiveness of the audit process.

7.2 Purchasers

Purchasers are mixed in their views of audit partner rotation, which is discussed in the context of the stability of audit teams mainly, but also in other contexts. These first few quotations are positive about it. The first purchaser's comment raises the issue of having sufficient 'depth' within the accounting firms to cope with rotation.

> [Rotation is] the right thing to do...If you think about the principle of independence and how you execute against it...the principle is right for partner rotation. The consequences are that if the accounting firms don't have enough depth...it all comes down to cost...because are they really recruiting...the expertise that they need in order to service the requirements of the market?

Another purchaser raises the benefit of bringing in 'fresh ideas'.

> I can understand why [rotation is] there because...we've seen a number of bad examples where there's too close a relationship between a CEO and an audit partner...And...if the CEO moves to another company, the partner shouldn't be allowed to move as well...because we've [had] some very bad practice in the past... what tends to happen is that senior partners will just swap around and they'll give some examples of where that's happened. I think it brings a fresh idea. Most of the big firms are big enough now to be on the big companies to be able to swap partners and have enough.

Another purchaser thinks it is a positive thing that a new partner might be able to provide insights from other companies or industries:

> I'm actually quite okay with the need to rotate partners. First of all, we don't replace [a] partner every year, so...some seven years is [a] pretty long...time to make sure that it's a fresh mind...besides, as I understand, the more senior you [are, you] actually do not participate in...detailed work anyway. They are more there to make sure that everything's okay, give the advice, present to the board and they make the decisions. They're not the one doing the audit. So in that sense...rotation is a healthy thing because they're not too close, they're not seeing the same people all the time. They may be able to bring in some fresh idea that is seen in [an]other company, [an]other industry, whatever...it is actually a healthy thing.

The danger of impaired objectivity when too close to the organisation is brought out in the next quotation:

> [Rotation] certainly hasn't caused any sort of disruption, but... I can't think of anything where it's made it improved either. Maybe at the operational level, it's had an impact...I don't necessarily think it would be a bad idea...if you audit the same firm for a lot of years then you can become very close to the organisation, and even...

> [the] perception could be [that you are] close to the organisation, and maybe some of your objectivity might be impaired, and as a partner, you'd probably want to get off and do some other things and maybe come back in a couple of years.

The fresh pair of eyes that comes with rotation is the subject of another purchaser's comments:

> That's really a governance issue, isn't it...to make sure that there's a fresh set of eyes and things...that's better...because if there were mistakes made, that would be caught out. You could have a diversity of view...you don't have the same person looking at the same thing and glossing over the same thing again.

According to another purchaser, an auditor who stays too long 'practically becomes the accountant for the company':

> [T]he organisational knowledge is always there...if it's from partner to partner, I won't say there's an issue because there'll always be audit files, audit papers and all the rest of it in the company...so the facts and figures would be easily obtained, but the overall assessment... it's done by a second person or a different person that really just adds to the...independence and the external part of it. In other words, it's done by an external party. So...if you've been doing the same audit for the last 10 years...you're no longer really an external party because you're so close to it...rather than an auditor, you've practically become the accountant for the company...because your relationship has grown and grown and grown, so you've lost that objectivity and you don't have that independence.

In the context of the stability of the audit team, the two next purchasers' comments reveal how seamless a change of audit partner can be.

> [T]he experience we've had with our previous auditor and the partner rotation worked well...they're not so much succession planning, but the way they planned that it did work well, and we didn't find that had an impact [on] the overall knowledge. Obviously, [there is a new] relationship and the new style and culture that comes with the change, but apart from that we didn't find that an issue. I'm...a believer of certainly putting out to tender your audit services on a regular basis. Now if that was the culture, would you be needing this partner rotation...that's up to individual companies and where they're heading.

> What we've had is a situation where we had a manager for a number of years and then he became a partner and he was on the job for a number of years...he became a consulting kind of regional partner and not responsible for the job. Then they brought someone else in. But he was providing that continuity, probably in the background in their offices explaining things. So the questions didn't necessarily always come through to [us]...in that case, they've managed that rotation process really well.

Another purchaser alludes to the fact that a partner formerly on the job is available for advice if necessary:

> Generally speaking, they have different levels of people involved anyway. So when they rotate off it's not a big loss...because everybody has somebody in training...I can understand the reason for it because you don't want something like HIH again where people become too embedded in the company. It's good to understand the company without being too sympathetic; [you need] balance. And that partner's always available anyway if they haven't left the firm.

Another purchaser speaks about the positive experience of a 'good' audit partner being replaced by another 'good' audit partner:

> [W]e were quite fortunate. We just had our audit rotation for the first year last year, and we were quite fortunate that we had an extremely good auditor replaced by what, on every indication after his first year, is also a very good auditor. However, you could imagine that must work in the reverse, that as an auditee...you could have a fairly good audit partner and [they are replaced by] someone...[with whom] there's too much of a ruction, or [who is] too potentially disruptive, even as a visibility thing, to try and move on. But you can breathe a sigh of relief once the five years have come up and you get someone better.

Another supportive purchaser discusses audit partner versus audit firm rotation:

> On balance...I'm probably for mandatory audit rotation...a new set of eyes as a principle must be quite a good thing, and also must militate against the risk of getting too cosy with each other, which I felt was the essence of the HIH problem. Now, of course, there's not mandatory rotation of firms, which was that whole discussion,

> but I didn't feel that was necessary...people of that integrity and reputation mean that they're going be willing to take a pretty strong look in their first year for anything that their predecessor might have missed...whether or not it's the same firm. So I don't...see that as poor regulation.

Other purchasers, however, disagree with the idea that audit partner rotation has merit. In the first quotation, attention is drawn to the potential for other senior people involved in an audit to be able to remain on the engagement without interruption.

> [E]ffectively, you might have your signing partner or your engagement partner who rotates off, but your tax partner and your IT audit partner, they might be sitting on there for 10 years... because they're not the...lead partner per se.

The difficulty for highly industry-specific partners when the firm has no other clients in the same industry is eloquently expressed in this next quotation.

> Yeah, it is a bit of a problem...[when] the partner has to go. Our last audit partner...is leaving [our industry]—his time's up, he's had to leave. To stay in the sector and for the firm to utilise his knowledge and capability, he's gone to the UK, he's had to rotate off this. He doesn't get to stay here, there is no job here he can do...because the firm doesn't have any other audits [in the same industry]—as they shouldn't—and so he's had to leave the country...is that really smart? If Australia has let a good auditor skill go because of some rules then I don't think it [is] appropriate really. And what we've actually got back as the audit partner is the audit partner of [several] years ago. And that's okay. He's been out into...other industries, and so at least he knows us. But it's [several] years-old knowledge, right? And that's one of the reasons why, when we got him back, we asked for some more up-to-date skills...as part of our engagement, instructional or directional guidance. So it is a problem. It's creating a problem for...the Big Four firms. But I'm just giving you a preparer's experience; we've lost a good audit partner, and [he's] not in the country now and can't be because he's [industry] specific.

The next purchaser also alludes to this problem of not having a critical mass of clients in the same industry:

> 'Five years sounds [like] a long time, but in a large company it's not such a long time.'

> It has an impact because you don't get the longer-term relationships out of things and it's still a learning curve for people and how to handle it because it hasn't been applying for all that long, so it's making it difficult at times. Five years sounds [like] a long time but in a large company it's not such a long time. [With the] top-50 companies in Australia, arguably it takes a couple of audits for someone to fully understand all the ins and outs of the business, so you then get the situation if you're only there for five years, it's taken you two years before you learn it and it doesn't give you much time to...be in the saddle fully operational...in the large companies, it's probably helpful. It's predicated on the basis that you've got to have turnover so that people can be independent and not get consumed...by the client. I don't subscribe to that view...Seven years would make it operationally a lot easier to manage. But...you get to a problem where you say, well, you want expertise but...if you've got a client in a particular industry, the only way you can get expertise in industry is by working on similar companies. So it's almost as long as you have three companies in the same industry, you won't be able to develop the rotation of people to build that expertise.

This next purchaser, who feels the requirement is 'artificial' and has no impact, brings up the loss of understanding and continuity when a partner has to rotate off.

> '[I]t's a shame that you lose some of that knowledge...some things are complicated and having that continuity and that understanding is important.'

> [T]he whole thing with...partner rotation is... artificial and this idea that after four years or five years or whatever the number is you have to change...is totally artificial. And I understand it means you can demonstrate something, but... it makes no impact at all...it's a shame that you lose some of that knowledge...some things are complicated and having that continuity and that understanding is important and then you have to go through this whole education process all over again and even very capable people who can deal with that level of ambiguity and complexity and moving things, it takes a year or so just to

> immerse, so you've constantly got this one or two years catching up in that period...they do a good job of it, but I don't think it adds a darn thing, this rotating...my experience with auditors is that, there's that 99.9 per cent of them [who] are ethical, are extremely professional and the fact that they are on a job for six years rather than five years is not going to change one jot how they view that company.

7.2.1 Summary

The purchasers express a diversity of views about the issue of audit partner rotation. Often the issue arose in the context of conversations about audit team continuity and knowledge of the client. Several purchasers could see the benefit of a 'fresh pair' of eyes and the dangers of becoming 'too close to management'. Other purchasers provide insight into the seamless way in which their audit firm manages the rotation situation. Negative views of rotation are, however, also forthcoming. One purchaser sees the rotation as 'artificial' and as having no real impact. Another points to the potential for inefficiency and ineffectiveness of audits because of the time it takes to get to know some clients. Also raised as an issue is the difficulty for rotated audit personnel when their firms do not have a critical mass of clients in industries that require a high degree of knowledge specificity.

7.3 Suppliers

Like purchasers, suppliers express diverse views on the merits or otherwise of audit partner rotation. These first few quotes are supportive of the requirement to rotate, with later quotations expressing more negative views. The first supplier expresses the idea that rotation can contain boredom that might arise from familiarity with a client.

> [For] small clients, five years is fine...10 years on a small client would be really boring, so it's...nice to have the excuse to get off them... most people have actually liked rotation from a client perspective, if it's properly managed...it's not so much a nuisance in that we go and do something else...it's quite attractive that after five years I go on and have a new challenge.

'Removal of familiarity' with the client and adding 'fresh eyes' are pointed out as benefits of auditor rotation in the next three quotations:

> It certainly does remove, or has the ability to remove, familiarity and things like that, which I agree with. I can understand that.

> [R]otation's quite good; you get fresh eyes, new thinking, all of that.

> It has some impact but it's offset by the benefits of a fresh set of eyes looking at things from a different angle...partner rotation is a good thing. What is the best time frame? Five years is probably reasonable.

Speaking from a client's perspective, this next supplier points to the complexity of business and the need to 'retrain' the new partner in the two years after rotation.

> '[T]here's an issue from the partner [and] the client point of view... that they're now going to go and retrain that person for the next two years.'

> [T]he five-year period, while I can understand it in principle...[it] doesn't help. I can understand why it's done in terms of familiarity and stuff like that, but whether it's five years, whether it's seven years, I don't know...if you're really looking at it from a better audit process, I'm not sure the drive is right, because what they're saying is that I get too familiar and therefore I overlook, I don't challenge them enough, and therefore it has to go to someone else, who's going to have a fresh eye and look at everything. That's fine, but then there's an issue from the partner, [and] the client point of view...that they're now going to go and retrain that person for the next two years...while the audit process is the same, the...complexities of businesses...are quite different and it takes time to get on top of it...I don't have a solution, but, yes, I can imagine that would be quite frustrating for clients. And it's starting to manifest itself into people going out to tender more often too.

Another supplier raises the issue that audit partner rotation is not a new requirement, given that the period of partner engagement has been reduced from seven to five years.

> The Big Four also had...a type of rotation in place, before it became mandatory, and you always had your engagement partner...the terminology might change, but there was always the engagement partner or the signing partner, and there was always a review partner or a quality-control partner, whatever you wanted to call them...generally, even on the smaller clients, the firm's internal

> risk-management process was such that, if I wasn't a partner, I was a director, but…before I signed off on anything as a partner on a set of accounts, you'd have to have that review discussion with another partner in the firm. And that's probably where it's made it easier for the Big Four to do the rotations, because they always had a couple of partners who were involved in most of the audits.

The next supplier provides insights into managing the rotation situation so that clients are not affected adversely.

> [I]t hasn't [had] a huge impact from how we manage it as a firm. When we rotate partners, it's never just a cut-off…there's a period of transition so that the partner rotating on has had sufficient experience with the client before that rotation [for it] not to be an issue. More rotation…used to happen when partners retired and it's now…standard practice that it happens, so that the individual that's rotated off is, if ever there were an issue, they're there as a resource, as a sounding board…in jobs that are complex, the partner rotating on would have had comfortable experience generally in the industry, but certainly in regards to the accounting issues, it's a big deal for a rotation to occur. But as far as it creating an issue from an ability to provide service to the client or provide an audit opinion that is robust, it shouldn't be a problem.

This next supplier's comments also address managing the rotation, with shadow partnering necessary in order for the new partner to come to grips with the complexity, global reach and sheer size of a big client.

> Five years isn't very long. [Company X] is my biggest client and they've got operations in 50 countries around the world and I came on to the audit the year before I rotated and just shadowed the partner. And we've had to do the same thing on all those really big clients, otherwise…you're not that exposed compared to changing auditors in the first year…[In] my first year at [Company X], if I hadn't done that year of shadowing…I can't come up to speed with operations in 50 countries round the world all in one go. So…most people wish it was seven years, not five. And I find it odd that most companies would say, and most processes [would] say, [that]

'I find it odd that most companies would say, and most processes [would] say, [that] after 10 years you should think about whether you should come off as a non-exec. director, but after five years, you're not independent as the auditor.'

> after 10 years you should think about whether you should come off as a non-exec. director but after five years, you're not independent as the auditor. I find that disconnect wrong. I would have thought we could do seven or 10 years on a big client.

The same supplier continues, stating that, from a personal view, rotation has attraction because it creates new challenges:

> They do think that they see a benefit from fresh eyes [and] that… five years is too quick and, from our point of view, it's frankly a nuisance….it's a nuisance from the firm's point of view—for two reasons: 1) just managing people's partner careers and…managing client expectations…[Company Y] comes up for rotation. They will have a view that they can have whoever they want out of our partners. And the same would be true for any top company in the top 50 so you're…having someone who's got the flexibility to take on a client of that size…a very senior experienced partner, [which] is quite hard for us to manage in a partner capacity.

This supplier admits, however, the extent to which rotation is 'stretching' partners who are in high demand across multiple clients. He or she also feels that partners might be lost to the firm at these points of rotation.

> '[O]ther partners are getting very frustrated because they can't get their first step into a big role and…it's going to become quite an issue for all Big Four firms.'

> What we're tending to find is that we've got partners who are in high demand who are stretched across multiple clients and have a team of people underneath them and other partners are getting very frustrated because they can't get their first step into a big role and…it's going to become quite an issue for all Big Four firms—just managing their pool of partners coming through on the cusp of being okay to take a senior position, whereas in the past, before rotation, they'd have come through as the junior partner and become the senior partner [and that gave them] a board that knew and trusted them…It's quite hard to make that step up now for…the young guns. And…the other thing that will become quite hard for us to manage as a firm with partner rotation is that…it's actually refreshing to stop and think, 'Okay, do I want to stay on and do another five years as an auditor on another client or should I go and do something else?' And we will lose partners who will do that.

The next quotation highlights the difficulty of managing rotation in highly regulated, complex industries with few players, such as authorised deposit-taking institutions.

> '[I]f you are the audit partner on [Bank 1], [Bank 1 understands] at the end of five years you've got to go, but will they let you go and be the audit partner on [Bank 2]? Well, over their dead body...so it becomes incredibly hard to manage the senior partners, sustaining the position in the industry that they see themselves in. The clients [have] the opportunity to select the best partners, but also protect their views and their understanding and knowledge of the business they've shared. Protecting all of those things does become quite hard.

Several suppliers express their preference for seven-year rather than five-year rotations, as exemplified by the next quotation. The view is that it can take two years to really gain a sound understanding of a highly complex client, which leaves too few years before rotation to take advantage of that learning.

> Seven years is certainly better. If you take an ASX top-100 or an ASX top-50 client, these are very, very big businesses, they are very complex businesses, they have multiple processes, multiple operations, they generally operate in more than one geographic location. Whether it be in Australasia, they're generally operations in [a] foreign jurisdiction. It probably takes two to three years for an audit partner really to get up to speed, and...you're through your three-year mark and you really hit your straps in year four and year five and then you've got to rotate. And you start the process again in year five of re-educating the next person...there is definitely some learning and some handover of knowledge, [but] it takes a couple of years for them to get up to speed, they really get in their straps and you change again. Where at least if you had seven years you've got three years to get things, you then get three or four really good years, and...that's the time when your audit quality's at its peak.

Another supplier voices similar views and is clear that, in his or her opinion, the disadvantages of partner rotation outweigh the advantages:

> What it's meant to do is, you plan succession a lot earlier and in a more formalised way. It's unlikely that what you're going to do

is bring a partner on after the rotation period and say well, here it is. You're more likely to introduce a partner in the last year of somebody's rotation program, in the last year as partner before they rotate off to familiarise themselves with the key issues of the business, the industry, the style of reporting, because otherwise it's very difficult to pick it up in a short…time and…having come off two of my large public companies this year, I think five years is too short…And the disadvantages outweigh the advantages and the advantage is that they're not getting too close…the disadvantages are that it doesn't matter how good your succession program is and your knowledge transfer…there's a lot to be said…of building of the knowledge. It usually takes you a couple of years to build it up…and then as soon as you've got there you're starting your succession plan…it's just too quick…something like seven years would probably be more reasonable. Seven years is nothing and a more realistic period. Five years is…very short and what does it achieve?

The same supplier continues, explaining how a firm's view becomes intertwined with a partner's view.

'The only thing with interchanging is the knowledge: you can't just create it overnight, that knowledge is valuable; it does mean something.'

[W]hat tends to happen with particularly the large clients is not just the view of that individual partner that's being expressed; it's usually the view of the firm, because the way that you've got a quality-assurance partner on major engagements, you might have more than one partner, you'll have a lead audit partner and another partner. You'll have your technical partner [work with] somebody on your national technical group, you'll have PSR, which is our professional standards review process, so by the time you've signed an opinion, it's less likely [to be a partner] by himself and having reviewed the work of his staff, it's usually representative of the collective view of the firm because of the process that you've undergone to get there. Now, I have to make judgment calls on all the things that I do, but ultimately I'm doing it within a context of the way the firm operates, so could you interchange me and somebody will come to the same conclusion they would? The only thing with interchanging is the knowledge: you can't just create it overnight, that knowledge is valuable; it does mean something. And in some industries, it's the knowledge of the industry; you can't sit down and read it in a book...in a day or even a month. You have to deliver, you have to understand it, you have to go to [the] site, you have to look at these things...I understand if you're making that kind of investment...the period over which you want to use that...could be longer than five [years]...five is an arbitrary period that really doesn't mean anything.

Another three suppliers lament the loss of client knowledge that occurs with rotation:

> [I]t doesn't really help your client business side of things because once a partner rotates off, the knowledge—whilst we obviously talk as partners and we'll pass on knowledge. That part of the partner rotation doesn't help because all of your knowledge goes off with the job...from a knowledge perspective...I don't think it helps... Having knowledge of a client's business is very critical...I've got clients—not in a listed environment—that I've been doing for 14, 15 years and I know exactly where their issues are, and I communicate those to my team on a regular basis. So it's absolutely critical.

> I understand where the partner rotation comes from, but...over time, you do build up a fairly significant knowledge base of the organisation and how it operates, and then you just walk away. And then effectively your partner has to go through build[ing] up [the] process again, because it just comes from interacting with the people and relating that to the numbers and the systems and the industry...the five-year period, while I can understand it in principle...[it] doesn't help...there's definitely an educational process that goes on for...the first 18 months. So you've gone from a very experienced—sorry, a quite experienced—person to helping to develop another partner. And...that doesn't help.

> ...there is a critical shortage of qualified, highly talented people within the industry at the moment and all of the Big Four—and... probably...the second-tier firms as well—are struggling to hold on to their young qualified accountants, particularly where you have demand in the US and UK markets for your young chartereds, and your young CPAs to head over there.

The same supplier goes on to discuss the frustration that clients experience when an audit partner with whom rapport has been developed is changed:

> '[T]he chemistry that operates between people [is] not always able to be replicated, because each partner is different.'

> I can understand why it's done in terms of familiarity and stuff like that, but whether it's five years, whether it's seven years, I don't know. I can imagine that some of the clients would get quite frustrated because every five years you're going to be looking at a new face. And just the chemistry that operates between people [is] not always able to be replicated, because each partner is different. And while you try to pick the partner that's going to work well with that client, there's still an element of training. So…it must be a bit frustrating, because as an experienced person, I can have a conversation and get a comment, and I can understand why, that's because I know that over here they're doing that and then that. A new person, they make the same comment and…it has no meaning because they don't understand all of the elements of the business.

The same supplier raises the personal career considerations that rotation among a small number of players in a single industry might necessitate. In such circumstances, where the client is not comfortable about a partner moving to a competitor's audit, the only way to continue to utilise expert knowledge might be to move interstate or overseas.

> 'When you come to the end of your period, the stars have to align or the planets have to align for you then to transfer onto a job or another engagement in that same industry, where you can use that same knowledge, which previously you couldn't work on because it was going to provide a conflict issue.'

> Sometimes the thing…about the question of specialisation is, if you're working on a large organisation, it's very, very unlikely that you're going to be working for another large organisation that competes with that organisation. So your specialist knowledge is dedicated to that entity. When you come to the end of your period, the stars have to align or the planets have to align for you then to transfer onto a job or another engagement in that same industry, where you can use that same knowledge, which previously you couldn't work on because it was going to provide a conflict issue. And even if the stars align and you can work on that job, sometimes that creates a conflict in itself because your client who you're just coming off

> doesn't want you to go onto their main competitor in the year that you finish...so it's taken out of your hands. You're now in a position where, okay, if I really wanted [to stay in the industry] and it's [a] small market anyway, it's a niche, I might have to go overseas—that's the only way that I can really go to the next level without... from a career point of view, going backwards. And...that gets lost at times, and what tends to happen, at the end of the day, if you're a partner, you're obviously trying to progress, and you're trying to get to the next level. If you're coming off public companies, they don't always line up the way that you want to, you might end up having to take a backwards step because at that particular point in time the next available job wasn't there. You might go back and just do...a set of referral clients out of subsidiaries out of the UK where the complexity is not as margined and all this billable skill that you've developed in dealing at the top end of town and dealing with boards and dealing with difficult issues and public company reporting gets lost, because you can't easily take that type of a company.

The same supplier does provide insight into the type of strategic thinking his or her firm engages in to maximise skill utilisation:

> [W]e're a little bit better than that at doing it; we're strategic. You've got a team of partners that do work at the top end of town and we tend to think in advance as to how we're going to shuffle things around [and] where people...sit, but obviously it's a lot of effort for little gain...I don't think it was really thought through that this perceived benefit of the rotation was going to be delivered—and I just don't know that there'd be any difference at all if you went to seven [years] or even longer.

7.3.1 Summary

Some suppliers consider that rotation is worthwhile in bringing that 'fresh pair of eyes' and upheaval in what might otherwise be a growing familiarity. Several suppliers, however, reinforce one another's quite independent comments in arguing that five-year rotations are too short, and that seven-year rotations would retain the advantages while minimising the disadvantages of too frequent rotations. For complex, global clients, a view is frequently expressed that 18 months to two years is needed to ensure a new auditor is 'on top of things', leaving only two years before the next partner needs to be trained—perhaps through a 'shadowing' process. Several suppliers allude to the manifest frustration for clients having to build a new rapport with a partner and 'train' the new partner. One supplier speaks eloquently of the potential personal difficulty in terms of continuing an upward career trajectory and utilising and extending specific industry specialist skills, especially in a complex, regulated industry with few participants.

7.4 Standard setters

One of the standard setters would like to have seen some research into whether partner engagement length was a problem before the reduced rotation period was introduced.

> [There were] probably other ways of doing it…that was a legislative answer to a situation which was perceived to happen with the HIHs, so…in reality…it may well have been able to be done in other ways. In certain areas where you've got expertise…you've got to replicate that out, and is the period appropriate or could you do it and still achieve it another way? So…that would have been a good thing to do some research on and then come up with some ideas in seeing whether in fact it is a problem—to the extent it's been there. But… we're there now so we've got to live with it, but it was a legislative change, so it probably didn't go through the rigour as to what our processes have done.

The same standard setter continues, expressing his or her view that seven years would be more appropriate than five for rotation:

> [S]even years…would be a far more appropriate period for a rotation…without a doubt and certainly I would support that…it would allow a…better period…for a person to be on an assignment, to have the learning bit at the start, the bit in the middle where they knew all about the job and then you have the transition bit at the end to the next period, to the next partner coming on, and…that would be a more manageable process to use that period.

Following inappropriate rules at the expense of quality is the danger with the current situation, according to this next standard setter:

> [T]he area of independence…is really not a regulator issue; it's a policy decision and a government decision. But I have heard people

> say that mandating a five-year rotation, for example, would mandate that 40 per cent of audits were ineffective because it takes two years to get up to speed and to acknowledge things…corporate knowledge is important as well, so we need to make sure—that's not a regulator issue but it's a law and a policy issue—that we don't put ourselves in a space where we sacrifice quality for following inappropriate rules…it's not an issue that…we have with the regulator, but in the Australian market, something that…needs to be focused on is the size of the market for listed companies or the number of listed companies and the pool of audit resources that we have.

The same standard setter explains why, in his or her opinion, seven-year rotations would be more effective than five-year rotations:

> [E]ven though I'm in a very large firm, five-year rotation for lead and review partners will really start to bite into the available talent pool to effectively conduct audits across the pool of entities for which rotation is mandated, which is the listed entities. But also the principle in following the ethical principles around independence is there and so therefore rotations [are] inherent in any audit done under the *Corporations Act*…how do you deal with the familiarity threat? So…something that we're certainly watching closely is, if five years isn't any good for our market, what is a better measure given that we need to be independent—which I still think is absolutely important, I'm not downplaying it. But would perhaps seven be a better answer for the Australian market than five?

The next standard setter alludes to the implications of rotation for competition in the market for audit services, and the need for a critical mass of partners:

> [I]n terms of [the] size of a practice, in terms of doing listed entities, you need to be a minimum size. You need to have a minimum number of partners to allow rotation to take place…the minimum you [could] get by with [is] three, but…it's better to have four or above. So it means that audit practices which do listed work need…to grow to a minimum level…[There are] advantages in that because as firms get bigger, the quality—that's not to say that when they're smaller they don't have quality—but…it helps with the quality aspects of both the firm itself for the quality control it needs to put in place and also the audit quality, so in that respect it's a good thing.

7.4.1 Summary

Standard setters, many of whom are also suppliers, reiterate the view that five-year rotations are too frequent, with consequential dangers for audit quality. One standard setter speaks about the implications for competition of needing a critical mass of partners if auditing listed entities.

7.5 Regulators

Regulators, perhaps somewhat surprisingly, reveal some ambivalence about the merits of audit partner rotation. While supporting rotation, this regulator's comments reveal doubts about its effectiveness because of the countervailing issue of the time it can take to get to know a complex client such as a bank:

> Partner rotation is a good thing but...I don't know if it's really been that effective because the more they rotate the partners, the more the problems you create. It takes a partner two years to learn a bank, for instance, over a five-year term. So where's the value add in the rotation...I don't have a problem with independence... independence is not the right question. The issue is more about compromise of professional judgment. If someone's judgment gets impaired—like a partner could do the same client for 20 years and he could always be seen as someone who is a straight-up-and-down guy. He produces a good-quality product because he's a thorough professional, year in and year out. The other partners will get sloppy as the years go by.

The next regulator, asking a question of the interviewer, points to a potential way of evading the rotation requirements:

> What's the ruling in respect of if partner A is partner of the client, that's a Big Four, number-one client, partner A goes to Big Four number two, the client magically has tender six months later, and oops—they go to Big Four number two?

The next regulator alludes to the difficulty of maintaining audit quality with initial audit engagements:

> Inexperienced in terms of coming to grips with the industry and coming to grips with the entity for the first year, most of the firms will say to you, or an experienced practitioner will say, '[The] greatest risk of me getting something wrong is probably in the first year or two.'

A differential approach by the audit firms to the issue of rotation is the concern of another regulator:

> [W]e've gone onto the public record around rotation, because we could see parts of the profession responding to it in a more assiduous way than others who are just going, 'Oh, what does all this mean?' Tough.

7.5.1 Summary

Somewhat surprisingly, the comments by regulators reveal that not all are unquestioningly convinced about the merit of audit partner rotation. Regulators, like purchasers and suppliers, raise the fact that it can take up to two years to effectively understand, for instance, a banking client. One regulator observes that not all firms approach the issue of rotation with the same seriousness.

8.0 Issues and implications

While there was no specific questionnaire information about auditor rotation, this was an issue that arose frequently in response to prompts and was volunteered in the interviews with purchasers and suppliers and, to a lesser extent, with users, regulators and standard setters.

There were mixed views with respect to the desirability of the amended mechanisms used for auditor rotation, with many interviewees indicating that they agreed with auditor rotation in principle but there had been unintended consequences with respect to the implementation of the amended regime. Among those who raised concerns about the current requirements, many spoke of the fact that the five-year time horizon was an insufficient period in which to build up knowledge of the client and to obtain a reasonable return for the investment in that knowledge before mandatory rotation occurred.

Those who spoke in favour of rotation included a large number of purchasers and suppliers as well as a number of users, regulators and standard setters. They articulated the desirability of having a 'fresh pair of eyes', a 'diversity of views' and for rotations to ensure a reasonably frequently refreshed relationship between the client and the audit firm. More than once, interviewees made reference to the damage that an inappropriately close relationship could create and cited the case of HIH. Purchasers raised the fact that rotation was in place in many audit firms well before the current regulatory framework, but noted the period was typically longer than the current five-year period for other than exceptional circumstances. Purchasers also expressed some degree of anxiety about the existence of a formal rotation process and that there was always some degree of uncertainty about the quality of any partner rotating in.

Among the purchasers representing companies within the top 50 or so companies listed on the ASX, there was deep-rooted concern about the speed of rotation. There are instances in which a new partner in a large complex client, which might have branches in many jurisdictions across the world, undertakes the formidable task of understanding the nature of the business and its risks and then has to assimilate this knowledge, build up expertise quickly and acquire a pay-off from that expertise before the rotation of the next partner. Purchasers also express concern that when such a senior partner rotates off, the next logical client might be a major competitor in the same industry. They typically see the logic in such movement of a partner, but discomfort exists about the potential unintentional transmission of client-specific knowledge to the new client.

Suppliers also agree with the principle of rotation but have concerns. Several suppliers, particularly within the Big Four, comment that rotation is a trigger point for some clients to consider, if not implement, a tender process. Suppliers also note that there is a significant trade-off between the notion of independence—real and perceived—and the erosion of the knowledge of the client. Again, it was common to suggest that a five-year period was too short—particularly for large and complex companies. In some cases, complexity is linked to the regulatory framework within which certain companies operate.

One supplier inquired whether there should be a counterbalancing requirement that executive directors rotate off after, say, 10 years because they too could become stale in their view of the company and require a refreshed outlook and new challenges.

Suppliers to larger clients also make the observation that the large clients feel they have the power to demand a partner of their choice. As a consequence, there is increased pressure exerted on the most expert partners in the larger firms and somewhat less ability to train up more junior partners to be the senior partners of the future.

While some suppliers noted that the five-year rotation was a 'tipping point' for clients, it was also a tipping point for some of the individual partners and firms that we interviewed. Some of these partners used a five-year cycle to reconsider their own careers and whether in fact they wished to undertake another cycle. The notion of staying one or two years in a client is now seen by many as unacceptable so that their entire careers now consist of a series of five-year cycles.

Firms spend a good deal of time and energy managing the process of rotation, with partners coming on to an engagement as either senior managers or directors and in some cases even secondary partners a year or two ahead of the process of handing over to a new partner. The downside to this process is that it can sometimes be a very lengthy period of apprenticeship. There was one instance in which the same person was involved with a firm in the order of a decade before rotating off as engagement partner. This cuts across the notion of a fresh pair of eyes every five years.

It seems, however, that firms that have developed or are developing high-quality processes to ensure that the handover from one partner to another will have a significant structural advantage going forward. There is clearly diversity in the level of sophistication of the handover from one partner to another among those client representatives with whom we spoke.

Regulators, standard setters and users all agreed, by and large, that rotation was good in principle, but also acknowledged that there was a substantial trade-off between knowledge of the client and independence. Suppliers and standard setters recognised that, as a generalisation, the quality of an audit in the first year or two was at a lower level than the quality of an audit after the partner had been engaged with the client for three or more years. There was therefore near-universal agreement that rotation had consequences for the knowledge base and quality of the audit as well as the real and perceived independence of the relationship between the supplier and purchaser of audit services.

We would also note that it was difficult for the authors to unpick this repeated request for a longer period from the genuine concern about the loss of knowledge and therefore a lower-quality audit due to the inherent normal human behaviour of resisting change. Every one of the interviewees who mentioned a longer period referred to a seven-year rather than a five-year period. This reflects the previous regime that most of the interviewees operated within. There was, however, the authors believe, a genuine desire to find the right balance. This balance between time and perceived independence might need to be crafted conditionally on the size, complexity or regulatory framework within which the auditee operates.

9.0 Concluding remarks

With respect to auditor rotation, various stakeholders have well-constructed and thoughtful arguments for and against partner rotation for longer or shorter periods. One way of systematically adding some structure to this is to consider what might explain, rationally, why a longer period might benefit the efficiency of the capital market compared with a shorter period.

On balance, by examining the arguments for and against, it would seem that organisations that are large in size or are particularly complex or operate in a highly regulated and therefore complex industry are those that might command longer periods of audit tenure compared with other organisations. Essentially, the argument driving this is that the nature, complexity and rigour of those audits require the opportunity to have critical members of the audit team working on the audit for a longer period. It is also the case that in these instances there are questions about the critical mass of the supply of partners and other senior staff in sufficient numbers to be able to handle the rotations that will occur. We saw instances of partners leaving either the profession or the jurisdiction simply to obtain appropriate work after rotating off large, complex clients. This practice will dissipate the pool of talent available to undertake large, complex audits in Australia.

Related to this is the concern that at present the regulatory structure of the operation of registered company auditors means that there is no-one with the responsibility for public oversight of the quantity or nature of those who are registered company auditors. We have few data and no policy position about the supply of registered company auditors, the quality of their expertise or their ability to undertake expert audits in particular industries in particularly complex clients. This is in stark contrast with the clear policy oversight of the supply of medical practitioners, for example.

Additionally and not unrelated, there are insufficient publicly available data to undertake any research of any depth on the effect on the careers of individuals who rotate off auditing engagements. Does it indeed become a breaking point in careers, which causes auditors to leave the profession?

DIVISION E

REGULATORY REFORMS TO AUDIT THEIR IMPACTS 10

I'm not too informed about what the regulator has...done. For example...I didn't know that they're now legally enforceable auditing standards, rather than self-regulation by the industry. My general experience with the regulators is that, if anything, it creates...more work for the lawyers and...a more inhibited view about statements that are made by anybody, including auditors...What happens if...something becomes legally enforceable that was...[previously] regulated by a professional standards' body is that the first thing you do when you make that kind of statement is [to]...check it with your lawyers because of the potential legal liability that's attached to it. And, let's face it...when a company...collapses, if we take the extreme case, the first thing that any litigation funder looks [for is]...'[Is] there an auditor with good professional indemnity insurance that we can go after?' And so the more prescriptive the regulatory response is...in some ways...it's counterproductive. It works against what's supposed to be achieved.
— User

1.0 Key issues

This study explored in depth the impacts created by the regulatory reforms of the audit function put in place in the period after the corporate collapses of the early part of this decade. Some of the issues surrounding these impacts include:

- what are the costs and benefits of legal backing for auditing standards
- have the reforms after the corporate collapses earlier this decade reduced the likelihood of unexpected future collapses

- have these reforms improved the general public's confidence in the capital market
- have these reforms enhanced the credibility of financial statements
- have these reforms enhanced audit quality
- have these reforms added value to a company's business operations?

2.0 Introduction

The period after the high-profile corporate collapses of earlier this decade—internationally and nationally—saw major legislative reform through the ninth instalment of the Corporate Law Economic Reform Program: the *Audit Reform and Corporate Disclosure Act 2004*, effective from 1 July 2004. Under that act, among other things, the responsibility for the setting of auditing standards was moved from the profession to the Financial Reporting Council and the standards became statutory instruments with legal backing under the *Corporations Act 2001*.

The issue of reforms to the regulation of the audit market elicited many lengthy comments from stakeholders, especially from suppliers, and many of the comments could fit within multiple subsections of this and the next chapter. The structure of this division is that this chapter examines survey and interview responses related to questions about the legally backed auditing standards and the reforms more generally and takes a primarily demand-side perspective. The next chapter deals with the impact of the reforms and the regulatory process primarily on the supply side of audits and the third deals with the conduct of the regulators and quasi-regulators in monitoring compliance with the auditing standards. The interconnectedness of the themes and contexts that arise around regulation makes it necessary to read all chapters in this division with this in mind.

3.0 Introduction: legal backing for auditing standards

Under the *CLERP 9 Act* (2004), a reconstituted Auditing and Assurance Standards Board (AUASB) was created and charged with revising the existing auditing standards such that they could be enforced legally. A two-year grace period was given from the effective date of the act until the revised standards became operative for reporting periods beginning 1 July 2006. All of the data that we report on were gathered after this operative date. The AUASB, in revising the standards, elevated much of the guidance material, which contained implied obligations, to mandated essential procedures and also downgraded some previous 'black-letter' paragraphs to guidance material. During the grace period and for some time before, the International Auditing and Assurance Standards Board (IAASB) continued to update and issue its standards, on which the Australian auditing standards are based. Changes in the newly issued AUASB standards were therefore a combination of Australian revisions and IAASB amendments. The survey and the interviews with stakeholders addressed the issue of legally backed auditing standards. Discussion of each source of responses follows.

4.0 Survey

Responses to the survey question 'Are you aware of the following specific changes that have occurred in the regulation of audit services in Australia?' are reported in Table 10.1.

As might be expected, suppliers of audit services are near-universally aware of the standards. Approximately three-quarters of all purchasers and just more than half of all users are aware of these changes.

Table 10.1 Responses on awareness of the introduction of legally enforceable auditing standards (per cent)

	USERS				PURCHASERS				SUPPLIERS		
	Total	Accounting expertise	Professional users	Private investors	Total	Directors/ audit comm.	CEO/CFO	Other	Total	Big Four	Non-Big Four
Are you aware of the following specific changes that have occurred in the regulation of audit services in Australia?											
The introduction of legally enforceable auditing standards	54	68	52	38	77	79	76	77	90	93	90

Percentage of respondents answering 'Strongly agree' or 'Agree' on a five-point scale.

5.0 Interviews

Interviews with stakeholders revealed their various perceptions of the impact of legal backing for auditing standards.

5.1 Users

Generally, comments from users were favourable about the advent of legal backing for auditing standards. Users felt that with legal backing came a perception that things had been done correctly. Illustrative comments follow.

> [T]o a degree…having an outsider arbitrate or adjudicate on doubtful situations where the question is whether the professional standard has been met or not can be a positive…If the professional bodies [are] too lax on their members then outside legal enforceability is some progress.
>
> I would imagine it's increased costs to a point. But it probably also allows litigation…to be a lot more effective and enforceable. There's a threat there…for people to be in compliance with these accounting standards.
>
> It's probably going to improve the credibility of financial statements.

There was, however, recognition of some pitfalls of legal backing among the users. For instance:

> [I]t also…means that you run the risk that somebody who really knows the details of the ins and outs of the profession will make a judgment that, in almost unanimous opinion of the practitioners, is unrealistic given what the practices were, and potentially sets through the legal process a new standard that again goes into that prescriptive regulation by the courts that inhibits the auditing process rather than provides more insurance…Too many times have we seen that if something goes wrong the response from regulators, lawyers, the courts is to set new standards without considering the wider implications. And that kind of ad hoc legislation…[is] dangerous and it creates a maze of things that are inefficient.

Some comments from users, however, conveyed scepticism that legal backing should make any difference.

> I just can't see where [it has made any difference] in terms of the market generally. Certainly, if people were expecting...on day one... that...everyone...[would] go 'Oh, yeah, that means the financial statement's credible'—I can't see that...just because they're legally enforceable now...the market continues to expect and believe that the auditors are doing what they need to do behind the scenes, irrespective of whether it's legally enforced or not to get the right outcome.

> Would it resolve concerns of the credibility of financial statements? I can't answer that question. It really is a question of whether those enforceable auditing standards go beyond what was previously in the professional standard—one. And two, whether we get examples in the future where the enforcement of those standards is better than it was in the past through the professional bodies. There are certainly examples where you would say professional bodies are too lenient on their members.

> [H]ave they improved what's out there and available? They'd probably catch a few that otherwise wouldn't have got caught—but broadly, no.

> [I]f we did have any concerns in the past then having a legally enforceable standard that everyone follows would, should, reduce those fears of them not being credible.

> I don't think it's hurt the credibility of financial statements, but I don't think it's done a...necessarily huge [thing].

> It wasn't as if we didn't feel assured prior, I wouldn't have thought, from our perspective. [I don't know] whether we feel more assured.

> [I]f the expectations gap is what an auditor should intuitively do versus what they're prescribed to do...[legal backing has] widened it because a good auditor would probably do both: they would follow the prescriptive rules and then they'd apply their own auditing skills.

One person feels that it should reduce the audit expectations gap:

> [I]f we've got a legally enforceable law that says that an audit must tick off these...points then there should not be an expectations gap over time as we're educated.

Another user is somewhat disparaging of what is involved in audit judgment, as revealed by the following quotation:

> '[T]hat's where auditors need to be tougher: to be saying to clients—and remember, these are people who are paying their bills—"Look, I'm sorry".'

> I don't know how much judgment auditors have or need. There [are] only four accounts—asset, liability, income and expense—and the only debate...ever seems to be as to whether the debit goes in the P&L or the debit goes in the balance sheet. And then on the other side, whether you really should be recognising the income or not. And the majority of companies are not overly aggressive with those two issues: capitalising expenses and bringing forward income. I don't think anyone—any shareholder—ever got too upset. And...when I talk shareholder, I mean someone who is the mythical shareholder, who's there for the long time, not some guy who just buys and sells within a month—that's not what we're running the company for. I'm running a company to try and optimise returns for someone who's there for the long haul. And if a company were a little conservative—even far too conservative in terms of expensing too much and not recognising income fast enough—in the long term, no-one's going to be upset about that. Whereas people do get upset when you're not expensing things and you're capitalising expenses and when you're bringing income forward that's really not income.'

The same person enunciates the conflict implicit in saying 'no' to those who pay the audit fee:

> [T]hat's where auditors need to be tougher: to be saying to clients—and remember, these are people who are paying their bills—'Look, I'm sorry, you shouldn't be capitalising that expense, and you shouldn't be recognising that income.' Because on the other side...if you're being too conservative, no-one's going to get upset, because the income will eventually come through and if you've understated the expenses, in the next period, you won't have the expenses. Or if they're exploration costs, five years down the track you won't have a big write-off to clear it out, because you haven't found the ore. But it's tough to—I haven't had to do it myself—but to sit down someone who's paying your bills and say 'sorry'.

5.1.1 Summary

Responses from users vary from no knowledge that auditing standards have become legally enforceable to a sound understanding of this reform. Similarly, responses vary between those who are enthusiastic about this change and those who can see little merit in the idea. Two comments relate to perceived laxity on the part of professional accounting bodies and legal backing being an improvement. The notion of having a 'threat' to encourage compliance is attractive to at least one user. There were, however, also comments foreseeing problems—for instance, with the law and lawyers becoming involved in a way that created unintended consequences. There is even a suggestion that legal enforceability might increase the expectations gap since prescriptive rules might militate against the application of auditors' skills. Notably, responses by users refer to the audit explicitly as 'insurance' and to the importance of professional indemnity insurance in 'going after' auditors. Scepticism is expressed that legal backing will result in increased credibility for financial statements or any difference in the conduct of audits, since legal enforcement should not influence the auditor's behaviour and it is not as though major doubts exist about the work of auditors.

5.2 Purchaser

Among the purchasers, there was little support for legally backed auditing standards, with comments relating to potential detriments to the auditor–client relationship and increased costs, as seen in the following quotes.

> [T]he auditing standards were already existing and auditors are professional people so there's already an expectation that they'll be doing the appropriate bits from those standards. As I understand it, all of the legally enforceable aspect of it is going to do is to require more documentation...and laying a paper trail for what you've done, and I just see that as an increase in costs.

'[W]e're moving away from a process in which the auditor and the client work up a relationship...to one in which the auditors are very conscious of the fact that they must comply with legislation otherwise they leave themselves and their firm exposed.'

> [I]t's not so much that I'm concerned if they have the force of law. Well...the long answer to it is, yes, and the reason why is because... we're moving away from a process in which the auditor and the client work up a relationship where they're receiving advice

> based on their opinions and assessments that they've made and the judgments that they've made, to one in which the auditors are very conscious of the fact that they must comply with legislation otherwise they leave themselves and their firm exposed...so... it's shifting the priority away from what...was the essential relationship between client and auditor. That's the danger I see. I notice that on audit committees that I have now...quite often when a query comes up, I'll be informed by the auditor that that's required under the legislation. It's kind of become...the priority; you've got to comply...the danger is that in that process we might lose what would be...an opinion which would otherwise be given, but there's reluctance there because of this new requirement... In other words, we're starting [to] see the disempowerment of sovereign governments in the process, and business direction being dictated by these regulations...this is a little off the track, but it's kind of related because it's becoming a pervasive force...in the way in which the administration of these processes take place. So it's a concern I have that we're going to lose something that...is really quite essential to the process. Inadvertently, I mean—everything has been done with the best of intentions.

The same person goes on to comment on the loss of intellectual property in terms of the accounting and auditing standards that has occurred with the move to statutory regimes for each:

> [I]n that decision that the accounting profession took to handover... it's in the first instance [that] the accounting standards had lost intellectual property rights and...the same thing has now happened with the auditing. But it's because it was an initiative taken by government, because it was perceived that this was what was necessary to fix the problem. So it's a shame because...it's a step backwards...[Legal backing] makes no difference at all...there's a hidden problem here for government in that if there is another failure then who does the government look to as a scapegoat? It's responsible now.

Further, concern was expressed about the increased prescription brought about by legal backing for auditing standards, as illustrated in the following quote:

> [T]he way in which the US approaches everything is by prescription—that is, they operate by rule. Whereas everything that is done basically under the British-related systems, in which we're part, aren't based on principles. And so our whole legislative base is supposed to be based on principles, but here what is now happening is that our regulatory agencies are then interpreting those principles and putting out guidance, which effectively is regulation. And so we're moving...more and more towards that rules-based approach. And my difficulty with rules is that no matter how well they're formulated...circumstances change and the rules become out of date, and they're very hard to fix because they tend to get set in stone once they're made. But also...people then use them as a substitute for judgment.

5.2.1 Summary

Purchasers' views range from perceptions that legal backing for standards should make no difference to auditors' conduct to perceptions that it will interfere with the auditor–client relationship. The former view is justified by the stance that auditors, as professionals, are assumed to be in compliance with the auditing standards—with or without legal backing. The latter view is justified by the perception that the auditors' opinions, assessments and judgments are likely to be coloured by the legislation. One purchaser sees this, taken to its extreme, as potentially affecting even the direction of business. Another purchaser observes that legal backing for the standards means that the government has to take responsibility for future corporate failures, which are seen as inevitable. A purchaser laments the loss of the accounting profession's intellectual property rights, which occurred in the transition to a new statutory standard-setting body. The merit of principles versus rules-based standards is raised with an observation that Australia has moved closer to the US approach and not only does this cause a risk of the rules dating, it risks replacement of judgment with rules. The potential impact on costs is mentioned in some quotations from the interviews in this section, but a dedicated section on costs appears later in this chapter.

5.3 Suppliers

Among the suppliers, no-one expressed the view that legal backing for the auditing standards would make a difference. Typical comments included:

> [I]f an audit is supposed to focus on the risks then having to do a lot of other stuff around other areas that are no risk doesn't make the audit any better. It might mean it's a more pretty file...but I don't necessarily think it's going to mean that you're going to identify problems any sooner, any better, anymore frequently than you would've under the old system, where you used your judgment.

> No. I don't think it changes [things]...from the external perspective, I don't think it changes [things].

> It's done nothing for that because the public don't read the auditing standards. So, no, from their point of view, they would have no idea...it's done nothing for the expectation gap.

> I don't think the general public would know any different...I don't know if you asked the general public whether they would be... aware that there's actually been a change...Even [with] a lot of our clients that we talk to, it's an interesting discussion to have. You go in and you say that there's been a change in the auditing standards and they're, 'Oh, really?' So I don't know whether that's [their] area. So whether it's changed the perception, I don't think it has, because people aren't really aware.

Again, among the suppliers, the divide between the Big Four and non-Big Four can be seen:

> I'm looking at it from a Big Four point of view, because we see a lot of clients in a lot of industries. So you do gain a lot of experience and you have [a] bigger, broader base to have that professional judgment. Maybe when you're talking [about] a small firm who don't have the breadth of experience or the depth then it might be a totally different issue. But from a Big Four point of view, I don't think that making them law has helped us particularly.

5.3.1 Summary

There is scepticism among suppliers of the degree of awareness among the general public and even by their clients of the change to legal enforceability of the auditing standards. There is even greater scepticism evident of this change being associated with higher-quality audits; at best, it is seen as potentially creating a marginal difference.

5.4 Standard setters

One standard setter, in a comment pertinent to competition in the market for audit services, noted that legal backing for auditing standards had heightened the barriers to entry and he or she alluded to the difficulty of having auditing standards—whether legally backed or not—capture the essential skill that creates a good auditor.

> [T]he concept behind [the legal backing of standards] is that it's improved the quality...so that has a flow-on effect to the companies, but more importantly...to the ultimate users...that takes you back to the debate about what is a good audit.

When pressed further, the same person continues in response to the observation that 'the politicians...would say that we wouldn't have done this unless this added value to the market. Why have a law unless it does some good?'

> [T]his is a difficult area because the difficulty here is you're trying to put a level of precision over something which can't be measured... the really difficult thing is that...really high-quality auditing is about really understanding the issues and the risks and being able to...take indicators in places and join them together to actually understand the implications of something before it gets...too far down the road.

5.4.1 Summary

Doubt about the ability of auditing standards, whether backed by legislation or not, to encapsulate the essence of a high-quality audit is expressed eloquently by a standard setter in this section.

5.5 Regulators

Unsurprisingly, the regulators defended legal backing for the auditing standards.

> The only difference is if an auditor gets it wrong, it's more visible that you can penalise them for that...That's the only difference, but you [could] penalise an auditor previously anyway...under negligence or duty of care because there've been so many legal cases with auditors.

The same regulator argues that the legally enforceable standards require no more audit work than had already been the case:

> [W]hat's changed? Nothing. The only thing is one's been quantified as a legal instrument and then the other case is that was not as enforceable, right, we'll add another legal path to make them accountable. I don't think it's such a big change...What worries me is that when the auditor runs the argument [and] thinks the force-of-law standards make [them] do more work. Now if that means it focuses their minds...prior to that they should have been doing it anyway.

5.5.1 Summary

The potential to hold auditors more accountable for the conduct of audits as a consequence of legally backed auditing standards compared with previously, comes through in the comments of a regulator.

6.0 Issues and implications

Users, purchasers, suppliers and standard setters were all interviewed on the issue of legally backed auditing standards. A number of helpful insights were gained from these discussions. Some users took the view that as soon as a crisis emerged in what would otherwise be a free market, the political response was to increase regulation. While this is a natural response, there is concern about the unintended consequences, which could in fact damage what would otherwise be appropriate public policy settings. Additionally, some users take the view that this set of legally enforceable auditing standards might catch one or two undesirable incidents that previous processes did not, but that broadly the market will not be well served by these changes to the status of auditing standards.

Purchasers were split between whether or not this was a positive initiative for the Australian economy. Some purchasers suggest that if it results in a better outcome for the capital market then this is worthwhile, while others are concerned that the legal enforceability involved will result in auditors essentially withdrawing from offering opinions and judgments and moving to fulfil compliance requirements. This, it is argued, will reduce the value of the relationship between auditor and client. One purchaser laments the loss of the setting of professional accounting standards as a loss of intellectual property rights for the profession and the same is true for auditing standards. He also observed that there could be an unintended consequence for government in these shifts and that the government had no-one to blame but itself and its own processes if and when there was another round of corporate failure.

While there were remarkably few positive views on the general issue of legally enforceable auditing standards offered by the users interviewed, standard setters took the view that this initiative was good because it would give rise to improved quality. This is important to companies and the ultimate users of financial statements: the shareholders.

There were diverging views about the motivation that gave rise to legally enforceable auditing standards. One regulator indicates this is something the accounting profession wishes to have in order to give substance and support and a more clarified approach than was previously the case.

In conclusion, while there is a high level of appreciation of the legal enforceability of auditing standards, there are mixed views about its benefits and, indeed, some scepticism. It would be reasonable to say, however, that it is difficult to systematically observe the effects on the capital market in a practical sense of the benefits of legal enforceability. Therefore, some interviewees are guarded about concluding one way or the other on the value of legally enforceable auditing standards.

7.0 Introduction: quality consequences of the reforms

Specific questions about the impact of the reforms on the auditing regime were asked in the survey and the interviews. Given the inevitable cost of implementing the reforms, the responses make interesting reading.

8.0 Survey

Recipients of the survey were asked five questions pertaining to the impacts of the reforms on financial reporting and audit quality after the corporate collapses of earlier this decade. One question asked for perceptions of whether there would subsequently be less corporate failure. The second question related to whether there would be an improvement in the capital market. The third question asked whether the reforms would improve the credibility of financial statements. The fourth question concerned expected improvements in audit quality and the fifth asked about value added to companies' business operations. The tabular reporting of results is given in Table 10.2, followed by analysis.

Table 10.2Responses to the impacts of changes to the regulation of audit (per cent)

	USERS				PURCHASERS				SUPPLIERS		
	Total	Accounting expertise	Professional users	Private investors	Total	Directors/ audit comm.	CEO/CFO	Other	Total	Big Four	Non-Big Four
The regulation of the market for audit services will reduce the number of corporate failures occurring in Australia	28	22	31	34	15	14	13	21	15	7	17
The recent regulatory and market responses to high-profile corporate collapses have assisted in:											
Improving the general public's confidence in the capital market	21	22	16	23	19	14	20	23	20	34	17
Enhancing the credibility of financial statements	25	29	22	22	21	23	21	33	22	34	20
Enhancing the quality of an audit	33	34	31	34	34	29	34	40	42	52	39
Adding value to a company's business operations	37	34	38	41	18	20	18	17	20	21	20

Percentage of respondents answering 'Strongly agree' or 'Agree' on a five-point scale.

Responses to the survey with respect to the question about whether the present regulatory requirements would reduce the number of corporate failures occurring in Australia showed considerable scepticism. They ranged from a peak of approximately one-third of those among private investors agreeing to this statement to a low of 7 per cent among Big Four suppliers. There is also scepticism about whether the regulatory and market responses to corporate collapses would improve the general public's confidence in the capital market. Again, responses typically were about one-quarter of all respondents indicating that they agreed with the proposition. Similar responses were received from each of the user, purchaser and supplier groups with respect to the capacity of the recent regulatory and market responses to enhance the credibility of financial statements.

With respect to the capacity of those regulatory and market responses to enhance audit quality, there was a more positive response, with approximately half of the Big Four supplier group respondents agreeing with the proposition and typically about one-third of all other respondents agreeing. There was scepticism about whether these responses would add value to a company's operations among suppliers and purchasers, with a somewhat more optimistic response from user groups.

On balance—and with a rare exception—user, purchaser and supplier groups were sceptical about the positive contribution these regulatory and market responses would have with respect to the issue of corporate failure. It can be said, however, that there is at least some belief by several in the market of a more positive outcome from these responses.

9.0 Interviews

In the interviews with stakeholders, the discussion about regulation elicited many lengthy responses, especially from suppliers. The issues that arise under the theme of 'regulation' are extremely intertwined and difficult to separate. Many of the comments in the next chapter (Chapter 11) are also pertinent to audit quality and hence to financial statement credibility.

9.1 Users

In their comments, users tended not to differentiate between the impact of the reforms to audit and the reforms to accounting through adoption of IFRS, so their comments need to be interpreted in that light. In general, users' comments reveal their scepticism of the general public or shareholders being aware of the reforms. Users showed a lack of confidence that the number of corporate failures would be reduced as a result of increased regulation of the market for audit services. This section begins, however, with the few more positive comments we received.

Not all users were sceptical, as the following comments reveal, with responses affirmative about the enhanced credibility of financial statements.

> Yes [there is greater credibility than before]...as an investor in companies...I tend to rely on them and we've had a couple of big-name collapses...and it's probably going to happen again, but...[with] the...amount of regulation that there is around now...they're going to be fewer and fewer as time goes on. So yeah, I rely on them and...others could too, more so than in the past.

> [Y]es [there is greater credibility than before]. But the general feeling...is that it was always assumed that the auditors were doing their jobs and...largely that...was assumed and is still assumed now, and that sometimes there is and will always be errors. But...it doesn't ever come up really in my discussions with the capital markets that the audit...information may be incorrect. It just doesn't come up; it's assumed to be right. No-one knows what's going on behind the scenes, but they just assume it's right...So I'm saying...that people did assume it was right before anyway.

> [There is greater credibility than before]...in some senses, creating more complexity or more regulation can be counterproductive. So these things go in swings...you do have a period of perhaps excessive tension when the companies post these sorts of collapses, but inevitably these sorts of situations will come back. So it's very, very hard, in my experience, to guard against outright fraud or distortion of the truth because those sort of companies invariably will find a way to present their statements in a way that's not accurate.

The same person goes on to recall how blunt an instrument regulation can be in attempting to make dishonest people honest:

> [I]n a sense...and...we've seen this from the US, adding to the complexity can be... counterproductive in a lot of ways. You have to rely to a certain extent on the honesty of directors and no amount of regulation necessarily is going to ensure that dishonest people are going to be honest. But to the extent that more onerous financial information can be useful, that's probably right. But...domestically...most analysts are struggling with the international accounting standards. And in fact they've said previously that that information has... made it harder to understand a lot of accounts as opposed to easier. So that's talking to a lot of CFOs and even CEOs, and a lot of those people struggle with the presentation of their company accounts, so what hope does an ordinary person reading those accounts have? So...that's overshadowed some of the...moves to greater disclosure.

'You have to rely to a certain extent on the honesty of directors and no amount of regulation necessarily is going to ensure that dishonest people are going to be honest.'

Another user, obviously thinking more of international financial reporting standards than reforms, states:

> The ordinary shareholder with international standards and greater comparability and just more and more disclosures, they probably assume that they do have a greater degree of credibility. But I have the opposite view with the analysts, because the more sophisticated the rules get, the more unintelligible that they become and they become a bit 'What does it all mean?'

Turning now to the more negative comments, this first quotation points to the perceived lack of knowledge among ordinary shareholders of the legislative and other reforms in response to the corporate collapses of earlier this decade:

> No, I don't think they'd have a clue about those changes and I certainly don't think that they perceive any [difference in credibility than before]. Maybe in the US, with Sarbanes-Oxley and all that kind of stuff, but I wouldn't think so in Australia.

The same person goes on to question whether the general public cares:

> [D]oes the general public care...they have an expectation of what the financial statements are and I don't think that that will have changed. Maybe there was a bigger gap before in that expectation and maybe the gap has closed a little now...I don't think the general public would perceive any difference in the accounts these days than previously, other than they'd probably find them harder to understand.

Another user expresses a similar view about ordinary shareholders' indifference to the changes:

> [T]hey're indifferent [to whether financial statements have more credibility than before]...if you're working in the industry, and with my limited experience, companies are much better and certainly providing better-quality reports. So...that standard's gone up. At the financial statements level, you might argue most investors are indifferent—certainly from our experiences.

Commenting in the context of accounting standards, another user observes their complexity, before moving on to the implications for the credibility of financial statements brought about by the reforms:

> I don't think that a lot of small shareholders—a lot of shareholders—have a real issue with how things are reported...a lot of them do struggle to grasp on to the reporting...they struggle as a result of the different changes, especially in Australia. I don't know whether there's another country in the world that changes accounting standards as much as Australia do[es], or have as many onerous accounting standards as what Australia does...it becomes rather complex for individual shareholders to actually make head or tail of what's going on in the reporting.

Continuing with the theme, the same user goes on:

> [I]t basically just passes everyone by...the reporting...shareholders rely much more heavily on analysts' reports from broking houses on the current state of play in a company, the reports and how they've been reported in terms of results, and what the analysts think in terms of the forecast going forward that the company's got over the next 12, 18 months.

The same user implies that the financial statements are the least-read section of annual reports:

> [I]n my experience, a lot of clients will draw a lot from the annual reports of a company, basically from the chairman's address or the CEO's address, and from AGMs, as opposed to the reporting of the accounts...there's such a big focus on the reporting of numbers by the accounting firms, but in reality when you...go to an AGM, or whether you have a company presentation, the finances are really at the end of the presentation, and they're brushed through fairly quickly, and no-one really understands...exactly what's being reported and why it's being reported.

The same user anticipates that an economy that is less buoyant will again reveal concerns and questions about the quality of accounting and auditing:

> [W]hen the economy turns the other way, and companies start going broke, that's when people start looking at [auditing and auditing standards] and start questioning why something was done and why it wasn't done.

The same person goes on to say something that is quoted in Chapter 3 dealing with the expectations gap, but which is worth repeating here:

> [I]n terms of what is debated as the audit expectation gap, if anything, those collapses have lowered the public's perception a little bit and thereby closed the gap in terms of lowering their expectations. But I don't think that they've got more confidence in the auditing standards than they had before. And...I don't think the broad public is that aware of the regulatory responses, the tightening of regulations, and rather would...if you mentioned to them an Enron or an HIH, they would mainly see that as a failure of the audit profession, and it would undermine their confidence rather than say, 'Okay, this has led to a regulatory response and a tightening up of standards that now...makes us actually more secure than we were before. We just didn't know how unsecure [sic] we were.' But in terms of perception, I don't think it's improved really.

One interviewee sees the check-list approach as auditors 'protecting their own backs' and clearly sees little role for reliance on auditors as an early warning mechanism for problems:

> '[M]aybe auditors have failed in the sense that they're just not relied on as the early warning signals of problems within companies.'

> [I]t limits the ability of auditors to provide information that's really going to be critical of the company…in a lot of ways…auditors are protecting their own backs, just like a lot of other professions, in the sense that they can meet a certain standard, but in terms of material issues…from time to time they do have to use their judgment and…alert investors to certain issues. So if it's just a narrow approach to information they present then the information's not that useful. Not many people rely on auditors as the first point of identifying issues within a company; they're normally relying on something else. So to that extent, you've got to say that maybe auditors have failed in the sense that they're just not relied on as the early warning signals of problems within companies.

The same person goes on to explain why he or she thinks shareholders are not assuming the financial statements have greater credibility after the reforms:

> Firstly…the ordinary shareholders are confused by…the extra reporting that's come with all those things, particularly in the US. It's worse there obviously than here, but financial statements are getting bigger and thicker and harder to read, so they'd be confused with that…and that's what happens in markets: for a short time, shareholders got sceptical about what they were given and that…just gradually dies away, new regulation comes in, usually the crooks still aren't very honest and the good people who were always honest are still honest and the world moves on and you wait for the next cycle…I've been in this game for 20-odd years and I've seen it about five times. So no, I don't think they would…naturally assume that the financial statements are more credible today than they were five years ago.

> No, I don't think people would feel as if [financial statements] had greater [credibility]. I don't think that most shareholders would be aware of the legislative change. They wouldn't understand what impact it has…there'd still be a certain degree of distrust out there

> in the community…Perhaps it's waned a bit now, but…I don't think people would be surprised when things get uncovered. So I don't think they're aware of the legislation…that's true for any legislative change in the community. The government doesn't communicate these things very well at all.

The same person elaborates in response to the question 'Do you think it's possible to communicate them well?':

> Yes, I do…I don't think they make an attempt at all, so any attempt would [be better]. What have we got now? We've got about 10 ads every night on terrorism. They've resurrected terrorism, resurrected the super changes, which actually came in last year, over a year ago, so any ad at all on explaining what action they've taken for the community to rectify some of those sort of issues…is one way of doing that. They're certainly willing to spend the money on promoting what they believe they've done for the community, so why not [spend] on something like that?

'They're certainly willing to spend the money on promoting what they believe they've done for the community, so why not [spend] on something like that?'

> [A]n Enron or a WorldCom can happen again. You can regulate until you're blue in the face, but if somebody wants to…commit fraud on that scale, there will be others…I'm not sure [that] increasing the regulation, increasing the disclosure and all the rest of it [will work]…it's just added cost to the system.

The same person goes on to explain his or her view that the increased regulation makes it easier, not more difficult, for problems to arise:

> [A]ll the things I've seen ASIC do in the Australian market, and all the rest of it, it's resulted in policies, guidelines, not regulations, to a large extent, and…they've found that the market here is relatively robust anyway, with all our existing checks and balances. So are our investors any safer? No, I wouldn't have thought so… unfortunately…increased regulation makes it easier for people to get duped, because you probably become too reliant on [the fact] that the boxes are ticked, rather than going, 'Is this a fundamentally sound investment proposition?' And you can't take that away from an investor or an investor's advisor on working that out…it would probably make it easier for more problems to…arise.

9.1.1 Summary

Few among the users express a view that, for ordinary shareholders, financial statement credibility has increased as a result of the legislative and other reforms that followed the collapses of earlier this decade. Several users respond more from the perspective of changes to accounting standards (that is, the adoption of IFRS) than from the perspective of reforms to the auditing regime. These comments are relevant, however, in that, generally, they claim that the complexity of financial statements adds to the difficulty of increasing investor confidence and of having the public in general and users of financial statements in particular know about and have an understanding of reforms—to either accounting or auditing. More than one user is of the view that, from a broad perspective, the reforms could be counterproductive. One user sees negative media reports and high executive salaries as contributing to a generally pejorative view of business among the public.

The next chapter, dealing in depth with stakeholders' perceptions of the operationalisation of the reforms specific to audit, and regulators' and quasi-regulators' conduct in monitoring audit quality, needs to be borne in mind as being of relevance to the material in this chapter.

9.2 Purchasers

There was little support among purchasers for the notion that regulation of the market for audit services would reduce the number of corporate failures occurring in Australia. Remembering that the interviews were conducted before the global financial crisis or even the full extent of the sub-prime credit problems became known, some of the comments are ominously prescient, as this first quotation demonstrates.

> [L]et's say that we take the [sub-prime] market...that's collapsing right now. Well, 12 months ago, I bet you all the guys who were...auditing them were saying the financial statements are fine but if there's a rising...reliance upon sub-prime lending for that organisation that's changing its risk profile considerably. So they've basically got a much higher sensitivity to a decline in...or an increase in credit spreads on that kind of lending then that's not very transparent when it comes to the way the financial statements are put together. That should be the kind of thing that organisations are highlighting in their risk management and limits of their broader

> sustainability-type reporting...which emphasises the risk to the organisation and how it's being managed and contained and what the profile is, et cetera. But that piece, that ain't audited right and if I was a regulator...what I'm more concerned about is what's there.
>
> [In general,] the auditing firms, their standing is reasonably good... I don't have that feeling that there's a huge amount of criticism over the accuracy or the professionalism of auditing work.

A theme common among the purchasers is the view that more corporate failures are inevitable as part of the risk of business:

> [W]e've encouraged this view that failure is not permitted to happen, whereas in fact failure is a normal part of business...when we talk about expectations, the public has been either encouraged or lulled or whatever, unrealistically, into the view that [an] audit [is carried] out wall-to-wall and picks up all errors, and well it's supposed to, and the businesses aren't allowed to fail, which is wrong.

One purchaser, however, is more optimistic that the reforms have added to confidence in greater financial statement credibility:

> [I]t's probably a reasonable assumption that the market thinks that all these feathers up in the air must've ended up with improvements [in financial statement credibility].

The same person goes on, alluding to the changes to the independence rules, which are discussed in the preceding chapter, to infer that retail investors are more aware than they are perhaps generally given credit for of events in the marketplace:

> [T]he granularity would not be well known, no. It's very clear that...it's well known from just attending AGMs...the mums and dads certainly know about non-audit services and quite regularly will ask questions about non-audit services. And at one stage, going back three or four years ago, we used to have some quite big non-audit ratios...And that stuff was getting called out and it wasn't getting called out necessarily because the market or the analysts were calling it out; it was getting called out because people were reading it...the mums and dads were going to the trouble of reading the accounts. So...that is well known...some of the other *CLERP* changes are probably less well known...the Sarbanes-Oxley stuff

> to Australians...is almost a black art. Yes, I suspect the public knowledge and understanding of why every now and then... someone gets in terrible trouble...with an audited client deriving out of Sarbanes-Oxley is...non-existent...However...the HIH Royal Commission, in an Australian context, would come absolutely at top of mind and they'd know that the relevant judge made a lot of recommendations, many of which were taken up. And...the corporate governance guidelines would be quite well known as well. That's obviously a bit broader than auditing but...it's probably seen as [being in] the same strand.

The same purchaser continues on this theme, but moves to those internal to the company—board and audit committee members—in terms of their awareness of changes in the audit regime:

> [T]here is also [a] more sophisticated thought process about auditing. Even talking about it as a niche part of the capital markets—as the assurance market of listed companies...in our questionnaires now, we provide quite a lengthy section regarding our own audit committee, the independence of the audit committee, the qualifications of the board members, the details of the audit relationship with the external auditor, detail of the internal auditor...that's quite an interesting example...that there is a broader knowledge and reliance on audit principles than there were prior to those collapses.

The following comment from a user, an accountant, reveals his or her perception of how the complexity of the financial statements is militating against regaining a sense of confidence in the financial statements:

'Even I have trouble with financial statements and I'm a trained accountant.'

> [T]he media's sensational reporting and...constant criticism of the 'big end of town'...[have inflicted] significant damage to the credibility of the business sector. And the difficulty is that financial statements at the same time, in an attempt to try to provide more information, have grown enormously, along with general corporate governance statements...it's reached the stage where the complexity of the report is not assisting people in regaining that sense of confidence. So... it's...a good example of how regulation and direction and more and more of this information has...actually made the situation slightly worse, because it's become so complex that if you wanted to hide

> anything, firstly a board could easily do it. And secondly...[for] most people, it's beyond their capacity to be able to absorb it all. Even I have trouble with financial statements and I'm a trained accountant.

The same person continues, referring to media reporting of business, high executive salaries and some spectacular failures as factors that keep the public on edge, contributing to discomfort, not comfort, with the financial statements:

> [W]e're in a bit bind here, this is between a rock and a hard place. And there is this innate criticism, supported by some spectacular failures...the Enron-type situation and HIH have all left this feeling that big business is able to take out the small investor and... the media keep it going. And with high salaries that are paid at the moment to CEOs...I don't see any progress towards a feeling of comfort and feeling that all of this is now leading to a greater credibility.

The next two comments from purchasers illustrate again the connection between this and the next chapter in that they deal with the perceived direct impacts of the reforms, which in turn influence audit quality. They appear here to remind the reader to view Chapters 11, 12 and 13 as having a common theme. The first points to pressure on fee margins and potential audit-quality implications.

> [B]ecause they've got budgets on each job and they've only got a certain amount of time for each job, it's how much time is going towards [it]...and that's always a danger of where the industry may head. Does it go to a point where it gets so tight with margins and these sort of things...does the quality drop off really in the objective of the audit? Does it get to a point where it's quite dangerous?

The second sees a check-list approach as a bad practice leading to bad outcomes:

> [O]ne of my views over a long time is that the more you develop a check list-type approach, the danger is that someone says if you can actually tick all the boxes on the check list then you are deemed to have complied even though you get to a wrong answer...So when you get to a situation where check lists drive behaviour and...where people just get concerned about what the answer on the check list

> is then...that's bad practice and it leads to bad outcomes. And the best example of all that is...if you look back to the governance requirements that applied and you look at Enron. Enron could tick all the boxes for good corporate governance because everybody just focused on what was [on] the check list as opposed to what was the substance of what was happening.

9.2.1 Summary

With one exception, purchasers do not express optimistic views of the likelihood of the ability of the reforms surrounding audit since the corporate collapses of earlier part of this decade to enhance confidence in the credibility of financial statements. Mention is made of the perceived inevitability of future corporate collapses associated with business risk. One purchaser, however, is more positive about the interest and knowledge of retail investors in general aspects of financial reporting and audit, albeit with little knowledge of the detail. This same purchaser comments positively on the knowledge level of board and audit committee members about matters surrounding the audit function. Once again, examples are provided of responses that deal with the impact of the reforms on audit processes and the implications of that impact on audit quality, which in turn influences financial statement credibility, to remind the reader of the link between this chapter and the next.

9.3 Suppliers

Among the suppliers, there was no perception that the level of regulation of audit services would prevent future collapses. Two suppliers mentioned that a focus by regulators on documentation and especially that of a check-list nature was an ineffective approach to regulation that would not prevent corporate collapses:

> I'm not sure that just handing out check lists and stuff to say that we have to fill them out will...reduce the amount of corporate collapses anyway.

The same supplier goes on to allude to the inappropriateness of the content of the check lists if the prevention of corporate collapse is the aim:

> 'The company is not going to collapse because someone didn't tick a box.'

> [Y]ou do…waste a lot of time in the wrong places because a regulator is going to come in and they're not necessarily going to know the client. All they're going to be able to do is look at the form. So you might've filled out all the forms and totally missed the key risks and issues in a client…they're not going to know that. They're going to see you did your form. They're going to say, 'Yes, well done, the file is great.' Then three years down the track, when the whole thing falls to pieces, it's not going to be because of the form. It'll probably be because someone missed one of those key risks…Or the technicality around one of those accounting issues was dealt with wrongly, or whatever it will be at that level. The company is not going to collapse because someone didn't tick a box…It'll collapse because of some very high-level absolutely fundamental, all consuming-type event, like an Enron. The revenue just wasn't there or whatever. They're the things that will bring you down, not some of the things that these regulatory check lists focus on.

Another supplier believes that the reforms could create a marginal difference in terms of belief in the credibility of financial statements:

> [W]ould it resolve concerns over the credibility of financial statements? I don't think it will resolve them, but it will help a little in that all sides are aware that you have the legal enforceability angle to it…in each case…it's a marginal difference rather than a quantum leap.

One supplier alludes to the difference between audit failure and corporate failure:

> Is the current approach giving greater guarantee that there won't be audit mistakes? [It's] hard to say, but it would be a case, and I don't think that's the case of whether the standard of the individual was always right or wrong…I don't think the odds have changed probably as much. You'll always get entities failing…on pure financial grounds. Now that doesn't necessarily mean that there's been an audit failure.

One supplier believes ordinary shareholders derive comfort from the reforms, but then goes on to question the understanding by investors of the emphasis of matter paragraph in the auditor's report:

> [Shareholders] probably do [believe financial statements have more credibility], but…they're all still pretty sceptical…people worry enormously when they see something as large as Enron go under… who would've thought HIH [would go under?]…I remember clearly when you got the stock market reports on the radio…and they [would say], 'HIH is up 23 cents today'…it was a very large organisation. And then when they bought FAI, which had a very high profile in the insurance market, which was probably punching above its weight in terms of profile compared to how big it really was, but it was a very well-known, very large enterprise. And we've seen an enormous level of mismanagement there, and we think, well how could they not have known?
>
> I remember at the time…speaking to a manager at Arthur Andersen about it, and he was very defensive about the whole thing and said, 'Oh, we've done everything that we should've done'…but he said to me at the time they had an inherent uncertainty [about] going concern[s]. Well, I don't recall that. But even if AAs had put that opinion on HIH's financial statements, I don't think the investor would've understood exactly what that meant. And we've got this strange situation with the standards whereby if you think that an entity is not a going concern, if you think that there are serious difficulties with it, you…have to give a clean opinion. It's an unqualified…an unmodified opinion, but with an emphasis of matter.

Another supplier expresses belief that ordinary shareholders do assume more credibility, but he or she goes on to allude to perceived inconsistency by regulators shaking that faith:

> Yes…they would assume that there's more credibility. And… part of me says…there's definitely been a tightening up in the environment…the expectations now are a lot more stringent, yet you have events [*an example is provided of what the interviewee perceives to be an inconsistency*]…that sort of inconsistency would put doubt into the shareholder's mind. But…overall, they would expect that with all the disasters that have happened that someone

> is now more accountable. That someone typically tends to be—they tend to look towards the auditors a lot more...that's the wrong place to look because...managers and directors have the ultimate responsibility for the financial statements, and notwithstanding that we're obviously attesting of them, so there is responsibility on our part too. But...inconsistent behaviour of the regulators would put some doubt into their mind...they'd like to think that they can rely on them more.

Several suppliers differentiate between ordinary and more sophisticated investors in terms of the likely level of credibility they attach to financial statements:

> [T]here would be a split between...people who are more involved in looking at financials closer to companies that would understand that it probably isn't [more credible] verus maybe the general public out there that would have the perception that because of all of this the rules have been tightened...The top end of the capital markets, people that are dealing with companies all the time and [are] involved with them, I don't think they really see that there's any difference.

Several suppliers, however, see little to no likelihood of the regulatory reforms giving rise to enhanced belief in the credibility of financial statements.

> I don't necessarily think [shareholders assume financial statements have greater credibility]...the perception probably is that things have been shaken up a bit...we've had the collapse [of] Andersen's, which has obviously been quite a high-profile thing. And... a large number of the public, and therefore your readers of financial statements, have understood what happened in that instance at a high level...things like that have probably created the prominence that therefore there are things being done to rectify it. Obviously, the Sarbanes-Oxley [issue]—it depends on who's aware of it—but it certainly has been given a bit of profile. So how does that feed into whether they think they're getting anything different from what they were [getting] previously? I don't necessarily think...things have...changed from what I saw.

The same person goes on to say that directors and audit committees have changed in their approach to the audit, but not the 'average reader':

> [W]hat you're finding is it's more about directors in particular, and audit committees. I've certainly seen a significant change in their attitudes and their level of diligence in the way that they deal with us and what they're expecting out of us. Absolutely, there's been a change there. But as to the average reader of financials, I don't believe there's been a significant change. But I have certainly seen, particularly from non-executive directors, a very different change in attitude over the last three or four years.

The next supplier states that stakeholders and the general public think that the auditor is a regulator. Regulators themselves have referred to the audit as delegated regulation (for example, Knott 2002).

'The stakeholders and the general public think that the auditor is a regulator, so…we're losing credibility all of the time, but it's really the regulator that needs beefing up and more money spent [on it].'

> I…don't believe the shareholders have [belief in greater credibility of financial statements]. I don't think that they have any real feeling of credibility in the processes at all…a lot of people have been shocked by the regulators with the perception of not effectively regulating places like HIH and the crowd in Western Australia…Westpoint, and One.Tel. And there's a whole raft of companies come and go and fall on their sword and the regulator tends to run for cover and then strengthens the regulations after the collapse. The Enron affair was a perfect affair. And the auditor is in there, and even though the auditor might not be to be blame for any of this, because the auditor is looking at things after the horse has bolted (the auditor might not be to blame in all cases, or very few cases), [but they] would…be blamed. The stakeholders and the general public think that the auditor is a regulator, so… we're losing credibility all of the time, but it's really the regulator that needs beefing up and more money spent [on it]. And the ACCC is another—I know that's not a regulator—but just the fact that they've got their hand tied with trying to regulate petrol prices. They can't, so the general public thinks that the ACCC is a toothless tiger.

Another supplier points to the trade-off between the reforms raising belief in financial statement credibility and the raised cynicism created by the collapses themselves:

> I don't know [whether shareholders now assume financial statements have greater credibility]...it will be patchy...some people will... assume they have greater credibility...there will be many people whose levels of cynicism have been raised by the experience and not necessarily assuaged by what happened since those experiences. So I really don't know. The only way I could find an answer to that question would be to get some empirical data by survey...I meet a range of people who have a range of different views, and I just don't know.

Another supplier speaks about the fact that there will always be collapses:

> [S]ome of the collapses will unfortunately continue to happen... But there's always going to be that small one that for some reason something goes wrong—the collapses this week in property development schemes; the water gets muddied with that. There's, 'Oh, well, the auditor should've picked it up.' 'The regulator should have picked up'—whatever.

The same person goes on to allude to the relationship between the quality of audit and the quality of information in the context of the transition to Australian Equivalents to International Financial Reporting Standards (AIFRS) that occurred in a similar period to the reforms:

> [T]here'll always be that scepticism around it. If people believe there were problems previously...they'll still think that happens because things go on. I don't think that perception has been helped by the AIFRS, the new accounting standards...people, particularly firms...they're bruised from the experience of bringing those in... it's a mute point as to whether that improves the overall credibility of financial statements on that. So...people would have difficulty separating quality of audit from quality of information...people are still struggling until that settles down and that'll be a way to go. And...those people who thought that audits were pretty good anyway will probably continue to think that there will be collapses, but they're the exception to the rule.

The same person continues, expounding on how the wider public has little understanding of the difference between an audit that is poorly executed and one where the auditors could not have been expected to detect the problem:

> I'm not sure that the fact that these standards are legally enforceable [will make] people…think [that things have changed], until effectively a firm is hauled over the coals for not doing it, and that's in the public arena…it's behind the scenes. Analysts… believe the financial statements have less credibility, not through the audit process, but through what's disclosed in there. Ordinary shareholders—it's a difficult one…[With] the HIH…[and] each of these, when you pick apart the bones of it, you can see that it was an audit generally that wasn't properly executed, or the problem was something that the auditors would not have been expected to pick up. So there's always a reason for it, but I'm not sure that reason necessarily gets seen by the wider public and understood.

The same person continues, going to the issue of public trust and the auditor:

> It's difficult. I don't know what the general public's view of what an auditor does or doesn't do is…if anything, it's reduced because of those collapses and people are suspicious. They probably don't know what's going on behind the scenes. So…a big agenda for us is this whole question of trust…some auditors haven't covered themselves in glory, but it's a little bit like the umpire: you only ever see the umpire when he's made a bad decision. Sometimes a guy can…make terrific decisions and he doesn't get much credit for it. Regulators…are the same.

Continuing on this theme, the same supplier alludes to the publicity received by 'colourful' corporate characters:

> [M]anagement are always the bad guys…particularly in Australia… I notice coming from the UK, where corporates have somewhat faced much bigger [issues] and so on…the Australian interest, or cult of celebrity, extends well into the corporate arena, so there are some fairly colourful characters. And…the more you have those people paraded through in the context of HIH—the sort of people who are put on trial and so forth…people tend to extrapolate that and just

> have their views, and an element of talk probably comes in. But I don't believe the financial statements have greater credibility. It's either unchanged or people are suspicious.

9.3.1 Summary

Suppliers are in the main sceptical that the reforms will enhance the credibility of financial statements, although one or two believe that the general public, but not sophisticated investors, could be of this view. Suppliers have no belief that corporate collapses will be reduced as a consequence of the reforms, and allude to the fact that the regulators and check lists do not focus on audit issues pertinent to this issue. The suppliers tend to see collapses as a business risk, not an audit risk, and hence view a corporate collapse as not being an audit failure. There is questioning of the public's understanding of the meaning of an emphasis of matter section in an audit report. An observation that the public sees the auditor as a regulator is interesting in that at least one regulator is on record as labelling audit as delegated regulation (Knott 2002). Some of the suppliers' discussions reveal beliefs about the harm that the collapse of HIH has done to the trust that the public places in auditors, which has been exacerbated by the publicity given to colourful corporate characters.

9.4 Standard setters

Standard setters are realistic about how much of the reforms to the auditing regime is known to retail investors and how legal backing for auditing standards is but one aspect of the reforms. The first standard setter's comment illustrates both of these points:

> [T]he average off-the-street investor probably doesn't know [about the regulatory changes]. In fact, they probably didn't even know that there were auditing standards before that, [which is] somewhat unbelievable, but if they don't read audit reports, it's probably a reasonable conclusion.

The same standard setter continues, explaining that if more confidence has resulted it is in association with the sweeping nature of reforms beyond the mere legal status of auditing standards:

> [I]t's likely that they do have more confidence [in the credibility of the financial statements]...the issue becomes one of what's the confidence built on? It's probably not just built on the changes in

> the auditing standards; it's probably more a fraction of the whole change in the regulatory framework: the ASIC's rules have changed, you've got your continuous disclosure...auditors have got to go to the AGM and answer questions relevant to the conduct of the audit—probably more feel-good factors than tangible factors. But the real test will be [whether] there will be more corporate collapses and there have to be because people make decisions that don't always turn out the way they think they will—and that doesn't mean someone signed a report and it's fallen over. What it means is [that] business couldn't operate with the cost structure it had with the changes that are occurring in the global economy.

Continuing, the same standard setter makes a most prescient comment about how confidence is a function of not only the regulatory regime, but the economic fundamentals and expectations regarding the future.

> Perhaps one of the more fundamental questions becomes one of, if things tighten up, it may not be...the financials; what happens if the pressure goes back into the financial statement process because people are then trying to get to the forecast? And that's when your whole integrity issue comes back in and maybe some businesses have had it easy, and auditors, because the results are there. They don't have to work harder to deliver, but as we go forward, if things tighten up, interest rates rise, exchange rates move...books aren't necessarily as effective as people thought they would be, then we might see a different outcome. And then you might see a change to that answer, because...the confidence probably comes from forecast versus actual.

Another standard setter comments on any enhanced credibility of the financial statements in the following way:

> [I]t's very, very difficult for ordinary shareholders...to have any real understanding of what happens [in relation to regulation activity]. And how would they? If you haven't had any exposure to it, how would you have any real understanding of what goes on?

The same person goes on to imply that although ordinary shareholders might have a low level of understanding of what goes on in the auditing space, directors' understanding has improved markedly in recent years:

> [T]rying to get the directors to understand it...is extremely important...the directors' attention and...desire to understand and depth of understanding, has probably increased quite a lot in the last few years...it's still got some way to go. And it obviously varies very much by individuals...But...it is much better than it was, say, 10 years ago...the broader understanding of the process and how far it can really go, how much assurance has really been given... that's come up some notches.

The next standard setter also alludes to the issue of just how much knowledge of the changes in the auditing regime exists among less-sophisticated shareholders:

> I wonder even how much the less-sophisticated shareholders would even be aware that there's been a whole lot of change in the regulatory environment, and therefore would necessarily think that there's a greater level of assurance. The more sophisticated investors would be somewhere between aware and vaguely aware of there having been change without necessarily perhaps understanding it a lot.

Another of the standard setters comments on research conducted by the AUASB with small practitioners that shows less than optimal awareness even among this group of the auditing standards.

> We've done a little bit of market-based awareness, an awareness survey where a worrying level of knowledge, awareness and let alone understanding of the new audit standards [were seen] at the smaller end. But that was the very small end of the practitioner market. Less than 10 is where we pitched it, down to much smaller ones. And a number of the practitioners surveyed were only spending 20 per cent of their time on audits, which is an issue in itself...And is that a bad thing?

The same standard setter continues, explaining his or her view that audit quality is not necessarily improved by creating an auditing regime that is easier to regulate:

> Those things...are the real core of really quality auditing. So it really is about understanding the risks; it really is about being able to stop and [identify] them. And a lot of what we have in auditing standards doesn't really go to those sorts of issues. It's more around

> saying you need to do particular things in different circumstances. And it's now much more around explaining what you're going to do and explaining what you have done, and documenting what you have done, which creates trails of what work has been done, which makes it easier to regulate what's been done, or review what's been done. But it doesn't necessarily improve the quality.

9.4.1 Summary

Standard setters are at pains to differentiate between the various levels of investor sophistication in the marketplace, which in turn influences knowledge of the reforms to the regulatory regime in an auditing context, especially of their extent and nature, which extends to more than legal backing for auditing standards. In the context of whether the reforms are likely to have enhanced the credibility of financial statements, some positive views are expressed, but these views are qualified. One standard setter notes the importance of the economic fundamentals to public confidence, no matter what the regulatory regime, and the global financial crisis reminds us of how relevant such a comment is. Another standard setter reminds us that changes that create a regime that is more conducive to regulation do not necessarily translate to enhanced audit quality.

9.5 Regulators

Regulators' responses convey a lack of conviction in any belief that reforms to the regulatory regime have resulted in enhanced confidence in financial statement credibility or in the confidence of the share market.

> I don't really know [whether shareholders assume there is greater credibility in financial statements]...I'm not sure how much... ordinary people would be reading financial statements...So...a lot of the information about...listed companies is coming out through annuals and journals and they're probably better able to assess documents...I'm not sure whether ordinary people really pay a lot of attention to a lot of the documents which are produced by companies in the sense that...[they] really rely upon the analysis of experts.

The same person continues, emphasising how the analysts on whom this reliance occurs receive much of their information from company presentations:

> [T]hey're probably not aware of the detail of them...because you see a much heavier level of disclosure and comments about all of these things in annual reports, but whether or not they're across the [detail]...of it is another thing...what I mean about analysts is that one...of the key things analysts are getting information from is company presentations and things like that, when they're actually questioning the executives of the company, even there in a live environment and that's probably where the information which people perhaps put the most credence on comes from. But others say the audited accounts are a fairly important starting point.
>
> My sense of the situation is that the market tends to be reactive rather than proactive so that investors really haven't got any further comfort from what they've seen as a result of Enron and HIH.

9.5.1 Summary

Regulators are sceptical that the reforms have added to confidence in the capital market and doubt that 'ordinary people' read financial statements, relying instead on analysts who attend corporate briefings. Of course, under the continuous disclosure regime, briefings to analysts are made public through the Australian Securities Exchange Announcements, but the implication is that 'ordinary people' don't read these either.

10.0 Issues and implications

Responses from users, purchasers and suppliers all suggested that there were very modest levels of agreement with the proposition of enhanced confidence in the capital market as a consequence of reforms after Enron and HIH. Indeed, of each of these three groups approximately 20 per cent gave a positive response and 80 per cent did not agree.

There were widely differing views with respect to responses to the question about the value-adding capacity to a business's operations, with users much more positive compared with purchasers and suppliers, who were very sceptical. Interestingly, about 80 per cent of purchasers and suppliers responded negatively to this question and those responses were reasonably uniform between different types of purchasers and different groups of suppliers.

The interviews conducted with these three stakeholder groups supported the overall conclusion from the survey. Users suggest that the market will continue to believe that auditors will undertake what they need to do to form their audit opinion. Others support a belief that the market will not see much impact from the changes. One more sophisticated set of responses suggests there could be a change, but only if two conditions are met: 1) that current auditing standards really are different from their predecessors; and 2) that enforcement will be better. This particular respondent is somewhat critical of the profession's ability to enforce standards, implying that a high level of regulated enforcement will give rise to a higher-quality outcome.

With respect to purchasers, few observations suggested there was a clear increase in confidence in the capital market and suppliers too shared the scepticism that the market would be any different to what preceded it.

Users, purchasers, suppliers, standard setters and regulators were all interviewed, with one of the questions in relation to enhanced credibility of financial statements as a consequence of the reforms. In general, all of the groups had members who either agreed or disagreed with the premise within this question, with surprisingly little insights or innovations produced by the question. One of the most intriguing results from the interviews was that users believed they had quite a sophisticated and complex understanding of the work of an auditor and what the current regulatory requirements entailed, as well as past practices.

Some users praised the current regulatory requirements, suggesting that they provided a floor level of quality. Various users described the present regulatory system as giving rise to audits that were 'standardised', 'consistent', 'unbiased', 'objective', 'comprehensive' and 'methodical'. There seemed to be an implication in the minds of some that these requirements would give rise to higher-quality auditing and they took the view that this would mean that the auditors would be better able to comment on the credibility of financial statements. A few users suggested that the auditor needed to go beyond this and be inquiring and innovative in their understanding of a business and the risks that business faced.

Some purchasers feel that while the audit might not change much of what is done, the current regulatory requirements add considerable robustness to the audit, which might not have been present before. A number of purchasers suggest that, fundamentally, the audit they observe has not changed with recent amendments to regulatory requirements; however, it has driven up costs. Few purchasers were able to identify how the audit had been changed or whether the auditors provided new and valuable insights into the business. Those who were able to make direct comparisons between Australia's current position and the Sarbanes-Oxley legislation in the United States spoke favourably of the Australian position and somewhat harshly of the more prescriptive and compliance-driven US position.

Various purchasers discuss their need for a balance and the fact that the 'check-list approach' is really just a minimum floor level, which returns to the point that audits that fulfil all the regulatory requirements are a floor level and there needs to be innovation and insight beyond this to achieve a high-value audit. One purchaser suggests that auditors have an obligation for and on behalf of their clients to push back against regulatory requirements if they think there is a better way for the audit to be achieved and for the outcome of the audit to be better delivered to the capital markets.

11.0 Introduction: cost consequences of reforms

The survey and the interviews canvassed the issue of the cost consequences of the regulatory reforms brought in after the corporate collapses in the earlier part of this decade. This section examines responses directed specifically to cost, but, as with previous sections in this chapter, several of the comments could be placed under multiple headings. It is important to bear in mind that this and the next chapter should be read in conjunction with each other.

12.0 Survey

User, purchaser and supplier groups were surveyed about their perceptions of the additional audit procedures required as part of the revised, legally enforceable auditing standards in terms of increasing costs and adding value to the company's business operations. Results are reported in Table 10.3.

One can observe from the responses to the surveys that users, purchasers and suppliers all share the view that costs have increased, with 81 per cent of users, 90 per cent of purchasers and 92 per cent of suppliers agreeing with the proposition that costs have increased.

Table 10.3 Responses on the cost impact of regulatory reforms to audit (per cent)

	USERS				PURCHASERS				SUPPLIERS		
	Total	Accounting expertise	Professional users	Private investors	Total	Directors/ audit comm.	CEO/CFO	Other	Total	Big Four	Non-Big Four
In response to high-profile corporate collapses, regulation now requires auditors to comply with additional mandatory audit procedures. In your opinion, complying with the additional mandatory procedures will:											
Increase the costs of conducting an audit	81	85	80	76	90	86	93	87	92	96	91

Percentage of respondents answering 'Strongly agree' or 'Agree' on a five-point scale.

13.0 Interviews

Users, purchasers, suppliers, standard setters and regulators were asked to express their views about the cost implications of the enhanced regulatory regime surrounding audit. Quotations from their responses follow.

13.1 Users

All of the users' comments reveal that an increase in costs is expected to accompany the increase in regulation of audits, and mostly there is unhappiness about this eventuality, as the following quotations reveal.

> [T]hat's often the hard sell for the auditors: to demonstrate to us that there is an increase in the service provided, or an increase in our ability to rely on the service that is being provided to compensate for the increase in costs, and it's hard to see...[T]he auditors try and sell it as a value add to our organisation, but their perception of

how they're adding value to us is quite different to our perception of where the value has been added. So they're kind of saying, 'Yes, but we were able to do this for you', and we're thinking, 'Well, hang on, did we want that done or do we really think that they have done what it is they say they've done?' So…it's hard for us to see the additional costs as any value added to us.

[L]egal enforceability…increases costs because there's now…that legal opinion attached to it. So, if anything, the auditor is forced basically to check that they are within the limits, or that they work within a template that's been provided by their legal counsel.

It'd probably increase costs…I'm not sure how much is involved with the old system, but for a smaller company to have to go through that 150-page check list, the cost as a percentage of their revenue would be a lot greater than BHP or someone like that, so it probably does increase costs.

[I]t has definitely increased costs. People are complaining about it.

Two users, however, do not see increased costs as necessarily a negative thing, as long as the quality of financial statements improves too:

[I]t's all very well and good worrying about costs, but if it results in a better outcome and you have to pay a slightly higher cost then that's not an unreasonable outcome; that's a win-win situation…the aim should always be to get the best set of financial statements, the most reliable…set of financial statements that gives you the best indication as to where a particular company is positioned at that point in time.

I…feel for the auditors there. It's probably hindering a more lateral approach and…deeper exploratory think[ing]…the regulations probably also put more…walls around what they're doing. Whereas if an auditor fronts up and they're wanting to explore it more, but it might increase the cost of the audit and all the rest of it, it gives the board more things to say, 'Well, you've done what you have to do.' 'We've ticked all the boxes, why do you want to go and do that? We're not going to spend that money'…there are obviously issues around that…it's always what

'It's probably hindering a more lateral approach and…deeper exploratory think[ing]…the regulations probably also put more…walls around what they're doing.'

regulation does, which is trying to react to things that happened where people lost lots of money, but, equally, it's [a question of] what do investors expect of an audit...that's probably been lost a bit. And it is [a] comfort that the numbers are accurate and the auditors should be able to explore that as much as they need to.

I don't know that it's hindering the efficiency of the capital market. It may well be making the audit a more costly exercise than it should be. But the capital market is so far in the future that the reporting of historical information is, whilst important, the efficiency of a capital market is its ability to digest information that occurred today and price it. That's what makes a capital market efficient... the regulators and auditors would do well to...make the whole process as efficient as possible, and that's not just the procedures, that's also the reporting, but I don't know that it's hindering the efficiency of the capital markets...I'm a bit out [of] the loop on what happened with the regulatory processes, but I don't have any issue with [it]...by and large, irrespective of the regulatory requirements that now...exist...the auditors were doing behind the scenes what they needed to do to get the right outcome, and if they could add value in other ways then good on them.

13.1.1 Summary

Users' comments reveal some scepticism of value adding when auditors' fees increase, and recognition of a disproportionate impact for smaller companies. One user, however, expresses the sentiment that auditors should explore as much as is necessary—regardless of cost—and another seeks to balance increased costs against improved quality of financial statements.

13.2 Purchasers

Purchasers are aware that auditors are being requested by the standards and regulator to undertake additional procedures in terms of documentation. Their comments reveal that some are prepared to pay for the incremental time involved, but some are not.

> '[M]ost organisations wouldn't allow an absorption of an extra 10 per cent pass-on.'

[I]t just means things are a little bit...tighter...or, their costs have gone up to allow for it, so we've had that discussion over the last few years...they're presumably hiring more people to allow for it because it means more people on each audit team. So in other words...they've compensated for it... What we're really talking about is that it...either eats into the margin that the audit firms make—so they have to absorb the extra cost of now adding an extra 10 per cent on to every auditor's times that probably document—or to some extent they'd defray the costs...most organisations wouldn't allow an absorption of an extra 10 per cent pass-on...surely the key thing for a partner is to make sure the substantive work is done because they're signing the bottom line. So it's a bit like [a] plane, isn't it? You've got to do the maintenance otherwise you've probably lost your business if one of them comes out of the air.

[T]hey cannot...officially charge clients just because their internal documentation now is much better than before, because, to the clients, it's not...that value add from a direct marketing perspective.

Every document that is prepared costs money...it costs money not for the client but for the auditor because someone has to review it, someone has to check it, someone has to reference it and tick... the box. And it's every single document because, in the end, that document could be hauled up in front of a court.

[T]he process that is forced by the regulator, and this check-box approach that we're talking about, really just drives [up] costs for us.

[O]ur audit costs have gone up and it is because there is a requirement to do more work. My expectation of the auditor is the longer you're here, the more you know about us and that should result in some productivity, and they say they factor that in...I went back to ASIC, [the] government's requirements, IFRS requirements, the more you have to do and disclose, the more audit work you're going to get. But it's just one follows the other...So what's driving audit activity, and therefore costs up, is the amount of disclosures that are being required by those two elements...well, three, I suppose: corporate law, the ASX, the governance...and again IFRS.

[F]rom a customer's point of view, we see that as coming through discussions with the auditors about why the fee's gone up this year, purely because there's paperwork to be filled out and things to be documented. When they haven't been done in the past, it's not really a good reason for doing it, but they're being forced down this path by the expectations of the regulator. And...the PCAOB in the US, which...apparently...you can call them up at any time and send someone out to examine the audit work papers they've done on our business and haul them over the coals for weaknesses or inconsistencies in those. So...that's the biggest expectation gap.

[T]hat's a worry overall with all these things, but invariably the way it's being played out is that because of the regulatory approach being adopted...the general response of the auditing firms [is that] they are saying to the clients: 'We have to do more work to meet the requirements of the regulator.' So therefore the client has to pay more money and that doesn't mean that they're not doing other things...They're doing more time in...filling out the check list-type thing and the clients are having to pay for it.

[S]itting where we are, thinking all right, we've got to shell out large amounts of money for their supported process, it'd be pretty good if it was valuable towards our organisation and provided a framework going forward or provided a lot of handy tips or incentives or whatever...a different set of eyes looking at things. But with this new check-list approach that's less likely to happen...they're more focused on ticking the boxes and making sure that they're covering all the bases and providing useful information.

[I]t's stuff that they tell us they have to [document], but [for] me as a client, why would I pay for it? They're asking me to pay for work that I've not asked them to do and whose benefit I don't see, so... when it comes to fee negotiations, we always just knock that out as a legitimate factor.

> Very rarely do they tell us something that we didn't already know or we weren't already aware of. They try to, because they try to make themselves valuable to us, but...the process that is forced by the regulator, and this check-box approach that we're talking about, really just drives costs [up] for us. In our specific example, I don't think we'd lose much. But I...stand back and try to imagine a broader industry type of approach. I could see how people could come to that conclusion, how this check-box approach would mean that the auditors have got X amount of time to spend on this because they've got a capped fee. They go through the check-box approach and don't look at anything else. In our case, I don't think it matters that much. I don't think we'd lose much because of that, but I can...see a situation where other companies would.

> '[T]hey try to make themselves valuable to us, but...the process that is forced by the regulator...really just drives costs [up] for us.

> I don't see a risk as long as the partner's still on the hook. It's just a time waster. It just adds to cost and inefficiency. And...it has the potential to distract from the main game, because the check list's filled in, the pat questions are answered and all of a sudden, no, there's no budget left. Oh, well, we can't look into this area, which is a bit of an issue.

13.2.1 Summary

Purchasers' comments reveal their reluctance to pay extra for additional audit procedures around documentation that they perceive as not adding value to them. Some purchasers do not hide their refusal to pay extra in this situation, making their auditors absorb the increased time requirements without charge. Purchasers reveal some concern that the auditor's focus moves from what can add value to them to ticking boxes, which is perceived as being of no value to them.

13.3 Suppliers

Suppliers concede that an increase in costs has accompanied the revised auditing standards—whether or not those costs are capable of being passed on.

[W]e have had some change in our methodology, but fundamentally, what we do hasn't really changed that much. It's just that we've got to put a lot more—whether it be paper or whether it be documents on an electric file—significantly more time...for example, when we're doing our quotes for audits going forward, not for maybe existing clients, but certainly for prospective clients, the section it takes up in our budget document for administration, what I would consider to be administration-type tasks, is almost more than...the section that deals with the actual guts of the audit. It surprised me in going through our budgets now and plotting time and how long do we think it's going to take how much time is in that administration area. It's just amazing.

> 'I have some clients who understand and are willing to bear part of that cost, if not all. And I have other clients who say, "Well, tough, that's the market you're operating in, we assumed you were always doing a quality audit."'

[T]he cost varies depending upon the type of client and the types of things you're having to do and whether you could spread it across a client...I do a lot of audits of funds and quite often some of the prescriptive measures are in the set-up, the planning phase and the completion phase. But a lot of the work you're doing at the individual fund level hasn't changed greatly. So you know those costs would be heavy if you were just doing one fund, but if you were doing 60 funds, it's spread across those. So it might be a relatively modest increase. On a corporate it can be a significant increase, it could be 10 or 15 per cent. And that's difficult...I have some clients who understand and are willing to bear part of that cost, if not all. And I have other clients who say, 'Well, tough, that's the market you're operating in, we assumed you were always doing a quality audit.' If something changes, you've got to absorb the cost, but it's certainly a cost. To what extent this year and last year—it's a cost of the fact that...our files should have been tighter, but weren't as tight as they should be, so it's costs we should always have been incurring to have tight files...My guess is that cost is...anywhere between 5 and 15 per cent of an audit depending on quite how it's done, which is a pain.

From the point of view of costs...making those standards black-letter law [means that] a lot of it's become a lot more prescriptive of yourself, so a lot of areas that were like you should do this or you should do that have now become you must do this, you must do that. So, yes...It does add another layer of costs, because ordinarily you'd use your judgment to focus on areas of risk and potentially areas that didn't have any risk you could tone down or cut back on the level of work...it's fairly standard, you could probably get through it pretty quickly...Now, you can't. The minimum level of document[ation] requirement is higher than what it was because... you used to be able to use your judgment to decide whether you should do something. Now, irrespective of your judgment, you must do things. So...the costs will go up.

[Costs have gone up]...there are some things that we probably would've done, but on some engagements may...not have done, because it was a 'may'. 'The audit may use its judgment to do this', whereas now it's the auditor should. And so a lot of our internal work programs, check lists, et cetera, are now you can't put a 'not applicable' or say 'partners' judgment'; we don't need to do this, you have to do it. So the second you have to do something then there's an extra, whether it's a half an hour or an hour or whatever it needs, then you do have an increase in costs. And it still doesn't take away from any of the other bits of the audit that you were doing; it just means that some of things that you may have determined that weren't applicable now are. So, yes, [there is a change] cost-wise.

I'd like to think that ultimately it doesn't distract the auditors from the objective of the audit...you do end up with assurance on the credibility of the financial statements...the objective is there and the auditors get there. Do they get there by the most perfect critical path? Probably not. Does it add to the cost? Obviously, it must. Is it a massive issue? To listen to my audit colleagues, it's getting more annoying, so that the weight of extra cost and burden is higher.

13.3.1 Summary

Suppliers' comments reveal that some of their clients are more prepared than others to pay increased costs as a result of increased documentation and regulatory requirements, confirming some of the purchasers' revelations. The increased time for 'administration' is clearly sizeable given the comments of some suppliers. Comments reveal that at least some of the increased cost is performing tasks that were previously considered unnecessary given the risks, but which have now become mandatory regardless of the risk.

13.4 Standard setters

Standard setters provide a broader perspective of the increase in audit costs than the other stakeholders tend to do. Their comments follow.

> [T]here's no doubt that it heightens the barriers to entry. Yes, the cost of getting the fundamentals in place has gone up.

> [T]here can be no denying that to deliver what the capital markets today consider to be a quality audit costs more money than it did before we had the changes in regulation and auditing standards in law and regulator oversight. For a whole variety of reasons, we've had IFRS as well in that space. There [are] a lot more disclosures. There's a lot more fair valuing involved, so skill sets needed to have changed. So there are lots of reasons driving cost [and] it is costing more, but I'm not blaming that on the regulatory process.

> The commercial issues...press down on that...because if you increase the underlying cost base by additional documentation-type work, process work, then your clients are unwilling to [pay]. If the total cost of doing the documentation plus the other risk—the real risk-thinking piece—blows out a bit then there's pressure to squeeze it. So if you can't squeeze a documentation piece then it's the other piece that gets squeezed...that's the commercial reality that happens a bit. But that's...one of the quirks of the auditing world, isn't it: the pressure that the audit is put under to minimise the amount of work that's being done.

> Yes, the audit inspections by the regulator, and all the costs that that imposes...the regulator view of the need for documentation and, at the same time...the tightening of audit standards coming internationally anyway, versus the firms having a somewhat more pragmatic [view], or wanting more flexibility perhaps than...the regulator was giving.

'[A] lot...of the additional cost is... around documentation and process, rather than additional work, because the standards didn't really change.'

[The] standards were amended to make them enforceable, but at the same time there'd been two or three fairly key updates to the underlying ISA and particularly around documentation. So that...happened at the same time...It was the increased requirements which had come out of updates to the ISA which were going to come through anyway, and particularly around documentation. That would've in itself lifted the scope of work. On top of that, [the standards being] legally enforceable pushes you...down the road of being even more careful about documentation and doing more documentation. So it's a bit of a combination of those things. But a lot...of the additional cost is... around documentation and process, rather than additional work, because the standards didn't really change. The fundamentals of it didn't change...there's no doubt that it heightens the barriers to entry. Yes, the cost of getting the fundamentals in place has gone up.

Yes, there is a paradox there that isn't admitted. And I don't think directors necessarily have too much of a view about this. The discussion you have with other directors is more around the auditors are coming here saying the standards have changed therefore they've got to put the fees up by 20 per cent. Tough, that's their problem. [I] don't want to know about it. [It's] not our issue... that their administrative costs have gone up because of regulation. Join the rest of the world with everything; that's what's happening to everybody. In every sense, we don't want to know about it.

13.4.1 Summary

Standard setters point out that some of the changes to auditing standards that have added costs are attributable to changes in the underlying International Standards on Auditing, which occurred before the release of legally enforceable standards and were incorporated into those standards. One standard setter makes the interesting observation that barriers to entry to the carrying on of an auditing service have been raised, which has implications for competition. Another supplier points to factors besides the changes to auditing that have added to costs (for instance, IFRS adoption). Another points to the constant pressure to minimise the amount of work that is done in an audit in order to contain costs.

13.5 Regulators

Regulators, as might be expected, are unrepentant about required additional procedures and costs.

> [L]eaving it in the hands of the auditors, you've got this commercial approach where...they're constrained by costs and they can only charge so much in fees, and I wouldn't want it to be left totally to the auditors to decide how much work to do.

The same regulator goes on to say:

> I'm not sure that the...mums and dads in the market are all [aware that] there [are] legally enforceable standards around...there has been a lot of publicity about it and a lot of training, which of course I would have received unpublished notification about. I'd say, on balance...it has made no difference in the expectation gap...it has increased costs.
>
> Even without [the legal backing for auditing standards], they're still liable under negligence and duty of care...if they don't do an audit properly. This whole idea of force-of-law standards increasing the cost of an audit, it's just a fee-grabbing exercise.

13.5.1 Summary

Regulators have mixed views on the justification for legally enforceable auditing standards increasing costs.

14.0 Issues and implications

With respect to the individual interviews, users, purchasers and suppliers all acknowledge that costs have risen as a consequence of these changes. For users who are somewhat sceptical of the value-adding capacities of an audit, these added costs only intensify the irritation. Purchasers also acknowledge that costs have risen, but there appears to be some acceptance of these costs being passed on—at least in part. Suppliers have acknowledged increased costs and in some instances margins have been squeezed.

One purchaser makes the interesting and insightful comment that auditors are acting like any private-sector supplier providing a service to a market: they seek to provide that service in the most efficient means possible, whereas regulators have a different imperative—the delivery of a certain quality of service in a particular way. The clash between these two is an obvious and not uncommon difference between regulators and participants in a competitive market.

The changes in costs because of these regulatory changes reinforce the views of those in the market who are cynical about the value-adding capacities of an audit. None of the interviews reveals great insight into the public policy value of having an effective and efficient audit process. This is an issue that we will return to elsewhere in this report.

So, while users, purchasers and suppliers are generally of the same view—that costs have moved up as a consequence of the introduction of various regulatory changes—some of the regulators interviewed are less sympathetic to the increased underlying costs for auditors.

A number of standard setters were interviewed with respect to this question and their responses were interesting and insightful. Some standard setters appreciated that, while there was going to be a gravitation upwards with respect to legally backed auditing standards, several of the costs associated with increased documentation came not from the changes to the Australian regulatory environment or legally backed auditing standards; they in fact came about because of changes in the international standards, which called for higher levels of documentation. Because of the policy position of the standards board in Australia to hold back the introduction of these international standards until such time as legally backed auditing standards were introduced, the legal backing and changes to the international standards were introduced simultaneously in Australia. This would have exacerbated the increase in costs and likely resulted in the market concluding that the regulatory regime was the root cause of these elevated costs, when in fact it was a more complex situation. One standard setter also made the observation that the change to legally enforceable auditing standards could in fact substantially increase the threshold costs of becoming an auditor to the corporate sector—thereby limiting competition. He or she observes that this could be an unintended consequence of this shift in the status of auditing standards.

Related to but not directly connected with the increase to operating costs of conducting an audit under the new regulatory environment is the issue of the costs or potential costs to auditors with respect to litigation risk.

One observer speaks eloquently about what is referred to in the auditing literature as the 'insurance hypothesis'. The insurance hypothesis states that a significant component of the value of an audit is the fact that when something goes wrong and a company fails or goes into liquidation those who sustain an economic loss because of this will seek to recoup some or all of that cost through litigation against the auditor, whether an audit failure has occurred or not. The observation made by this particular user is the fact that the change in regulatory environment will exacerbate this potential cost to audit firms. If this is true, it will add to the cost of conducting an audit, albeit in an indirect way, without necessarily adding any legitimate value to the audit process, and it will perhaps not be observable until the professional indemnity insurance premium is affected.

A second observation with respect to litigation came from a regulator who took the view that the presence of legally backed auditing standards would change the environment in only a relatively minor way. One specific way it will change the environment is to add another legal pathway to enhance auditor accountability.

15.0 Concluding remarks

In each of the chapters thus far, the concluding remarks have focused on the policy implications—in particular the implementation of policy—and the accountability for potential future action to some authority or person. This chapter documents in considerable detail the consequences of the legal backing of auditing standards and the effect on the quality and the costs of the audit of companies listed on the Australian Stock Exchange, among others.

While the description of the present state is detailed, the potential policy actions of participants in the market for audit services are limited to one single issue. Whereas some users accept that the present regulatory framework and its additional impositions mainly on the suppliers of audit services are beneficial in terms of the standardisation and development of a minimum quality, it is a fact that there is no evidence from suppliers, purchasers, regulators or standard setters that the change in the regulatory regime and, in particular, the legal backing of auditing standards, has enhanced the quality of the audit product and specifically enhanced the efficiency of the capital market.

One policy outcome and action could be that the relevant public policy institution, the Financial Reporting Council (FRC), be mandated and perhaps even required to systematically gather evidence that demonstrates that capital market efficiency has been enhanced by the requirement to legal back auditing standards. That is, rather than assuming this public policy enhancement has given rise to added benefit to the economy, we should gather empirical data that demonstrate or indeed refute that these changes to the regulatory regime have had a consequence on the Australian economy. We note there is a direct parallel with the legislation in the United States (*Sarbanes-Oxley Act 2002*), which requires a number of evidence-gathering processes to demonstrate this public policy position has been of benefit to the US economy.

While it seems apparent to the authors that the FRC has the overarching responsibility for this process, it is an issue that could also be relevant to those in the Treasury in the Federal Government and to those responsible for research and gathering of evidence in the Australian Auditing and Assurance Standards Board.

INCREASINGLY PRESCRIPTIVE AUDITS A DISTRACTION FOR AUDITORS? 11

> [D]oes it distract? Look, it's like people driving cars with mobile phones. I'd like to say that everybody is sensible enough not to use their mobile phone when they're driving, but some people get distracted by mobile phones. So...it's brought an element of risk into it, and you have to make sure you don't get lost in the detail and ignore the issues...the really good professionals will make sure they get the issues right, and if that means that for some reason something gets missed on the documentation...they'll feel more comfortable in that than being absolutely watertight on the documentation and having missed the issue. But there will be a number that go the other way because they're that worried... we've had it drilled into us for a while now that ASIC will come in and inspect a file if [it's] not right, so people have spent...massive time on that.
> — Supplier

1.0 Key issues

The regulatory reforms to the auditing regime of earlier this decade were pervasive, once the revised, legally backed auditing standards were included. This chapter explores the impact of the changes in terms of the auditors' work conduct.

- Is the increasingly prescriptive nature of auditing a distraction to the auditor?
- To what extent, if any, has the increasingly prescriptive nature of auditing, including increased documentation, resulted in a check-list mentality that is to the detriment of auditors' judgment and the quality outcome of the audit?

- Given the additional audit procedures now required, do audit budgets give less scope to: a) understand the client; and b) delve into issues that arise?
- Will the additional audit procedures encourage over-auditing?

2.0 Introduction

A common question across the surveys and the interviews related to whether or not the increasingly prescriptive nature of audit acted as a distraction for auditors, so interfering with their task. Survey responses appear below and interviewees' responses in the section after. While the increased audit documentation requirements arose separately from the creation of legal backing, owing to concurrent changes in International Auditing Standards, the complexity of this has been heightened by the presence of legal backing. This means that there is an inexorable link between legal enforceability on the one hand and documentation on the other. This section examines some of the comments devoted specifically to the issue of the impact of additional procedures as a result of the reforms on the audit. The next chapter examines stakeholders' perceptions of the way in which regulators handle their oversight responsibilities.

3.0 Survey

The survey question was framed in the context of the additional mandatory audit procedures imposed in response to the high-profile corporate collapses of earlier this decade. It read: 'In response to high-profile corporate collapses, regulation now requires auditors to comply with additional mandatory audit procedures. In your opinion (on a scale of 1 = Strongly agree to 5 = Strongly disagree), complying with the additional mandatory procedures will distract auditors from the objective of a financial statement audit, which is to give assurance on the credibility of financial statements.'

Interestingly, a majority of respondents, including those closest to the production of audit opinions, do not believe that the new regulatory requirements cause a distraction from the major objective of the audit, as can be seen in Table 11.1. Importantly, however, there is a noticeable differentiation between the typical responses of those who might be seen as less technically expert and those who have a greater level of expertise. Users, whether they are seen as professional or retail users, are the least likely to believe that there is a distraction arising from these new regulations. Of the two groups of producers of audit opinions, it was those from non-Big Four firms who viewed the new regulatory regime as most distracting. One might speculate that this is a consequence of the documentary requirements, which could impact more on firms outside the Big Four.

Table 11.1 Responses on regulatory changes as a distraction (per cent)

	USERS				PURCHASERS				SUPPLIERS		
	Total	Accounting expertise	Professional users	Private investors	Total	Directors/ audit comm.	CEO/CFO	Other	Total	Big Four	Non-Big Four
In response to high-profile corporate collapses, regulation now requires auditors to comply with additional mandatory audit procedures. In your opinion, complying with the additional mandatory procedures will:											
Distract auditors from the objective of a financial statement audit, which is to give assurance on the credibility of financial statements	19	24	15	14	27	28	38	23	37	33	38

Percentage of respondents answering 'Strongly agree' or 'Agree' on a five-point scale.

4.0 Interviews

Most interviewees were asked to respond to a question similar to that posed in the survey protocol explained above. That is, did the stakeholder perceive the increasingly prescriptive nature of auditing to be a distraction? Responses from users, purchasers, suppliers, standard setters and regulators to this question are canvassed below, together with discussion of these responses. Parts of the responses that touch on observations about the regulatory process and regulators themselves appear in the next chapter.

4.1 Users

There was a frequent perception among users that there had to be procedures in place for an audit, otherwise things would be missed, and that check lists assisted with this process in providing a minimum base for requirements. The following four quotations demonstrate this theme.

> I don't know whether they're becoming any more or any less [prescriptive]...to a certain extent, there's always going to be that check list.

> [I]t's not having a huge influence on this organisation as an investor...Regulators don't always achieve the desired outcome and prescribing rules and approaches is often limiting the scope that might be applied.

> [T]here is a minimum [needed]...[For] the current...required regulatory processes and procedures, you need something as a necessary minimum, because...not every audit firm is [one of the Big Four firms]...I can be reasonably confident that...all those Big Four firms, in 99 per cent of the times, have got it covered, [and] are doing the right amount of work. But I'm certain that a lot of the small firms are not. When you've got a one-partner firm doing an audit, the level of documentation that he might...have could be very different to what [one of the Big Four firms] would need.

> No, I don't see them coming around...but they probably have check lists that we never see, but I don't see them coming around with check lists wanting this and that. They'll be coming around, they'll be taking your documents, your emails or your working papers and...that's what I see of it and testing and checking those.

Two users looked at check lists as providing consistency and standardisation in the audit 'product' and so, by implication, adding to audit quality, as the following two quotations reveal.

> [T]hey've probably given you a different answer, especially if they love their job or they've been around for a while...[In] the old days...they might've been able to do what they wanted to...but... a check list and a standard way of doing things is good, and as long as it covers that area of credibility then it shouldn't really distract... I'd rather see them be consistent...I don't have much to do with this, but...I'd rather see them have that consistent approach with the check list. Now, the auditors may be able to provide an additional service to their client by providing advice that's paid for separately, but...in terms of the audit, then [with] that check list...you know that you're getting the same quality of audit across the board.

> [There are] benefits of having a common approach across the auditing fraternity because it gives us as investors some comfort that the quality of audit is consistent and of a certain level, otherwise you get the chance where you've got some rogue auditing firm who might think they've got the latest whiz-bang concepts, and they really aren't providing a very good level of service at all. But, by the same token, if they've got ideas and if they are clearly of the view that the current standards are far below where they should be then...they have an obligation to the rest of the investing community to do something about that and to lead the way, and to try and push changes through with the regulator. So...there's a need to be proactive.

> [T]here is the real fear...from the auditor's perspective, that they're being asked to provide assurances to the validity of the statements—and they are. There's no doubt that they are being asked to do that... there's no value at all having an audit statement that's just a general tick-off. But that is what the expectation is...from the professional community, and I don't think it's unreasonable for companies to have to pay for that.

Others view a check-list approach in a more sinister light, with one user finding similarities with the financial services regulatory reforms in a very negative way.

> The check-list approach...makes it easier for companies that perhaps people are going to lose money on to exist. We've certainly found that in financial advising, with the FSR [financial services regulation] reforms, because now there [are] such huge compliance

> requirements…the poor advisors can sit there and say tick, tick, tick, tick, tick, tick, tick, we've done everything. The advice is still poor.

There was, however, acknowledgment among users that a check-list approach exacerbated by reforms could inhibit 'innovation' and 'that inquisitive investigative attribute', resulting in 'narrow-minded' or blinkered thinking. This next quotation discusses the potential for inhibited innovation:

> '[M]ore than likely, you're going to get people just staying within the scope of what they need to do to meet the requirements, rather than be[ing] innovative and go[ing] beyond that.'

> [T]hat is one of the dangers [of] the check-list approach versus inhibiting innovation… there will always be…that legal opinion that will say if you go outside the check list, you're exposing yourself, and some people will eventually do it, but more than likely you're going to get people just staying within the scope of what they need to do to meet the requirements, rather than be[ing] innovative and go[ing] beyond that…that's the inherent danger of too prescriptive regulation…there is a real risk that a 'tick-the-box' approach and requirement does detract from that main objective and…as a user of financial accounts, my overriding aim is to have as much assurance as is possible that I can rely on these numbers, that they are a fair representation…If you're forced to choose always the prescriptive approach then we're probably missing too much. And this [is] where, if anything, a commentary would come in useful. But there is…a real risk that too prescriptive an approach takes the eye off the main game, so you're fulfilling the legal requirements but the rest gets left behind.

The person in the next quotation speaks of check lists as discouraging the exploration of issues:

> [T]here might be certain things that you might've been more biased [about] because of your personal experiences, whereas a check list can avoid it. But, by the same token, if they meet that requirement, and you as a person or professional feel that may be not the true indication, but they've met that requirement, then it's away from that level, isn't it? You won't get somebody sticking out their neck or saying, 'Look, I think, based on experience, that they meet these boxes but maybe down [further] they've got some other issues.'…

> And going back—maybe these organisations that we saw going bust—maybe they met the boxes at that time, but deep down people involved know that that's not the right way to go.

Another user comments on the danger of a check list impeding on the time spent gaining an understanding of the client:

> You've been here for three weeks and you're asking questions that indicate that you don't really know what we do and this is the problem, because they don't have the time. In an ideal world... week one would've been spent [finding out], okay, what...these guys do, what is their business about, because the auditors have never been there before. But that doesn't happen because they've got to get straight into it and start...ticking the boxes. So when we're reviewing the process at the end, we're thinking, 'Well, how much credence can we put on the non-financial assurances that these guys are giving if they don't fully understand the business?'

Users did not comment on documentation specifically, with the exception of one, who differentiated between the Big Four and non-Big Four in terms of the perceived quality of documentation.

> [T]here is a minimum [needed]...[With] the current...required regulatory processes and procedures, you need something as a necessary minimum, because...not every audit firm is [one of the Big Four firms]...I can be reasonably confident that...all those Big Four firms...99 per cent of the times have got it covered, [and] are doing the right amount of work. But I'm certain that a lot of the small firms are not. When you've got a one-partner firm doing an audit, the level of documentation that he might...have could be very different to what [one of the Big Four firms] would need...But does it distract the audit firm's objective? I don't think so...[at] the small end, it's a good thing that they have to think about documentation and check lists and procedure and, at the big end of town, they've got enough infrastructure and support to do it.

'[A]t...the small end, it's a good thing that they have to think about documentation and check lists and procedure and, at the big end of town, they've got enough infrastructure and support to do it.'

4.1.1 Summary

Some among the users are concerned that increased attention to check lists is eating into budgeted audit time, so that other issues might not be investigated. While concerned about the time it takes to attend to check lists and the potential for the check-list approach to create form-over-substance audits, some users feel that a standardised approach creates a minimum floor for required audit procedures.

4.2 Purchasers

Among the purchasers, several expressed concerns about a check-list approach.

> [P]rocess and demonstrative compliance—that's what an audit has become. We've got to demonstrate that we comply with the auditing standard.

Comment was made about the potential costs and inefficiency of spending time completing check lists that not only might mitigate against recognising other issues—'seeing the wood for the trees' or 'form over substance'—that need investigation, but might deplete the auditor's time budget for little value, ultimately impacting on audit quality. Three of the purchasers captured these concerns eloquently when asked if the increasingly prescriptive nature of auditing was becoming a distraction.

> [E]verybody talks about over-regulation, ticking the boxes. I can understand the reason for it because of what happened a few years ago and the regulators want to be on top of everything. Like anything, if you go too far with it, it becomes very, very difficult.

> I definitely see that risk [of an auditor seeking to follow only the check list] and...the auditor would need to be very wary of that... to the extent that the regulator is empowered to require the auditor to follow their check list or submit information to them [and that] is separate and distinct from the auditor's responsibility to the other shareholders of the company, and maybe [that] should be seen as... one element of the audit, but not the core element of the audit—not the core driver.

> [A narrow view in terms of responsibilities and roles given a check-list approach is] a definite risk...when you've got more rules and

> you've got less time, what are you going to do? You're going to play it safe, right? And then if you do have a lot of inquiry, how much time and confidence do you have to break out and pursue it? [I] don't know...in audit—and I say this to my team on the other side of the fence here in finance—professional scepticism is very important, but when you've got scarcity of time and abundance of workload, a large part of it regulatory driven, you may well let that go or you may well trade it off or run it down...your professional scepticism is also borne by how well you understand audit, how well you understand...the industry that you audit and how well you understand that business. If you've got good understanding across all three of those, your professional scepticism is at its peak, but if you don't have a lot of time or a lot of training, or [you haven't] had...the time or the stewardship or the supervision to build up that commercial nous, then you're going to miss things and that's where the value add comes in.

Other purchasers, however, do not see the requirement to complete check lists as necessarily harmful:

> [W]hether that's...beneficial or not is quite hard to form an opinion [on], in my position—not being in an auditor's role, not really having full knowledge on exactly what is in those check lists. But... to the extent where [in] past practice there were gaps, or it was easy to forget things or to overlook things—and this [is] a tightening up of that process—I couldn't see that as a bad thing. But whether a lot of this ticking the box is peer reviews and then these sort of things...maybe it's after the event and it's not going to be equivalent to signing the dotted line on those accounts...I've got to have faith that where it's heading is helping the standards of the profession... It's methodical, it's consistent.

One purchaser thinks the Australian model is superior to that of other countries—no matter what its flaws might be:

> '[I]n a sense, it's an insoluble model, but... it's produced a far better economic outcome than other models in other countries, so...it may be flawed, it may have its gaps, but it has worked.'

> [I]n a sense, it's an insoluble model, but...it's produced a far better economic outcome than other models in other countries, so it may be bad—sorry, it may be flawed—it may have its gaps, but it has worked...the last five to

> 10 years...[for me] as an individual, as a personal investor, has been positive. It's created a greater distance between an auditor and the company because the auditor is afraid of losing their job and their livelihood...but it's come at a cost of process and autocracy and box ticking. Would it free them up to do more work if they [didn't have] to do that...the primary role of the auditor is to challenge what's in the financial statements, to be sceptical.

Another purchaser sees check lists as potentially lessening the audit expectations gap:

> [I]t's much more of a check-list approach than it used to be. So... the auditors...[are] certainly bringing in those check lists to satisfy the regulators...more than anything, it's probably lessening the [expectations] gap because they're coming onboard to that approach.

The next purchaser feels that increased documentation associated with check lists is something that was already being done before the reforms:

> [E]ven our internal audit team are facing the same...issues, as in we are doing a lot of internal documentations...For example, you'll be done documenting, half the things we do we probably [would] be able to finish the audit quicker [without the documentation]...that probably is one way that people...[could be used to add] more value [by being] out there doing another audit...external auditors [are] probably...facing the same issues because I understand nowadays external auditors are also subject to audit, [and] external audit firms are subject to audit, so obviously they would have to make sure that the quality and the extent of the documentation has to be present...I don't disagree with the concept...it is...good. They should be already doing it anyway. I can't imagine they'd just go in and scribble two lines and somehow just give an opinion on a financial statement, though they should be already doing it. So hopefully this is not something that is causing too much grief...[for] any of the Big Four firms because they should be already doing it.

The same person goes on to express perceptions of a differentiation between the smaller and larger audit firms:

> For example, [with] the smaller size firm...there might be a bit of an issue because they try to do a similar thing to adopt a best practice, but then...hopefully if it's a smaller client they're looking at...the

> time required perhaps is proportionately reduced as well in terms of trying to match the best practice...the concept is definitely... a worthwhile one. Now whether people would take it to the extent to be able to draw a balance, I'd probably have to wait and see. Maybe...the pendulum is now swinging a little bit because...[there were] some possible past incidences...and people were not sure, so therefore [they] may have drawn to the extreme and the pendulum perhaps might swing back a little bit when people are a bit more balanced in terms of what they're looking for...[There shouldn't be an issue] on the bigger sized firms anyway, because they should already have the practices or the normal day-to-day practices... already more or less there.

Another purchaser similarly sees no difference from what has been practised in the past in terms of check lists:

> [G]enerally they [have a] check-list approach anyway, regardless of whether it's prescriptive. And if...parts of the thing [are] prescriptive, well just send your juniors out to do it. I don't think that's particularly an obstacle at all...we'd rather see check lists than no check lists.

Yet another purchaser does not see the check lists as a distraction:

> [T]here are partners who I've bumped into who would be very, very prescriptive on issues and it's to check to the last detail...others take a more commonsense approach...that's probably going back to the principles involved rather than trying to drive through exact rule[s]...But on the whole...they've got the balance pretty right... but...we're dealing with big companies [audit firms], we're dealing with [one of the Big Four] and that's been our experience. It's been pretty good.

Another purchaser discusses the level of prescription as just a further evolution of the audit process along a continuum from less to more regulation and prescription.

> I was an auditor for 17 years and so when I started auditing, I started... in the internal control era...we used to look at internal controls... A year or two into my training, we went fully substantive...And that was very check-list oriented, but it was very focused on the balance sheet and analytics and the like...Then we went back to

> 'I don't think the auditors have found their feet yet in terms of the balance between controls and substantive...cost.'

a more controls-based business orientation. And... in hindsight...it's fair to say that was fairly well focused towards a consulting additional services kind of offering. And now we've come back a bit on that to a post-independence world, where we're still controls focused, because people want value in recommendations around controls. But I don't think the auditors have found their feet yet in terms of the balance between controls and substantive...cost, because the controls that they're looking at, I don't think they've worked... out yet...the moving of the audit models over time perhaps demonstrates—I don't know what it demonstrates, to be honest; the market or the regulator or the evolving nature of business...[is] a big part of it...business is more complex and sophisticated now.

One purchaser questions objections to an enhanced documentation or check-list approach, querying whether auditors are reluctant to disclose their 'true' opinions:

> Let's just look at it [from] two points of view. One is because of the regulations and because of all the governance issues that everybody has to go [through]...auditors obviously have to check more, et cetera. That's one thing, but what could be the negative connotation of that? Could it be that they're not willing to perhaps disclose their gut feel[ing] or their perception on a particular item because it could perhaps be challenged and it cannot be substantiated sometimes? And therefore, if it can't be substantiated and it could be challenged...it won't be brought into the forefront if it's just a suspicion or a doubt?

The same purchaser argues that the check-list approach will not constitute a distraction because auditors must still complete their 'bread and butter' audit work:

> I don't think that there's distract[ion] from what their job is. At the most...it adds to their workload...but if it adds to their workload, they've just got to spend so many more hours on it...it's not that they're going to have to reduce the amount of effort that they do for their bread and butter in audit stuff and then say, 'God, I've got to do this additional impostor work, so, well, look I've done one part of it.'

Another purchaser takes a broader perspective about the relativities of this issue between the United States under the *Sarbanes-Oxley Act 2002* and Australia under its reforms:

> [A]ll our experience with our auditors is that it's very much still a risk-based audit. If I was to show you the audit plan, they do start off with identifying the risks and the point in our processes that those risks can occur. I don't feel...[that] as a preparer, that it is just a tick-the-box audit that they do. [Companies] have just deregistered from the SEC because the impost of SOX costs [is not] worth the registration and the listing in the New York Stock Exchange. And SOX actually takes you down a path of ticking off boxes...if you're not a SEC registrant, [we're] back to a more commonsense, risk-based, not the tick-the-boxes-based audit.

Three purchasers comment specifically on audit documentation. The first two have some sympathy with auditors' disquiet about the extent of regulatory prescription:

> [F]rom what I hear from our auditors...and some of the discussions we have...the gap in expectations between the regulators and the auditors at the moment is around the area of documentation. The auditors are basically saying...they would like to be in a position where they [can] say, 'Once we've formed our opinion, that's our opinion. We issue that opinion and, if it goes wrong, if something happens with that company, we're still stuck having to stand by our opinion and we'll be the ones in court over that.' But they're being forced down this path...by the regulators of saying, 'No, you have to substantiate how you formed your opinion. You have to have all of the paperwork in place.'
>
> Does it...distract them from the objective of giving reasonable assurance? I'm not sure it does...the question is: 'Does it add value to the audit process?' I'm pretty sure they'd reach the same conclusions without it all. The question is whether...it would be as robust in terms of documenting how they got to that conclusion if you looked at it two years later.

The third purchaser sees documentation in a more positive light:

'[T]hat's an intellectual challenge for them, and it's really ensuring that they've done their job properly rather than just a form-filling exercise.'

[T]hat probably [also] depends on the nature of the documentation...[if] it enforces a discipline around their conclusions then...that's a good thing. The concept of the auditor having a casual discussion with management in the corridor or in the coffee room or something and drawing conclusions from that discussion that just enabled them to sign off a set of financial statements... that's not acceptable. And if...you're saying that we're requiring them to...address [the issue of] have we thought through this, this, this and this, and let's lay out logically what... our conclusions are and why we've drawn them, then that's a positive...It just enforces some discipline around their process, providing it's succinct and productive and not bureaucratic...that gets back to the question of the nature of the paperwork. If it's filling out exactly the same form for 10 clients for a year then that would be soul destroying...I don't know exactly the nature of the paperwork...but hopefully it's intended to enforce some discipline in making them think about aspects of the client's business, and draw conclusions from that, and actually document why, or reasons why, they've drawn those conclusions...that's an intellectual challenge for them, and it's really ensuring that they've done their job properly rather than just a form-filling exercise.

4.2.1 Summary

Purchasers observe that the regulator is auditing the auditors, but there is scepticism expressed about whether this can be successful, with a claim that what is recorded cannot capture adequately exactly what has happened. Among those from the purchasers who feel that the level of prescription faced by auditors does not present a distraction to them, a major reason for this is the perception that the audit firms should already have been complying with the documentation and other requirements, especially among the Big Four. Some look on it as adding rigour and discipline to the audit effort. The observation is made that in terms of internal audit, increased requirements for documentation are happening too. One purchaser with experience of complying with the *Sarbanes-Oxley Act* comments on the check-list approach under that act as being much more extreme compared with the approach under the Australian auditing standards. Two comment on whether the Big Four and non-Big Four are equally equipped to deal with the level of prescription, especially in terms of documentation. The comments about documentation from purchasers reveal the essence of the debate about this required audit procedure: documentation as inflexible and inefficient versus documentation as a worthwhile discipline that contributes to audit quality by compelling a reflective approach.

4.3 Suppliers

Among the suppliers, many interviewees felt that the level of prescription created a concern for the quality of the audit. Indicative comments appear below and range from those that documentation provides evidence of a job well done to comments about added cost. The first few quotations from the interviews highlight that, to partners, there is a need to maintain professionalism in the face of increased time pressures because of check lists and enhanced documentation requirements, and to ensure that audits continue to entail substance over form.

> [Prescription has] the potential to [distract]...I'm the partner signing off on my clients. Is this heightened regulator risk actually going to change my own view about what...things am I worried about, what are the major things from a shareholder's perspective in these financial statements? I don't think it's going to change that. Does it change my focus a little bit internally on me specifically reviewing areas of our files, rather than relying on, as in any organisation, delegating some responsibility to...the manager or the director on the engagement? Will it change my focus on those things? Probably, in some ways, because...if I am the one [who's] the partner on the engagement, it crystallises some of those things.
>
> But in terms of the external [audit]...I've got to do what I've go to do to get to an audit opinion. And just because there may be another regulator who can look at my files or who can require this or that or put extra things in, those are just part of things that you've got to get on with. I don't think it affects my approach to it.

Remembering that at the time of the interviews, there had not been a great deal of experience with the new requirements, the following quotation speaks to any distraction being only until familiarity takes over, but then goes on to imply it will lead to consumption of time with no apparent productive outcome.

> Yeah, it is a distraction...until we get comfortable with it and understand how it's done, there is a risk. The reality is...[that] the way that it happens is, instead of people working 100 per cent of the time, they work 120 per cent, because the last thing a professional will do is let the form get in the way of the substance. It means that we have to ramp up and get the form right. And, yes, there's a risk of distraction, but I would like to think that we are still nailing the substance things.

The same person goes on to elaborate on the risk of prescription creating inefficient audit practices to the extent of over-auditing:

> [W]hat it will do for a little while is...bring back the double audit, which is basically the audit that's done...by the senior members of the audit team...around what are the issues and what are our calls on those, and are we comfortable with those, and flushing those out, which is to make sure we get the right answer. And then [there's] the other bit of the audit, which is documenting that, making sure we've done enough detailed work to support that, the cycles and so forth...before this great focus on quality, they were quite nicely integrated. You were having the top-down driving of the risk approach to audit and flushing that out, and they all neatly linked through...it's brought back a little bit of the dual audit.

Another supplier voices a similar concern:

> The processes can be very prescriptive in terms of form filling and that can distract an auditor from applying his time in terms of the judgment areas, and that does become difficult when you are forced down a track of form filling. And often those forms can be fairly detailed. And to do it properly, it does take time, and often that time cannot then be spent in relation to the judgments, better knowledge of a client, better further analysis on the risk areas.

One of the suppliers expresses concern about the impact on auditors' business models of the requirement for greater documentation and the difficulty of being recompensed by clients who see the audit as a commodity, as illustrated in the following quote:

> The users of the accounts don't quite understand what an audit is or what the regulations are, so they're saying, 'Well, why should an audit cost?' They don't...particularly see the value in an audit,

> which is ironic, because if anything goes wrong, usually the auditors are the first people that they try and sue. Notwithstanding that, they don't seem to place too much value on an audit in terms of the cost of an audit. So…trying to marry up the regulators' requirements, and trying to marry up our obligations and our own business models, and trying to get the consumer, or the users of the accounts, to understand, is quite a challenge.

The majority of suppliers, however, did speak in negative terms of the increasingly regulated approach to audit and in particular its potential to distract them. These next two quotations speak about what is perceived as auditors' fear of non-compliance.

> [W]e auditors are so intent on complying because of what can happen to us if we don't, we tend to have a very narrow vision of what our responsibilities are. So it does distract the auditor.

> Yes, absolutely [it is a distraction], because they've got all auditors gun-shy now. They're just saying, 'You've got to strictly do each of these different things.' And the only way to properly combat the way that we're being talked down to effectively is to check list things and just to simply say, 'Oh, well, we did that, we did that', instead of…having more of a holistic approach to the audit. And when you look at the language, the way that they're treating auditors, and then when you look at things like they've tripled the size of the CALDB in the past year…you go 'hello?'. They've got new auditing standards, they've got force of law, you've got three times the number of people on the CALDB and they're basically telling us that we must be very prescriptive, we must do all these things. Yeah, it has to have an effect on auditors, who are just simply going to tick a box: yes, we've done that; yes, we've done this… We've only got so much time to do things and clients don't expect us to increase the audit fees by 25 per cent to account for all these sorts of things. So we're the meat in the sandwich.

This next quotation highlights just how many reviews—internal and external—audits are subject to:

'If you're looking at a small-tier firm that might not have those internal policies, then the regulators probably have a job to do there, and a check list might...be quite helpful.'

> The regulated approach [is] horses for courses. You have audit firms that have a lot of expertise and...crudely trying to group them into groups: the Big Four...we have technical expertise with high-quality standards already internally; we're regulated in turn; we have our own self-review policies; we have every man and his dog coming in looking at our files. So we...have that basic foundation sorted. If you're looking at a small-tier firm that might not have those internal policies, then the regulators probably have a job to do there, and a check list might...be quite helpful. It might make sure that they're all a little bit more in line with at...least a basic standard. But where we have the real skills... and what we like to focus our audit on, and where the value comes in, is when you...look at the...financial risks that are involved in the business, and trying to focus on understanding the client's business; understanding where likely problems are to come up... once you've identified those—usually, they're very highly technical areas—[you can focus] your audit time on those aspects, as opposed to ticking and bashing and getting a nice, neat, make sure the boxes are crossed. Because we already have our work programs, our systems already have a lot of that built into it.

Some of the comments about the content of the check lists were quite scathing in terms of the perceived harm to audit quality that could ensue.

> [T]he second aspect of it is documentation. Whilst...it is a very good thing, [it] is, however...starting to drive people to behave [differently]...there's a lot of time being spent on documenting, and my big concern is that, whether we like it or not, we're moving to auditors spending time behind their machines documenting rather than talking to clients and actually getting out and understanding the business and the business processes. And...there's a balance somewhere in between, where it is important to document, but it is also important to make sure that we spend time in the client's business understanding the processes, understanding the commercial reality of transactions.

Since increased documentation requirements most affect suppliers, it is not surprising that several of them comment specifically on this issue.

The first few comments are in a positive vein, acknowledging that audit files are in a better state as a consequence of the emphasis on documentation; however, some negative comments follow.

> Our audit files are better because of...getting sufficient documentation...I started in the late '80s with the firm—and I'm not sure if the audit opinions would be different now—but...we probably are better in documenting how we got to that opinion, but maybe there was more in the partner's head, for instance, and it should have been in the file. So, to that extent, that's a good result... certainly, the compliance burden is...far more significant than even within the last few years; it's grown.

> Where we've probably not been good, as all firms in this profession, is in the form and recording that...that's very much the focus [of] these legally enforceable [standards]...getting it written and properly documented for the record [is] where... we've been less good historically as a profession than we should've been...Yes, we have to make sure we cover everything and there's more prescription in certain areas, and more rule[s]...in applying that, but I don't have major concerns over that philosophically. Others of my partners would have...The fact that we've now got them as legally enforceable, we could have a debate one morning about whether that's right or wrong. The fact that they're there and legally enforceable...creates a very small expectation gap...between the regulators and the auditors. They are as well equipped as anybody to know what we do.

'Where we've probably not been good, as all firms in this profession, is in the form and recording that.'

The same person goes on to imply that the standards have usurped much of what was previously involved in the auditor's task:

> [I]n [the] pecking order, another firm will understand exactly what we're doing on an audit because that's what they're doing. The regulators will be just a few steps behind...management and boards are a little bit away from them...And then...the general public and investors are quite a way behind that as to our responsibilities around full audit and so forth. But...it's crystal clear now in those standards; it's set out. All that's left to the firm to do [is] an interpretative notice perhaps, design sample sizes and how it's documented and so on.

In the next two quotations, suppliers raise the fact that in the past documentation was not always adequate around judgments, creating a need for some assumed knowledge.

> [O]ne thing that's happened certainly within [Big Four firm named] and…within the Big Four [generally] is [that] our focus on documentation has really increased…the audit files have always existed, but to document it to the degree that you need to so that somebody could come in independent [of] yourself and reach the same conclusion based on that information—that hasn't always been there. You've always had to have some assumed knowledge… you couldn't just pick up the information and come to a conclusion because sometimes the judgments weren't that well documented. So from that perspective, I haven't had too many issues where questions have been asked around 'where's this check list', because it's usually been there in some form. It's been more the emphasis, the focus.

> [I]t means you've got to document your judgment…that's really what it comes down to. And it's a hard one because judgment is exactly judgment. I make a decision on my professional judgment on something that I do. There [are] so many different factors that I'm taking in to potentially make a decision on something, make a call on something, and sometimes to document [that is] very difficult. So therefore I don't necessarily think it's taking the judgment out, but what it is doing is it's making you justify your judgment. So if [you] could say [that] by virtue of those actually taking some of the flexibility away in relation to what you would consider to be professional judgment…what they're saying is… it's taking away…your capability to…make a judgment call…I've probably gone a little bit around in circles there, but…you can still use your judgment, it's just that you've got to justify your judgment and sometimes that is difficult to do.

> [Prescription has] certainly added value for the record...it's there, it is written, the evidence is there, whereas before the evidence wasn't documented. The work has been done but it wasn't documented. It is causing partners particularly to spend a lot more time in the files...a lot of that energy is [consumed in asking] 'Have we constructed it correctly, dotted the Is, crossed Ts, documented it?' My getting into the file...isn't flushing out any more issues than you knew were there, because...if the youngsters don't get them and bring them to your attention anyway, or through the file, you're not always going to flush them out. So I'm hoping it'll settle down...it certainly has over the last few months. I feel much more comfortable around the quality—that it's there, that we're across it. But we've a way to go before...it's in the stream. So there's a little bit of a risk [that] it is a distraction, but I'd like to think we still stay focused and we say 'Well, okay, we've got these additional constraints. We thought we were policing ourselves pretty well, we thought our professional judgment was pretty good, but if you guys want to police us and you want to be prescriptive, well, okay, that's the regime; we'll live with it.' But we'll still do the substance of an audit as we've always done [it] before.

'[Prescription is] certainly added value for the record...it's there, it is written, the evidence is there, whereas before the evidence wasn't documented. The work has been done but it wasn't documented.'

Increased cost and a trend towards a more prescriptive US-style regulation are issues raised in the next quotation, even though there is acknowledgment of an improvement to the quality of documentation.

> One of the issues...in audit files over the years has been the quality of documentation...[I]n recent times and [with] the level of regulatory reviews that we've had that have really made us focus and improve the type of documentation that we have [have] improved the level more. It will continue to improve the level of documentation, which...is important...we need to continually keep...making [those files] better...But I don't necessarily think that sort of prescriptive American-style regulation is where we really want to be...It will add more cost and...at the moment, the problem that we find is that regulators are pushing down and saying you must do all this sort of stuff.

The next supplier comments on the increased documentation compliance burden:

> '[W]hat's happening now is that things that we have...physically done [previously] but perhaps haven't printed on paper, we now have to put on paper.'

> [T]he biggest distraction is the necessity to do check lists, et cetera. The regulators are very much pushing a documentation side of things. And largely I don't disagree with the principle [of] what they're trying to achieve. But what's happening now is that things that we have... physically done [previously] but perhaps haven't printed on paper, we now have to put on paper... it's distracting because you've got to spend so much time doing check lists and all that sort of stuff now. We've mandated those...they've got to go on our files so that the staff have no choice, the audit team has no choice in completing them. And they're time consuming, and they're really just putting on paper things you've already done...that is one of the biggest challenges.

4.3.1 Summary

Many of the supplier interviewees make negative comments about the increasing regulation of audit. Several highlight the merit of the disciplined approach to documentation that is now in place, however, they lament the amount of time it takes. One mentions the difficulty of being in a transitional period between the previous and the new auditing standards—which was the case at the time of the interviews—as representing a potential distraction. Overwhelmingly, however, the comments related to the consequences for auditors of not thoroughly documenting, not only what was done, by why alternative methods were not adopted, and the risk that this incremental documentation requirement would detract from a holistic approach to the audit. Disturbingly, this check-list focus was mentioned as pervading internal reviews of audit documentation too. Several suppliers allude to documentation before the advent of the legally backed standards as being of a quality below optimal. Terms or phrases such as 'focus', 'improvement', 'better audit files', 'record of key factors', 'recording in the file rather than in the partner's head' all appear in this section. Nevertheless, there is acknowledgment of the increased prescription, the compliance burden, the increased cost and doubt expressed about the expertise of regulators in monitoring in terms of their focus on the appropriate issues.

4.4 Standard setters

In applying the auditing standards, the standard setters themselves admit to difficulty in implementing documentation requirements, as the first quotation from the interviews reveals. Reference to the PCAOB requirements as a benchmark is raised as a misunderstood comparison in this first quotation from the interviewees.

> We hear fairly regularly from the regulators, and...these days they're reviewing the audit firms annually and they are looking at our audit files as well...they pick up things, they feedback to us... [Something I've been] hearing a lot about it the last 12 months is the level of documentation...[For] most things they feedback, we'd say 'Yes, okay'; perhaps [there is] a question of degree here and there, [but we] acknowledge it. Documentation is quite a problematic issue for the auditing profession right now...I'm trying to come to grips with exactly what level of documentation is required by auditing standards. Reference is made to the PCAOB requirements quite often, but...possibly [it is] misunderstood...the profession's trying to look at how to interpret our own auditing standards, our own documentation requirements and our reasonable reference point is the PCAOB requirements. And this has been a major concern to the smaller practitioners. I hear it around the board: the representatives of the smaller firms get very concerned around documentation. The larger firms are more relaxed about it in principle, but we are aware that we probably don't totally meet the standard the regulator would like to see across the board for documentation.

While acknowledging the increased cost to create enhanced documentation, the comment from another standard setter reveals faith in the profession to document well, without detracting from time spent on the quality of the real audit.

> [T]he bottom line is that [prescription]...shouldn't [be a distraction]...human nature is that it probably will [be] in certain circumstances, but in reality it shouldn't. There's no reason why you can't do the documentation and still do the risk assessment and proper thinking. I don't think the two are...mutually exclusive...the question is more around [whether] there [is] real value in the work that's associated with

'There's no reason why you can't do the documentation and still do the risk assessment and proper thinking.'

> the documentation and the costs that are put on the community as a consequence. And I know the profession would say—I'm sure you'd probably find people who would say—'Well, the documentation stops us from doing the real work.' Well, I...don't think that's right...there's no reason why you can't do both.

Two standard setters raise the issue of tension between a risk-based audit approach and a prescriptive approach that demands attention to events and transactions even of low to zero risk.

> [M]any in the audit profession would say auditing is about risk assessments and determining where the issues are and resolving the issues. That's...what good auditing is about. It's not about documentation, it's not about quality of documentation, it's not about doing particular steps, if you are legitimately of the view that [there] isn't risk attached to that area. So [it's] that ability to... be truly risk-based versus having to do what's required, what's described in certain things. It's a constant tension between those two points of view. Now, the reality is you're never going to have one or the other...It's going to be whatever model we have in whatever country you're looking at; it's...a combination of both. Different sets of standards, different jurisdictions. It's different places on that spectrum. The debate is often about principles versus prescription, as patent as that...that's oversimplifying it, actually. What we have everywhere is a mixture...a spectrum and it's really a question of where you're sitting on that spectrum, because there is nothing that's purely principles based and there's nothing that's purely prescriptive...We would normally say that we have auditing standards in Australia which are principles based, but they...have a fair amount of prescription in them.

> [N]ow...you document [the procedure to be used], but you've also got to document why every other way which you could have done it was not appropriate...that's what's adding a lot to the documentation as well as just...[having] everything on the file. So...there is going to be an increased cost in terms of the documentation and...that probably goes to the check-list approach. Whether that will lead to any better audits...probably not.

None of the standard setters feels there is a serious problem with the level of prescription, as the following quotations reveal.

> In theory, it shouldn't [distract]...because they have their own audit methodology so they do have a tried and tested way of doing an audit and if they've got the right quality-control processes within the firm they should be isolating these regulatory requirements as additional to the audit and add-ons. Now, where there's a lot to deliver in a short space of time then [it] could [distract] because you've got limited resources now to spread across a larger requirement. But...there is potential too for it to improve the audit in that the fact that they have to do a lot of other regulatory things [that] will increase their knowledge of the organisation and also the compliance risk associated with that. So there are benefits in doing all this regulatory stuff because you do...improve your knowledge of the business rather than just the financial statement information flows.
>
> I couldn't go through any of the auditing standards and disagree with anything behind any of the intent in any of those standards.

Another standard setter sees the situation as positive:

> [W]hat's going on at the moment overall is a positive, not a negative. I don't think it's detracting. You can definitely see the argument and could mount the argument that the focus on documentation and being form driven and demonstrating that you've done what the standard requires, or what a regulator wants you to show, can lead to a check-list approach, but being part of a profession that—I know we had our HIHs and our Harris Scarfes and our Ansetts here, when Enron was happening overseas, et cetera—the call to the profession was to say, 'Well, look, we...being the capital markets, need some evidence that you know what it is to be objective and independent and that you're capable of exercising that independence and objectivity and that we've got some mechanism for understanding that you're doing it'—hence all the oversight.

'[W]hat's going on at the moment overall is a positive, not a negative.'

Continuing, the same standard setter goes on to support ASIC:

> [W]e're in an era where the profession is responding and wanting to put up their hand and say, 'Yes, I understand what it is to do a decent job'...what I read in here by the required regulatory processes and

> procedures—yes, we've got auditing standards in law, but it's not so much that, it's the oversight. And people are saying look, we want people to know we're doing a good job. So that's...focusing people very much on what sort of a trail do I feel I need to leave behind to demonstrate I've done a good job. That of itself then requires you to make sure you have addressed all the right areas. So, where are we in the cycle? I don't see we've created a problem for missing the reasonable assurance piece. Depending on the reaction of our regulators and how they enforce compliance, or their interpretation of compliance, [that] might get us into a different spot, but I'd be supportive of where ASIC has been to date and don't see that they're doing that.

The same person comments on whether the use of check lists is the most efficient way in which to audit:

> There'll be more done but...there's going to be more check lists in it...there's going to be a principle-based approach but behind that there will be a lot more to the check list and so therefore...the audit...[will] be more expensive, it will require more documentation and bigger files and more people on the job, but we'll get to the right answer...the real question is could that be done [in] a more efficient way? Probably, it could have.

4.4.1 Summary

Standard setters give nuanced responses to the question of prescription as a distraction. They acknowledge the risk of it leading to a check-list approach, but can see the potential for it also to improve the audit and argue that, in a normative sense, increased prescription, especially around documentation, should not lessen the more judgmental aspects of an audit. Generally, there is support for what the regulator is attempting to achieve and the increased documentation is seen as a positive in that it provides an evidence base for a claim of a job well done. The anomaly of many auditors' claims to a diminished role for judgment in the face of their calls for greater clarity, which can be interpreted as a call for more explicit rules, is raised also. Standard setters, many of whom are also suppliers, comment on the use of the onerous US PCAOB requirements as a reference point, much to the likely chagrin of smaller firms. The issue of prescription or rules-based standards versus principles-based standards and the tension between these two positions on a continuum are raised also.

4.5 Regulators

Interestingly, some regulators recognise the potential pitfalls of encouraging an approach to auditing that is too prescriptive, as in the following quote:

> I'm uncomfortable with the check-list approach to auditing...I realise how much professional judgment is involved when you're assessing risks in auditing a company and in terms of finding problems and dealing with problems and discussing them with management. A check-list approach doesn't suit that kind of environment. The problem with a check-list approach, like the standards, is that there are certain people in the industry who will try to find ways around it. They'll try to find shortcuts and they may just defend themselves in terms of having ticked something but not having done the work satisfactorily. In audits, I find that as you work through the job, you get triggers and there are certain triggers...or [alarms that] are going [off] which make you chase down different burrows and perhaps find things that you wouldn't have found if you had just complied with a check list. So I am uncomfortable with the check-list approach and I don't think it's constructive or reflects the professionality [sic] of what an audit does.

In other respects, however, there is little empathy for the auditor's plight as revealed in the following quote:

> [O]ne of the standard complaints you get from business people now is well, we've got to do all of this extra work and it doesn't achieve anything because for legitimate people it's just extra work. If you're determined to do the wrong thing, well, something like that probably isn't going to stop you. So...it's probably a similar issue...I've noticed in my travels this whole issue about Sarbanes-Oxley that some people view...as imposing...[requirements in a] prescriptive manner, which doesn't take account of their particular needs.

The same person goes on to say:

> If you have a check list, then the auditors will treat that as the maximum. Well, that's unfair. Some auditors, some audit firms, may treat that as the maximum work that they need to do whereas really...in a lot of cases, it's the minimum....If there is going to be a check list, it has to be emphasised to investors and the people in the

profession alike that this is the minimum...standard that you have to reach and there is an expectation that you move beyond that and deliver better results in terms of your professional judgment and experience.

We're not distracting them. They may actually distract themselves because it all comes down to fees from clients, right? No, but the auditors themselves ask for [a check list]...when they talk...in public policy forums, they want professional judgment, but when they go to the Institute of Chartered Accountants or somewhere else, they're always looking for an audit practice guide. They can't have it both ways.

I agree there has been a loss of focus...when you've got so much regulation and you've got so many hurdles to get over in delivering a satisfactory audit, you can lose sight of...what you're supposed to be doing...and you get bogged down in nitty-gritty-type stuff, which...is necessary in certain circumstances, but does distract. I'm talking now in terms of delivering the product at the coal face and...the engagement partner, the audit partner, should always have a big-picture approach and...be able to rely on his... supervisors to do the nitty-gritty stuff, the managers to draw up the problems on [the]...big picture and deliver them to the audit partner as the big picture...recently the audit partners are getting increasingly bogged down in detail because of...the prescription in terms of regulation...My sense of working in an audit team is that you've got the people actually doing the hack work and you've got supervisors who see a larger picture and are able to draw back and feed up the chain...the...important problems that need to be brought to the attention of the next level...that feed-up process is being stunted as a result of the amount of hack work you have to do to meet the regulation, the provisions in the law.

[T]he regulators are a bit inclined to say...that for all that you get this objection [that] the concept that audit standards have to be principle based and judgments paramount, that equally the auditors, the firms, are actually forever asking for greater clarity, which really means more rules.

4.5.1 Summary

Most of the regulators who commented on the appropriateness of the level of prescription placed on the audit function justified the level required. As with the standard setters, regulators point to the anomaly of some auditors asking for more guidance while championing the need for judgment. They also express the view that it is up to auditors to decide how much work to do. The prescription and compliance requirements are seen as a minimum benchmark for the conduct of the audit with scope for judgment or additional work not inhibited.

5.0 Issues and implications

Users, purchasers, suppliers, standard setters and regulators were all interviewed with a query about whether the additional audit procedures required as a result of the reforms distracted auditors from the objective of a financial statement audit. In general, in all of the groups, some members agreed and some disagreed with the premise within this question. That is, no group of respondents was unanimous in its response. One of the most intriguing results from the interviews was that users believed that they had a relatively sophisticated and complex understanding of the work of an auditor and what the current regulatory requirements entailed.

A number of users—in particular those who are professional investors—take the view that the current regulatory requirements, with their heavy emphasis on compliance and documentation, have shifted the focus of the auditor away from the need to spend time understanding the business and the risks of the business. There were several representations suggesting that users were concerned that auditors were now forced to 'get on with ticking boxes' rather than spending time reflecting on and coming to grips with the business, its processes and its risks. It was interesting to observe that many of the users claimed to have a quite sophisticated understanding of the time taken to undertake these processes.

Some users have a very different perspective, suggesting that the current regulatory requirements are not a distraction from the main objective of the audit and that in fact an audit might be largely irrelevant anyway. There was also a suggestion that the market was constantly assessing and reappraising the value of securities and that the contribution made by an audit was modest. One user suggests that auditors have an obligation for and on behalf of their clients to push back against regulatory requirements if they think there is a better way for the audit to be achieved and for the outcome of the audit to be better delivered to the capital markets.

Other users praise the current regulatory requirements, suggesting they provide a floor level of quality. Various users describe the present regulatory system as giving rise to audits that are 'standardised', 'consistent', 'unbiased', 'objective', 'comprehensive' and 'methodical'. There seems to be an implication in the minds of some that these requirements will give rise to higher-quality auditing and they take the view that this will mean that the auditors will be better able to comment on the credibility of financial statements. A few users suggest that auditors need to go beyond this and be inquiring and innovative in their understanding of a business and the risks of a business.

In terms of policy implication, the descriptors used ('standardised', 'consistent', and so on) and enunciated by the users above might represent a necessary but not sufficient condition for there to be a high-value audit that attests or gives assurance to the credibility of financial statements.

Purchasers are also split between those who believe that the current regulatory processes are a distraction and those who believe they are not. Those who are critical of the current proposals suggest that for the audit to be of value it really needs to look at the substance behind the transactions and behind the documentation. Those who believe that regulation is not a distraction tend to share the view of users that the current regulatory requirements are there to ensure an appropriate job is done and that they represent 'demonstrable compliance'. Those who speak positively about the current regulatory requirements also add that these requirements have helped ensure there is greater distance between auditors and their clients. Some note that this distance comes at a cost, including the cost of possibly unnecessary documentation and over-auditing, but nonetheless the benefits outweigh the costs.

Further, some purchasers add that while the requirements might not have changed much of what is done, they have added considerable robustness to the audit, which might not have been present to a sufficient level before.

A number of purchasers suggest that, fundamentally, the audit they observe has not changed with recent amendments to regulatory requirements; however, it has driven up costs. Few purchasers are able to identify how the audit has been changed or that the auditors provide new and valuable insights into the business as a consequence of the regulations.

Those who are able to make direct comparisons between Australia's current position and the Sarbanes-Oxley legislation in the United States speak favourably of the Australian position and somewhat harshly of the more prescriptive and compliance-driven US position.

Various purchasers discuss their need for a balance and that the 'check-list approach' is really just a minimum floor level, which returns to the point that audits that fulfil all the regulatory requirements are a minimum standard and there needs to be innovation and insight beyond this to achieve a high-value audit.

One purchaser questions why auditors might find increased documentation requirements a negative development, alluding to an unwillingness to convey their 'true' beliefs. In view of this, when commenting on the increased requirements, auditors and audit firms need to be careful to explain the reasons behind their concerns and not give an incorrect impression of an unwillingness to commit their thoughts into writing.

Similarly, suppliers are divided between those who believe the current regulatory requirements are a distraction and those who believe that they are an enhancement. Those who are critical of the current regulatory requirements point to the ever-increasing amount of time spent on documentation, which has distracted them from the time they are able to commit to understanding the business. This point runs in tandem with observations that clients are reluctant to absorb substantially increased fees, so the number of hours available to an audit is a 'zero-sum game'. Those who are critical suggest that some audit partners are becoming 'gun-shy' of the possible penalties and that they have to change their approach from being less principles based and reliant on judgment to being much more check-list oriented. Other suppliers suggest a 'heightened regulation risk'.

Those who believe that the current regulatory requirements are positive point to the fact that the regulations really represent the enforcement of a minimum level of quality. Often these observations come from larger audit firms with an accompanying implied criticism of the quality delivered by non-Big Four firms. The implication is that the Big Four firms do not require these regulatory requirements, whereas other suppliers might need them.

Standard setters see the current regulatory requirements as a useful part of the quality control of an audit and not as a distraction from the real, continuing operation of the audit. They observe that the requirements give rise to demonstrated evidence that a good job has been accomplished. Standard setters understandably take the view that all of the auditing standards have an important role to play in the quality of auditing and its role in the capital market.

One standard setter interviewed proposes the dilemma that is sometimes seen in the market where, with respect to public policy, auditors call for audits to be judgment driven and principles based, whereas when interacting within professional bodies or associations, they seek greater 'clarity', which inevitably becomes something akin to a check list. Another standard setter observes that the biggest single change the current regulatory requirements have made relates to the whole issue of objectivity and independence.

Other regulators acknowledge that the current requirements could give rise to a loss of focus and audits might indeed become bogged down in some of the tedium, which in turn has consequences for the nature of the work undertaken in audit firms. Given the scale of the change in the nature of the work, it has consequences for the working lives of many individuals who might be attracted to and retained within the profession (refer to Chapter 8). There was, however, also an observation that for an auditor and an audit client going to do the 'right thing anyway', the new regulatory requirements, particularly the requirement for documentation, would add cost without deriving any economic benefit for that particular client. The implication is that there will be an increased cost for all participants in the audit market to protect outcomes across the entire market for the public good.

Across all the stakeholder groups interviewed, there were those highly supportive of the current regulatory requirements and those who believed that the changes had not been a step forward. Almost to a person, everyone called for the need for a balance between highly prescriptive compliance-driven audits and those involving professional judgment. The observation comparing the Australian requirements with those of United States would suggest that we are much closer to principles-based auditing than the more compliance-driven auditing elsewhere.

There is no doubt, however, that users, purchasers and suppliers all have insights into the amount of time taken by the documentation requirements of the current regulations. Observations suggest that this documentation is either a benefit because it helps demonstrate compliance with necessary minimums in the quality of an audit or is wasteful of time and distracts an auditor from understanding the business.

While not expressly included in the survey material, the debate between rules-based and principles-based standards triggered comment from some of the interview participants.

One standard setter observes that the whole debate of rules versus principles has not been particularly helpful. Although Australia has come from a background of a principles-based environment, even principles-based standards have included an amount of prescription. He or she went on to say that the IAASB would argue that its standards were principles based, but again, there was an element of prescription in many of those standards.

One purchaser observes that the US jurisdiction is very focused on prescription with a rules-based environment, whereas the United Kingdom (and other jurisdictions influenced by this country, including Australia) is conceptually founded on a principles-based environment. The commentator went on to observe that in Australia, regulatory agencies had gone on to interpret those principles to create guidance, which was then in turn interpreted as rules. This is not meant to be a criticism of regulatory agencies because sometimes they create this guidance at the behest of participants in the market to assist them. The commentator also observed, however, that the difficulty with rules was that they could become outdated as circumstances changed or even irrelevant because of environmental changes. The second difficulty with a rules-based regime is that rules can be used as a substitute for good judgment.

6.0 Concluding remarks

The essential focus of this chapter has been to demonstrate the belief among various stakeholder groups that the new public policy position pertaining to the regulation of the market for audit services has brought with it a significant cost—specifically documentation and other requirements have distracted the auditor from the key focus of the audit, thereby lowering the quality of the audit.

As indicated in the previous chapter, the change of the regulatory regime and the public policy settings that drove that change did not contain within them any requirement that the change of position was ultimately to the benefit of the economy, the efficiency of the capital market or any of the participants in the market for audit services. Again, the action that can, and one might argue should, occur is the systematic gathering of real world evidence of the effect on the capital market of these changed regulatory arrangements. Given that they have now been in place for some time, it is possible to pursue this and it would provide some degree of accountability of the legislature's decision to introduce this requirement on participants in the market for audit services.

Additionally, there is some evidence from the interviews that a shared understanding of the minimum documentation required between each of the suppliers that are subject to oversight (and inspection) of the regulator is missing. This will be discussed at greater length in the next chapter, however, having some open and transparent discussion about what the minimum documentary requirements should entail and that this minimum platform be shared among all suppliers and agreed with the regulator seems to be a useful and accountable action that the regulator could undertake immediately. This might be augmented by the oversight or indeed direct involvement of the Financial Reporting Council and the Auditing and Assurance Standards Board.

The transparency of this process could assist in ensuring that the minimum requirement necessary has not been unintentionally lifted beyond the requirements in Australia by reference to the practical use in certain firms of the PCAOB documentation or by an intentional or unintentional desire to make the documentation internationally comparable. At present, the Australian regulatory environments are based on our jurisdiction and, while we might be sympathetic to international needs or requirements, as yet there has not been internationalisation of the legislative framework.

THE APPROACH, OPERATION AND RESOURCES OF REGULATORS 12

> [There are] a lot of audit partners out there who haven't kept [up] technically as well as they should. It's not meaning they're incompetent, but they just haven't kept up as technically strong as they should have. And I would question where ASIC's come from, because I don't think…[there are] too many people, or any people, doing those reviews that are ex-partners of firms. And I just have a problem…it's like me…coming and telling the doctors how they should operate. I'm not actually sure, unless you've been there, that there's…full appreciation. And I'm not saying that a lot of things they're doing [aren't] good…improving the documentation and making sure that there's a real good tie up probably makes sense, but I…don't think it's the be-all and end-all…there's also a very dictatorial [attitude]…if they think you've made a mistake, they just go after you like a dog after a bone…the bulk of people out there don't stuff up because they're bad or devious…it's a slip or it's just an oversight…we're humans, and yet their approach is if they get a sniff of anything…they just go in there…some of the treatment is a bit over the top.
> — Supplier

1.0 Key issues

The operationalisation of the changes to the regulatory regime in the early part of this decade gave rise to many comments from the participants in this study. From their comments, the key issues that arise include:

- have the approach and operational aspects of regulators' oversight of auditors and the audit process been effective
- is communication with the profession by regulators adequate

- have ASIC's inspections of auditors been conducted effectively
- how have ASIC inspections been received by auditors
- how adequate is the resourcing of the regulators
- how can the expertise of regulators be enhanced
- should the Big Four and non-Big Four be treated differentially by ASIC in its oversight function?

2.0 Introduction

Many of the face-to-face interviews included comments about the regulators' approach and operational practices, mainly in terms of ASIC, but also in terms of the Australian Prudential Regulation Authority (APRA). This section explores stakeholders' perceptions of the regulators' attitudes, approach, competence and resourcing. Comments specific to ASIC inspections of audit firms are included as a separate section.

The next section provides analysis of stakeholders' comments about the issue of whether a prescriptive approach to audit is a distraction and whether it hinders or helps the capital market.

2.1 Users

The first user responds in relation to whether the prescriptive approach helps or hinders the capital market:

> [I]t certainly helps, but in general the regulator is about three steps behind—certainly [in] equity markets—and in general, they're always playing catch-up. So…to the extent that auditors can be more prescriptive…that would be useful, because it really isn't a lot of help to have standard-format audit opinions, which everyone just glances at for 30 [seconds], provided the key points are there. The actual information people need is more in the accounts…certainly, it's useful…having a more prescriptive approach, but generally the problem areas [where] people have [trouble] interpreting…accounts are where those companies are one step ahead of accounting standards, let's put it that way, or other reporting requirements… from an investment point of view…the issues are where you're caught napping in terms of a company that's not disclosing something they should be.

The same person is somewhat disparaging of the conventional auditors' role and goes on to explain his or her perception that regulators are acting reactively rather than proactively:

> In my experience...the regulators are three steps behind...[B]y the time they've identified...the problem [it has] already blown up. So to the extent that auditors can be more commercial in providing... useful information to investors...that would be a great help, rather than in a technical sense just looking at the accounts...the accounts are living documents that I need [in order] to understand the company...what's really happening from an operational point of view and that's how I look at accounts. So when I've got something that's camouflaged in the accounts in terms of what's happening from an underlying commercial point of view, then I can't, or investors can't, understand what's really going on. And to the extent that auditors can...throw light on it, that's what I would find useful.

Another user comments in response to the question: 'Do you think perhaps there's a gap between the regulators and auditors, and is that affecting the capital markets in investing?'

> [*Referring to a recent collapse*] [I]t seems like ASIC was aware of the situation but only towards the end [did] they put the brakes on. And it's something I've then questioned because I'm not sure when ASIC's supposed to come in and say, 'Guys, you don't meet certain requirements'...what I can't understand is they'd been monitoring them for some while. And yet even a couple of the property guys, the specialists, were saying, 'Look, be careful of these kinds of investments', and nothing was done. And you would've thought... would an audit have helped or did they have an audit? So...there's a gap there. [In] the last couple of months...there's [been] a big gap.

Some users give the impression that they believe it is ASIC that is responsible for the framework under which auditors conduct their work.

> If I can use ASIC in this case as a regulator, as far as we're concerned and the auditors [are concerned]...our experience of the audit process is that...if you have...the framework of ASIC in place, which obviously we're aware of and the auditors are aware of... the auditors generally follow that framework of the regulators as closely as possible, and probably in some extent to the letter.

> ASIC might have a statement which the auditors then interpret literally instead of tailoring it towards each individual company. So I wouldn't have thought...that there is much of gap between the auditors and the regulators in that sense.

The same person, when pressed on whether there is a gap between auditors and regulators, goes on to say:

> Do auditors really look beyond the check list? And is the check-list approach valid for the audit process? I would've thought that perhaps there is a gap there, but...it's certainly not one that we're particularly aware of.

One user sees a commonality in the aim of both auditors and regulators:

> [F]rom the angle we see it, from the auditors coming in and from what we see that the regulators want, we see that they're both after the same thing...the auditors aren't completely off on a tangent looking at different areas and displaying concern for different risks compared to the regulators. So in that respect, they're not that far apart.

One of the users sees it as being up to the auditors to negotiate with the regulators to have things changed if a better way exists:

> Absolutely, it's the case of the horse before the cart, isn't it, really? And...that's where auditors have an obligation to their client base to push back against the regulators. If they think that there is a better and a more innovative way of doing something then surely they should be coming together to try and make those changes...as an investor, I don't just sit and listen to what everyone is telling me about buying a particular stock; I will look at it and I will make my own judgment based on the knowledge and information I've got. And if I have got information or the knowledge to be able to make an informed decision then I should, in the auditor's case, be able to push back against those regulators or approach them and try and get changes put through.

Another user is positive about the role of the regulator:

> [T]he regulators are there to ensure there is a robust regulatory environment and to do that it's a lot of work and a lot of cost and so those costs are always passed on.

The *Sarbanes-Oxley Act 2002* (US) featured prominently in the interviews of users as regulation that was too prescriptive—perhaps because these representatives were having to comply with that act within their own entities.

> I wouldn't have a clue whether it's distracting auditors...it probably is a bit. And...the payback of that is an auditor either decides that they have to do their job the way they feel [it] is best done as well as following the prescriptive rules, in which case the cost of the audit would probably...be higher than it would...need to be. Whether... it gives more credibility to the assurance statement, I don't think it really does...people look at the regulations that came out... the US is the most glaring example, so it's a good one to use, and the initial reaction to the *Sarbanes-Oxley Act* was: 'Oh, fantastic, everything's going to get better.' Now the reaction is the absolute opposite...we've got all this prescriptive regulation; it's become almost impossible to be a public company. A lot of people in the investment business are attributing the increase in private equity bids for listed companies to [the fact that] listed companies don't want to be listed anymore because it's just too hard these days. So...it's having a lot of influences that...and...I'll stick with the US because it is the most glaring example [of] regulation over the top...a lot of that regulation will be scaled back in emphasis over the years ahead. It was way too draconian from the start. It didn't need to be that strong. And things like ENRON and HIH and all those things will happen again no matter what the regulators do; it will happen again.

> [T]alking to the US people...their reporting requirements certainly amongst the companies, and I presume amongst their auditors, [have] made their life so difficult that...they're subverted by regulation...you have to have the right balance. And...the focus... should be [on] clarity, presenting financial information with clarity so people can understand it, as opposed to having overweight... rules and regulations that everyone can tick the box [on], but [which]...doesn't [necessarily] enhance their ability to understand what's going on.

One user draws a link between accounting standards and audit complexity:

> [S]ometimes the...complexity of these audits can take away from the materiality of what they're...trying to achieve, which is trying to make sure that these companies report accurate and material reporting...a couple of the accounting standards—employee accounting standards, those type of things, with the owners reporting on employee expenses...that [is] a necessary evil...to a point. If you're going to do an audit, you need to have all the checks and ticks...your Is...dotted, otherwise you'll tend to find that there [are] holes.

The same person goes on to query what happens at the end of an audit:

> [G]oing back to...having your blinkers off, potentially...I'm not too sure how an audit's done, whether an audit is performed and then completed—but when an audit's completed, is there...an audit review back in the office...do they do a...general overview of the audit? [Do] you have someone go out and do the finite pieces...is there a final check in terms of a general overview of the feeling of the business, management's credibility, a number of different things that might just raise a few other questions, rather than the stock standard audit year in, year out? Is there a review meeting post-audit? I assume there is, where various questions are asked...of the individuals that undertake these.

Another user compares the resourcing of the Australian regulator with that in the United States:

> When I was at [a merchant bank], we had all these different licences and you deal with the ASIC...with half a dozen matters at a time from licensing to a query. They never give you a case officer. You have to deal with six different people because they were so fearful that you may be able to coerce or influence one person. It was that bad. So they are terrible and unlike the US...where some of the best and brightest from the accounting firms would take fellowships at the SEC or the Federal Reserve and they'd work there, not on their own clients, but to learn and also add to the intellectual capital—albeit temporarily—of those venerable regulators. Nothing like that happens here for ASIC. So ASIC suffers two capital shortfalls: real capital and human capital. And structurally, I just don't know how they work.

The same person continues with a suggested solution in terms of resourcing the regulator's required expertise:

> So you know how you close the gap? You get them to share the resource; they cop a tax break for sending some people across and you...take out the non-essential rules.

2.1.1 Summary

In discussing whether increasing prescription has become a distraction for auditors, users often allude to accounting standards as well as or instead of auditing standards. They tend to respond to interviewers' questions about prescription through a much more generic perspective than the other stakeholders. Bearing this in mind, there are positive comments by users about the Australian regulatory regime in comparison with what is seen as the overly prescriptive US Sarbanes-Oxley regime. Users speak of regulators as being three steps behind companies that use questionable accounting methods or fail to disclose what should be disclosed. There are implied accusations of regulators at times failing to take action in situations that appear to be in obvious need of activity. The standard-format audit report is viewed as not helpful and at least one user appears to wish to have the role of auditors changed radically to help interpret the accounts. There is a perception that it is up to auditors to negotiate with regulators if there are aspects of the regulatory regime that auditors consider should be improved.

2.2 Purchasers

Purchasers' comments reveal how well informed about the regulatory regime imposed on auditors they are. In the first quotation, the purchaser questions the need for the regulator to take a punitive or form-over-substance approach and asks just how many real audit failures occur.

> My sense of the way the regulator...is performing at the moment is that there's an element of heads on sticks. So no matter if an auditor does go through a process and some audits fail...what should be the result of an audit failure? How should the regulator respond to that? And you know what? In terms of the numbers of audits that fail, it's questionable; it's quite subjective. But in terms of a proportion, it'd be interesting to know what that would be...I do sense that there is an element of form creeping in here versus the substance. So the regulator says: 'Well, you didn't circularise debtors and that's a problem with the audit.' Well, who cares in most cases?

At the time of the interviews, there were some well-known inconsistencies between regulatory frameworks (in this instance, between the *Corporations Act* and accounting standards). The next purchaser calls for more collaboration between regulators.

> We have some areas of conflict between corporations law and accounting standards, and therefore duplication of disclosures or subtle differences in disclosures—like key management personnel reporting...[So] auditors are being placed in this position of... audit both or I [will] form a different view of one or the other... accounting boards are a regulator too...so regulators learn to—we need to...get the act together. And it's getting better, by the way.

The next purchaser accuses ASIC of taking an excessively legalistic approach:

> I don't think auditors and regulators...do have that big a gap... [but] there are sometimes specifics of differentiation on that...ASIC can sometimes take a much more legalistic view as opposed to a commercial view or a commonsense approach, whereas...auditors... do have a huge amount of commonsense in their application of things, although with the regulations and it being incorporated into corporations law and all of that, that obviously ties your hands...If that's the law, that's the law, but...they do have quite a commonsense approach, whereas...ASIC on occasions...reverts to the legalistic.

The next purchaser highlights the danger of a 'regulate first, ask questions later' approach:

> [I]n a review of the regulatory framework for the Federal Government...one of the issues that came through strongly was that any type of failure or perceived [failure]—whether by [the] media or the public's concern over failures in a corporate sector—tends to lead to a knee-jerk reaction to create more regulation. It's perceived to be the only way in which politicians can properly respond—[by] being seen to do something. And as a consequence...we've got a bit of a culture in this country of regulate first and...ask questions later...there have been some spectacular examples of that recently where the existing systems, which were perfectly adequate to deal with matters which arose, were hijacked by the political process and sent off into royal commissions of various sorts...what's happening

> here [is] there's a tendency to see this as going somewhat in the same direction. The whole scene in which these regulations are made [is] increasingly becoming more and more prescriptive, whereas I've always viewed audit as being a process of forming judgment, which then gives rise to an opinion...we're in danger of losing that judgment and opinion process by going down this route of more and more prescriptive approaches to what are perceived problems. The difficulty being, I don't think you can prescribe precise actions for every possible eventuality. So that's the background [from] which I come to these things.

The same person goes on to argue that regulators are trained to think prescriptively:

> [I]f there's an expectation gap between regulators and auditors... regulators understand what auditors do...[the] people I've spoken to in ASIC and APRA [seem to] understand that. The problem... [that] arises is that regulators, and particularly the legal profession, are trained to think in a prescriptive sense. They do not think in terms of generalities or principles—at least, that's been my experience. And...that's where the difficulties arise, in that they look for prescription and they tend to not see the value as much in informing judgments based on subjective information.

The same person continues to enunciate what to him or her is almost a 'sixth sense' held by good auditors:

> [A]ll of the really good auditors that I knew had a sort of sense of things. It wasn't something that...you could easily put down in a textbook; they had a feeling. I was always struck when I was in Victoria that the number of frauds we detected were, I don't think there was one instance where they [were] picked up by system audits; they were picked up by other means. And I kept on asking myself why would that be the case, and...it's partly because good auditors who are alert will see some anomaly and that will lead through with their investigation to some issue that they might identify...this goes...to the heart of the process of auditing, which increasingly is looking at risk assessment...I'd hate to see us looking to get so far away from the prescriptive approach that we start to lose those other facilities. And if they turn into technicians, which is what...the pressures are [going] to do...we will lose significantly

> in the process...this would be a significant loss...[With] that sort of approach, you tend not to see the freight train coming at you; you're too busy counting the nails on the rails and all those things... it's a distinction between a profession and what is essentially a bookkeeping-type of role. So that's the danger...if there's such a thing as a gap, it's not so much an expectations gap; it's just both have a different approach to things.

Another purchaser refers to the trend towards greater emphasis on risk management and sustainability and the reporting on those aspects of a business:

> I'm sure regulators would be [saying], you can have a financial audit that delivers the result that says the financial statements are okay, but then you can end up having an organisation that collapses down the track...in other words, it's reported its risk-profile fine, [and its] financial statement audits reflect everything that's going on, but there's actually a very huge inherent risk in the organisation... [W]here this actually comes out is probably [in] a new wave of reporting, which is all around sustainability and organisations basically starting...you're seeing now everybody looking to understand how an organisation is going to ensure that it's going to exist for the long term, not in terms of its own survival but as well as its contribution to the environment overall. And...the big debate at the moment is the certification of stuff that's outside the financial statements [which] performs the other half of the annual report, which is all to do with risk-management statements, government statements, basic issues around social and community responsibility and those kind of issues...[they] have become more prevalent.

The same person goes in response the interviewer's prompt about whether this issue of risk management—for example, around the sub-prime issue—is more the regulator's or the market's concern:

> [I]t's both...a regulator obviously is concerned about systemic risk, so they're concerned if a big person goes down...we've seen all of that with some of the collapses of Fincorp and the like, and you ask well, what view would the auditors have had a year before? The same questions I would have imagined would get asked around Enron, HIH—all those things. So it seems...there's still somewhere...a gap, isn't there?

The same purchaser goes on to comment about a retrospective versus future-oriented view:

> [T]he real challenge is—and what probably a lot of people don't get is—that unfortunately the review of the financial statements is very much a historical up-to-today view. It's not really a very well thought out view of the future. And this comes back down to the resourcing issue, because it's easier for less-experienced people to verify what is [rather] than to have the experience to think about what may be—and this is the big dilemma...it's looking at the future view...[and] the question is, and the profession will probably say, 'Well, we don't have an obligation to report that.'

The same purchaser goes on in response to a comment about litigation risk, in the context of the previous quotation:

> Exactly...It's probably an area they wouldn't want to touch...and that's why, of course, nobody certifies risk-management statements and things like that. It's hard. Nobody does it at the moment. There [are] no requirements.

The same purchaser expands on the importance of transparency—in terms of financial statement disclosures and the audit:

> [T]he key thing is, [has the audit client] been open in their disclosure? And for that you still need a fair degree of expertise to understand what a bank or an insurance company or a mining company should be disclosing. What are the relevant issues that need to be put into that kind of report?

One purchaser sees the emphasis on compliance and governance as strengthening the end result:

> [C]ompliance and governance [are] becoming more important everywhere, so...if there is a demand [from the] regulator, it would just be in addition to...what the normal duties are. So at the most, it can strengthen the end result rather than weaken it...I wouldn't have any issues with regulators, say...having an impost on saying do this or do that, as long as that just enhances the overall audit or the transparency of the audit.

The same purchaser continues:

> [The amount of time that auditors might spend on checking lists and documentation for regulatory purposes] would depend on how much wealth the company themselves knew on governance. So... if the company's got their own department doing compliance and governance for the auditor, it will be a cursory check...on whether everything's working properly or not, and if it isn't being done by the company then...it's better for them to be doing it anyway.

The next purchaser raises the issue of dealing with multiple regulators for international operations:

> [T]hat isn't a problem to me because the auditors have to look at the regulations and ensure that we do comply with the regulator. And where there's a particular issue, they point it out in terms of an interpretation. Where it does become a problem is...where you have to deal with a different regulator, and you have a different account and you talk about the fact that it's so unnecessary to have so many different accounts to comply with a different regulator.

The same person explains further:

> [I]t's just that all the different financial accounts have to be audited. But that's more in the line of what else...the finance director has to deal with. We only deal with the Australian accounts, so it's up to the Australian regulator. We have close relations with the Australian regulator. It's just that...he has to do so many different versions of it to suit other regulatory authorities. And it would be much easier if the standards were global rather than to have the US gap versus [the others]. You know they're trying to get uniformity—and that is the issue.

The same purchaser responds to the interviewer's query about whether there is a perception that what auditors do now is just a requirement to pass the regulator's test rather than the primary focus, which is to provide an audit for the end user.

> [E]verybody talks about over-regulation, ticking the boxes. I can understand the reason for it because of what happened a few years ago and the regulators want to be on top of everything. Like anything, if you go too far with it, it becomes very, very difficult.

The same purchaser then responds to the question: 'Are you happy with the level of regulation?'

> [T]he red tape committee has tried to, for example, bring back the level of regulation…there is a view that…apart from having different regulators with different jurisdictions…we are too heavily regulated. But I'm not sure exactly what needs to [be] taken back.

2.2.1 Summary

Purchasers make some interesting observations about the attitude and approach of regulators in the audit space. A legalistic, reactionary, punitive approach is generally not supported, whereas greater cooperation and collaboration between the various regulators, including at the international level, is seen as desirable. Purchasers recognise the role of judgment in the audit process, and prescription that discourages application of good audit judgment is seen as a definite negative. One purchaser urges a rethink on reporting to include more disclosures around risk management and sustainability over the long term and the assurance provision on those disclosures. In comments that are eerily farsighted in terms of what has since become the global financial crisis, this same purchaser asserts that what is currently not audited in terms of risk exposures is as important as, if not more than what is audited.

2.3 Suppliers

Few suppliers' comments are positive in relation to the attitude and approach of regulators—predominantly ASIC, in its oversight role of auditors. This first quotation is indicative of some of the frustrations that are voiced:

> '[T]hey tracked me down on holiday overseas within an hour of finding out.'

> I had something that looked like a breach on one of my clients and…they tracked me down on holiday overseas within an hour of finding out and said there's a potential problem and [these are] the steps we're taking and don't do anything with your client until we find out. Now fortunately, it was a misunderstanding and there wasn't a breach, so I know our system works well and I, as a board member, have been through that process. But I had that discussion with ASIC and he was adamant that I should've had a whole system of checks that I needed to undertake personally before I sign an

> independence declaration. Well, that's just inefficient use of audit time and if we, in a firm this big…jolly well ought to have a system set up that works and then we ought to be able to rely on our system and we audit our own system and ASIC, when they came in, audited that system as well as auditing a selection of our files.
>
> '[S]hould their aim be to have a witchhunt or should their aim be to make auditors do a better audit?'
>
> [B]ecause they've got a check list which says that I ought to have done something and I hadn't, they thought I'd done something wrong in my audit… that kind of approach is symptomatic. They've got check lists and…if something's missing on a check list, they will tell a small firm that they've not done a good job, but [to] tell them how to fix it—I don't think they will be able to. And…that is the only point of them doing that thing…you would hope to lift the quality of audits, not to pick on bad auditors. If you step back and say what are they trying to achieve in that…should their aim be to have a witchhunt or should their aim be to make auditors do a better audit? See, it ought to be to make auditors do better audits.

The same person goes on to question what it is that ASIC, through its reviews, is attempting to achieve:

> I don't think [ASIC] know [what ASIC is actually trying to achieve] yet either…they're very much in 'suck it and see' mode and this is new law for them and they'll go and look and reflect on what they found and then hopefully think about what they do need to try and achieve from it. And commonsense to me would be what they should try and achieve from it is spend some time helping the smaller firms, particularly in an environment where they're saying we don't like it…we want more, we want the second tier to step up. That should be where their focus is, but that's probably an arrogant big-partner view, isn't it? But…[we] as a firm just invest so much time and effort in supporting our partners to do the right thing that…and I realise this does sound arrogant, I find it hard to think that ASIC will help us improve our process across any of the Big Four, whereas the poor one and two-partner practices out in the field would love some guidance and whether it's from the Institute [of Chartered Accountants] or from ASIC, we could do a lot to help them. But…I can't imagine ASIC is going to help me personally do a better audit…and that might sound arrogant…And it's not because

> I think I'm great…it's because…I have a great firm structure behind me to support me and train me and give me guidance and have our own internal quality reviews and all that stuff.

The same person continues, expressing his or her fear that the current approach by the regulators will lead to audits becoming unhelpful and not useful:

> [I]n terms of different perspectives, the regulators are in the tick-the-box mentality and their chances of getting an audit wrong if you just go to a tick-the-box mentality are high. The chances of getting sued over it may be low if you've ticked all the boxes, but… ultimately, if we take that approach to doing our work, we will become un-useful and unhelpful…my experience in the US is that that's where the US firms have gone…I've seen [the files of] two of the Big Four firms in the US recently…and they're…just useless. You pick the files up, you can't understand the business, but there [are] piles and piles and piles of forms saying that things have been done and things have been checked at different times, but can you get a sense of what drives the business from reading an audit file in the US? No, you can't. And do we want to go that way? I hope not. A), you can't keep staff, but b)…it is us becoming unhelpful and just focused on our own [processes] to the extent that, well why would you bother having that service provided? It's not useful.

Another supplier dismisses the prospect put by the interviewer of a government agency performing audits:

> I'm not convinced that's useful, but then the value add's gone and it just becomes something that you have to have. And then you go and get the other help and guidance and thinking from some other service…maybe that's ultimately where the government wants to go, but I don't. I'm not convinced that that's useful…if you were to go down that track, that would have all sorts of implications for capital market transactions because of the ability of a government-owned audit to go and report investigating accounts, reports to go in prospectuses and things like that would be zero and at the end…you'd have to have a huge fundamental rethink in the whole capital market…I've been doing a couple of US transactions recently and they have this concept of giving comfort letters to the underwriters where only the auditor can give a comfort letter

> and I can tell you that no government auditor would be able to do that, so you'd then have a massive rethink of that whole approach to [the] capital market. It would just be really fundamental and I can't see any of that's value add[ing]. So I can't see [that] it would drive more efficient capital markets or greater independence or anything useful.

Another supplier points out that in the United States, the rigorous regulatory regime imposed by the *Sarbanes-Oxley Act 2002* is in the process of being unwound to some extent.

> [T]here is a gap…the nature of that gap is that the regulators are looking for a very rules-based audit, so it's very much driven by sample sizes, tick and dash, follow a methodology and follow it rigidly. Whereas…a good audit on a financial statement is far more complex than tick a box, fill out a form, follow a set of standard procedures. It involves large amounts of judgment. It involves understanding commercial realities within transactions. So…the US is probably a really good example of where a regulator has come and they've imposed in the Sarbanes-Oxley framework, which they are now busy trying to unwind, because in some ways they imposed an overly onerous system, which was really driven around looking at an individual financial statement, and people say, 'Well…if we stand back from that, we start to look at substance, and understand commercial reality, we…may get a better outcome than necessarily going and ticking every single box or selecting 50 transactions.'

The same person goes on to imply that in Australia, too, the trend towards prescription has become excessive:

> [A]uditing's started to move towards being…much more regulated, taking out some of the judgment…so you have auditors now who complete an audit and really don't understand the business, or look at a transaction and audit it according to the standards, but really don't understand the commercial reality. And, in some ways…that level of sophistication that we're getting in the financial markets… we're…trying to audit to another level. And that's not necessarily good…we do need to change…we need to go back to saying that not everything can be addressed through rules; there is judgment. The auditing game is primarily based on judgement, and yes, we need to put [in] frameworks [on] which judgment can be based…no

> matter how many rules you have, no matter how many things you follow, you only ever test a sample of transactions, and if you've got a rogue management team or a management team that wanted to deceive or defraud shareholders and auditors, it is going to be very difficult to stop that.

Another supplier concedes that regulators are influencing audit practice, but not yet to an unreasonable extent.

> I don't think it's just become a plain old watchdog on behalf of the regulator...the regulator's taking a much more active interest in the audit and the audit process, and...the initial reaction by regulators globally has been to make sure that policies, processes and procedures are followed...therefore, what they are doing is they are driving change in the way audits are being done through the way in which they are reviewing the files, the way in which they are dealing with the firms...the regulator is influencing what is happening out there in auditing practice, but I don't think that we've got to the stage where the audit is done on behalf of the regulator...auditors understand fairly clearly that the relationship is with the shareholders.

The tension between cost pressures and the tendency of the regulator to expand requirements is evident in this next supplier's comment:

> [O]ne of the problems is—and I'm finding this all time, just on a superannuation audit—you go into...audit a large fund and... there [are] cost pressures involved because you're dealing with the members' money ultimately. And the administrators...and the trustees are trying to force the costs down all the time...yet the regulator is all the time broadening the extent of the audit requirements. So...this year we've got to audit risk-management statements, risk-management plans, derivative plans as well as the financials, as well as member statements, to comment on with compliance aspects. So the length of time that an average auditor will take is going to be increased probably 10 or even 20 per cent... yet we can't increase our fees 10 or 20 per cent. That tends to then cause a shortcut of the process and the taking of the audit risk, and that can't be good.

The same person goes on to explain how, in his or her view, auditors are working for regulators:

> [T]he regulators are looking to the auditors to do their job for them, and that's becoming much more apparent...we'll take...[as an example] a simple self-managed superannuation fund audit where the regulator, being the ATO, is expecting now that the auditor is going to be the eyes and the ears of the ATO, similar to the role that a tax agent may play as being a tax agent almost of the ATO. So we're almost working for the regulator now rather than the stakeholders, who are the members and trustees in the superannuation fund context...that's being translated through the whole of the...audit profession, where the regulator expects the auditor to comply with the requirements of the regulator primarily, and then worry about the stakeholders, the readers of the financial reports, almost as a secondary issue. Now if the readers and stakeholders are the capital markets, I'm not sure whether that process is making the capital market more robust, or the safety of the capital markets more robust. It's certainly satisfying the regulators, who if they get it wrong, they're being fired upon by the capital markets and everyone, like the HIH issues and so on. So...the regulators are tending to use the auditor processes as satisfying their own requirements more than looking at the end users' requirements.

The same person explains how prescription can be counterproductive:

> The concept of materiality and risk assessment and all these things [is] being funnelled down into a much more a prescriptive approach. And the more we have to follow absolute prescription, the less ability we've got to broaden our brains to look at what's really going on in the company, because we're not being asked to comment on that, we're being asked to comment just on that very narrow field. Again, using superannuation as an example, if you're just looking at something like...a self-purpose test...you're only having to comment on that and you're focusing your attention only on that, there could be lots of things happening around in the fund which are not proper, or which may expose the capital markets or the fund to risk, which aren't being commented on because of the prescriptive nature of the assignment.

An obviously non-Big Four supplier discusses the pressure of work at peak audit season and how, while audit files might not be completed at that time, as expected by the regulator, it does not make any difference to the appropriateness of the audit opinion rendered.

> I get the impression that the regulators have a very definite view that an audit is very much a complete process, that you've got all of your forms and check lists and everything else. And their approach is designed [so that] everything is completed and ticked and every box is completed, then you can sign off the audit report...in a nice world, that might be possible. But when you're at the busy time and you're trying to clear about three or four audits in a week [that's not possible]...the way we operate...in the mid-tier is that we really focus very much on the risk and material items...and, as long as we're comfortable that they're right then we get the rest done. But the housekeeping and the tidying up of that file [aren't] always as good as [they] could be. And there's a combination of reasons for that...they're now saying I've got 60 days to [tidy up the file, but] it won't...alter my opinion. So, in other words...I've covered what I need to cover to be satisfied my opinion is reasonable. Doing all of the ticking the boxes and putting the bow around the file, while it makes sense, it never alters [the outcome]...the regulators really believe that if you don't do all of that, how can you issue your opinion. Where a lot of that is...we just haven't gone back and ticked the box because the box wasn't there to tick when we were talking to [whoever].

The same person goes on to explain his or her perception of a difference in philosophy between the Big Four and non-Big Four:

> [T]here is a [disjunction]...it was explained to me one time...that the Big Four expect to be sued because of the nature of the work, and therefore they're very compliance driven and form driven and they do tick the box. And then if someone challenges them, if they've got all of the boxes ticked, it's very hard to prove negligence. The mid-tier really doesn't want to be sued because...we don't have the resources to be able to defend them, and therefore there's a very heavy focus on material items and the risk items, and the risk areas, to make sure that the numbers are going to make sense.

The same person laments what he or she sees as the lack of consultation over the reviews by ASIC:

> [T]hey've kind of been chasing cats up trees, which in a sense isn't going to change. It would've been better if they had come out beforehand and said, 'Well, this is our view of life and how auditing should be done.' And let's sit down with a group of people and find out if that's the way it is…done, and if not, why not, and how can we work together. And then to say well this is what we expect. Now you need to have all of these things in place, because they're very document driven…all of the firms are going through and getting quality-control manuals and…tying it all up in the process and making sure everything is cross-referenced…it doesn't really change what we do…I'm not saying that it shouldn't be done, but…I don't…think it necessarily improves the audit process.

The same person continues with the theme of the lack of consultation:

> [T]here would've been more effective ways of saying 'This is what you need to be looking at doing, and this is the training that needs to be done…by an auditor to keep himself current, and these are the key areas that really we want to see.' But they didn't…So everyone's rushing around now and getting all of the compliance stuff done, which is going to be there…the staff [is] going to be aware of it and everything's going to be tied in, but I'm not…sure that it improves the audit process.

Lamenting the role of the regulator as judge and jury, the same person continues:

> I don't know who set them up as judge and jury…I'm not aware of any consultation that they had with the firms before they started the process. And I still have a problem with the process because I don't believe that a tick-the-box approach is an appropriate way of doing an audit…you've got to be thinking, you've got to be really looking at things. And just because I tick the box did that box consider everything that I should've considered…therefore it's a lot more…like an art rather than a science. And they're treating it very much as a science. And I'm not…sure that's right with the complexity of transactions, the changing accounting standards… there [are] a lot more grey areas. And a tick-the-box approach won't

> necessarily result in [a] satisfactory audit...there should be a bit more pressure on the training and how the auditors keep up-to-date and how they keep current. And while they look at that, that's not a big part [of it]...as long as the firm's got a training process to record that, they have a quick look at that...[yet] that's...quite important.

The same person goes further in criticising the current approach of the regulators, calling for more cooperation and education:

> They seem to be very much focused on achieving targets of 'we'll knock a few auditors off and then we'll be seen to be doing our job'. And I'm not...sure that that's...smart...it just annoys people... rather than what we should be [doing, which is] working together and making sure that the education of everyone is up where it should be; making sure that there [are] proper review processes and quality review processes in the firms...that's where you're going to improve the tenor of audit, so that I then have to make sure that all my jobs of a certain category have a quality review, which looks at the accounts and looks at the audit and makes sure we've done it right. And that'll pick up more than me ticking all the boxes...I just have a different way of looking at...that communication and where they're going, they're saying that that's going to lift the auditing standards, [but] I'm not convinced...you've got to get the education requirements really strong and meshed and...if you're going to be an auditor...this thing's out there, but let's drive it, and let's make sure that the quality reviews on the jobs are done on a timely basis and are good, because that will pick up things that the one partner may not.

In the continuing conversation with the same person, they suggest that the regulator does not understand the role of the non-Big Four.

> ASIC have been very critical of the mid-tiers and...unfairly... they need to understand that it's a relative issue. The mid-tiers, in my experience, do a pretty good job auditing businesses which are of the right level for them, perhaps with turnovers of $10 to 200 million, that sort of thing. Yeah...there's an expectation. I don't think the regulator properly understands their role.

The same person comments on the resourcing of the regulator:

> ASIC [are] probably under-resourced...someone [said] to me recently, who's a tax specialist, 'Well, why do ASIC vet all these

> things?'...they don't have the ability to do it and that's why the Australian Taxation Office moved to self-assessment. They...said look basically it's all up to you. You all look after your own tax returns and everything else. We're going to have teams which go out and do audits and checks on various taxpayers. We'll have various other means of determining whether people are complying with the law. It seems to me that the regulator is half pregnant; they don't know whether they're meant to be approving things or whether they mean to be saying to the marketplace you just do it, you know what the law is, just do it all yourself and from time to time we'll check if we become aware of things...they're stuck between...being the judge and jury in their role of regulator. I don't think they quite know exactly what their own scope is...so when they come to the auditors...they're really struggling with that.

The same person continues with an example:

> I received a letter once on a client of mine where they did surveillance, and they wrote to me and said your programs have not been tailored according to—this was under the old auditing standards. But they specifically said that the audit program should've been tailored. Well, there were various things which were done in the audit which were quite specific to that particular audit without necessarily being documented as tailored procedures in the actual programs. But the point was they couldn't even point to where it said in the auditing standards that that was a mandatory requirement. That was their own expectation. And their own expectation was based on the software that the Big Four use where they select the procedures per company in their own computer software. And the practical reality nowadays is that we use *CaseWare*. And *CaseWare* comes with standard-type programs. And whilst you will do separate procedures which are peculiar to that industry or that client, sometimes you don't necessarily document it in the actual audit program. And it's getting down to a really nitpicking-type of situation now. And given that the audit standards carry the force of law...auditors are quite rightly saying...why is it that we have so much scrutiny on us...[W]ho looks at the work of architects and...[asks] why did you put that beam in that place, and so on and so forth? No-one does it for architects. No-one's...looking over the shoulder of doctors and surgeons to make sure that everything that

> they're doing is appropriate...there needs to be an element of self-reliance there, and then they just simply conduct their checks. And I know they are doing that, but...we're all confused as to what in fact they are doing, and what their level of expertise is.

Another supplier articulates what he or she sees as overcompensation by the regulatory regime for the corporate collapses:

> [T]here's been an overcompensation [by the regulators] for corporate collapses, a knee-jerk response to some high-profile collapses...in Australia and the US as well. And as a result of that, the regulation of the industry has just grown astronomically...everyone has the same goal in mind, but...we might be at the stage that it's...[like] using a mallet to crack a walnut...I don't know an auditor that doesn't want to give a good, strong audit opinion that's based on sound audit evidence based on an audit that's been conducted complying with the auditing standards, and that they know their accounting standards—and I assume that's all the regulators want as well. But it's unfortunate that because of collapses we're now spending more and more time on the compliance part of our role...I don't think we spend less on the audit...[but] the total hours have increased...it's a distraction to the extent that there's more to do, but I don't think it's a reallocation of time; it's just adding to the time partners and all of our staff now need to [take] to comply.

Another supplier raises the issue of legal liability that auditors need to contend with, and which might not be appreciated fully by regulators:

> [T]here is a difference there. The regulators will apply the specific wording of the auditing standards, whereas, within the profession, an auditor might be more focused towards the potential liability that's involved in doing an audit, and that's something the regulators may not take into account in their application, or in their review of the auditing standards applying to an auditor's work... They are looking to see that the auditing legislation, as it is now, is being applied. And that's clear that they're following the auditing standards in its application...The added pressure that an auditor has is in terms of potential exposure...of the work from third parties. So, yes, we have got the requirements to comply with the law. We also have to factor in judgments that are inherent in our work that may expose us to liability. And that is a difficult one, where

> the regulator may be applying specific auditing standards...With the exposure that comes from doing an audit, the regulator may be focused on applying the black letter of the auditing standards, which has to be done. It may not be factoring in that an auditor is also exposed to outside pressures in terms of many stakeholders in doing his work. So from that perspective, they're coming from one angle. An auditor within a firm has to consider many other aspects as well. So that is possibly something that is...not probably factored into the review by the regulator.

The same person goes on to emphasise the role of auditor judgment:

> The regulator is focused on compliance with the law, compliance with the auditing standards, and that may not be enough in terms of [the] judgment calls that the auditor has to make, and how they're making those judgments calls is something that may not be looked at enough in doing their work. Their focus may be more on prescriptive check lists rather than [looking] at the judgments that were made [and asking] are they the correct judgments?

One supplier is quite pejorative about regulators, calling them an irritant to auditors:

> [T]he gap between [the regulators] and the auditors in terms of expertise, knowledge, even commonsense quite a lot of the time, is large and, I fear, growing...the auditors are probably getting better and ASIC might even be getting worse...this Westpoint investigation I fear will turn into another Yannon and...they will have any number of excuses as to why this is. But...the regulators are an annoying irritant at the backsides of auditors without... adding very much...I'm talking about ASIC in that context, but... there [are] a lot of regulators. We had a diagram in this room of how many people regulated the audit practice and...it got up to eight different regulators through a variety of internal and external [means]...some of them global, some of them national. So if the Institute of Chartered Accountants and ASIC are just going to go round and peer review people's files, you can...hear the sighing of 'Oh, my God, what is the point?'.

The same person expresses a need for less but more effective regulatory scrutiny:

> [I]deally, what you want is less but more effective regulatory scrutiny and picking off the auditors who do not have the infrastructure or the ability or the resources to...stay in the game. The natural result of that in unfettered capitalism will be either a Big Four or a big three or a big five or whatever it ends up being, there for a long time until...one of them makes a mistake. So you get concentration of audit power. It's questionable whether that's a good thing, but the regulators at the moment aren't helping...in terms of the...audit process itself, there's a lot of box ticking that goes on and I question its value.

The same person, no longer an auditor, but still with a supplier, continues, implying that the purpose of the increased prescription is to build a wall of process behind which the actors can hide if a failure occurs:

> [T]hat is a big problem, and the regulators just keep on building the wall. It's very rare that you hear a regulator say, 'I wouldn't... remove that tick off the check list because that's not relevant.' Their ideal process improvement is to build an ever-larger wall, and when you stand back at the end of several years of putting extra bricks in the wall, you're going to have a really ugly wall. But it makes it more standard and consistent and boring and it takes all the judgment out of auditing that used to be there...I used to quite enjoy it, [but] I wouldn't go back to it. Now, yes, it becomes standard, it becomes consistent. Would that have stopped Enron, would that have stopped WorldCom? Would that have stopped nearly all the things that it's allegedly in place to prevent? I don't think so... the public response to any...problem is to build a wall of process, which you can hide behind. It doesn't address the underlying issue, but it means that everyone is safe when they get to court.

The number of regulatory or quasi-regulatory bodies conducting audit reviews is the subject of the next quotation.

> [With] the current regulatory process and procedures...and I'm talking in the broader context...within a Big Four firm now, 12 months a year, round the clock, you have somebody reviewing the audit files. Whether that be ASIC, in their role as regulator in

> the market, whether it be the AQRB, which is the Big Four-funded quality review board, whether it be a global practice office review, which all the Big Four run, an internal practice office review, or an institute review through the ICAA. That's five layers of review all looking at, broadly speaking, the same things...therefore, as a partner, you can end up being reviewed four or five times a year. It means you can have your files looked at—and often it can be the same files looked at—by a number of different people. That is not efficient in any way, shape or form, and it certainly does detract from the time you have available.

Another supplier takes up the theme of inefficiency:

> [A] lot of the doubling up and the inefficiency comes in [when] you've got four or five different regulators who all have four or five different views on something, and then you end up with a check list that might cover the same thing four or five different ways so that you can make sure that everyone is happy with what you've done. And...that... becomes more of a form-filling exercise and it isn't really focusing on what an auditor is there to do. The auditor is there to make sure the financial statements aren't materially misstated. Where...[are] the material misstatements are likely to come from? They're likely to come from areas of complexity, or...unusual transactions, risk areas. So let's focus on those instead of doing...what I would call, in some cases, some silly form-filling exercises.

The same person expands on the idea in terms of the futility of ending up with a 'beautiful audit' file at the expense of a quality audit:

> [There are] the market issues around competition and the lack of [competition] with the Big Four, although I can't see a workable alternative at the moment. There's the ineffectiveness of regulators and yet they're sort of irrelevant and yet still annoying. It's like the mosquito effect almost—the regulators in this country. Overseas... it works a bit differently. Probably the one that we've talked about but not emphasised too much is the effect of all of that on audit methodology such that it becomes such an inexorable legal defence document. So do you end up with sufficient judgment in there? Do you end up with all the partners really thinking about what they are saying and standing back from ever being able to say something, or do you end up with the world's most beautiful file?

The same person continues, expanding on the danger of audit firms taking on engagements for which they are ill equipped:

> We do…some audits of negligence cases, usually defence rather than attack, when people accuse auditors of not doing the right thing. So I've got a fair bit of knowledge from that perspective. And most of the ones that I see are the smaller firms, or even sole practitioners, who take on jobs that they just shouldn't have done, and clearly weren't capable of doing…and [they] end up relying on…management representations, if not hearsay…one of the risks of having junior staff, who aren't enjoying it and don't really understand, and audit partners, senior people, who are too frazzled, is that you end up relying too much on what the client tells you, and that isn't really the role of auditing. So that [doesn't work].

The next comment by a supplier implies that check lists can reduce the volume of documentation:

> [I]t's interesting when you look at the [evolution] of the procedures in the Big Four. I can remember [when] I was a partner in [one of the Big Four] for a while and we went from a heavily documented process to having a book, which kind of indicated the types of controls and different systems…so you then determine what testing you did and documented those and then went about your audit. But they were finding that that wasn't as efficient, so therefore they then went back to tick the box as being…more efficient…there's always been the concept of the phantom auditor and people just ticking. And…whenever you have a tick-the-box approach that lends itself to that. So if you're under a budget constraint, you'll tick the box when you may not have done something. And there's no need to document…it further; you just simply sign off the box.

The same person goes on:

> [I]t's interesting…when you look at where the Big Four are within methodologies—they've kind of [had] a go at [it] both ways…And there's no doubt…[that if you are] trying to get the auditor to think, ticking the box is not the best way…because they're driven by process, not by the content…you've got to be very careful that you're pulling that all together and challenging the numbers… unless you do that, I'm not sure that you've got a lot of confidence or assurance that things are all right.

The same person says, in response to a comment about the relationship between a check-list approach and staff retention:

> [I]t's interesting because even in the mid-tier you don't have that as much. The auditors are required to think and challenge and this is the best way. And when some of them...leave and see if they can make it in the Big Four, they're...quite surprised that their ability to think through stuff is quite often at a better level than their compatriots at the Big Four because they've been driven by this [as] the way we do it. So we just do it this way without even thinking about whether that's the most appropriate way to achieve that audit objective.

Another supplier states:

> [The risk of being fixated with prescription and check lists] is definitely there...what tends to override it is that you've always got the experience and the use of your professional judgment and the fact that you've had to exercise [that] on numerous other occasions gives you what you need to move beyond the prescriptive tick the box...the tick-the-box [approach] is still there, but...that's [not what is] going to get you there. You have to do all these other things, you have to manage the tensions that are within organisations as to how you get information [and] how you decipher that. You might be able to tick every single box and it all looks okay, but it still falls over. It's the exercise of professional judgment and... it's underestimated...You look at the way...the legal professional looks at that. There's professional judgment exercised all the time in judicial cases...and that seems to be accepted that...you get facts and, on the balance of what's presented to you, you apply the law and you come to a conclusion. Our job's not that dissimilar...I get presented [with] the facts and I fit them all in the holes and if I colour in all the right boxes it gives me the answer. What tends to happen is I'm given something and it doesn't quite fit and I have to work out what the range of outcomes is and how do I narrow that range of outcomes and what [do] my standards say—my standards, which are principles based rather than prescriptive.

The same person expands on the degree of judgment auditors invoke:

> [In] the US...things aren't as black and white. There is a degree of interpretation required: that's what we do...[and] you can't substitute that...we're moving now to having to document that. It's not that easy to document at times, the exercise of judgment, so that somebody can come in and exercise exactly the same judgment based on the facts. But that's what we'll move to and, in the end, to get down and say well I can see that [I've] considered that on the balance. I've thought this and I've thought that and the standard allowed me to do this or allowed me to do this or that and gave a range...I've then looked at external expert's advice...you have to piece all that together and...it's a little bit more than...tick the box.

The verdict of another supplier is that the intellectual input is diminished when a check-list approach is used:

> Yes...it's a generalisation isn't it, but form filling as a way of...audit is not...going to give you the outcome you should have because staff then aren't learning...it's not an intellectual [exercise]...it's the issue of some [of those]...working in the US that the greater the intellectual input into the audit process, the better the outcome... is going to be...[The] reality is, even in accounting more frequently than not, [that] there isn't a black and white answer to any given circumstance, so if you don't have an ability to exercise your intellect in those circumstances, how can you deal with conflicts of accounting?

Another supplier gives an analogy of the check list that pilots must work through before a plane may become airborne. Few would question the necessity of such a routine procedure before flying, despite the challenging nature of qualifying as a pilot and the skill and judgment involved.

> I've been [with] the firm [many] years. In that period, we've moved from highly prescriptive check lists that we had without any legislation backing them to getting rid of those and having blank sheets of paper and working it out, which actually was a worry...to selective databases of master steps that people work out which ones they want to use. And in working that out...they look at the client, what we may have done last year, plus what's the prescription. So...it's a little bit more prescriptive but sometimes it helps people

> to have a bit of a check list because that's the way...you execute. Does it stop an airline pilot flying an aeroplane because he or she has that check list they go through...they need the check list, they know it's right, but you know they're doing it so that they know it's happening, and I think that's sometimes what we're doing here.
>
> When you get reviewed, we get reviewed internally, we get reviewed externally; they look for the forms. They're not as focused on what judgments you've made. There is some of that, but if you haven't got those forms, you feel like you're exposed.

2.3.1 Summary

Suppliers overwhelmingly lament what they see as a 'tick-the-box' approach to ASIC's audit firm reviews and believe the reviews are conducted with insufficient consultation. Some see this approach as militating against high-quality audits, with auditors resorting to 'blind adherence to documentation without much thought'. There are several pejorative observations about under-resourcing of ASIC, particularly in terms of the level of expertise of the personnel charged with undertaking the reviews of audit firms. Claims emerge that the regulator has been 'shocked' at what has been seen in the smaller firms, but non-Big Four suppliers are concerned that the regulator's opinion on the design and implementation of what is seen as a sound audit methodology has been benchmarked against a Big Four approach when the smaller firms do not have the same level of critical infrastructure, technical advisors or critical mass. Non-Big Four auditors would argue that they achieve quality audits, but in a way different from that of the Big Four.

2.4 Standard setters

There is some trepidation among standard setters about the approach of the regulators:

> [A]uditors—certainly those who have been doing it for a while—have got a view that it's...an expression of the opinion on the financial reports. I'm still a bit...nervous with what I've seen [that] from the regulator's viewpoint...it's more a compliance thing. Have you complied with every standard and I don't know whether they've taken in the relevance of a particular requirement to the circumstances of the audit engagement or doing the audit of a particular entity...They take the view [that] you do it if it's

> required. If it's there, it's a black letter rather than is it relevant for the entity. There may be a black-letter requirement which... [means] you go and do it, but it has so little impact on it...so...that's probably the disconnect between the two of them at the moment... the audit profession is now coming to the [point] that...maybe it is a check-list approach and...even if it is probably...not...relevant, if it's a mandatory thing, well then we have to do it...that's the view which is being taken...ASIC takes the view that if you've complied with everything, you've ticked it off...then the outcome should be right.

The same standard setter articulates what he or she sees as the role of judgment in the audit process:

> [E]ven if an individual did all those things, you still need the professional judgment...to say does this look good, do you agree with what's there...there is a component part of that and it's that professional judgment bit which I sometimes have...a concern about...[which is] how much the ASIC put themselves in the shoes of the individual...in the relative short space...between year end and when you're signing off the accounts. With all the information you have available, you're signing off an opinion with that evidence at your hands...The ASIC reviews after the event are a lot more penny-in-hand and...that's where some of the differences are arising, so it's an interesting stage...the style of audits will over time—because of the way it's set up in Australia...[and] even though I think it's a wrong way...there will be a lot more of a check-list approach to it. I still don't think it will go 100 per cent to the American way, but... there's going to be more of a gradual movement to that end of it.

The same person goes on:

> [O]verall, it will be principle based, but...within that principle base, there will be certainly a lot of check lists. Have you done everything? Yes or No? But...I don't think we'll get to the stage that if you've done everything and it's fine, yet you give a clean audit report...there'll be more of that looking at the totality of it and saying are we comfortable with that? Yes or No? And therefore you might find that will give the more principle-based thing, but... within it...it's going to be a principle-based regime with a fair bit of check lists attached to it.

Another standard setter addresses the tension between principles-based auditing standards and prescription as the extremes of a continuum:

> [O]ne of the real issues between the profession and the audit regulators—if we can call them that—is the relative importance of documentation in particular, but also in…following out or completely closing out the prescriptive requirements in auditing standards…there's this constant tension between…saying auditing standards are principle based and the level of prescription that exists in there.

The same person continues along the same theme, arguing that there has to be a balance between principles-based standards and prescription:

> [T]he IAASB would argue that it is principles based, but there is a hell of a lot of prescription in that as well. So…it's missing the point a little bit to have that debate [over] one or the other…it's a question of you…have both; it's a question of getting some balance.

One of the standard setters points to the use by regulatory authorities, especially APRA, of auditors in an explicit delegated regulator role.

> [E]xternal auditors obviously know…that their job is to express a reasonable assurance opinion on financial statements…deep down, regulators know that as well, but you take any particular entity, whether it's HIH or any bank or whatever that's heavily regulated in a heavily regulated industry. The auditors and the regulators have risks and responsibilities in relation to that organisation and those risks are quite different…but there is a concern…within probably the accounting profession and the auditors that should anything go wrong then there'll be a number of serious questions from the regulators. So it means there'll be a lot more scrutiny on the audit and the actual quality of the audit both from ASIC and from APRA, if it's an APRA-regulated entity…regulators like APRA, they [also] try and outsource regulation to the external audit profession, so it's difficult for a regulator to get highly skilled and sufficient highly skilled resources to regulate effectively. So what they do is they engage the external auditors to do a lot of their work for them and the examples of that are…when APRA engages the external auditors to do targeted reviews on particular subjects and…then they require auditors to notify them of all breaches…Now I'd understand how

> regulators expect auditors to do that if they understand the nature of an external audit. There's no way an external auditor, as part of the audit, is...going to know all breaches.

The same person goes on to argue that regulators are in danger of expecting more than auditors can achieve:

> [T]here is an expectation gap with regard to an external audit between the accounting profession and the regulator...the regulator's trying to draw as much as possible from an external audit that's probably not really there...so, there is danger in that for the accounting profession in that if something does go wrong then the regulator will try and draw more from the audit than it should do and it will also try and defend itself and use the accounting profession to defend itself, to deflect blame...and HIH is probably a prime example. Things have tightened up considerably since then as well.

The same person continues with this theme of an audit being 'outsourced regulation', pointing out that there is a limit to what an audit can achieve:

> [O]ther things that external auditors do are outside the scope of the external audit, but they have to report on compliance with a risk-management strategy and there [are] other compliance statements they have to do and there [are] compliance reviews and [so on]. They're all outside the scope of the external audit...[as well as] compliance with prudential standards. It seems to suggest that more and more, the regulator's trying to build up the onus on the external auditor as opposed to the onus on itself to regulate...it's outsourcing regulation to the accounting profession and every time that we come up with a new one of these things, I...think of it in terms of here we go again; here's the regulator trying to outsource regulation to the accounting profession. The danger is that because they do a lot of that then they will try and draw more from the external audit than is reasonably there.

Later in the same interview, the same standard setter explains a perceived difficulty in engaging with regulators:

> [W]e, as an auditing profession, try and engage the regulators in a lot of things and they don't want to be engaged because of their perception of conflict of interest, that when we're developing

> standards or whatever, if they give their opinion on an exposure draft or they contribute to the process in any way, then it compromises them when they come back and have to regulate. In other words, they don't want anybody turning around to them and saying, 'Well, you said this was okay. You gave it a rubber stamp and now, in your regulation, you're saying it's no good.'

Another standard setter points to an anomaly that he or she sees in the incentives for auditors to be provided with accurate information by clients compared with those existing in relation to regulators:

> I don't think the gap [between auditors and regulators] is...as obvious as perhaps it might appear...by that I mean the gap that I see is that the regulator has a view that the auditor is a quasi-regulator and I don't have an issue with that; that is a role of the auditor to form an opinion under the *Corporations Act* and report breaches of [the] *Corporations Act* and so forth, so it's not... implied; it is...a physical obligation. Where I do have an issue... is that the auditor is afforded no protection under the corporations law in respect of management, directors, employees of a business who deal with the auditor providing that auditor with true and correct information. Yet the regulator has the powers that enable it to obtain any information and to prosecute anybody who gives it false information and yet we've got a situation where you've got an auditor who's operating in a quasi-regulatory role who isn't even supported by a legislative requirement that the entity and the people that they audit should give them correct information.

The same standard setter goes on to compare the responsibilities of auditors with those of the companies they audit:

> [W]ith the *CLERP 9* changes, one of the issues I raised was...[that] the changes in auditing standards, black lettering, enforceable by law, arguably increased documentation requirements, et cetera, are very akin to the US auditing standards and requirements of the US. Look at the parallel with the US with what they require business to do as well. What we've done in Australia is we've probably implemented, to an extent, part of the US auditing standard-type requirement around documentation, archiving files, et cetera...put that costing to the auditor and left the businesses alone to a fair degree in terms of their obligations and what they should do. Now

> we say that bearing in mind that the US have recently reviewed how they approach [surveillance]...and how people document their patrols and how far they have to go...they've eased off, but they haven't taken the whole process away and...we're seeing a situation where there's more onus...back on to the auditor, and the businesses, supposedly under the spirit of entrepreneurial spirit and being able to trade freely without too much restriction and cost of doing business, but there's a cost of doing business on the auditor and has that all been passed back to companies? And is there as much responsibility on companies? And you mentioned continuous disclosure; is there as much responsibility on companies as perhaps there should be around some of those areas?

Another of the standard setters questions whether what it is that regulators want auditors to do is consistent with quality auditing:

> I don't know that the auditor's duty is to give value to the end user, being the client, because you'd say who is the client? The user[s] of the audit opinion...if we're talking about a financial statement audit under the *Corporations Act*...are prima facie, the shareholders. And there might be debates around who else is entitled to rely on it and whether vulnerable people are entitled to rely on it...or there's a duty of care that comes out of vulnerability. So I don't think that it's the value to the company...to the end user...the focus needs to be on getting a quality opinion, which is that nothing has been omitted that shouldn't have been or nothing's in there that's incorrect. And again, you'll come back to materiality, but the financial statement's taken as a whole and that sort of point...is doing what it is that the regulators' think we ought to be doing going to result in us missing what we need to do to deliver a quality audit?

The same person continues with the theme, pointing out the danger of emphasising the audit trail at the expense of dealing with the issues uncovered:

> I don't see it being a danger yet in terms of where we are—but...the regulators' behaviour when they oversight audits and the reviews is relevant here—[one of the dangers] is this concept of a check-list mentality...so much focus goes on documentation and leaving the trail as opposed to...identifying and dealing with the issues... I don't see a problem at the moment appearing or anything that's

> irreconcilable, but a lot of effort and a lot of discussion does go into the fact that increasingly, [more] time is being spent on the trail of documentation that's left than was being done previously and...if fees don't increase, costs are absolutely increasing. So if fees don't go up in a commensurate fashion, then might quality suffer because you're focused too much on the documentation trail...that's definitely a space to watch.

Another standard setter says:

> I don't see [the check list] as the mechanics that affects the day-to-day audit...it's more in the back end in just demonstrating to the regulators that they comply, but if you've got a requirement black letter that says the auditor shall understand the risks associated with the business of the client...then they've got to do some work to understand those risks...you can't adopt a check list-style approach to that. Black letter says this is what you've got to do, so it creates activity for the auditor, but activity in the right thing.

The next standard setter raises the importance of auditors being able to write and communicate well:

> The funny thing is it is a bit of a challenge for our profession because so many of the newer requirements are almost what I call social requirements. They're around communication. They're not... around how you ensure you find problems or deal with them; they're around just how you communicate generally and clarify your engagement and...the skill of your communication, and it is very difficult to get people to write well in this profession. [It is] very rare to get a junior staff member who can...string words together articulately on a piece of paper...our most technically competent people are probably our best communicators as well.

Education of users is the key, according to this same standard setter:

> [T]he emphasis should be on the education of the user of the reports and just let the audit process settle down as much as possible without imposing too many changes on that process, but educate people as to how to get the best out of the audit process.

The alignment of interests between regulators and auditors is the subject of another standard setter's discourse:

> They're experts in accounting standards and they're obviously going to become experts in how to apply auditing standards because they're taking that on...I hope...they recognise that ultimately they're not at war with the accounting firms. They...have very much aligned interests.
>
> [T]here is a perception that the regulatory view of the world is that if it hasn't been documented it hasn't been done, and that there is a need for prescriptive rules. Even...saying that, the firms like prescriptive rules, for all that they complain about it, because it's easier to demonstrate that they've done the job they need to do, rather than...relying on judgment...there [are] clearly some dissenting views around that space between the regulators and the auditors. Equally, my sense of the regulators is that they are quite concerned—particularly as you cascade down the scale—about more quality control. Although...based on their private conversations, there would also be an argument that even within the large firms, there have been pockets of less than adequate performance. And there's perhaps been a bit of a cleansing process in some of those firms in the last few years that's been necessary. Equally, if some of that process has moved people to other firms, rather than to retirement, you're...just shifting the problem rather than removing it...So the risks are...greater, although you're then perhaps working on smaller assignments that are less critical in the event of a failure; they're not having the impact in the marketplace of a large collapse.

The same person goes on to lament the perceived lack of communication by the regulator in the lead up to legally enforceable auditing standards:

> [T]ake the *CLERP 9* changes...I don't think the main regulator has done themselves any favours early in the piece of those changes in terms of not being very communicative with...the audit stakeholders...there was quite an extended period of enormous anxiety about the changes that were occurring around them without communicating much at all, let alone adequately, with the firms being impacted by the changes...that was probably unfortunate... [but] that's been turned around in the last six or 12 months...there's

> perhaps a slightly different attitude. We've played...probably a small, but nonetheless...a part in that, just in terms of the dialogue that this organisation's had with both firms and ASIC itself...there's an enormous anxiety out there; you need to communicate with them, explain how you're going to approach the work that you're going to do, that the changes to the systems aren't necessarily going to mean they're all about to be put into jail.

2.4.1 Summary

Standard setters add some perspective to the debate surrounding regulatory oversight, pointing out the alignment of interests that exists between auditors, audit firms and the regulators. There is, however, some concern about an exaggerated focus by regulators on compliance itself as constituting the basis for a quality audit. The anomaly in having allegedly principles-based auditing standards alongside regulatory check lists is raised. Even though the standard setters lament the trend towards a check list-based audit, they seem to see it as inevitable. Also raised is the difficulty for regulators of reviewing documentation that retrospectively attempts to provide insight into the conduct of the audit.

3.0 Inspections

In the interviews with stakeholders, few issues triggered more vehement responses—among suppliers at least—than the issue of regulatory inspections of audit firms. The next section focuses on stakeholders' perceptions of this regulatory oversight and the resourcing and expertise of regulators. This section focuses on comments directed specifically to inspections. No users made comments relevant here, so the section begins with comments by purchasers.

3.1 Purchasers

The purchasers featured in comments in this section are very aware of the regulatory inspection process that has been imposed on their auditors, as their comments reveal.

> [P]ossibly there is [an expectations gap between regulators and auditors]. Anecdotally, I [have] heard of some ASIC surveillance of some of the big firms, probably going back one and half [to] two

> years ago...some onsite inspections of files, interviews of audit partners. And it sounded to me—again...the risk here is that I come from such a small experience base because I only have one corporate—but the sort of things that ASIC were putting to the accountants, who were telling these kind of stories of the onsite visits, were...relatively paranoid and unrealistic...I would think that...showed that ASIC really had some quite negative views, even of the big firms, and were quite suspicious of the audit firms being compromised in some way by their clients. As I say, it's some time ago...But I know if they've started to become enriched with actual information, they've started to become less antagonistic...while I... confessedly start from an example of one...they perhaps had really come straight off the HIH Royal Commission and [were] starting from a bad example of one.

One purchaser is somewhat sympathetic to the impossibility of the role allocated to the regulators, who are charged with retrospectively determining from documents the course and adequacy of the conduct of the audit:

> The regulator at the moment is trying to audit auditors, that's number one. And how do they do that? By going through their working papers and trying to understand what happened in the real world. They weren't there! What's on a piece of paper can never substantiate what happened. It's like a performance assessment; you put down somebody's performance, but unless you're present when the discussion took place, the piece of paper is totally unrepresentative of the situation; it just cannot capture it all. So the regulator is coming in and auditing the auditors and then after the event they look at the annual report and they come and talk to management or the directors about the way something's been presented and they try...[to] understand something that might have taken weeks to discuss and debate, so the regulator's...placed in an impossible situation.

In a more general context—and not necessarily associated with the reforms specifically—the next comment addresses perceptions of the value added of an audit from one purchaser's perspective (although the comments are made more from a user's than a purchaser's perspective).

> As an external party...I can't really comment...in terms of whether it should be [prescribed] or not...we would like...some sort of prescription, because...there's always the relationship issue with a head partner and the company. There might be too much pressure on the audit partner to skipper, then at least if there's a list of things to check off...that forces the auditor to do that. So...as a user of information, we'd rather have a little bit more [prescription] than not enough.

The same purchaser is disparaging about the value of the audited financial statements:

> [I]n terms of information...the usefulness of the disclosures in statutory accounts isn't great for the financial companies... therefore, rather than the companies giving us a set of accounts, quite often we...never look at the actual statutory accounts. What we're given is an investor report rather than a set of statutory accounts...we're...not looking at auditor numbers here, so the final P&L [profit or loss statement], the statutory account, is audited, but the numbers we're given are quite often not audited...to us, it's a failure of what...the regulators are doing in terms of what should be disclosed. So the bit that's...regulated, audited, is something... we don't bother to look at if...the numbers add up.

Another purchaser comments:

> We have a fairly homogenous business, very similar products... So we have fairly stable and long-established processes...[Audit firm X has] come in every year and done their audits. They raise things from time to time, but the general issues that the business has thought about and concluded on 10 to 15 years ago, we're not operating [in] a really dynamic changing environment in terms of the product and the service that we offer. So very rarely do we get value add from the audit process.

3.1.1 Summary

Some purchasers make pejorative comments about the value of audit to them as they discuss regulation, which tends to be taken to refer to the audit itself.

3.2 Suppliers

The passion with which suppliers spoke on the issue of regulatory inspections was revealed in many of the interview quotations included below.

> I've had the misfortune to have ASIC review one of my files recently. It just came up in the random cycle and [I] have also just been through IQP review internally. My impression of ASIC...is that their approach is a tick-the-box [one]. They're looking at our audit files to see if the right boxes have been ticked...so I don't think it's...a good use of a regulator's time to come and look and say, they may have got their audit opinion right, but did they get there the right way...that's not useful...the questions that they asked me... were quite silly. [*An example is given, but the details are withheld because of potential client identifiability*] We've clearly, from all the documentation on file, done all those things, so the fact that there's not a check list there is a ridiculous thing...to say. I just felt like that was indicative of their whole approach to the review of the file...where I get frustrated with the regulator is they...are using too junior people to be able to apply professional judgment. If it's the right information on file...they [fall] back to a check-list mentality and if they're going to do that and cause difficulties for firms if that hasn't [been] done, then you will force us to [do] what I see a US firm [doing], which is blind adherence to documentation without much thought. Does that produce good audits? No. Does it make it harder to sue us? Potentially, but does it mean that we'll... get things wrong more often? Yes, I think it does. And does it give useful information to the endholder? No, it doesn't...I expected to be disappointed by ASIC's approach to [the] review [of] our files and I was resoundingly disappointed...that my expectations were fully met.

The same person goes on to differentiate between the Big Four and non-Big Four in terms of the regulators' findings:

> I've been overwhelmingly disappointed by the regulators and that's what I expected...my problem—and don't take this the wrong way—the informal feedback we get from the ASIC review is [that] they've been quite pleasantly surprised by the standard of audits in the Big Four firms. They've been shocked at what they've seen in

> the smaller firms, so it may be that this prescriptive way of doing things is a good way of getting the small firms to lift their game... therefore, they might think that they're doing a good job and they might be doing a good job when you look across the board, potentially, because that doesn't overly surprise me that they've been quite surprised at what they find in the smaller firms...due to a couple of transactions I've been involved in the last two or three years, I would have looked at files for all Big Four firms...[and] the standard's pretty good. Smaller firms, I don't know.

Another supplier is ambivalent about the potential impact of the regulatory review:

> As far as going through various firms now...we haven't been subject to review as yet, but we will be and we know that. I'm not sure what they're trying to achieve out of it. I've been to sessions where the regulator has discussed the process and I really haven't come away with anything as to what their outcome is as far as this is concerned. So as to whether it's hindered or helped, I don't think it's done either...I don't think it's...hindered; there [are] other factors that hinder the capital markets. I don't think the way the auditors are behaving or the way the regulators [are] viewing auditors [have] any impact...it's really between those two parties where the issues are.

The same person goes on to claim there is inequity in applying Big Four methodologies as the benchmark that non-Big Four firms must live up to:

> [T]hey have been through a process on a number of stages with the Big Four. And they've certainly given them a bigger tick compared to...non-Big Four firms—absolutely, I agree with that. The resources is one of the issues...but the concerns that I have are more...that they have...formed an opinion on how an audit methodology should be...designed and implemented, and their opinion seems to be formed on what they've seen primarily at the Big Four. Now... they've got more resources than the non-Big Four have in relation to things like technical support, all those sort of areas which obviously underpin how we do things...technically, how our methodology is developed, et cetera. And we don't have those resources, and none of the non-Big Four firms [has] those resources; there's no question about that.

The same person expresses the inappropriateness of regulators applying their opinion of how an audit should be conducted:

> [T]o form an opinion on how an audit should primarily be done is...not the role of the regulator. And because they've taken what I would almost describe as this high moral ground then they're going to be disappointed...But that doesn't mean that what we're doing is wrong or is not the right way to conduct an audit. And that's the problem...this is where I say you've got this almost expectation gap because they're saying this is the way we think you should do things. But we're also saying...you're not actually doing it wrong, but this is the way we think you should do these things. And... that's the problem.

Yet another view, quite damning of ASIC's approach to the reviews, follows:

> There's a mid-tier group that's started and they've had the ASIC accountant there. But it is still hard...They're very aggressive when they come in and review the firms. And I'm not sure that too many of them have ever been in the firing line in terms of having to sign off, having to pull things together, to have a real appreciation [of] some of the issues, and therefore what is important and what isn't important...the issue then becomes if they think they've got a big issue then they just go through you like a dose of salts. And I'm... not sure that that's the right approach...it would've been nice to learn what their way of life is before they started doing these reviews, because I'm not too sure who set them up as judge and jury. Who said that ASIC's way of thinking about how auditors operate was the way to go...they just started the inspection program...talking to some of the firms [that have] been reviewed, some of [ASIC's] approaches have been a bit cute and totally lacking in understanding about how the firms operate.

The views of another, obviously non-Big Four supplier, in terms of ASIC using the Big Four processes as the benchmark, are expressed in the next quotation:

> [O]ne of the things which I have enormous difficulty with is [that] ASIC will go in and have a look at the Big Four and they'll come out with their report, which says essentially that they're all doing

> a really good job, that they had a few nitpicking points, which were really minor about the Big Four. And they really do things very well. The Big Four have got excellent procedures and quality. Occasionally, there are slip–ups, which we find out about later... then they've gone into the mid-tiers and they've looked at those procedures and what they appear to have done—and...a lot of the people I speak to...agree with me—is they've said okay the Big Four is the standard...the benchmark, now let's have a look at the others. And they've gone, 'Oh well, you're nowhere near as good as the Big Four.' Well, surprise, surprise; the mid-tiers don't have the same critical mass and ability [and] infrastructure around the auditors and so on, and technical advisors and all that.

Yet another supplier laments the fact that ASIC is all too willing to point out what is wrong, but loath to provide guidance on addressing the issue:

> [I]t would be part of [regulators' expertise to question audit methodology]. Do they have the expertise? That's a hard one. It depends on the situation. One of the issues I have when the regulator comes in on the inspections is that they will tell you what you're doing wrong. They won't give you the guidance on how to address it. They'll say that you've got weakness in a certain area; you ask for guidance as to what they expect and often you don't get that...it's from a protection point of view from the regulator that they don't want to be seen to dictate what the best practice is. They would rather not hold themselves to be that kind of benchmark in terms of how to do an account. It does make it difficult though for the firms to know what the benchmark is.

Another supplier enunciates the importance of how regulators go about their role:

> I don't think it's...confusion about what their role is...they're regulating the audit profession now and that's clear, and that's under law and so on and so forth...the query is the way in which they do it. And I don't know whether these stories are true or not... and you inevitably get the horror stories about this, that and the other...[There are] tales of PCAOB inspections [where]...people are spending more time performing the inspection than was spent performing the audit, and deliberately looking to find things. You

> know, these rumours that the PCAOB is staffed by disgruntled ex-employees of the Big Four, who are looking to get some payback. All that stuff has gone into urban...legend.

On the same theme, the same person goes on to eloquently explain the difference between a regulator who acts collaboratively versus one who acts in a more aggressive manner:

> [W]hether you philosophically accept or not that an independent body should regulate the profession, that's where we're at. That's where we're at in the US. It's where we're at in the UK. That's the way it is. The rules are set and [are] there to apply to. But...it's in how you interpret and deal [with] those rules. And that's a mirror with ASIC in its dealing with clients. I've done a lot of work under the *Managed Investments Act* with compliance plans where ASIC have swung in the pendulum from being very tough enforcers, because they needed to be with some things, to more helpful in terms of helping people construct these things, so that people are more willing to come and discuss issues, and they work through collaboratively.

The same person suggests that ASIC could afford to rely on other review processes within the firms themselves, especially within the Big Four:

> [I]t's a policing discussion. Are you a community policeman or are you an enforcer...you've got to be both. And I'd like to think that within the Big Four...we have some pretty rigid quality ourselves. We have real-time quality reviews [in which] our files [are gone] through independently...We have global risk reviews and so on, which are pretty damn tough. And those global reviewers are themselves reviewed as they're carrying out the task. So we have some pretty strong processes and some pretty tough disciplinary measures...way before ASIC get in there. So you'd think that ASIC would—and maybe they are—be comfortable with some of that, rather than putting another layer on top.

3.2.1 Summary

Suppliers hold generally negative views of the way in which regulatory inspections are approached and conducted. There is incredulity that a retrospective examination of the audit files and documentation alone can give accurate insight to the nature of the judgment calls made during the conduct of the audit. There is a lack of respect for the knowledge and expertise of the regulators charged with the task of conducting inspections. There is frustration over the perceived lack of communication about the way in which the task is to be conducted and from the non-Big Four there is resentment that the methodology of the Big Four is used as a standard that must be lived up to in order for it to appear that a quality audit has been conducted.

3.3 Standard setters

In a context pertaining to any expectations gap between regulators and auditors, a standard setter says:

> [Y]es, [the tension between audit firms and the regulator is] quite real...it perhaps has diminished in more recent times, but the tension was very real...[with] the introduction of the audit standards having the force of law and that potential for criminal sanctions...there was huge anxiety. And then overlaid with the other *CLERP 9* changes of the reviews being undertaken...the audit inspections by the regulator, and all the costs that that imposes. And...the regulator view of the need for documentation, and at the same time...the tightening of audit standards coming internationally anyway, versus the firms having a somewhat more pragmatic [approach], or wanting more flexibility perhaps than the regulators were...giving.

4.0 In defence of regulators

It is important to understand that many stakeholders expressed empathy for the difficult task that regulators must carry out. This section brings some of these comments together to emphasise the constructive nature of the discussions with interviewees.

4.1 Purchasers

> I don't think [the prescriptive approach] adds a thing to the shareholder...I understand the thinking behind it and I understand the politics behind it in terms of...politicians being seen to do things and not to be soft on this issue and that's why it's gone to the law. But...Australia on the whole's got it pretty right.

The next purchaser, who has worked on both sides of the regulatory divide, eloquently explains the pressures experienced by regulators:

> I've had the privilege and benefit of working within a regulator... I can tell you now regulators are removed from the real world. They do not have to exercise the professional judgment that auditors and preparers have to exercise; they're very process driven. They almost cannot put themselves in the shoes of the directors or management or the auditors, but by dint of the nature of the regulatory world, they end up doing that...they do not face the day-in and day-out judgments that have to be made on provisions, impairments, measurement of items, interpreting accounting standards that [are] the meat and potatoes of management, preparers and auditors. So the regulator sort of parachutes in and looks at things in an ex-poste clinical way and has the benefit of hindsight and expects to see a perfectly laid out answer. It doesn't happen that way. Making sausages is not clean; it is messy. But judgments are made along the way and typically they're made in good faith and on reasonably good evidence and [they can be substantiated]...there are different perspectives because the regulator is...[under] enormous ex-poste pressure to justify why they didn't do something ex-ante.

The same person puts into perspective the need to weigh the costs and benefits in deciding on the level of resourcing to be attributed to regulators:

> The resources will always be inadequate to capture all the issues. There will always be a cost–benefit judgment made about which cases [to take on]...A regulator is not about regulating every event; it's about sending signals, it's about putting in place mitigation control to stop the market going berserk. Now that's an over-exaggeration, but it's trying to stop behaviours at the far end of the normal distribution curve—well one end of the normal distribution curve—because the number of false evil criminal activities is probably less than 5 per cent...the regulator is really trying to send signals...so it has to make strategic interventions...the question about resources is...a cost–benefit [one] and it's about managing it at the margin rather than doubling the resources.

The same person also expresses some sympathy for the position in which regulators are placed: unable to countenance failure.

> [J]ust a word in defence of the regulators here too. Part of their problem is that they can't tolerate failure...regulatory bodies have to report to parliamentary committees where you've got all the dynamics of opposition and government fighting it out in that political environment. So [the principals] at ASIC and at APRA have to go before parliamentary committees on a regular basis. If any of their charges fail, if any of their companies—particularly in APRA's case—have failed then there's all hell to pay. So all of their incentives and [all of] their emphasis [are on] prevent[ing] failure at any cost...'drive risk out of the system' is [essentially] the mantra. And in the process, unfortunately, what that does is it destroys businesses...this is the reason why...we've got to just be a little vigilant in this area.

4.2 Suppliers

One supplier questions whether the focus is on the really key issues:

> [T]he focus hasn't always been [on] what I see as the key issues, but I can understand it as well, because unless you're out there and you're having the discussions and you're seeing it first hand, and you're dealing with boards, and you're dealing with management, and you understand the tensions that often exist there, the complexity of transactions, the timing of certain things, you don't always get an appreciation of what the key factors that you should be focusing on are.

The same person goes on to comment on the expertise of the regulator:

> That goes to our own risk assessment, that goes to how we determine where we're going to focus our efforts and...it comes down to materiality. It's not all materiality, but you will look at certain areas and not look at others in as much detail because that's riskier, because of incidents of anomaly of error in the past, because you know the business. You can't understate that...that is important. Somebody coming in cold to review it, whilst they might try to come to the same conclusion as you based on the documentation that's there, you can't get that same feel[ing] and so when you start looking at it you can understand why the focus might be on something else rather than [on] what you think is the key issue...

> it's very difficult to get that level of confidence in expertise within the regulator up to that same level, unless they're out there...doing their own detailed work.

One supplier expresses a positive view of what could be achieved if more was done to include forensic auditing in audit processes:

> The other thing that I...want to mention is innovation...and the way audits are done, and particularly technology and data, and a lot of the work that we do in forensic now is beginning to migrate into audit practice. So, for instance, I've just finished doing a job called 'forensic audit systems'...when we help, in this case, a US company to have a look at its operations in the Asia-Pacific area...a lot of that involves technological taking of data, analysing it and looking at things that at the moment aren't really looked at. So...there are a lot of useful things that could be done that at the moment are not done, but within five years probably will be...the forensic side to it will become a huge element of auditing...I'd like to see...the human judgment side of audit partners who've come up through a more enjoyable profession and learnt how to do it well combined with the technological data analysis, which is much more objective. So you have the subjective side and the objective side. If you marry those two together...you would get a much better audit process than the current one, which is really there to protect the auditors and to satisfy the regulators...the tick ticking...Will it happen? There'll be elements of it, but it will never be as pure as I've just described because you'll always have regulators nagging away and auditors trying to make a buck and make sure they don't get sued.

Another supplier points to insolvency practitioners being able to provide insights to auditors as a potential way to improve audit quality:

> I'm sure there [are] a lot of...fraud and investigative accountants, insolvency practitioners and that sort of thing [out there]... and that's another thing I found quite strange...that a group of accountants would go into a business from the insolvency field, to try and investigate...why a company failed and...how to restructure a business, yet there was never any input from auditing, which I would have thought would have been a fairly natural progression, that when you go in and you investigate what's happened to a company and why it's failed, why it hasn't succeeded...you don't

> consult the auditing group to come in and say, 'Well, let's go through these accounts; why have they accounted this way?' [There is] none of that—not in my experiences, anyway…And…vice versa…with auditing…the skill set that insolvency practitioners [have], their investigative powers, could be utilised in the audit field…in saying that check lists are great…you probably need to keep an eye on [them], because…if there is a check list in place, it's easy to learn the check list, potentially, if someone knows what the check list is.

4.3 Standard setters

One standard setter welcomes the signal it sends to less than compliant clients to have ASIC involved in the oversight of an audit:

> [T]hat sends a very clear signal that there is a difference, that if someone is dealing with ASIC, for example, there is a higher level of responsibility than if you are dealing with an auditor…that ultimately does send a message—albeit it may be subtle—because a lot of people probably have never sat back and thought about it like that…perhaps if companies knew that [by] providing information to an auditor that was a half-truth, or maybe not quite the full picture, you might get a different level of commitment, a different level of communication…The discussions I've had with various regulators have said, 'Well, if we did that, perhaps companies would tell you things they might otherwise not do', but it's somewhat counterintuitive that that would be a breach of the act anyway. So…what we're trying to deal with here is…the exception, not the rule. We're dealing with the people who should be doing the right thing, not those that are because…it won't apply to them. But, typically, where things go wrong, and then people get upset, is where people haven't been doing the right thing. It doesn't mean putting something in the act will make it happen, but at least it sends a very strong signal that the auditor is somebody that…[the] entity should deal with, with integrity and responsibility, and it's not a process that some may see as tick the box. Yes, we've had an audit and we've got the audit report; we can move on…that's where I see the gap…the red tape issue is a part of it as well.

5.0 Issues and implications

Through the interviews we have learnt that users, purchasers and suppliers are all highly aware of the regulatory changes, which in Australia have included the creation of an inspection process conducted by ASIC of audit firms and the processes within those firms. This inspection process triggered a series of comments from purchasers and suppliers in particular. Users, purchasers and standard setters, however, also commented on the whole issue of the resourcing of regulators.

Both purchasers and suppliers recognise the need for inspections and their benefits, which provide quality control and potentially useful information to the capital market—albeit that the regulators' reports tend to highlight negatives only. Nonetheless, purchasers and suppliers were sceptical not so much about the concept but the delivery of the inspection process. One purchaser makes the observation that depending on how the inspection is undertaken, there is never an opportunity to gain an understanding from the documentation in any working paper file of the events as they unfold in the real world. Indeed, these purchasers make frequent reference to the inspections and the disconnection between inspections and the purported 'real world'.

Those suppliers interviewed who were members of firms that had been inspected through the ASIC process were mixed in their evaluation of the inspection process and some were overtly negative. One Big Four supplier indicated that the informal feedback he received suggested that the Big Four emerged on the whole feeling pleased with the overall evaluation of their systems and processes, but the processes in some of the smaller firms left ASIC 'shocked'. Observations from the non-Big Four supply side were that the inspection process had been contaminated by the inspectors observing the resources available to the Big Four and expecting—and indeed requiring—the non-Big Four to operate at the same resource level. There was, in the view of one non-Big Four supplier, a lack of empathy for the fact that they did things differently.

There was also considerable criticism that the inspectors do not have any or sufficient 'real world' auditing experience and that inspection services are limited because of this deficiency.

Users, purchasers and standard setters make the observation that the regulator is inadequately equipped to undertake inspections and indeed to more generally operate in an effective and efficient environment. One user expresses disappointment that there is a need to obtain greater interaction between practice and regulators and to attain more practical experience for those in regulatory environments. One purchaser makes the insightful observation that the resources assigned to regulators in economies such as ours are almost by definition inadequate for fully undertaking the task entrusted to a regulator. This person also acknowledges that the efficient operation of a regulator is to be selective and strategic about the work they undertake rather than attempting to be comprehensive. He suggests that Australian regulation is of this type. This purchaser also notes the beneficial use of secondments and sabbaticals from private-sector suppliers into regulators, which is common in the United States but until very recently has been rare in Australia. The authors of this report note that the ASIC review document strongly proposes to engage in this form of secondment program starting in 2009. Evidence the authors have gathered from purchasers, suppliers and users suggests this is a very positive step forward.

Finally, one standard setter observes that audit is in fact an outsourced form of regulation, but there is a potential disconnection between the achievements and the outcomes of the audit and what the regulator might ultimately wish to be reported. This is not the responsibility of the auditor per se, but suggests a subtle re-engineering of regulatory objectives and outcomes.

With respect to documentation generally, it is interesting to observe that while participants in the market have their criticisms of documentation, users, purchasers, suppliers and perhaps particularly standard setters all observe that there is a benefit in enhanced levels of documentation. While there are considerable concessions that the work is being done anyway, there is a popular belief that there is value to be found in documentation. One theme among suppliers is that the documentation will provide an opportunity for replication of the judgments made. This adds rigour and substance to the judgments made during an audit and provides support for the argument that the judgments are not simply arbitrary but are based on a substantiated context.

There is little doubt that on the demand and supply sides of the market, the observation is that larger firms are able to adapt to an environment where greater levels of documentation are obligatory. While not specifically observed, this might have consequences for those who supply into the market for audit services—at least with more economically substantial clients.

Again, while not often directly referenced, there is a belief that efficiency in documentation is a necessary part of our future.

6.0 Concluding remarks

Many of the issues relating to the regulation of auditors have been dealt elsewhere in this report; however, there are a small number of actionable items arising from discussion in this chapter to which one might give consideration.

The chapter reveals considerable tension from suppliers in their consideration of the approach, operation and resourcing of regulators. With this in mind, it might be useful, particularly with regard to such topics as inspections and quality control, for ASIC and APRA (as appropriate) to establish an open and transparent forum between suppliers and regulators and possibly other important stakeholders, including the AUASB. Such a transparent but potentially informal forum could help resolve tensions and misunderstandings. This forum may or may not have the possibility of operating under Chatham House rules; however, the importance of having some degree of opening in these interchanges is seen as important and will contribute to the efficiency of the capital market if successfully pursued.

A common theme within the chapter is the quantity and quality of resources available to the regulator—particularly ASIC. With the introduction of secondments into ASIC, this will assist principally with respect to gaining highly skilled and particularly experienced auditors into the task. There is, however, evidence that the level of resources in quantitative terms is still modest and consideration might be given to the scale of resources available to ASIC, especially as it builds and enhances its inspection service through these current times of considerable financial strain in the world economy.

As indicated in the first recommendation, there is a need for support, interaction and communication between the regulator and those who represent all of the suppliers of audit services—that is, all registered company auditors and, in some circumstances, beyond. As the market has emerged, there is no single peak body that can represent this entire group. At one point, it might have been seen as the Institute of Chartered Accountants in Australia, but that group has gone beyond representing the supply side of this particular market. How one structures a market so there is one clear unambiguous peak body for the supply of the audit market is a challenge that is not easily resolved. Clearly, it cannot be the AUASB that sets auditing standards; it cannot be the organisation that maintains the register of company auditors because that is the regulator (ASIC); and it cannot be the Companies Auditors and Liquidators Disciplinary Board, because it has the task of dealing with inappropriate behaviour of people who are registered company auditors, among others. It would therefore be useful to have a peak body that is created from other interested parties to represent this particular group.

One issue with respect to the inspection services is that there is some evidence that the inspections are 'one size suits all'. No doubt, those close to the inspection process will feel this is a harsh and unreasonably generalised observation. It is, however, the case that there is evidence that inspections are forcing 'check-list approaches'. The sophisticated business models of those suppliers with whom we communicated tended to hold the audit as a two-part process. One part is largely transactional, with a considerable quantity of work that is relatively menial and standardised, but through that process and supplementary to other processes, there is an opportunity for particularly important, unusual, innovative, risky transactions or events being highlighted and being put off into a secondary process, where considerable judgment is required. This second part of transactions and events cannot be subjected to a check-list approach in the same way that the bulk of the transactions might be. At this point, inspection processes that are more forensic than procedural in their approach might be useful. Having inspections that can capture the need for routine procedure and check lists as well as being insightful, forensic and tolerant of ambiguity would be a useful step forward and would no doubt assist in the inspection process.

Finally, the inspection reports that are published tend to be negative in orientation without providing the other side of the equation—that is, praise for particularly good practice. The capital market is not being informed of the total outcome of the inspections. The inspections to the extent that they can be a 'window' on the quality of the audit work done by each of the suppliers are the key to providing information to enhance the efficiency of the capital market. If these inspection reports can be written as windows on the quality of the work then there will be enhancement in our market.

DIVISION F

COMPETITION 13

> They really do dominate, the Big Four. And it's very hard for the medium and...the small firms...to compete with the ongoing educational input those guys have all the time available for their staff, and all those sorts of things. It's hard for them to compete and stay at the same level and...it wouldn't be entirely healthy to have four or three mega-firms governing an industry, because once...you dominate something, you can control...the way things are done [and] the degree of quality to which they are done.
> — User

1.0 Key issues

The issue of competition within the market for audit services raises important issues for the profession, including:

- is the level of competition in the market for audit services optimal in terms of its association with the quality of services provided
- does the disparity in size between the third and fourth of the Big Four and also between the largest of the mid-tier and the smallest of the Big Four matter
- is it feasible to expect enhanced competition to come from growth in the mid-tiers that could bring any of them to a level comparable with the fourth in size of the Big Four
- to what extent are unnecessarily restrictive auditee company's self-imposed constraints on the purchase of joint audit and non-audit services to blame for a perceived lack of choice among the Big Four
- to what extent are constraints imposed on the growth of firms by a shortage of skilled personnel?

- if it is believed that it would be unhealthy to have less than four large audit firms, how best can we deal with the moral hazard for regulators in monitoring and acting on any transgression by a member of the Big Four accounting firms
- to what extent do the rules around rotation of audit partners trigger consideration by auditee companies of a change in audit firm
- is the level of competition in the market for audit services such that radical alternatives should be considered—for example, nationalising the audit function or allowing other professions to provide audit services?

2.0 Introduction

The degree of competition within the market for audit services is important to audit quality, audit fees, auditor tenure, auditor change, industry expertise, client knowledge, non-audit service provision and to regulation of the market, among other things. The structure of the Australian market consists of the Big Four firms, among whom three seem to be larger than the fourth, and the non-Big Four firms of national mid-tiers and smaller firms. The survey and interview data in general convey perceptions of a highly competitive market. In what follows, the survey results and stakeholder interviews are analysed and insights are drawn.

3.0 Survey data

As indicated in the interviews discussed later in this chapter, there seems to be evidence of effective competition in the market for audit services for smaller and medium-size auditees at least. In the minds of some, however, there is a question about the extent of competition for larger company clients. This led to a survey question about the level of competition for this part of the market, the results of which are reported in Table 13.1.

Responses to a question about the level of competition for larger company clients, averaged across the users, purchasers and suppliers, showed that a little less than half of the respondents believed there was a competitive marketplace for larger companies. Among all types of users, approximately 57 per cent agree with the statement 'For larger companies in Australia there is a lack of competition in the market for audit services'.

Of the purchasers, directors and audit committee members are clearest in their view that there are concerns about the lack of competition, with 61 per cent of that group of purchasers agreeing with the aforementioned statement. Among the suppliers, the group that clearly believes there is a competitive market is respondents employed within the Big Four firms. The various discussions with individuals provided support for these positions and showed there was much complexity with respect to the issue of competition, with differentiation between competition for the larger clients and the more modestly sized clients and between price competition and competition for quality, which for many respondents represented different issues.

Table 13.1 Responses on competition and auditor brand names (per cent)

	USERS				PURCHASERS				SUPPLIERS		
	Total	Accounting expertise	Professional users	Private investors	Total	Directors/ audit comm.	CEO/CFO	Other	Total	Big Four	Non-Big Four
For larger companies in Australia, there is a lack of competition in the market for audit services.	57	58	58	56	52	61	50	43	55	27	62
An external financial statement audit is of value to you because of the brand name of the audit firm conducting the audit.	32	32	33	30	34	36	31	36	30	82	16

Percentage of respondents answering 'Strongly agree' or 'Agree' on a five-point scale.

With the obvious exception of Big Four suppliers to the market for audit services, no stakeholder group had a strong positive view that the brand name of the audit firm conducting the audit was of particular value. This view by purchasers and users is consistent with the proposition that it is the Big Four classification that adds value rather than simply the brand name of the individual firm. The highly differentiated view between non-Big Four and Big Four suppliers can probably be explained by sharply differing views on the effect of a brand name on competition (Table 13.1).

4.0 Interviews

Stakeholders consisting of users, purchasers, suppliers, standard setters and regulators were asked in face-to-face interviews whether they felt there was sufficient competition in the market for audit services. Additionally, in conversations, issues about competition were raised in a context not necessarily responsive to a specific question on the matter. Responses appear in the following sections, together with a synthesis of the insights and policy implications that flow from these responses.

4.1 Users

Among the users, none spoke positively about there being sufficient competition in the market for quality audit services; rather, concern was expressed about insufficient competition. Indicative quotes follow.

> [I]f you put your audit out to tender, you've also got your current auditor, you've typically got at least...one other Big Four firm... doing tax, due diligence work, valuation work—something for you—which excludes them. You may well have two firms excluded, because one's done your tax work and one's done valuation work for you recently...so when you go to put your audit to tender, if you can find two of the Big Four to give it to, and one second-tier firm, you're doing well. And for a whole bunch of reasons, a lot of Australian companies don't want to go to a second-tier firm.

'I'd have concerns about seeing a second-tier audit firm on a...major global company.'

> [I]t's constrained at the top, because...particularly with companies going international, they really have only got a choice of those big firms...we've seen some rotation of audit firms within those big companies, and...you'd normally take that as being a reasonably healthy sign that they do have to change their auditors. But the reality is that second-tier firms... are [not] big enough. I'd have concerns about seeing a second-tier audit firm on...a major global company. They're okay for a domestic-type company—smaller ones, but...investors want the comfort of having one of those big firms on the line should anything really go wrong.

> [There is] not enough competition, especially when you're looking at big jobs that only a couple of big firms could possibly do.

> You see even in Melbourne there would only be certain firms that have enough depth to do a bank or a large insurance company.

One user asks why niche audit firms have not emerged.

> [W]hen I first started working, it was the big eight, and the trend's only been [in] one direction. There is no reason why the accounting profession can't do what the legal profession has done, much better...in that if I've got a big job in legal advice, there's Mallesons, Freehills, Robinsons, Clayton Utz, these big firms, but...beneath them...are specialist boutique law firms that might not cover every aspect. Like Freehills can cover everything. Whatever your problem is, Freehills can handle it. And a small boutique firm may not be able to handle everything, but [it] will handle some things better than Freehills...I can't understand why there isn't room for an audit firm that just specialises in doing mining companies—and just audit. No tax work, no advisory work, no valuation work, just say, 'Look, we're going to be the number-one boutique firm in Australia for mining companies. We've got 500 mining companies listed in Perth, it's a real market, and I can make myself the number-one firm in Australia, and I'll do it a lot cheaper than the Big Four, and I'll do it better, by really being a boutique and...never putting my hand up to audit BHP or the National Bank; it's just not in my interest.'

'I can't understand why there isn't room for an audit firm that just specialises in doing mining companies—and just audit.'

> [T]hat...lack of choice...has created the conflicts, so...how does the industry react to it...we've already seen...the receiver side... splitting off...Should you...be hiving off, which...is the ultimate way you go, hiving off the audit part of the firms, so there is no conflict? It's going to be [something] the accounting profession really has to think about and deal with, because I cannot believe with the size of these firms now that there are these fantastic synergies. They're just monoliths, bureaucrats; how in hell does someone in Brisbane who's auditing some weird and wonderful industry...access that information net somewhere else in the world, five time zones away...And how are they going to make that an efficient process...it's nonsense.

4.1.1 Summary

Among the users, concern is raised that it is difficult for large companies to find sufficient firms to tender for audit when one of these firms is the current auditor and another might be doing tax, due diligence or valuation work, leaving only two and perhaps one second-tier firm eligible to win a tender. The banking and insurance industry sectors are noted as particularly problematic for competition among audit firms. Several interviewees commented on the difficulty for the smaller firms to compete with the continuing educational input and training that the Big Four can provide. Suggestions for remedy include the creation of boutique, industry-specific audit firms.

4.2 Purchasers

Some among the purchasers felt that competition in the market for audit services was quite adequate and that, for large-company audits, the presence of four large audit firms was sufficient, with scope to use the non-Big Four for specific advice, as exemplified in the following quotes.

> [W]e've got four key firms, obviously large firms that we'll go to... that will provide decent enough competition...for us...So, I'm... okay with that...from a competitive perspective...From an audit perspective at the big end of town, you've got the big firms there.

> [B]ecause I've got an auditor, what it unfortunately means is the auditor can't give me advice on various bits and pieces that I need. So then the only thing about that is it comes down to your comment earlier about the fact that some of the small firms, and I have gone down to small firms...to get particular advice. In fact when there have been conflicts with any of the big guys and I've...found that you can get good advice because essentially you're not looking for a big audit team to come and do a big audit.

> [F]our is competitive enough...they're big...they're scaleable enough and you don't want too many because then you...come back to the situation...we had...where...too much competition tends to cut margins...the quality's better; you don't get competition and you don't lower the standards.

Several people, however, commented on how difficult it was to avoid conflicts of interest with only four big audit firms in the market, and there was concern about the future if another of the large firms did not survive.

> It's becoming a problem…it used to be the big six, and…if it ended up as the big three or the big two…that would be a very major issue…with four we're probably still okay. But…we've got four major banks in Australia, so it would be interesting, and I… don't know who their auditors are, but the concept of one auditor auditing a number of those major banks would be interesting in terms of whether the clients would be happy with that…there's a potential conflict there.

> [Y]ou also need enough scope to be able to have an accounting firm as an auditor, another accounting firm who provides tax advice and maybe a third one that provides other sorts of advice…four's about as tight as it could get and still work effectively. But…it works reasonably well.

> [I]f we had to go out and tender our job out, there'd be enough interest…the other firms would be interested in doing it. I don't think we'd end up with a situation where we just couldn't find people interested in taking on the work. When you get down to three, well it starts to get a little bit tight then. But the other thing I'm not aware of, because I don't follow it closely enough, is the extent to which some of the second-tier firms are starting to try and ramp up a little bit to fill that gap.

The insight the next purchaser offers is that requests for a partner change can occur:

> [I]f we have a problem with [one of the Big Four], we could always ask for the partner to be changed. And that's a high degree of influence.

The next purchaser identifies competition in advice in international tax as a problem area:

> Where…we are finding there is very little competition is in specialised tax areas—for example, international tax. This is not really an auditing question; this is an ancillary thing…This is where the Australian Tax Office and other jurisdictions have made the…

> international tax so complex and so specialised that you haven't got a hope…[of] doing it on your own. You absolutely have to work with advice and because of the nature of it, there [are] probably only two or three companies that can do it and each company will probably only have two or three people involved in it and they're charging like wounded bulls. It's just awful…[and] there's not the market for competition because it's so specialised and it's very, very difficult…But in terms of straight audit, fine…there's quite sufficient competition in the market.
>
> The trouble is that in the last six months so many of the smaller–medium ones have been swallowed up by the big guys…and you look at letters in the mail, off and on, just saying from partners of small firms that now…we've been taken over…we've joined as partners with XY and Z and now we can bring you…all of these other services, which we couldn't bring you in the past.

The next purchaser points to the mobility of audit partners:

> [W]hat you are seeing is the firms getting smarter around… transferring and recognising global accounts. So you might end up with a partner that comes from the US or comes from the UK for a period. I don't see that as something that's out of the question. However, in Australia, I don't know whether we're necessarily big enough to attract quality ones from those markets. But… competition really rests in the individual partner, and that's about the only thing you can really tie it down to, because in terms of a process and methodology, they're all the same.

One purchaser sees so little competition that nationalising the auditing function is 'just one step away':

> I believe we're about one step away from nationalising auditing… there isn't any competition really, [there is] no differentiation, so why not just make it one and it's the government? And the regulator's frustrated with the quality of audit, so why doesn't the government take it on? That's the sort of way you're tending. If you look five years down the track, 10 years down the track, with all this tension that's going on…I can see nationalisation is a real—not a threat, it's probably the wrong word. It may be an outcome.

If you've got your regulations set such that your auditors can't provide consulting services, certain tax services and so on, you already need to have a relationship with two of the four. You're down to three and it...just makes it hard. The same people are going to be doing the work for everyone.

The concentration of the profession's gone too far... we'd be better off if we had maybe six firms, and one of the reasons for that is [that] when you get involved in significant corporate transactions, often there [are] not enough firms to enable you to have someone acting independently for you. I've been involved in transactions where individual firms are acting on both sides of the transaction. So we talk about having the need for independence and confidentiality and getting proper advice, but it's simply [that] you can't do it. And everybody says: 'Oh, we'll have our Chinese walls', but...you've got hundreds of millions of dollars riding on a transaction, how much do you want to trust that some guy in one of the firms is not going to talk to the guy in the office next door to him because he said he's got a Chinese wall?

'I've been involved in transactions where individual firms are acting on both sides of the transaction.'

[T]hat stuff's been going on for [the] 30 years that I've been involved in the profession and it goes in cycles. The big firms think they're going to get into smaller clients and grow them into big clients and the smaller firms want to hang on to their clients that are growing and they aspire to [do] the big accounts, but invariably it's the margin. And the way to test that is you have a look at an analysis of the auditors of the top-100 companies, effectively now and 10 years ago, [and] let's see how much difference there is in the type of firm doing the audits.

[T]he trend typically in commerce [is] organisations get bigger, not...fragment to be smaller, and that's happening at the company level as well as at the accounting services level. It's also happening in the legal fraternity. The legal firms are consolidating and getting bigger, as are the accounting firms, as are the financial advisors in the investment community. That's the trend.

Several interviewees expressed the sentiment that the market would not cope with the failure of another of the Big Four and one commented on the problem that presented for regulators.

> [I]t's just the nature of where society's heading…with the way it's consolidating…[H]ave a look at the amount of products on the supermarket store now—that's shrinking, isn't it? That'll keep shrinking…you'll have less diversity…whether you have four or five firms…[Y]es, an extra one perhaps would be better. The collapse of Andersen's…it shakes everyone for a while; everyone's on their toes for five years, 10 years, and then does it drop off again until there's another shake? And then is it just a cyclical type of an arena that we're in?

> [F]or a run of the mill corporate company, medium to small scale, there's really no issue because there are lots of auditors you can go to out in your local suburb…to get it done, but at the higher end of the scale, if you're in global markets and if you're in a large listed company, especially with overseas ambitions or any connections offshore…you don't have much choice but to use the large top three or four firms, which are internationally recognised. Only because, if you use one of the smaller ones, which are very local perhaps, or which are only recognised, say, in Sydney or Melbourne or in Australia, that level of confidence…and dealing with overseas banks, [and] overseas stakeholders…becomes that much more difficult.

Some speculated that two or more of the non-Big Four might step in by merging if another of the Big Four was to collapse.

> Andersen's going down was a big wake-up call to a lot of people. But there again, the market always corrects itself too, so…if one of the current Big Four were to go under—like an Andersen's, EY obviously picked up Andersen's and brought them into the fold—would one of the remaining three be big enough to pick up a Deloittes, let's say…and bring them into the fold, or would one of the second tiers, a PKF or…an RSM Bird…would they just come in and all of a sudden they become a Big Four, because they take over part of Deloittes? It may not happen overnight, but in two or three years one…of the second tiers might step up and become one of the so-called Big Four.

One interesting comment relates to the double standard applied to the financial reporting of the auditing firms themselves compared with what is required of incorporated entities.

> '[T]he worst joke of all is [that] for all the disclosures that the Big Four firms and all the accounting firms support on AIFRS, none of them publicly report[s] their results.'

> It is an absolute joke and the worst joke of all is [that] for all the disclosures that...the Big Four firms and all the accounting firms support on AIFRS, none of them publicly report[s] their results. None of them [is] subject to the same level of scrutiny that's inflicted on their clients. What a joke. And they should be. Do you know why they should be? Because in substance, as far as ASIC and the SEC and the others are concerned, they are the outsourced regulators to a large extent. Think about the opinions and work that they render, which is a material part of what ASIC or the ASX or other regulators would depend on...And you cannot afford for one of them to fail. We're locked into four now. You have no view of their solvency or their financial [viability]. You have nothing. [It's] the ultimate hypocrisy.

4.2.1 Summary

Purchasers are generally, but not unanimously concerned about insufficient competition in the market for audit services, although they comment on international tax being more of a problem than audit. Their solutions to the audit competition concern include using the non-Big Four for a specific type of advice if conflicts arise in using a Big Four firm and asking for an audit partner to be changed if this is needed. Often the comment is made that it would be better to have six rather than four big firms, but this could be because some of the more senior interviewees still have fresh memories of there being six or more firms. Purchasers recognise the trend to consolidate and grow, perhaps because it is so common in their own sector. The failure of Andersen is commented on as a wake-up call to the profession with the implication being that it was not necessarily a bad thing.

4.3 Suppliers

Interviewees from the supplier group frequently commented on how competitive the market was, even among the Big Four. Some typical comments follow.

[I]n the top ASX 100, there [are] three firms that are serious, but... that's probably enough and...from our point of view, it always seems to be enough. It was seen to be a hard-fought battle whether you win, lose, come second, first, second or third. It always seems to be a pretty close call, so...there probably is enough.

[E]very audit tender that we participate in is highly competitive. I don't see any fat in the margins; I see tenders being very competitive, prices being incredibly tight and those are the characteristics of a highly competitive market...there is probably a view around certain companies and directors that there is a limiting choice in that they feel that there are only four and they can only choose out of the Big Four if they're a large listed entity. But...is there competition? Absolutely. And what some of the top 100 might feel if they were limited to four...certainly some of the smaller listers, there is still a range of firms that they can choose from.

I find it very difficult to go below four...we're finding with some of the larger organisations that use all four in different capacities—tax, internal audit, external audit and maybe valuation and advisory—that they're at the limit...at times...they can't find anybody, any of the four or they might find one of the four that's independent or not conflicted and that gives them a limit of choice—[of] that there's no doubt. So I don't think that we could ever get to...three unless it happened through one of the existing Big Four going down the Andersen's path, which...I'm not sure that's going to happen. So is there enough competition? Probably just enough, because...I've participated on a lot of tenders and they're still very price competitive...so it's still...competitive in terms of value and providing a top-notch service. I don't think there's complacency or anybody that would say that we've got a monopoly.

> 'You really always want to have one at least outside and hungry to come in if you want to maintain your position, and...[there is] probably one too few.'

It's less of an issue...from an auditor's perspective. It's more of an issue [for] the other services, because, depending on the board's view of independence and multiple service providers, once you've got, let's say, Ernst & Young as the auditor and you might have someone else as your tax advisor, if you want to do a deal...not that many people are finance providers. You, almost by default...if you're a decent size organisation, end up using all four of the Big Four. You really always want to have one at least outside and hungry to come in if you want to maintain your position, and...[there is] probably one too few...I don't have a resolution [for] that and I can't see how that could work in the short term. I can't see how you could build one.

In terms of the competition...you look at it at two levels. One, at a general level: are there enough firms? I'd like Deloittes to be stronger. I'd like it to be a Big Four in Australia...the difficulty is [that] by the time you've...driven with independence, you use one firm to be your auditors, another firm to do something else. If you want to do something else, you're left with a choice of one or two, plus the broader specialists; it's quite narrow...when you get below that in particular industries then you find that the competition becomes tighter. You might find it's a competition between only two, which...is not always helpful.

The trouble with some of the competition at the moment [is]...the Big Four are the world's least successful cartel in terms of prices and all that sort of stuff...we're cutting our throats left, right and centre, which...is another topic, but [it] isn't helpful competition, because it makes it very difficult to attract and retain the good staff when you're doing big jobs at a huge discount because you need to secure your mark in the audit space, in the market...[T]hat competition is unhelpful, but...if it went down to three, we'd have a real problem...four's a good number. Five or six—I don't think you need six. I don't think you need five.

'[I]t makes it very difficult to attract and retain the good staff when you're doing big jobs at a huge discount because you need to secure your mark in the audit space.'

[I]f you say, 'Our auditors need to be independent'...that's one firm [down], we then want to have tax advice and strategic advice and maybe that is another sort, and then you have a third firm that maybe does the other services. Now if there are only four for a multinational and then...you start to rotate audit, that then is complex to manage.

Structural shifts in the market were also commented on, with the Big Four setting up separate sections with lower cost structures to penetrate the smaller-company markets and the non-Big Four and the smallest of the Big Four consolidating. Illustrative comments include:

[T]here's a huge amount of competition, particularly within second-tier firms. The competition in the top-200 listed companies, which is the domain of the Big Four, is absolutely intense, and because of the rotational nature of auditors…that competition is starting to spill into the second tier. And the Big Four now are reducing their prices substantially to try to knock people like ourselves off. So… the audit profession is subject to intensifying cost pressures…that's a bad thing because it just leads to shortcuts and a lowering of the standards…We're finding it more and more difficult and more and more competitive to win jobs because of the Big Four coming into our space.

'The mid-tier are going up a little bit more and the Big Four are coming down a little bit more.'

I think it's going both ways…the mid-tiers are penetrating a bit up into what was traditionally a Big Four-only zone…there's a level of…audit clients that will always be Big Four because they're just too big for the mid-tier, the mid-tier just can't service them. And whilst…just about all of the mid-tier firms around Australia are generally federated models… they're individual[ly] owned…there's a bit of movement in that at the moment in integration, but until they're… fully integrated, their ability to…service those really large national clients is just not there. And they will always be the domain of the Big Four. So then there becomes that kind of grey area in between, where they've either been previously serviced by the Big Four or by the mid-tier. And…what you're seeing is it's a bit of both: the mid-tier are going up a little bit more and the Big Four are coming down a little bit more.

[W]e do undersell ourselves because the risks are getting higher. We're required to do more work in fraud and regulatory compliance and the quality control and all the rest of it. So we should be charging premium rates, but we're not as a market. So you'd have to say it's competitive because if it wasn't competitive…audit fees [would double] overnight, and the companies would just have to pay. But it is competitive and therefore it's key keeping audit fees at a more moderate level…the big firms have now all got their mid-market groups, which is really trying to compete [in] the market that's been the mid-tier…interestingly enough, the write-offs that they experience on that work are huge. And they're undercutting mid-tier firms…for instance, my charge rates would be probably 30 per cent less than the Big Four, so you'd think that I'd have a distinct advantage. But when you're putting in a tender for a reasonable client and you find your competition [is] one of the mid-tier divisions of the Big Four, they'll quite often undercut you.

[W]e take clients off the Big Four ourselves. We've taken clients obviously off a lot of other mid-tier firms and vice versa. In many respects, we're all swimming in the same pool. And the Big Four on the one hand are keen to drill down very much to the SME market and that's why Ernst & Young have got their enterprise section, which is specifically designed to take on smaller clients. It's almost a Jet Star operation to Qantas, it really is. And Deloittes have also got a Jet Star operation, so they're using different charge-out rates… It's a completely different cost base.

The next supplier observes intense competition at the point in the market for which the Big Four and the non-Big Four compete:

[W]e've got…a bit of a scramble among the mid-tiers in Australia to get themselves to the size that they can take on these bigger audits. And then you've got this competing irony of the Big Four… coming down into SME level because there's not enough work for them at the top end. And there's not enough work for them at the top end partly because they've had to hive off their management consulting divisions. So they're going 'What else are we going to do?'…then you've got Baring Point and all these other businesses out there, which are taking work off the Big Four. So the Big Four are having to compete in other ways.

'[Y]ou've got this competing irony of the Big Four…coming down into SME level because there's not enough work for them at the top end.'

[T]here will be a lot of structural issues for the mid-tier as they continue to merge and they'll have all these corporate culture clashes as they merge…it's not necessarily healthy for the marketplace, but ultimately…we're going to see some, let's…call them 'supersized mid-tier' firms…after that then there'll be a distinct third tier. That's the way it's going.

[They do so] at their peril though, because they will target a larger client, but…they may be at risk of providing poor service to some of their own clients. And the middle-market, mid-tier firms have picked [up] a fairly large number of audits from the Big Four for that reason. So it works both ways. But there is competition from the Big Four too for our larger clients, yes.

'[W]e've had enough of the fees and we don't see what value we get out of being with the Big Four.'

[T]he Big Four have got their limitations. They cannot service certain clients because the overlay of the way they do things is just too costly and...they get to a certain level and they can't afford to do those audits any longer. Or if [they] are doing them, their fee quotes are so high that those clients are dropping down into the mid-tier...And I'm seeing a lot of that happening lately. We're quoting a lot of jobs which were previously Big Four clients...they've just said, 'Look, we've had enough of the fees and we don't see what value we get out of being with the Big Four.' So...it's in that grey zone where you're getting all the movement.

One supplier comments on the danger of smaller firms accepting engagements for which they are not equipped:

[N]o-one really wanted Arthur Andersen to go the way that it did. It was pretty horrible, particularly for the people there. Ideally, you'd want more competition, but this is the real world. I don't know how you fix that...the bigger danger at the moment is small firms trying to audit things that they just can't really do.

[P]erhaps you could still do it with four, but...the regulator pushing the way he's pushing means that there is no ability to differentiate. So there's no reason to compete in that space. The only reason to compete is at the individual level.

Several suppliers commented on the difficulty that would be presented if another of the Big Four failed, and of the moral hazard this would create for regulators.

[F]our's adequate. Obviously, it would be better with more firms. To service those type of clients you've got to have the resources, you've got to have the expertise. So I don't see it as a huge issue at the moment. You wouldn't want one of those firms to merge or disappear.

The theme emerging from the next quote is that some good might have emerged from Andersen's collapse:

> Absolutely—far too much competition in the marketplace from our point of view...the Andersen's one, it's very regrettable that we lost that firm...and I feel dreadful for the 95 per cent of people who were doing the right thing in that firm, but there were some not good things going on, allegedly. And if it was the collapse of a firm that needed to bring that out and get houses put in order, and sort out anything that wasn't right that was happening in the other firms, then that's good that comes out of bad.

The theme of the next and subsequent comments is that three large firms would simply be insufficient:

> [F]our is probably still okay. The concern I would have is, is any regulator around the world going to put another one down if something happens, because we can't have three.

> [I]f you take the Andersen example...it was proved that they didn't have a case...the case went away three years afterwards, but because of the action taken, that firm went down pretty quickly. If that was to happen again, would any regulator...do that? Because what are you going to do, are you going to knock another firm over and only have three? That...starts to become a problem. And the problem with that is that the one that goes down will go to the other three, which will make them even bigger, which makes the gap between them and the next level even bigger. So you're miles away from ever getting another one joining...there's a big gap now, but the more you take one out, the top one isn't going to splinter and go into these little ones to create another one. It's going to go to three big ones.

'[T]he one that goes down will go to the other three, which will make them even bigger, which makes the gap between them and the next level even bigger.'

> [T]he number's okay, but the concern would be [whether] a regulator somewhere [is] going...to be able to act as they would act and... put another one down, if it came to that because of the particular circumstances?

The next supplier comments on the increasing barriers to entry:

> [T]he risk profile, the cost of audit, PI insurance, the fallout [are]... making it harder and harder, and all this regulation that's been put on to the profession is making it harder for some of the smaller firms to...be in audit...you'll find at the bottom end of the market there would be a lot of smaller firms who are...getting out of doing audits because the cost of...being accredited, the cost of running the appropriate quality-control systems, the cost of managing the regulator just doesn't make it an efficient business model for them.

Perceptions of the role of regulators in driving the Big Four market are obvious too, as exemplified in the following quote:

> [T]here's reasonable competition, but it's stratified. In other words, any big listed company is going to go to the Big Four...the mid-listed and even smaller are going to be comfortable with a mid-tier firm, but once they get [to] a certain size then they're naturally going to go to the Big Four...There's certainly a lot more competition at the mid-tier level with the size of the firms, but...in the back of my mind [I] get the feeling that ASIC thinks that all listed companies probably should be done by the Big Four, and...that's a silly approach to have. And I'd say who have been the auditors of the major corporate collapses? It's the Big Four.

> [I]f somehow those smaller firms were able to package their product and enter into some sort of agreement with each other, it would maybe go somewhere towards it, but that's the only solution I can think of.

4.3.1 Summary

Suppliers, both Big Four and non-Big Four, tend to see the market as very competitive—so competitive that despite increasing cost pressures, audit pricing is seen as cutthroat. Non-Big Four suppliers see the increasing penetration of SME divisions of the Big Four into the smaller-company market as a relatively new phenomenon designed to take market share from them. They tend to see this as a new business model on the part of the Big Four pitched at capturing both premium paying audits and the next tier of more price sensitive audits. At the same time, the mid-tier firms are seen to be competing heavily for smaller listed clients with the Big Four. A perception emerges from the interviews with suppliers of convergence of Big Four competition penetrating from the larger clients towards midsize clients and of non-Big Four competition penetrating from the small to mid-sized clients towards larger clients. At the point in the market where these two forces overlap, it can be expected that clients are experiencing exceptionally heavy competition for their custom. Additionally, at the lower end of suppliers, there is a view that more of these firms are ceasing to supply audit services. A view is expressed that it is due to constraints on the supply of non-audit services to clients that the Big Four has been driven to seek market share elsewhere.

On another theme, several suppliers comment on the moral hazard problem for regulators should another of the large international audit firms fail in the way of Andersen. The sentiment seems to be that four major firms is just enough, but a reduction to three would severely stress the market in the view of the suppliers.

4.4 Standard setters

One of the standard setters pointed out the need to be clear about defining the lens through which competition was viewed; was it just the Australian market for audit services or the global market, was it on an industry basis or total market basis and was it just audit services or the wider assurance market that should be assessed in terms of competition? While defining the scope of the market was important, most of the standard setter group responses looked only to the Australian market for audit services and, as with the users, purchasers and suppliers, most comments were reflective of a high degree of competition in that market, but some concern was expressed about the lack of choice between the Big Four in certain situations where potential conflicts existed.

> It's quite fierce competition...all auditors are quite proud of the quality of the service and the audit they do and they're taking it from the point of view of...providing that assurance service to the best of their ability for the clients so that the clients get value for undertaking the audit. So it is quite a competitive marketplace... in certain areas, they always do overlap...so in that area [there will] be competition, but...in the mid-tier, the competition doesn't alter whether the Big Four are involved or other mid-tier firms...in other words, we find there's just as much competition if an assignment comes up and there's only mid-tier people who are going for it as well as...a situation where there's mid-tier plus Big Four. It's always competitive and...it always has been and probably always will be

and I don't know whether the merging of firms in the mid-tier will lessen the competition. It might be one or two of them probably and they will perceive greater advantage and that would be about the difference.

The next standard setter comments on the fact that often the choice even among the Big Four is restricted:

> '[T]he choice in a practical sense comes down to one out of two because of different factors that might be present.'

[I]f you look at some of the regulator requirements around the number of previous members of firms that can be on boards or in financial reporting roles, as the US rules set them, in clients, means that there may often be a firm precluded for whatever reason. And similarly, if there may be a particular service that is incompatible with an audit being provided by a firm then you've got another firm perhaps knocked out, so you've got a choice of two...[P]eople feel perhaps locked in and I've heard that many, many times—that the choice in a practical sense comes down to one out of two because of different factors that might be present. Sometimes those issues have come about through entities...creating a rod for their own back through...interpretation very narrowly of what is or isn't compatible with conducting an audit. So you've got policies that just say [that] dealing with...any tax matters are incompatible, et cetera. So, if you've only got four to start with, it's not hard to knock out two and...that's where there might be limited choice. But looking at it from the point of view of a partner and a Big Four audit firm, when audits are put out to tender, it is very, very rare to see the...outcome of that tender not result in a lower fee. So, what does that tell you about competition?

Restricted choice is the theme of this next quotation, too:

[W]e don't have a monopoly or even an effective oligopoly because... the concentration's [not] here. So there's competition when it comes to fees when this work comes up, but you've probably got limited choice. At best, you'd be choosing one out of four for skill sets generally...and probably one out of two in a lot of instances.

A standard setter alludes to the gap between the third and fourth of the Big Four:

> [At] the large end of town...there is real concern about there only being four firms, and that even in a market of the Australian context there are not enough providers, and there's such a gap between... even three and four, let alone four to five, six, let alone further down. So further consolidation to the extent of trying to perhaps have fifth and sixth alternatives that are larger would be desirable.

Among standard setters, some interesting comments were made about the role of regulation in relation to price pressures.

> [W]hat's driven [price pressure] has been external pressures, rather than necessarily what the profession has done. I don't think price pressures ever completely go away...they will reappear more strongly in the coming period than they have been in the last few years. It's been because of the responses to the failures and the additional requirements put not just directly on auditors, but... pressures that have been put on, directly and indirectly, directors that have been a big part of those changes.

In terms of keeping the market competitive, the following comment from one of the standard setters advocates systematic testing of the market at a time aligned with the signing audit partner rotation requirement:

> There is always price pressure. You...can't escape that. There is still tendering happening in the marketplace and...[there] always will be and it's in the listed company environment, which is where the big firms really want to focus their audit practices. Audit partners rotate every five years, so companies are starting to accept [that] they have a five-year change in relationship. Well, if you're going to have that change, perhaps we build in a five-year testing of the market as well so there will always be competitive pressures.

One interesting comment compared the recent competitive pricing pressure with that when audit tendering first became common in the 1980s, reflecting that the pressure to keep costs low was now coming from the purchasing side rather than the supplier side.

> [L]et's say that we go back to the '80s where we went through that...tender process. A lot of audits [were] put out to tender, a lot of fees [were] cut. Arguably, that was done at a time where firms were buying audits because they could provide other services. So we're in a slightly different environment, but what they might be

> doing this time is building a bigger base with a view of taking out competition...it was the profession last time that probably...created that tender situation, with some firms going out and aggressively buying work...you'd probably see it more from the corporates this time round, trying to lower their costs...the issue then is, is there sufficient competition in the market...Audits have invested in these large corporates what is a tiered-type approach and delivery of service...there probably is sufficient competition...what will happen is the definition of quality will change because the regulator will form a view and an assessment of what it believes is quality and nine-tenths of reality is perception and if that's plastered all over the reports, the papers and whatever else then presumably that will have some effect.

Several comments reflected the difficulty of creating more firms truly able to compete in terms of the availability of skilled personnel and of building sufficient scale.

> [There are] only a certain number of firms in the marketplace, but there [are] only a certain number of skilled people in the marketplace. So if there were more firms, those people would be spread across more firms. It doesn't mean there [are] less skills available to you, but it may mean that you have a better framework for engaging those skills if you've got more competition. So now if you can access skills from five, six, seven, eight good firms then...that's definitely healthier and definitely better for you as an organisation than being tied to two, three or four.

The difficulty in ensuring a supply of appropriately skilled staff before engagements are won is alluded to in this next quotation:

> [E]conomically, that will be tough for [the non-Big Four] to compete with the Big Four for skills...In other words, [to] pay the money they need to pay [to attract staff] before they get the jobs to support it. That's not a catch-22...in the Big Four; it's not quite like it used to be in that a partner could leave and take no clients. These days, you engage the firm more than the partner. So if you wanted to attract a consolidated middle-tier firm wanting to attract skills from one of the Big Four, they're not likely to necessarily acquire clients that way.

> [C]onsolidation of middle tier might be one [way to create more competition]. You're not going to increase competition through new entrants to the market...It couldn't have the scale.

The difficulty of building scale by having staff break away from one of the existing firms is pointed to in this next quotation:

> You won't find people breaking off...to do a general audit practice. It's possible. It's happened in the past, but they haven't really built the scale and the trouble is, to do it and build scale, you could build scale in an industry space. Build scale across the board, no, it would be very tough.

That there has already been a close call with regulators for at least one of the Big Four firms since the Andersen collapse is the point of this next quotation:

> Four is trying to gollop up bits of five and six, or five, six and seven, or however it plays out...to play catch-up. So...that's unrealistic for all that it might be seen to be desirable. It was a terrifying prospect that you might've had some serious damage done to [one of the Big Four] in the US so soon after the Arthur Andersen debacle and that was even seriously contemplated. You wonder if sometimes the regulators learn anything from their past transgressions.

Other appropriate courses of action beyond bringing an auditing firm down exist in the case of transgressions and should be explored, which is the subject of this next quotation:

> I would...agree that a regulator, the last thing they could afford to do would be to put down one of the Big Four. So in other words, that...does have some ramifications as to how the situation got treated, but...I don't think the process of bringing down a Big Four is really...they're losing sight of what the reality of the situation is. That was just sensationalism, maybe from the regulator's point of view. I don't think that really achieves what you want and there are other ways of doing it without effectively destroying a firm...the thing is...people need to be more aware of what is an appropriate course of action in that area...I don't see it happening as much now...people are a bit more aware of what the obligations are and there'll be other more appropriate courses of action taken.

In terms of potential ways to increase competition, ideas included allowing other organisations (for example, legal firms) to undertake audits and mergers between two or more of the non-Big Four:

> [A]nother way to increase competition in the market...is to allow other people to do audits...I don't think we really want to go there, but...do you allow other types of organisations to do audits? Then you can increase your choice. But who those would be? They've got to be qualified accountants, certified, registered company auditors...I don't know that they exist.
>
> Could a legal firm set up an audit division...it's a left-field thing. I don't see why not. Make your professional services fit.

A standard setter muses about how some of the non-Big Four might build scale to create a firm to rival the Big Four:

'There's always the catch-22 [with]...industry specialisations because you can't get the experience and the skill without the jobs, and you can't get the jobs without the experience and the skill.'

> Is it a bit like the four banks and the two supermarkets because it's what barriers to entry are...you're not going to break the Big Four up—not that I can see. So how do other players in the market become more competitive in their space in terms of building scale...the ways of doing it would be consolidation of the middle tier into two or three super audit firms, which is a possibility, but people like Grant Thornton, BDOs, PKFs have been trying to do that. You could put two of those together, a Grant Thornton and a BDO...Grant Thornton are quite big in the UK and the States and they're generally number five behind the Big Four. So if you got mergers of number five and six or five and seven...then you might get more serious. There's always the catch-22 [with]...industry specialisations because you can't get the experience and the skill without the jobs, and you can't get the jobs without the experience and the skill...so if you're going to create more competition by merging middle-tier firms then they've got to start attracting talent from the other Big Four to get the skills to enable them to compete.

4.4.1 Summary

Standard setters leave little doubt that in their opinion competition has historically been and remains fierce in the market for audit services, whether it be within the Big Four or between the Big Four and non-Big Four. Further, there is a view that current attempts by the mid-tier firms to grow naturally or through acquisitions will not impair competition, although the supply of skilled labour is seen as a constraint on growth. Nevertheless, standard setters acknowledge the lack of choice for companies in need of large, international audit firms. Standard setters, several of whom are also suppliers, comment on the exacerbation of this situation by companies that constrain their own choice, perhaps overly conservatively, because of perceived independence or potential conflicts that might arise in purchasing joint supply of audit and non-audit services. Such a large gap between the third and fourth of the Big Four firms and then between fourth and fifth is seen as not generally desirable, but difficult to change. Standard setters acknowledge the delicate balancing act for regulators between maintaining competition and effectively monitoring and acting on any transgression by any of the Big Four.

4.5 Regulators

One interviewee from the regulator group commented on how difficult it would be if another of the Big Four did not survive.

> A classic [example] was [one of the Big Four] in Japan...which 'failed', and one of the ramifications that came out of that was [that] even though [this firm] was suspended, there was a concession given so they could...get back to doing audits for a period because...the financial system couldn't work otherwise.

5.0 Issues and implications

Overall, among users, purchasers, suppliers, regulators and standard setters, there are few concerns expressed about the amount of competition either between the Big Four and non-Big Four or within these sectors. There are interviewees within each group, however, who express concern about the paucity of choice for large corporations, or those with extensive international structures, among the Big Four and fears for what will happen if one of the Big Four does not survive. Other comments are made about the difficulty of attracting a sufficient number of skilled audit personnel if an expansion or merger of the non-Big Four is used as a vehicle to create a true addition to the top tier of suppliers, and the difficulty of building scale if personnel within the Big Four break away.

A significant number of users believe that with only four major audit firms there is a lack of competition. Observations were made that once one had Big Four suppliers in certain tax and valuation work, there remained perhaps one or two outside the group that would comprise the competitive field for an audit engagement. Users also observe that for a significant portion of the market, the Big Four are really the only potential suppliers, and certain investors seek out and give preference to global brand names such as the Big Four. One user makes the observation that the sheer scale of the Big Four is an advantage not matched by the smaller firms and, in particular, the scale provides the opportunity for training and skill development, which in turn means that there is a lack of competition and potential dominance and even market control by a small number of players. This in turn could indicate that the quality levels are dictated by a small number of firms.

Purchasers are more mixed in their views and make observations that are both positive and negative with respect to the presence of competition. A positive view expressed by some purchasers is that the quality of the non-Big Four suppliers in Australia is such that one can turn to them for specific advice on certain matters, which makes the potential field for audit suppliers, even if one is restricted to the Big Four, more competitive. Other purchasers believe that the Big Four for the big end of town are sufficiently competitive and there are several observations that there is significant competition in Australia once one looks beyond the larger ASX-listed companies.

One of the more complex observations is that too much competition has the effect of driving down quality; however, this comment makes evident the dilemma that some users believe is present in which too much competition drives down quality while the purchasers suggest that too many purchasers drive down quality. Finding the appropriate number seems to be difficult if not impossible. Other purchasers observe that in Australia there is no sense of market failure at the larger end of town. There always seems to be someone able to take on the audit and execute it to the satisfaction of the purchaser. Other purchasers suggest that for some services the non-Big Four are stepping up and becoming more competitive. There is a notion across a large number of purchasers that, at the margins, between the Big Four and the non-Big Four, there is considerable competition, with the Big Four establishing 'enterprise' or 'middle-market' divisions that compete fiercely with non-Big Four firms—particularly with respect to price.

Another feature of this middle ground is that members of the Big Four are seeking to integrate into their practices some components of the non-Big Four firms; this in turn lowers competition. While some purchasers believe that the market for audit services has normal market self-correcting mechanisms, there are other observations suggesting that the sheer scale of suppliers in the market for audit services signifies that structurally it is hard to see how a large audit firm can develop through natural market forces.

While there is some scepticism of the present circumstance and indeed one observer suggests that we have so little competition that we could give consideration to the nationalisation of the audit industry, there is an observation that much competition exists, particularly at partner rather than firm level. Indeed it is observed that the Big Four have such a global presence that they have the ability to move partners around even from outside Australia in order to provide competitive service to clients on a qualitative basis rather than just looking at competition on a fee basis.

Suppliers from the Big Four and the non-Big Four firms are quite vocal on the issue of competition. Several suppliers make the observation that there is quite extreme price competition and every time an ASX-listed company comes up for tender, the battle is intense. There are repeated suggestions of very tight margins and considerable fee pressure.

Frequently, suppliers suggest that competition for all but the very largest of clients is intense from a number of alternative suppliers. On the other hand, suppliers recognise that purchasers feel that at the upper end the amount of choice available is limited. Similarly, one senior member of the profession representing a supplier perceives that for one to have a market in which there is seen to be competition, that competition can be generated where a large listed company might have an inner circle of three of the Big Four in one way or another, but must have one not supplying it. That is, if one of the Big Four is outside this inner supply circle then there will be some degree of hunger and interest to enter it.

Several suppliers observe that for some clients Australia effectively has a market comprising three rather than four large suppliers and that some of the behaviours of the fourth-largest supplier in Australia involve the integration of some parts of the middle-tier suppliers.

Suppliers also recognise that some of the mid-tier are moving up and some of the Big Four activity is moving down into smaller audit purchasers.

There is also a belief that structurally it will be hard to see another big player in the audit supply market. Perhaps one of the only feasible ways would be to have an integration of two of the mid-tier firms on a national or even global level. The probability of that happening is not high.

One supplier suggests that the presence of the Big Four with work divisions that cater for middle-market clients effectively creates a second brand name for the Big Four, with potentially different standards of quality and cost structure.

Other suppliers indicate that, in fact, the Big Four are ending up competing with firms in non-audit work areas that were once part of their parent organisations. The presence of these consulting firms competing in some of the areas in which the Big Four are working has meant there is less work for the Big Four, which in turn places pressure on all parts of the organisation, including on staff retention (refer to Chapter 8) and the ability to interchange between audit and non-audit work.

If indeed there is to be a further large supplier, it will imply some degree of merger activity and all the costs and difficulties involved with mergers.

While some suppliers acknowledge that the presence of more competition would be healthy, one effect would be that some firms engaging in audits might not have the expertise or skill set to undertake them. The potential costs to the economy of this possible quality issue could be significant. Other suppliers express concern that the regulatory environment and the expectations of the standards of quality for audits have meant that some suppliers are moving out of the market, thereby lowering competition. Related to that is the issue that the level of regulation has meant that the ability of each Big Four firm to differentiate itself on quality terms from other members of the Big Four is limited and in fact the quality differentiation comes at partner not at firm level. This represents a challenge due to mandated audit partner rotation requirements (refer to Chapter 11).

Several comments from suppliers discuss other aspects of regulation and how the regulatory environment has in fact been changed by the relatively small number of large audit suppliers. Specifically, one comment was that the Arthur Andersen collapse presented a shock to the system relating to audit quality and had therefore reinforced a message throughout all of the remaining large suppliers that quality was important and minimum quality standards needed to be maintained. Additionally, there are repeated comments that the presence of one failure of an audit firm has meant that regulators struggle to ensure the non-recurrence of the collapse of another accounting firm. Put bluntly, there is a moral hazard for regulators. If they do find reason to make another audit firm not commercially viable, the number of large suppliers will be restricted even further. One specific comment was that if another firm went down then the staff and clients of that one firm within the Big Four would probably reposition in the remainder of the Big Four, making a Big Three and extending the gap between that larger audit firm group and the next tier. As economic circumstances adjust with the global financial crisis, the potential moral hazard might be more real—at least in some jurisdictions around the world.

There is a common belief that competition, particularly at the mid-tier level in the audit market, is intense but recognition also at the larger end of corporate Australia that there is more limited choice. Limited choice, however, is not seen to be having an effect on the existing intense fee competition, at least in much of the market where interviewee organisations are represented. Additionally, there are repeated observations about the substantial gap between the Big Four suppliers and others and the fact that the number of providers is limited. Another observation relates to the presence of partner rotation and the fact that this might inject behaviour into the market in which audit partners are rotated every five years, then auditees might seek to 'test' the market each five years or so, as the relationship with the incumbent auditor is forced to change anyway through rotation.

One standard setter also observed that, in the 1980s, audit firm fee competition was intense and initiated essentially by the audit firm in order to win consulting activity. Through regulatory change, this is now not possible, but there is still considerable price pressure in fees, driven this time by clients rather than audit firms. Their motivation appears to be the desire for cost efficiencies.

Another observation by a standard setter is that although there are a limited number of larger firms, there are also a limited number of skilled individuals working within the entire market. A structural situation in which there are more firms and those skilled individuals are more evenly spread gives more potential to access the right people. Certain regulators also recognise there is a moral hazard with respect to the behaviour of the existing Big Four and a need to be careful not to downsize the number of large players. When asked how the number of large suppliers could be increased, there were several creative suggestions, but in reality the likelihood of this happening was seen as relatively modest. Also, there was an observation of something akin to a 'catch-22' situation in that an audit firm needed to have the 'right' clients to develop the appropriate skills sets but also required the appropriate skills sets to gain the 'right' clients.

One regulator made the observation that the moral hazard problem already existed and had already occurred in Asia: while one firm was subject to regulatory sanction, sufficient concessions were given so that it continued to trade.

The remaining quandary is that despite the presence of sometimes intense competition, the majority of purchasers do not currently see financial statement audits as a value-for-money service provided to the market.

6.0 Concluding remarks

While sensitivity exists, particularly around the big market capitalisation levels, there is not inconsiderable evidence of the presence of competition in the market for audit services. This competition exists with respect to the quality of differentiated products and also to prices.

In terms of public policy matters, there is an issue that we have not been able to resolve about whether the ACCC has jurisdictional rights over a group of partnerships that operate within a particular market within Australia, and clarification on this matter would be useful. If there are regulatory processes to oversee competition, it might be to the advantage of the Australian economy and the efficiency of capital markets in Australia.

Second, there is considerable nervousness among many stakeholders that the number of large-end suppliers (repeatedly viewed as the Big

Four, although in some cases in Australia it is seen as the larger three firms of the Big Four) is really the minimum number that makes for a competitive efficient market in the supply side of the market for audit services. The fact that this number seems to be at the very edge of what is acceptable to ensure a competitive and efficient market means that it places the regulator in a position of 'moral hazard'. That is, the regulator has the power to inflict considerable damage on an audit firm such that it might dramatically downsize or even fail (as we have seen with Andersen). This regulatory power may in fact be exerted not only within its own jurisdiction but by other regulators in other jurisdictions, and the consequences could be quite profound for one or other of these Big Four practices within Australia. This places pressure on the regulator, at least the one within their own jurisdiction, to exercise care in their dispensing of penalties or criticisms. If those penalties or criticisms are such that it could cause one of the larger firms to downsize or fail, it could be that the regulator has to pull back to ensure that there remains a minimum number of suppliers in the market.

The second point intertwined above it is that we operate in a global market and even where great care is exercised in managing and monitoring each of the larger Big Four audit suppliers, the effects on the viability of those suppliers could come from jurisdictions outside their own and where they have little control or ability to manage the circumstance. In this case, it seems inevitable that ASIC will need to develop a contingency plan in the event that one or perhaps more of these larger Big Four firms collapses or is not always able to supply audit services in the Australian market. It is possible that ASIC already has this contingency plan in place, but that is not known and we are not able to verify its existence. If it does in fact exist, it is such an important public policy document that it probably should be open to some degree of inspection.

As we know, the importance of having a market for deposit-taking institutions is important in the Australian economy—for economic efficiency and social reasons. The importance of this public policy position is such that a regulatory body, APRA, was created to oversee these institutions. APRA is able to access the financial data to determine the continuing viability of these institutions on a month-to-month basis. Given that we are at the very limit of the large suppliers of audit services, some parallel ability to observe the financial viability of each of those large suppliers in the market for audit services now seems warranted. Unlike many organisations, the Big Four do not publish financial statements and therefore neither the clients nor the market generally are able to make their own assessment about the continuing financial viability of these partnerships. The ability to assess their viability could be an important structural benefit to the Australian economy and would give assurance of the continuing viability of each of these large players. Such a mechanism would be seen as invasive, but it could be conducted on a confidential basis, possibly by ASIC.

The level of competition has been discussed essentially at firm level; however, underlying all of this is the viability of staffing levels and, for our purposes in regard to this chapter in particular, registered company auditors. There is some evidence that this pool of registered company auditors can be divided into those that are genuinely active and those that might be seen as barely active or inactive. The exact number of active registered company auditors is not known to us, but is believed to be ageing and/or shrinking and poses a serious medium to long-term threat to the competitive environment within the market for audit services in Australia. No single body seems to have responsibility for ensuring the viability of this pool of active registered company auditors. This is a matter that could be attended to by the Financial Reporting Council, which has oversight of this general area but not this specific issue. Related to this issue is the ability to assess the competency of the pool of registered company auditors and their capability to in fact actively participate at the relevant level of activity within the market for audit services. A parallel and equally concerning fact is that the APRA-approved auditor pool is also small—perhaps too small—for the tasks it is required to undertake to fulfil the legislative requirements required by APRA. This too is an efficiency matter and has consequences for the efficiency of the state of the capital market.

DIVISION G

DIFFERENTIAL AUDITING STANDARDS 14

> I wouldn't advocate that you make it easier to stay private [unlisted] necessarily because there are other…issues…For the country as a whole, it would be good if more companies did step up to that plate and had access to capital markets…there are stock exchange requirements in terms of continuous disclosure, for example, that already create some differentiation between listed companies and private companies and there are the public requirements of lodging accounts that already create that differential. To differentiate it any more in terms of audit requirements…would be rather dangerous.
> — User

1.0 Key issues

While the issue of differential auditing is one that intermittently elevates in profile, at the time of the interviews, it was prominent. The key issues around this topic include:

- if there are to be differential auditing standards, what is the best basis for differentiation—listed–unlisted, small–large, public–private or some other distinction even within these sectors
- to what extent, if any, would the move from private to public company be discouraged if it involved also moving to a higher level of auditing standards
- how would those dealing with listed and unlisted companies in terms of, for instance, credit worthiness evaluate financial reports audited to different standards
- are calls for differential auditing standards misplaced such that the call should really be for a differential reporting framework incremental to that currently existing

- should cost be a primary driver for decisions about differential auditing standards
- would differential auditing standards add to or detract from the audit expectations gap?

2.0 Introduction

Stakeholders were asked about differential auditing standards in the context of listed versus unlisted companies. Note that this differs between questions on the audit mandate, which go to the issue of whether or not the company is a small proprietary company. Responses, especially from users, sometimes confuse this issue of differential auditing standards and differential mandates. Note also that if there are differential standards for one class of audited entity, there is a need to understand what criteria one uses to create a framework for these differential standards. In the minds of some interviewees, their responses were more about the quality of the audit delivered than the auditing standards and this was based on an assumption that the outcomes were heavily influenced by the standards.

2.1 Users

The notion of differential auditing standards appealed to some users. From a cost point of view, this first user likes the idea; however, there is some confusion evident in terms of differential auditing standards versus differential audit mandates.

> [I]f you've got two different types of businesses—one being a listed business—you've...potentially a number of different stakeholders... and they don't have access to...the reports...like you might do in an unlisted company or private business, where shareholders have probably got more of a say in the running of the business. So...the audit standards over a business which is listed would potentially be a lot more onerous than an unlisted business...it probably would, from a cost point of view, be a fairly...good thing to have. However...trying to keep it all standardised...maybe potentially the audit requirements for a listed company could be clarified a little further, rather than being so complex and changing so often, that they can tend to be confusing...you could potentially have different sets of reporting, because there is a different end user.

A qualified 'yes' to differential auditing standards is received from this next user:

> [Y]ou're basically saying that the non-listed companies should maybe have a bit more relaxed standard because they don't have the capital behind them? Yes, I agree. Especially if the non-listed companies have got a small amount of shareholders and those shareholders might be really close to the company anyway, and the general public isn't being offered equity in there, or...[isn't] able to buy into those non-listed companies, then definitely. But any company that has...a public offer...should keep the same set of auditing standards because you need to [be] able to rely on them. So I guess a yes, but depending on the make-up of the shareholders of that non-listed company.

One user points to the cost burden imposed on entities that are mandated to purchase audits, implying that the status quo of a differential mandate is preferred, without really addressing the notion of differential auditing standards:

> The cost burdens are a bit of a sore point at the moment, but...one of the main points as far as the standard of auditing is concerned is the cost...where do you draw a line? You don't want to have to force some non-listed companies that might not have the financial clout to have...an audit to the extent that it's going to cost them such a large amount of money that it's going to potentially bankrupt them... if the auditing standards are set across the board then it becomes a case in the auditing firms [of] what processes they had in place to ensure that the minimum standard is applied across the board and then there [are] only varying degrees for the more regulated entities...I would've thought that happens in practice already.

The idea of differential auditing standards does not, however, appeal to several other users.

> I just don't think that it's really focused on by the capital markets.

The subject of this next quotation is that it will become much more attractive to stay private if public companies require a higher level of auditing than private companies:

'[I]f you make it more attractive to stay private, that step into the public arena becomes that much more of a hurdle.'

> I don't think it would be helpful. I can see a rationale why you would have maybe a lesser auditing requirement for [an] unlisted company, because all the stakeholders presumably have privileged access to the accounts and often more direct involvement in the company itself. But I'm covering the small end of the market, those companies that have just made that step from a private company into the public sphere, and when you make that step there are a number of hurdles that you have to overcome. The reporting requirements in the public arena are much more onerous than they are as a private company. [As a] private company, you don't have to give any details of your accounts. In the public sphere, not only do you have to publish regular accounts with some detail, but you also have to spend a lot of time with various stakeholders. So if you make it more attractive to stay private, that step into the public arena becomes that much more of a hurdle.

Another user, who does not believe in differential auditing standards, sees it as being up to users of the auditor's report to determine the level of assurance they want to take from that report:

> [That] falls to the users of the accounts, and the users of the accounts in the unlisted sense can be anything from a private individual putting money into a private company to support a mate or a good idea all the way up through the banking system to somebody like [name of company]. We invest in unlisted companies as well. I... don't believe in different audit standards for different levels...the auditing standards are applied in the assurance statement given by the auditor; what work have they done? I'm not a professional investor so it's difficult, but as a professional investor, I would like to know what they do...the scope of what they do, to guide me with how much assurance I can take from the statement.

The same user voices a personal view that, in his or her mind, it is the more naive investors who are likely to invest in unlisted companies, implying that it is inadvisable for them to be investing in companies audited to a lower level.

> [T]he risk you run in unlisted companies, if there was a...lower standard applied to the auditing of those companies, the people who potentially could invest in them [are] potentially naive to some extent...[there are] a lot of listing rules that apply to listed companies, which make the whole governance issue more robust. Those rules don't apply to unlisted companies so...I don't think there's a right and wrong answer. I can understand what the push is for, but...it depends on what the users of the auditor's recommendations...want from them. If users are willing to accept a very much lower level of auditing standard and consequently a very much lower confidence assurance on the company's accounts then maybe it's fine.

The next user observes that there is already differentiation of entities that are not as regulated, but a single level of quality is preferred:

> [I]f you had differential standards then there [are] going to be different perceptions out there in the market as to the relative value of an audit of this entity compared to the value of an audit of another entity. So aren't you better off having one standard across the board, but with lesser degrees for entities that aren't as regulated...that already happens in practice, doesn't it?

The difficulty of comparing companies—for instance, for loan worthiness—when differential auditing standards are present is pointed out:

> I suspect this will come from the burden of auditing costs on the unlisted sector. If you're talking about the capital markets as a whole, I would have thought it would cause problems...banks are lending to unlisted and listed companies that are in the same sector; they like to be able to compare them. If you can have different audit bases, I would have thought that's a major problem.

One user raises the increased cost burden with differential auditing when a company moves from private to public:

> I wouldn't be looking at differential [standards]...you've got to get back...from small to big companies, listed to unlisted companies, that very similar information and similar veracity of that information...There are a lot of public unlisted companies. Why should they have different audit standards to the listed public companies?

'[T]hat's going to increase the cost of capital, so...it would be inefficient.'

> Similarly, [with] the private companies...it would also increase the burden of cost when a company moves from private to public, which many do. If they've got to change the numbers, the fastest way to get it through is that you've got a constant set of numbers. We're involved very actively in raising new money in IPOs [initial public offerings], in floating companies. Everybody goes back to the last three or four years' results. If they've got a different level of audit applied to them, you're going to have a different level of costs [and] comfort on them, and that's going to increase the cost of capital. So...it would be inefficient.

The user argues that for the sake of efficiency, the capital market needs one set of reporting across the listed and unlisted sectors:

> '[I]f you want to make an efficient capital market, you really should have the same reporting across both areas.'

> [W]e've created this two-tier approach...the regulated market is probably too regulated, but the unlisted [market is] not regulated enough. And then you have things like we're seeing in the current marketplace, where it's ludicrous to think that a private equity investor can make money purely and simply by taking a listed company and taking it into the unlisted area...there's absolutely no sense in it. And yet they can, because you don't have all these requirements from a compliance perspective. So it's something that I've been finding it difficult to get my head around. It seems to be a bit of nonsense really...if you want to make an efficient capital market, you really should have the same reporting across both areas.

The comments from the next user reveal indifference to the issue of differential auditing standards:

> I don't think [there should be different standards] and the reason... [why is] we're kind of indifferent. The assumption still remains that the auditor behind the scenes does a job which fulfils its objective, which is fair and true information. Whether the standards or the procedures behind there change whether you're listed or non-listed, I don't think the market's really focus[ed] on.

2.1.1 Summary

Users reveal some confusion about the existing situation with respect to the audit mandate for listed and unlisted versus public and private companies. Bearing this in mind, their comments reveal the full range of responses for the notion of differential audit between listed and unlisted companies: indifference and positive and negative sentiments. Those who support the idea of the application of differential auditing standards cite the cost of an audit as an issue, plus the difference in accessibility to the accounts. Those who prefer the status quo cite the implications for the cost of capital, the incremental hurdle to become listed and the fostering of an efficient capital market as reasons for their support.

2.2 Purchasers

Only one purchaser is interested in differential auditing standards, and even then, the response is qualified to a preference for size distinction rather than a listed/unlisted distinction:

> [A]uditing is a little bit different than accounting standards, but... it does seem...that [with] some of the depths and level of assurance that auditors need to take...large organisations [and] complex organisations could be differentiated from those which are very small and perhaps fairly simple organisations. So...it's more size rather than whether they're listed or not listed.

The interviewer then comments: 'So you don't subscribe to the argument that one of the costs of being publicly traded is the cost of a more substantial, more detailed level of audit because you're in the public arena?' The response is:

> No, I don't...it's wrong to think that way...there's a presumption that when it's not listed that somehow the capital is raised by a form of big business which should be able to look after itself.

The same person adds:

> My difficulty is that many of those people draw on funds that are from the community, or the public as a whole—you know, superannuation funds and so on. So...if there's a differential standard which perhaps led to a failure of a company, it's going to equally impact on the community as if it were a publicly listed company...there's some sort of unofficial view out there that if you're publicly listed then it's mums and dads, and if it's not then it's only big business. But it's all mixed up, and it's not as simple as that.

'[I]t's all mixed up, and it's not as simple as that.'

Other purchasers, however, were not supportive of the desirability of differential auditing standards for listed versus unlisted companies.

'[W]hether they're listed or not doesn't do away with their need for accountability.'

> [W]hether they're listed or not doesn't do away with their need for accountability, and I understand that when they're listed...they've got a broader public support for their capital, rather than perhaps a tighter level. But...the auditing standards basically give an assurance, and my preference would be not to differentiate between listed and non-listed. However, I'm very comfortable about differentiating on...economic size.

The same person continues, deviating somewhat from the question in shifting the conversation to differential accounting standards:

> On the Australian capital markets, we've got about nearly 2000 stocks listed, but it's only the top 200 to 300 perhaps that are meaningful in any market capital sense, and they would represent something like about 96 per cent of the total market capitalisation. So there's a whole tail of very, very small companies [for whom] the cost of producing full sets of accounts with full auditing processes become fairly prohibitive. It's for that reason that IFRS is moving, for example, to produce scaled-down accounting standards for SMEs. And...there is a case to argue for SMEs having some form of differential standards, and...I would see that as being a subset, rather than a completely different set of standards.

The negative view of the proposition of differential auditing standards is continued in the next quotation:

> [P]articularly in our view as stakeholder to unlisted companies, we'd want very high standards on both. No, we wouldn't be differentiating.

2.2.1 Summary

No purchaser is supportive in an unqualified way of differential auditing standards based on a listed/unlisted criterion; however, some confusion between differential auditing and accounting standards is revealed. A size distinction does, however, receive some support. The need for accountability by both listed and unlisted sectors is cited, as is the pervasiveness in both sectors of superannuation investments.

2.3 Suppliers

Overall, suppliers are not supportive of the notion of differential auditing standards, especially once reflection on the issue takes place.

> I would support anything that would [close] that...expectation gap between what...people think auditors do and what auditors actually do. Anything that would make that smaller...is a good thing, and... commonsense would tell you [that] yes, the requirements of a big listed entity are not the same requirements as a private company that needs an audit or whatever. So yes...if that could be made practical that would be a worthwhile project.

Continuing, the same supplier comments on potential confusion that could arise:

> I'd presume that there would be a set of guidelines for whether you fall into a category A or a category B, [which would be okay] so long as everyone consistently applied the categories. The only downside to that is then you're introducing a different set of rules [and] if you're an outside observer...there could be a little bit of confusion as to which rules the auditors are applying. So in some ways, that might...make the expectation gap even worse if people don't know which category a particular entity falls into...I would...be concerned about...I don't know whether that would make it easier for us or not. Certainly, from an efficiency...[and] cost point of view, that would be great because we could...then cut down on a lot of the more specific detailed procedures that you have to do on a listed entity that you might not necessarily need to do on a non-listed entity. But in terms of the confusion, it might...make it a little bit more confusing for the users.

'[I]n some ways, that might...make the expectation gap even worse if people don't know which category a particular entity falls into.'

Another supplier is similarly negative about the idea:

'[A]n audit is an audit.'

> I don't think we're talking about the level of an audit...an audit is an audit. Obviously, the audit gets more complex depending on the nature of the entity and their operations, but...the underlying audit requirement should be the same.

Two suppliers, however, see it as a marginal issue:

> I can see the argument, but...it's such a complex issue and I... wouldn't think that auditing standards are the key matter there... For instance, there is already a flight from some jurisdictions of listing because of the onerous nature of the listing requirements, which really has very little to do with auditing and a lot to do with the way the capital markets run themselves. So...this is a marginal issue. The answer to many of these questions...will be does it increase cost? That will often be my answer. Clearly, for non-listed companies, there is some differential cost in that, yes. Do I think that matters? Not much.

> I don't have a strong view. I could probably argue it both ways and it doesn't really impact upon me very much...the principle of keeping it as simple as you can is a good one, and obviously listed companies have different stakeholders to unlisted companies. But again, I don't really have a strong view and I'm probably not the best person to ask.

The challenge of complying with the auditing standards and having smaller clients see the value added is articulated in this next quotation:

> One of the challenges that...mainly the auditing profession is going through is a concept of...[the] size of organisations and how we overlay the requirements of the auditing standards—and particularly now that they...form part of the law...how we apply those standards down to smaller organisations...It's a big challenge because the cost benefit to the shareholders and directors and management of having to overlay such an extensive audit methodology into smaller clients—they don't see any value of that at all...we're going through it at the moment with our clients... Absolutely, methodology has got to be applied to all companies regardless of the size, but it's a challenge because we're having to do

> all this additional work, and the client doesn't see any cost benefit out of it.

2.3.1 Summary

Suppliers are not supportive of the prospect of differential auditing standards, although two are somewhat ambivalent. Potential confusion for users is cited as a genuine concern and the proposition that 'an audit is an audit' is put, indicating that this could be a minimum standard that needs to be maintained.

2.4 Standard setters

One standard setter responds to the issue of differential auditing standards and is not supportive of the proposition:

> The short answer is no. I...have strong views from seeing stuff from a different perspective...the way of doing that is around [the] reporting framework, not around the auditing, not around the assurance framework...you get to the nub [of] that issue by thinking about what information is really required to be reported, and by implication, it's scaled down for non-listed or certain... different categories. And then...you'd look to have assurance over that scaled down.

The same person continues:

> [A] lot of the debate around differential auditing standards is getting mixed up between the reporting framework and the assurance framework...it's a reporting framework issue predominantly... there might be some stuff on the edges, but...it's predominantly a reporting framework issue.

'[A] lot of the debate...is getting mixed up between the reporting framework and the assurance framework.'

2.4.1 Summary

The one standard setter commenting on the issue of differential auditing standards points to the reporting framework, not the assurance framework, as the source for change in relation to this issue—if change is desired.

2.5 Regulators

Some support for the proposition of differential auditing standards is received from one regulator:

> I'm looking at it from the perspective of being an investor and... there is a lot of danger for an unsophisticated investor, investing in unlisted shares and there should be some kind of...disclosure to ensure that they...know what they're getting into and they probably can't get out of [it]...there should be some kind of differential there.

The same regulator continues:

> [A]udits can be very costly and you can get more assurance if you know the company is listed and is a disclosing entity and is required to jump through the hoops of the standards—all the standards.

Another regulator is opposed to the idea because of the variety of size and importance of companies within the unlisted sectors, although he or she seems to be more amenable to the concept if it is based on unlisted, public company turnover.

> '[T]here are some very substantial unlisted businesses [and] some people who are dealing with them will... want to rely upon the accounts.'

> The only reason I'd be a little bit wary about that...is that there are some very substantial unlisted businesses [and] some people who are dealing with them will...want to rely upon the accounts, like financiers and...other people...the whole concept of having a differential auditing standard in the sense of saying...you're not going to audit those accounts as closely...There [are] a lot of very small listed companies who really aren't all that important from an economic standpoint and you could probably have differential auditing standards for them and it wouldn't make a lot of difference. But there are some major unlisted companies [for whom] it probably would make a lot of difference and people would in fact be concerned about that...The irony of this is...it may even be better to do it more in terms of turnover or something, rather than being the distinction between listed and unlisted. It's probably a bit arbitrary in some respects.

2.5.1 Summary

While one regulator is somewhat supportive of the notion of differential auditing standards, based on a cost argument, it is not clear whether he or she has more of a differential disclosure regime in mind. A second regulator is troubled by a listed/unlisted criterion, arguing that many unlisted entities are major entities, and that turnover would be a better distinction. There seems to be an argument that even among public companies, differential auditing standards based on a size differential could be of benefit.

3.0 Issues and implications

The very notion of 'differential auditing' causes confusion in the minds of at least some participants in the market for audit services and in particular users, who confuse the issue of differential standards with differential mandates. From users, we can see that there are mixed views with regard to the advantages and disadvantages of differential auditing standards. Some of the motivation for the positive view comes from the perception that they will cause cost savings. Some users, however, are adamant that differential auditing standards are not appropriate and that differential standards will cause inefficiencies to the capital market because of the enhanced attractiveness of remaining private as opposed to going public. Also, there is concern that differential auditing standards will cause confusion and decreased understandability in the capital market. The risk that the capital market faces and the lack of genuine understanding of the issues involved here are behind many of the views expressed.

Purchasers, on the other hand, show little support for the idea of differential auditing standards. They note that the criterion of listed versus unlisted is inappropriate. There are positive suggestions that a size-based criterion would be more functional. Perhaps least supportive of all were suppliers. They describe a genuine concern about the ability to effectively communicate the level of assurance that is being given as a reason not to pursue this as a policy initiative. Standard setters (who are often drawn from the supplier side of the market for audit services) are also not supportive of differential auditing standards, although one standard setter draws a sharp distinction between differential auditing standards and differential accounting standards and suggests that the debate might be confused because of the intersection of the two.

Regulators do provide some support for differential auditing standards. Again, much of the motivation seems to be focused on the costliness of obtaining assurance. A further rationale is around the fact that there are some large unlisted businesses operating in the Australian economy and this difference would mean that certain companies operating within the economy would be audited to a differential standard. On balance, while there is some support by regulators, there is concern that the criterion of listed/unlisted is inappropriate and that size (possibly measured by way of turnover) would be a more relevant criterion. One might speculate that the discussion of differential auditing standards is also confused somewhat because of the existing availability of an audit firm-delivered 'review'. Existing standards on the preparation and execution of these assurance services already exist and are well developed and in a mature state.

All things considered, there is only limited support for differential auditing standards and if there is to be a discussion around this issue, it should focus on the size-based criterion rather than that of listed/unlisted.

4.0 Concluding remarks

There is no doubt that some confusion exists between the audit mandate and the issues around differential auditing standards. The discussion and debate around differential auditing standards seems to wax and wane as an issue of priority, and there is no clear agreement on the criterion to be used to distinguish between different levels of audit requirement; some argue for listed/unlisted because of the presence of the public in the capital market, while others note that the distinction should be drawn along the scale of auditee as the economic substance of some unlisted companies is significant.

There is no policy action or operationalisation that is evident from this as the debate does not appear to be conclusive. There are, however, actions that can occur for certain organisations that face the need for an audit as a possibly unintended consequence of legislative action in years or even decades past. Unincorporated associations sometimes based on state or territory legislation find themselves subject to the requirement to undertake an 'audit'. One might argue that, in terms of the criterion listed/ unlisted and in terms of the criterion large/small, these organisations do not warrant an audit and the participants in these organisations would be fully satisfied with a review performed by an audit firm. This is not necessarily a call for differential auditing, as the presence of reviews is well established with clear levels of assurance being provided. Removal of these auditees from the debate might assist in clarifying the issues involved. One might argue that the audit requirement for these organisations is an 'accident of history'.

INTERNAL AUDIT 15

> Do I think the shareholders are getting value? Yes...a strong internal audit function and a well-planned one would provide benefit to shareholders and to non-exec. directors, and to a lot of people... because they are, effectively at least, eyes and ears for people that aren't involved on a daily basis. But from an audit point of view at this point in time, and maybe it's just until we settle in a little bit more with the auditing standards as law...I'd be using it as an indicative mechanism.
> — Supplier

1.0 Key issues

The issue of the external auditor's reliance on internal audit and whether that had changed from the past and to what extent the capital market valued internal audit was raised with stakeholders. While this was a second-order issue in terms of the future of audit, responses raised the following issues:

- how frequent is the presence of an internal audit function in organisations
- what benefits can an internal audit function provide to an organisation
- can the market assess the value of internal audit
- does the market value internal audit
- do boards of directors and/or audit committees value internal audit?
- is the external auditor relying more than was the case in the past on the internal audit function?

2.0 Introduction

Stakeholder groups were asked questions about internal audit—in particular, variations of the question: 'Do you think auditors are perhaps placing more reliance on internal audit than in the past, and do you think the market might be looking more at the value of the internal audit?' Analysis of the responses by users, purchasers, suppliers, standard setters and regulators is presented next.

2.1 Users

This first quotation reminds us of the fact that not all entities maintain an internal audit function:

> Not as far as my companies are concerned, the companies that I research, because they're generally too small to have a real internal audit function.

Several users say that the internal audit function is worthwhile. For instance, the first quotation speaks about its role in ensuring compliance and building an ethos of what is and is not acceptable:

> [A]n internal audit is fairly important...in the broking industry... we have internal audits quite often, from a compliance point of view of what we do...they're an important part of just building an ethos through a whole organisation that certain things are acceptable and certain things are not...an internal audit procedure is highly important because it stops any impropriety during the year, potentially, rather than just once a year. It's probably cost effective, to a point, for a company to have internal auditors.

The same user goes on:

> [There are] certain things where they could rely on an internal audit...it all comes back to materiality and that sort of thing. Obviously, large issues...need to be reviewed by the external auditor as well, but smaller certain issues [can] probably...be assumed correct under an internal [audit]...[I]s internal audit now compulsory? I think there [are] certain cases in the US whereby they're stating that it is.

In this next quotation, the idea is put forward that internal audit can potentially save companies money or a corporate collapse:

> It's probably an expensive operation for certain businesses to have internal audits, but...it potentially could save a lot of dough, or a corporate collapse as well, over time. It's just one of those things... in this day and age that you probably need to have.

The fraud-detection potential of an internal audit function is raised in this next quotation:

> [Y]es, for the larger companies, risk management [and] internal audit are an issue that the market is more concerned about, and that they are looking to for companies to have. That is certainly something that my fellow analysts would probe when they're looking at a company. What are your arrangements, and what is the internal audit, how is it organised? So...there is an awareness, at least in the analyst community, about the limitations of external audits. The fact that it's not continuous audits, that in itself places more value, more responsibility, on the internal audit function of the company. And I'm thinking back [to] National Australia Bank, for example, [and] the Homeside debacle...there was a failure of the internal audit... to really understand the implications of valuation models that were being used, and the people there were content to just sign off on black box-type...justifications. You know, 'We've got the formula but...it's too complicated for you to understand', or it's a trade secret...So yes, the internal audit function...is becoming more important for the larger companies in particular, and...the internal audit is the front line for fraud detection. It's not the external audit...that's the last line of defence.

'[T]here is an awareness, at least in the analyst community, about the limitations of external audits.'

Another user sees the external auditor reinforcing the work of the internal auditor, rather than the other way around:

> I would be worried if external auditors were relying totally on internal auditors, because...I see the external auditor as being almost a second check against the advice in the role that the internal auditor is giving...it's almost like a back-up...just a second opinion to make sure that something hasn't been missed, so that we can rely

> 100 per cent on our financial statements at the other end. And it gives us that extra level of comfort…internal auditors are important, and…you can rely on them to a point, but I wouldn't like to see the situation where you had external auditors putting together an audit opinion purely based on the internal audit situation.

The same person continues, emphasising the regularity of input that internal audit provides:

> [T]hey both have an important role to play. And the internal audit should be more of a…regular input to the process. Whereas the external auditor is really a one or twice a year, come in and just do their spot checks to make sure, just to confirm in their own mind, that what the internal auditor says is happening, is happening. But they do need to make their own assessments.

There is not a great deal of enthusiasm for the propositions that external auditors are placing more reliance on internal audit than in the past or the market valuing highly the internal audit function.

> [I'm] not sure about the external auditors. I would hope that they're still doing what they need to, to get their assurance done. I'm sure that they're testing the processes of an internal audit and to the extent they're satisfied. I don't mind the fact that they rely on the internal audit perhaps, but…I would hope that it's not to the exclusion [of] doing their own work. And in terms of the market placing the value…I don't think that it really comes up…the assumption is that between the auditors and the internal auditors, what people are looking at on the financial statements is true and correct.

Some users, however, are more firmly of the view that the external auditor is not relying to a greater extent than in the past on the work of internal auditors, as these next few quotations reveal:

'I don't even know whether the market does even think about internal audit.

> I haven't seen any evidence of external auditors changing the reliance that they're placing on internal audit…it doesn't seem to have changed…in the 12 years or so that I've been doing this kind of job…I don't even know whether the market does even think about internal audit. I've not ever had any discussion with anyone about that kind of thing or seen any indication that the market even thinks about it.

I haven't seen any evidence of an impact.

> [T]he expectations of the external auditors [are] to check that that internal audit process is efficient and working, and not compromised...the example of that most recently is National Australia Bank, where hindsight was something very poor in the internal audit process that linked into management processes and all the rest of it. And you would hope an external auditor would have looked at that—which obviously again wasn't the case—and said, 'The way it works is not actually going to achieve what everybody, internally and externally, thinks it is achieving.' So... there's probably more focus on them as a very external third-party, independent checker of internal audit processes.

The interviewer prompts: 'So more so in the past?' The response is:

> I suspect NAB and HIH and Enron and WorldCom and all the rest of it have increased that expectation.

'How about auditors?' asks the interviewer. The response is:

> But they should have been doing it in the first place.

One user is more certain that there is greater reliance by external auditors on internal audit and the justification for this response is given as cost pressures.

> [F]rom the external auditor's perspective, they probably are being forced to rely on the internal audit processes more than they would in the past and that would be the pressure on costs more than anything...that's perception; I haven't got evidence to support that. And I'm not sure there is exactly a problem with that, provided the governance of the internal audit function is appropriate, the skills of the people that are doing the job [are] appropriate. And the external auditor can verify [it] by testing what approach they've taken and what the outcomes have been and what the recommendations have been...I'm not too sure that there is...a problem with it. In a badly governed internal audit environment...it would be a huge risk to rely on the internal audit function, but generally speaking, certainly the company we look at, that doesn't seem to be an issue... it is happening and...it's happening because of the cost of audits these days...the real implications are the external auditor needs to

> do that work on the internal audit function to satisfy themselves; it adds to the reliability of the work done by the internal auditors and how much comfort they can take from that work.

The same person continues:

'[T]he market... of institutional investors has never really focused on the internal audit function at all.'

> [T]he market...of institutional investors has never really focused on the internal audit function at all. I've had analysts who, obviously quite a few of them...work for me, and we would rarely ask to see internal reports or do anything like that...[In the] the marketplace, [there is] probably not a huge amount of interest or following [of] the internal audit function. Maybe that should change, I don't know. I doubt it. I don't think it will change.

There is not a great deal of enthusiasm from users for the proposition that the market values internal audit:

> [I]n terms of the market placing the value...that...doesn't... really come up...the assumption is that between the auditors and the internal auditors, what people are looking at on the financial statements is true and correct.
>
> [T]he market, myself included, assumes that the audit process is... working as it's intended.
>
> In terms of [the] market placing more value [on it], I don't know... the actual companies would place a lot of value on it. The market probably wouldn't know or care.
>
> [A]s far as the market placing more value on it...it's more of an internal quality-control process than anything...any external parties are aware of. I don't think the market is that aware of the internal audit procedures other than it's something that...most people within our market do, but obviously the better that you do perform that internal audit it, should assist you in the audit process at the end of the year. I don't know whether they're placing more reliance or less on it.

2.1.1 Summary

The comments of users show that many value the internal audit. Specifically mentioned are its roles in ensuring compliance, building an appropriate ethos and in fraud detection. There is little support from users for the proposition that external auditors are relying more than in the past on internal audit. One user argues that cost is driving auditors to increase this reliance, but there is little agreement. There is virtually no support for the proposition that the capital market places value on the presence of an internal audit function and, in fact, an assertion is made that institutional investors ignore it.

2.2 Purchasers

Purchasers see internal audit as a valuable function, as is evident from these first two quotations:

> [T]he external auditor is absolutely crucial and the work that they do and the final assurances they give are absolutely critical. But if I want to look at whether my systems are working well in the company, and whether or not some of the areas...[in] risk management are operating properly then I would expect internal audit to be targeted to do that work.
>
> [In industry] that relationship [between internal and external auditors] has been always very close...So my long-term picture of that is that external audit and internal audit worked together very closely...looking at each other's audit plans.

The same person continues:

> [T]he function of internal audit has always been—within this [company] and I suspect within all [companies in this industry]—of critical importance, and I doubt if that's changed all that much; maybe the sophistication and the talent within it, but not the actual role.

There is, however, no support for the proposition that the market is placing more value on the internal audit function:

> I don't even know whether the market does even think about internal audit. I've not ever had any discussion with anyone about that kind of thing or seen any indication that the market even thinks about it.

'The market probably wouldn't know or care.'

> Is the market placing more value on the internal audit function? I think it is…we do as a private company. But in terms of listed companies, you know you can't afford to make any mistakes, and especially large mistakes that are going to be picked up as part of an audit, so to have that internal process in place, whether it be in the form of a set procedure like a check list…most would do it.

The purchaser continues, pointing out the importance and usefulness of internal audit as a training ground within financial institutions:

> [T]hat is essential. It is essential that the internal auditor be protected…I also follow a view that…this is one of the most effective and useful training grounds for rising young executives… so internal audit…is not something which is sort of [a] lowly job within the organisation; it's something which is really important… it's a really, really good tool. It's very hard to achieve though because most people perceive this role as sort of a backwater…but you get a lot out of it if…it's done properly. This is not to get away from the basic tests of fraud and all those things; you still need that capability. But…you need more these days and it's essentially under the heading of risk management.

2.2.1 Summary

The purchasers who comment on the issue of internal audit tend to see a close relationship between external and internal audit. Purchasers see value in internal audit, not least because of its potential for training in risk management and other aspects within financial institutions. No purchaser, however, perceives that the market values the internal audit function. In fact, there is doubt expressed that the market even thinks about internal audit at all.

2.3 Suppliers

The first supplier reminds us of how few entities have an internal audit function:

> I still haven't seen the trend back towards having fully fledged internal audit functions for a lot of our clients…you'll find that the majority of our clients, out of this office, don't have an internal audit…if you go back in history that was probably when this

> market was...not doing so well, with the cost cutting, et cetera. From a commercial perspective, that would have been one of the areas [that was cut] and I haven't seen it come back yet. I do have a number of US-referred clients that have an internal audit...so there is a function...The first observation would be I don't think entities themselves, the ones I deal with anyway...are placing a huge value on internal audit, otherwise [they would] be putting that function in place in some way. So... I don't see it impacting external auditors at this point...because I don't have a number of clients that have internal audit.

'I don't think entities themselves...are placing a huge value on internal audit, otherwise [they would] be putting that function in place in some way.'

The same supplier continues, explaining how for the one client with an internal audit function with which he or she is familiar, there is some reliance on the work of that auditor:

> The one that I do, there is a critical assessment of how good that internal audit function is, the quality of the people, the scope of work that they do. And then based on that assessment we will reduce the level of work we do in some areas. Now if we make that assessment and we feel that that internal audit isn't...to the standard that we would like then we'll do work over the top of it. Again, if you think about the key...judgment assessments of an audit, it's unlikely that an internal audit function looks at those areas anyway. They look at more the underlying, lower processes. So...from a material issue on an audit perspective, whether there's an internal audit function there or not, there'll be the same effort on those issues because they tend to not get involved in those; it's more on the process...side.

The next supplier, however, even though positive about the role of internal auditors, does not rely on their work, justifying this by the additional procedures that need to be carried out if such reliance is made.

> '[A]t this stage, I'm not placing full reliance on it...I'd like to because it would save me work, but... any time you place reliance on a third party there's a whole heap of procedures that you have to do.'

> [I]f I was looking at internal audit, if I thought it was just reviewing their results, seeing what they came up with, it would give me a better feel[ing] for what the internal audit environment was like, but at this stage, I'm not placing full reliance on it...I'd like to because it would save me work, but...any time you place reliance on a third party there's a whole heap of procedures that you have to do. And I would've done those before they were law as well, but the cost saving is not 100 per cent...you can't just chop off a whole heap of work, because you still have to do some work to make sure that the people doing the internal audit are appropriately qualified and the program is appropriate and covers all the risk areas. So it would ultimately be more efficient for me to be able to rely on internal auditors, so long as they plan their work properly and they reported to the right level of the board, and I thought their work would cover what I would see as all the risks.

The next supplier also points to the additional work required before reliance on the work of internal audit can be forthcoming:

> In terms of...external audit placing more reliance on internal audit, [I've seen] very little...I was expecting more...an external auditor always has to make up their minds about how far they want to rely on any expert, but particularly internal audit...in practice, I haven't seen any visible change in that over the last few years or even months. And I was expecting them to do a little bit more of that. Perhaps in the public sector there's some increased reliance...[but] in the private sector, not really...So yes...the market does and external auditors perhaps surprisingly don't. It may be that the external audit methodology is now so standardised, consistent and inexorable a methodology that there isn't room to rely on internal auditing. Why would you do that? It'd be more effort to do the work you need to rely on an internal audit than it would be to go and do it yourself. So the fact that I see a difference in the answers to those two questions—do the external auditors know the market: yes—may actually be driven by some of your previous questions about the need for external auditors to change under regulatory pressure...ironically, that leads to less efficiency, not more, in that particular context.

One supplier who had been an internal auditor implies that the time available to an internal auditor, unfettered by fee constraints, permits a depth of checking that external auditors cannot always achieve:

> I started life in the profession as an internal auditor and we used to work hand in glove with the external auditors and we both relied on each other...the external auditor could say to me, 'Why don't you check such and such.' And I used to do operational auditing mainly...And I would not have any time constraint on checking such and such because I was employed by the company. I would check, go through that program and then report back to the managing director at the same time as the external auditor, so that the three of us could work collaboratively to make robust the whole audit process, internal and external. And that had the result of significantly reducing the audit fee to the company—and this was a major company...or ensuring that the external audit fee didn't go up as much as it would normally have gone up if the internal audit process was not hand in glove for the externals. And we used the ACA and the CPA standards, relying on the use of another auditor... and it worked extremely efficiently.

The same supplier, currently a board and audit committee member, goes on to discuss the level of cooperation between the external and internal auditors that can be observed in that organisation, and he or she obviously values the relationship.

> I'm on the board of a company at the moment which also has an internal audit process. I'm on the external audit committee representing the directors on the committee along with another fellow, and we work hand in glove with the internal auditors and we have nothing leaving us. And the internal auditors are working with the external auditors and it does work very well.

Another two suppliers point to the board of directors as particularly valuing internal audit, the second one commenting also on the value of internal audit to the market.

> [B]oards of directors particularly are looking at internal audit functions quite often as a useful ally in the organisation to... go through and have a look at things, and of course using things like the auditing committee, they have a direct conduit to that...

'[P]erhaps because external auditing has become so boring, internal auditing seems to be able to attract more people to it.'

> I've also noticed that executive management, although...to some degree that has always been the case depending on the personalities, are also more inclined to use internal audit to do things.
>
> Is the market placing more value on the internal audit function...yes...that's partly cyclical. It has gone through some ups and downs... perhaps because external auditing has become so boring, internal auditing seems to be able to attract more people to it. It seems to be a more prized role.

The same person continues:

> [I]t may be that internal audit has also had a bit of a boost to its morale by its role in uncovering some of these United States corporate collapses—WorldCom particularly—which if it hadn't been for the heroism of the internal audit people that wouldn't have come out as soon as it did...So yes...the market does [value it] and external auditors perhaps surprisingly don't.

2.3.1 Summary

Suppliers remind us that not all their clients maintain an internal audit function. When that function is present, suppliers appear to value internal audit, yet surprisingly few state definitively that they rely on the work of internal auditors. Two offer the additional procedures necessary to investigate the internal auditor and his or her work as potential reasons for this. The experience is, however, mixed since another supplier, who had been an internal auditor earlier in his or her career, and who is currently an audit committee member, obviously values the close working relationship between the internal and external auditors in that company. Other suppliers support the value to boards of directors, especially non-executive directors.

2.4 Standard setters

Only one standard setter, who is also a supplier, is asked a question in relation to current reliance on internal audit compared with before the recent regulatory changes.

> I wouldn't say there's more reliance. Well, cut out stocks for a moment, because that's different. But I would've said it's similar, if not slightly less.

The same standard setter continues in response to a question about whether or not the market is placing more value on internal audit:

> Yes...well the directors are...their focus, similarly as their focus on external audit has gone up and they've acknowledged [it]...boards are, as a generalisation...much more focused around internal audit and what they're doing than they were before.

2.4.1 Summary

Standard setters confirm the suppliers' view that boards of directors are placing more value on internal audit than in the past. There is, however, no support for the proposition that external auditors are relying more on internal auditors than in the past.

2.5 Regulators

Regulators are confident that external auditors are placing increased reliance on internal auditors, but think that the market cannot assess what internal auditors do.

> [T]he external auditors are placing more reliance on internal auditors. Of course, it depends on their quality, but once they've been assessed as being solid and, turning out high-calibre work, yeah, there is reliance on them. I'm not sure about the market... I don't have an opinion on that. I can't see how the market can assess an internal audit function without...looking at what they do.

The same regulator continues, explaining that cost pressures are driving this perceived increase in reliance:

> [S]ome of the market would be because of cost pressures. They'd know that external auditors are getting increasingly squeezed and would expect them to rely on internal auditors, but some of the market...the institutions, would be aware of that. I'm not sure whether the rest of the investing community would be aware of that though.

Another regulator agrees that external auditors are placing more reliance on internal auditors:

> '[T]he true position is that the whole concept of internal audit has become increasingly more important.'

> [I]nternal audit is a very big issue in the securities industry and [the] major players...have very aggressive internal audit teams, often on an international basis, major security brokers...I don't know whether or not they're placing more reliance on the internal audit function...the true position is that the whole concept of internal audit has become increasingly more important in a sense...as part of the internal audit is the whole...compliance function, which is very big in financial services...I know that boards of directors are very concerned to ensure that they're getting the compliance function...[and] audit functions operating properly. So to some extent some of the things which probably would've been picked up by an audit are now being dealt with internally...Because...now it's not just you being good enough just to make the audit; you've got to be having procedures in place to deal with things in advance...it's probably right that they're placing more reliance on the internal audit function...you've got a proper internal audit, or internal audit function...some organisations do.

2.5.1 Summary

Regulators believe that external auditors are placing more reliance on the internal audit function. There is no firm view about whether regulators believe that the market values internal audit. One regulator points out how difficult it is for the market to value audit when it cannot see what that function does in an organisation.

3.0 Issues and implications

While it is clear that there are organisations of substance that do not have a well-maintained or substantive internal audit function, it is the case that many of the users expressly value the presence of internal audit capacity, whether it is outsourced or in-house. Despite the fact that users value it, they see little interaction between the work of external auditors and the role of the internal auditor. Additionally and importantly for the issue of the role of audit in the capital market, there seems to be little support for the proposition that users value the internal audit as part of the value of a company in the sense of its appreciation in the capital market. Purchasers on the other hand see a relationship between the internal and external audit functions. Additionally, purchasers also value the role of the internal audit function and see it as an important part of the risk-management profile of an organisation. Consistent with users, purchasers do not see the internal audit function as having a positive consequence for the presence of the organisation and its participation in the capital market. There is some scepticism about whether the capital market thinks about or has a view of the role and value of the internal audit function.

The suppliers of the external audit function surveyed on this matter also take the view that not all clients maintain an active and substantive internal audit function. There appears to be little evidence that external auditors rely on the work of internal auditors as a valuable contribution to the external audit process, despite the fact that they recognise its value. Regardless of this, suppliers recognise that boards of directors and audit committees as well as executive directors and management appreciate the importance and value of the internal audit function. Consistent with certain others, standard setters do not support the proposition that external auditors rely on the work of internal auditors no matter how valuable or substantive that contribution might be.

Regulators do see external auditors as placing more reliance on the internal audit function, but they do not necessarily recognise that it is perceived as valuable to the market. A critical issue here is that the capital market might not discern the value, substance and significance of the work of an internal auditor.

On balance, the work of the internal auditor is, for those who are able to distinguish it, perceived as valuable, substantive and a contribution to the economic wealth of the organisation. There is considerable scepticism about whether it is observable to the capital market and the issue then becomes how the value and contribution of the internal audit might be better appreciated, potentially by the external auditor and, more importantly, the board of directors and those who participate in the capital market.

4.0 Concluding remarks

The evidence of the lack of observability of the internal audit function provides a challenge for internal audit to add to the efficiency of the capital market. Because of the need for careful validation of the work of internal audit, there are significant cost pressures on external auditors being able to use the work of internal auditors. If, indeed, it is believed that the work of internal auditors could be of value in determining the credibility of financial statements, care might be given to reconsidering how the validation by the external auditor of the work of the internal auditor might be undertaken in an efficient way. This might require organisations such as the Auditing and Assurance Standards Board to reconsider what are the appropriate threshold requirements to determine that validation.

Additionally, and possibly more importantly, because the work of the internal audit is essentially unobservable to the capital market, consideration needs to be given to how that work can be provided with greater transparency. It is noted, for example, that the ASX Corporate Governance Guidelines recommend the existence of an internal audit function be disclosed to the capital market. An important advance on this would be if those guidelines were also able to describe the nature of the work and the scale of the undertaking in any given listed company. In that way, there would be a window on the quality and extent of the work of the internal audit that might be more satisfying to the information needs of the capital market.

OTHER ASSURANCE SERVICES AND REPORTS 16

> [T]here is scope for auditors to give assurance around other things... particularly [on] the topic of the moment: climate change. We've been looking at triple bottom-line reporting and this sort of stuff for the last 10 years, but only in specific circumstances has there been an appetite for that...we'll see a lot more general appetite [for] that. We do give opinions around internal controls and so forth, so...there will be broader and deeper, or more shallow, assurance being given generally...we're comfortable...we know what we're doing on that. The question is: we know we're doing [it], but how do other people interpret that and see it?
> — Supplier

1.0 Key issues

Provision of assurance on various types of non-financial information has long been mooted as a potential growth area for public accounting firms. This chapter examines this issue in the context of questions about the demand for, willingness to supply and regulation of specific types of non-financial information and the assurances provided for it. The generic challenges surrounding these types of reports and assurance on them include:

- is there a demand for assurance provision of non-financial information
- given the range of types of non-financial information, is there a preference for assurance to be provided on some types ahead of other types
- what level of assurance is appropriate for the various types of non-financial information; are some types unsuitable for audit or review-level assurance

- is there a likelihood of confusion if assurance is provided on many different types of non-financial information or at several different levels
- can an entity's auditor provide independent, objective reports on directors' or management's integrity and judgments when he or she has to work so closely with those personnel during the external audit?

2.0 Introduction

Assurance provision of non-financial information is the subject of this chapter. It reports on stakeholders' perceptions, elicited through the survey questionnaire and face-to-face interviews, on a range of reports over which assurance could potentially be provided by external auditors. The list of these includes assurance on:

- the presence of material fraud in a company
- a company's internal control procedures
- the integrity of senior executive managers in a company
- the risk-management approaches of a company
- the performance of senior executive managers in a company
- the environmental and corporate sustainability performance of a company
- the quality of corporate governance in a company
- conflicts of interest of directors of a company
- senior executive managers' projections for the company
- the reasonableness of non-financial information contained in a company's annual report
- the environmental and corporate sustainability performance of a company.

Analysis of the survey and interview data follows in subsequent sections.

3.0 Survey

Participants in the mail and telephone surveys were asked to indicate whether they believed provision of specific services involving reporting on various non-financial data was best provided by an external auditor and, if so, the extent to which they believed that the value of this service warranted an additional fee. Responses are reported in Table 16.1.

From Table 16.1, there seems to a high degree of shared and positive agreement with respect to the auditor providing certain reports. These include reporting on: the presence of material fraud, the company's internal control procedures, risk-management approaches in the company, the quality of corporate governance and conflicts of interest in the company. For each of these, the users, purchasers and suppliers took a more positive than negative position. On some other matters, purchasers were more conspicuously differentiated from the other two groups. For example, while about one-third of users reacted positively to the auditor reporting on the performance of senior executives, purchasers and suppliers were much less positively disposed to such reports.

Table 16.1 Responses on services best provided by an external auditor (per cent)

	USERS				PURCHASERS				SUPPLIERS		
	Total	Accounting expertise	Professional users	Private investors	Total	Directors/ audit comm.	CEO/CFO	Other	Total	Big Four	Non-Big Four
For each of the following services, please indicate whether you believe this service is best provided by an external auditor by placing a cross in the appropriate box in Part (i).											
Report on the presence of material fraud in a company.	81	75	79	89	66	67	66	62	70	67	70
Report on a company's internal control procedures.	80	76	81	85	79	84	78	75	81	77	82
Report on the integrity of senior executive managers in a company.	50	46	51	53	33	33	32	38	27	34	25
Report on the risk-management approaches of a company.	75	73	77	76	70	70	72	64	63	66	62
Report on the performance of senior executive managers in a company.	34	32	32	37	14	16	12	19	12	11	12

	USERS				PURCHASERS				SUPPLIERS		
	Total	Accounting expertise	Professional users	Private investors	Total	Directors/ audit comm.	CEO/CFO	Other	Total	Big Four	Non-Big Four
Report on the environmental and corporate sustainability performance of a company.	44	45	48	40	31	22	31	43	32	46	28
Report on the quality of corporate governance in a company.	77	77	79	75	74	63	80	76	68	66	69
Report on conflicts of interest of directors of a company.	74	73	74	74	61	56	60	70	53	34	58
Report on senior executive managers' projections for the company (for example, sales growth, earnings potential).	40	38	41	42	32	33	30	36	30	25	32
Report on the reasonableness of non-financial information contained in a company's annual report.	49	52	55	40	48	43	47	59	47	56	45

Percentage of respondents answering 'Strongly agree' or 'Agree' on a five-point scale.

Generally, for the other questions, there was ambivalence (for example, the report on the reasonableness of non-financial information contained in a company's annual report) or a generally negative reaction (a report on senior executive managers' projections for the company).

Overall, users seem to be the most positive with respect to the availability of these reports. It might be important to note that of the three stakeholder groups—users, purchasers and suppliers—it is only the users who do not have direct contact in the transactions that create these reports and who might have the least clear understanding of the cost and complexity of obtaining and using these reports. In other words, for users, these reports could be thought of as a free good.

4.0 Interviews

Not all interviewees were asked about every potential report listed in the introduction and hence not all categories of stakeholder are represented in the interview analysis below. By the same token, some stakeholders' comments cover a number of these potential reports. In such cases, the comments are not repeated but are included under the category first mentioned by the interviewee. The types of reports on which comment is made are presented in the same order in which they appeared in the survey instrument. Each of these relates to the auditor providing a report on the issue at hand.

4.0.1 The presence of material fraud in a company: users

Among the users who discussed the issue of whether a report on the presence of material fraud in a company would be valued, the response was positive.

> In terms of fraud, it's a tricky one, because where do you...draw the line in terms of what auditors can...sign off [on] and that they've provided comfort on...the markets would probably appreciate it. I...can't get my head wrapped around how you'd do it.

> Fraud assessment...I'm a trusting person. I'd assume that...most CEOs and directors of public companies act in the best interests of the shareholders and the company. I assume that's the case, but I know it doesn't always happen. So maybe, [auditor sign-off] would...be helpful.

4.0.2 Report on the presence of material fraud in a company: suppliers

This supplier sees fraud and risk assessments as within an auditor's ambit, and adds internal controls to that list, pointing out that the US *Sarbanes-Oxley Act 2002* requires auditors to certify client reports on internal controls:

> On a couple of those things...like fraud, risk assessments, even if you go as far as internal controls...that effectively is what's happening with Sarbanes-Oxley in the US. So there are entities here that have to comply with Sarbanes-Oxley and therefore auditors are already making those extra assurances on some of those things. So

> a Sarbanes-Oxley-compliant client has to confirm themselves that they've got adequate internal controls and the auditor has to certify that that is the case. So some of those things around controls—fraud, risk management—are already in place under Sarbanes-Oxley. They're not really here from an Australian perspective. So there are some benefits to that.

The same supplier continues, explaining that these assurances are not necessarily going to prevent fraud and manipulation:

> 'If someone wants to be fraudulent then it is very difficult for any of those processes to stop that anyway.'

> Some of my concerns...around that would be that... Sarbanes-Oxley and that sort of assurance and reporting...came in because of the likes of Enron and WorldCom et cetera...it's still not going to stop the ultimate manipulation. If someone wants to be fraudulent then it is very difficult for any of those processes to stop that anyway...[so] there's got to be a balance there...the Sarbanes-Oxley stuff has gone to...too low a level on individual controls rather than focusing on that bigger picture.

4.0.3 Report on the presence of material fraud in a company: regulators

The one regulator who commented on a report on the presence of material fraud in a company was enthusiastic about the idea:

> Definitely. When we invest, we want to make sure that the companies that we invest in are doing what they say they're going to do, and that they've got good systems and processes in place to protect against fraud, for instance. That doesn't mean that any of us would think that fraud won't potentially happen, because it's probably quite hard to set up a system that is going to prevent fraud. But if you've got enough checks and balances, you should be able to pick it up pretty quickly if it does happen, and then let the market know about it. So yes...you need the safety mechanisms put in place to prevent against those one-off fraudulent-type effects or other risks in a particular business to try and get some comfort...[about] what the risks are to invest in that particular company.

4.0.4 Summary: report on the presence of material fraud in a company

Users commenting on the desirability of auditors providing a report on the presence of material fraud in a company are positive. Suppliers, however, see some obstacles, even in the area of fraud, which is acknowledged as having a nexus with the financial audit. Auditors' legal liability is raised as an issue. A supplier notes the reality that such an auditor's report will not prevent fraud or other manipulations. Another supplier fears that users will not understand the message intended by auditors in such reports. Sarbanes-Oxley (SOX) compliant companies are, however, already in receipt of assurance on their internal control reports, and of course internal controls have a relationship with the propensity for fraud to occur. The single regulator to comment on this area is enthusiastic about the idea.

4.1.1 Report on a company's internal controls: suppliers

As with one of the suppliers in the previous section, this next supplier reminds us that the SOX regime is already requiring auditors to provide assurance about management reporting on internal controls:

> I'm not a fan of the SOX regime, but...more and more people want to understand things about companies' controls and therefore they would like to know what we're doing in relation to controls and see information about that...Because of the whole background of SOX, people want to have confidence in company controls and therefore want the independent sign-off, but also because accounts these days are so complicated, most people don't understand them...mum and dad shareholders don't understand them. They are more likely to want to be able to rely on a whole lot of information which is peripheral to or falls outside of the financial statements and therefore some general comfort that the company systems are reliable and therefore that any financial information that's spat out is reliable is quite useful for them...[That's] why...there probably should be more information disclosed around controls and outcomes.

The same person continues:

> Also, people are less interested in historical information and therefore more real-time stuff is of interest...we'll never audit real-time information and release it [in] real time, so...if you could get

the position where we'd audited controls and therefore people knew information was reliable because it had come out of that controlled environment, that would be useful...that's probably the main thing where...people would...find it useful and the market ought to find it useful to say our work's done, more can be disclosed...in terms of how it can be disclosed...it is a SOX-style of sign-off, but it would want to be much more tailored...my observations on the SOX process is that most people have said yes, it's had some use, but the costs far outweigh the use. The way the law's been interpreted has just been so over the top and there's been far too much work, so I haven't given a lot of thought to how it should be disclosed... whether it's certification of the CEO, CFO certification or something much more prescriptive, I don't know, but I would have thought something around controls would be the main thing that...people [would be] wanting to see disclosed more...in relation to work that we...do at the minute.

4.1.2 Summary: report on a company's internal controls

Bearing in mind the suppliers' comments in the previous section on reports on fraud, a single supplier further reminds us of the US SOX regime and the fact that assurance about management's reporting on internal control has been found to be useful—but costly. Suppliers perceive that there is demand for this type of assurance.

4.2.1 Report on the integrity of senior executive managers in a company: users

There was concern among some of the users about the type of expertise and the subjectivity that would be involved in auditor-provided reports on the integrity of senior executive managers. Potential conflicts of interest between auditors and management were raised in light of the current auditor-appointment model.

> 'I'm asking myself how long would an auditor survive [who] gave a critical or an unfavourable opinion about the integrity of management?'

[T]hat comes down to one auditor's view on someone else, and...that's a bit dangerous.

[T]hat's really hard...[auditors are] not trained psychologists.

I'm looking at the small companies that I mainly deal with and I'm asking myself how long would

> an auditor survive [who] gave a critical or an unfavourable opinion about the integrity of management...there's an inherent conflict of interest that is hard to resolve under the current appointment process of auditors, because auditors do get appointed by the companies; they don't get appointed independently. If that were the case, if there was an independent panel allocating auditors to a company, then the situation would be different.

One user, however, is in support of a report on management integrity:

> [A]s an investor in listed companies, I'd find that more valuable than reading the financial statements. An analyst can wade through the financial statements and provide a research note for us, but to have an opinion on the management and the way they go about business...would be helpful. Something a little bit more tangible than just reading numbers...would be good.

4.2.2 Report on the integrity of senior executive managers in a company: purchasers

The purchaser group also raised the notion of a potential conflict of interest.

> How would they know? I can't possibly imagine an auditor saying that management didn't have integrity...it's just too conflicted, the relationship, the way it's set up at the moment between management and auditors, who pays the bills and all that kind of thing. It's the kind of thing that I, as an audit committee chair, ask the auditors in a private session without management. I wouldn't expect them to go public on their views on that kind of thing.

> '[I]t's just too conflicted, the relationship, the way it's set up at the moment between management and auditors, who pays the bills.'

4.2.3 Report on the integrity of senior executive managers in a company: regulators

The view from regulators coincided with users' and purchasers' sentiments that the relationship between management and auditors was too conflicted for auditors to be able to provide such a report.

> [T]hat's a good idea...there is a serious obstacle in the fact that management appoints auditors[9] and have some influence and leverage over their dismissal and the ability to appoint someone else who is more malleable. So unless the system of recruitment or appointment of auditors changes...auditors will be in a very invidious situation and it might be hard for them to be objective when assessing management's ability. I like the idea of assessing management because it's one of the principal risks of investing in a company, but I can't see that idea could work in practice unless the structure of the industry is changed.

4.2.4 Summary: report on the integrity of senior executive managers in a company

The potential conflict of interest in having an auditor provide a report on the integrity of senior executive managers, when managers have influence over auditors' dismissal and replacement, is seen as too great by users, purchasers and regulators.

4.3.1 Report on the risk-management approaches of a company: users

Opposing views were expressed by users about auditor provision of a report on companies' risk-management approaches, as can be seen in the following two quotations. One was enthusiastic and could see value being added, but the other felt there was a problem if companies were not already aware of their risks and that to have an auditor opine on this issue would be 'dangerous'.

> I do see merit in comments—for example, about the risk-management processes—because here it is easier to develop a framework against which to evaluate what's happening in the company. And looking again at the small companies that I research mainly, this would be... beneficial to those companies because a lot of them don't have that kind of...formal risk-management process. If they were forced to look at it, the company, from that perspective, it would...in many cases improve their business. So I can see a rationale for that.

9 In fact, members appoint auditors under the *Corporations Act 2001*.

> It's in a consultation paper about potentially having auditors audit the top-five risks that a company is exposed to. And that kind of thing... would be a really bad idea...if it's the kind of non-financial information that auditors have some idea about, then possibly, but otherwise... we could be expecting auditors to be opining on something that they really don't know much about or don't understand, and...that'll be a very dangerous situation. If you're going to rely on your auditor to tell you...whether you've got it right in terms of your top-five risks for the company...there's a problem there.

'If you're going to rely on your auditor to tell you...whether you've got it right in terms of your top-five risks for the company...there's a problem there.'

4.3.2 Report on the risk-management approaches of a company: regulators

While the only regulator to discuss an auditor-provided report on the risk-management approach felt that there was merit in auditors providing more assurances generally, there was doubt about the merit of this issue.

> It's very difficult because a lot of the audit statements these days don't tell you a lot. But then you can't expect an auditor to be sitting on the shoulder of every director either...it's a really hard one...what auditors provide today is probably on the light side. It would be better to have more assurances, but I haven't given a lot of thought...to what the nature of those assurances should be... expecting them to be looking at everything that a director says is ridiculous...[there are] benefits of regulation, or stipulations that auditors do certain things, but the onus can be quite phenomenal and you may not get a lot of benefit out of it.

4.3.3 Summary: report on the risk-management approaches of a company

Bearing in mind the comment from a supplier in the first section of this chapter on fraud, which covers risk-management reports too, there is some support for this type of assurance being provided by auditors. One user takes this from the perspective of the entity, rather than of other users, and comments that it would be dangerous for companies to rely on such reports. The regulator who commented saw merit in auditors being required to provide more assurances but he or she had not thought through the nature of those assurances.

4.4.1 Report on the quality of corporate governance in a company or on conflicts of interest of directors of a company: users

There was little support among users for an auditor-provided report on the quality of corporate governance and on directors' conflicts of interest. Quotations from the interviews reveal the extent of opposition to this proposition.

> I don't see why you would need that...I get back to the powers of the corporations law, particularly where you're dealing with listed companies that now under corporate governance [guidelines] should have a balance of independent directors. I would have thought that burden rests with them, not an audit process...to have it as a standard reporting requirement...is unnecessary...it's just going to add to the whole cost of the system in an already overregulated system.

> [W]e should rely on independent directors...[and] under the corporations law...there is enough to ensure that there are those checks and balances internally in the company as it is.

4.4.2 Report on the quality of corporate governance in a company or on conflicts of interest of directors of a company: suppliers

The following supplier feels that auditor-provided assurance reports dealing with statements made by directors would not be appropriate, because it would mean providing assurance on directors' judgments and assessments.

> In terms of directors' statements...that gets very difficult from an assurance perspective, because...it will be about judgment and assessment...you could get 10 people around this room and a director could make a...comment about the future or its business, or its assessment, and you could have 10 different views. So how do you provide assurance on something that nearly everybody is going to have a slightly different view or take on...that area is fraught with difficulty. And then how would the capital markets or the investor group perceive that assurance? Because...what would you be saying? Are you saying that he's right or he's got a reasonable

> basis to say that...I'd be concerned about what you're trying to say. At least if he says something like we have a specific fraud detection program in the company then that's something I can assure people that it is in place, because I can go and say well what have you got in place to do that? If it's factual about what's there then that's okay, but if it's views about things or where things are going...it's very hard.

4.4.3 Summary: report on the quality of corporate governance in a company or on conflicts of interest of directors of a company

There was no observable support at all among users for an auditor's report to be provided on the quality of corporate governance or on conflicts of interest of directors. The predominant feeling is that the responsibility for these aspects of corporate life lies with directors. Suppliers also show no support, with concern about the subjectivity involved in such assessments.

4.5.1 Environmental reporting and sustainability performance: suppliers

One member of the supplier group commented positively on an auditor-provided assurance report—specifically on the environmental and corporate sustainability performance of a company, as long as

> [if was] relevant and provid[ed] assurance in areas that are relevant to users...I see this whole area of sustainability and CSR [corporate sustainability reporting] as an area that is relevant because one thing that I see happening in the sustainability space...[is] market participants seeing that there's value in having some attestation attached to a sustainability report, or some sort of corporate social responsibility measure, but then going out and getting that attestation from people who don't have a framework from within which to provide the attestation. So you've got engineers—and I'm not saying engineers don't know about engineering—but do they know about auditing? So that's an area that the profession needs to think about...it's a logical [outcome]. You need to have the skill set to provide the assurance, but you need the assurance framework, so that's a place for the future.

4.5.2 Summary: report on the environmental and corporate sustainability performance of a company

The single supplier who directly addressed assurance provision on corporate sustainability performance information was positive about this type of auditor reporting, noting that auditors had an appropriate framework within which to conduct these assessments, but that this was not necessarily the case for other categories of report providers.

4.6.1 Report on senior executive managers' projections for the company: users

Among the users, there was scepticism about whether auditors would be willing to provide assurance on forecasts and about the value of providing such assurance when no convincing or persuasive list of criteria against which to evaluate the forecasts existed. Two illustrative comments follow.

> I'm dubious about the value of providing audit opinion on those kind of statements, and the key question I ask...[is] what are the standards that you would evaluate the forecasts against, or those statements against, those non-financial statements?

> I'd be surprised if you would find auditors willing enough to stake their reputation on potential forecasts. I don't think really that's their job...their job is to make sure that what's being reported is compliant and being reported correctly and...to a certain standard so that everyone's comparable...Forecasts can tend to be a little bit of the unknown...it would be helpful, but I just don't know if that's the job of the auditors to do that.

Several felt that it would be valuable to have the auditor provide assurance on forecasts and that the capital market would value such assurance.

> [T]here is certainly some scope for the forecast stuff, most definitely...capital markets would be very happy...[with that] as a service.

When pressed on the type of report provided by the auditor, the following comment ensued, drawing attention to the auditor's legal liability:

> It's just got to be clear what's being done [in giving certification on those forecasts or perhaps a review]...if it's going to be done...if it's completely disclaimant away [sic] there's no point. Do you know

> what I mean? And reviews tend to be disclaimant away [sic] a bit. By the same token, I can't get my head wrapped around how you'd deal with the liability of certifying something.

Assurance about explanations of why forecasts were not met also featured as a potentially valuable exercise.

> [C]omparatives are fairly interesting—potentially comparative to a forecast—and why [they did] or why they didn't meet their forecast projections. It could be something that would...provide some assurance that what they've said in the past has come to fruition... it gives...an indication of credibility on behalf of the management, that they've...done what they said they were going to do...and if they don't...achieve it, why they haven't done it...And it's pretty important to relay that back to clients.

The issue of legal liability for the company providing the forecast was, however, a concern expressed by one person:

> [T]he concern...is...if these statements suddenly become [the] subject of an audit report that attaches a different level of liability to them. That, in my experience, means that the companies will consult their lawyers before they make any announcements whatsoever, and that really works against the interests of the financial markets... the purpose of such an audit opinion on non-financial statements would be to test the veracity, the content, the reliability of the forecast. But in the absence of very clear and set measurements, or a stance against which we could compare it and evaluate it...the financial markets, the press, the analyst community, [do] a better job of probing how much of that is real, how much of that is baloney, than the auditors could achieve, keeping in mind that if there is an auditable report, or an audit report on those statements, in the first instance, the information flow would be reduced. So at this stage, no, I would not advocate it...it would do more harm than good.

'[T]he financial markets, the press, the analyst community, [do] a better job of probing how much of that is real, how much of that is baloney, than the auditors could achieve.'

Another of the users was worried also about legal liability, but this time from the auditor's perspective:

> [A]s an outcome, it's the right idea how it kind of lands...it's got a cost benefit reality to it. It's just so costly to get over the liability that maybe that outweighs the benefit.

One of the users felt that such assurance would be of little value because auditors would not have the required industry knowledge to be able to credibly provide it.

> Generally speaking, I don't think that will add a lot to the audit process...they'd struggle to come to grips with what that meant...I don't necessarily think the assurance would be of any value at all...it sounds okay to us, because there [are] suppositions in all those forecasts—like certain level[s of] economic activity, certain industry dynamics. It's not necessarily an auditor's place to [do]... no-one understands those things.

4.6.2 Report on senior executive managers' projections for the company: purchasers

Only one of the purchasers responded in the specific context of forecasts. That comment, similar to one from the user group, related to the legal liability of the entity in providing such forecast information.

> [B]efore anything like that happens, I'd like to see the business judgment rule extended for directors of companies to be able to make some kind of meaningful commentary about future performance without being exposed...it's exactly that forward-looking information that would be much more useful to use as a financial statement than this backward-looking stuff we've got at the moment. So if we did get to that point and if companies weren't providing that kind of information then you could have something that says yes, it's been compiled from this or it seems reasonable in those circumstances, but it's always quite fraught trying to get those kinds of opinions on forecasts.

4.6.3 Report on senior executive managers' projections for the company: suppliers

Two of the suppliers commented explicitly on the provision of assurance on forecast information. The reactions were mixed, with one in support and the other not so.

'I can't see how it would provide any value whatsoever to a shareholder, or to the market, because we'd basically put every caveat on it that we could.'

No, absolutely not. Forecasts, any comment that an auditor—and I'm speaking about it from an auditor point of view—that we could make on forecast would be so heavily qualified that I don't know what benefit it would provide to the shareholders. It would add another layer of cost that they'd [have] to pay for and...they'd end up with something that said, 'Well, you know we can't guarantee this will happen; we can't guarantee that will happen.' If these five limited assumptions happen exactly as they're said, and exactly in the same order and whatever, then yes we can. But...anything that we could provide would be too limited. I can't see how it would provide any value whatsoever to a shareholder, or to the market, because we'd basically put every caveat on it that we could...It's too risky from a forward-looking point of view.

[F]inancial information that is not strictly part of the financial statements...auditors can play a valid role there. Looking at forecasting...evidently you're into the future, auditors can certainly make sensible comments on the assumptions and bases on which that forecast is being prepared, as you would for instance in a prospectus; proper disclosure statements and all that sort of thing. So they could certainly add some value there. Are they the best people? I don't know; there are probably others who could [do] it as well or better. If you start applying the corporation finance disciplines of a Big Four firm to it, it becomes very expensive, very quickly. And...you'd have to ask is the...benefit of that greater than the cost. I'm not convinced it is for future forecast information. Also, if management are making forecasts, people need to understand [it] is their prediction of the future, and it has inherent uncertainties, and everyone should make up their own mind about that. And if it later transpires that management have made up these numbers then they should pay the price...So, [auditors are qualified to handle] financial information in the past...[but] into the future, less so—although...they could sensibly comment on assumptions and bases.

4.6.4 Summary: report on senior executive managers' projections for the company

Users are troubled about the legal liability issues—from a company and an auditor perspective—if auditors provide assurance through their reports on projections for the company. The single purchaser commenting specifically on the projections or forecast issue wants to see some attention paid to the business judgment rule to limit directors' liability before this type of report is supplied. One supplier feels that auditors would place too many caveats on such a report for it to be of any value, while the other feels that such reports could add value, but they would be very costly.

4.7.1 Report on the reasonableness of non-financial information contained in a company's annual report: users

There were mixed feelings among users in relation to auditors' provision of a report on the reasonableness of the non-financial information in a company's annual report.

This next user comments on how hard it would be to expect auditors to provide assurance on statements that are inevitably forward looking when the financial statements themselves are retrospective.

> The most crucial thing...is reviewing the non-financial information to ensure that it's not inconsistent with the...financial information. So when you're referring to in your spiel about how the company has performed for the year, your results that you're talking about aren't inconsistent with the results that have been shown in the financial information...Where the difficulty lies is when you look at the non-financial information there's a tendency to talk about performance this year and where you're going from there, so that's where the difficulty would be for the auditors...how to verity that information. And certainly you wouldn't be able to do it to the same level of assurance that you've provided financial information. So you couldn't sign an audit report on financial and non-financial information because there's often talk about markets, talk about future expectations and future performance—that sort of thing.

One user felt that for companies where such assurance would be the most use, little voluntary non-financial information was likely to be disclosed.

> [I]t's a hard one in terms of what companies are prepared to pay for. Obviously, companies seek the law and they say, 'Well, if we comply with accounting standards, that's what we should pay for.' So it would probably take an exceptional company to go to the... further stage where they'd provide even more disclosure...it would be useful in cases, particularly where companies are at the financial edge or when there are accounting/financial problems. But in those cases, my experience has always been that those sorts of companies are less likely to try and disclose information.

One user is sceptical that such assurance would be useful because it is likely to be surrounded by disclaimers if provided:

> [W]e've already got enough obligations around disclosure and the accuracy of information provided into the public domain and all the rest of it. Is an audit of that going to increase any more? I wouldn't have thought so...So no, I'm not sure you need auditors clearly involved more in that space, given you should already have enough comfort about it, given the current structures under the corps law and all the rest of it.

4.7.2 Report on the reasonableness of non-financial information contained in a company's annual report: purchasers

Purchasers were generally against assurance being provided on the non-financial information in an annual report, worried that it would lead to the second-guessing of management. Two illustrative comments follow.

> I have reservations about that...because...it can take the form of second-guessing of the board...The board is accountable and the board should be required to make its reports in those areas. If the shareholders wanted assurances, they're really saying, 'Is the board basically reporting honestly to us?' And...that takes us down a different track...if a board makes its assurances and is reporting to the shareholders then it's held accountable to those, and there are regulatory mechanisms in place to punish them if they mislead their shareholders...I'm not really...keen on the auditors going in and giving an assurance. The other worry...is that I saw what happened in the NSW Government when it established the Independent Commission Against Corruption...in the end, because the ICAC became involved in ruling on whether the government had

> made appropriate decisions or not, the government has got into the habit, before they'd made a cabinet decision, of shooting the stuff off to the ICAC to get it checked to see if it was okay. And what was happening effectively was a transfer of authority from an elected body to an unelected body. So I feel the same way about directors of companies…it's a kind of slippery slope when they start to move things away and say, 'Well, the auditors are going to check to see if that's okay.'

> [T]hat could be within danger of being quite subjective. And no, I didn't find it a particularly appealing idea from the point of view of the audited company. From the point of view of a stakeholder into other audited companies as discussing customers, et cetera… it would be quite a potentially useful prism, but it's one that we attack ourselves anyway.

4.7.3 Report on the reasonableness of non-financial information contained in a company's annual report: suppliers

Suppliers were generally sceptical that clients would be willing to pay for assurance services provided on non-financial information.

> They've got to see value out of it…one of the challenges from an audit perspective is…about all this additional work that we've got to do, that we've to actually communicate to not only the directors and management, but…to the shareholders as well…[that] they're… getting some value out of that. And that's a challenge sometimes… in the end, some of them just want to see the report…But for those who [are] genuinely [interested], you can…communicate somewhat what they would consider to be value items out of it, then it becomes a little bit easier to pass that cost on. But it's a hard one.

Others from the supplier group made it clear that they were not comfortable with providing assurance on non-financial information.

> I definitely would not want to be putting my signature on that sort of stuff…as a normal part of events, I would read certified financial statements and I would read the directors' reports obviously. And it doesn't form part of my opinion, but I would always make sure that it's consistent with what's in the financial statements and [that it's] consistent with my understanding of what's happened in the entity. So I always…make sure that that's the case. But in terms of

> risk assessment and those sorts of things...the level of expertise and the level of in-depth knowledge that you need to have about the company, which management obviously would have to be able to conclude on those sorts of aspects of the business...would be beyond what we would ordinarily gather from a normal audit relationship...that would be stretching our role quite far. And... the costs would become quite prohibitive if we [had]...to do that.

Suppliers raised questions about whether the level of assurance being provided on non-financial information would be understood by users of the assurance.

> [T]he auditors can properly give assurance on the financial information, but to give assurance on non-financial information... we're getting into areas where the auditors would have to have the expertise for us to be talking about a whole range of things. I don't know where you stop with...stuff like that.

The same person continues:

> [Part of the rationale for my answer is that the business acumen of auditors has a limited focus as opposed to a more generalised one], because they will be looking, as they must do, to [give] an assurance within a degree of confidence, which means that it automatically would mean that you take a conservative view.

4.7.4 Report on the reasonableness of non-financial information contained in a company's annual report: standard setters

The one general comment from a standard setter on the issue of assurance provided on non-financial information was positive.

> [C]onceptually...it would be helpful...my understanding from talking to analysts [and]...the research suggests that some of the more meaningful information is non-financial...it's not included in the financial statements, and it may well be still...financial...so if some of those things are...reasonably important as indicators of value then conceptually having the receivers of that information or... encouraging some more of that information being made available, and then putting some sort of assurance over that framework would seem to be a logical extension of what we currently have, which is...focused...on what [is] required by [the] accounting standards.

4.7.5 Report on the reasonableness of non-financial information contained in a company's annual report: regulators

There was a view from regulators that assurance provided on non-financial information would not be of great value to the capital market and would present an 'onerous' burden on auditors.

> The reality of it is that announcements are price sensitive at the time made, so...there's [not] much point going back and...[having] an auditor maybe trolling back over statements which are made a year previously...also fundamentally...the auditor is [not] going to have the level of expertise...because...[those are] commercial judgments about things and [I don't know] whether or not you're really going to be able to say a lot of sensible things about it...The reality...is that that information has got to [be] right when it's released and I'm not sure an audit process some time after it's really going to achieve a great deal.

> [T]his is a very difficult area now...quantifying and assessing whether something should be disclosed or not would be quite an onerous burden on an auditor. I can't see how it could be regulated or proscribed so, can you get me an example of non-financial [information?]...I can see it's a good idea, but...it would be difficult to implement in practice.

4.7.6 Summary: Report on the reasonableness of non-financial information contained in a company's annual report

Users have reservations about auditor provision of assurance on the reasonableness of non-financial information in annual reports. Concerns are expressed about the difficulty for an auditor of providing assurance on statements likely to be future oriented. One person feels that companies most in need of providing non-financial information are the least likely to provide it and another feels that companies would feel compelled to pass such information past their legal counsel first, which could inhibit disclosure. One user feels there is a role for compliance plans to receive such treatment, but overall there is little enthusiasm from users. Purchasers are not supportive—one because he or she sees it as second-guessing management and the other because of the degree of subjectivity involved. Suppliers are sceptical that there is demand for this type of assurance, given its cost compared with the value likely to be derived from it. Another supplier feels that the depth of knowledge required to give such assurance would be beyond that acquired through the normal audit relationship. Suppliers are concerned too about whether readers of reports would understand adequately exactly what it is that auditors are providing assurance on. Regulators are very negative about the prospect of auditors providing this type of report, arguing that it would be very difficult to regulate, that it is not clear that auditors would have the requisite skills and that the dated nature of the information would make assurance provided on it of dubious value.

4.8.1 Assurance on information outside the financial report: general comments—users

Several stakeholders made comments that were more general in their perspective of auditor-provided assurances beyond the financial report. Users' comments appear first, with the next quotation pointing to the benefits of such assurance.

> [Auditors] probably should [provide some sort of assurance on non-financial information]...the auditors probably have expertise in different areas rather than just numbers these days, and...as far as we're concerned, looking more at the compliance plans [of] audit...it's important that those processes are audited other than the financial numbers being audited...There [are] a lot of internal processes and procedures, and...compliance plans et cetera that we have to adhere to...Even though it can be painful at times, it does... provide a benefit to us [in the long term] because it's another set of eyes looking at things and they're interpreting things in a different way than we are and they might look at things [from] a different angle. So there are benefits.

Not all users, however, are supportive, as the next two quotations demonstrate:

> I'm dubious about the value of providing audit opinion on those kind[s] of statements... If somebody can come up with a convincing... or even a persuasive list of criteria that could be applied to evaluate those non-financial statements then maybe I would change my mind. But at the moment I really see that as a problem of what kind of measurement do we

'If somebody can come up with a convincing... or even a persuasive list of criteria that could be applied to evaluate those non-financial statements then maybe I would change my mind.'

apply, what kind[s] of criteria are the basis of an audit opinion on non-financial statements.

'I don't...think it's something that an auditor covers or needs to cover and doesn't have the experience and depth to cover.'

[*'Would the capital market find it helpful if auditors provided some assurance on non-financial information?'*] No, I don't...think the work that they do—this includes the Big Four firms—helps them in any way understand how a board would work. If you were talking about the structure of the board, on the SRI issues...it's not really their game, that's not what they're about...providing assurances on non-financial stuff leans to a specialisation in something—SRI or governance or whatever it might be. I don't...think it's something that an auditor covers or needs to cover and doesn't have the experience and depth to cover.

4.8.2 Assurance on information outside the financial report: general comments—suppliers

Suppliers generally felt an assurance report on information outside the financial report was feasible for the auditor to prepare, but they could see some drawbacks in terms of the time it would take. This first supplier does see a report on fraud and risk management as having a nexus with auditors, but is still ambivalent about whether or not auditors should be supplying the service.

'[A]uditors are quite often not very good at reviewing non-financial information.'

I'm generally keener on auditors focusing on their strong suit, which is financial information. And auditors are quite often not very good at reviewing non-financial information...some of the ones you mention—fraud being one and risk management perhaps as being another—do have some nexus with the auditors and it does make sense for them to make some comment on that. I'm not strongly in favour. In fact...I would quite like it to be someone other than the auditors who does that, but someone should do it. Should it be the auditors? I'm in the middle. I neither agree nor disagree on [fraud and risk management]. It's very hard to give a high level of assurance on intangible things, and if you do attempt...to give even a reasonable level of assurance on non-tangible items you have to do a lot of work, it takes a lot of time and that adds to the cost.

The same supplier discusses the likely impact of this type of reporting on auditors' legal liability:

> The other example I'd put on record is the [state X] Auditor-General's Office, which is one of the few that has to comment on KPIs [key performance indicators] and achievement. Now that's perhaps a little more tangible even than this, and it's questionable how much value that adds in the great scheme of things. I'm also reluctant to take away the responsibility from management and [the] board for delivering on those less tangible matters. And whilst no doubt everyone will say that they are still responsible, but the auditor expresses an opinion, this will no doubt create a degree of expectation gap where people rely on the auditor to get it right. And in practice I see that quite often, but the auditor has looked at this, the auditor has looked at these KPIs. But it turns out that they weren't right. So whose fault is it? People think the auditor. Now the only thing that saves the [state X] Auditor-General is that the [state X] Auditor-General cannot be sued. Once you get auditors who do not have that legal immunity from prosecution, you have a completely different legal dynamic. So, I'm probably tending on the negative to doubtful.

The same supplier comments:

> Even just a review will cost. Auditors, particularly Big Four auditors, are not good at just a quick review. It's not what they're geared up to do; it's not what their methodology is designed to do; it's not what intuitively they want to do...the type of people who work in audit division in [the] Big Four tend to bring the whole sledgehammer to crack the nut, and the legal and regulatory framework has encouraged...that position. To just do a review of those things, sure they could. Would it help? I don't think so... These views will probably be a very individual and dissenting minority and not shared by most of the rest of the Big Four, but nonetheless that's what I think.

4.8.3 Assurance on information outside the financial report: general comments—standard setters

On the matter of providing comparative non-financial data between companies, one standard setter comments:

> [T]o get comparability if you're going to get—just to pick a simplistic sample, sales pipeline-type information. To get comparability then you need all the relevant companies to be doing basically the same thing. So…you probably need some encouragement in some form or another in the reporting framework to get them to do that. And… if you build that, expand that reporting framework, then it's just a question of what assurance.

The interviewer then comments: 'So, in the circumstance where you have a client in one industry and there is no mandate to disclose certain things, but they want to and then they want assurance around it?' The response from the same standard setter is:

> That has happened. It goes back to these investor reports…to some extent. That is what is in some of those investor reports, although they have probably got less information in them, less of that type of information in them now than what they probably had a few years ago. And there are some limited examples…of those investor reports having some assurance put over them.

4.8.4 Summary: assurance on information outside the financial report: general comments

In general comments about the notion of auditor-provided reports on information beyond that included in financial reports, there was a range of views. Users tended to be supportive but suppliers were generally not—arguing that the Big Four would tend to bring a 'sledgehammer to crack the nut' mentality to such engagements. The one standard setter's comment in this section refers to his or her perceived need for a mandated approach and a formal framework for such assurance to be provided. The reader is reminded that the issue of assurance that goes beyond the statutory audit is addressed in Chapter 17.

5.0 Issues and implications

With reference to the survey, certain positive results with respect to additional and/or enhanced assurance services are observed. Positive results relate to potential reports on material fraud, internal control procedures, risk-management approaches within the auditee, the quality of corporate governance and reports on conflicts of interests of directors, specifically with respect to users. Purchasers and suppliers show some scepticism, although there are positive responses in relation to reports on material fraud, internal control procedures and, to a somewhat lesser extent, risk approaches of the auditee. Suppliers and purchasers also received relatively positively the idea of the auditor reporting on the quality of corporate governance. Some of the more detailed comments from various stakeholder groups, however, suggested that a considerable amount of conditionality exists around the positive responses observed in the survey.

On the issue of providing assurance on non-financial matters generally, a number of mixed views are expressed within the interviews. Even among users, there are mixed views on the positive/negative aspects of these potential additional assurance services. The point is made that if there is additional assurance around these disclosures then this might inhibit the provision of enhanced disclosure by directors and/or management. The mere fact that there is an assurance process around a further statement, irrespective of the topic or content of that statement, changes the nature of the statement itself, it is argued, and therefore might limit or inhibit as full a disclosure as would otherwise be made. In other words, the presence of assurance could change the statement itself and the propensity to make such a statement too. Additionally, users express some scepticism about the level of disclaimers that would be placed on these assurances and whether, as a consequence, the assurances given would be useful. Another suggestion is that there is adequate regulation around many of these additional disclosures and, as a consequence, assurance services on these disclosures are unnecessary. Purchasers also take the view that assurance around some of these additional statements would represent 'second-guessing of the board', which is there to oversee company management on behalf of the shareholders. Suppliers also see various positive aspects to additional assurance being provided to statements made to the market, but are sceptical about whether purchasers are prepared to pay for that assurance and if there is value in its provision. There is also some question about whether these additional assurance services would be well understood by the market and if indeed it would be possible to provide assurance when some of the additional disclosures could represent subjective statements, which, given different perspectives, could be either 'right' or 'wrong'. Standard setters are more positive about the possibility of assurance on additional statements, but suggest the need for universal reporting and a framework within which to report. Regulators are more sceptical, questioning whether there is value in these assurance engagements other than in the unrealistic circumstance of provision of real-time assurance.

With regard to certain additional assurance services, there are some quite positive views among particular stakeholders. With respect to reporting on material fraud, users believe that the market would appreciate these additional assurance services, but questions remain about how it would be best achieved. Suppliers believe that assurance around issues such as fraud and risk management would have a nexus with the existing audit framework and therefore the auditor would be a credible supplier of these additional assurance services. Others believe that auditors might not be the 'right' people to provide even reasonable assurance. One suggests that the audit technology used might not lend itself to the provision of additional assurance services, equating it to bringing 'a sledgehammer to crack a nut'. Regulators are quite positive about auditors providing additional assurance around the presence of material fraud. Regarding internal controls, more positive than negative views are expressed and, again, suppliers see a nexus between their current role and the provision of additional assurance around internal controls.

Users, purchasers and regulators openly question providing assurance about the integrity of senior management. The nature of these concerns revolve around two aspects: 1) whether the type of expertise an auditor possesses is appropriate for the provision of such assurance; and 2) more generally, the view that there is an inherent conflict of interest between the appointment of the auditor on the one hand and the assessment of the integrity of management on the other hand.

Risk-management approaches by the company also attracted some scepticism. Suppliers see that there is some nexus between what they currently do and the provision of additional assurance. Users have more mixed views, as do regulators.

With respect to a report on the quality of corporate governance, users support the general notion that the provision of independent directors is the appropriate mechanism to ensure there are adequate checks and balances, rather than an assurance mechanism of the type that might be provided by auditors.

Another possibility for the provision of assurance is on reports about environmental and corporate sustainability, but the observation is made that whoever provides the assurance needs to have the relevant expertise (such as that required in the climate change area) as well as an appropriate assurance framework. Therefore, the provision of one of these in the absence of the other would represent an inadequate solution for the provision of that additional assurance.

There are more extensive observations about management forecasts. On the one hand, users question whether suppliers are willing to provide assurance and the nature of the appropriate framework or criteria on which these forecasts would be judged. An alternative might be to provide a commentary on the adequacy of previous forecasts, thereby adding to the understanding of the quality of forecasts in the past. Users suggest there are issues around the legal liability of the company in making these forecasts and indeed legal liability for auditors in providing assurance around them. Purchasers too raise the issue of the legal liability in making forecasts. Suppliers have strong but mixed views. Some argue that the conditions around such an assurance would be so qualified that the assurance could be of questionable use. An alternative would be to provide assurance around the assumptions made in the construction of forecasts rather than the forecasts themselves, and the authors observe this is already the case in relation to initial public offerings (IPOs).

With respect to the provision of non-financial information in company annual reports, suppliers are comfortable with ensuring that the non-financial information contained in annual reports is not inconsistent with conventional financial reports as already mandated by the auditing standards, but are somewhat sceptical about stretching that role further. Additionally, there is some question about whether the market would understand such assurance.

While generally there is a considerable amount of questioning of the value of these additional assurance services, a common observation is that the market would not understand such assurances. History tells us that new information in the market might not be well understood and there is a need to be patient so that the market can be educated.

Many but not all of the additional assurances services that generated discussion represent, at least in part, information that is captured by the auditor in the process of formulating the background information used within the audit process. For example, the determination of the presence of material fraud, the understanding of internal controls, the assessment of the integrity of senior management in understanding the approach used by the auditee in risk management and the quality of corporate governance generally are inputs into the audit process and, some would argue, are necessary conditions for the completion of an adequate audit in many instances. The distinction here is that rather than being inputs into understanding the background of the audit so the audit can be completed competently, these assurance engagements represent outputs that would be used to inform the market rather than inputs used to inform the auditor in completing the audit process. The important distinction between inputs and outputs is that outputs would be used to inform the market. The auditor would be held accountable for those assessments and therefore would require clear subject-specific guidance within which those judgments might be made and clear expertise in making them.

6.0 Concluding remarks

There is the potential for positive action in relation to provision of the types of assurance raised in this chapter, which could provide utility to the capital market. As indicated in the survey and the interviews, there is positive sentiment towards the provision of assurance on some matters beyond the statutory audit. For example, there is support for assurance on reporting of the sustainability of entities. It is noted that while a framework exists within which this assurance can be provided, what is potentially missing is subject-specific guidance that would provide clear pathways for assurance on specific areas. These specific areas could include sustainability and topics such as conflict of interest of directors, internal control (which already conspicuously exists in the United States) and corporate governance.

In fact, each of these three topics could be subsets of the more generalised area of the risk approach of the auditee. It is the last of these topics—the risk approach—which could be one of the most highly value-adding assurance engagements for the capital market. Provision of this subject-specific guidance could be undertaken by the Auditing and Assurance Standards Board, perhaps in combination with other stakeholders including the ASX, the professional accounting bodies and the Australian Institute of Company Directors.

With respect to the issue of sustainability, the International Auditing and Assurance Standards Board is already tasked to provide this topic's specific guidance. Additionally and as an important motivation to those in Australia who engage in these actions, the international board—while it recognises the importance of these specific areas—does not see them specifically as fitting within a generalised framework of the risk approach of the management of the company. This provides Australia with an opportunity to provide leadership on this matter.

DIFFERING LEVELS OF AUDIT ASSURANCE 17

> The profession itself has been unable to define a systematic framework that...defines what reasonable assurance even is. At best, it's better than nebulous, but it is a concept that's not well articulated.
>
> — Standard setter

1.0 Key issues

One of the issues that the auditing profession has grappled with for some time is the notion of differential levels of audit assurance. The auditing standards have settled on one level of assurance for audit (that is, reasonable assurance), with the other level for assurance being a review (not an audit—that is, limited assurance). This chapter examines stakeholders' responses to the proposition that audit engagements could result in either higher or lower levels of assurance than is 'reasonable'. In doing this, the key issues around audit, as opposed to review, include:

- could there be circumstances in which auditors might be able to sign off on an audit at a level of assurance different from 'reasonable assurance'; and, if so, what might these circumstances be
- if circumstances exist for audit where deviation from reasonable assurance can be given, is that assurance to be provided at a higher or lower level than reasonable assurance
- is it possible for auditors in an audit engagement to provide a higher than reasonable level of assurance such that it constitutes a guarantee
- is there demand for levels of audit assurance higher than reasonable assurance at the price it is likely to cost
- what would be the consequences for auditors' legal liability if either or both higher or lower levels of assurance in an audit existed

- would readers of audit reports be confused if differential levels of audit-level assurance existed in the marketplace
- is there confusion in the marketplace about audit and review levels of assurance provided?

2.0 Introduction

Stakeholders were questioned in the face-to-face interviews about their view of whether scope existed to sign off on audit engagements (not review engagements) at a level of assurance different from that currently in place—that is, reasonable assurance. This chapter provides analysis of responses to this line of questioning.

2.1 Users

Some users are enthusiastic about the possibility of higher or lower levels of audit assurance than is currently provided by an auditor: reasonable assurance.

> [*Is there scope to sign off at a higher level of assurance?*] For sure. It may be at a lower level too...When we saw the audit report of this particular organisation that went down, on the face of it, you would've thought they were confident in their numbers...they had a couple of provisos, but I would've thought if they had an option to maybe a lower level, they might've taken that where you'd think, okay maybe you need to be careful of this organisation. And...by the same token, if they're really confident then obviously they're staking their reputations on it.

The same person continues after more probing by the interviewer:

> [F]rom the limited experience that I've had at looking at the audit... you go back and say look I'm interested in the financial health of this organisation. If they're just saying we are satisfied, that's one level. But it could be we need...more information, or we have limited satisfaction or whatever. Maybe it's a signatory to say, 'Look maybe you need to be careful.'[10]

10 One could argue, however, that this already exists with the emphasis of matter.

The same user continues:

> [*Would companies be prepared to pay for different levels of assurance?*] For sure. And you know if you're doing damage to the investor market, capital markets, say, 'Well, why do we need to do that?' So you're right. And it always goes down to one versus the other… what you're trying to do, which you may not be able to…those companies that you think are not going to be around for a while, people are aware of them. So it just speeds up their death. But who would be willing to provide the death certification is another story, isn't it, and [it] can be quite expensive too. Or people say, 'Well, we won't bother with it.'
>
> Yeah, that's right [one level of assurance and no variation perhaps], no matter what you're looking at. It's not an absolute level of assurance…otherwise just the costs that get imposed on organisations.
>
> [*In response to the question: 'So you don't feel they would be willing to pay extra because of all those added costs, if there was a variation?'*] [T]he need would have to be demonstrated about what it is. I'd need to see what the question or the issue was that needed that extra level of assurance, rather than just simply be saying that we should be providing a higher level of assurance for the sake of it.

2.1.1 Summary

One user is enthusiastic about the possibility of levels of audit assurance other than 'reasonable' being provided on financial information. This user appears to argue that auditors could base the level of assurance on the confidence they have in their report and the continued viability of clients. Another user, however, wants a single level of assurance across financial and non-financial information. There is modest evidence provided that users would be willing to pay for differential levels of assurance.

2.2 Suppliers

This first supplier speaks about audit clients seeing the audit as a necessary evil and, as such, the likelihood of these clients being prepared to pay for a higher than 'reasonable' audit assurance level is unlikely.

> '[G]enerally, users of financial reports regard the audit as being a necessary evil.'

> [T]he average small company and SME who might require an audit sees the audit process as being purely a reactive necessary process to satisfy the regulator, and is generally very reluctant to go and ask the auditor to broaden their scope and pay for broadened scope. If the auditor has to strictly comply with the financial reporting for the requirements...under audit, it's very difficult for the auditor to broaden their scope under the prescribed climates...Taking superannuation audit, we have to comply with the auditor's report and we can't necessarily even narrow our scope to say that we can't comment on an item or an issue which we're obliged to comment on; we can't narrow that scope. And similarly, we can't broaden the scope under that report unless it's a special-purpose audit which the client, the trustees, are asking us to do. And then there's no formal audit report to cover that...generally, users of financial reports regard the audit as being a necessary evil, or the management regards the audit as being [that].

The same person continues, implying that the threat of legal liability impedes auditors providing many potentially value-adding services:

> [A]s soon as an auditor is trying to value add—and we all do try to value add—but as soon as we say something is good in trying to add value to the process, or something is enhanced to add value to the process, if it turns out that that's wrong...we're dead... consequently, even though we'd love to value add, because of the competitive nature of our profession, we're scared to do it half the time. Like the regulator in superannuation wants us to write positive management letters as well as negative management letters...I'm loath to put my hand up and write a positive management letter and say the industry fund that I'm auditing is all hunky-dory and there's nothing wrong with it, because you know that there is going to be something wrong with it within the confines of materiality.

Another supplier expresses doubts about the potential for provision of a higher level of assurance:

> [W]hether you go for a higher level of assurance...that depends on the circumstances. If we talked about a listed environment, would the readers of financial reports get some comfort out of it, or is there

> scope to do a higher level of assurance? I have some doubt whether you could. It would vary from organisation to organisation.

The same person continues, discussing a lower rather than higher level of assurance:

> [A]s you get down into the lower forms...there's probably some scope to have different levels of assurance down at that level, particularly where...you've got private family companies that are being audited by virtue of the fact that they pass the thresholds under the *Corps Act*. You're effectively reporting to—it might be two shareholders, both family members—so therefore what are they looking for? Well, they're primarily getting the audit done because they have to under the law, but they don't necessarily always see much value out of it. So potentially there's some scope for some lower level of assurance there. I don't know how far you'd bring the bar down...that would be questionable...[but] there is some scope for that, particularly down the track.

The same person continues, making it clear that explanation of the scope of a higher-level assurance engagement would need to be given in the report:

> A higher level? Look, as long as you scope it out properly as to what...constitutes that higher level of assurance you're giving. Now does that mean that there's more concentration on work around the internal controls and we report more significantly on internal controls? Yeah...there's some scope to do that. But...you would need to make sure that what that higher level of assurance is has been properly scoped out and is understood, certainly in the report as to what you've done there...You'd need to be very careful of that one.

> [W]e have the three levels that are clear at the moment. We have the positive assurance, the negative assurance and the agreed upon procedures,[11] which...give us enough scope to move around financial statements generally. I would not be averse to giving an opinion on a specific aspect, because at the moment...if you get a question on goodwill or debtors or something in the financial

11 Some would argue that 'no assurance', as is the case with an agreed-on procedures engagement, is not a level of assurance.

> statements, our stock standard phrase before we get into that is, we give an opinion on the accounts as a whole et cetera.

The same person provides some examples of when directors might want to have additional assurance provided:

> I can see some scope where...the directors would want to have additional assurance when we're doing our audit in particular places. And that's commonplace...we'll do some extra on tax. Or we only have to do three stocktakes around your 10 sites, but we'll do five to give you extra comfort. If you're doing that, you know there are ways in which that can be disclosed as having to give some extra comfort around those. So I don't think it's a problem on that.[12]

The same supplier then discusses the prohibitive cost of high levels of assurance:

> The only way you could get further positive assurance across the financial statements as a whole, I'm not sure what the mechanisms [are] because we're doing that and it's a reasonable assurance. Whether we get into territory [where] we can give absolute assurance is beginning to get into the realms of statistical stuff. So...there's scope for it, but...the price would be so prohibitive that people wouldn't choose to do it. And...the only purpose to do it would...be to try and get the auditors on the hook if there was something wrong with it. And there'd always be test cases around that. Goodness knows what it would do to the PI [professional indemnity] market and so on.
>
> No...we should all have the same level of assurance and the same standards because that's the only way you're going to get uniformity in terms of reporting in opinions both nationally and... internationally. You start playing around with that one and then you might start saying well which standards are we going to apply? No...we've all got to have an agreed upon type of procedure for the level of assurance that's requested, and it shouldn't be a question of money or anything else.

12 The existing auditing standards framework does not facilitate public disclosure of such assurance, but it could be provided to directors and/or audit committees.

2.2.1 Summary

Suppliers are mixed in their views of varying the level of assurance provided in an audit engagement. The views range from a certainty that one level only is appropriate in order to ensure uniformity in reporting options to a view that such engagements and reporting would be viable and that demand would be present. One supplier gives an example of where a higher level of assurance might be given as directors seeking to have more audit work done around a specific account balance than the auditor considers necessary—albeit the outcome would be communicated privately to directors. Another supplier raises the fact that the cost of absolute assurance would be prohibitive, because of the professional indemnity premiums required.

2.3 Standard setters

This first standard setter, as per the overarching quotation at the beginning of this chapter, points to how difficult the profession has found it to articulate even how the well-accepted 'reasonable assurance' level is defined, implying that until that definition is under control, other levels of audit assurance are problematic. The same standard setter, in response to the interviewer's comment, 'Is it not well defined?', responds:

> Well, certainly not well defined and therefore on the side of recipients, it's not well understood.

The interviewer comments: 'So, you're saying the supply side of the market doesn't define it well?' The same standard setter's response is:

> It doesn't define what it's providing.

The interviewer comments: 'So there's no hope?' This same standard setter responds:

> No hope for those on the demand side being really clear about what they're getting...if they think about it, [they might] have some notion of there being an audit sign-off and that's part of the job that needs to be done as a director, or as a shareholder you might vaguely understand. Well, the sophisticated shareholders would have some understanding of the process presumably and know that it's got to be there, and probably think that it's valuable much of the time, or most of the time. Would they be willing to pay more for

> a higher level? Possibly. And it may be much more in the context of a very explicit assignment, rather than the general financial statement audit.

Another standard setter speaks about the difficulty of providing higher than reasonable assurance:

> [T]he guarantee issue is probably very difficult to obtain because you're dealing with information provided by a third party which, in turn, you are then expressing a view on. And…if you go to most things…do you know what most…'guaranteed' means? You'd rarely see 'guaranteed' on anything other than, 'We guarantee that if you bring this back within 30 days, we'll replace it with a new one.' Well, that's pretty easy to do, isn't it?

The same person continues, giving examples of how it would be virtually impossible for an auditor to provide a guarantee:

'[U]nless directors were prepared to guarantee something then the auditor or the assurance practitioner's not.'

> If you…go through the concept of what it is that we see in the marketplace that's guaranteed, even these rental streams that are guaranteed, they're guaranteed as long as there's sufficient funding in the vehicle that's providing the guarantee…Go and read the fine print—they're not guaranteed at all, so you then turn around and say, well how might an assurance practitioner provide a guarantee? And again, you get to the fine print and…you'd find that you'd be back to the reasonable assurance or moderate-type levels again. And you say well what areas would people want guarantees on? No-one's going to guarantee that the value of fixed assets or non-current assets is recoverable because it's dependent on future outcomes and assumptions. No-one's going to guarantee that the tax benefits are recoverable…the reasoning being that if you…go through the standards, they're all based on probability anyway…they're not even at a guaranteed level, so you'd be asking somebody to sign off on something at a higher level than it's…being presented under anyway in the first instance. So…unless directors were prepared to guarantee something then the auditor or the assurance practitioner's not.

Using another example, this time non-financial, the same standard setter emphasises the difficulty of an auditor providing a guarantee:

> Probably the closest thing you could ever get to a guarantee would be—and even then you'd have to be dealing with pretty good governments—would be government bonds where someone had some [debtor] fees and [could] swear there was an investment in the government bond that was going to provide the cash-flow stream. But then you probably wouldn't need the guarantee because of the nature of the investment. So you go through some of the other examples around management integrity, objectivity, corporate governance, environmental, I don't think anyone's going to provide a guarantee. Let's say someone wants a guarantee that X-company's emissions outputs are so many tonnes of carbon a year...you'd be relying on an engineer's assessment of the output, which could change depending on whether there was a breakage in a gas tube somewhere or something else that could happen.

The same standard setter continues, implying that even with almost 100 per cent re-performance of the transaction processing, a guarantee would still be difficult to elicit from an auditor:

> Guarantees are absolute, and the funny thing is you... look at the audit reports that a lot of government entities want on various matters and they...ask for a certification, which is effectively a guarantee. Those reports typically get wound back from a certification to 'and in my opinion' or 'in our opinion', and an audit or assurance-type report because a guarantee is absolute. And...you'd say well, most investors would love it if someone can say, 'Yes, we guarantee these accounts are free of error'...you'd have to almost do a 100 per cent re-performance and then you'd probably want your work audited.

'[Y]ou'd have to almost do a 100 per cent re-performance and then you'd probably want your work audited.'

The same standard setter invokes moderate assurance available under review engagements against which to juxtapose the concept of reasonable assurance:

> [W]hen you put it in perspective...what an audit is predicated on is [that] someone's got adequate systems to generate reliable financial information, which if you test over a sample basis you

> get to a reasonable conclusion that the outcome that's presented is reasonable. That's...the gist of it—and that there are processes to deal with the judgmental factors outside of that. But that's why the moderate level of assurance sits there because really what it's saying is: 'You presented me with this information; based on that, nothing's come to my attention.' Really what someone's saying when they say that is: 'There may be something else outside of that which I haven't been made aware of and if I was, I [would] have a different view.'

2.3.1 Summary

Standard setters are not positive in their response to the interviewer's question about the possibility of levels of assurance other than the reasonable assurance for audit engagements. One standard setter points out that even that well-accepted concept has not been defined. A second standard setter provides examples—financial and non-financial—to illustrate what he or she sees as the virtual impossibility of auditors being able to provide a higher level of audit assurance that constitutes a guarantee.

2.4 Regulators

The first regulator comments on the confusion that he or she perceives will be felt when unsophisticated audit report readers find another level of audit assurance to comprehend:

> [*In response to: 'How do you communicate the relative levels of assurance?'*] Good question. [I] don't know because...people who aren't attuned to audit are even going to get more confused. Because as soon as I try and say: 'This is not just the product which we've tried forever and a day to explain what it is, that now my product's actually this bit, and this bit, but this bit isn't this bit.'

Another regulator, however, can see a place for differing levels of audit assurance, depending on the nature of the subject matter:

> I'm not saying this is my view, but opining for a minute, that the assurance provided within the financial statements on the robustness of the numbers is as we know it now. The commentary by the auditor in another section of the annual report around management's commentary on its performance might be at a lower level of assurance.

2.4.1 Summary

Confusion among audit report readers if more than one level of assurance is provided on an audit engagement is how one regulator sees it. Another, however, can see that reasonable assurance could be provided on the financial information with a lower level of assurance around management discussion and analysis.

3.0 Issues and implications

The field of differential levels of audit assurance evokes some thought-provoking observations from various stakeholders, including users, suppliers, standard setters and regulators. Users demonstrate on the one hand a desire for higher levels of audit assurance, but only relative to a demonstrated need for that assurance, and on the other hand some not inconsiderable confusion as to what is presently available and communicated in the market for audit services. On the part of one user there appears to be confusion about differential levels of assurance as opposed to the differential information conveyed in an audit opinion.

Suppliers by and large are relatively guarded against higher levels of assurance and there are multiple reasons for this. First, they observe that, from their perspective, users are not necessarily enthusiastic about the current audit product let alone something that is enhanced. Repeatedly, the audit process is described as 'a necessary evil' or is seen simply as a compliance commodity that is not necessarily high value adding—at least for some stakeholders. Second, there is concern about higher levels of assurance attracting the threat of legal liability, which might attach to audit reports set at this higher level. One supplier observes that there are circumstances where a lower level of audit assurance might be viable—that is, where the stakeholders or recipients of the audit opinion have lower levels of information need and the audit opinion adds lower information value than would otherwise be the case (for example, where a company is a closely held family concern). Higher levels of assurance might be possible, but the need would have to be clearly defined and clearly scoped. There was an assumption by suppliers who believed higher levels of assurance were possible that this higher assurance would in fact be communicated privately to directors as opposed to communicated openly to shareholders and other parties. An observation is made that extremely high levels of assurance would come at a prohibitively high cost so the market for it could be limited, if it exists at all. Another limitation to differential levels of audit assurance is around the fact that there needs to be uniformity, if not complete consistency, in the calibration of levels—nationally and internationally.

Standard setters believe that it is hard to articulate—or perhaps more correctly, communicate—the current level of audit assurance to the market for audit services in Australia. Having differential levels would add to the confusion in the market. There is also a very lengthy enunciation that higher levels of audit assurance in the form of a guarantee or a near guarantee would be impossible. Even if those words are used, there would be limitations and conditions on them that would in fact mean that the 'guarantee' would cascade down to reasonable assurance anyway. Generally, standard setters are not positive about differing levels of assurance. This viewpoint contrasts with one regulator, who believes that it is possible to have differential levels of assurance where those differential levels attach to different components of what is communicated to shareholders. Here, reasonable assurance could attach to financial information and a lower level of assurance could attach to the management discussion and analysis component of an annual report. Another regulator is concerned that the differential levels of assurance would give rise to misunderstanding in the market and then questions how easy it would be to communicate with the market on these differential levels of assurance.

Across these various stakeholder groups, there is only limited interest in differential levels of assurance, although there is a prospect of it in specific circumstances. Consequently, in certain conditions, differential levels of audit assurance might be possible, but otherwise, there is little if any enthusiasm for differential levels of audit assurance.

4.0 Concluding remarks

There is some evidence that demonstrates that for all stakeholders in the capital market, having differing levels of assurance for audits has considerable cost in terms of potential confusion, without great enhancement to the efficiency of the capital market or informing the participants within that market. It is important to remember of course that the framework within which auditors operate allows for review engagements and audit engagements where review engagements provide only 'limited assurance' and audits provide 'reasonable assurance'. The one potential anomaly here is that reasonable assurance, which is included as black lettering in the auditing standards, thereby becomes an upper-level cap on the amount of assurance that may be obtained, at least for statutory audits. This is so despite the fact that boards of directors may seek much higher levels of assurance over particularly controversial, high-risk or pressing matters.

At present, to use one contemporary example, if a board of directors desired higher than reasonable assurance on an executive termination package then it could not ask for it as part of the statutory audit opinion and obtain anything other than reasonable assurance. If the board was to ask, not unreasonably, for a special report to be distributed to only the board and/or audit committee comprising such information then that would be seen as either 'agreed-on' procedures or an additional assurance assignment that is outside the framework of the auditing standards. Agreed-on procedures bring no assurance. So if the engagement was conducted as agreed-on procedures, a board would be unable to receive assurance. If the engagement was an additional assurance assignment within the framework of the auditing standards, the board would not be able to seek assurance beyond 'reasonable' and if the engagement was taken as additional assurance to some level beyond reasonable then it cannot be conducted within the auditing standards. Put bluntly, reasonable assurance becomes the cap of the level of assurance that can be provided under the auditing standards, which might be unsatisfactory to the purchasers in the market for audit services. While this might be broadly acceptable, there could be instances where there are issues of high value or high risk where greater than reasonable assurance is needed by the client and can be provided. Policymakers need to consider whether 'agreed-on' procedures engagements may in fact give some level of assurance, including higher than reasonable assurance and whether this would be useful beyond traditional agreed-on procedures engagements, or alternatively, that, where feasible, further audit engagements may give assurance above the level of reasonable. We note that there might be considerable potential confusion with the public reporting of the outcomes of these engagements. There are, however, some stakeholders, including audit committees and boards of directors, who seek from time to time such assurances and who presently have no way of having them delivered under the auditing standards.

DIVISION H

CONCLUSION AND RECOMMENDATIONS 18

1.0 Introduction

A market values no product or service unless the underlying characteristics and contributions made by the product or service are known to that market. Markets act efficiently and will price goods and services according to the value that the buyers in the market see exhibited by the product or service. The price paid for the product or service will be the intersection of the price demanded by the suppliers and the price the purchasers are prepared to pay.

Goods that are seen as 'compliance' goods are invariably subject to price minimisation by purchasers. Typically, a compliance good is one that is required by regulatory authorities and is not valued inherently itself. There are those in the market for audit services who believe that auditing is a compliance good. There are others who believe auditing provides substantial benefit to shareholders, to the board of directors of a company and generally to the community. This benefit extends to the capital market and to the quality of information used in that market. Whether or not it is seen as something of value, it is the case that the inherent characteristics of the audit are not well exposed or necessarily understood to all in the capital market. This, in some circumstances, has given rise to a mismatch between the value delivered and the value expected. This mismatch has been called an 'expectations gap'.

Auditing is in a class of goods and services that is referred to in the economic literature as an 'experience good'. An experience good is something that you cannot fully understand the characteristics of until you have experienced the delivery of the product. Many services, such as dental, medical and legal services or even airline travel, can also fall into this classification. The essential characteristic of these products is that you have to experience them to understand their qualities. You might have some prior description or review of the service. You might even have family members or colleagues who have experienced them, but, unlike physical goods, these products need to be experienced by the individual for the individual to have a full understanding of the nature of the product. Compare, for example, the purchase of a new motor vehicle with the purchase of audit services. One can test-drive the motor vehicle and one can choose colours and options, but one has the opportunity to see the product before purchasing it. The purchase of an audit is based mainly on reputation and the promise of delivery of something of a quality and a nature that is desirable.

Audit is therefore difficult to understand without experience of it. Further, even if there is experience of it, key stakeholders see little of the experience. For instance, directors know little of what transpires during their company's audit. This means that compared with, say, dentistry, full understanding is doubly hard. At least with dentistry you get to live and feel the experience.

It is in this context that the comments in the next section and the recommendations that follow it should be read. Many of the recommendations seek to assist in overcoming the level of information asymmetry existing between audit and those who cannot experience it directly.

2.0 Where, then, will the future of audit take us?

During the early years of the twenty-first century, policymakers and certain participants in the market for audit services have taken important steps to map out the future of audit. In Australia, the changes to the regulatory regime (*CLERP 9*) after the spectacular corporate collapses of the early years of this decade have seen some important 'big-picture' changes. We have seen changes in auditing standard setting, with greater representation in the process from those outside the supply side of the market; the legal backing of auditing standards; more detailed requirements over the independence of the auditor; a reduction in professional self-regulation and co-regulation; together with an increase in regulation and oversight by Australia's principal regulator in this area. There have been similar changes in other jurisdictions around the world to a different extent and with a different nature, but regulatory change has been one of the hallmarks of auditing in the past several years in many parts of the world. The unresolved question remains whether these changes have had their intended effects.

2.1 What were the intended effects of the regulatory changes?

There were many well-intended changes to the regulatory regime in the earlier part of this century that could have provided value to the market for audit services, enhanced the audit attestation function and enhanced financial information that was crucial to the efficient operation of the capital market. It is difficult, however, to conclude that all these regulatory changes have had the intended effect. The intended effect can be gleaned from the six overarching principles for the Corporate Economic Reform Program in general, reproduced in the *CLERP 9* Discussion Paper as:

- analysis of the costs and benefits of the proposed changes
- development of a consistent, flexible, adaptable and cost-effective regulatory and legislative framework
- reduction of transaction costs for firms and other market participants
- achievement of appropriate balance between government regulation and industry regulation
- removal of barriers to entry for service providers
- improved harmonisation between Australia's regulatory framework and those applying in major world financial markets (Corporate Law Economic Reform Program Discussion Paper, no. 9, 2002:14).

The stated objective of *CLERP 9* is useful also: 'The underlying objective of the reforms is to improve the operation of the market by promoting transparency, accountability and shareholder activism' (Explanatory Memorandum to the CLERP 9 Bill 2003:Clause 1.4). The relevant portion of the introduction to the CLERP 9 Bill states that the bill sets up a framework that includes measures designed to improve the reliability and credibility of financial statements through enhanced auditor independence (for example, partner rotation and disclosures around non-audit services), improved enforcement arrangements (for example, legally backed auditing standards) and measures to better allocate and manage risk (incorporation and proportionate liability) (Corporate Law Economic Reform Program No. 9 Bill [2002]:2–3).

2.2 Have the regulatory changes affecting auditing brought a positive cost/benefit outcome?

Some would argue strongly that the enhanced regulation has meant that the documentation requirements have been strengthened and have resulted in better quality auditing. The extent to which decision making is now documented and thus defensible is stated by several interviewees as a positive. It has, however, not come without cost. In some instances, this cost has been difficult to separate from other costs because of the existence of other contemporaneously timed changes in financial reporting, including the introduction of AIFRS.

The costs of these changes are evident at many levels. Some have argued strongly that these changes and the documentation requirements in particular represent a distraction from the primary objective of the audit and have meant more time and effort have been spent on documentation rather than dealing with the substantive issues of the audit. The changes have also meant that many see there has been an extension in the routine nature of much of the work, which might not suit the present generation of audit firm recruits—that is, generation Y.

The withdrawal of co-regulation as the primary policy position and the creation of separable regulatory frameworks have produced potential separation between those who regulate the audit market and those who supply into it. In effect, this could have exacerbated a second expectations gap that runs parallel to but is separable from the expectations gap between users and audit suppliers. Interviewees discussed an observable gap in expectations between regulators and suppliers.

The changes have also given rise to a potentially unintended consequence. The remuneration and rewards for members of the auditing profession have been seen to decline in relative terms while the risks and the level of scrutiny and potential penalties have increased. If true and sustained, this development has a consequence for the long-term recruitment and retention of staff interested in and passionate about auditing. The nature of the change in the work and the increase in the mechanical and routine aspects also mean that there are potentially less opportunities for auditing staff to develop their business acumen and gain an understanding of their clients more broadly.

We have found evidence that auditing staff has not only acquired more limited reward opportunities and faces higher risks, they have severe limitations on alternative income possibilities through investment because of the changed independence requirements. These independence requirements also have the effect of potentially causing inefficiencies in the supply of consulting services to audit clients. Similarly, the rotation requirements mean that potential inefficiencies are introduced especially where an audit client is in a particularly complex or highly regulated industry; the five-year cycle could give rise to inefficiencies in the conduct of the audit, although it could provide enhancements in independence.

With the changes, we found no difference in the frequency or extent of reading of the audit report compared with before the regulatory changes. It is noted, however, that the audit report remains standardised and has not been substantively altered, adjusted or elaborated on with the regulatory changes.

In the interviews that were conducted, we did not find many who believed that the legal backing of standards added to the value of an audit; indeed, we found few individuals independent of the audit standard-setting process itself who believed that legal backing would make much difference. We found no-one who was prepared to say that the capital market had been enhanced by the legal backing of standards. Perhaps there are others who we did not interview who would be prepared to take such a position.

We have no evidence that the change in membership of the Auditing and Assurance Standards Board has not had a positive consequence in making it more accountable to a wider group of stakeholders within the market for audit services. There is no evidence that the legal backing of standards has in fact enhanced the credibility of financial statements, the quality of auditing and its role in the capital market or reduced the likelihood of unanticipated corporate collapse. The introduction of regulatory changes related to independence has been important and has caused structural change in the market. We do not know if we have avoided an independence catastrophe as a consequence of these regulatory changes, but we might have. We can conclude, however, that the changes have given rise to considerable cost—financial and non-financial. The changes to oversight, including but not limited to regulatory inspections, have also had costs and have, we would argue, profoundly changed the structure of the work, which will have considerable continuing consequences for audit firms and their staff.

Despite the potential negatives listed above, we still see a market that does not seek to change a mandate to the auditing profession that makes it obligatory for all listed companies as well as many others to undertake a statutory audit of one form or another. The key to the value of the audit is to ensure that the market sees the characteristics it brings and chooses to value them. The future of audit is all about ensuring that value is delivered, the alternative being the 'compliance good' philosophy and driving down of costs and fees as a consequence. One interesting outcome of recent regulatory change has been the dissipation of auditor concerns about legal liability.

2.3 Responses by a market that is increasingly under pressure

The recent past has seen considerable pressure applied to audit firms and indeed the market for audit services generally. As suggested above, these pressures come in many forms but, when viewed from the supply side of the market, there is evidence of pressure with respect to the price of the services delivered. There are also pressures related to the inspections and regulatory oversight—sometimes, we are advised, from many different sources; pressure in terms of recruiting appropriate staff at junior and more senior levels and a loss of opportunities to deliver auditor-provided non-audit services; and pressures from changes in the expectations of work patterns and scale of work by generation Y employees. This list is not comprehensive.

One component of the strategic response by at least some in the market for audit services has been to 'commoditise' the audit work. Commoditisation is a common mechanism used in industries where there is a provision of a service to respond to price and other pressures. Its application in auditing could therefore have been entirely predictable. Parallels can be found in the transport industry, the pharmaceutical industry, in such practices as conveyancing and even in the delivery of medical services in some parts of the world. Commoditisation has the effect of driving down costs but it has been shown to remove some of the 'glamour' or intrinsically satisfying aspects of service delivery. Consider, for example, the airline industry and the comparison of airline travel a quarter of a century ago with the 'low-cost carriers' of today. The same basic functional service is delivered but the removal of the prestige or mystique of the service is apparent.

The commoditisation response also has the effect of making the work more standardised and formulaic and, as a consequence, it is easier to document the processes that have been undertaken in the work. While this commoditisation response might have occurred with or without the regulatory changes of recent years, it seems likely that these changes have at least exacerbated these responses. We saw no evidence that this trend was reversing or perhaps reversible. Given this, policy settings need to minimise any potential adverse consequences of commoditisation so as to maximise the net benefits of this trend.

The intersection of the commoditisation response (and the consequential effect on the nature of the work), together with, as noted above, the reality that much of the quantity of the more procedural work is undertaken by generation Y employees results in what might be seen as a 'perfect storm': the expectations of the nature of work have gone in one direction and the reality of much of the work available to be undertaken has gone in the other. We have evidence that there have been attempts by audit firms to deal with the symptoms that have arisen here. This includes the creation of variety by rotation of clients to provide diversity of work (including the creation of 'middle-market' work), giving staff exchanges and facilitating graduate studies. These methods, however, all deal with the symptoms of commoditisation but the trend towards commoditisation itself remains unchanged and probably unchangeable.

What are the other responses to a market that is increasingly under pressure? These responses could come from firms, regulators or those who set policy.

One strategy could be implemented by a cooperative engagement by firms and regulators at least and would involve creation of a mechanism for the market to observe the value of the inherent good or service being provided. If the value of the product or service can be better displayed to the purchasers of that service, the drive-down in costs and the understanding of value are made more possible. Put another way, this would ensure the transparency of the value of the product to the client. There have been previous attempts to provide transparency of value and the accounting firms PriceWaterhouseCoopers and KPMG in recent years have attempted to make more evident the processes that go on within major audit suppliers.

Perhaps in ensuring that the market sees value, we need 'windows' on processes and outcomes so that auditing is more observable by the market. When was the last occasion you saw a newspaper report with the headline, 'Auditor does good job', or when were we informed of the number of audits conducted in the past calendar year that were successful and aided the efficiency of the capital market? Where we do have a window on audit outcomes including positive ones? Where we have them, they are invariably 'bad' news stories. The very inspection service that the regulator has set almost inevitably means that only bad news is ever revealed. No evaluation exists of particular processes within accounting firms as being 'above satisfactory' or 'equal to world's best practice'. One can understand why a regulator might not want to do this, but it does not add to the efficiency and competition to drive up the value of the audit and, in that sense, it does not aid the efficiency of the capital market.

2.4 Where to from here?

What, then, is the future of audit? If the market increasingly becomes suspicious of and even cynical about the value of the audit, the ultimate prize of a mandated audit could be at risk. We observed no evidence that the removal of the mandate, which would make audit entirely voluntary, was on the minds of market participants.

Throughout the chapters in this report are policy suggestions that might assist in addressing some of the challenges we infer from participants' observations. For example, one suggestion is recruitment of staff who are better 'fit for purpose' given the commoditisation trend. Is it the case that particularly intellectually able graduates, who will expect, indeed demand, variety and challenging work, should be the targets of recruitment? Are the current selection criteria in graduate intake processes optimal?

There are other policy recommendations—for example, the area of materiality (or tolerance for error) has not been exposed to considerable debate in the wider market for audit services. Providing information, transparency and communication vehicles—at the very least between auditors and audit committee members—increases the value of the audit and permits a more informed discussion on the matter. One can see value in the audit by simply changing the materiality level and understanding the consequences of that to cost and to the quality of the audit. The need for more flexibility in audit reporting, for more dialogue between regulators and suppliers, for peak bodies with overarching responsibilities where currently non-comprehensive arrangements mean that overlaps or underlaps occur, for more research into the efficacy of regulatory changes and for plain-English, widely available explanations of audit processes and the role of audit in enhancing capital market efficiency—these are some of the actionable recommendations made within each chapter that arise from studying the responses of the many participants in this project. The next section summarises in full these various suggestions, before final 'concluding remarks' are made.

3.0 Summary of recommendations

Below is a summary of each of the recommendations that is drawn from the individual chapters. The table is provided as a summary of the individual recommendations and their specifics. The recommendations, however, should not be read out of context of the wider discussion. In particular, we emphasise that many of these matters are not new and, for some of the recommendations, it is not the first time that they have been made—but this does not reduce their validity or their importance. In a number of instances, progress towards achievement of the ultimate recommendations has been made. We do not imply that in all cases, ineffective or inappropriate progress has been made. We would assert, however, that progress towards achievement of the recommendations might have some way to go. Additionally, in a number of cases, we have made suggestions that have not been pursued previously or arrangements that are not presently in place.

These conclusions, recommendations and potential action items might be of use to the reader as a summary, but we again remind readers that they need to be considered within the context of the wider discussion in this report. The authors have expressly not ordered these recommendations with a view to priority or specific importance. They appear in the same sequence as they appear in the text, with reference to the chapters in which the words of the various participants either explicitly or implicitly gave rise to the suggestions.

Some of the recommendations are more easily implemented than others. Some require legislative change, which some might consider too difficult to achieve. The recent furore over executive remuneration, however, demonstrates that where there is a will, legislative change can be made quite quickly.

3.1 Summary of recommendations

Ch.	Issue	No.	Conclusion/policy/action	Suggested responsibility
3	The audit expectations gap continues to exist, is complex and multifaceted (existing at least between users and suppliers, purchasers and suppliers and regulators and suppliers) and at the least is costly to the efficiency of the market for information within the capital market and could have many other costs associated with it.		Minimise the audit expectations gap to the extent possible.	All parties in the market for audit services.
3	Differential incentives on the part of suppliers and other stakeholders to create or maintain an audit expectations gap, even to the extent of 'manufacturing' it, depending on the circumstances. Diversity among users and purchasers (and even some regulators) in terms of the sophistication, capability and motivation to fully understand the audit process and outcomes.		Recognition that the audit expectations gap will never be closed and that eliminating differential incentives for a gap to exist and 'educating' all stakeholders are not possible. Focus on stakeholders who are motivated and have the capability to have their knowledge and understanding of audit and its outcomes raised and focus on specific topics known to be the subject of misunderstandings (for example, materiality, use of term 'test basis'). Because of shared objectives and sophistication level, the gap between suppliers and regulators should be given the highest priority in terms of gap minimisation.	All stakeholders in the market for audit services
3	Perceived complexity of financial reports limits potential for communication solutions for auditors.	3.1	Policymaker recognition that enhancing the readability and understandability of financial reports is a multifaceted, multi-agency responsibility with no single body taking overall responsibility for monitoring more than technical compliance with accounting standards and so on. A body, likely the FRC, should take on explicit responsibility for monitoring aspects of the quality and understandability of financial reports.	FRC (possibly using round tables jointly chaired with ASIC)

Ch.	Issue	No.	Conclusion/policy/action	Suggested responsibility
3, 4, 5	Audit report wording is standardised/ commoditised, which hides the degree of auditor judgment involved in relation to a specific auditee, ignores the diversity of the audience in terms of the motivation for and capability of understanding of audit outcome information and uses terms that can be misconstrued (for example, material misstatement, test basis).	3.2	Amend audit reporting standards to encourage more nuanced and auditee-specific audit reports in order to encourage reading by target audience. Perhaps this should be in the form of appendices to a standardised report (refer also to Recommendation 3.5).	AUASB
		3.3	While audit reports need to fulfil minimum legal requirements, there should be positive encouragement by regulators to allow auditors to include nuanced and subtle explanations and observations in a way that adds value to the report for interested readers.	ASIC
3	Generalised non-reading of the auditor's report creates potential to miss emphasis of matter paragraphs.	3.4	Consider the current guidance on location and highlighting of emphasis of matter paragraphs to ensure they are conspicuous.	AUASB
3	The standardised audit report wording uses terms that can be misconstrued and that could therefore contribute to the audit expectations gap. In particular, there is evidence of misunderstanding of the use of the terms 'reasonable assurance', 'material misstatement' and 'test basis'.	3.5	Change wording within the auditor's report to minimise the audit expectations gap (for example, 'This audit is a certification of the X percentage probability of the absence of misstatement in the financial report above an absolute aggregate dollar value of Y', or 'We are X per cent confident that there are no misstatements in the financial report above an absolute dollar value of…').	AUASB

Ch.	Issue	No.	Conclusion/policy/action	Suggested responsibility
3	Several suppliers' comments indicate that they do not understand that authorities in Australia view the external audit as a form of 'delegated regulation' (Knott 2002). In Australia, audit is privileged by a mandate in many cases (that is, is required by legislation); it has the shareholder at its centre as the client and always is the beneficiary of restraint-of-trade policies (that is, only appropriately qualified people can sign an audit report). These aspects of the current framework are not well understood by some suppliers.	3.6	Creation and wide dissemination of an overarching, high-level, educational piece on the role of audit in Australia's society, including content in plain English on for which types of entities audit is mandated, the audit process and, for suppliers, a section reinforcing the privileged role that audits hold and the rights and responsibilities that level of privilege brings with it.	FRC? AUASB? Joint professional bodies?
3	Regulators allegedly sometimes do not practice 'delegated regulation', but instead dictate 'detail' to a point that interferes with audit efficiency, and even more seriously, with audit effectiveness.	3.7	Despite acknowledged existing mechanisms for communication, greater communication between regulators and supplier representatives from both larger and smaller audit suppliers and wider dissemination of feedback to the population of audit suppliers is needed to enhance communication of what each party (regulators and suppliers) is seeking to achieve.	ASIC Joint professional bodies AUASB

Ch.	Issue	No.	Conclusion/policy/action	Suggested responsibility
4	Many of the aspects of audit are not well understood by some users and purchasers.	4.1 4.2 4.3	Provision of collaboratively written, widely available educative material about auditors' work and process, focused on users as the audience, written in layman's language and spelling out important things such as the fact that the work involves sampling (arguably a less ambiguous word than 'testing'), it might be particularly risk focused, it deals with substantive issues pertaining to that particular industry or entity and describing what levels of materiality are used and how these are determined. For consideration is whether these descriptions should be specific to the company or might be more generalised for a particular audit firm. Provide educational materials in plain English in relation to use of the words 'material' and 'materiality' in an audit context. Consideration to be given to a government-funded public education campaign of the type administered to encourage understanding of the importance of superannuation contributions.	AUASB Joint professional bodies AICD ASA Individual audit firms Legislature
4	Information search costs for auditors' reports are high since these documents are currently available only by acquiring, and searching within, individual company annual reports.	4.4	For listed companies, auditors' reports should be mandated as a separately filed ASX document (as well as located within the annual report) so that they can be searched in aggregate as publicly available information individually or for a particular class of company or type of report. Caveats would need to be drawn with the filing to the effect that the auditors' reports should be read in conjunction with the related financial reports.	ASX (listing rule) or ASIC

Ch.	Issue	No.	Conclusion/policy/action	Suggested responsibility
5	The concept of 'materiality' as it is used in an auditing concept is not well understood outside the profession and is a previously under-emphasised part of the audit expectations gap. As such, costs are imposed on the market for information within the capital market.	5.1	Apart from the inclusion of generalised information about materiality and its role within audits (refer to Recommendation 7.1), create specific guidance for audit committees in terms of their need to inform themselves about audit materiality and their right to request disclosure by the auditor to them of the level of 'tolerable error' used in the audit.	AICD IIA
		5.2	ASX to include in its Corporate Governance Guidelines and Recommendations a recommendation that audit committee members undertake structured education programs that include content related to the statutory role of audit, audit processes and audit outcomes and audit committee member rights and responsibilities in relation to these features. This could be a recommendation that such requirements be included in corporate audit committee charters.	ASX
		5.3	Consider the integration of audit-related concepts wherever relevant into subjects/units within tertiary and professional business qualifications (as many institutions do with ethics education).	AFAANZ Universities/ TAFEs Professional accounting bodies
6	The personal attributes of maturity, tenacity, self-assertiveness, resilience and integrity—many of which feed into the notion of 'emotional intelligence'—might be as important to successful audit outcomes as technical auditing skills, yet are seldom targeted explicitly as graduate attributes by tertiary institutions and beyond in their teaching programs.	6.1	Collaboration between relevant parties to assess the best way to build the development of key personal attributes into subjects/units and courses.	Suppliers, professional accounting bodies, AFAANZ, universities

Ch.	Issue	No.	Conclusion/policy/action	Suggested responsibility
6	Based on participants' comments, the present audit business model in some practices is under stress. It is seen in some instances as heavily pyramidal, tending to overly rely on junior staff, who are least likely to possess the ideal 'personal emotional intelligence' attributes, at the interface between the client and the auditor, and depending on retention of staff with the appropriate personal and technical skills for future leadership.	6.2	Consider whether the current widely used business model is sustainable and optimal in the longer term.	Audit firms
		6.3	Consider whether audit practices' current recruitment techniques test appropriately for the personal skills required in a successful auditor.	Audit firms
		6.4	Consider developing more effective systems and processes for the management of client-specific knowledge and ensuring its continuity despite changes in audit team membership.	Audit firms
		6.5	Consider developing more effective workplace flexibility practices to retain staff at points of major change in their personal lives.	Audit firms
		6.6	Alter recruitment policies to encourage hiring of many more honours graduates (and others with higher-level analytical skills).	Audit firms
6	Some stakeholders noted that opportunities for development of business acumen and industry knowledge in junior auditors have become more limited with increased independence requirements.	6.7	Consider development of a national database divided by industry groups and also geographical distribution including data that relate to audit, governance and risk issues relevant to auditees within the Australian market for audit services.	Professional accounting bodies Universities
		6.8	Enhance the adequacy of the teaching of auditing at tertiary level and in continuing professional education by developing high-quality, realistic multimedia and case-based teaching and learning materials.	Universities/TAFEs Professional accounting bodies
6	Remuneration schemes that reward client accounting staff based on the number or extent of audit adjustments exist and can usurp the role of the audit committee and encourage conservative accounting rather than accounting that reflects the economic reality.	6.9	Include in the ASX Corporate Governance Guidelines and Recommendations a recommendation that audit committee members be advised if such a scheme is in place and, if so, how it operates.	ASX

Ch.	Issue	No.	Conclusion/policy/action	Suggested responsibility
7	Many participants' comments indicate that in their view, higher levels of prescription have led to more 'menial' work for junior auditors.	7.1	Consider greater use of mechanisms other than Year 12 score for entry to university accounting degrees (for example, as has been done for entry to medicine) since the competitive forces to maintain university entrance scores as high as possible might not create circumstances for suitably disposed students to enter into accounting degrees.	AFAANZ Universities
		7.2	Conduct research into whether the presence of alternative pathways to the professional body programs (to CPA Segments and CA Program) has a negative effect on entrance standards or on the quantity of accounting graduates entering or exiting universities in Australia. If there are other alternative pathways then what would be the likely consequences?	AFAANZ Universities
		7.3	Consider whether the 'best and brightest' really represent optimal audit firm recruits for the majority of appointments.	Audit firms
7	Auditing has an 'image' problem and has become less attractive as a career than it once was. The global financial crisis could mask this fact in the short term, but it will resurface as an issue.	7.4	Consider how the profile of auditing can be made more widely known as an attractive career option.	Professional accounting bodies

Ch.	Issue	No.	Conclusion/policy/action	Suggested responsibility
8	Widespread observations by participants at the time of questioning result in the conclusion that the retention of staff is becoming more of a challenge than in the past.	8.1	Given feedback from more junior auditors, consider_ reorienting human resource performance systems to work optimally (for example, taking into account the audit readiness of assigned clients) to reward merit and potential.	Audit firms
		8.2	Consider secondments to regulators (and others such as 'policy' officers) since secondments to clients are no longer as possible, presuming any potential conflicts of interest can be minimised or eliminated.	Audit firms
		8.3	Inform staff not just about employment opportunities and career development that exists within their firm but give benchmarked objective comparators to other alternative employment.	Audit firms
		8.4	Engage with audit firm alumni not just as potential clients but as potential returning employees.	Audit firms
9	Discouraging auditor-provided non-audit services (APNAS) for all sizes of clients creates inefficiencies and costs for shareholders.	9.1	Apply the ethical rules covering APNAS differentially according to some criteria such as listed company size (for example, S&P ASX 500).	ASIC
9	Companies' disclosures regarding non-audit service fee categories are inconsistent, reducing comparability.	9.2	Provide guidance as to appropriate detailed services that fit within specific classifications.	AUASB
9	Audit division staff has reduced freedom with respect to investment opportunities compared with other public practice staff, but generally might not be as susceptible to losing employment in economic downturns because of the mandated nature of audit.	9.3	Investigate whether stability of employment characteristics compensate for forgone investment opportunities and, if not, compensate accordingly.	Audit firms

Ch.	Issue	No.	Conclusion/policy/action	Suggested responsibility
9	Although members of the three professional bodies in Australia (CPAA, ICAA and NIA) are bound by the IFAC-compliant APESB's APES 110, there remain registered company auditors who, as a question of fact, are not members of these bodies and hence who are not necessarily bound by an ethical code based on IFAC's code through membership of a professional accounting body.	9.4	Include ethical standards within the AUASB's legal mandate or else the FRC provides the AUASB with a strategic direction to issue ethical standards for auditors.	Legislature FRC
9	Five-year audit partner rotations are reported as creating problems for large, complex, highly regulated companies.	9.5	Consider differential application of audit partner rotation requirements rather than a 'one-size-fits-all' approach.	Legislature ASIC
9	Several participant suppliers commented on the point of audit partner rotation as being a trigger point for decisions regarding whether to leave or remain in the auditing profession. No data are available as to whether partner rotation has increased the rate of exit from the profession.	9.6	Conduct research into movements of registered company auditors per capita both before and after the introduction of the five-year rotation requirement, controlling for other factors likely to affect these movements (for example, retirement).	ASIC Professional accounting bodies Accounting firms University academics (would need to be provided with de-identified data)
10, 11	Increasingly, the prescription of audits is seen to 'distract auditors' from their tasks.	10.1	Evidence should be gathered as to whether the regulatory reforms of earlier this decade have been cost beneficial.	FRC AUASB

Ch.	Issue	No.	Conclusion/policy/action	Suggested responsibility
11	There appear to be no agreed minimum documentation requirements between the regulator and auditors. It appears that, by default, PCAOB documentation requirements have been adopted by the Big Four in internationalising their audit processes and applied to PCAOB and non-PCAOB regulated audits alike. In turn, suppliers interviewed advise that they believe that Australian regulators have seen this as the minima and onerous when applied to Big Four and non-Big Four auditors in relation to the bulk of audits inspected.	11.1	Greater dialogue between auditor representatives and regulator representatives should take place.	ASIC Professional accounting bodies
12	There was evidence of tension and misunderstandings between suppliers and regulators at the time of the interviews. The authors note that current forums such as the ASIC Chairs Committee and various task forces, the Regulatory Discussion Group, APRA's Superannuation National Auditors Consultative Committee (SNACC), ASIC Accounting Liaison meetings, the Research Group and other informal as well as formal meetings and discussions did not all exist at the time.	12.1	Establish a new forum or make more effective existing forums for communication between suppliers and regulators and create wider dissemination of outcomes of those communications to ensure transparency and a comprehensive understanding of these communications by the supply side of the market.	ASIC APRA
12	It is difficult to encourage communication between suppliers and regulators when there is no peak body for registered company auditors.	12.2	Encourage formation of a peak body for registered company auditors or alternatively adapt existing structures to achieve greater communication and then dissemination of outcomes.	CPA Australia ICAA NIA

Ch.	Issue	No.	Conclusion/policy/action	Suggested responsibility
12	It is noted that there has since been increased funding to ASIC, but at the time of the interviews several participant stakeholders perceived continuing under-resourcing of ASIC, in monetary and expertise terms.	12.3	Adequate resourcing of and training in audit-related matters of regulatory inspection staff so they hold relevant expertise and experience.	Federal Government ASIC
12	An alleged 'one-size-fits-all' approach by ASIC to inspections.	12.4	A more nuanced and informed approach to inspections, which might include engagement with peak body for registered company auditors.	ASIC
12	Reports on ASIC inspections tend to focus on negative aspects.	12.5	A more balanced approach to ASIC reporting on inspections.	ASIC
13	In the unlikely event that there is a failure of one of the Big Four accounting firms, it is probable that there will be adverse effects on the market for audit services and particularly for competition in that market. The continuing viability of these partnerships, however, cannot be observed and there appear to be no contingency plans by those who regulate this market.	13.1 13.2	If not already in existence, a contingency plan to deal with the threatened failure of one of the Big Four should be established. Regulatory oversight, perhaps on a confidential basis, of the financial statements of the Big Four accounting firms.	ASIC APRA ASIC
13	There is no single regulatory body responsible for oversight of the 'wellbeing' (for example, number per capita, level of activity, level of maintained competence) of the pool of registered company auditors.	13.3	Establishment of a body responsible for oversight of the wellbeing of the pool of registered company auditors. Alternatively, existing mechanisms could be adapted to deal with this matter. As a minimum, continuing registered company auditor accreditation should be dependent on carrying an appropriate amount of professional indemnity cover, complying with minimum annual continuing professional education requirements and subject to appropriate quality review processes.	FRC

Ch.	Issue	No.	Conclusion/policy/action	Suggested responsibility
14	Entities that require what might be called 'micro-audits' often are required by their constitution or by legislation (for example, incorporated associations) to be subject to audit, when a review would suffice.	14.1	Consider reviewing with a view to amending (often state and territory) legislation so that the term 'review' rather than 'audit' is used, or indeed a choice between both, where appropriate.	Legislature
15	Reliance by the external auditor on the internal auditor requires procedures to investigate the competence and level of independence of the internal auditor that tend to negate any efficiencies involved in reliance.	15.1	Consider ways in which external auditor reliance on internal audit can be facilitated. This can emanate from the internal or external audit sides of the market.	AUASB
15	It is difficult for the market to perceive the value of internal audit when present in a company.	15.2	Companies should be encouraged or required to disclose detail about the internal audit function, what level it reports to, the type of work it engages in, the number of personnel involved, and so on.	ASX G100
16	There is demand for assurance on various non-financial information types, much of which falls within a 'risk-management' framework.	16.1	Provide thought leadership by developing subject-specific guidance for assurance on certain types of non-financial information within an overarching framework of 'risk management'.	AUASB
17	The auditing standards constrain the level of assurance to 'reasonable' even where there is client need for something above this level and where the circumstances exist in which it can be delivered.	17.1	Provide a framework whereby higher than 'reasonable' assurance can be given within the auditing standards, in circumstances where there is client demand and an ability to deliver at that higher level. It is acknowledged that this suggestion would mean a departure from the assurance framework of the IAASB unless changes were also made at the international level.	AUASB

Ch.	Issue	No.	Conclusion/policy/action	Suggested responsibility
17	Agreed-on procedures engagements cannot provide any assurance.	17.2	Consider whether 'agreed-on' procedures engagements should be able to provide a level of assurance. It is acknowledged that this suggestion would mean a departure from the assurance framework of the IAASB unless changes were also made at the international level.	AUASB

4.0 Concluding remarks

A key outcome of this research has been to make inferences from the invited opinions of many different stakeholders in the market for audit services. These invited opinions suggest a number of challenges in that market and ways in which such challenges might be addressed from the viewpoint of contributing to capital market efficiency. Although challenges are identified in this report, the innate 'stress testing' of auditing brought about by the GFC bears witness to its present robustness.

By faithfully incorporating the words of participants who contributed to this project, we have left the power of their words untouched. At the same time, using this 'window' to the views of participants in the market for audit services at a point in time, we have sought to synthesise and distil themes and common perceptions. These perceptions, we judge, are interpreted as 'fact' by those who hold them, but we have come to learn that 'fact' is in the eyes of the beholders and might not be shared by others.

We have concluded that various stakeholders see that the external financial statement audit is valued and that there is no call to reduce or eliminate its mandate. We conclude, however, that the audit expectations gap survives. We are of the view also that it is not possible to close this gap completely and that to aim to do so is an unrealistic expectation. Our view is that efforts to minimise the gap should focus on where they have most likelihood of success and, for a number of reasons, this likelihood does not lie with a focus on retail investors. Suppliers and regulators share a similar advanced level of sophistication in understanding financial information and share also a common motivation to minimise any expectations gap between them. We conclude that this might be where efforts should focus, while simultaneously generating relevant educational materials for more general use. Efforts, we believe, should focus on specific topics our research has led us to believe contribute to misunderstandings, such as materiality.

In terms of reforms to the regulatory regime in the past several years, we find some evidence of unintended consequences. There is a recognition that audit documentation quality has improved, but at a cost.

The apparent 'commoditisation' of the audit has multifaceted consequences. We point to some of these consequences and provide suggestions as to how they can be managed. We also observe that the audit opinion provided across a whole range of auditees is almost identically worded. This in and of itself could have contributed to an undervaluing of the financial statement audit in the market for information. We suggest amended audit report wording and reporting formats to address this issue.

We infer from participants' comments that some audit committee members and even directors exhibit less than complete understanding of matters relating to the external audit and we make recommendations for ways that these cohorts might be better alerted to address this.

We observe many challenges relating to the staffing of suppliers to the audit market. These relate to more junior staff and generation Y issues, as well as the challenges for providing appropriate incentives for more senior staff and the limitations some of the regulatory changes have caused there. Some of these issues might be suppressed by the GFC, but the core underlying characteristics seem unlikely to change.

The working title of this research project has been 'The Future of Audit'. While it is always the case that the future is what you make of it, this is true in particular for the market for audit services in Australia and beyond. The absence of a call for the reversal or reduction of the audit mandate is a powerful starting point for the future. The absence of reference to auditors' legal liability in statutory audits, as could have been expected to arise as a concern from prior research into the expectations gap, is noted also.

There are no doubt challenges, many of which are noted in the preceding 500 or so pages. Importantly, we find evidence of unintended consequences of recent regulatory changes. Lessons need to be learned before further changes and implementation of such changes. The forthright views of participants in the market have been documented here. These might be useful in informing policy positions and changes to those positions by a range of stakeholders, including those who set public policy, those involved in the supply of audit services and those who set auditing standards and give guidance to the audit market.

The authors have attempted to avoid platitudes or 'motherhood' statements in writing this report. Those who were expecting them will be disappointed. Similarly, those who choose to 'cherry pick' more critical observations in this report will not be representing its contribution faithfully or in the spirit in which it is intended.

The 'future of audit' is not without its challenges and there are actions that can be taken by key participants in the market for audit services. Auditing is now and can be expected to remain a key part of the delegated regulation within the Australian economy.

Bibliography

Knott, D., *Protecting the Investor: the Regulator and Audit,* Speech, CPA Australia Congress, May 2002.

APPENDIX

QUESTIONNAIRE
A NATIONAL STUDY ON THE FUTURE OF AUDITING

SECTION A

Please place a cross in the box that you feel best describes the stakeholder group to which you belong:		
Users of external audit services:	**Purchasers of external audit services:**	**Suppliers of external audit services:**
☐ Accounting professional ☐ Financial advisor ☐ Financial analyst ☐ Financial lender ☐ Financial planner ☐ Private investor ☐ Senior equity investment manager ☐ Stockbroker ☐ Other. Please specify: __________ __________	☐ Audit committee member ☐ Chief executive officer ☐ Chief financial officer ☐ Company director ☐ Other. Please specify: __________ __________	☐ Auditor (Big 4) ☐ Auditor (non-Big 4)

SECTION B

The following questions seek your opinion on issues relating to the scope and value of external financial statement audits.

1. For each of the following services, please indicate whether you believe this service is best provided by an external auditor by placing a cross in the appropriate box in Part (i).

   If you indicate "yes" in Part (i), please specify the extent to which you believe that the value of this service warrants an additional fee by placing a cross over the most appropriate response in Part (ii).

Services:		**Part (i): The service is best provided by an external auditor.**			**Part (ii): The value of this service warrants an additional fee.**				
		Don't Know	**No**	**Yes**	**Strongly Disagree**			**Strongly Agree**	
a)	Report on the presence of material fraud in a company.	☐	☐	☐	1	2	3	4	5
b)	Report on a company's internal control procedures.	☐	☐	☐	1	2	3	4	5
c)	Report on the remuneration received by directors of a company.	☐	☐	☐	1	2	3	4	5
d)	Report on the remuneration received by senior executive managers of a company.	☐	☐	☐	1	2	3	4	5
e)	Report on the integrity of senior executive managers in a company.	☐	☐	☐	1	2	3	4	5
f)	Report on the risk management approaches of a company.	☐	☐	☐	1	2	3	4	5

Services:		Part (i): The service is best provided by an external auditor.			Part (ii): The value of this service warrants an additional fee.				
		Don't Know	No	Yes	Strongly Disagree			Strongly Agree	
g)	Report on the performance of senior executive managers in a company.	☐	☐	☐	1	2	3	4	5
h)	Report on the environmental and corporate sustainability performance of a company.	☐	☐	☐	1	2	3	4	5
i)	Report on the quality of corporate governance in a company.	☐	☐	☐	1	2	3	4	5
j)	Report on conflicts of interest of directors of a company.	☐	☐	☐	1	2	3	4	5
k)	Report on senior executive managers' projections for the company (e.g., sales growth, earnings potential).	☐	☐	☐	1	2	3	4	5
l)	Report on the reasonableness of non-financial information contained in a company's annual report.	☐	☐	☐	1	2	3	4	5

2. Would you like the external auditor to report on any other aspect of a company's activities or operations? If so, please specify what these are in the space provided below, and indicate the extent to which you agree or disagree that the value of this service would warrant an additional fee.

Other services:	**The value of this service warrants an additional fee.**				
	Strongly Disagree			**Strongly Agree**	
a.	1	2	3	4	5
b.	1	2	3	4	5
c.	1	2	3	4	5

3. Please indicate the extent to which you agree or disagree with the following statements:

Statements:		**Strongly Disagree**			**Strongly Agree**	
a)	An external financial statement audit provides direct assurance about:					
	(i) the integrity of senior executive managers in a company.	1	2	3	4	5
	(ii) the prudence of the business decisions made by a company.	1	2	3	4	5
	(iii) the adequacy of the internal control system of a company that is relied upon in the preparation of financial statements.	1	2	3	4	5

Statements:		Strongly Disagree			Strongly Agree	
b)	An external auditor has a responsibility to:					
	(i) detect all material fraud in a company's financial statements.	1	2	3	4	5
	(ii) detect all material errors in a company's financial statements.	1	2	3	4	5
	(iii) warn the audit committee of a company about early signs of risk areas.	1	2	3	4	5
	(iv) act as a whistleblower to the appropriate regulatory authority.	1	2	3	4	5
c)	An external financial statement audit is of value to you because:					
	(i) of the business acumen that the auditor brings to the audit.	1	2	3	4	5
	(ii) of the specialist industry knowledge that the auditor brings to the audit.	1	2	3	4	5
	(iii) the auditor provides an unconditional guarantee about the truth and fairness of a company's financial statements.	1	2	3	4	5
	(iv) the auditor has a good understanding of the company's business.	1	2	3	4	5
	(v) the audit opinion issued is an expert opinion.	1	2	3	4	5
	(vi) of the brand name of the audit firm conducting the audit.	1	2	3	4	5
d)	Audited financial statements are too complex to understand.	1	2	3	4	5
e)	The notes to the financial statements are too complex to understand.	1	2	3	4	5
f)	The audit report is too complex to understand.	1	2	3	4	5

4. For the following question, please place a cross over the most appropriate response to each part:

Questions:		Poor				Excellent
a)	In general, how do you rate the business acumen of:					
	(i) audit partners?	1	2	3	4	5
	(ii) junior auditors?	1	2	3	4	5

5. Using a scale of 0% to 100%, please provide the most appropriate numerical response to the following questions:

Questions:		Please specify numerical response (0% - 100%)		
a)	How confident are you that an auditor will detect all material fraud in a company's financial statements?		%	
b)	How confident are you that an auditor will detect all material errors in a company's financial statements?		%	

The following questions seek your opinion on the legal and regulatory environment for audit services.

6. Please indicate the extent to which you agree or disagree with the following statements:

Statements:		Strongly Disagree				Strongly Agree
a)	The recent regulatory and market responses to high profile corporate collapses have assisted in:					
	(i) improving the general public's confidence in the capital market.	1	2	3	4	5
	(ii) enhancing the credibility of financial statements.	1	2	3	4	5
	(iii) enhancing the quality of an audit.	1	2	3	4	5
b)	The regulation of the market for audit services will reduce the number of corporate failures occurring in Australia.	1	2	3	4	5
c)	In response to high profile corporate collapses, regulation now requires auditors to comply with additional mandatory audit procedures. In your opinion, complying with the additional mandatory procedures will:					
	(i) distract auditors from the objective of a financial statement audit, which is to give assurance on the credibility of financial statements.	1	2	3	4	5
	(ii) increase the costs of conducting an audit.	1	2	3	4	5
	(iii) add value to a company's business operations.	1	2	3	4	5

7. For this question, please place a cross in the most appropriate box for each of the listed changes:

Questions:		Please place a cross			
a)	Are you aware of the following specific changes that have occurred in the regulation of audit services in Australia?				
	(i) the introduction of legally enforceable auditing standards.	☐	NO	☐	YES
	(ii) reforms pertaining to auditor independence.	☐	NO	☐	YES

The following questions seek your opinion on general questions relating to the provision of audit services.

8. Please indicate the extent to which you agree or disagree with the following statements:

Statements:		Strongly Disagree			Strongly Agree	
a)	External financial statement audits currently represent value for money.	1	2	3	4	5
b)	For larger companies in Australia, there is a lack of competition in the market for audit services.	1	2	3	4	5

9. Can you suggest no more than three issues that the audit profession in Australia has to address to ensure that auditing is highly valuable to you?

____

____

10. Is there anything else that you would like to comment on in relation to the way audit services are provided and regulated in the future?

____

____

Please complete Section C.

SECTION C

The following questions seek some general information about you. The information you provide will only be used for analytical purposes.

1.	Do you read annual reports and audited financial statements?	☐ No			☐ Yes	
2.	Do you use or rely on audited financial statements in your decision-making?	☐ No			☐ Yes	
		If yes, please specify the types of decisions: __________ __________ __________ __________				
		Poor			**Excellent**	
3.	How do you rate your understanding of financial statements?	1	2	3	4	5
4.	How do you rate your understanding of the external financial statement audit, which includes the level of assurance that the audit provides?	1	2	3	4	5
5.	To which of the following age brackets do you belong?	☐ 18-24 years ☐ 25-34 years ☐ 35-44 years ☐ 45-54 years			☐ 55-64 years ☐ 65-74 years ☐ 75+ years	

<table>
<tr><td>6.</td><td>What is the highest level of education you have obtained?</td><td>☐ < grade 10
☐ grades 10–13
☐ TAFE or equiv</td><td>☐ Undergraduate degree
☐ Postgraduate degree
☐ Other. Please specify:
____
____
____________</td></tr>
<tr><td rowspan="2">7.</td><td rowspan="2">Are you a member of an accounting or finance-related professional association?</td><td>☐ No</td><td>☐ Yes</td></tr>
<tr><td colspan="2">If yes, please specify which associations:
____
____
________________________</td></tr>
</table>

Thank you for participating in this survey.

Two reply-paid envelopes have been supplied.

Please return the completed survey in one of the envelopes, and use the other envelope for the prize draw.

ABOUT THE AUTHORS

Keith A. Houghton, PhD (WA), FCA, FCPA, is Dean of the College of Business and Economics at The Australian National University (ANU). Professor Houghton is the Professor of Business Administration at The Australian National University. He is the author or co-author of four books and dozens of research and professional articles. These have been published in journals ranging from the *Journal of Accounting Research* (US) and the *Journal of Business Finance and Accounting* and *Accounting Organizations and Society* (UK) to *Abacus* and *Accounting and Finance* (Australia). Dr Houghton is or has been on the editorial board of *Auditing: A Journal of Practice and Theory*, *The Accounting Review* and *Journal of Business Finance and Accounting*. He is or has been the chief investigator of a number of Australian Research Council grant projects in the fields of accounting and auditing. He (together with Ken Trotman) undertook an assignment to inspect and report on 'The Process and Policies in respect of Independence, Conflict Resolution and Quality Controls' of the Australian assurance practice of KPMG from 2002 until 2005.

Christine Jubb, PhD (Melb), CPA, CA, is a Research Fellow with the Australian National Centre for Audit and Assurance Research at The Australian National University. She has been a member of the Australian Auditing and Assurance Standards Board since its reconstituted inception in 2005. Her co-authored auditing textbook, *Assurance and Auditing: Concepts for a changing environment*, is widely used at undergraduate and postgraduate levels. Dr Jubb has published in research and professional journals. She has been a chief investigator on three Australian Research Council grant projects in the fields of accounting or auditing. Prior to joining The Australian National University, she was Professor of Accounting in the Deakin Business School, Deakin University.

Michael Kend, PhD (Melb), has been a Lecturer at RMIT University since 2007. He is a former accounting lecturer at The Australian National University (2003 to July 2007) and former convenor of the Australian Auditing Research Forum, held annually at The Australian National University since 2003. Dr Kend has published in the areas of segment reporting, auditing expertise and corporate law reforms. He has been awarded several research grants, including from the CPA Australia grant scheme, ARC Linkage and the AFAANZ research grant scheme.

Juliana Ng is Professor of Accounting in the Business School at the University of Western Australia. Her research has been recognised in journals including *Auditing: A Journal of Practice and Theory* and *Advances in Accounting* (US), *Management Accounting Research* and *The British Accounting Review* (UK) and *Accounting and Finance* and *Australian Journal of Management* (Australia). She is currently on the editorial board of *The International Journal of Accounting*. Professor Ng has secured research grants, including funding from the Australian Research Council.

INDEX

www.ingramcontent.com/pod-product-compliance
Lightning Source LLC
LaVergne TN
LVHW052111210926
848482LV00025B/539
* 9 7 8 1 9 2 1 6 6 6 5 0 6 *